FROM ELECTION TO COUP IN FIJI

FROM ELECTION TO COUP IN FIJI
The 2006 campaign and its aftermath

Jon Fraenkel and Stewart Firth (eds)

THE AUSTRALIAN NATIONAL UNIVERSITY

E PRESS

IPS Publications
University of the South Pacific

Asia Pacific Press
The Australian National University

ANU

E PRESS

Co-Published by ANU E Press and Asia Pacific Press
The Australian National University
Canberra ACT 0200, Australia
Email: anuepress@anu.edu.au
This title available online at: http://epress.anu.edu.au/fiji_citation.html

First published in Australia by
Asia Pacific Press/ANU E Press
Crawford School of Economics and Government
The Australian National University
Canberra ACT 0200 Australia
Email: books@asiapacificpress.com
Ph: 61-2-6125 0178 Fax: 61-2-6125 0767
Website: www.asiapacificpress.com

First published in Fiji by
IPS Publications
University of the South Pacific
Private Bag Laucala Campus
Suva, Fiji Islands
Email: editorips@usp.ac.fj
Ph: 679-3232248 Fax: 679-3231524
Website: www.ipsbooks.usp.ac.fj

Asia Pacific Press ISBN 978-0-7315-3812-6   IPS Publications ISBN 978-982-01-0808-0

National Library of Australia Cataloguing-in-Publication

From election to coup in Fiji : the 2006 campaign and its aftermath.

Bibliography.
Includes index.
ISBN 9780731538126 (pbk.).
ISBN 9781921313363 (online).

1. Fiji. Parliament - Elections, 2006. 2. Fiji - History -
21st century. 3. Fiji - Politics and government - 21st
century. I. Fraenkel, Jonathan. II. Firth, Stewart, 1944- .

324.99611

Cover photo: Litiana Waqalevu
Cover design: Annie Di Nallo Design

Contents

viii

Tables

Figures

Maps

Symbols used in tables

..	not available
n.a.	not applicable
-	zero
.	insignificant

Acronyms and abbreviations

ACCF	Assembly of Christian Churches in Fiji
AGOFI	Apostles Gospel Outreach Fellowship International
ALTA	Agricultural Landlord and Tenant Act
ANC	Armed Native Constabulary
AOG	Assemblies of God
APS	Arya Prathinidi Sabha
AV	Alternative vote
BKV	Bai Kei Viti
CAMV	Conservative Alliance–Matanitu Vanua
CBC	Constituency Boundaries Commission
CEDAW	United Nations Convention on the Elimination of All Forms of Discrimination Against Women
CEO	Chief Executive Officer
CMF	Christian Mission Fellowship
COG	Church of God
COIN	Coalition of Independent Nationals
CRC	Constitutional Review Commission
CRWU	Counter Revolutionary Warfare Unit
EU	European Union
FA	Fijian Association
FAP	Fijian Association Party
FBCL	Fiji Broadcasting Corporation Limited
FLP	Fiji Labour Party
FML	Fiji Muslim League
FNP	Fijian Nationalist Party
FSC	Fiji Sugar Corporation
GCC	Great Council of Chiefs (Bose Levu Vakaturaga)
GDP	Gross Domestic Product
GEA	General Electors Association
GVP	General Voters Party
JFP	Justice and Freedom Party
MP	Member of Parliament

NAPF	National Alliance Party of Fiji
NDP	National Democratic Party
NFP	National Federation Party
NFU	National Farmers Union
NGO	Non-Governmental Organization
NLTA	Native Land Trust Act
NLTB	Native Land Trust Board
NLUP	New Labour Unity Party
NUFP	Nationalist United Front Party
NVTLP	Nationalist Vanua Tako Lavo Party
PANU	Party of National Unity
POT	Party of Truth
PIAS-DG	Pacific Institute of Advanced Studies in Development and Governance (University of the South Pacific)
PIANZEA	Pacific Islands, Australia and New Zealand Electoral Administrators
PM	Prime Minister
PR	Proportional Representation
RAMSI	Regional Assistance Mission to the Solomon Islands
RFMF	Republic of Fiji Military Forces
RTU Bill	Promotion of Reconciliation, Tolerance and Unity Bill
SAS	Special Air Service
SDL	Soqosoqo Duavata ni Lewenivanua
SDS	Shree Sanatan Dharm Pratinidhi Sabha
SLMP	Social Liberty Multicultural Party
SVT	Soqosoqo ni Vakavulewa ni Taukei
UGP	United General Party
UK	United Kingdom
UN	United Nations
UNIFIL	United Nations Interim Force in Lebanon
UPP	United Peoples Party
USP	University of the South Pacific
VAT	Value-added tax
VLV	Veitokani ni Lewenivanua Vakarisito

Authors' biographies*

Kylie Anderson – Lecturer in Politics and International Affairs in the School of Social Sciences, Faculty of Arts & Law as well as coordinator of a number of courses in Pacific Island government and politics at the University of the South Pacific. She has published previously on human rights, gender, and security. (anderson_k@usp.ac.fj)

David G. Arms PhD – Priest of St. Columban's Mission Society who, since 1970, has worked mostly in Fiji. He has conducted various elections for the Church and written extensively about Fiji's electoral system, especially on behalf of the Citizens' Constitutional Forum, of which he is currently a Director. He was an authorized observer at the Fiji elections of 1999, 2001 and 2006.

Mosmi Bhim – MA student in governance at the Pacific Institute of Advanced Studies in Development & Governance (PIAS-DG) at the University of the South Pacific. She was part of the University's observer mission to the 2006 Fiji election. (bhim_ms@usp.ac.fj or mosmi_bhim@hotmail.com)

Jeannette Bolenga – Fellow in Electoral Studies, PIAS-DG, University of the South Pacific. She has observed parliamentary elections in Vanuatu, Cook Islands, Solomon Islands and Fiji. Vice president of the Pacific Islands Political Studies Association and formerly the Vanuatu Principal Electoral Officer and a policy advisor to the Vanuatu Ministry of Internal Affairs, she holds a Master of Development Administration from the Australian National University. (bolenga_j@usp.ac.fj)

Apolosi Bose – From the Yasawa Islands in Ba Province, he previously worked as a Business Development Consultant and Corporate Services Manager for the Ba Provincial Holding (BPH) Group. He has been involved with the BPH Group since 1996. He holds an LLB and a Graduate Diploma in Legal Practice from New Zealand and a Post-Graduate Dipoma in History/Politics from USP. (boses@connect.com.fj)

Mahendra Chaudhry – Leader of the Fiji Labour Party. He was Fiji's first prime minister of Indian descent until deposed in the coup of 19 May 2000 and held captive at gunpoint for 56 days. A trade unionist, he led the Fiji Public Service Association for three decades and heads the National Farmers Union. A strong human rights advocate, committed to social justice, democracy and the rule of law, and multiracialism in Fiji.

Alumita Durutalo – Lecturer in the Division of Politics and International Affairs at the University of the South Pacific. She has a number of publications on contemporary Pacific politics and her research interests include political representation and customary leadership in the Pacific, contemporary politics in Melanesia, regionalism and globalization in the Pacific. (durutalo_a@usp. ac.fj)

Michael Field – Journalist with the Fairfax Media in New Zealand; he has covered South Pacific politics and culture for over 30 years. A former press secretary for the then Western Samoan Government, Field spent the bulk of his career with Agence France-Presse. His publications include *Speight of Violence* (with Tupeni Baba and Onaisi Nabobo-Baba) and, most recently, *Black Saturday*, an account of New Zealand's colonial occupation of Samoa. (mjfield@clear.net.nz)

Stewart Firth – Head of the Pacific Centre, College of Asia and the Pacific, The Australian National University, and Professor of Politics at the University of the South Pacific during the period 1998–2004. He has written widely on the history and politics of the Pacific and is the editor of *Globalisation and Governance in the Pacific Islands*, published by ANU E Press.

Jon Fraenkel – Research Fellow in Governance PIAS-DG at the University of the South Pacific. Author of *The Manipulation of Custom: From Uprising to Intervention in the Solomon Islands* (Victoria University Press & Pandanus Books, 2004). (fraenkel_j@usp.ac.fj)

Paul Geraghty – Director of the Institute of Fijian Language and Culture from 1986 to 2001, and Associate Professor in Linguistics at the University of the South Pacific. Author of several books and numerous articles on Fijian and Pacific languages, culture, and history, he is also well known in Fiji as a newspaper columnist and radio and TV presenter. (geraghty_p@usp.ac.fj)

Graham Hassall – Professor of Governance at the University of the South Pacific. He has been an accredited observer at general elections in Indonesia, Cambodia, Cook Islands, Vanuatu and Fiji Islands. (hassall_g@usp.ac.fj)

Brij V. Lal – Professor of Pacific and Asian History in the Institute of Advanced Studies at The Australian National University where he has taught and researched since 1990. Lal previously taught at the universities of the South Pacific, Papua New Guinea and Hawaii at Manoa. He has written widely on the history and politics of Fiji. His latest publication is *Islands of Turmoil: Elections and Politics in Fiji* (Asia Pacific Press, Canberra). (brij.lal@anu.edu.au)

Graham Leung – Chairman of the Electoral Commission and a partner in Howards Law firm in Suva, Fiji. He was born on Levuka, and has previously worked in the Office of the Solicitor General, as Deputy Ambassador to the United Nations and at the Pacific Islands Forum Secretariat. Former Chairman of the Fiji Law Society. (gleung@howardslaw.com.fj)

Ratu Joni Madraiwiwi – Vice President of the Republic of the Fiji Islands and Roko Tui Bau, one of the chiefly titles from the influential island of Bau, off the coast of Viti Levu. He trained as a lawyer in Australia and Canada, and worked in the Attorney General's chambers as a solicitor from 1983–1991, before becoming Permanent Arbitrator and then a High Court judge. He resigned in 2000 following the coup d'état of that year and worked in private practice until his appointment as Vice President in January 2005.

Lynda Newland – Lecturer in Anthropology in the School of Social Sciences at the University of the South Pacific. For her PhD, she conducted fieldwork on the state's family planning program in rural Muslim villages in West Java, Indonesia, but since arriving at USP in 2001 has engaged in research on Christianity in Fiji. (newland_l@usp.ac.fj)

Rae Nicholl – Lecturer in Political Leadership, Media Politics and Women's Politics in the School of Social Sciences at the University of the South Pacific. Before joining USP, she worked at Victoria University of Wellington, New Zealand, and spent a period as a Fulbright Scholar in the United States Congress. She wrote her PhD thesis on women and candidate selection in New Zealand, Guam and South Africa. (nicholl_r@usp.ac.fj)

Robert Norton – Honorary Senior Research Fellow in the Department of Anthropology at Macquarie University in Sydney, where he taught from 1969 until 2004. He began researching the politics of race and ethnicity in Fiji in 1966. His book *Race and Politics in Fiji* was first published by University of Queensland Press in 1977, and in a revised edition in 1990. He has also published numerous papers on Fiji in various academic journals. (robert.norton@scmp.mq.edu.au)

Samisoni Pareti – Writer for the regional magazine, Islands Business, and is the Fiji correspondent for ABC's international radio service, Radio Australia. He began his career at national radio in 1986 and covered the two coups in Fiji. He has also worked at *The Fiji Times*, commercial radio FM96, the Pacific news service, Pacnews, and the *Fiji Sun*. He writes about politics in the Pacific as well as about issues such as HIV/AIDS and the environment. (spareti@unwired.com.fj)

Biman Prasad – Associate Professor and Head of the School of Economics at the University of the South Pacific, Manager of the Employment and Labour Market Programme at the University and a Director of the Fiji Islands Revenue and Customs Authority. He has a PhD from the University of Queensland. He has extensive experience in the Pacific region, and has published numerous articles on Pacific Island economies. (chand_b@usp.ac.fj)

Jonathon Prasad – PhD candidate and tutor in Hinduism at Lancaster University, UK. His research examines the construction and uses of Hindu identity in Fiji. He previously conducted research in Fiji on the 1996 constitutional review process. His other research interests are the relationships of both economics and mental health to religion. He was previously employed as a social policy consultant by the British government, and a political researcher for the BBC. (jonathon.prasad@gmail.com)

Laisenia Qarase – Prime Minister of Fiji. He took up the post on 4 July 2000 and subsequently formed the Soqosoqo Duavata ni Lewenivanua (SDL) to successfully contest general elections in 2001 and 2006. He was born on Vanuabalavu in the Lau Group, and educated at Suva Grammar School and Auckland University. He served as Managing Director of the Development Bank (1983–98), and then the Merchant Bank of Fiji (1998–99), before becoming a Senator and then Prime Minister.

Steven Ratuva – Political sociologist and Senior Fellow in Governance at PIAS-DG at the University of the South Pacific, and also President of the Pacific Islands Political Studies Association. His areas of research and publications include security, civil–military relations, political parties, political thought, affirmative action and development. (ratuva_s@usp.ac.fj)

Robbie Robertson – La Trobe University development historian, Professor and Director of Development Studies, PIAS-DG, University of the South Pacific. He is co-author of *Government by the Gun: The Unfinished Business of Fiji's 2000 Coup* (Pluto, 2001) and author of *The Three Waves of Globalization* (Zed Books & Fernwood, 2003; Alianza, 2005). (r.robertson@latrobe.edu.au)

Baro Saumaki – Senior analyst with the Capital Market Development Authority, Suva, Fiji. He has a BA in Economics and an MBA from the University of the South Pacific.

Kesaia Seniloli – Senior Lecturer in the School of Geography, Faculty of Islands and Oceans, at the University of the South Pacific. She previously served both on the Fiji Constituency Boundaries Commission (1996–97; 1997–1998) and on the Electoral Commission (December 1999–December 2004). (seniloli_k@usp.ac.fj)

Suliana Siwatibau –Volunteer for general community services through membership of governing and advisory bodies of several national and regional NGOs and intergovernmental bodies. She is also a freelance consultant on issues of resource management and community development, and has a long-term interest in women's development and rights issues. (siwatibau @connect.com.fj)

Morgan Tuimaleali'ifano – Lecturer in the Division of History, Faculty of Arts and Law, University of the South Pacific. His research focuses on chiefs and the chiefly system in the Pacific, especially in Samoa, Fiji and Tonga, and his most recent book is *O Tama A 'Aiga: The Politics of Succession to Samoa's Paramount Titles* (IPS Publications, Suva, 2006). (morgan.tuimalealiifano@usp.ac.fj)

Anare Tuitoga – Instructional Designer with the University of the South Pacific Distance and Flexible Learning Support Centre and also a History lecturer. He previously taught at the University's Marshall Islands Campus, and has an MA in History-Politics. He is a native of Nasau village and belongs to the *mataqali* of Colata in the *tikina* of Naloto in the *yasana* of Wainibuka in Northern Tailevu. (tuitoga_a@usp.ac.fj)

Piccolo Willoughby – Legal Officer for the Citizens' Constitutional Forum, an NGO based in Suva. He is also a Barrister and Solicitor of the High Court of Fiji. Piccolo came to Fiji in 2004 as a volunteer with Australian Volunteers International. He holds an LLB (Honours First Class) and a BA (Major in Philosophy), from the University of Sydney in 2002 and 1998, respectively. (piccolo_willoughby@ccf.org.fj)

The 'yellow bucket' – A weekly column on Fiji politics and national affairs that can be found on fijivillage.com. Inspiration for the column is found, like many things in Fiji, around a yellow bucket of *yaqona* or kava – hence the name. Launched early in 2003 it has gained a reputation for providing astute observation of Fiji politics and its forecasts have proved remarkably accurate in recent years. Authorship of the column is credited to an editorial board that gathers regularly around the yellow bucket.

* Author information current at December 2006.

Acknowledgments

The editors are grateful for financial support from the British High Commission and the Australian High Commission. Wendy Tubman worked painstakingly on copyediting the various chapters, and the Executive Director of the Pacific Institute of Advanced Studies in Development and Governance at the University of the South Pacific, Professor Ron Duncan, gave ongoing support to the project, as did Maree Tait and the staff of Asia Pacific Press at the Australian National University. Michael Govorov kindly produced the maps in the book. Thanks to all participants at the initial post-election workshop in June 2006 and to contributors to this volume. The views expressed herein are exclusively those of the authors.

Fiji's perpetual legitimacy crisis

Stewart Firth and Jon Fraenkel

This book was born out of the need for greater scrutiny of Fiji's elections. Not since 1963 had a Fiji election been subjected to any book-length scrutiny. In comparison, for example, neighbouring Papua New Guinea had earned itself a book for each election since independence. We were determined to redress that literary imbalance. There had been a significant number of substantial, and often excellent, event-specific documentary accounts of post-independence elections, but no broader exploration of the social context of electoral politics. Owing to the odd mix of communal representation and the new-fangled post-1997 voting system, Fiji elections had became a focus of considerable international commentary amongst political scientists and international electoral systems specialists. From within the country, also, elections posed repeatedly awkward challenges. Indeed, that was what had sparked the international debate. A constitutional crisis had dislodged Fiji Indian-backed elected governments in 1977, and coups had done the same in 1987 and 2000. Elections had, in each case, sparked the controversy. Could Fiji's 2006 election find some way out of that starkly polarized history? Would the power-sharing, or the multiparty cabinet that ensued from the 2006 election, prove the master-key to ethnic accommodation, and enable Fiji to re-orient itself away from the debilitating politics of ethnic polarization?

That much was the theme of our originally intended book; its relevance has been modified but not obliterated by subsequent events. We knew that the passage of time would change the significance of the May 2006 election. We also knew that the military commander believed the government corrupt and wanted it defeated. But when the election came and went, and the government was re-elected, and the commander fell silent, we hoped that Fiji had averted the threat of military intervention. The formation of a power-sharing cabinet, for the first time bringing together representatives from the two starkly polarized political parties, backed respectively by the bulk of ethnic Fijians and Fiji Indians, seemed to offer a unique solution to Fiji's perpetual political impasse. That was the perspective offered by then Vice President Ratu Joni Madraiwiwi, included in this volume, and rightly so. And it was a viewpoint embraced, for a time, also by the commander of Fiji's military forces. Popular optimism abounded, and Fiji – for the first time – seemed to have found a home-grown strategy for the supersession of ethnic fractionalization.

Under these circumstances, the important task was to gather together a diverse group of people to comment upon and analyse the election from a wide variety of perspectives. In a workshop held at the University of the South Pacific in June 2006, we gave an opportunity for prospective contributors to share thoughts and tackle various election-related themes, and the proceedings of that event form the backbone of this book. Few anticipated at that time that, less than seven months after the election, yet another coup, on 5 December, would breach the banks of Fiji's democracy, transforming the 18 May election into a last gasp before the country lurched once more into military government. Yet, coups do not easily obliterate the significance of their preceding election. That was true of the 1987 and 1999 polls which, albeit annulled by subsequent coups, commanded an enduring historical interest. The difference, as regards the 2006 poll, was oddly that the boot was on the other foot. This time, unlike 1987 or 1999, it was a coup that dislodged a government elected on the basis of majority ethnic-Fijian support.

Fiji has established two methods of changing government since 1987: elections and coups. Neither is fully accepted as settling the matter. In the last two decades, the democratic result has determined the formation of governments on three occasions (1992, 1994 and 2001) but it has not done so, or done so for only a short time, on another three occasions (1987, 1999 and 2006). The army did not accept the outcome in 1987, and staged a coup. When the 1999 election brought to power the country's first prime minister of Indian origin, many indigenous Fijians refused to accept the result and welcomed his overthrow by George Speight a year later. The army then took over, and installed an interim administration. And when an election returned the Qarase government to office in 2006, the army seized power once again, claiming that the election result was not in the national interest and dismissing democracy as a mere 'numbers game'. None of Fiji's previous coups has resulted in a lasting military government: Fiji is not Burma. Instead, both domestic and international pressures have encouraged a return to constitutional democracy as each wave of rulers seeks to consolidate its legitimacy.

Therein lies the crux of Fiji politics; each social force that claims unilateral power for itself almost visibly struggles for a broader public consent, and cringes in the face of its unacceptability to one or other section of the community. That perpetual legitimacy crisis owes its origins to the 1987 coup; no subsequent elected government commanded a broad popular consensus. Rabuka's governments in the 1990s failed to do so. So did the short-lived Chaudhry administration of 1999–2001. And so it was also for Qarase, first after the 2000 coup, as the courts found his interim regime unconstitutional, and then, again, after 2001 when, despite election victory, the courts found his government unconstitutional because it failed to follow the power-sharing rules in the constitution. In the dying days of the 2001–2006 Qarase administration, that search for legitimacy remained visible, as the re-elected government – under the threat of impending military overthrow – sought to bolster and sanctify its legitimacy by vain appeals to the Great Council of Chiefs, and, although the response was disappointing, to the Office of the President.

Neither elections nor coups, then, enjoy enduring legitimacy in the Fijian political system. Nor do constitutions. Fiji has had three constitutions since independence (those of 1970, 1990 and 1997), and, owing to the legally precarious position of the post-January 2007 interim administration, there is now talk of a fourth. The extraordinary constitutional justifications of the commander, as relayed to the nation on 5 December and again on 5 January, the appeal to the 'doctrine of necessity' or various supposed 'reserve powers', seem destined to fall on deaf judicial ears, at least if these retain any semblance of independent authority. Yet, leaving aside the supposedly pristine legal debates, the political realities are clear enough. Fundamental rules and institutions in Fiji are accepted up to a point, but not if they threaten vested interests too directly or they deliver the 'wrong' outcome. Under these circumstances, principle counts for less than power. Mahendra Chaudhry, the prime minister overthrown in the 2000 coup, is a minister in the military-backed interim government. The victim of one coup, Chaudhry is the beneficiary of another, back in power but through the agency of armed force rather than the popular vote.

Commitment to democracy and constitutionalism seem, then, to sit more lightly with Fiji's political leaders than the desire to reclaim a place at the top of Fiji's public life. That much was true also of the host of politicians who hoped to gain from Speight's coup in May 2000 or, perhaps more pragmatically, from the military takeover that superseded it. And the switch to serving the 2007 military government – for such it is in all but name – is all the easier for those who chose to participate in the Bainimarama-led cabinet because the December 2006 coup was undertaken in the name of anti-corruption. They claim to be a part of a clean-up campaign, sweeping away corruption, nepotism and inefficiency and to be acting in the national interest. But then all Fiji's coups have been justified by appeals to the greater good – the protection of 'indigenous rights' in the case of the 1987 and Speight coups, 'national security' in the case of the army's intervention on 29 May 2000, and, in December 2006, 'anti-corruption'. The labels may change but beneath lie the ambitions of individuals and groups who want political power and are not willing to wait for the cumbersome, and often messy and difficult, process of electoral democracy to get it.

Books about elections are habitually, and necessarily, about political parties, political deal-making, campaigns, candidates, platforms, policies, issues, the media, the role of women, voting systems, electoral boundaries, and regional political peculiarities. This book covers all these issues, but it also does more than that. It includes chapters by the major protagonists at the polls: Laisenia Qarase, the prime minister who won the election, and former opposition leader Mahendra Chaudhry, who lost and claimed it was tainted by ballot-rigging. That argument subsequently became a major part of the case of the Republic of Fiji Military Forces and, bizarre though that was, of the Fiji Human Rights Commission, which sought to justify the coup of December 2006. This book also addresses many of the unique nuances of Fiji politics: how Christian, Hindu and Muslim religious organizations responded to the election, the role of traditional chiefs, the regional peculiarities in electoral politics (in Rewa, Tailevu, Rotuma and Ba Province), the backwash of earlier events in Fiji's political history, especially the 2000 coup, and, most importantly, the campaign against the sitting government by the military commander, which proved ultimately decisive in reversing the course seemingly set in stone by the 2006 election result.

We offer this book, then, as a study of a moment in time in the jagged course of Fiji's modern history. The contributors wrote their chapters before they could have known that the military would annul the election result. Their perspective, and no reproach is due to them for this, is inevitably from within the pre-coup democratic and constitutional order. We have not sought to revise those contributions. If those chapters turn out to be primarily of historical interest, so be it. They are no less important for that. But this book is also much more than an interpretation of past events, forgotten players or defeated social forces. Elections will return, and – at the time of writing – the political players examined in this book are already climbing back onto the stage, assuming positions in the interim order or staking out their claims and perspectives for the anticipated contests of the future, whether these be legal, political or ideological. The supposedly cathartic intervention of the military in government rests inherently on force, even if buttressed by the persuasive sirens of a 'clean-up campaign'. Legitimacy crises, which figure as such a perpetual accompaniment to the orchestra of Fiji politics, will not easily be discharged by gunpoint. And, as the absence of consensus makes its presence felt, the social forces, ideals and political players investigated in this book will resume their roles, no doubt in transfigured but still recognisable forms.

Fortunately, we had not gone to press when the commander of Fiji's military forces seized control in December 2006. So we were able to include several contributions to the interpretation of that enigmatic event, and the odd reconfiguration of Fiji politics that followed it. Robert Norton, in a postscript to his concluding chapter, asks whether the coup might prove a means of transcending ethnic divisions, although emphasising also the inherently coercive nature of military intervention. Jon Fraenkel has sought, in an addendum, to weigh and balance the initial conflicting interpretations of the December 2006 coup. Ours will not be the last word on Fiji's latest coup, and nor should it be. Here was a sufficiently perplexing event to warrant a host of analyses and investigations. We offer our own as a contribution to that ongoing debate, one buttressed and backgrounded by a far-reaching and detailed survey of that era when constitutional power-sharing was attempted as a productive way forward in the ever-turbulent history of post-independence Fiji.

February 2007

A note on the Fiji electoral system

Jon Fraenkel

Fiji adopted the alternative vote (AV) system as part of the 1997 constitution, and its finer details are set out in the 1998 Electoral Act.[1] Previously, the country had used an Anglo-American style first-past-the-post (or plurality) system. The new AV system, like its predecessors, reserves a substantial number of seats for members of specific ethnic groups, although now accompanied by 'open' or common roll seats. There are 46 reserved constituencies – 23 are for the ethnic Fijians, 19 for Fiji Indians, 3 for 'General' electors and one for those from the island of Rotuma.[2] In these communal constituencies, eligible citizens from Fiji's distinct groups vote for candidates from their own ethnic community. In addition, there are 25 open constituencies, where all eligible citizens vote together. Every eligible citizen may complete two ballot papers – one for a communal seat and one for an open seat. The boundaries of the various communal and open constituencies are not coterminous. Every geographical area in Fiji will be, in some way, covered by all five different types of constituency. All constituencies return only a single member to the 71-member *Bose Lawa* (parliament).

The alternative vote system is a preferential voting system. Voters are required to rank candidates. If no candidate gets a majority (50 per cent+1) at the first count, the lowest polling candidate is eliminated and his or her ballots are recounted to ascertain voter second preferences. If there is still no candidate with an outright majority, the next lowest polling candidate is eliminated and

Table 1   Outcome in the 2006 North Eastern General Communal
           constituency

| | | Number of counts | | | | |
Candidate	Party	1st	2nd	3rd	4th	5th
Harry Robinson	UPP	528	545	561	941	Excl.
Nawaia Touakin	Independent	357	361	Excl.		
Rebo Terubea	FLP	383	391	423	Excl.	
David Christopher	SDL	1,467	1,478	1,511	1,547	1,639
Rocky Billings	NAPF	289	Excl.			
Robin Irwin	Independent	629	873	1,158	1,165	2,014
Informal votes		389				
Total votes		4,042				
Total valid votes		3,653				
Votes required for a majority	1,827					

Notes: UPP = United Peoples Party; FLP= Fiji Labour Party; SDL = Soqosoqo Duavata n Lewenivanua; NAPF = National Alliance Party of Fiji; Excl. = excluded.

his or her votes are again redistributed in accordance with preferences to the remaining contestants. This process of elimination and redistribution continues, if necessary, until there are only two candidates remaining.

Table 1 shows the outcome in one of the three General Electors' communal constituencies in 2006, where the outcome was ultimately decided at the fifth count. The total number of valid votes was 3,653, so the required majority threshold was 1,827 (50 per cent+1). No candidate achieved this at the first count, so the lowest polling candidate, the NAPF's Rocky Billings, was eliminated. Redistribution of his preference votes failed to yield a winner, and it required the elimination of three further candidates until, in a two-horse race, Robin Irwin passed the threshold by obtaining 2,014 votes, although he had received only 629 first preference votes.

Fiji's voting system uses a split format ballot paper, with an 'above-the-line' and a 'below-the-line' section. Voters are required to choose which section of the ballot paper they complete, but they may not complete both. The 'above-the-line' section of the ballot paper requires the voter to place a single tick next to a favoured party or candidate. Such ticks are taken to endorse the preferences lodged by political parties or candidates with the Fiji Elections Office shortly

before the polls. The 'below-the-line' section of the ballot paper requires the
voter to rank candidates him or herself. Parties may lodge preferences with the
Elections Office even in constituencies where they do not stand candidates. In
such cases, they must list another party as first preference. Around 95 per cent
of ballots at the elections of 1999, 2001 and 2006 were cast 'above-the-line'.[3]
The consequence of this was that in constituencies where there was no winner
at the first count, political parties had substantial control over outcomes.

In the case of the North Eastern General communal constituency, Robin
Irwin's victory owed much to party preferences, which controlled the
redistribution of ballot papers that had been cast 'above-the-line'. When the
first candidate (Rocky Billings – NAPF) was excluded, most of his votes were
transferred to Irwin because, as shown in Table 2 (column 5), NAPF had
listed Irwin as second preference. The residual Billings votes that went to
other candidates were 'below-the-line' ballots. Similarly, the second eliminated
candidate, Nawaia Touakin (independent) gave second preference to Irwin.
When the final two candidates were eliminated (FLP and UPP), Irwin
benefited from having been placed as penultimate preference (5th) ahead of
his major rival, the SDL's David Christopher (6th), as shown in the first and

Table 2   Preferences lodged by political parties for the 2006 North Eastern
              General Communal constituency

	Party/candidate lodging preferences									
	UPP	Touakin	FLP	SDL	NAPF	Irwin	NVTLP	NFP	JFP	COIN
	(1)	(2)	(3)	(4)	(5)	(6)	(7)	(8)	(9)	(10)
Robinson (UPP)	1	4	2	5	5	4	4	5	4	4
Touakin (Ind)	4	1	4	3	3	2	2	3	3	3
Terubea (FLP)	2	6	1	6	4	6	6	6	5	5
Christopher (SDL)	6	5	6	1	6	5	1	4	6	6
Billings (NAPF)	3	3	3	4	1	3	5	1	2	2
Irwin (Ind)	5	2	5	2	2	1	3	2	1	1

Notes: UPP = United Peoples Party; FLP= Fiji Labour Party; SDL = Soqosoqo Duavata ni Lewenivanua;
NAPF = National Alliance Party of Fiji.

third columns. As a result, Irwin leapfrogged ahead of David Christopher at the 5th count and took the seat. Four parties (shown in columns 7–10) lodged preferences for this constituency even though they did not stand a candidate, hoping to use these to trade for better preferences from other parties in other constituencies.

Fiji's AV system is a compulsory system in two senses. First, eligible citizens are required to register and cast a ballot, and may face fines if they do not do so. Second, they are required to rank at least 75 per cent of candidates in order to cast a valid (formal) ballot (either by inserting numbers themselves or by voting 'above-the-line' and thereby endorsing party preferences). Ballots completed by a tick below the line are invalid. Research by the Fiji Elections Office has shown this to be the commonest reason for casting an invalid ballot. In total, 8.7 per cent of ballots were invalid in 1999, 12.1 per cent in 2001 and 9 per cent in 2006.

Notes

[1]   The full 1998 Electoral Act is available online at http://www.undp.org.fj/elections/Elections/law/electoral_act_1998.htm

[2]   General electors are all those who do not fall into the Fijian, the Indo-Fijian or the Rotuman categories. The Rotuman constituency covers all of Fiji.

[3]   The exact share of 'above-the-line' votes is uncertain because the Elections Office has never been able to release the full set of forms which show the detailed records of all votes.

Editors' note

Throughout this book, in accordance with common usage, the term 'the Promotion of Reconciliation, Tolerance and Unity Bill' has been abbreviated to 'the RTU Bill'.

Note also that, throughout this book, different authors use different terms to describe those descended from the Indian subcontinent. No attempt has been made to standardize this usage.

INTRODUCTION

1

Changing calculus and shifting visions

Stewart Firth and Jon Fraenkel

The mood in Fiji following the 2006 election was positive. Not only had the two major parties performed strongly and confirmed themselves as the unequivocal representatives of their respective communities, but Fijian and Indian ministers were working together at last. If those who drew up the 1997 constitution were right, such cooperation could be expected to bring stability and harmony to the country. Unexpectedly, the constitutional provisions for power-sharing were implemented with the entry into government of a group of ministers from the largest losing party. Given the worsening state of the country's foreign reserves and the decline of the sugar and garment industries, the election outcome and its aftermath seemed to be another of those good strokes of fortune that the people of Fiji have come to expect. The 1987 coup, after all, could have ended in brutal dictatorship, but it did not. The 2000 coup could have split the army down the middle, but instead it isolated a small group of military rebels, leaving the commander in control and making possible a return to constitutional government. Twice on the edge of disaster, Fiji twice avoided it.

Fiji had seemed doomed to increasingly frequent instability when George Speight and his followers seized control of parliament in May 2000. Each of Fiji's three constitutions had lasted a shorter time – the 1970 constitution for 17 years, the 1990 constitution for eight years and the 1997 constitution (which came into effect in 1998) for fewer than two years until it was abrogated by the Republic of Fiji Military Forces in the wake of Speight's so-called civilian coup. But a series of court judgements set Fiji back on the path to constitutional democracy. In the Chandrika Prasad case of March 2001, Fiji's Court of Appeal declared that the 1997 constitution remained the supreme law of the land and had not been abrogated. A High Court ruling later approved the president's dissolution of parliament, opening the way for elections in August 2001, when the prime minister, Laisenia Qarase, led his newly formed Soqosoqo Duavata ni Lewenivanua (SDL) party to its first victory. Remarkably, the judicial system retained its integrity and continued to command the respect of political leaders. On the heels of his arrest by the military, George Speight was convicted of high treason and sentenced to death, although this was commuted to life imprisonment by the Prerogative of Mercy Commission. Ironically, the forces responsible for saving Fiji democracy – the military and the law courts – were both un-elected institutions.

But where did that leave democracy in Fiji? The 2001 election established majority rule – of a sort. The SDL won, although the Fiji Labour Party (FLP) gained the larger share of first preference votes. Majority rule had never sat easily on Fiji's communal soil. Three times, mainly Indian-backed parties had won elections; the first time the consequence was a constitutional crisis and, after that, the result was in both cases a coup. The outcome was always the same – a reversion to Fijian-controlled government. Indian leaders seemed perpetually relegated to sit on the opposition benches. The 2001 election put the politicians back in charge, opening yet another era of fraught top-level inter-communal rivalry. Not for the first – or the last – time there was a successful bid for indigenous Fijian unity in the face of the 'Indian threat', echoing the experiences at elections in the 1970s and 1980s.

So too at the 2006 election. Democracy seemed to work, but not many people wanted to ask whether or not democracy had in fact been put to the test. Would the mood have been so positive if the FLP had won, and Labour leader Mahendra Chaudhry become prime minister for a second time, even supposing he had invited members of the defeated Fijian party into his cabinet? Had that happened, Labour would have risen to power without anything resembling the coalition with Fijian allied parties that it had built at the time of its previous victory in 1999. If so, would people have expected stability, or would they have feared another 2000, when Chaudhry's Labour government was overthrown in the name of the rights of indigenous Fijians? In other words, does democracy work in Fiji only so long as the indigenous Fijians win the elections?

The answer to that question has historically been yes, although whether that was inevitably so is more difficult to judge. The historical reason for the affirmative answer lies in Fiji's colonial past as well as in its political experience since independence. The British transformed Fiji politically, economically and demographically, but they did not obliterate all that was distinctively Fijian. They created a modern state with a modern bureaucracy, the most effective in the South Pacific, but they also enshrined within it an indigenous Fijian state-within-the-state that resonated with the echoes of an older order. They created a modern economy, underpinned by the sugar industry; and they brought so many plantation labourers from India that, by the time the Union Jack was lowered for the last time in 1970, the descendants of those labourers were in the majority. In the Fijian villages, life was much changed compared with the pre-cession years, but ancient affiliations and practices survived in a manner interlaced with superimposed British versions of Fijian tradition: the provincial council, the Roko Tui and the Buli.[1] As the certainties of the old order began to crumble, the church also played an increasingly powerful cohesive role for Fijians.

Protecting Fijians had been the leitmotif of British colonial rule. The number of Fijians fell continuously for the first 45 years after cession in 1874, and the early colonists feared the indigenous peoples would disappear completely unless cushioned from the harsh impact of market forces. Protecting Fijians meant keeping them in their villages under the authority of traditional chiefs until well after World War II. British rule had not always been so benign, only periodically so. In the first 20 or so years of the 20th century, an alliance between the colonists and the Indians seemed distinctly possible, and likely to lead to ever-increasing encroachments onto Fijian lands.[2] But when, under pressure from colonial India, continued bonded labour migration from the subcontinent became clearly impossible, the calculus changed. When the no-longer indentured Indian labourers went on strike in Suva, and when their leaders began to demand greater political rights, the temporary rift between the colonists and the Fijians was gradually mended. World War II cemented that marriage, at least for Fiji's towering 20th century chief, Ratu Sir Lala Sukuna.

For Fijian commoners, life in the colony was less hospitable. But Fijian soldiers fought hard for the British cause during the Pacific War. For their services, Ratu Sukuna was entrusted with reinventing the Fijian administration, or a bowdlerized version of it. The *tikinas* were amalgamated and villagers were pressed into new towns. The late 1940s and 1950s was an era of restraint for the indigenous community, and frustrations grew. By the 1960s, educated Fijians were earnestly demanding change, and the dismantling of Ratu Sukuna's Fijian order hastened indigenous movement into the towns and into the formal sectors of the economy.

For the Indian community, the 1920s and 1930s had been years of advancement. The era of indenture had ended, and advancement in the schools and a flowering of religion proceeded apace, along with a continuing movement of Indians towards the towns. Defeat of political demands, as for minority communities elsewhere in the world, served to invigorate social and economic advancement. Yet, by the mid-1940s, the Indians were no longer a minority. And with the coming twilight of the colonial order, as debates began to rage about suitable post-colonial institutions in the mid 1960s, the calculus of demography played a central role. With a common roll, the Indians might take control of government. With a communal roll, embellished with the old rhetoric of Fijian protectionism, the indigenous community might feel safe. The British colonists were not wholly insensitive to these sensibilities, but they had no workable answer. Land leasing by Indian farmers from Fijian landowners, for example, was made subject to statutory renewals, generating a periodically inevitable conflict in the legislature that echoed down to the 2006 election.[3] At the London conference of 1965, a highly elaborate 'cross-voting' system was introduced, in the hope of elevating politicians of national standing, able to draw on support from both the major communities.[4] It did not work. And, as with land leasing, the debates about Fiji's electoral system proved to be perpetual sources of contention.

By the 1960s, the stage was set for Fijian politicians to adopt a highly defensive posture in their approach to national politics. A minority in their own country, and only recently acquainted with the concepts of elections and voting, the Fijians were determined to ensure that democracy, if that were unavoidable, should work in favour of the indigenous community. More than that, it should work in favour of the high chiefs, who had, since 1904, nominated Fijian representatives to the Legislative Council. They lost that monopoly in 1963, when commoners for the first time were allowed to vote. But in the finally agreed constitutional arrangements left behind by the British in 1970, the Council of Chiefs remained recognized and powerful by being able to appoint eight of the 22 members of the Senate and veto any legislation affecting Fijian interests. In sympathy with Fijian sensitivities, communal representation remained the bedrock of the post-colonial constitutional arrangements, lest the Indians take control by virtue of superior numbers.[5] Fiji's three post-independence constitutions all left a substantial space for communal representation, gently moulding the conduct of elections into a basically race-based experience for which, as Paul Geraghty notes in this volume, one wears one's Sunday best. Fijian chiefs did not easily settle back into a ceremonial role, a mere decoration on the new order, but dominated post-colonial national politics through the governing Alliance Party, under the leadership of Tui Nayau, Ratu Sir Kamisese Mara.

The vision of a multiracial Fiji espoused by Ratu Mara rested on the Alliance Party bringing together its Fijian, General Voter and Indian associations in a multi-ethnic government rather than a multiparty government. The first post-independence election, held in the context of a search for unanimity in the new and difficult post-colonial circumstances, gave that party its strongest ever showing. None of the later Fijian mainstream parties was ever able to repeat the Alliance's 1972 achievement of obtaining 25 per cent of the Indian vote. Yet Ratu Mara, like Laisenia Qarase in 2006, was constantly disappointed that Indians would never vote in sufficient numbers for his party. He felt betrayed. The Alliance never picked up a single Indian communal seat, and its great rival, the Federation Party, never picked up a single Fijian communal seat.

Still worse, Ratu Mara's shift to the political centre in search of Indian votes gave birth to a threat on his other flank. In the mid-1970s, the Fijian Nationalist Party emerged, demanding a 'Fiji for the Fijians' and condemning Britain for saddling the country with a multiracial constitution instead of reciprocating the honourable generosity of the high chiefs in giving Fiji to the Queen in 1874. At the April 1977 election, Sakeasi Butadroka's Fijian Nationalist Party split the Fijian vote, with the unexpected and unwanted consequence that the National Federation Party narrowly won the election, with 26 seats to the Alliance's 24. Cold feet, indecision among party members over who should be prime minister, and the reaction of indigenous Governor General Ratu Sir George Cakobau ensured that the largely Indian-backed party was never to govern. Ratu Mara was returned at the head of a minority government. When minority government proved unworkable, the Governor General called for fresh elections, which were held in September 1977. The Alliance won.

This was an experience repeated, without the constitutional niceties, a decade later, when Lieutenant Colonel Sitiveni Rabuka seized control in a bloodless coup to depose the government of Dr Timoci Bavadra. In power for only a month, Bavadra's Labour government had won the 1987 election in coalition with the National Federation Party, inauspiciously bringing together the two major Indian parties and, probably forever, undermining Labour's claims that it could or would supersede the politics of race.

The 1987 coup shattered the country's second vision of a multiracial future, centred on the coming together of Fijians and Indians in the towns and in the cane belts of western Viti Levu and the 'friendly north', the Macuata region around Labasa on Vanua Levu. The 'facade of democracy', as Asesela Ravuvu put it, had been cracked.[6] The idea that Fijians would ever accept an Indian prime minister, or a government in which the largely Indian-backed parties had a majority, had been exposed as an illusion, or so it was said around the *yaqona* bowls. What would have happened if the Indian population had kept climbing? Would the loss of illusions have entailed dictatorship, spearheaded by the overwhelmingly indigenous Republic of Fiji Military Forces? That we shall never know, for, by the mid-1980s, the Fiji Indians started leaving in large numbers to live in New Zealand, Australia, the USA or Canada, where their race counts for little and where talent is amply rewarded.

Mahendra Chaudhry's rise to power in 1999 was on the back of a third vision of a multiracial future, but it was not his own. The 1997 constitution had been principally the dream of Fijian coup leader Sitiveni Rabuka and opposition leader Jai Ram Reddy, although Labour's Krishna Datt played an insufficiently acknowledged role. In Jai Ram Reddy's speeches, the new vision was quite explicitly counterpoised to the class-based party-building approach espoused by the Labour Party:

> You can have multiracialism in two ways. You can ... have multiracial parties ... That kind of multiracialism is, maybe, a bit premature for Fiji, perhaps we are not ready for it ... The communal pulls are extremely strong ... we are locked into a situation where we will continue to look into the indefinite future in terms of race ... There is another kind of multiracialism ... Let us each be in our separate racial compartment ... Let communal solidarity prevail ... Let everyone be united, but from our respective positions of unity, let us accept that we must co-exist and work together ... It may be ... that that is a more realistic approach.[7]

Communal seats were thus retained in the 1997 constitution. Indeed, there were now 46 of them as opposed to the 27 under the 1970 constitution.[8]

Other tensions emerged between the political leaders' views and those of the Constitutional Review Commission (CRC) entrusted with preparing the proposal for Fiji's fundamental laws. The CRC wanted fewer communal seats, and looked not so much to the emergence of multi-ethnic political parties, but rather to sophisticated electoral mechanisms to deliver inter-ethnic compromise and a multiracial government. The politicians were, perhaps rightly as it turned out, not convinced that this would necessarily happen. They superimposed the power-sharing provisions on top of a basically Westminster-based constitution, in ways that jarred and creaked at times under the heavy weight of controlling government formation. More than once, the courts were to be transformed, effectively, into law-makers. Disquiet about those various provisions was still notable in the aftermath of the 2006 general election, when Mahendra Chaudhry found he could not assume the position of Leader of the Opposition because his party was in government, and when Prime Minister Qarase, as he explains in this volume, found that backbenchers from the now allied Fiji Labour Party could not legally function as a check and balance in the legislature.

During 1997–1999, the Labour leader had been transformed from critic to strong advocate of the 1997 constitution, but he never quite mastered the style of leadership it required. Rising on the crest of a wave of dissatisfaction with the government of Sitiveni Rabuka, his party obtained an absolute majority at the election in 1999, aided in no small way by the new electoral provisions. The overthrow of Chaudhry's government a year later seemed to confirm, yet again, the notion that democracy works only as long as the indigenous Fijians win. But there is room for reasonable doubt. In 1987, the Bavadra government had lasted just a month before it was overthrown. The 1999 People's Coalition government faced down the initial challenge within days of the announcement that Mr Chaudhry was to become the country's first-ever Indian prime minister, and lasted a full year in office. President Ratu Mara came to the Labour government's assistance in the early days, and calmed the disquiet of the leaders of the small and fractious Fijian parties that had so helped Labour to win.

Labour had an unshakeable mandate, Chaudhry would continually say during that turbulent year, but Fijian allies were indispensable if one recognized the security threat. When the dam finally burst on 19 May 2000, it was called a 'civilian coup'. But civilian coups are never quite possible in a country with as large an army as Fiji's. A small squad of crack soldiers from the élite Meridian Squadron supported the coup, and its ultimate fate rested critically on provoking wider military support. Given the role the military played in ultimately defeating George Speight, perhaps a more solid alliance between the commander of the military forces and the government might have seen off the threat in May 2000, or put Labour back in office in its aftermath. The refusal of Ratu Epeli Ganilau, himself a former military commander, to take the position of Home Affairs Minister in the Chaudhry government, weakened the link with the military and left that crucial ministry unable to respond effectively to the gathering storm clouds of Fijian discontent. As the 2006 campaign commenced, military commander Voreqe Bainimarama gave a lot more than just the impression that he would back the re-election of a Labour government, and made it clear he would defend such a government to the hilt. Back in 2000, the military's position was less clear.

The multiparty cabinet forged in 2006 differed in three critical respects from that formed in 1999, all of which undoubtedly improved the former's prospects (even if the arrangement, despite those advantages, was still to prove highly precarious). First, it was the Fijian party that had the premiership and that was in the ascendancy. Given the Fijian majority in the population, a multi-ethnic government led by a mainstream indigenous party was always more likely to succeed. Second, the other participating party, the Labour Party, was the undisputed majority party of the Indian community. By contrast, the 1999 elections had not met Jai Ram Reddy's expectation of two triumphant robust communal parties, each retaining solidarity in their own racial compartments. Labour had obtained strong Indian support, but the Fijian vote had splintered. Rabuka's Soqosoqo ni Vakavulewa ni Taukei (SVT) had obtained the largest share of the Fijian vote (38 per cent), but the new preferential voting system had worked against it. The SVT won only eight seats, well below the 18 it might have had if the election had been conducted under the former first-past-the-post system. With those eight seats, it only just qualified for inclusion in cabinet in accordance with the multiparty cabinet rules. But this inclusion was not to happen. The former governing party was deeply disappointed by its electoral defeat, and put up conditions for participating in the Labour cabinet. Chaudhry did not negotiate, and the courts later found the prime minister's exclusion of the SVT from government to be in accordance with the constitution. Looking back later, other judges – as they struggled with the complexities of the multiparty cabinet provisions after the 2001 elections – were less certain.[9]

The third critical difference distinguishing the 2006 post-election setting from that of 1999 affected the fundamental calculus of Fiji's electoral politics. Changing proportions of the major ethnic groups in the population had secured the position of the indigenous Fijians, and perhaps moved Fiji away from those troubled years when minor variations in the turnout or vote-splintering could make a major difference to electoral outcomes. In a system in which most Fijians vote for one party and most Fiji Indians for another, demographic shifts in ethnic populations assume great importance, as a number of contributors to this volume point out. And as more Fiji Indians than Fijians are emigrating, the arithmetic of demography is working relentlessly against the Fiji Labour Party, especially in the open constituencies where everyone can vote together, and where outcomes are often determined by which group has the slight majority. The ironic effect may be to enhance inter-ethnic cooperation in government as the Fiji Indians, losing numbers all the time, recognize that power-sharing offers the best chance of a place at the table. By a demographic route, has Fiji reached the destination envisaged by the architects of the 1997 constitution? More doubtful is whether or not communal solidarity can and will prevail, in the way the constitution-framers envisaged, as the forces that bound both communities into a bipolar two-party system dissipate. If communal solidarity fades and the people of Fiji begin to divide along different lines, the mechanics and campaign strategies at future elections will be very different from those of 1999, 2001 and 2006. That will complicate matters, and may, by that odd, long and painful route, make the victors in future elections those who are less steeped in the communal politics of the past.

Notes

[1]   The Roko Tui were chiefs installed as salaried governors of the provinces. Within the provinces, local government was organized through the *tikinas*, districts made up of several connected social groups (the *vanua*). Those who took charge of these groups, often also chiefs, were called '*Buli*', and were responsible for levying taxes, maintaining the order of villages, implementing provincial council resolutions and ensuring provision of services (*lala*) for higher chiefs (Macnaught, J. 1982. *The Fijian Colonial Experience: A Study of the Neotraditional Order under British Colonial Rule Prior to World War II*, ANU, Canberra, 1982, pp.4–5.)

[2]   Colonial controls over the Fijian administration were strengthened; restrictions on Fijians entering contracts were eased; and the former taxation-in-kind scheme was replaced by a more flexible system allowing cash payments. Crucially, however, full-scale land privatization was halted by Sir Arthur Gordon in the British House of Lords. Had the Edwardian boom and the accompanying heyday for Pacific plantations continued, pressures for opening up Fijian lands might have been much greater.

[3]   One of the key issues in the election was the SDL/FLP conflict over whether the Native Land Trust Act or the Agricultural Landlord and Tenants Act was the appropriate legislation covering land leasing.

[4]   All voters had four votes – one in their own communal constituency (either Fijian, Indian or General) and another three in 'cross-voting' or 'national' constituencies, where eligible citizens of all races voted together but for candidates whose ethnicity was specified as Fijian, Indian or General.

[5]   Norton, R. 2004. 'Seldom a transition with such aplomb: from confrontation to conciliation on Fiji's path to independence', *Journal of Pacific History*, 39(2): 163–84.

[6]   Ravuvu, A. 1991. *The Facade of Democracy: Fijian Struggles for Political Control, 1830–1987*, Institute of Pacific Studies, USP, Suva. See also, Scarr, D. 1988. *Fiji: The Politics of Illusion*, New South Wales University Press, Sydney.

[7]   *Hansard* (Suva: *Parliamentary Debates, House of Representatives*, Fiji, 24 July 1992), pp.730–731.

[8]   Parliaments under the 1970 constitution had 52 seats, whereas under the 1997 constitution they had 71 seats, but the percentage of communal seats under the 1997 constitution was larger (65 per cent compared with 52 per cent).

[9]   The Supreme Court later reviewed these issues emphasizing greater scope for different interpretations depending on circumstances: '…even an invitation or acceptance expressed to be subject to conditions may not represent a failure to invite or an act of declining. Allowance must be made for the possibility that, in political negotiations, the forceful assertion of a requirement may not represent a final position. This Court construed the letter of purported acceptance under consideration in the 1999 Supreme Court opinion as a final non-negotiable position. That was a finding of fact 'in the circumstances' of the case. In other circumstances, even a similarly expressed "acceptance", or "invitation", may lead to a different conclusion. We should add that rigid stances are not readily reconciled with the Compact and the spirit of the Constitution as a whole'. (Qarase v. Chaudhry, Supreme Court, 18 July 2003, paragraph 134, p.46). We are indebted to Jone Dakuvula for highlighting the significance of this later comment.

2

Chance *hai*: from the campaign trail

Brij V. Lal

Balata, Dabota, Tagi Tagi, Garampani: these are distant, even vaguely exotic, names to this Labasa-born lad. They are, in fact, names of hauntingly beautiful places, evoking the sight, sound and smell of growing up in a rural settlement more than half a century ago. The same sprawling, rippling sea of cane fields, people going about their business on horseback or bicycle, weather-beaten faces of sons of the soil, their leathery skin cracked by excessive kava drinking. People show the hospitality and humanity that rural folk everywhere will recognize instantly. A hot cup of tea materializes quickly even in the poorest of homes, along with the invitation to stay over for a meal. These touching gestures remain with you long after you are gone.

I am travelling through western Viti Levu, trying to get some sense of what rural folk think about the election, the stories they might have to tell of what they have seen or heard. Everywhere, I am greeted with respect and affection, even, or especially, by those who think I am with the enemy, meaning the National Federation Party (NFP). At least you haven't become independent, one man says with a chuckle, a not too subtle reference to those who, unable to secure a party ticket and for one excuse or another, are standing as independents. Astoundingly, in this election there are more than 60 independents. What impact they will have on the final outcome is causing concern to party strategists. (None, as it turned out in the end).

In rural areas, the normal rhythm of life continues largely undisturbed by what is happening in the country at large. A few pocket meetings[1] here and there, the occasional talk by a visiting politician or the local candidate, but little more than that. In urban areas, it is a different story. There, the campaign in its early stages is full of talk of betrayal and treacherous preferencing, about intimidation and fear and vote-rigging. Both the SDL (Soqosoqo Duavata ni Lewenivanua) and Labour (the Fiji Labour Party or FLP) accuse NFP of reneging on preference deals, which the NFP vehemently denies – but not to any great effect. The party recognizes its minority status, a far cry from its glory days when it was the major party of the Indo-Fijian community. It gives its first preferences to Labour in predominantly Indo-Fijian areas and to the SDL in several winnable open seats in southeastern Viti Levu. Labour accuses NFP sarcastically of not knowing whether it is 'Arthur or Martha', that is, whether it is a party of and for the Indo-Fijians first and foremost or whether it has multi-ethnic identity and aspirations, while the SDL uses NFP's preference distribution to rally the Fijians behind it, telling them that both NFP and FLP are secretly consolidating Indo-Fijian support between them and that Fijians should do the same under the SDL's broad umbrella. Divide and rule is the name of the game, and all the parties know it: unite your own ethnic constituency and divide enough of your opponents to win. I find the charge of betrayal hollow.

I listen to the radio, religiously watch the evening news on television, buy and read all the newspapers. There are so many issues lurking in the background that desperately need to be discussed, but they aren't. It's as if everyone is avoiding hard, controversial topics in the campaign. The Promotion of Reconciliation, Tolerance and Unity Bill (RTU Bill) is one of them. The government says it wants to use the RTU Bill to bring closure to the painful events of 2000, but its opponents see it as a barely veiled attempt to grant amnesty to the coup-plotters whose support the SDL needs, especially among the nationalist sections of the Fijian community. The fact that some (notably former vice president Ratu Jope Seniloli) have been released from prison on compulsory supervision orders raises doubts and nurtures suspicion about the government's true motives. There is massive objection to the Bill from community and non-government organizations. Petitions are sent in the hundreds and protest marches are organized, reminding me of the 'Back to May' movement against the May coup in 1987. The Fiji military forces commander, Frank Bainimarama, thunders ominously that the RTU Bill will simply 'not happen'. To emphasize his point and to remind the country of his authority, he joins 500 of his fully armed men on a march through Suva the day parliament is dissolved. Bainimarama is angry, he says privately, because the government is not really in charge and the country is being run by two unelected men: Jioji Kotabalavu, the chief executive officer of the prime minister's office, and Senator Qoriniasi Bale, the Attorney General.

The country is deeply divided over the rift between the military and the government. There are some who applaud Bainimarama's tough, no-nonsense approach. FLP president Jokapeci Koroi, asked on television about her views on the army's confrontational attitude to the government, says that she would have no qualms about the army overthrowing the Qarase government and putting Labour back in power to continue its 'unfinished business'. I am astounded by the utter brazenness of the statement from the head of a party which itself had been a victim of the army's intervention in 1987. Later, seeking to deflect the issue, she says she was quoted out of context, but I have seen the interview with my own eyes, and she was not misquoted. The government calls for her resignation, but the matter is not followed through. As the campaign progresses, the issue quietly slips away. In many places, I hear Indo-Fijians actually supporting the army's stance. As one person tells me, in Hindi, 'We will take aim at them [meaning the SDL] by placing the gun on the shoulders of the soldiers'. 'You need steel to cut steel', another says to me in a tone that I find somewhat disturbing. 'The army is with us', Labour tells the electorate. 'There will be no coup. Don't be afraid. Vote for us without fear.' The message is repeated in pocket meeting after pocket meeting. It is effective in rallying wavering supporters to the party in the dying days of the campaign.

On the Fijian side, there is genuine discomfort about the army's increasingly confrontational statements. Many feel the army is overstepping its constitutionally defined role. In newspaper advertisements and on radio and television, Laisenia Qarase makes this point repeatedly. He wants the Supreme Court to rule on the proper constitutional position of the army in a Westminster-type democracy. There are some who are calling for the government to discipline the commander and cannot fathom the government's reluctance to move. But there is confusion about the proper procedure to use for this. On the eve of the elections, the widely admired Vice President Ratu Joni Madraiwiwi, a high chief in his own right, convenes a meeting between Qarase and Bainimarama to cool the temperature of the public spat between them. A vaguely worded accord is negotiated, and there is a palpable sigh of relief in the country, accompanied by a foreboding sense that things could go wrong at any time. As the campaign concludes, the army's strident intervention in the public arena has pushed many Fijians to the SDL side. Ironically, the army has achieved a result it wanted to prevent in the first place: SDL's increased popularity among Fijians.

In a radio interview, I am asked about the army's antics. My view is clear, and directly opposite to the military's, which sees an increased role for itself in the public life of Fiji. 'It is better to prevent the mess at the outset' one officer tells me, 'than to be called in to clean it up after the event.' Pakistan is cited as a model. I don't think it is the army's role to interpret the public's will, I say. Its role should be to enforce the public will, not to interpret or pre-empt it. My words are published in the papers and, for a brief moment, I wonder whether I should be so incautious in my public statements. 'Watch out, Doc', a Fijian nationalist candidate says to me at the Dolphins Foodcourt in Suva, slapping me playfully on the shoulder. He was the same person who had staged a public confrontation with me at a Reeves Commission hearing in Suva and had called on television for my resignation. He made the headlines. But when I met him in Korovou a few weeks later, he said politely that he hoped I did not mind what he had said about me. He was standing for a by-election, and wanted some free media attention, which the episode had given him. But I am troubled for a brief moment only: I have to be true to my convictions.

Another issue burning in the background is the expiry of agricultural leases under the Agricultural Landlord and Tenant Act (ALTA). The leases began expiring in the late 1990s. Now, there are thousands of farmers whose leases have not been renewed, who are uprooted and beginning new careers as casual labourers, small vegetable growers and domestic hands, crowding the already clotted Suva–Nausori corridor. I am told that in the Nasinu constituency contested by Labour's Labasa-born Krishna Datt, fully 40 per cent of the voters are displaced Labasans. There is quiet resentment against them – resentment about their industry and enterprising spirit, their preparedness to work for any wage. 'This place stinks of Labasa'; 'Labasa, Labasa *gandhaye*', a taxi driver tells me as we drive from Kinoya to Tacirua via the Khalsa road, not knowing that I too am from the 'friendly north'. There is intense competition for the squatter vote. But about a major cause of that problem, the expiry of leases, nothing much is said. SDL wants to renew the leases under the Native Land Trust Act (NLTA), which gives the landowner more say and greater flexibility on the renewal of leases, while Labour prefers the ALTA, whose tenant-favouring 'hardship clause' places greater onus on the landowner to prove that his need to reoccupy his land is greater than the tenant's.

The NFP proposes the concept of a 'Master Lease' under which the government would lease land from the landlords under the provisions of the NLTA and then lease it to the tenants under the terms of the ALTA. The idea was first proposed by Jai Ram Reddy and Wadan Narsey in the late 1990s, but it goes nowhere in this campaign. People are reluctant to engage seriously with ideas and alternatives, I begin to realize, preferring instead the comfort of the simple slogans. As I travel through the countryside, I see displaced tenants by the roadside selling root crops, vegetables and fish. The look on their sun-bathed, anguished, furrowed faces touches the heart. Through no fault of their own, they have become refugees in their own homeland. I see formerly productive cane fields slowly reverting to bush. A Fijian farmer, deep in the heartland of Viti Levu, tells me about the situation in his area. Many leases were not renewed and tenants had to move to the town. 'NLTA or Calcutta', some village wit had remarked. But after a few years, the landowners realized their error in the absence of the income that the lease rents brought, and pleaded with the former tenants to return. Most refused.

The land issue is closely tied to the uncertain fortunes of the country's ailing sugar industry. The preferential access to the European Union markets will soon expire, forcing Fiji to sell sugar on an internationally competitive market. The sugar mills function on ancient machines habitually prone to repeated breakdowns. The increasing cost of transporting cane to the mills and of hiring labourers is being felt by the growers. The uncertainty of renewal of leases creates its own problems. The government has talked about re-structuring the sugar industry, following the advice of an Indian team of experts, but the precise details are not spelled out. Strangely, it is not an issue in this campaign. Just as certain as night will follow day, Labour will oppose any solution proposed by the SDL. The reason? Politics. Keep politics out of the industry, people say, but that is naïve. Politics drives the sugar industry, always has. Mahendra Chaudhry's power base is in the cane belt; and he is the general secretary of the National Farmers Union. Farmers are slowly, visibly descending into poverty, while their leaders play politics and manoeuvre for political advantage, like vultures hovering eagerly over a mortally wounded animal.

Every major party has prepared a manifesto, a grab-bag of ideas and proposals about how they will address the social and economic problems facing Fiji. These are attractive documents, professionally produced, accessibly written and widely distributed. Though there are vernacular versions, the main one is in English. But these are for show really. Many candidates with poor English wave a copy furiously before their audiences, with all the pretended passion they can muster, urging them to read it when they themselves are innocent of its contents! Prepared speeches, rehearsed several times over, are the standard campaign fare. Politicians glibly tell people what they want, not what they ought, to hear. But manifestos have to be launched, a politician tells me, because without them, people would not take the party seriously. The ones loudest in their demands for manifestos are those who don't read, a candidate says to me slightly cynically. Complex ideas are reduced to laughter-inducing slogans. Voters want entertainment as well as (some) enlightenment.

The method of campaigning in Fiji has changed dramatically over the years. When I first began writing about elections in the early 1980s, large rallies were the order of the day. People travelled miles to listen to speeches. There was no television in Fiji then, and the video revolution was just beginning. So people turned up for rallies because these were a major item in their limited social calendar. By the late 1980s, cassettes began to be mass produced, carrying the party's ideas into distant rural areas, where people could listen to their leaders while sitting around the *tanoa*. Sakeasi Butadroka, the fiery Fijian nationalist, was among the first to use this medium. By the 1990s, pocket meetings had come to prominence and were used very effectively by the FLP. And with good reason too. Labour's organizational machinery, well-oiled and functioning efficiently, reached out to the grassroots. A handful of diehard supporters in each constituency was briefed – brainwashed may be a better word – to carry on the party propaganda while the candidate moved elsewhere. In the late 1990s, video cassettes were used, especially by the NFP to carry party leader Jai Ram Reddy's message on the constitution, but that trend did not catch on.

More recently, radio and television debates, phone-in programs, live interviews and, especially, advertising on television, have come to dominate election campaigns. SDL led the way in 2006 with slick advertisements – the white dove, the party's symbol, flying majestically against a light blue background – reminding the people of all it had achieved in the past five years and asking them not to jeopardize their future by voting for other parties. Labour focused on the real and alleged failures of the SDL government, highlighting the problems of poor water supply, unemployment and increased cost of living. Its advertisements, featuring despairing down-and-out people needing food, shelter and clean water, were pointed and hard-hitting in the characteristically Labour style. The NFP, strapped for funds, dusted up its 2001 campaign video for the 2006 election, screening exactly the same images but with a changed voice-over. No one noticed, which caused some bemused puzzlement among party leaders! The National Alliance launched a surprisingly well-funded media campaign, highlighting its connection to the legendary lights of the Fijian establishment: Ratu Sukuna, Ratu Edward Cakobau, Ratu George Cakobau and Ratu Mara, with a gently smiling party leader Ratu Epeli Ganilau holding up a lighted torch, marching towards a rising dawn. Slickly packaged television campaigns will be the order of the day in the future.

Campaign styles vary. Among Fijians, especially in rural areas, there is an acute awareness of cultural protocols governing public discourse. Voice is not raised and insulting language avoided. Un-chiefly conduct is frowned upon. I vividly recall a National Alliance meeting at Syria Park in Nausori. I was invited to the meeting. Ratu Epeli arrives in a new, rented four-wheel drive. Making a good impression is important. About two dozen people, mostly Fijian women from the neighbouring hinterland, are seated in a temporary corrugated iron shelter. At the appointed time, Ratu Epeli enters the speaker's shelter with his chiefly wife. They are seated on two elegant chairs facing the audience. Ratu Epeli is introduced. He reads a prepared speech, some of it in English. He is a dignified man, chiefly, well-spoken but wooden. He is critical of the SDL's policies, but never once does he directly attack the party or its leader. He talks about the need for the various ethnic groups to work together. He eschews racial politics. He talks about Fiji as a multiracial family. He is against racial discrimination in any form, including race-based affirmative action programs for Fijians. People clap politely when he finishes. *Yaqona* is served in the traditional Fijian way. He mingles with the crowd rather awkwardly. Style and status count as much as the substance of the speech. Snippets appear on the evening news and in the following day's papers.

After Ratu Epeli finishes, he asks me whether I might like to say a word or two. This catches me completely by surprise; I am unprepared. I realize quickly that Ratu Epeli is not inviting me, he is actually asking me to speak, in the traditional chiefly way. What to say? I begin with something I had read in the papers recently, some politician saying that racially polarized politics were inevitable, necessary even, because Fijians and Indo-Fijians could not, could never, work together. History was proof enough of that. I said in response that our history showed the contrary to be the case. Fiji had encountered seemingly intractable problems in its recent history, but our leaders had been able to resolve deep-seated difficulties through discussion and dialogue. Independence was a contested issue, but it was eventually achieved amicably. Our leaders were able to work together to devise ALTA, which had brought decades of prosperity to the country. Again, after the coups of 1987, they were able to retrieve the country from the brink of a precipice and conflagration. In the 1990s, Jai Ram Reddy and Sitiveni Rabuka, once bitter foes – Reddy was, after all, the chief target of the Taukei Movement in 1987: 'Reddy the Gun, Bavadra the Bullet', the placards had proclaimed – had been able to join hands to give the country the best constitution it ever had. We can work together, I said.

Meanwhile, the Prime Minister was telling his campaign audiences that Fijians were are not ready for a non-indigenous prime minister. And some SDL politicians were suggesting that the constitution should be changed to reflect the Fijian wish for the country to be led by Fijians. I said that I myself did not have a problem with a Fijian leader of government, provided that arrangement was the outcome of a political negotiation rather than a constitutional requirement. If race were further entrenched in the constitution, specifically the requirement that the prime minister should be a Fijian, we will once again court international sanctions. We will be expelled from the Commonwealth and strain our relations with our neighbours. With the population trend favouring Fijians – they would be about two thirds of the population in a decade or so – it was likely that a Fijian would always head government. Repeating my oft-spoken words, I said that this preoccupation with race was a prescription for political paralysis.

My words, echoing the sentiment Ratu Epeli had aired a few minutes earlier, received a warm response. He shook my hands in appreciation, and the women sitting in the shed clapped gently. I was moved, but wondered how much of what I had said was understood by the audience, for I had spoken in English. How I wished then that I could speak fluent Fijian, rather than communicating with my fellow countrymen in a language that none of us own or are truly comfortable with.

A week or so after the Nausori meeting, I attended an NFP rally in Suva. I had gone there to observe the proceedings and to catch up with old friends. I was a bit late and sat at the back of the room. Much to my surprise, the chairman announced my arrival to the audience and said, without my permission, that I would be speaking towards the end of the meeting! The speakers were full of fire and with a bagful of ideas about how to resolve the problems facing the country. Labour's strategies of 'boycott and high court' (someone mischievously added paraquat) were derided to quiet applause. In other meetings, as the campaign heated up, the rhetoric got hotter and more personal. Indo-Fijian audiences love chest-thumping, *masala,* talk.

After the last speaker had finished, I was invited to the front, still unclear in my mind about what to say. Then, all of a sudden, I remembered something I had read – or was told. In one of the meetings a year or two back, Mahendra Chaudhry had said that NFP stood for 'Not Fit for Parliament.' I began by reminding the audience that NFP had, in fact, played a very large role in Fiji's recent history. I asked the audience to name four of the most important achievements of Fiji in the last half-century. People look blankly. They are not used to this kind of interactive meeting. Achievement of independence, I suggest, is one. People nod in agreement. The Denning Award of 1969, which led to the departure of the Colonial Sugar Refining Company and brought prosperity to the sugar industry, is another. People are listening intently now. The successful

negotiation of the Agricultural Landlord and Tenant Bill after independence
– also a milestone achievement. And finally, I ask people not to forget the
promulgation of the 1997 constitution, a momentous achievement considering
the circumstances prevailing in the 1990s. I then make two concluding points.
In all these four achievements of national importance, the NFP had played a key
role: that was a matter of historical record and no trimming of the truth could
alter that fact. And second, I say these achievements came about as a result of
dialogue and discussion, patient negotiation and sensitive appreciation of the
fears and aspirations of Fiji's different communities. People clap warmly as I
sit down. I hadn't said anything terribly profound, but I realize as I ponder the
event later that our people, even political leaders, have a poor understanding
of history, even the recent history of their own party.

The NFP puts on a brave face, but even the most optimistic assessment by
party insiders gives them just a handful of seats, anywhere between three and
eight. They can't be kings, its leaders realize, but they could be king-makers
by distributing their preferences wisely and perhaps, as a bonus, get a Senate
seat or two. Its most critical handicap in this election is that there is no clear,
and in the public's mind clearly identifiable, leader; no one face of the party.
Attar Singh, Pramod Rae and Raman Singh take turns to represent the party
in various fora, but that only serves to compound the problem. On this front,
Labour has a considerable advantage. Mahendra Chaudhry is the public face
of the party, its brand name. For many, Chaudhry *is* the Labour Party.

In the Fijian electorate, Laisenia Qarase enjoys a similar advantage. He
is no longer the shy, awkward campaigner of 2001, unsure of himself and
dependent on others for advice. In 2006, he is relaxed, confident, skilled at
public speaking, engaging. He is the undisputed leader of the SDL, which
he has, over the course of five years, built into a cohesive, well-oiled fighting
machine. His most prominent Fijian challenger, Ratu Epeli Ganilau, is also a
well-known name from a distinguished family, but his base is limited and his
platform of multiracialism drowned out by the politics of racial polarization.
Qarase's advocacy of race-based affirmative action policy and his frequently aired
view that Fijians must continue to lead the country fall on receptive ears. The
fear of Chaudhry returning to lead pushes many Fijians into the SDL camp.
'Do you want Mr Chaudhry to lead this country?' Qarase asks his audiences

repeatedly, and the response always is a thunderous 'No'. A Fijian taxi driver tells me that he admires Chaudhry for his courage, but he does not trust him. To him, the Labour leader is politically too smart for his opponents; he always has something up his sleeve. He was not alone in thinking that.

Personalities certainly matter, but both SDL and Labour have done their homework. Qarase has made sure that in his policies and programs no province is left out. The provincial link is assiduously cultivated, and the party's network reaches deep into the Fijian hinterland. The SDL is not officially endorsed by the Great Council of Chiefs, as the Soqosoqo ni Vakavulewa ni Taukei (SVT) was in the 1990s, but people know that its blessing is with it. Any opportunity to 'explain' the government's policies – the RTU Bill, for example – to the provinces is seized to strengthen the party's connection with the grassroots, reminding them of what the government has accomplished. With the disestablishment of the Conservative Alliance–Matanitu Vanua party, SDL became the umbrella party of the Fijian community. The SVT is a ghost of its former self, fielding only one candidate, that too an Indo-Fijian! Like the SDL, Labour's machinery is strong. The National Farmers Union, the Fiji Public Service Association and the Fiji Teachers Union are all identified with Labour. Parliamentarians are regularly required to keep in close touch with their constituents. Chaudhry himself sets the example that others can ignore only at their peril.

Voters have become more sophisticated over the years. Now, they are keenly aware of the power they have in their hands. They know that they own the vote. They expect the candidates to come to them, to sit down with them, serve them kava and cigarettes, attend their marriage and funeral functions. They expect to be picked up from their homes and transported to the polling booth – at a time convenient to themselves. Candidates from all political parties complain about the expense incurred in entertaining voters. Many say that they have spent more than $10,000 of their own money during the campaign, most of it on providing kava. I am amazed at how much kava is drunk these days. Any excuse to mix a bowl. A party worker tells me that in his constituency, meetings go well into the night. 'That's good', I say, thinking that people are really engaged with the campaign. 'No, Doc, nothing like that. They want long meetings so that they can drink more free grog.' In Fijian meetings I observe, *yaqona* is drunk, but protocol and rank are recognized. The spirit of the *vanua* is honoured and outsiders are formally welcomed. But among Indo-Fijians, *yaqona* is consumed in copious amounts, without decorum or dignity. Excessive *yaqona* drinking among Indo-Fijian men is a major cause of domestic problems and extramarital affairs, which sometimes end in tragedy. The sad thing is that *yaqona* drinking is becoming increasingly popular among younger people.

Politicians try hard to meet their public obligations, but sometimes things go wrong. A man tells me that when his wife died in a tragic fire accident, the politician representing his constituency felt obliged to make an appearance. He walked up to the bereaved husband, and asked him if he knew who the dead woman was! The man decided there and then not to vote for that parliamentarian ever again. Another candidate told me that when she visited one particular household, an elderly lady told her that she would vote for her provided she increased her monthly allowance. She was honest enough to say that she would try but could not promise. The old woman abruptly shut the door on her. The changing voter behaviour, at least in the Indo-Fijian community, is producing a new kind of politician, one who is attentive to the needs of the constituency almost to the exclusion of any other consideration, who spends most available time and energy mixing with constituents, ministering to their personal needs. Whether the candidate would make a good parliamentarian and legislator capable of handling complex national policy issues is, sadly, a secondary matter.

I encounter a range of opinion as I travel the countryside. Most talks are depressing: non-renewal of leases, unemployment, discrimination in the public sector, people waiting hopefully for their children to emigrate so that they, too, could go. But there are light moments as well. Without humour, it would be difficult to cope, I realize. A middle-aged man in Tavua town assures me over a bowl of grog that there has been real progress in Fiji since 1987. Progress? How? 'Look, Doc', the man says, 'in 1987, our government lasted one month, in 2000 it lasted one year. Next time, it will last two years, no?' A thigh-slapping laugh follows. 'Let's hope it lasts much longer', I reply, joining in the laughter. A man in Rakiraki tells me he will vote Labour. Before I am able to say anything, he says, 'If Labour wins, there will be trouble. We will then have a better chance to migrate'. This reminds me of an incident in Sydney when some protestors hoisted a banner saying 'Speight *ke Maro Goli*'. This could read as 'To hell with

Speight' or 'Shoot Speight'. The protestors had the latter in mind. A man tells me, 'We will get ourselves photographed in front of parliament house and will use the photograph to claim political asylum in Australia!'

Other stories. A man says he will never vote for NFP because it is a rich man's party. Another replies: '*Arre*, you should vote for a rich man's party: what can a poor man's party do for you?!' At another place, a man relates a story which has been around for a while. Someone says he will never vote for NFP because NFP is not known outside Fiji. There is a Labour party in the UK, and in Australia and New Zealand, but there is no NFP there. 'How can you expect help for a party no one knows about overseas?' A candidate in Tavua says they should vote for Mahendra Chaudhry because he is a man of courage. 'I was a hostage for nearly two months. I saw with my own eyes the terrible beating the soldiers gave to my leader. I saw blood on his face. His ribs were broken. But he did not flinch.' People are impressed. But a week later the local headmaster visits the area and is told the story. He is puzzled. How could the candidate have seen Chaudhry being beaten 'with his own eyes' when he was not in parliament and never incarcerated? Trimming the truth: everyone seems to be doing it.

People devise ingenious ways of getting their message across to the people. At one meeting, a candidate asks people to vote for the *vara*, the germinating coconut tree which is the FLP symbol. Why? Because coconut is offered to the gods in Hindu religious ceremonies. 'Coconut water is the purest form of water, untouched by human hands', he says. What that has to do with politics is beyond me. But at another meeting, an NFP candidate responds to this by saying that, yes, coconut water is the purest form of water, but we offer it to the gods using the mango leaf. The mango tree is the symbol of the NFP!

There is much talk about the poor calibre of candidates standing in this election. How can candidates with limited education be entrusted with making decisions about the country's future, people ask. Many are barely able to put two sentences in English together: how will they be able to digest complex bills in parliament? The point is taken, though it is easy to say this while sitting on the sidelines. The calibre of Fijian candidates is better than the calibre of Indo-Fijian candidates. Fijians see a future in politics for themselves. Indo-Fijians don't. Some of them are standing because they are retired, have nothing useful to do, and are looking for a bit of fame and fortune before the flame is finally extinguished. Some are standing because they believe passionately in some cause or because their party has asked them to. Their sense of loyalty and perseverance commands respect.

At the beginning of the campaign, almost every candidate I speak with is hopeful about his or her prospect. 'Chance *hai.*' We have a chance. But hope begins to vanish as the campaign proceeds. It is a sad spectacle. The saddest though is the fate of those who, having done their arithmetic, know from the very beginning that they have no hope of winning at all. But they put on a brave face, go through the motions and campaign house-to-house. How they can muster the energy and enthusiasm to go on the campaign trail in humid heat and dust, day in, day out, over several weeks defies easy comprehension. I suppose hope springs eternal in the heart of every prospective politician. Some hope to make enough acquaintances to help their business. For others, this is a trial run, an apprenticeship for the next time around. At least one candidate tells me that the exposure he has gained in this campaign will help his chances for selection in the municipal elections.

As I travel around the countryside, usually by myself, I often think how things have changed over the years. I published my first Fiji election analysis in 1983. There was no internet then, no websites, no email, no googling, just the radio and the newspapers. Gathering data – about the demographic and ethnic composition of a constituency, for example, or getting hold of party manifestos or profiles of candidates – was tedious and time consuming. Luck played a large part in acquiring the election marginalia so essential to understanding the mood of the campaign. But all that has changed. All the data you need are now posted on the official election website. Both SDL and Labour have their own websites, displaying their manifestos and speeches by their leaders. All the major newspapers have their own websites, carrying analysis as well as information. Expert commentary is copied and carried far and wide. It is possible now to 'know' what is happening on the hustings without leaving your computer desk. The kind of detailed analyses I wrote earlier seems inappropriate now because everyone who wants to can have access to the same data set. I have become a remnant in my own lifetime!

As the day of reckoning draws near and all the campaign propaganda have been distributed, attention turns to the logistics of manning the polling booths: sheds will have to be erected, transport arranged, food and grog organized, trusted party workers found to look after the booth. And the waiting, the endless waiting for the D-Day. As I say goodbye to the campaign trail, with some sadness I have to admit, I know in my heart that the friendships I have made with people in once exotic and unknown places, such as Balata, Dabota, Tagi Tagi and Garampani, will remain with me for a very long time, reminding me of the world I once knew so intimately, but of which I am no longer a part. Fate has dealt these folk a cruel hand. Often they suffer through no fault of their own, victims of other people's envy and avarice. I hope and pray that, whatever the final outcome, the verdict of the ballot box will be respected and that citizens of this most beautiful of lands on earth will be given an opportunity to fashion the future of unity and prosperity that they so richly deserve and which is within their reach.

Notes

[1] Small meetings with a handful of supporters in the constituency, largely away from the media and usually around a *yaqona* bowl.

3

The pre-election 'cold war': the role of the Fiji military during the 2006 election

Steven Ratuva

The military's role during the May 2006 election was largely in the form of participation in political campaigns against the incumbent Soqosoqo Duavata ni Lewenivanua (SDL) government for the purpose of protecting 'national security interests'. While the 1987 and 2000 military interventions involved deployment of armed troops, the 2006 deployment largely involved public relations – and at times psychological pressure – to attempt to influence the election results. This was the first time in Fiji's history that the military was openly involved in electioneering and associated activity. The issue of contention then is: by such involvement, to what extent did the military exceed its constitutional limits? Are the limits clearly defined – as the ruling government argued – or are they meant to be interpreted in a utilitarian way, depending on the security circumstances – as the military contended? Another pertinent question is whether or not the military's campaign influenced the election result. Indications are that it may have – but in an unexpected way; rather than diminishing Fijian support for the SDL, it strengthened it.

The military's election campaign was linked to its attempt to affirm its post-2000 coup ambitions to 'cleanse' Fiji of trouble-making ethno-nationalists. Had the SDL lost the election, it would have vindicated the military's stance and given it the moral high ground that it wanted to occupy. There was some general public fear that if the SDL won there would be a reprise of the pre-election 'cold war' between the SDL and the military; yet, in fact, the post-election formation of the multiparty cabinet quickly eased the tension, enabling the two sides to re-engage in a peaceful way. In fact the military commander pledged his support for the Prime Minister and the multi-party government. However, the post-election honeymoon period between the SDL government and the military did not last long. In September, the military commander went back on his words, started denouncing the government and demanded that two controversial bills, the Qoliqoli Bill (which was for the purpose of returning ownership of the traditional fishing grounds from the state to the indigenous landowners) and the Promotion of Reconciliation, Tolerance and Unity Bill (RTU Bill) be withdrawn. This created a new phase of hostility and tension, leading to speculations of another military coup in Fiji. This chapter examines the extent and possible impact of the pre-election 'cold war' between the military and the government. The battle for moral and political supremacy between the two institutions provided the backdrop to an otherwise peaceful and reasonably fair election.

Fiji's military plays a pivotal role in shaping the culture, configuration and dynamics of Fiji's politics. The primary role of the Fiji military since its inception in the 1870s has been that of 'internal security', although there were overseas deployments during the Boer War, World War I, World War II, the Malayan campaign and during various international peacekeeping operations since 1978.[1] Nevertheless, apart from its involvement in the 1870's colonial pacification process of coercing rebellious Fijian tribes to submit to British rule, the most direct interventions of the military in political affairs in recent times were the two coups in 1987 and when it moved to remove the coup makers and impose martial law in May 2000. Since 2000, the relationship between the civil state and the military has gone through a turbulent phase; this had a significant impact on the role of the military during the 2006 election.

The evolution of a fighting force

The genesis of the Fiji military is to be found in the years prior to cession to Britain in 1874. Cakobau, a warlord from the powerful chiefdom of Bau, had an army, dubbed the 'Royal Army', that was part of his pre-cession government. The Royal Army, together with servicemen from the Royal Navy (Australian Squadron), formed part of the ceremonial guard during the deed of cession ceremony in Levuka, the old capital of Fiji, on 10 October 1874. After cession, the Royal Army was converted into the Armed Native Constabulary (ANC). The ANC consisted largely of local Fijians under the command of British officers.[2] It was used extensively to suppress the anti-colonial and anti-Christian rebellion of tribal groups in the interior of Viti Levu, the main island of the Fiji archipelago, and in Seaqaqa on Vanua Levu, the second largest island, until it was abolished in 1906. A paradoxical characteristic of the ANC was the technique of using indigenous troops to suppress indigenous uprisings. This was an effective method of 'divide and rule' deployed by the British to maintain its hegemony.[3]

In 1897, as a result of rumours of New Zealand's intention to annex Fiji, the Governor, Sir George T.M. O'Brien, signed an ordinance providing for the establishment of an all-European Volunteer Force 'whose task would be to repel invasion [and] quell local disturbances'.[4] The ordinance was repealed in 1906 and was replaced by the Fiji Rifle Association Ordinance, which required that all the rifle clubs be mobilized under the Fiji Rifles Association in the event of an invasion. During the Boer War (1899–1902), a number of local European residents of British descent volunteered to join the British forces.

It was not until World War I that Fijian troops were sent overseas as a coherent force. They were mostly involved in the Labour Corps because they were not allowed full infantry status by the British. World War II provided the opportunity for Fijians to prove their fighting prowess. Two battalions were sent to the Solomon Islands when the Japanese invaded the Pacific, and fought with distinction under US and New Zealand commanders. It was during the Solomons campaign that Fijians won high praise as 'the best jungle fighters in the world'. During the communist uprising in Malaya (now Malaysia) in 1950, Fijian commandos were mobilized with other Commonwealth troops to crush the anti-colonial rebellion. Again, a significant paradox in this case was the use of colonial troops by the British to quell an anti-colonial movement by other colonized people. Inspired by the exceptional Fijian soldiers' performance in Malaya, the British government recruited 200 Fijians into the British Army in 1960, many of whom joined élite regiments, such as the British Special Air Service (SAS).

Since 1978, Fijian soldiers have been active in peacekeeping operations overseas. These have included the UNIFIL mission to Lebanon as part of the United Nations-sponsored buffer between Israeli and Lebanese-based anti-Israeli groups, and to the Sinai Peninsula as part of the United States-sponsored multinational force to keep peace between Egypt and Israel over the disputed peninsula. Fijian soldiers were also sent to Rhodesia to be part of an international observer group during the first election after independence. After the end of the Cold War, Fiji participated in UN peacekeeping missions in Croatia, Somalia, Cambodia, Afghanistan and Pakistan, Kuwait, Iraq and East Timor, and sent troops to Bougainville as part of a regional peacekeeping force following the end of hostilities there in 1997. Fijians have served in the Regional Assistance Mission to the Solomon Islands (RAMSI) since 2003, under the overall command of the Australian military.

In recent years, a number of Fijian officers have joined the New Zealand and Australian armies, but the largest number have joined the British Army. Since 1997, about 2000 Fijians have been recruited by the British. Many were already trained soldiers in the Fiji military. Private security companies operating in Iraq since the US-led occupation of that country, such as Global Risk Strategies, Homeland Security Limited and Triple Canopy, have recruited close to 1000 former soldiers, serving soldiers (who had to resign) and non-soldiers to perform a variety of security tasks.

The Fiji Navy, an important component of the military, was set up in 1978. The first ships were purchased from the United States and subsequent ones were provided by Australia and Israel, as military aid. The navy has been used mainly for policing the 200-mile Exclusive Economic Zone, and in emergency operations relating to rescues and national disasters. The military's Air Wing was formed after the 1987 coup, when the French provided two helicopters as part of its military aid package to the Fiji military. It was disbanded after both helicopters crashed and after subsequent revelations of huge debts incurred as a result of the aircraft. The profile of the navy was raised as a result of the appointment of its commander, Commodore Frank Bainimarama, as commander of the Fiji military.[5]

Institutional and ideological transformation

The military coups of 1987 brought to the surface a whole series of contradictions that characterized Fiji's post-colonial state. By and large, the contradictions centered on the tension between national identity and civic nationalism on one hand, and communal identity and ethno-nationalism on the other. Theoretically, at the professional level, the military was an institution representing civic and national spirit – but at the ideological and political levels, it was a guardian of indigenous communal interests. The institutional and ideological shift from the former to the latter became the basis for transformation from the 1990s to the post-2000 coup period. By 2006, the military, led by Bainimarama, had aligned itself firmly on the side of national identity and civic nationalism.

The coup in May 2000 was engineered by civilian ethno-nationalist politicians using a small group of élite soldiers from the Counter Revolutionary Warfare Unit (CRWU). Although some soldiers were involved in taking the government politicians (including the Prime Minister) hostage, the military, as an institution, was not. The military intervened to thwart the takeover, firstly through negotiations and then, when negotiations fell through, by way of force. The situation in Fiji was precarious, to say the least, with executive and legislative authority neutralized, the judiciary and police rendered ineffective and the President as head of state powerless to take control of the situation. The military, as the last bastion of state power, intervened to salvage the situation by firstly asking the President to 'stand aside' and then suspending the constitution. These were the two major barriers to the military's intention of dealing with the coup perpetrators directly. The actions by the military were contentious and were seen by some as tantamount to staging a coup. However, to the army, these were the only means to deal with the coup perpetrators in a direct and effective way and to maintain order and rebuild security in a new, chaotic situation.

Upon the removal of the President and the suspension of the constitution under the 'doctrine of necessity', the military proceeded to put in place a re-democratization process, starting with the setting up of a ruling military council, followed by a caretaker government and an election a year later. Meanwhile, the coup perpetrators – consisting of nationalist politicians, former military officers, members of the CRWU and other civilian ethno-nationalist agitators, and including some chiefs – were rounded up and imprisoned. A final attempt by the nationalists to complete their unfinished business and reclaim lost glory, by removing the military commander in a mutiny on 2 November 2000, failed. The plan was to remove the commander and take over the military, release George Speight and the coup perpetrators, and establish an exclusivist ethno-nationalist state called the *Matanitu Vanua*, outlined in a document called the Deed of Sovereignty.[6] The military had vowed to put an end to any attempt by indigenous ethno-nationalists to implement their political agenda and, since 2000, has been campaigning hard against ethno-nationalist ideology. This was a sudden change in the ideological and political orientation of the military – from its role as guardian of indigenous nationalism to one which advocated multi-ethnic statehood. The military made use of nation-wide public relations programs to articulate these changes.

The military public relations machine in motion

While the military had been involved in public relations exercises – such as the use of its band and sports (especially rugby) teams – for many years, it was really only after the 1987 coup that there was large-scale concerted effort to mobilize public opinion and re-create an acceptable public image of the military. Since then, public relations has grown into a professional priority for the military – a priority that has seen it deploying its troops around the country to carry out a variety of integrated tasks. Since the 1987 coups, three phases of image-making can be discerned. The first was the post-1987 coups extensive image re-creation process, the second was the post-2000 coup public relations exercise, and the third was the 2006 election campaign. Each had its own specific objectives, characteristics and methods, although there were basic similarities in terms of the ultimate motive: to win the hearts and minds of the citizens.

The post-1987 coups image reconstruction

The coups in 1987 undermined the Fiji military's international and local image in a significant way. Internationally, the Fiji military was highly respected as a fighting and peacekeeping force and this image took a battering as the international and local media vilified the Fiji military in ways that were unprecedented. From a heroic outfit the military became a demonized mob. While the military was hero-worshipped by indigenous nationalists, it was vilified by other ethnic groups, especially Indo-Fijians, who felt that the coup had victimized them and relegated them to the status of second-class citizens. There were also many Fijian supporters of the Fiji Labour Party (FLP) who were openly critical of the military.

The response of the military then was twofold. The first response was to use force, torture, imprisonment and psychological coercion to intimidate opponents of the coups. The second was to engage in an extensive public relations exercise to convince people of their goals in uniting the country.

There were two audiences for the public relations exercise. The first was the local Indo-Fijian community, which had to be convinced that Indo-Fijian political rule had led to instability and that the coup was to provide the political environment for 'political stability'. The second audience was made up of Fijians who were opposed to the coups and who were seen by the military as probably the biggest barrier to their attempt to unify Fijians under the military's ideological spell. After the coups, a large number of Fijians, especially from the western side of Fiji, had mobilized behind Dr Timoci Bavadra, the deposed prime minister (also from the western side), and the ensuing tension led to various violent incidents.[7] To the military, the Fijians were seen as a greater threat to their designs than the Indo-Fijians because Fijians could easily 'melt' into the Fijian community without being identified, unlike Indo-Fijians who were more 'visible' as a group.

In these circumstances, a number of varied but complementary approaches were used by the military to change its public image and provide legitimacy to its post-coup political consolidation. These included direct community public relations use of sports, entertainment by the military band, introduction of the school cadet scheme, expanded recruitment, establishment of the auxiliary unit, use of symbolism, 'civilianization' of military personnel, and extensive use of the church and of the *vanua*. The details are shown in Table 3.1.

Post-2000 coup public relations

The public relations approach after the 2000 coup was different because of the different circumstances of the coup. The coups in 1987 were direct interventions in which all branches of the military were involved. In 2000, although the élite CRWU of the military was involved in the coup, the entire operation was largely supervised by civilian politicians and nationalist activists. As in the 1987

Table 3.1   The nature of the military's public relations exercises after the 1987 coups

Public relations activity	Purpose and approach
Participatory approaches	
Sports	Organization and involvement in rugby as a public relations tool.
School cadet scheme	Setting up of military cadet schemes in schools as part of the curriculum in order to inculcate military values into young minds.
Auxiliary unit	Setting up of a maritime unit involved in marketing village produce. This was a way of projecting a good image of the military in the rural areas.
'Civilianization' of military and militarization of civilian life	Senior officers were recruited into senior civil service positions and many civilians were absorbed into the military, where they held military rank. They could operate both as civilians and military officers
Expanded recruitment	Expansion of the army under the justification of 'security' and 'employment', and facilitation of Rabuka's promotion to major general.
Rural infrastructure projects	Use of the engineering unit for infrastructure development in rural areas.
Ideological/sentimental approaches	
Brass and rock band	Bands used in concerts and on public occasions to whip up pro-army sentiments.
Use of church	Use of Methodist Church to mobilize Fijian support for the military.
Use of *vanua*	Use of traditional sociocultural links to consolidate military support amongst Fijians.
Media	Use of newspaper and radio (both English and vernacular) to propagate military values and ideas
Symbolism	Use of military, political and cultural symbols (e.g. wide use of military uniform, songs, dances, promotion of warrior mythology etc.) to promote military discourses.
Public show of force	Use of parades and public shows of force to keep the public reminded of who has the power.

coups, the public justification was political paramountcy for indigenous Fijians, although there were complex economic and political factors associated with the coup. The military as an institution intervened to thwart the coup and free the members of parliament who were held hostage. The military succeeded in doing this after weeks of cat-and-mouse negotiations with the hostage-takers, culminating in the use of force by the military to neutralize the coup makers.

At the height of the hostage drama, the military and the coup makers were engaged in an intensive propaganda and counter-propaganda warfare never before seen in Fiji. The coup makers produced dozens of leaflets making allegations – ranging from deposed Prime Minister Mahendra Chaudhry's conspiracy to get India to take over Fiji, to President Ratu Mara's blood-drinking antics. The coup makers deliberately planted rumours to keep the public in a state of fear and panic, hoping that this would work in their favour, especially in terms of the military bowing down to their demands. George Speight, the self-styled coup leader and international public image of the coup, was the major official mouthpiece through which the 'aspirations' and 'cause' of the coup were articulated. The military responded by attempting to nullify the coup-makers' claims and vilifying their leaders.

Meanwhile, the military engaged in active public relations throughout the country (discussed in further detail later in this chapter). The exercise continued even after the coup rebels were overpowered. There was an increase in the media blitz, with the military frequently making public statements, and a special Fijian program on Sundays for the commander, Commodore Frank Bainimarama. The military bands (both the brass and rock bands) were used extensively for public entertainment to provide a 'feel-good' factor during the depressing times after the coup, and also to project an image of the military as defender of public interests. However, political developments after the coup saw the relationship between the government and the military deteriorate and the military's public relations stance took a different twist, both in style and intensity.

The post-coup/pre-election military–government power struggle

Unprecedented tension between the government and the military preceded the 2006 election and provided the backdrop to the military's pre-election campaign. From 2003 onwards, Frank Bainimarama directed sustained criticism against the government on a range of issues, including his own reappointment as military commander, reconciliation policy, the size of the military budget and the performance of politicians and public servants. But he reserved his greatest censure for the government's attitude towards those involved in the 2000 coup. That attitude, in his view, was revealed by the RTU Bill introduced into parliament in 2005. He thought the government too lax, and demanded that the rule of law be upheld so as to ensure that no more coups took place.

Military objections to government policy first appeared following attempts by Qarase's government to reduce the sentences imposed on soldiers convicted of mutiny at the Sukunaivalu Barracks in Labasa during the 2000 coup. Some government members also called for the release of George Speight and his accomplices. The military resisted this move, arguing that the rule of law should take precedence over political emotions and that those who had been found guilty must serve their full sentences. The war of words caused some public anxiety, compelling Bainimarama to publicly state on 15 April 2003 that there was not going to be a coup.[8]

Things came to a head some months later when Bainimarama's contract expired and the government threatened not to renew it. Bainimarama called for the removal of Jeremaia Waqanisau from his post as CEO of the Ministry of Home Affairs, and was alleged to have threatened him personally. Bending to the pressure, the government appointed Waqanisau as ambassador to China soon afterwards. To mobilize support within the military, Bainimarama asked his senior officers to pledge allegiance to him. Five senior officers refused, saying that their loyalty was to the military not to the commander. The officers, Colonels Ratu George Kadavulevu, Alfred Tuatoko, Samuela Raduva, and Akuila Buadromo, and Commander Timoci Koroi, a naval officer, were asked to resign as a consequence. The five alleged that, during the stand-off with the government, Bainimarama had asked the senior officers to organize a coup. The government requested President Josefa Iloilo to establish a commission of inquiry into the case, but he refused on the grounds that Bainimarama had given assurances that the military had no intention of overthrowing the government. Because Bainimarama was the biggest obstacle in the government's attempt to free the 2000 coup rebels, the government – from 2001 to 2004 – had been pursuing indirect methods to replace him.

Bainimarama was offered diplomatic positions in the UK, Malaysia and New Zealand, all of which he turned down. The government even promoted him to vice admiral and backed his unsuccessful application for the post of UN field commander in Kuwait. At the end of the day, Bainimarama opted for a contract renewal to enable him to see through the conviction and punishment of the coup rebels. With considerable reservation, at the end of January 2004, the government eventually extended Bainimarama's contract for another five years.[9]

The government soon discovered it had reappointed one of its greatest critics. From October 2004 onwards, Bainimarama engaged in repeated public criticism of government policy; it continued until the election was held in May 2006. He criticized the government for organizing Fiji Week for the purpose of inter-ethnic and inter-religious national reconciliation. The ceremonies included public apologies by some chiefs – some of whom were involved in the 2000 coup – to the Indo-Fijian community for the suffering they had endured during the crisis. The military refused to take part in the ceremonies, saying that the apologies were meaningless without justice taking its course.[10] The military again condemned the government for the early release of the former vice president, Ratu Jope Seniloli (who was convicted of coup-related crimes), and argued that it made a mockery of the judicial process and was a threat to national security. This drew criticism from a number of government politicians, who accused the military of meddling in political affairs. Moreover, after the resignation of Seniloli, Bainimarama publicly supported the idea of having a non-Fijian take over Seniloli's position, saying he favoured someone with excellent leadership skills for the post, regardless of race. The government saw his statement as unjustified interference with the affairs of the state. The tension reached a level of seriousness that raised widespread public concern in late 2004 and early 2005. Bainimarama sent out a series of warnings to the government that the RFMF 'would put pressure on anyone' who dared tamper with national security, saying that 'if we don't act, this country is going to go to the dogs and no investor will want to come here'. He likened the military to a tiger sitting in a corner. 'You have to give it [the tiger] room', he warned. 'If you don't give it room, it will bite you.'[11]

In April 2005, two convicted coup plotters – Ratu Naiqama Lalabalavu (now Minister for Fijian Affairs) and Ratu Josefa Dimuri (now Minister of State for Agriculture, Alternative Livelihood and Outer Islands Development) – were given early release after serving just eleven days of their eight-month prison sentences. Bainimarama delivered a salvo of criticism against the government, provoking an equally fiery reply from Home Affairs Minister Josefa Vosanibola, who warned the commodore that he would be 'disciplined' if he spoke to the media without consultation with him. A public argument between the two followed. And more conflict came with the non-renewal of the contract of Australian lawyer Peter Ridgeway, the Deputy Director of Public Prosecutions, who, on 20 June, was ordered by the government to leave Fiji. Bainimarama saw this as an attempt to undermine the coup investigations, especially because Ridgeway had made significant inroads into the coup investigations and prosecutions.

The most important source of military–government tension, however, was the controversial RTU Bill, which the government hoped would settle the post-coup matters once and for all. Amongst other provisions, the Bill proposed to set up a Reconciliation and Unity Commission with powers to grant compensation to the coup victims as well as provide amnesty for the coup perpetrators as part of the process of national reconciliation. The military argued that providing amnesty would undermine the rule of law and would encourage future coups. The military was adamant that all convicted coup perpetrators were to serve their full sentences. When the earlier draft of the Bill was being discussed in parliament, the military sent a number of officers to watch and listen to the proceedings and at the same time provide a show of force to tell the government and parliament that they were serious.

Other issues also soured the relationship between the government and the military. Amongst them were allegations by the military in August 2005 of plots to remove the president, with some alleged plotters having links with the government.[12] In October of the same year, the military spokesperson, Lieutenant Colonel Orisi Rabukawaqa, made scathing allegations regarding corruption in the Registrar General's office involving illegal Chinese immigrants. In the same month, the military publicly opposed its budgetary allocation, stating that it wanted more autonomy over its finances rather than having to go through the CEO for Home Affairs. The military saw the bureaucratic control of their budget as tantamount to 'political control' of the military by the Ministry for Home Affairs. Bainimarama was further infuriated by the fact that, although the military budget announced on 4 November had been increased from F$67 million in 2000 to F$76.4 million for 2006, it was still short of the F$84 million the military wanted. Due to the shortfall, the military was forced to apply cost-cutting measures. Earlier, in October, the commander had been fined for overspending the military budget, but this was later overturned by the Supreme Court.

The situation grew tense in December 2005 as the military demanded the resignation of the CEO for Home Affairs, Lesi Korovavala, because of the delay in the re-trial of the 20 soldiers charged with mutiny during the 2000 coup, resulting from difficulties in sorting out the contract for the judge advocate, Graham Leung. Bainimarama threatened to 'send his boys' down to the CEO's office to 'secure it' if nothing was done quickly. The stand-off led to the intervention of Vice President Ratu Joni Madraiwiwi, who stepped in to cool down the situation. On 31 December 2005, Bainimarama stated that the military no longer recognized Josefa Vosanibola as the minister responsible for the military, stating 'The Military now is on its own and is not answerable to anyone'.[13] He further stated that legislation being proposed by the Qarase government was 'racist' and based on self-interest, not on the interest of the nation. In a related pronouncement he reassured the nation that, 'I am the one who is standing for democracy and the rule of law because the Government and its officials only want the laws to be made to suit them'.

The 2005 tensions spilled over into 2006 and intensified. Towards the end of January, the Auditor General, Eroni Vatuvoka, accused the military of contempt of court for refusing to follow the Supreme Court order to open up the military welfare fund, about which the military has been protective, arguing that the fund is a private one not a public one.

In addition to the RTU Bill, the other Bill which attracted the wrath of the military was the Qoliqoli Bill, which was meant to legally enforce indigenous ownership and control of traditional fishing grounds currently under state jurisdiction. The military commander saw the Bill as a threat to security, on the grounds that it has the potential to cause dispute and conflict within the Fijian community. He assured the country that there was not going to be any coup, in response to widespread rumours of a possible takeover of the government.

In early January 2006, Bainimarama called on the government to resign because of its inability to resolve the 2000 events and also because of its 'racist' legislation. He claimed:

> They have let people out of jail on one excuse or the other. How can they [the Government] sleep at night – do they have a clear conscience?…This government is incompetent…It's better that they resign so that better people can do the things that [are] supposed to bring us good.[14]

The tension was worsened a few days later when the military learned that the government had approved a shipment of arms for the police. The military stated that they were not consulted and it appeared that the government was deliberately arming the police against the military. This was denied by the government as well as by the police and the matter was laid to rest after the Commissioner of Police visited the military headquarters to explain that the arms were standard police equipment, were only for use in confined places, and were needed to replace dilapidated old police weapons.

One of the most high profile incidents was when the military issued a media release in which it threatened to take control of the country if the government failed to 'continue the good fight'.[15] This was in response to a newspaper-reported comment by Pita Nacuva, the acting Foreign Minister and now Speaker of the House of Representatives, that the attitude of the military was based on 'sour grapes'.[16] When the president of the FLP, Jokapeci Koroi, appeared on Fiji Television supporting a 'government take-over', the incident created a political crisis that saw the intervention – and resolution of the conflict – by the Vice President, Ratu Joni Madraiwiwi, on 16 January. Nevertheless, the impact of Bainimarama's outburst had consequences within the military itself. The land forces commander and deputy to Bainimarama, Colonel Jone Baledrokadroka, confronted his boss about his outburst. This led to a stand-off between the two that culminated in the dismissal of Baledrokadroka from the army.

In responding to criticism regarding his anti-government stance, Commodore Bainimarama stated, 'I really don't have any business in the political running of government. My outbursts are not political. It's about national security…

Security to me and the RFMF means a clean and corrupt-free country'.[17] In a meeting between the Prime Minister and the Commodore convened by the Vice President, it was agreed that both Bainimarama and the commissioner of police be invited as observers in the Security Council and also that there be more direct communication between the Prime Minister and the Commodore through regular meetings to discuss issues of common concern. The Prime Minister also assured Bainimarama that the next election would be conducted fairly, without government interference. The Vice President urged the two parties to be more responsible in their dealing with each other, saying, 'It is critical that elements in the Government and the military exercise circumspection and discretion in their dealings with each other at all times'.[18]

However, that was not the end of the matter. The Minister for Home Affairs lodged an official complaint with the commissioner of police against Bainimarama for his threat to overthrow the government and asked him to determine whether or not the commodore's words were seditious or treasonous.[19] The Minister for Home Affairs told Bainimarama that he would withdraw the complaint to the police on the condition that Bainimarama apologize for his threat of 8 January to depose the government. As expected, Bainimarama refused to apologize, saying, 'Asking me to apologize for making that statement is an insult to the working people of this nation because, simply, it is my job...No one is going to attack the military without any retaliation from the military – not even under any agreement'.[20] On the advice of his senior officers, he retaliated by withdrawing commitment to the agreement made with the Vice President on 16 January; in particular, any further talks with the Prime Minister were to be put on hold.

Pre-election psychological warfare: The 'truth and justice' exercise

As the tension between the government and the military increased in tempo, and as the election approached, the military embarked on a nation-wide program to combat what they saw as 'lies' perpetrated by 'opportunists' in government. The announcement for the commencement of the campaign was made by Bainimarama on 10 March:

> We will go into villages and tell them the real truth of what happened and what is being
> done...I will advise the people because they cannot continue to advise a government that
> continues to make it okay for those that went to jail to get back into society. By not educating
> the people about doing what is right, it is willfully lying and misleading them.[21]

The proposed campaign was supported by the FLP, which by that time had aligned itself with the military. The leaders of the Conservative Alliance and the New Nationalist Party called for Bainimarama's arrest for fomenting instability. The SDL saw the proposed campaign as an attempt to undermine its power base while some, like former prime minister Sitiveni Rabuka, saw it as a perfectly constitutional process.

In response to accusations of interfering in elections, the military stated that what they were involved in was an 'exercise' not a 'campaign'. The military's confrontation with the government even extended to the Supervisor of Elections, Semesa Karavaki. The military commander attacked the election preparation as being disorganized; Karavaki, himself a territorial soldier, reciprocated by saying that Bainimarama should not interfere in the election process. In fact, Bainimarama had initially opposed the election date, saying that it was too early given that the registration process had a lot of anomalies.

The military's strategy in the election campaign was twofold. The first element, the 'truth and justice' exercise, was focused largely on re-educating the public about the 2000 coup; the second element of the strategy was direct campaigning against the SDL party. The two were closely linked because the SDL was seen as supportive of the 2000 coup, both its ideological justification and its political execution.

Bainimarama openly spoke of his campaign to discourage his soldiers and friends from voting for political parties and candidates he deemed 'racists' and 'discriminatory'. This attracted flak from SDL campaign manager Jale Baba, who urged Bainimarama to stand for the election to prove his worth, as well as from Alexander Downer, Australian Minister for Foreign Affairs, who warned Bainimarama about interfering in politics.[22]

Bainimarama's campaign was very direct. He urged voters not to listen to fearmongers and 'opportunists' who claimed that a victory for the FLP would spell instability for Fiji. He then asked voters to keep an open mind, saying, 'Don't choose a party just because it's a Fijian party. Choose an Indian or Chinese if his policies are for your benefit'.[23] The military defended its campaign saying that it was not against any particular party or politician; it was primarily for the purpose of asking the voters to vote with their conscience.

A case which further infuriated Bainimarama was the sacking of Sitiveni Raturala, a popular Fijian radio host who, on 9 March, hosted a show with Bainimarama. In response to allegations by the military that the government had a hand in the sacking, the CEO of the Fiji Broadcasting Corporation Limited (FBCL), Francis Herman, said that Mr Raturala had breached his contract. It later emerged that the issue had to do with Raturala giving the whole air time to Bainimarama without allowing time for the public to ask questions live on air. The military warned the FBCL against muzzling its voice and, in a surprise move, Raturala was quickly drafted into the military's public relations team.

The military public relations team

The military public relations team consisted of 30 to 40 soldiers – in teams of three to four – who visited various provinces in Fiji. To make sure that they were welcomed, men from the provinces were deployed to carry out the public relations tasks. The normal approach was for the soldiers to ask, traditionally, for permission to enter the village to carry out their exercise. Often, the presentation was accepted, although in some cases the soldiers' requests were ignored. Fijian protocol usually demands that visitors are welcomed, no matter how disliked they are.

After the *sevusevu* ceremony (welcoming ceremony), a request would be made for *veitalanoa* (discussion) to take place. The soldiers would explain the purpose of their visit and would then proceed to make their verbal presentation. Questions and answers would follow. The whole process would take place in the presence of the chiefs and other leading members of the village and often involved kava-drinking. Upon completion of the task, the soldiers would head for another village.

Although the military said that their campaign was successful, it is not easy to provide evidence for this. The fact that they were readily accepted into the villages and given the chance to make their presentation did not mean that people were convinced by their message. Furthermore, even if the messages were convincing there was still doubt about whether or not the impact was sufficient to sway the people's votes away from the SDL. The landslide victory of the SDL could mean that the military's campaign had very little impact on Fijian voters' behaviour.

Conclusion: implications of the military's public relations activities

The direct participation of the military in the 2006 election shows that the aftermath of the coup of 2000 still shaped, to a great extent, the political and ideological climate in Fiji. The post-coup public relations effort by the military sought to undo the 'lies' which justified the 2000 coup, and the effort intensified as election fever heated up. The military was bent on ensuring that the political trajectory before and after the election was based on the principles of multiracialism and transparency – although the approach used was highly questionable in the context of modern liberal democratic norms; in particular, the line of demarcation between the civil state and the 'non-political' military was blurred.

Normally, in a parliamentary democracy, the military operates under civilian authorities so that its coercive power is manageable and accountable. A military with special interventionist powers may not be good for stability and democracy. The role of the military is one of the dilemmas of post-colonial militaries, in which there have been difficulties in making it align with and accountable to civilian rule. This dilemma is partly historical because, since the colonial and post-colonial period, many post-colonial militaries have been used as active components of political governance by colonial and post-colonial élites. During the colonial days, as we have seen in the case of Fiji, the role of the military was to help maintain internal security. The Fiji military was groomed as part of the Fijian élite power structure, and its intervention in 1987 on behalf of Fijian nationalism was a violent manifestation of this.

The 2000 coup was not strictly military, but a civilian intervention undertaken by civilian nationalists with the help of some soldiers. Moreover, the military intervened to smash the coup, imposed martial law and helped put Fiji back on the road to democratic governance. The military was of the conviction that the coups of 1987 and 2000 were not to be repeated, and that all possible steps should be taken to ensure this. The military saw their public relations exercises as ways of educating the people about the 'evils' of coups. The SDL was seen as an institutionalized supporter of the 2000 indigenous nationalist ideals.

While the government and various foreign governments, such as those of Australia and New Zealand, denounced the public relations exercise as 'political interference', many people in Fiji, especially the Indo-Fijians and other ethnic groups, saw the military as a saviour, as the only institution that would protect their rights and well-being from extremist Fijian hegemony. The country was divided into two groups of citizens; those who felt that the military had overstepped its authority, and those who believed that, despite the extra-legality of its actions, the military was right in terms of ensuring political stability.

The military's public relations effort may have driven Indo-Fijians into the FLP camp – as they felt confident that the military would provide them with the sought-after security if the FLP won – and driven Fijians towards the SDL – as they felt alienated and threatened by the military's perceived alignment with the FLP.

The tension between the military and the government took an unexpected turn. After the SDL party won the election, it offered the FLP nine cabinet seats and, consequently, a multiparty cabinet was set up. This had an immediate effect on the political perceptions and behaviour of the citizens, as well as those of the military. People of all ethnic groups welcomed the move and the military made a commitment to support the multiparty government. The political tension that had characterized the pre-election and election period suddenly disappeared. Most of the issues of contention between the military and the government suddenly became obsolete. And, as a result, the military disbanded its public relations group and, in its place, created a small but professional public relations team of six people, and shifted its effort from direct propagation of views to the public towards community service by its service arms, such as engineering, and naval search and rescue.

The question then is, will the new political climate be sufficiently sustainable to see the blossoming of a new civil state–military relationship in which the professional lines of demarcation are respected? Or will future political developments re-create the conditions that led to the pre-2006 election 'cold war'?

This all-important question, however, became somewhat superfluous when, in September, the 'cold war' between the military and the government reared its ugly head again. The military demanded that the government withdraw the Qoliqoli and the RTU Bills, spawning further tension between the two institutions; by November this had developed into a national crisis leading to speculations about a possible military coup.

Notes

1   See Ratuva, S. 2003. *Storm in Paradise*. Life and Peace Institute, Uppsala.
2   For details, see Brown, S. 1998. *From Fiji to the Balkans: History of the Fiji Police*, Fiji Police Force, Suva.
3   Sanday, J. 1991. 'The coups of 1987: A personal analysis', *Viewpoint*, 30(2).
4   Brown, 1998. *From Fiji to the Balkans*, p.24.
5   Ill feelings between the navy and land forces have existed, but not to the extent of causing tension and conflict. Bainimarama was born 27 April 1954, on Bau island. He joined the Fiji Navy on 26 July 1975. He was appointed acting chief-of-staff in November 1997 and confirmed in April 1998. He was named commander of the army on 25 February 1999, to replace Brigadier General Ratu Epeli Ganilau, who resigned to enter politics.
6   See Ratuva, S. 2000. 'Another failed coup attempt', *Pacific Journalism Online*, http://www.usp.ac.fj/journ/docs/news/nius3090shoot.html. This was confirmed by Captain Stevens, leader of the mutiny during the military court martial.
7   See Ratuva. 2003. *Storm in Paradise*.
8   Fijilive.com, 15 April 2003.
9   Fiilive.com, 1 February 2004.
10   Fijilive.com, 12 October 2004.
11   'Frankly speaking', *Review*, December 2004.
12   Fijilive.com, 24 August 2004.
13   Fijilive.com, 31 December 2005.
14   *The Fiji Times*, 4 January 2006.
15   Fijilive.com, 7 January 2006.
16   *The New Zealand Herald*, 10 January 2006.
17   *The Fiji Times*, 16 January 2006.
18   *The Fiji Times,* 16 January 2006.
19   Fijilive.com, 25 January 2006.
20   Fijilive.com, 29 January 2006.
21   *Fiji Sun*, 10 March 2006.
22   ABC television interview reported by Fijilive.com, 3 March 2006.
23   Fijilive.com, 9 March 2006.

4

Songs in sheds: some thoughts on the sociology of Fiji elections

Paul Geraghty[1]

The way elections are conducted in Fiji differs in many ways from the way they are conducted *ovasis* (a Fiji English term that usually means Australia and New Zealand, but can also include the United Kingdom and other places where *kaivalagi* – people of European origin or 'white' people – reside). These differences are, at least in part, due to indigenous Fijian customs. In this chapter, I attempt to answer such questions as why, in elections in Fiji, there is little or no heckling but lots of prayers and hymns, why people turn up for elections in their Sunday best, and the origin and function of that peculiarly Fijian institution, the electoral shed and the songs sung therein.

History

The first general election in Fiji was in 1963.[2] This was the first time that Fijians had universal suffrage and participated in a secret ballot. On the other hand, Indians in Fiji had been voting for representatives to the Legislative Council since 1929, and Europeans since 1904.[3] Fijians had taken little interest in national affairs, being more concerned with Fijian society and local Fijian politics, in particular the Bose Levu Vakaturaga (Great Council of Chiefs). However, they were not total strangers to the concept of elections. As with many aspects of the westernization of Fijian society, it was probably the Methodist Church that introduced the Fijians to electoral voting, with the Fijian administration not far behind. Some form of voting had existed in the

Methodist Church since 1866,[4] and the practice of electing office holders, such as *turaganikoro* (village headmen) and *mata ni tikina* (district representatives), by *laveliga* (show of hands) or by *vakaio* (acclamation) seems to go back a long way, probably to the 19th century.[5]

The Fijian word currently used for 'election' or 'ballot' is *veidigidigi*,[6] which is recorded as early as 1941.[7] Etymologically, it means 'many people choosing someone' – so is a very apt neologism, and whoever its coiner was deserves credit. The same word was used in the Bible – the current translation of which dates from 1900 – but there it seems to have a different meaning, translating as 'partiality' (1 Timoci 5:21) and 'make distinctions' (Jemesa 2:4). There is at least one alternative form, *veidigitaki* (literally 'one person choosing another'), which appeared in the Fijian language newspaper *Volagauna* in 1963,[8] but I have been unable to determine whether or not it had any general currency at that time. Certainly, it is not used today.

It is commonly believed that 'consensus' is the traditional Pacific way of making decisions, but this notion appears to be relatively modern. Before the arrival of Christianity and western government, decision-making was fairly exclusively by way of *lewa vakaturaga* (chiefly decision) – though if the people for whatever reason did not like the *lewa* of a particular *turaga*, they often found ways of getting rid of him or her and appointing another. With the westernization of political institutions, at least at a certain level, decisions were made by the will of the majority, and determined by voting. A now retired member of a certain provincial council told me that voting was only recently, within the last 10 or 20 years, replaced by 'consensus' – usually a steamrolling by the chair.

Politics is religion, campaigning is preaching

In the Fijian worldview, politics is, if not exactly religion, something very close to it. One indication – though I am always wary of reading too much hidden meaning into homonyms, as many anthropologists do – is that *vunau*, the word for 'preach', is also used for political campaigning. Indeed, political speeches are usually listened to with the silence and respect afforded a sermon, even when the 'congregation' patently has no intention of voting for the speaker.

Heckling is a *sine qua non* of campaigning in places like Britain[9] – but is very rare in the Fijian context, although it does occur to some extent among the Indian community. In nearly 30 years of living in Fiji and reading *The Fiji Times* daily (and other newspapers occasionally), I have, to my recollection, only come across the word 'heckle' once – and even then it was spelled 'hackle'.

The shed

To most native speakers of English, a shed is a small building for storing gardening tools or coal for the fire to tide you over the long winters. In Fiji, however, the word has a unique meaning. Essentially, it is a temporary open-sided structure, usually with bamboo posts and a corrugated iron roof, erected for many kinds of gatherings. In colonial times, there was a roaring trade in bamboo from the *bilibili* (bamboo rafts) that brought bananas down to Nausori by way of the Wainimala and Wainibuka rivers, precisely for this purpose; but this has all but ceased today.

The best-known Fijian word for the shed is *vakatunuloa* (sometimes shortened to *tunuloa*), on the origins of which there has been much speculation. It may have some connection with Tunuloa, on the Natewa peninsula in Cakaudrove, but the exact nature of the connection is obscure. The earliest reference is in Cargill's dictionary of Lakeba Fijian,[10] where *vakatuniloa* is defined as 'a porch or shade', and its Rewa equivalent is given as *vakatunuloa*. The 1839 definition suggests that it may have had a rather different meaning at that time. The word is not found in the first-published dictionary of Fijian,[11] but does appear in the most recent Fijian dictionary, in which both *tunuloa* and *vakatunuloa* are defined as 'shed'.[12] There are also a number of regional names for the same structure, such as *bolabola* and *covacova*.

In Fiji Hindi, the word for shed is remarkable in that it has at least four different forms. In most of Vanualevu it is *jhaap*, in most of Vitilevu it is *mad'haa* (the apostrophe after the 'd' indicates that it is retroflex), in some parts of rural Nadi and Bua it is *pandaal*, and the Fiji-English *shed* is used in Suva and Lautoka. It would be interesting to find out the original meaning or meanings of these terms. Given that none of them is a borrowing from Fijian, it would seem that this artefact was also present in traditional Indian culture, though some of its functions may well have been adapted from the use of the *vakatunuloa* in Fijian society.

The function of the shed is to shelter, fodder and ply with grog, visitors at a gathering, most frequently a funeral, but also weddings and, in Fijian society, *vakataraisulu* (the lifting of mourning for a chief) and, particularly in the islands, *vakatawase* – new year celebrations – when swarms of urbanites return to their villages for a week or two of celebration and feasting on fish and *lairo* (land crabs). The function of sheds at elections is similar, but they are erected by political parties or independent candidates, and function like the exclusive lounges run by airlines at airports, except that the customers are provided with the kinds of food and drink that are more popular in Fiji. The expectation is the same: that in return, the customers will continue to 'fly with that particular airline' – or vote for a particular party. No modern election is complete without some party complaining about the *agepije* or *liumuri*[13] of voters who go through their sheds and enjoy their *palau* and *yaqona* and then go and tick the name of some other party on the ballot form[14] – and complaining that the sheds are an inordinate drain on resources. But next election there they will be again, because voters have come to expect them. It could also be argued that they are symbols of the political power of the party or of the individual erecting and financing them. I believe that they are a relatively modern institution – certainly they seem not to have been present during the 1963 general election.

In Fijian custom, large gatherings – such as *tevutevu* (exchange of wedding gifts) and *vakataraisulu* – are subsumed under the name *solevu*, and I would like to suggest that, for Fijians, the election is a kind of *solevu*. Hazlewood[15] defines a *solevu* as 'a large number of people gathered together to present property to a chief, or to a town, on which occasion they generally *meke* (dance) and make *magiti* (large quantities of food); a kind of Fijian ball; feast, or fair'. The presence of the *vakatunuloa* or shed is one of the indications of this functional equivalence, but there are others. Clothing is one. Fijian dress codes are relatively strict (at least from the perspective of most westerners); when a Fijian goes out to a public occasion, he or she will dress appropriately. They will dress *vakavavalagi* (in the western fashion, e.g. trousers or jeans for men, skirts or jeans for women) if they are going to the cinema, or a concert of western music, or a western-type gathering, such as Suva's annual Hibiscus Festival. But if it is a *vakaviti* (traditional Fijian) occasion, such as most religious gatherings and *vanua*-based fund-raising events called *adi* (which are in many respects similar to the Hibiscus Festival), then 'traditional' Fijian dress is 'de rigeur' – *sulu vakataga* (pocket *sulu*) for men, and usually *suluira* (ankle-length under-skirt) and *jaba* (knee-length dress) for women.[16] For elections, Fijians typically dress in this traditional fashion. In many parts of Fiji, various groups of participants in the recent elections, including even groups of officials, chose to buy and wear specially tailored uniforms – *kalavata* or *puleta* – in much the same way as happens with *solevu*.

The songs

The songs that are sung in election sheds by Fijians, particularly when victory has been announced but often before that too, are taken from a very limited repertoire of songs that are associated with *solevu*. They could almost be numbered on the fingers of two hands: *Da mai laveta, Lomaloma, O Bau na yanuyanu, Liwavi au na tokalau, Noqu vanua*, and not many more. They are songs of *cibi* – triumph.[17] They are not songs that would normally be played on the radio, not songs that anyone would request on any of Fiji's numerous phone-in radio programs. They are patriotic songs, expressing pride in the nation or a particular region. Maybe not coincidentally, they all appear to have been composed in the 1950s or 1960s, so would have been popular at the time of the first general election in which Fijians participated. They belong to a very limited canon of songs that are appropriate in a very restricted context: *solevu* – and elections.[18]

Notes

1 My heartfelt thanks are due to Jon Fraenkel, Mosmi Bhim, Bruce Yeates, Adi Tiriseyani Naulivou, Vani Catanasiga, Jiaoji Rarubi, Andrew Thornley and Eremasi Tamanisau for their generous help with this chapter. Blame for any faults, however, is entirely my own.

2 Ravuvu, A. D. 1988. *Development or Dependence: The Pattern of Change in a Fijian Village.* Institute of Pacific Studies, University of the South Pacific, Suva. pp.80–81.

3 Meller, N. & James A. 1968. *Fiji Goes to the Polls: The Crucial Legislative Council Elections of 1963.* East-West Center Press, Honolulu, pp.11–13.

4 Thornley, A. 2002. *Exodus of the I Taukei: The Wesleyan Church in Fiji 1848–74.* Institute of Pacific Studies, University of the South Pacific, Suva. pp.481–483.

5 For instance, Native Regulations published in 1949 stipulate that village representatives to the district council should be elected by a show of hands (*A Lawa I Taukei* 1949:146).

6 Long vowels are often indicated by means of a macron – a straight line over the vowel. As macrons are not available with this typeface, for the sake of linguistic accuracy, in the following words the underlined vowels are the long ones: veidigidigi, lewa, solevu and puleta.

7 Capell, A. 1941. *A New Fijian Dictionary.* Australasian Medical Publishing Co., Sydney.

8 Meller & James. 1968. *Fiji Goes to the Polls.* p.145.

9 In a mock election held at my secondary school, Rugby School in England, the Tory candidate planted a pseudo-socialist heckler in the audience and had him shout out, 'What about the workers?' To which the candidate instantly replied, 'We are the workers – workers for a better Britain!'

10 Cargill, D. et al. 1839. Feejeean Dictionary. MS A 2065, Mitchell Library, Sydney.

11 Hazlewood, D. 1850. *A Feejeean and English Dictionary: With Examples of Common and Peculiar Modes of Expression.* Vewa, Feejee [Viwa, Fiji], Wesleyan Mission Press.

12 Capell. 1941. *A New Fijian Dictionary.*

13 Both mean 'duplicity' or 'treachery' – the first from Hindi, the second from Fijian – and both are used in Fiji English.

14 Lal, 'Elections' (n.d.:2) quotes a doctor who was defeated in an election as saying, 'The voters are treacherous bastards. They will drink your *yaqona*, eat your *palau* and vote for someone else'. Lal (n.d.:5) also reports that 'a Labour strategist tells his supporters to pluck coconuts (Labour symbol) by climbing the branches of the mango tree (Federation symbol). Translation: drink your opponents' *yaqona*, eat their food, go through their sheds, but vote for Labour'.

15 Hazlewood. 1850. *A Feejeean and English Dictionary.*

16 Geraghty, P. 1997. 'The ethnic basis of society in Fiji', in Lal, B.V. & Vakatora, T.R. (eds). *Fiji Constitution Review Commission Research Papers Fiji in Transition* 1:1–23. School of Social and Economic Development, University of the South Pacific, Suva.

17 Note that the so-called challenge of the Fiji national rugby team, the *cibi*, is not a challenge at all (which would be a *bole*) but a chant of victory.

18 Although this paper focuses primarily on the Fijian community, I would like to offer also a few comments on similarities and differences in the Indian community. Both emphasize prayer as part of election meetings, and in both there is a tendency to dress formally at meetings and during the elections, though there is overall more formality, and less noise, in Fijian meetings (Lal n.d. pp. 6–7; Mosmi Bhim pers. comm. June 2006.).

5

Election observation missions to the 2006 Fiji election

Graham Hassall and Jeannette Bolenga[1]

> Never believe what you read in the papers and particularly from observers
> who are paid a lot of money for a tropical holiday (Internet chatter)

The general feeling of unease in Fijian society in the lead-up to the 2006 general election made the presence of election observers of more than academic interest. In his statement of 1 March 2006, announcing that the election would be held over the period 6–13 May, Prime Minister Qarase extended invitations to seven potential observer groups. A media release from the Ministry of Information, Communications and Media Relations stated:

> The Prime Minister…announced that on behalf of Government, he would be extending invitations to the Commonwealth, the United Nations, the European Union, the Pacific Islands Forum, and, bilaterally, to Australia and NZ, to send Observers to monitor the Elections in Fiji. The PM will also write to the Vice Chancellor of the USP [the University of the South Pacific] to invite its School of Governance to monitor the Elections in close liaison and co-ordination with the Office of the Supervisor of Elections. Mr Qarase explained that Government was doing this because it has full confidence in the Electoral Commission and the Office of the Supervisor of Elections in independently conducting the General Elections in a free, open, fair and impartial manner, and with full transparency. [2]

The invited organizations undertook observer missions of differing scale and emphasis, although each in its own way in accord with the Electoral Act 1998 and a set of 'Guidelines for International Electoral Observers' supplied by the Fiji Elections Office. From the government's point of view, the presence of observers no doubt added to the transparency of the democratic exercise it was about to undertake. The invitation was both a sign to the international community that the government was confident of the ability of the Elections Office to implement the election, and an acknowledgement that some of Fiji's multilateral and bilateral partners had concerns about the election on the basis of Fiji's turbulent recent past (not to mention that Australia, New Zealand and the European Community had each donated substantial sums to help cover the costs of the exercise).

Others apart from the government called for observer presence at the 2006 election. For example, in September 2005, while the Commonwealth Parliamentary Association was meeting in Fiji, opposition leader Mahendra Chaudhry asked the Commonwealth Secretary General to send a monitoring group, citing election abuses of 2001 as a reason.[3]

Earlier Fiji elections

International observer groups had attended Fiji's general election in August 2001 following a request from the Fiji government to the United Nations (UN) – in response to which a UN Electoral Observer Mission was approved by resolution of the Fifty-fifth General Assembly '…as part of the effort to promote and consolidate new or restored democracies'.[4] Japan announced grant assistance of US$370,000 and ten support staff. At least 55 international observers were accredited for the 2001 poll – 40 represented the United Nations, 12 represented the Commonwealth Secretariat, and three represented the European Union (EU).[5] The UN report found the elections to be credible while expressing concern about technical problems '…including serious issues related to the electoral rolls'; about the 'unnecessarily complex' preferential voting system; and about the requirement of section 99 of the constitution for a multiparty cabinet to be established.[6]

The origin and purpose of observer missions

The practice of election observation has evolved rapidly in recent years, with standards emerging for long-, medium- and short-term observations. Among the lead agencies that have established guidelines are IFES[7] in North America, International IDEA[8] in Europe, and the UN Elections Office. In October 2005, 21 lead agencies gathered in New York to endorse the 'Declaration of Principles for International Election Observation'.

Within the Asia Pacific region, the practice of observation emerged in such divergent circumstances as the post-Marcos years in the Philippines and the relatively more staid political environments of Australia and New Zealand. The Australian Electoral Commission regularly invites electoral experts and practitioners to participate in observation of Australian general elections. The PIANZEA (Pacific Islands, Australia and New Zealand Electoral Administrators) network, which links the electoral commissions of Australia, New Zealand and the Pacific Islands, has also coordinated a number of election observation missions in the region.

The inclusion of a non-government international observer group, based in the Governance Program at USP, reflected the government's awareness of that program's interest in the development of electoral practices in Pacific Island countries. The USP had formally applied for status on 15 February, and this was granted by Supervisor of Elections Semesa Karavaki on 10 March, pursuant to the announcement made nine days earlier by the Prime Minister. In granting observer status the Supervisor commented:

> I am pleased to provide Observer accreditation to you and your team from the Electoral Studies Unit at the Pacific Institute of Advanced Studies in Development and Governance, USP …I fully support your Goal and Objectives. Independent observers have a vital role to play in any election and as outlined in Objective 7 of your Terms of Reference I am looking forward to your Report and any recommendations you may have which might improve the relevant Legislation and the procedures we use in the Elections Office.[9]

By the time of polling, 6–13 May, several additional observer groups had been given accreditation, and yet others came to Fiji to observe in an unofficial capacity. The PIANZEA network gathered a team of eight observers, from four regional countries – although there was no formal reporting process or coordination. Officials from the Papua New Guinea Electoral Commission came to learn any lessons in advance of their general election, scheduled for 2007. Transparency International sponsored a delegate from its Vanuatu branch. Due to the short time frame, the United Nations was unable to organize a mission.

In broad terms, each observer mission was interested in whether or not the elections were conducted in a 'free and fair' manner. No doubt the EU, following through with its interest in Fiji since 2000, had one eye on post-conflict restoration of democracy and the rule of law, and the other on ACP relations[10] and the future of the sugar industry. The Commonwealth, which has been monitoring the restoration of the rule of law in Fiji over a period of time, fielded a six-member team led by Keith Knight and including one Pacific Islander (Paul Bengo, Registrar of Political Parties in Papua New Guinea) and five additional experienced election-watchers.[11]

The 39-member EU observer mission was the best funded (with approximately FJ$2.4 million), most organized, and most visible (not least due to its accommodation at the Holiday Inn of its international observers and support staff). An advance team visited Fiji in March to gauge the viability of mounting an observation exercise and to determine its scope. Having decided to proceed, twelve 'long-term' observers arrived in Fiji on 10 April, and were despatched in pairs to six regions around the country. A further twelve short-term observers arrived prior to polling; they were also dispersed across the islands after an intensive period of induction and orientation. Nine members of the group were EU staff resident in Fiji. Additional staff were sourced locally to monitor media and provide logistical support. Local academics and specialists were engaged to provide background briefings at a pre-poll retreat. Chief observer Istvan Szent-Ivanyi, a Hungarian representative to the European Parliament, arrived on 3 May, shortly before polling commenced on the sixth. The mission announced that its report would be issued at the end of August.

The 23-person Pacific Islands Forum team was led by Forum Secretary-General Greg Urwin. Rather than organizing an independent program, the New Zealand government contributed nine observers to the Forum team. Although the Australian Government did not send an observer group, five diplomats from the Australian High Commission in Suva were registered as 'independent observers'. Fiji resident and New Zealand citizen Father David Arms was the single independent observer not attached to a diplomatic mission or university team. The United States Embassy accredited 15 observers and the New Zealand High Commission, three.

The Governance Program at USP organized a 16-member observer team, comprising faculty members, students and administrative staff.[12] Smaller teams of two or three persons had previously observed general elections in Cook Islands (2004), Vanuatu (2004), Solomon Islands (2006) and Samoa (2006), under a three-year EU-funded program, 'Transforming our Communities through Good Governance', run at PIAS–DG.[13] The much larger exercise in Fiji was made possible by the fact that all participants were living in the country, as well as by a general expectation that the Electoral Studies project at PIAS-DG would take on this civic role, particularly as no domestic observation teams were permitted. A budget of approximately $20,000 was established. Teams volunteered to observe in each of Fiji's four districts (although an effort to have an observer travel to Rotuma was thwarted – reportedly by excess rain on the island's airstrip).

Observer accreditation, orientation and coordination

The Supervisor of Elections commissioned a consultant to take responsibility for accreditation and coordination of observer missions. Only 'international' missions were allowed, and members of these missions were required to obtain formal accreditation.[14] This required their agreement to comply with guidelines for observers provided by the Elections Office.[15] No applications were denied by the Elections Office, and 121 observers were accredited.

Observation was defined to include observation and evaluation of the impartiality and functioning of the Office of the Supervisor of Elections and its team of electoral officials; the voter registration process and the establishment of the electoral roll; the voter education campaign; the election campaign; the voting process; the vote count; the determination of electoral results and their dissemination; and access to and use of the media.[16]

International observation was defined as commencing 'when International Electoral Observers have arrived in Fiji and have received their identity documents confirming their accreditation by the Office of the Supervisor of Elections' and ending 'with the departure of the Observer Group from Fiji'.[17] No Fiji citizens could participate in international observer missions.[18] Once accredited, observers had the right to obtain a visa, to move freely throughout the country, and to communicate freely with all parties involved in the elections in some way, including political parties, other social and political organizations, and officials involved in electoral processes. They were to communicate their findings to the Office of the Supervisor of Elections and seek his response before making these views public.[19]

In return for this access to all facets of the election process, international observers accepted a number of obligations: they agreed to respect the constitution and the laws of Fiji, to exercise their role with 'impartiality, independence and objectivity', and to wear their identity cards at all times.[20] While they could not 'interfere in, or impede, the normal course of the electoral process' and were to '…refrain from issuing individual statements about the electoral process to the media', they had an obligation to '… notify electoral officials of any action or conduct which they believe to be serious infringements of the electoral process'.[21] Diplomats accredited in Fiji and who were 'designated as International Observers', were free to '… exercise their functions without prejudice to the provisions of the Vienna Convention on Diplomatic Relations'. [22]

Upon accreditation, observers were provided with copies of all relevant legal and constitutional provisions, and with the Elections Office's policy manuals. The Fiji government's Information, Technology and Computing Department provided IT support to the Elections Office website (http://www.elections.gov. fj), at which information on constituencies, candidates, parties and electoral provisions was regularly updated. Immediately prior to polling, the Elections Office provided a one-day induction for international observers and, during the polling and count periods, observers benefited from the Supervisor of Elections' daily press briefings.

Shortly before polling commenced, observer missions met with each other and with major players in the electoral process, partly to share thoughts on how each group felt the process was proceeding, but also in an effort to collaborate and avoid duplication in fieldwork. However, while these meetings brought familiarity with each group's composition and strategies, they did not result in significant cooperation in practical terms.

Determining observer mission effectiveness

Radio New Zealand International reported that more than 100 observers 'from the EU, the Commonwealth, the Pacific Forum and the USP' had assembled to monitor the elections.[23] Given that one assessment put the cost of observer missions to the Fiji 2006 election at FJ$4.7 million (and the cost of the election exercise as a whole at FJ$48 million),[24] questions concerning the value of observer missions are clearly worth asking. At the same time, one may ask whether or not international observers had any particular training or expertise that would allow them to make pronouncements as to whether the elections were 'free and fair'. A related question concerns whether or not electoral actors have taken any lessons whatsoever from previous observation reports.

The impact of fieldwork

Although observer missions were not to interfere or intervene in any way in electoral processes and were to remain as neutral as possible, there can be no doubt that the presence of so many observers had an impact on political actors, if not on the election outcome itself. The major parties expressed their support for the presence of observer teams, each pointing to issues that required careful watching.[25] The National Federation Party, for instance, called on international election observers to 'observe the deliberate breaches of section 134 of the Electoral Act'; it was concerned about parties continuing to use the media to conduct campaigns, and at advertisements that included the Fiji Labour Party banner appearing in papers during election week.[26] Some parties and NGOs shared their concerns about aspects of the campaign by faxing letters to observer missions. Experience in the field suggests that some polling officials were more welcoming of election observers at polling stations than they were of the media, even though the media carried identity cards that gave them equal status. Does this point to the need for more civics education for officials on the role of the media during elections?

Observer missions and media

The observer missions were interested in how various media outlets reported the election, and in freedom of speech in general. The EU mission, in particular, undertook extensive media content analysis. On 19 May the *Fiji Daily Post* printed a small item in which the EU mission described the newspaper's election coverage as having 'a general tendency to report in neutral tone' – with 34.7 per cent of coverage going to the Fiji Labour Party and 28.5 per cent to the Soqosoqo Duavata ni Lewenivanua.[27]

For its part, the media reported the activities of observers and were keen to solicit opinions on 'the topic of the day'. Because voting proceeded over ten days and because observers were required to withhold judgemental commentary until completion of their observation period (and to avoid statements made as individuals, as opposed to the joint statement issued by the group as a whole), the observer presence was reported widely, but without substantial commentary. This did not stop the media from associating 'neutral' observers with political issues of the period. *Fiji Daily Post*, for instance, addressed the military commander with such headlines as "PSSST! WATCH IT FRANK!",[28] and used editorial space to urge observer groups to take note of attitudes expressed by the military.[29]

The impact of statements

The official and informal statements of observer missions had unavoidable impacts on public opinion. Virtually all groups observed a common set of problems (errors and omissions on the roll; inadequate supply of ballot papers; last-minute changes to polling-booth locations, etc), but no group reported evidence of intentional manipulation of rolls, ballots, or counts. Whereas some defeated candidates and parties offered their alleged evidence of (or at least hinted at motivations behind) intentional foul-play, such claims failed to gain support in the public mind, or in the views of the observer teams. The results that were announced, no matter how polarized they appeared in terms of ethnically defined voting patterns, were consequently accepted by the voters in general. The presence of so many observers in the field, paying particular attention to the manner of the opening and closing of polling stations, the security of ballot boxes during transportation to the count centres, and the integrity of the counting process, made it difficult for claims of ballot fraud to be sustained. The presence of observers seemed to have a similar effect on claims that ballots printed in excess of officially required quantities were somehow moved from the government printer and used in one or other constituency. Observers had full access to the premises of the government printer at Vatuwaqa and their presence, together with that of numerous other agents, including police personnel, made the prospect of ballot-smuggling highly improbable.

It is not clear which observer missions first directed their findings to the Supervisor of Elections, as required by Article 7 of the International Code. The Head of the EU's Electoral Observation Mission, Istvan Szent-Ivanyi, tabled a report on the election in the European Parliament's 'Committee on Development' on 30 May,[30] well ahead of the Mission's return visit to Fiji to make its final report at the end of August.

The Commonwealth mission's 'Statement on Voting' of 14 May suggested that while there were some shortcomings, the process was 'reasonably well managed'. The full statement, together with a picture of the team, appeared on page five of the *Fiji Daily Post*.[31] The Commonwealth mission's 'Statement on the Counting and on the Electoral Process as a Whole' of 19 May called the election 'credible' and, while expressing concern about shortfalls in electoral administration (notably problems with voter registration and with late distribution of ballot papers), focused on the 'challenge of representation based on ethnicity'.[32] On 20 May the head of the Commonwealth mission, Mr K.D. Knight, publicly requested the commander of the Republic of Fiji Military Forces to accept the results and to refrain from interfering in politics – mentioning at the same time his preference that the electoral system move away from its ethnic basis.

On 2 June, the final report of the Commonwealth mission was submitted to the Commonwealth Secretary-General, who forwarded it the following week to the Prime Minister of Fiji, the chairman of the Electoral Commission, the Supervisor of Elections, the leaders of the main political parties and Commonwealth governments. It was released to the media on 12 June 2006.

At the outset of its mission the Forum Secretariat team announced it would issue a statement to the Elections Office, to the government, and then to forum member countries.[33] It declared the results 'free and fair' on 15 May.[34]

The USP team issued a statement on 15 May that was reproduced in the *Fiji Daily Post* on 16 May.[35] Although small deviations from proper procedures were observed, the group commended the untiring efforts of election officials and the police who worked alongside them, especially given the short time frame between the date the elections were called, 1 March, and the date polling began, 6 May.

The EU mission issued a preliminary statement on 18 May that appeared in the press the following day.[36] In it, the EU commented on electoral administration, voter registration, electoral campaigns, media coverage, complaints and appeals, participation of women, postal voting, voting and counting. Amongst other things, the report noted that the Elections Office had received a total of 65 written complaints, but noted that the procedure for the hearing of these complaints was not clear, and the results of the hearings were not to be made public.

The broad outlines of each observer mission report contained similar themes and concerns: inadequacies in registration, ballot printing and distribution, and identification of polling stations; the high number of invalid votes; and the handling of postal and overseas votes.

After the election observation exercise, questions will continue to be asked about its utility and effectiveness. Did the presence of such a large collection of international observers influence the behaviour of any of the most significant actors? Did the army become more restrained after an informal information session between the commander of the armed forces and EU representative Szent-Ivanyi? Did losing candidates and parties limit their post-ballot protests on account of the 'second opinion' that observers were able to offer the public? Did individual scrutineers, returning officers and polling agencies alter their activities by reason of the fact that an observer might suddenly appear at the door? Answering such questions is not at all easy, but the reporting of some 100 observers, who had nothing invested in the outcome of the poll apart from concern for the condition of democracy in Fiji and for the integrity of the country's system of government, appears to have given the public a sense of ease about the outcome that made it possible to move to the next difficult item – formation of government.

Notes

[1] The authors acknowledge the research support of Mosmi Bhim and Amrita Nand, and additional information from Mark Borg and Gyan Deo.

[2] Ministry of Information, Communications and Media Relations. 'Prime Minister announces 2006 general election dates'. Media release, 1 March 2006.

[3] 'Fiji opposition to lobby for election monitors'. PACNEWS, 5 September 2005.

[4] United Nations. Secretary General. 2001. Support by the United Nations system of the efforts of Governments to promote and consolidate new or restored democracies. United Nations Electoral Observer Mission for the general elections in Fiji in August 2001, General Assembly. 56th Session. Agenda item 35. UNGA document A/55/L.90.

[5] UNDP project. Fiji Elections 2001. <http://www.undp.org.fj/elections/Media/index.htm> (accessed 15 August 2006).

[6] United Nations Secretary General. 2001. Support by the United Nations system of the efforts

of Governments to promote and consolidate new or restored democracies United Nations Electoral Observer Mission for the general elections in Fiji in August 2001, General Assembly. 56th Session. Agenda item 35.

[7]   International Foundation for Electoral Studies.

[8]   International Institute for Democracy and Electoral Assistance, an inter-governmental agency based in Stockholm.

[9]   Semesa Karavaki, Supervisor of Elections, pers. comm. 10 March 2006.

[10] The states of Africa, the Carribean, and the Pacific, in partnership with the European Union.

[11] These were Sheila Roseau, executive director, Directorate of Gender Affairs, Antigua and Barbados; Keith Knight, Rajabu Kiravu; Albert Mariner; Beta Tentoa and Canon Grace Kaiso. Administrative support was provided by Christopher Child. The Commonwealth team obtained immediate and extensive media coverage and promised to report by 22 May ('We're just here to watch', *Fiji Daily Post*, 2 May 2006, p.2).

[12] They were Mosmi Bhim, Samuala Bogitini, Jeannette Bolenga, Ian Campbell, Jon Fraenkel, Graham Hassall, Katayoun Hassall, Dolores Joseph, Mili Kaitani, Joe Ketan, Haruo Nakagawa, Rae Nicholl, Tui Rakuita, Sadhana Sen, Jagjit Singh and Etika Vulavau. Although no domestic observers were allowed, the USP team included Fiji citizens, who were granted the status of 'international observer' on the basis that the University is a regional organization.

[13] The Governance Program at USP is one of the programs run by PIAS-DG at USP.

[14] Available at <http://www.elections.gov.fj/press/20060324-2.html>.

[15] Election Office, Guidelines for International Electoral Observers, Fiji General Elections: 6–13 May 2006.

[16] Election Office, Guidelines for International Electoral Observers, Fiji General Elections: 6–13 May 2006.

[17] Election Office, Article 3. Duration of International Observation. Guidelines for International Electoral Observers, Fiji General Elections: 6–13 May 2006.

[18] Election Office, Article 4. Fiji Citizens. Guidelines for International Electoral Observers, Fiji General Elections: 6–13 May 2006.

[19] Election Office, Article 7. Rights and Privileges of International Observers. Guidelines for International Electoral Observers, Fiji General Elections: 6–13 May 2006.

[20] Election Office, Article 8. Obligations of International Observers Guidelines for International Electoral Observers, Fiji General Elections: 6–13 May 2006.

[21] Election Office, Article 8. Obligations of International Observers. Guidelines for International Electoral Observers, Fiji General Elections: 6–13 May 2006.

[22] Election Office, Article 9. Status of Diplomats. Guidelines for International Electoral Observers, Fiji General Elections: 6–13 May 2006. This right was not understood by some media outlets. When Ambassador Larry Dinger received headlines on 9 May for expressing concern at the number of names missing from rolls ('Poll Raises U.S. Concern', *Fiji Daily Post*, 9 May 2006, p.1.), his status as an 'official observer' was hotly contested in the press. *Fiji Daily Post*'s 10 May editorial, entitled 'Larry, Curly and Moe?' asked who had invited the US ambassador to 'go around observing our national elections and commenting on them while they are in process. Who gave Larry Dinger permission to snoop around the country untrammelled and without authorization? Our elections office? The Fiji Government? Or is

it the self-arrogating prerogative of Americans to just do what they please in other people's backyards?…There has been none of the same outspokenness from other foreign mission observers while the elections are on, but for some reason Larry has felt unencumbered by past protocols. His comments that deficiencies in the electoral process need attention and remedy are either gratuitous or designed to destabilize an already tense situation'.

23   'EU Official Arrives in Fiji for General Elections', Radio New Zealand International, 4 May 2006, < http://www.rnzi.com/pages/news.php?op=read&id=23899> (accessed 26 August 2006).

24   Coutman, B. & Chandra, J. 'Election Costs', unpublished seminar paper, University of Fiji, 2006.

25   *Fiji Daily Post*, 3 May 2006, p.3.

26   *Fiji Daily Post*, 6 May 2006, p.3.

27   'EU Chief Observer Praises Daily Post', *Fiji Daily Post*, 19 May 2006, p.2.

28   *Fiji Daily Post*, 2 May 2006, p. 1.

29   Editorial comment included 'How can the election be 'free and fair'? Isn't it already 'damaged goods'? How can Fiji have a 'free and fair' election when the commander is constantly interjecting his opinion into the democratic process – as though he were just another citizen, and without the weight of arms behind him? Are the EU and Commonwealth observers taking notes? Are they impressed with his coercive self-importance?' *Fiji Daily Post*, 6 May 2006, p.3.

30   Online at <http://www.europarl.europa.eu/news/expert/event_by_day_page/22-2006-150/default_en.htm> (accessed 26 August 2006).

31   'Reasonable poll says C'wealth', *Fiji Daily Post*, 15 May 2006, p.3.

32   The Commonwealth's statement on counting was published in Fiji Daily Post, 20 May 2006, p.5 under the heading 'Poll fair, now the challenges'.

33   *Fiji Daily Post*, 16 May 2006, p. 4.

34   Statement reproduced in *Fiji Daily Post*, 16 May 2006, p. 7.

35   'University of the South Pacific Observer Mission', p.7.

36   'EU Observers' verdict', *Fiji Daily Post*, 19 May 2006, pp.7, 9.

6

The cycles of party politics

Jon Fraenkel and Stewart Firth

Fiji politics runs through cycles of consolidation and fragmentation. For the Fijian parties, consolidation is the response to adversity, and fragmentation ensues whenever the heat of national politics cools down. The 2006 election, when Fijians united to back the main Fijian party, reflected such consolidation. But where was the adversity, and where the heat of politics? The truth was that the 2001 election campaign had never truly ended, but flowed almost seamlessly into that of 2006. Meantime, the political temperature had been kept high enough to command the attention of the Fijian voter. Otherwise, regional, provincial and *vanua* rivalries might have reasserted themselves more strongly, and more Fijians might have stopped to ask why they continued to live in villages and urban settlements where conditions were little better than decades before, and what the government had done about it.

For years after 2001, the dominant political issue was who should be in the government and who should not. The restored constitution required power-sharing, but the largely Fijian-backed Soqosoqo Duavata ni Lewenivanua (SDL) had not formed a multiparty cabinet after winning in 2001. The Fiji Labour Party (FLP) had taken the matter to court, and, for the next three years, debate raged over the legitimacy of the 2001 process of government formation. It became the central issue in Fiji politics. Not until November 2004 did Labour finally abandon its legal quest for inclusion in cabinet, and party leader Mahendra Chaudhry take up the position of leader of the opposition. No sooner had he had done so than the government launched the controversial Promotion of Reconciliation, Tolerance and Unity (RTU) Bill, causing the Republic of Fiji Military Forces (RFMF) to challenge the government's legitimacy and threaten a coup. As a result, the question 'who rightfully rules' – which elections are supposed in theory to settle – was never truly resolved by the 2001 poll, and Fijians were repeatedly reminded that the legitimacy of 'their' government and its legislation was in question. Under such conditions, what united the Fijians continued to be more important than what divided them.

Splintering of Fijian political parties occurs when the pressure is off, as in April 1977, in 1987 and again in 1999. Each decade's crisis triggers a countervailing rotation, in the latter years under the auspices of successive new political parties. The Alliance Party healed Fijian divisions at the polls of September 1977 and 1982, the Soqosoqo ni Vakavulewa ni Taukei (SVT) obtained the unanimous backing of the Bose Levu Vakaturaga (Great Council of Chiefs, or GCC) in 1991, and the SDL rose on the crest of yet another bid for Fijian unity in the face of adversity in 2001 and 2006.

For the Indian parties, by contrast, adversity often historically gave birth to internecine struggles. So it was in the 1930s, after the initial defeat of demands for a 'common roll', when a decade of struggles ensued between the Arya Samaj and orthodox Sanatanis, between those originating from south and north India and between Hindus and Muslims.[1] So it was in the wake of April 1977's constitutional crisis, when the 'dove' and 'flower' factions tore the National Federation Party (NFP) apart. And so it was in the wake of the 1987 coup, when the coalition between the FLP and the NFP broke down and was replaced by vigorous intra-communal competition. Yet this did not happen after the 2000 coup. Instead, the FLP went from strength to strength; it improved on its 66 per cent of Indian support in 1999 by obtaining 75 per cent in 2001 and 81 per cent in 2006. Had the FLP fragmented, in line with the previous cyclical experience, the 2006 election might have been very different. As a result, the events of 2000–2001 remained the crucible of party politics at the 2006 polls, and the 2006 election represented a sharpening of the political alignments already witnessed at the 2001 poll. This chapter explores that story.

The February 2001 Chandrika Prasad case proved a watershed in Fiji party politics.[2] Judges found that the interim administration had no legal standing.

One possibility was to reconvene the former parliament and so potentially restore the pre-2000-coup government. In theory, judges pay no attention to political practicalities. The law is the law, and constitutional interpretation stretches only so far as allowed by discerning the intent of the framers of those fundamental laws. In practice, the separation of powers between judges and legislators is often hazy, and so it was in Fiji. The Chandrika Prasad judgement was viewed by some as 'the case that stopped a coup'.[3] Yet, instead of requiring the reinstatement of the Labour-led government, the Court of Appeal ruling left space for the Fijian interim administration to repeat the process of selection of a new head of state and, thereafter, to re-legitimize itself by calling fresh elections. Not only had the military failed to issue the appropriate decrees abrogating the constitution, but President Ratu Sir Kamisese Mara had not, as everyone thought he had, resigned from office on 29 May 2000. Instead, it was a letter from President Mara enquiring about his pension entitlements on 15 December 2000 that became formally accepted as entailing his resignation. That meant that there were three months before a new president had to be selected, in accordance with the constitution.[4] And of those three months, only 15 days were left when the judges delivered their telling verdict on 1 March 2001. The no-longer-recognized interim president, Ratu Josefa Iloilo, thus had 15 days to repeat the process of his own selection via the GCC, which he successfully did.

In the wake of the Chandrika Prasad case, Fiji's political parties re-crystallized in new and unexpected ways. For the interim government, then Deputy Prime Minister Ratu Epeli Nailatikau appeared before the Court of Appeal to announce the government's acceptance of the verdict, so the alternative of defiance was straightaway, and fortunately for Fiji, rejected.

Three legal possibilities arose in the wake of the judgement: (i) the return of the Chaudhry government, (ii) the advent of a 'national unity' government or (iii) fresh elections.

Few thought the first option politically practical, and no attempt was made to restore Mahendra Chaudhry as prime minister. A majority of Fijians, roused to the defence of indigenous paramountcy by the events of 2000, would not have tolerated it. In any case, the former People's Coalition led by Chaudhry had splintered at the grass roots level even before the coup, and backbenchers

from the Fijian Association Party and Veitokani Lewenivanua ni Vakarisito had
been deeply implicated in the events of 19 May 2000. One was imprisoned on
Nukulau with George Speight.

The President's initial choice, reportedly, was the second option – a
'Government of National Unity', based on the 1999–2000 parliament, and led
by ethnic Fijian Deputy Prime Minister Dr Tupeni Baba, rather than Chaudhry
– but that did not eventuate either.[5] Moves to dislodge the FLP leader and
install Baba in his place commenced, spearheaded by veteran FLP members
Krishna Datt and Pratap Chand. However, Chaudhry supporters boycotted
the meetings, leaving them without a quorum. Meanwhile, the Labour leader
visited Fiji's re-installed President, Ratu Josefa Iloilo, and offered a dissolution.[6]
It was a tactically deft manoeuvre. If what was on the agenda was the formation
of a new unity government that would draw cross-party support, Tupeni Baba
appeared the most acceptable leader, particularly if he had the backing of the
majority of the 37 FLP MPs. If, instead, the outcome was to be a fresh election,
Chaudhry's strengths in rallying the party faithful and pulling out the cane belt
vote made him the likely choice for the leadership.

While the FLP argued, the President chose the third option, the one most
likely to calm ethnic Fijian passions. He dissolved parliament and swore in
Laisenia Qarase to lead the government until elections could be held. Having
been an 'interim' prime minister, Qarase became a 'caretaker' one, with the
advantage of incumbency to take into an election.

Chaudhry's triumph in the FLP internal battle was not without costs. The
defeated Dr Tupeni Baba formed the breakaway New Labour Unity Party
(NLUP), drawing with him a number of long-standing indigenous Fijian FLP
members, and some support from civil society activists and Gujarati businessmen.
Critically, however, Baba failed to retain the support of key moderate Indian
leaders. Both Krishna Datt and Pratap Chand were subsequently disciplined by
the party, although they remained within the fold and soon reappeared on the
front benches. At the 2001 poll, Chaudhry and Baba were fierce opponents: Baba
claimed a vote for Chaudhry would result in another coup; Chaudhry replied
that Baba was desperate to be prime minister. Baba's NLUP fought a spirited
campaign but it won only 4.5 per cent of the national vote, and secured only
two seats. By the 2006 election, it had vanished without trace.[7]

The Chandrika Prasad case also entailed a reconfiguration on the Fijian side of politics and the emergence of a new Fijian party, the SDL. To begin with, Fijian leaders were deeply divided. Efforts to unite Fijian parties in a 'Fijian Forum' to fight the impending election were plagued by faction fighting, as was the GCC itself. Verata chief Ratu Ilisoni Qio Ravoka described deliberations at the Chiefs' Council as marked by 'personal differences, backstabbing, *vanua* rivalry, political rivalry, jealousy and traditional power struggle'.[8] SVT leaders were reluctant to cede their position as the dominant Fijian party, despite strong indigenous criticism of their role in saddling Fiji with the 1997 constitution and precipitating the crisis of 1999–2000. The GCC withdrew its support for the SVT and declared an intention not to favour any one political party. That proved the death blow for Rabuka's SVT party, an organization originally invented as the chiefs' party. Schisms quickly became apparent in the SVT leadership[9], and even before the polls the party machinery was ebbing away.[10] The SVT was able to pick up only 8.6 per cent of the Fijian vote at the 2001 election, and vanished into oblivion in 2006.[11]

The launch of the SDL in May 2001 signalled both continuity and change in Fiji politics. In a bid to remain prime minister, Qarase initiated a constitutional review process aimed at providing a 'safety-valve' for indigenous discontent, and announced that government funds were to be spent on a pro-Fijian blueprint, including plans for the construction of a tar-sealed road through the rebellious province of Tailevu, near Speight's home area of Wainibuka. Qarase, himself a Lauan, received the backing of former president, Ratu Sir Kamisese Mara, and the Lau Provincial Council, mending what had been, in the Fijian tradition, a gross insult to the former long-serving prime minister, the Tui Nayau Ratu Mara, perhaps the last of Fiji's high chiefs with great political stature (*mana*) and a corresponding position in the legislature. Lauan, as well as Indian, shops and buildings had been destroyed in the unrest on 19 May 2000, Lauan houses had been stoned, and the notion that Lauans had for long captured and monopolized the resources of mainland Viti Levu had gained currency even in government circles. At the height of the post-coup crisis, Ratu Inoke Takiveikata, the Qaranivalu – highest chief of lowland Naitasiri[12] – had gone so far as to say that outer islanders (meaning Lauans) should not 'talk because you are visitors to Viti Levu' at a meeting of the GCC.[13] Yet peace was made among the Fijian leaders, at least temporarily. When the SDL was formed in Tamavua village, Naitasiri, its founding president was none other than the Qaranivalu (until he was later convicted and imprisoned for involvement in the mutiny of November 2000). The former president played his part in the new Fijian political reconciliation, despite animosities that festered beneath the Lauan surface. Now retired and at home on Lakeba, Ratu Mara ensured that his daughter, Adi Koila Mara, stood aside, giving Qarase a free run at the Lau Fiji Provincial Communal seat.

The SDL quickly became the new dominant mainstream indigenous Fijian party, despite scandals before the election. Chief among these was an 'agricultural scam' associated with the distribution of pitchforks, outboard motors and other agricultural implements to Fijian villagers, particularly in coup-supporting areas of Tailevu and Naitasiri. The 2001 achievement of the SDL in capturing 50 per cent of the Fijian vote, and winning 32 seats in the new parliament, was extraordinary, and saluted as such by defeated veteran SVT politicians, such as Jim Ah Koy and Berenado Vunibobo. The SDL captured all the urban Fijian communal seats, as well as Lau and most of mainland Viti Levu. Most remarkably, the antagonism between Fijian parties in western Viti Levu, the Party of National Unity and the Bai Kei Viti, had allowed the SDL to triumph also in that part of the country.

Another six seats were won by the Conservative Alliance–Matanitu Vanua (CAMV), a new political party formed by customary chiefs and politicians who were implicated in the 2000 coup. The leader of the CAMV, Ratu Naiqama Lalabalavu, was the Tui Cakau, the leading chief from the Cakaudrove area, and the highest-ranking chief in one of Fiji's three confederacies. George Speight himself was elected for the CAMV from his prison cell, although he soon lost his seat owing to his failure to attend three consecutive parliamentary sittings. He would not have been able to obtain the Tailevu North Fijian seat without the support of the Cakobau chiefs from Bau Island (see Tuitoga, this volume). The president of the Methodist Church publicly blessed both parties, offering Fijians the cohesion of shared faith in place of factionalization among traditional rulers.

The FLP also emerged triumphant in its communal heartlands, seeing off the potential threats from the NFP and the NLUP. In the open constituencies, it was able to repeat the 1999 achievement of capturing common roll seats in the cane belts. Beyond that, contests – as in 1999 – depended on the ordering of minor party preferences. Yet this time, the smaller parties' preferences did not favour the FLP. Prior to the polls, these parties had clubbed together in a 'Moderates Forum' – comprising the NLUP, NFP, SVT, UPP and FAP. These parties gave each other second, third and fourth preferences, but, critically, tended to place the FLP as last preference and the SDL in penultimate position. That decision gave the SDL nine of the open constituencies; CAMV preferences gave the SDL an additional three of these seats, and one was secured at the first count, without relying on preference votes. In addition, the SDL won the North Eastern General Communal seat, bringing the total to 31, compared with the FLP's 27.[14] The 'Moderates Forum' parties were left with only four seats in parliament, and soon lost two of those after Kenneth Zinck crossed the floor to join the government and after the courts overturned the Nadi Open result, giving an additional seat to the FLP.

The outcome left both large parties short of a majority, and there were brief rumours of a seemingly impossible coalition between the ousted prime minister, Mahendra Chaudhry, and his nemesis, the coup-supporting CAMV. The CAMV, however, wanted an amnesty for the coup convicts, including George Speight, a concession that presumably would have been a public relations disaster for the FLP. Predictably, it was the SDL and CAMV that joined forces to form a government. This was to prove a government plagued by controversy from its inception, both domestically and overseas. As prime minister, Qarase issued the constitutionally required invitation for the FLP to join the cabinet, but in a way that welcomed refusal. When Chaudhry accepted the offer, the Prime Minister responded that the conditions attached to the FLP's acceptance were too onerous, and that the FLP had rejected the Prime Minister's condition that cabinet be based on SDL policy. The court found otherwise, and a succession of high profile multiparty cabinet cases commenced that were used by Mahendra Chaudhry mainly as a method for de-legitimizing the government. Had the court been obeyed, Qarase potentially would have had to unwind his coalition with the CAMV, which was not entitled to participate in cabinet according to constitutional rules (except as part of the entitlement of the party of the prime minister). In addition, Chaudhry claimed vote-rigging at the 2001 polls, also pressing this before the courts.

From the 2001 election onward, the question of 'who rules?' in Fiji was kept permanently at the centre of Fiji politics, with another court case perpetually around the corner that would decide, again and again unfavourably, on the constitutionality of the Qarase-led government. No sooner had Mahendra Chaudhry finally given up and accepted the position of leader of the opposition in late 2004, than another issue emerged that again threatened the legitimacy of the government, and rekindled the 'who rules?' issue, albeit from a less familiar direction. The RTU Bill threatened, among other provisions, to provide an amnesty for coup-related prisoners. It brought to a head the long-simmering antagonism between the Republic of Fiji Military Forces and the Home Affairs Ministry (see Ratuva, this volume). Military commander Frank Bainimarama threatened to stage a coup if the Bill were passed. For the FLP, this seemed a blessing in an odd disguise. In the run-up to the 2006 poll, its party president, Jokapeci Koroi, in an ill-advised TV interview, astonished the viewing public by backing the military's threats to seize political power. Chaudhry refused to condemn the statement, despite having been part of the FLP government overthrown by a military coup in 1987. That the aspiration for political power could encourage such short-term pragmatism seemed extraordinary to most.

The perpetual centrality of struggles over the composition of government during the period 2001–2006, first due to the multiparty cabinet controversies and second due to the RTU Bill, gives some insight into the nature of communal party politics in Fiji. On both sides, parties mobilized around the race issue, even if the position of the FLP as the representative of the minority community and as the victim of the coups enabled it to couch its appeal in a more universalist doctrine. The SDL used race politics overtly. The 2001–04 multiparty cabinet controversies kept the need for 'Fijian unity' perpetually to the forefront and checked the potential for provincial splintering. The military's new threat to Fijian rule in the wake of the RTU Bill generated an unprecedented mobilization. SDL campaign manager Jale Baba brought busloads of Fijian villagers to demonstrate in support of the Bill outside the makeshift parliament at the police hall at Nasese in June 2005. Days earlier, uniformed military personnel had occupied the public gallery in parliament, and FLP MPs had staged a walkout. For the SDL, the RTU Bill, replete with its messages of Christian forgiveness and charity, proved a highly effective electoral tool (see Bhim, this volume). When public consultation on the Bill went out to the provinces, it generated overwhelming endorsement for government policy.[15] Had the SDL instead sent out a more direct request for electoral support for the party itself, it is doubtful that backing would have been so wholehearted.

The RTU Bill was also a concession to the CAMV, designed to subdue militant criticism over the continued incarceration of Fijians on coup-related charges. When CAMV president Ratu Naiqama Lalabalavu was himself imprisoned for 'unlawful' assembly during the mutiny at the Sukanaivalu Barracks back in 2000, it threatened to break the governing coalition. Yet, Ratu Naiqama and several of the other prisoners were released on compulsory supervision orders. As former New Zealand prime minister Geoffrey Palmer pointed out in a talk before the Fiji Law Society on 22 June 2005, scope to pardon prisoners already existed through the Prerogative of Mercy Commission under the 1997 constitution. What then was the intention of the Bill? The RTU Bill potentially achieved something that other possible responses did not, in the sense that an amnesty wipes out the damage to status in a way that a pardon or premature release do not. Was the Bill primarily a political device, rather than a practical measure? Was this a Machiavellian tactic on the part of the government? The Bill, after all, also played an important political role in other respects. In the run-up to the 2006 poll, the CAMV liquidated itself, with prominent ministers joining the SDL and, in most cases, keeping their seats. That political objectives played their part is also suggested by the shelving of the RTU Bill before the election, although an amended version was due to be put before cabinet thereafter.

Whichever way, the liquidation of the CAMV altered the calculus of Fijian politics. After the 2001 election, the presence in the governing coalition of a substantial ethnic extremist party helped to shape the basic direction of government policy. Government initiatives over the period 2001–2005 were nearly all aimed at placating the perceived threat from Fijian nationalists. Prime Minister Qarase's speeches regularly revisited the experience of the SDL's predecessor, Rabuka's SVT, emphasizing the danger of the mainstream Fijian party being outflanked by more militant nationalists. In reality, the most likely option was always that CAMV ministers would join the SDL. But could they carry the grass roots of the party with them in that transition? Would radicals who had been left out in the cold, like former Fiji Intelligence Services boss Metuisela Mua or the coup-prisoners themselves, vigorously challenge the new orientation? What would be the reaction in those villages in the Wainibuka area of northern Tailevu or in Cakaudrove Province on Vanua Levu, where the military clampdown in 2000 had left lasting grievances? The RTU Bill not only offered to wash away the stain of conviction for CAMV ministers, but also promised to soothe that festering resentment in the coup-supporting regions. That the RFMF was so opposed to the Bill only strengthened the perception of villagers in Northern Tailevu and Cakaudrove that the SDL was, in fact, *their* government.

The SDL was careful to avoid direct, and potentially damaging, competition with the CAMV. At the West Cakaudrove by-election in June 2005, the party withdrew its candidate at the eleventh hour, giving a free run to CAMV lawyer and former Native Land Trust Board official Niko Nawaikula, who later proved a key supporter of the CAMV liquidation. At the 2006 election itself, four of the previous six CAMV MPs were returned from constituencies in the former rebel regions, although now as SDL candidates. Those who rejected the new accommodation fared poorly.[16] The older Nationalist Vanua Lavo Tako Party was also badly defeated, ending up with only 1 per cent of the Fijian vote. The former threat to the SDL on the extremist Fijian flank, which had proved so important in moulding party policy during 2001–2006, had all but vanished. Nor was there any substantial new threat from the centrist parties, owing to the poor showing of Ratu Epeli Ganilau's revamped Alliance Party and the western Viti Levu-based Party of National Unity. What then would define the orientation of the new government?

With the election results announced, Qarase announced his intention to form a multiparty cabinet including members of the FLP.[17] Harried by journalists from Fiji TV, the Prime Minister at first emphasized his principled opposition to any 'government of national unity'. This was suitable only for war-time, he said, emphasizing the unbridgeable ideological gulf between the SDL and the FLP, and the absurdity of a constitution that left parliament with no substantial or effective opposition. Nevertheless, the portfolios offered to the FLP were to be substantial, initially out of a hope to avoid a rerun of the cycle of endless litigation experienced in the wake of the 2001 election by obeying the spirit as well as the letter of the law. Within days, Qarase had warmed to the new power-sharing arrangements, just as FLP leader Mahendra Chaudhry showed increasing discomfort at the thought of FLP ministers entering cabinet. The portfolios offered were those left in a 'mess' by the SDL, he said, and when Qarase refused to match the FLP list of nine ministers with the portfolios indicated, Chaudhry threatened to reject participation. It was the FLP Management Board that pushed for acceptance of the offer. The FLP leader chose to remain outside cabinet, even seeking to become Leader of the Opposition while his colleagues entered cabinet. Within days of the formation of the new multiparty cabinet, signs of a split emerged within the FLP, with the 'gang of five', including FLP ministers Krishna Datt and Poseci Bune, denouncing Chaudhry's decision as regards nominees to the Senate and submitting an alternative list.

Was Qarase's conversion to power-sharing a direct reflection of the difficulties this entailed for the rival FLP? There was an element of that, but there was also a more optimistic interpretation. Multiparty cabinet has inevitable attractions in Fiji, particularly for governments like the SDL 2001–06 administration, which had become familiar with the day-to-day difficulties of ruling without consensus. The new arrangements offered government a hitherto lacking legitimacy; also, as the new FLP ministers set about their work, the advantages of drawing on the reservoirs of talent in the Indian community became palpable. Above all, support among ordinary Fijians for the new accommodation was strong. The vast majority of indigenous Fijians might have voted for a party committed to upholding the interests of their ethnic group, but they liked the idea that, once so constituted, that party seek to collaborate with the big Indian party, particularly given that this was occurring from a position of strength. Qarase came to define the objectives of his second government by a commitment to make the power-sharing arrangements work, despite indicating a preference for a multi-*ethnic* over a multi*party* cabinet.

The 2006 election campaign witnessed some convergence in policy, despite the vigorous opposition of the two large conflicting parties and an outcome that entailed the eradication of all the minority parties. The SDL's manifesto focused on poverty reduction, and shortly before the election the government abolished value-added tax on essential food items – borrowing a key policy from the 1999–2000 Labour-led Peoples' Coalition. The government also promised to double $30 family welfare allowances to $60 per week, a move that galvanized Fijian support both in rural and urban areas. Nevertheless, in the wake of the 2006 election, the core policies of the new government – the Qoliqoli Bill, the RTU Bill, proposals for an Indigenous Claims Court and the shift from the Agricultural Landlord and Tenant Act to the Native Land Trust Act – all reflected that earlier incubus of the SDL as a party defined by the objective of placating indigenous discontent. Most of those core policies also entail potentially costly distributive exercises, likely to prove burdensome at a time when the Fiji government is spending more than it is receiving, and when budget deficits are ballooning. Economic growth is likely to slow from more than 3 per cent in 2006 to 2.2 per cent in 2007 as Fiji feels the impact of falling sugar prices and a contracting garment industry, and the outlook for 2008 is not much better.[18]

Postscript

The military coup of 5 December 2006 offered the possibility of a major break in the cyclical pattern of Fiji party politics. The RFMF was transformed from the major instrument upholding indigenous paramountcy into its nemesis, or so it, at least temporarily, appeared. FLP leader Mahendra Chaudhry and General Secretary Lekh Ram Vayeshnoi entered the interim cabinet, and the purging of the Qarase order led to triumphs for FLP MPs, members and supporters across the commanding heights of the state-run sectors of the economy. History appeared to have run full circle, with Mahendra Chaudhry taking the finance portfolio he had lost as a result of the military coup back in 1987. The new arrangement oddly mirrored the stillborn Qarase multiparty cabinet, except with the key FLP leaders now playing their part in an unconstitutional regime together with a group of Fijian leaders who had not secured substantial indigenous support at the time of the 2006 poll.

At the time of writing, the longer-run impact on party politics remains unclear, but the distinct historical communal responses to adversity surveyed in this chapter may, if given sufficient time, give way to a more complex pattern. 'Might is right' may become an indigenous focal point for political loyalty, and Fijians may rally behind a strong military regime. Bainimarama wants to delay elections for years – in part to allow time for a census and the redrawing of constituency boundaries, but mostly in order to entrench his revolution so that centrist politicians, with the multi-ethnic vision of those like Ratu Epeli Ganilau, can one day capture a substantial share of the Fijian vote. The interim prime minister wants to reconfigure Fiji politics in such a way that communal parties like the SDL no longer command the indigenous vote. Yet, international pressure is against him. The Commonwealth, the European Union, the Pacific Islands Forum and bilateral partners want a quick return to constitutional democracy. Fiji's economic prospects are against Bainimarama as well, as budget stringencies curb Fijians' access to the public sector and to a government that used to be 'theirs'.

If a party of the same hue and flavour as the SDL retains majority Fijian support, the survival of the new order will come to depend on Mahendra Chaudhry and the Fiji Indian vote. Here too the future is uncertain. As the economy slumps and as the honeymoon for the 'clean-up' campaign wears thin, Chaudhry may well lose Indian support for the new accommodation.

Whatever lies before Fiji following its most recent political upheaval, the coup of 5 December 2006 has finally laid to rest the exclusively ethnic interpretation of Fiji politics, not least because Fiji Indians can no longer see themselves, in good faith, as the solitary victims of Fiji's history.

February 2007

Notes

[1] Gillion, K.L. 1977. *The Fiji Indians; Challenge to European Dominance, 1920–1946*, The Australian National University Press, Canberra, chapter 6.

[2] On 4 July 2000, an Indian farmer, Chandrika Prasad, who had been displaced in the wake of the May 19 coup, filed an action claiming human rights violations with the High Court at Lautoka against the Republic of Fiji and the Attorney General. The case was first heard by Justice Gates in Lautoka in November 2000, who upheld the 1997 constitution and ordered 'the status quo is restored. Parliament should be summoned by the President' (Prasad v Republic of Fiji, 2001). The interim government appealed, resulting in the landmark case heard in February 2001.

[3] Williams, G. 2001. 'The case that stopped a coup? The rule of law and constitutionalism in Fiji', *Oxford University Commonwealth Law Review*, 1(1):73–93. For a contrary view, see Head, M. 2001. 'A victory for democracy? An alternative assessment of Republic of Fiji V Prasad', *Melbourne Journal of International Law*, 2(2):535–49.

[4] *Constitution of the Republic of the Fiji Islands*, 27 July 1998, s. 88.

5   'Baba was President's First Choice', *The Fiji Times*, 24 March 2001.
6   'Chaudhry wants fresh elections', Fijilive.com, 7 March 2001.
7   Both of the two 2001–2006 NLUP MPs contested as independents in 2006, and both lost.
8   *The Fiji Times*, 9 March 2001.
9   'Leadership Confusion', *The Fiji Times*, 23 March 2001; 'Fijian Parties to Unite', *The Fiji Times*, 23 March 2001; 'Nationalists withdraw from Fijian forum', *The Fiji Times*, 23 March, 2001; 'Northern Chiefs eye Break from SVT', *The Fiji Times*, 24 March 2001.
10 'SVT Group Breaks away', *The Fiji Times*, 23 May 2001.
11 Only one candidate contested under the SVT banner in 2006, ironically an Indian, Arvind Deo Singh, in Nadi Open constituency.
12 The Naitasiri title is one of the more contested in Fiji, and the occupant's authority certainly does not stretch across the modern-day province, which includes the bulk of the pre-war Colo East Province, which historically owed no loyalty to the lowland chiefs.
13 Cited in 'Splitting the Upper Echelon', *The Review*, June 2000, p.25.
14 The SDL's 31 seats do not include the Lau/Taveuni/Rotuma seat won by Savenaca Draunidalo. He stood as an independent, but was quickly identified as belonging to the SDL camp.
15 The GCC, although the recipient of those provincial consultations, expressed some disquiet and some support for amendment.
16 In the Bua Fijian Communal constituency, the incumbent Vula Josateki had opposed the CAMV liquidation and stood as an independent. He obtained only 146 votes, compared with the SDL's Mitieli Bulanauca's 4,321 (whereas in 2001, Josateki, standing for the CAMV, had won with 3,215 compared with Bulanauca's 2,049). The other former CAMV MP who refused to stand on an SDL ticket was Manasa Tugia. He had previously been MP for Cakaudrove West, but in 2006 stood as an independent for the North East Fiji Urban Communal seat and obtained only 353 votes, compared with the SDL's 11,548.
17 The initial public declaration by the Prime Minister to this effect had been during a leaders' debate broadcast live on Fiji TV, but most had interpreted this declaration as likely to entail a re-run of the token portfolios offered in 2003 in obedience to court decisions, in order to remain consistent with the letter of the law rather than the spirit of the constitution.
18 Reserve Bank of Fiji, *Economic Review* 23, 8 August 2006, p.2.

7

Defending the inheritance: the SDL and the 2006 election

Alumita Durutalo

Only five years after its birth, the Soqosoqo Duavata ni Lewenivanua (SDL) won a second general election on the basis of a promise to unify indigenous Fijians. The SDL's victory in Fiji's 2006 election signified an extraordinary achievement. The party showed that it had successfully inherited the mantle of its mainstream Fijian precursors, in the process renewing and reviving an ideological orthodoxy inherited from the Alliance Party and the Soqosoqo ni Vakavulewa ni Taukei (SVT). All three parties proved able to capture the majority of Fijians' votes. In each case, ascendancy has been based on successfully upholding platforms based on the trinity of *vanua*, *lotu* and *matanitu* (defined and discussed below). This chapter explores the emergence of the SDL after the crisis of 2000, the party's election strategies, its merger with the Conservative Alliance–Matanitu Vanua (CAMV), the role of the Methodist church, and the way in which the party is influenced by the traditional politics of the *vanua*. It concludes that, in 2006, the ideology of *vanua*, *lotu* and *matanitu* once again unified indigenous Fijian support behind the party most Fijians identify as being on their side.

The formation of the SDL

The SDL party was formed after a period of severe division amongst Fijian leaders occasioned by the coup of 19 May 2000. It was intended to fill a power vacuum within Fijian society and within mainstream Fijian politics. Although the newly emergent Fijian party differed in some respects from its predecessors, in its core philosophy it continued a long journey that was started by the Fijian Association in 1956. The Alliance Party had advanced an orthodoxy of *vanua*, *lotu* and *matanitu* between 1967 and 1987 and a similar fundamental ideological framework became the bedrock of the SVT from 1992 to 1999.[1] Like its predecessors, the SDL emerged as an eastern Viti Levu- and Vanua Levu-based Fijian political party. As with its predecessors, the link with the all-Fijian provincial councils provided the critical organizational underpinning for the party, and the backing of the Methodist Church proved of fundamental importance to the party's success.

The formation of the SDL was inspired by the need to unify indigenous Fijians once again under a single political umbrella, after the decimation of the SVT at the 1999 poll. That fracturing of the Fijian vote had ensured victory for the Fiji Labour Party (FLP)-led coalition in 1999, although that government lasted only a year. In the wake of its overthrow in May 2000, the Republic of Fiji Military Forces installed an all-Fijian 'interim' administration. Led by Prime Minister Laisenia Qarase, that interim government reconstituted itself as the SDL in the run-up to fresh elections held in August 2001, in the process reviving the staple orthodoxies of Fijian rule. The 2001 organizational structure of the SDL is shown in Figure 6.1.

The SDL proved a well-organized and well-funded Fijian political party from its inception. It was dominated by educated middle-class Fijians, of

Figure 7.1   Organizational structure of the SDL party

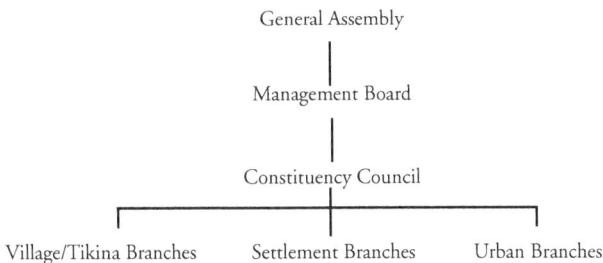

Source: Constitution of the Soqosoqo Duavata ni Lewenivanua (SDL) United Fiji Party: 3.[2]

whom current Prime Minister Laisenia Qarase is an outstanding example. Qarase and other ministers in the 2000–2001 interim government might instead have joined or taken over one of the already existent Fijian parties, such as the SVT or the Fijian Association Party or, most likely, the Veitokani ni Lewenivanua Vakarisito party. But these were all parties in decline, and Qarase eventually chose instead to forge a new party. From the start, the party faced a new rival, the CAMV, which was formed before the SDL. Perhaps the CAMV's close association with supporters of the Speight coup was a reason that Qarase preferred to form a different and seemingly neutral Fijian party to unite indigenous Fijians. However, the CAMV became successful in its own right, especially in Vanua Levu and in Tailevu North, Speight's power base.

Due to the similarities in political vision between the SDL and CAMV, after the 2001 election, the two parties coalesced and formed government between 2001 and 2006. Both parties stressed the need to address long-standing Fijian development problems, which they believed contributed to political instabilities in Fiji. The CAMV believed that Rabuka, as SVT government leader between 1992 and 1999, had not delivered on his 1987 coup promises to indigenous Fijians. Initial support for the formation of the CAMV was concentrated in the various *vanua* of the provinces of Cakaudrove, Bua and Macuata on Vanua Levu. Later, an invitation to join the party was extended to George Speight's supporters on Viti Levu. The CAMV was formed: (i) to ensure that Fiji would always be controlled by indigenous Fijians, and to incorporate that requirement into the constitution; (ii) to strengthen affirmative action for indigenous Fijians; and (iii) to introduce legislation to enable indigenous Fijians to be in full control of the development of their resources.[3]

The SDL had similar goals, but its early advantage was a more practical strategy for accomplishing these and a greater respectability (at least insofar as the link with the coup instigators was less clear). The SDL attempted to address Fijian issues through what it termed the 'Blueprint for Affirmative Action for Indigenous Fijians and Rotumans', which became a major plank of the party's 2001 manifesto. The 2001 SDL party manifesto explains affirmative action as:

> Special programmes of assistance to help remove the economic differences between the Fijians and other communities…These are…provided for in the Constitution…At

the moment the Fijians are falling behind in education, the professions, business and income…The affirmative action blueprint is about our vision of a country where different ethnic communities live in peace, harmony and prosperity. It is about creating a foundation for a stable and prosperous Fiji. It affirms our commitment to securing basic economic rights and a fairer division of wealth…Inequities and inequalities…pose a threat to our social stability. Failure to address these would put society at peril and deny social justice to a large section of the population.[4]

The point of convergence between the SDL and CAMV which led to their coalition between 2001 and 2006, and their merger prior to the election in 2006, was their common vision that addressing Fijian economic underdevelopment was a prerequisite for Fiji's future political stability. The overall SDL vision of a Fiji of 'peace, harmony and prosperity' could only be achieved by first finding solutions to critical Fijian under-development problems.

Background

Many Fijian political parties were formed between 1960 and 2006, reflecting regional cleavages and the sociopolitical diversity of Fijian society. However, the three most powerful ones, which emerged and were consolidated mostly in eastern and northern Fiji, but were usually weaker in western Viti Levu, were: the Fijian-dominated but multi-ethnic Alliance Party, formed in 1965; the SVT, formed in 1991; and the SDL, formed in 2001. After the two military coups in 1987, the SVT emerged to replace the Alliance and, subsequently, in 2001, the SDL emerged to replace the SVT. The parties have all given expression to a political ideology that proclaims the virtues of Fijian political paramountcy and unity.[5]

The three Fijian political parties sustained the dominance and ideological orthodoxy of the eastern and northern chiefdoms. The concepts of *vanua*, *lotu* and *matanitu*, upon which the orthodoxy was founded, have to be understood in terms of Fijian political evolution since the 19th century. *Vanua* identifies and demarcates a geopolitical boundary within which Fijian cultural practices and chiefly rule prevail. *Lotu*, meaning the new post-1835 Christian religion, replaced various forms of traditional Fijian religion and became grounded in the *vanua*. *Matanitu* is a Fijian word that denotes traditional government, and is associated with the country's three confederacies: Kubuna, Burebasaga and Tovata. Linkages between the *vanua* and paramount confederacy chiefs give political parties traditional sources of authority for indigenous Fijians. Legitimacy and recognition were enhanced by the employment of some eastern and northern chiefs in the colonial native administrative system of indirect rule. *Matanitu* became a symbol of the respect for authority and the new rule of law.

The dominance of the eastern chiefs was evident in appointments to the Legislative Council between 1904 and 1960. These were also the leaders behind the formation of the Fijian Association in 1956. This organization, which obtained around 75 per cent of Fijian support in its 30 years of existence, was formed to counter Indian demands for a common roll.[6] In the 1950s and 1960s, the divergent political demands of Fiji's three largest communities shaped the process of decolonization. On one hand, Fijians demanded the paramountcy of their interests. On the other, Indians wanted political rights that emphasized equality and were non-discriminating. In the middle, Europeans were adamant that their privileges be preserved and their special position be maintained.[7]

While other Fijian parties have tried to embody these three pillars in their party identity in one way or another, the Alliance Party, the SVT and the SDL have successfully maintained the orthodoxy as a common rallying point for their Fijian supporters. During the era of the Alliance (1967–1987) and in the first half of SVT leadership (1991–1994), political unity under the *vanua*, *lotu* and *matanitu* were accepted as givens within Fijian society. Challenges by western-based political parties in the early 1960s were not extensive enough to pose a threat to chiefs in the Alliance Party.

The formation of the FLP in 1985 and then the defeat of the Alliance Party in 1987 posed the first direct challenge to the orthodoxy. After the post-1987-coup formation of the SVT – another party intended to unify all indigenous Fijians under one umbrella – other Fijian parties, like the Fijian Association (FA) and the Veitokani ni Lewenivanua Vakarisito (VLV), emerged to pose a further challenge to the orthodoxy. The challenge intensified after George Speight's attempted civilian coup in 2000, in the sense that the coup leader did not readily accept the pronouncements of the Great Council of Chiefs. Rabuka's SVT had ushered in a new era in Fijian politics. In the process, the ideology of *vanua*, *lotu* and *matanitu* was modified.

Although the Council of Chiefs did not directly back the SDL party in the way that it had explicitly backed the Alliance Party and the SVT, support for the party emerged through the co-option of *vanua* chiefs as well as through the Methodist Church – as part of the *lotu ni vanua* – and through individual support. The party continued to express the collective political aspirations of the majority of indigenous Fijians as their representative in modern politics.

SDL strategy for the 2006 election

The SDL's principal objective of achieving 'Fijian unity' was, perhaps inevitably, not achieved. But the party's biggest achievement in this direction was its ability to persuade its coalition partner, CAMV, to join the SDL. The merger occurred on 17 February 2006, although a number of CAMV members and supporters did not sanction the move. Some supporters on Viti Levu complained that they were being marginalized by the Lau islanders in the SDL party.[8] Yet, the newly combined party proved successful in retaining under the new umbrella all six of the seats won by the CAMV in 2001. With 80 per cent of the overall Fijian votes, and 36 out of the 71 seats, the strategic readjustment of indigenous Fijian politics proved successful.

Strategic Methodist Church alliance

Central to the structure of the SDL was the use of *lotu* as a powerful uniting force amongst indigenous Fijians. The SDL emphasized the *lotu* and Christian morality as political virtues in its 2006 candidate line-up. Candidates seeking SDL nominations were required to show evidence of adherence to family values. Additionally, as seen in the curriculum vitae of a number of candidates, a number were Methodist lay preachers in their own churches.[9] While direct chiefly leadership in Fijian party politics has declined since 1987, the emphasis on the *lotu*, uniting both chiefs and commoners, was a most important factor in SDL victory at the 2006 election. The same strategy was attempted by the VLV in 1999, but it was able to secure only around 20 per cent of the overall 1999 Fijian vote. The key difference was that, in the intervening years, the SVT had collapsed, leaving space for a new Fijian party to emerge.

In the SDL primary elections for the 2006 election, Methodist Church membership was considered an important yardstick by which to measure a candidate's sense of morality and commitment to societal development. In large urban centres like Suva, where Fijians from the rural areas have relocated to work, and where the influence of the *vanua* is not as strong, the church was used to identify SDL candidates for the 2006 election. For example, within the Samabula Tamavua Open constituency, leaders of the local Methodist churches in the area – including Vunivau, Samabula East, Raiwai, and Raiwaqa – were in charge of local applications for the primary elections. After the primary elections in each constituency, the winning candidate's name was submitted to the management board, which had the final decision on SDL candidates for each constituency.[10]

In some cases, those who had won the primary elections were not ultimately selected. Instead, more prominent candidates were chosen by the management board. The party used customary methods of reconciliation to appease those who were eliminated. Conflicts were, in some cases, resolved amicably.[11] This political strategy by the SDL highlights the use of both modern and customary institutions of society to not only win elections, but also to maintain internal party peace in the process of electioneering.

Strategic *vanua* alliance

In 2006, the SDL considered the support of chiefs as fundamental to the success of the party, even if they did not compete as candidates. Chiefs, as traditional political leaders, are often nominated as office bearers in Fijian political parties. President of the SDL Ratu Kalokalo Loki, for example, is Tamavua high chief, who, through his chiefly influence, is able to attract people from the *vanua* in Naitasiri to the party.[12]

Furthermore, an addition to the new cabinet, appointed through the Senate, was Bau and Kubuna high chief Adi Samanunu Talakuli Cakobau. She became Minister without Portfolio in the Prime Minister's Office. The absence in government of any high-ranking Kubuna chief from Bau made Adi Samanunu's appointment a strategic one for maintaining the traditional balance of power and Kubuna support for the new SDL government. In addition, Adi Samanunu had been a strong rival to Qarase for the prime ministership back in July 2000, and one backed by the Speight group against the military's chosen candidate. Bringing her into the Prime Minister's Office was designed to heal that rift, and to quash a potential source of ethno-nationalist opposition to the new multiparty cabinet arrangements.

The Burebasaga fort has been maintained by the Minister for Education, Youth and Sports, Ro Teimumu Kepa, Roko Tui Dreketi (the leading title of the Burebasaga Confederacy). Her re-election, although hotly contested by her nephew, Ro Filipe Tuisawau, maintains some form of unity in Rewa (see Saumaki, this volume). The Tui Cakau, Ratu Naiqama Lalabalavu, head of the Matanitu Tovata or Tovata Confederacy, won in the Cakaudrove West Fijian Provincial Communal constituency. His cousin and traditional competitor to the Tui Cakau title, leader of the New Alliance Party of Fiji (NAPF), Ratu Epeli Ganilau, lost in the Suva City Open constituency. The Tui Cakau's inclusion in cabinet is intended to ensure the support of the Cakaudrove Confederacy.

On Viti Levu, Tui Namosi Ratu Suliano Matanitobua's re-election highlighted the support of the Namosi people for the SDL government. The SDL's hold on Fijians in western Viti Levu was strengthened by the inclusion of chiefs like Ratu Meli Saukuru of Nadi, who was formerly Vice President of the Methodist Church of Fiji, as well as Nadroga chief Ratu Isikeli Tasere and Navosa chief Ratu Jone Navakamocea.

The SDL managed to win all of the 17 Fijian provincial communal seats and all six of the urban Fijian communal seats in the 2006 election. The party secured 80 per cent of indigenous Fijian votes. In some constituencies, chiefly leadership contests were exacerbated by modern leadership competition in party politics, as seen in the Rewa Provincial Fijian Communal constituency. The SDL won a smaller proportion of Fijian votes (56 per cent) in this constituency than in any other Fijian constituency. Ro Filipe Tuisawau, who stood as an independent candidate after failing to secure the SDL nomination, obtained 41 per cent of the Rewa vote, perhaps also indicating continuing political dissent in Rewa. Since 1974, when the Fijian Nationalist Party was formed by Sakeasi Butadroka, the province of Rewa has been the power base of the Fijian Nationalist Party. Both Ro Teimumu Kepa and Ro Filipe Tuisawau were from the same chiefly household.[13] Within Fijian society, political parties are more than institutions for democratic representation; they also serve as vehicles for continuing subtle yet powerful ancient rivalries.

The SDL faced sterner competition in the open constituencies, where eligible citizens from all communities vote together. Ethnic voting was still observable in the open constituencies. For example, SDL won in the constituencies where Fijians predominated, such as the Lomaivuna-Namosi-Kadavu Open constituency. The FLP, on the other hand, won in constituencies like Labasa Open, where Indians predominated. Where an Indo-Fijian was fielded as an SDL candidate in a constituency with a strong SDL power base, the Indo-Fijian candidate won. The two Indo-Fijian SDL candidates in the Ra Open constituency and the Cunningham Open constituency both won their seats. Likewise, Fijians standing for the FLP in areas with a strong FLP power base also won their seats. This was the case for Fijian candidates in the Macuata East Open and the Yasawa Nawaka Open constituencies.

Neither the SDL nor the FLP had the unchallenged ascendancy in the open constituencies that they enjoyed in the communal constituencies. The open constituencies were shared almost equally between the SDL and FLP parties. The SDL won 13 of the 25 seats, and the FLP won the rest. Competition in some marginal constituencies was intense. For example, in the Laucala Open constituency, the SDL won with a margin of only 11 votes (7,856) over the FLP (7,845).[14]

Conclusion

The SDL's victory demonstrated the continuing political importance of the Fijian orthodoxy of *vanua*, *lotu* and *matanitu* as a unifying ideology for indigenous voters. In this context, any attempt by the party to concurrently promote Fijian political paramountcy with multiracial politics is a real challenge, unless non-Fijians readily accept the promotion of policies such as '50/50 by 2020: the blueprint for affirmative action for indigenous Fijians and Rotumans'.[15] As we have seen, the SDL attempted to present a multi-ethnic front in 2006 by including Indo-Fijians in its election line-up, and is likely to do so in future elections.[16] The SDL's strategy of facilitating policies for Fijian development has been a reaction to the long-term demands by some Fijian resource owners for greater government support in the development of indigenous resources.

The 2006 election reminds us that party politics for many indigenous Fijians is a means of expressing two sets of rights and demands – democratic and indigenous. Indigenous demands are being expressed through the electoral system against non-Fijian groups and as a means of extending ancient internal Fijian rivalries. In the long term, however, these indigenous demands may become problematic in a society of diverse sociopolitical and cultural realities, and the SDL's policies may, in the long term, be seen as offering solutions to some groups of indigenous Fijians only.

Notes

[1] The Alliance Party was not a Fijian party in quite the same sense as were its successors. While it relied primarily on the Fijian Association and on the votes of Fijians, it was nonetheless a coalition of different groups, and had substantial Indian support during the 1970s.

[2] At the lowest level, the branches report to the Constituency Council; the Constituency Council reports to the Management Board through the General Assembly. The Constituency Council comprises all branch presidents and secretaries. Each branch appoints its own president, secretary and treasurer. See Constitution of the Soqosoqo Duavata ni Lewenivanua (SDL) United Fiji Party (UFP): 2–3.

[3] Durutalo, A. L. 2005. 'Of Roots and Offshoots: Fijian Political Thinking, Dissent and the Formation of Political Parties (1960–1999)', PhD thesis, The Australian National University, Canberra: 315–16.

[4] 'Good Leadership for a Secure and Stable Fiji: Soqosoqo Duavata ni Lewenivanua, The SDL's Plan for Prosperous Fiji', Manifesto Summary 2001:8.

[5] I argue that the Alliance, the SVT and the SDL parties depict a version of Fijian paramountcy in order to unite the diverse sociopolitical groups of Fijian society. The chiefdoms in eastern and northeastern Fiji are similar to the hierarchical Polynesian types of chiefdoms, while those in western Fiji, where chiefs are regarded as 'first amongst equals', are more egalitarian.

[6] The common roll would have allowed for a one-person-one-vote electoral system.

[7] Ali, A. 1986. 'Political change: 1874–1960', in B.V. Lal (ed.). *Politics in Fiji*, Allen & Unwin, Sydney, p.9.

[8] In my discussion with some of the disgruntled members on the day of the merger, they voiced their concern about the way those in the top management of both parties forced the unity on grassroots supporters. There were quite a number of members from Tailevu North, for example, who voiced their concern about the future of their demands, such as the release of George Speight, in the new SDL party.

[9] For example, Ratu Peni Volavola, one of the two SDL candidates in the Suva City Urban constituency, stated that he had been a lay preacher since 1980; church steward in the Samabula East Methodist Church since 1999; representative to the 2006 Methodist 'Bose ko Viti' conference; and member of the Methodist Church of Fiji Working Committee. Likewise, the curriculum vitae for Misaele Weleilakeba stated that he was a confirmed lay preacher in the Methodist Church and Chairman of the Raiwai Methodist Church Financial Committee. See also the curriculum vitae for Ratu Mosese Volavola and Misaele Yadraca Weleilakeba, also SDL candidates in the 2006 election. (In the personal collection of the author.)

[10] Interview with Dr Tupeni Baba, SDL Candidate in the Samabula Tamavua Open constituency in the 2006 election, 16 June 2006, Suva, Fiji.

[11] *Ibid*. In Dr Tupeni Baba's Samabula/Tamavua constituency, the second SDL candidate, Pita Nacuva, responded to his party listing him as second preference by urging supporters to vote below-the-line, much to the frustration of SDL campaign manager, Jale Baba. In the event,

neither candidate was able to take this highly marginal seat, but Dr Baba was given an SDL Senate position, while Pita Nacuva became Speaker of the House.

12 Tamavua is a *vanua* in the province of Naitasiri. The *vanua* owns much of the land at the northern end of Suva city.

13 Durutalo, A. 2000. 'Elections and the dilemma of indigenous Fijian political unity', in B.V. Lal (ed.) *Fiji Before the Storm: Elections and the Politics of Development*. Asia Pacific Press, The Australian National University, Canberra, pp.87–88.

14 See Election Results 2006 – Fiji Islands, http://www.elections.gov.fj/results2006/Constituencies/47.html.

15 See *50/50 By Year 2020: 20 Year Development Plan (2001–2020) For the Enhancement of Participation of Indigenous Fijians and Rotumans in the Socio-Economic Development of Fiji*, Government of Fiji.

16 There were 19 Indo-Fijian SDL candidates in the Indian Communal constituencies and six in the open constituencies. Two of these candidates, Rajesh Singh, who stood in the Cunningham Open constituency and George Shiu Raj, who stood in the Ra Open constituency, were successful in the election.

8

The strategic impasse: Mahendra Chaudhry and the Fiji Labour Party

Samisoni Pareti and Jon Fraenkel

Leading the Fiji Labour Party (FLP) into its sixth general election, Mahendra Pal Chaudhry showed every sign of being a confident leader-in-waiting. Formed in 1985 on the crest of a wave of support from workers and the general public, resulting from a series of wage increases won from the stand-offish and aloof government of Ratu Mara, his FLP had, by the late 1990s, risen to a position of ascendancy in the Fiji Indian community. Chaudhry's overthrow in the coup of May 2000 served to cement his reputation as a die-hard fighter against injustice and a standard-bearer for the cause of Fiji's impoverished and oppressed citizens. He was a scourge to those who dared to cross him. Still vivid in the minds of those working in the Toorak office of the Supervisor of Elections during the run-up to the 2006 election was his verbal threat to the besieged incumbent, Semesa Karavaki, that Karavaki would be a 'sorry man' when the election was over.

A series of Tebbutt polls held in the lead-up to the 2006 general election confirmed that Chaudhry was the undisputed leader of the Indian community.[1] Harrying the government for 'incompetence' and 'racism', and drawing on the old cane field bases of FLP support, Chaudhry had won the backing of Indian professionals in the towns – even some bankers and businessmen – as well as many urban trade unionists. The only other Indian-led party, the National Federation Party (NFP), seemed like a spent force, not helped by its inability to find a successor with the charisma and the stature of its former leader, Justice

Jai Ram Reddy. Chaudhry thus had many reasons to feel that he would return as prime minister.

Chaudhry's FLP had also been buoyed by some significant successes in the battle with the Soqosoqo Duavata ni Lewenivanua (SDL)-led government, mainly the result of smart, strategic manoeuvres. Court victories in the landmark Chandrika Prasad case in March 2001, and successive triumphs in the legal controversies over the multiparty cabinet during 2001–2004 had, the FLP hoped, thrown into question the legitimacy of the Fijian-dominated SDL government. Labour had managed to block the Bill to transfer agricultural land leases from ALTA (Agricultural Landlord and Tenant Act) to NLTA (Native Land Trust Act) by denying the government the two-thirds vote majority it required as a result of constitutional protections connected to land legislation. A solution to the problem of expiring land leases remained elusive, with SDL policy on the issue meeting the same fate as had befallen that of previous administrations. As a result, Prime Minister Laisenia Qarase went to the poll smarting from the experience of parliamentary blockages, whilst Chaudhry had succeeded in reconsolidating his support within his power base, the Indian tenant farmer community.

There were other seeming triumphs in the propaganda war. The controversial Promotion of Reconciliation, Tolerance and Unity (RTU) Bill was introduced by Qarase in order to placate the SDL's junior coalition partner, the Conservative Alliance–Matanitu Vanua (CAMV) party. The amnesty provisions in that Bill might have made it possible to release from prison several CAMV leaders convicted of offences committed during the coup/standoff of May–July 2000 and the associated mutiny of November in that year. The SDL had wanted to bring the Bill into law before the 2006 polls, but Labour boycotted the parliamentary discussions. Many in the country were vehemently opposed to the proposed amnesty provisions, although the RTU Bill did have the backing, with some reservations, of the Great Council of Chiefs and the 14 provincial councils. In the end, time ran out, and the SDL went into the election with the political fallout of another unfulfilled promise tarnishing its reputation, while Chaudhry and his FLP registered yet another public relations triumph. As with the land lease bill, Chaudhry's tactics were to make Qarase and his SDL party appear ineffective, continuing what the Labour leader took to be a long legacy of failure of post-independence Fijian leadership.

Labour's strong support from Indian voters was not in doubt, as the December 2004 Tavua Open by-election result had shown.[2] Indian support alone, however, could give the FLP only around 23 or 24 seats, short of the 36 required to form government. Less certain was the extent of support from indigenous Fijian and general voters, which would be critical if the FLP were to win the additional 12 or 13 seats. The other alternative for the FLP was to build an effective coalition, but that depended on allied parties making strong showings in the open constituencies, or in the General, Rotuman and Fijian communal constituencies. Above all, what were needed were political parties that took votes away from the SDL, the other major contender for office.

Chaudhry hoped that repeating previous strategies would work well again in 2006. That meant taking the moral high ground by steering clear of the racial debate and focusing on 'bread and butter' issues. Labour's television advertisements, as well as the party manifesto, concentrated on such issues as the state of the economy, job creation, better housing, alleviation of poverty, cheaper education, better health services, prudent financial management, more appropriate rural development, infrastructure and utilities and the strengthening of law and order. Labour also campaigned on the supposedly great achievements of its 1999–2000 government – claiming credit, for example, for an increase in the GDP growth rate over those years – and contrasting this with alleged mishandling of the economy by the subsequent Qarase government.

Chaudhry repeatedly refused to discuss publicly the issue of leadership, in a manner reminiscent of his pre-1999 poll strategy. Back then, he had reportedly suggested to Dr Tupeni Baba that he would be the first choice for prime minister in the event of a Labour victory, while coalition ally Adi Kuini Speed had also entertained ambitions for the top position.[3] However, when the party obtained 37 seats in its own right, it seemed only fair, argued Chaudhry, that the FLP leader become prime minister. Yet, Chaudhry's assumption of the prime ministership back in 1999, the first ever Indian to assume the position, did not go down well with indigenous Fijians, many of whom felt hoodwinked by the move. It was then that President Ratu Sir Kamisese Mara came to Chaudhry's assistance, swearing him into office as well as seeking to placate Labour's unhappy People's Coalition allies. The initial storm blew over, but Fijian disquiet remained a source of both grievance and attempted political realignment during the period 1999–2000.

When George Speight seized control of parliament on 19 May 2000, Chaudhry's earlier assumption of the prime ministership and the associated affront to 'indigenous rights' featured centrally in the coup instigator's regular interviews on international radio and television.

Before the 2006 election, the issue of whether or not Fijians would accept Chaudhry's return as prime minister was as hot a topic as it had been at the 2001 polls. The idea that race should not be an issue in the campaign might have struck a positive chord amongst non-Fijian FLP supporters, but the issue of race remained much more controversial among the Fijian voters that Labour needed to win over. After all, even within FLP ranks, it had been indigenous Fijians who had been most likely to break away during Chaudhry's years as leader. Back in 2001, Dr Tupeni Baba's New Labour Unity Party (NLUP) had been a splinter party that drew support primarily from among the already small band of Fijian FLP candidates. After their departure, the FLP became even more solidly Indian in complexion. Prior to the 2006 election, some Fijian voters saw Chaudhry's efforts to steer clear of the leadership issue as evasive and suspicious, reflecting his inability to read accurately the mood of a section of the community that he desperately needed to win over.

The FLP strategy reflected the benefit of strategic partnerships under Fiji's alternative vote system. On the other hand, the SDL tactic of seeking 'Fijian unity' seemed misguided because, with victories in marginal constituencies relying on transfers of preference votes from like-minded allies, the best tactic for big parties is usually not to seek to merge with smaller parties, but for the parties to field separate candidates and give each other strong preferences. This was the strategy that gave the FLP an absolute majority back in 1999, and it was the strategy attempted again in 2006. At the intervening election, in 2001, it had not worked. Back then, a group of 'Moderates Forum' parties – including the NLUP, led by Dr Tupeni Baba, the former Deputy Prime Minister in the People's Coalition government – had emerged; this group was bitterly opposed to Chaudhry's leadership and blamed the FLP leader for exacerbating tensions in the run-up to the 2000 coup. Moderates Forum preferences favoured the SDL above the FLP, leaving Chaudhry's party able to capture only the 19 Indian communal seats and nine of the open seats in the FLP's cane belt heartlands of western Viti Levu and northern Vanua Levu.

In 2006, the FLP was determined not to repeat the 2001 experience of being left without substantial coalition partners. These were required for two reasons. Victories in the more marginal open constituencies required the FLP either to (i) obtain sufficient preference votes to win in its own right, or (ii) assist like-minded allied parties to win and then enter into coalition with them. This was what drove the FLP to enter into a pre-election coalition with the western Viti Levu-based Party of National Unity (PANU) and Mick Beddoes' United Peoples Party (UPP).[4]

Labour was unable to secure a similar arrangement with the new Alliance Party (NAP) led by Ratu Epeli Ganilau. Ratu Epeli, a former army commander and chair of the Great Council of Chiefs, adopted a 'multiracial' platform for his newly formed NAP, which seemed, in many respects, more suited to a coalition with the FLP than with the SDL. Aimed at resurrecting the earlier Alliance Party – which had been forged in the mid-1960s and been the dominant force in Fiji politics over the period 1966 to 1987 – Ratu Epeli's advertising campaign paid homage to the stabilizing influence of Fiji's key post-war traditional chiefs, Ratu Sir Lala Sukuna, Ratu Sir Penaia Ganilau and Ratu Sir Kamisese Mara. That the NAP remained formally neutral was indicative of their fear of the political consequences of too close an association with Mahendra Chaudhry – an association that would have limited the party's chances of winning Fijian support. This was a setback for Labour. Nevertheless, with some exceptions, the NAP preferences favoured the FLP, and enabled the party to win several of the highly marginal seats in the Suva–Nausori corridor.

Amongst the 13 parties that registered with the office of the Supervisor of Elections to contest the May 2006 general election was the rejuvenated PANU. PANU had been an important pillar of the FLP victory back in 1999, when its transferred preference votes gave the FLP four open seats. It had won another four Fijian communal seats in its own right. Chaudhry's close ally, Ba chief Ratu Sairusi Nagagavoka, was the party president, and two western PANU MPs, Meli Bogileka and Ponipate Lesavua, had joined the 1999–2000 People's Coalition cabinet. This episode caused some internal consternation. After his defeat at the 1999 poll, PANU General Secretary Apisai Tora broke away to join a rejuvenated *taukei* movement. He was among those who on 19 May 2000, aiming to create an atmosphere of destabilization, led the *taukei* march through Suva's streets while George Speight and his followers stormed Fiji's parliament. PANU had fared poorly in 2001, largely because Apisai Tora had forged a rival western Viti Levu party, the Bai Kei Viti, which split the Fijian vote and allowed the SDL to take the western Fijian communal seats. But, prior to the 2006 polls, Apisai Tora retired and his Bai Kei Viti party vanished with him. On the other hand, under the auspices of Ratu Sairusi, PANU reformed and contested all western Fijian communal seats, giving the FLP its second preferences. Together with the UPP and PANU, the FLP hoped to capture a larger number of the all-important 25 open constituencies.

Labour also hoped to translate the stand-off between the SDL government and the Fiji military forces into more votes for the party. Over the years of Qarase's 2001–2006 government, army commander Frank Bainimarama had skirmished repeatedly with the Home Affairs Ministry, and even threatened to seize control of the government. In particular, the commander was vehemently opposed to the RTU Bill, the amnesty clause of which he saw as undermining the military's work in stabilizing the security situation in the wake of the 2000 coup. Vice President Ratu Joni Madraiwiwi interceded to calm relations between Qarase and the commander, but the military continued to insist on involvement during the election campaign, even on several occasions marching through the streets of Suva in a show of strength. This was all grist to Labour's mill. Party president Jokapeci Koroi, in an interview on Fiji TV, professed to support the commander's threat to seize office, and her statement was subsequently defended by Chaudhry.[5] This was deeply ironic given the military's role in deposing the FLP government back in 1987. But Labour hoped that the military's newfound support for constitutionality and the rule of law would calm fears that a return to office of the FLP might precipitate another coup.

In the final stages of the campaign, Chaudhry sought to consolidate the FLP vote and dismissed the significance of smaller parties: the contest would, he argued, be a two-way tussle between his FLP and Qarase's SDL. In campaign meeting after campaign meeting, on sugar cane farm or in town hall, Chaudhry's message to voters was simple: 'the choice is not between 13 parties, but only two. If you aren't voting for Labour, then you are actually supporting SDL'.[6] When Qarase and his party fought back by pushing the leadership issue onto the election agenda, asserting that Fiji was not ready for a non-indigenous prime minister, Chaudhry again took the moral high ground and refused to descend to the 'gutter' of the SDL's racial politics, insisting on the FLP's intention to stick to the bread and butter issues that mattered most to the electorate.[7]

Two factors were critical in explaining the FLP's defeat in 2006. First, its pre-election partners, the UPP and PANU, did not perform as strongly as their counterparts in the People's Coalition of 1999. Beddoes' attempts to swing the general voters behind his UPP were partially successful in that the party managed to secure a second seat in parliament. Bernadette Rounds Ganilau won the Suva General Communal seat, pushing Labour Minister Kenneth Zinck into third place. The SDL candidate came second. Yet Beddoes himself only narrowly won the Western/Central General Communal seat, and the North Eastern General Communal seat fell to an independent, Robin Irwin, on the fifth count. The UPP candidate in that constituency obtained only 14.5 per cent of the vote. A West Country Liberal, originally from the United Kingdom, Irwin was vigorously opposed to Chaudhry's 'socialist' philosophy, and made it immediately clear that he could in no way be a Labour ally in the contest for the prime ministership. Although the SDL lost the only general communal seat it had gained in 2001, it is worth noting that it polled reasonably strongly in two of the three general constituencies, although less well in Suva City.

PANU also performed poorly, proving a faint shadow of its 1999 counterpart. The party had lost the all-important support of the Ba Provincial Council in 2005. Despite no longer having the Bai Kei Viti to contend with, it polled poorly in the west. Ponipate Lesavua managed 31.6 per cent of the vote in Ba East, but the SDL obtained over 60 per cent and thus took the seat on the first count.[8] Yasawa politician Meli Bogileka fared still worse. He obtained only 7.7 per cent of the vote in Ba West, barely denting the SDL's ability to secure its nationwide average of 80 per cent of Fijian votes in this part of the country.

Secondly, Chaudhry and Beddoes under-estimated the popularity of the SDL, and did not anticipate its strong performance in traditionally UPP and PANU domains in western Fiji.

The predicted splitting of Fijian votes arising from the emergence of many Fijian-dominated parties and independent candidates did not happen. All 23 Fijian communal seats went to Qarase's SDL, while Labour obtained all 19 Indian communal seats. Two of the 12 open seats obtained by the FLP had majority Fijian electorates (Nadroga and Samabula/Tamavua), but these were secured as a result of vote preferences from minority parties like the NAP and the National Federation Party. Much to Chaudhry's displeasure, Fijian voters were not attracted by Labour's painstaking effort to field more Fijian candidates. Nor did the decision to appoint several indigenous politicians – such as retired medical nurse Jokapeci Koroi and former ambassador and public service administrator Poseci Bune – to the party's top decision-making bodies noticeably boost the party's Fijian support.

The defeat of the FLP in 2006 was not solely a result of the weakness of their allies, or the unexpected strength of their opponents. There were also difficulties within the party; these exploded into the public domain after the election. In his years as party leader, Chaudhry had developed what many people, rightly or wrongly, took to be a tendency to surround himself with 'yes-men' – men generally not as well educated as their leader and definitely not as articulate when speaking English. After emerging victorious in the 1999 general election, Chaudhry, for this reason, found it hard to appoint competent ministers from his own party. Given the high number of Indian graduates and young professionals in Fiji today, Labour should have been able to choose from a huge reservoir of talent. Yet, the party has not proved very successful in attracting the new generation of younger professionals. By contrast, Qarase's SDL was able to select his ministers from a good mixture of young and matured professionals – qualified accountants, economists, technocrats, lawyers and academics.

Although Chaudhry's leadership style is often an issue of contention in Fiji, he never makes any concessions on this score. When asked by reporters whether he would re-consider his style in line with requests from the party 'dissidents', Chaudhry's standard refrain is to remark that voters have decided on his leadership by voting him back into office at the May 2006 poll.[9] This may be true as regards his Ba Open constituency, but not for the country as a whole. National leadership differs from that required to represent specific interest groups, trade unions or farmers' organizations.

In the wake of the poll, the speed with which Qarase moved to conform with the country's constitution and formed a multiparty cabinet left little room for Chaudhry to reveal publicly his distress at leading his party to another election loss. He did not follow normal protocol by conceding to or congratulating

Qarase. When confronted by a reporter about this on the day the Prime Minister took his oath of office and invited Labour into his cabinet, Chaudhry said he did not see the need to do so.[10] Writing a day or so after the elections results were declared, and after President Ratu Josefa Iloilo had sworn Qarase back into office, former *Fiji Sun* journalist Victor Lal called on the FLP leader to abide by Westminster conventions and tender his resignation for failing yet again to lead his party into an election victory.[11] Chaudhry did not react to Lal's public challenge. Close aides confirmed the party leader's disappointment about Labour's poor showing amongst the Fijian voters, a trend which some Labour members blamed on the party's Fijian coalition partner PANU. No longer could the party respond quite so easily to the experience of defeat, as it had done in 2001, with allegations of electoral fraud and with outrage over the illegitimate and unconstitutional process of cabinet formation.

If he wants to lead Labour into victory in the next general election, Chaudhry will have to come up with a new strategy that will enable Labour to maintain its Indian support while at the same time considerably strengthening its Fijian backing. Whatever that strategy turns out to be, Chaudhry will have to convince Fijian voters that in his determination to push the interests of his Indian supporters, he is not working against the indigenous community. For instance, fighting for the retention of ALTA offers (largely Indian) tenants the hope of security of tenure, but Fijian voters may want to see an increase in land rentals. However the Indian leader approaches the matter, history shows that Chaudhry is not, or is no longer, eager to jump into a coalition with a major indigenous political party. He witnessed the negative impact of such a manoeuvre after the 1992 election, when his minority Labour Party unexpectedly found itself holding the balance of power. Then, whoever it supported in the SVT party, which had secured the majority, would become prime minister: Ratu Mara's endorsed candidate, the late Josevata Kamikamica, or the charismatic Sitiveni Rabuka. Through deals that Chaudhry claimed Rabuka later reneged on, the trade unionist rallied behind the former coup leader, an action which came to haunt the Labour Party when, after the collapse of Rabuka's government two years later, Chaudhry and Labour found their vote slumping as the party was punished by an unforgiving Indian electorate.

Chaudhry had learned that lesson when the country prepared to go to the polls in 1999. This time, it was the NFP, the majority Indian party in parliament at the time, that brokered inauspicious alliances. Chaudhry's nemesis, Reddy, then the NFP opposition leader, ignored Labour's experience at the 1994 polls and decided to form a pre-election coalition with Rabuka's SVT. The two had earlier cooperated in a joint parliamentary select committee to produce the 1997 constitution. In the lead-up to the polls, Reddy agreed to become deputy to Rabuka in the event the coalition won. Rabuka's SVT was relegated to the opposition and the NFP suffered its worst-ever defeat in the polls – a defeat which, sadly, led to the premature exit from domestic politics of Reddy. The Indian electorate punished the NFP leader and his party for 'sleeping with the enemy'; the NFP did not win a single seat. It was to prove a long sojourn in the political wilderness for the NFP, with only its support in the municipal councils, amongst the older generation of sugar cane farmers and in some of the trade unions keeping the party alive. The NFP was again to find itself without seats after both the 2001 and 2006 elections. In the minds of Indian voters, the man who denied their party the right to govern the island nation when he led soldiers of the Fiji military forces into parliament on 14 May 1987 to stage a coup d'état and remove the late Dr Timoci Bavadra as prime minister should remain forever a foe, not a friend.

Owing to the 1999 annihilation of the NFP, Chaudhry was able to monopolize the Indian communal electorates and, with his majority bolstered by the support of minorities like the late Adi Kuini Speed's Fijian Association and Bune's Veitokani ni Lewenivanua Vakarisito (VLV) party, he was sworn into office as Fiji's fourth prime minister. It was to prove a short-lived administration. Precisely a year later, in May 2000, George Speight and a group of nationalists, with backing from renegade soldiers, seized parliament and took Chaudhry and members of his government hostage for 56 days.

Chaudhry's years of struggle had hardened his resolve. He looked back on his time as general secretary of the Public Servants Association that took on the might of the Alliance government with their austere financial measures – including wage freezes – in the early 1980s, and on his survival of two parliamentary takeovers, first as Dr Bavadra's finance minister in 1987 and then as prime minister in 2000. As many who have mustered the courage to challenge him only to seal their fate within the party will testify, the man is a strategist, a political animal and as much a fighter as he is a survivor. Serious allegations against Chaudhry's personal integrity have been made, some damaging – such as his alleged affair with a former journalist and the appointment of his son, Rajendra Chaudhry, as his private secretary in 2000. But, for the Indian community, these criticisms did not stick.

Former Labour stalwarts, like Dr Tupeni Baba and John Ali, report that picking a fight with 'Mahen' tends to be a daunting prospect for two reasons; firstly, because Chaudhry has overwhelming support amongst the grassroots supporters of the FLP, and, secondly, because he is a workaholic and as ruthless in internal leadership struggles as he is in battles against the Fijian government of the day. Fiji caught a glimpse of his tireless energy during the reign of the People's Coalition government in 1999–2000. As prime minister, Chaudhry kept for himself a cluster of critically important portfolios, including the crucial ministries of finance, public enterprise, sugar reform and information. He arrived at the office well before other staff in the morning and worked until late at night. Reporters had to get used to attending press conferences with the Prime Minister during weekends. This was a work routine that was hard to match even for younger members of his cabinet.

This industriousness is also reflected in the way Chaudhry worked to build on his support. In 2005, when Labour MPs walked out of the parliamentary chamber in protest against the tabling of the SDL's RTU Bill, the Labour leader was not in the house. He explained his absence to the Lower House the next day: 'I was attending the funeral of a well-known social worker in Ba', Chaudhry told parliament. The fact that the funeral took place in his own constituency was indicative of the FLP leader's retention of close links with his constituents. Whilst some of his members are content to remain within the cocktail circuit in town, Mahen would rather work in his office or visit the people in their homes and settlements.

Such diligence and grassroots support make any attempt to challenge Chaudhry's leadership seem like political suicide. Several Labour executives report that the dramatic 2006 post-election controversy between the 'gang of five' and Chaudhry was only the spilling into the public arena of a conflict that had been simmering within the party's management board for some time. 'Some of us have been battling Mahen all this while', said one executive Labour party member. 'There are a lot more challenges that happen behind the scenes and this challenge to Mahen's decision-making is not new. The only new thing is that this challenge has spilt into the public domain.'[12]

Internal conflict over the decision to participate in the multiparty cabinet was initially concealed from the public gaze. Several party executives reported that Chaudhry was clearly opposed to the idea, but did not oppose participation when he realised that the majority of his MPs wanted to accept Qarase's invitation. Chaudhry's constant insistence, during the 2001–2006 government, that he supported the multiparty cabinet concept made it difficult for him to avoid sending nine of his members to join Qarase's government. But the claim that he had personally authorized and inspired participation is unconvincing; Labour's participation was never the sole prerogative of the party leader but a decision for the entire party caucus. The intervening events – an outspoken FLP attack on the Prime Minister's choice of portfolios for the nine FLP ministers, coupled with a sudden climbdown and unconditional acceptance of those portfolios – reinforces the view that Chaudhry accepted this new direction for the party only under some duress.

Nadroga FLP MP Lekh Ram Vayeshnoi confirmed that he was reluctant to take up a cabinet position. 'I only decided to accept the position when Mahen asked me to', Vayeshnoi said.[13] A party executive later related that Vayeshnoi's performance in cabinet only confirmed the suspicion held by many party members that he was deliberately sent into Qarase's multiparty cabinet to do Chaudhry's bidding. Shortly after the formation of the new cabinet, Vayeshnoi's public denunciation in parliament of the government's affirmative action program triggered the debates directed toward establishing ground rules for the practical day-to-day working of the multiparty cabinet. When Labour's deputy leader Poseci Bune admonished his cabinet colleague Vayeshnoi for his parliamentary outburst on national television and asked Chaudhry to rein in the outspoken Nadroga MP, the Labour leader would hear nothing of the complaint.[14] Instead, Chaudhry told reporters he stood by the remarks of his more junior party member.

Chaudhry has the numbers. Vayeshnoi is deputy to Chaudhry, who is both parliamentary leader and general secretary of the party's National Council, Labour's supreme body. It was in the council, where he holds strong support,

that Chaudhry wanted the case of his 'renegade' party executives to be heard
and decided. On the management board, by contrast, the 'rebels' had five of
the nine positions. At the last count, Labour's National Council comprises 42
members, including 18 branch representatives – most of whom, according to
a party executive, are National Farmers Union (NFU) stalwarts. Chaudhry is
general secretary of the NFU. Urban-based workers have 13 representatives
in the council and there are two representatives each from women and youth
members of Labour. Party executives like Koroi, Chaudhry, Vayeshnoi, Bune,
Krishna Datt and Atu Bain are also members. Party MPs can attend National
Council meetings but have no voting rights.

With the numbers stacked against Bune and his allies, Chaudhry had two
clear options; sack the dissidents and throw them out of Labour, or take out the
olive branch and instigate reconciliation. At the time of writing, the outcome
of that potential split within the FLP is unclear. Chaudhry may even decide to
take up the unsolicited advice of Vice President Ratu Joni Madraiwiwi, who,
on the eve of Labour's first council meeting, held in a Nadi school in early June
2006, urged the Labour leader to reconcile with internal and external foes. 'Mr
Chaudhry is in a strategic position to destroy the multiparty government', Ratu
Joni told a meeting of the Fiji Institute of Accountants:

> This can be done by way of an ultimatum from the FLP to its members of
> parliament who are in cabinet. Alternatively, it will be a gradual erosion of cabinet
> cohesion by a series of sustained attacks on the government. The consequences will
> be serious for all of us. There will be recriminations and blame cast on all sides.
> They usually assume an ethnic hue in very short order. The resulting distrust will
> merely entrench the nay-sayers on all sides. So there are high stakes and failure
> has to be the last option available.[15]

On national television, a day after Ratu Joni's public address, Chaudhry
appeared taken aback by these precise and candid remarks, telling journalists
that he couldn't understand what moved Fiji's second citizen to make the
comments that he did.[16]

The day after Qarase had invited Labour to help form a multiparty
government, Chaudhry singled out a word that the Prime Minister constantly
used in their discussions: that it was his 'prerogative' as prime minister to decide
which Labour MP would be in his cabinet line-up. Interestingly, Chaudhry

used the same word when he defended his decision to finalize his list of eight senators, saying that it was his 'prerogative' as leader of the Fiji Labour Party to compile the senate list. Prerogatives are natural, sovereign or god-given rights, theoretically subject to no restriction.[17] They are exercised unilaterally, without consultation. As such, they are foreign to power-sharing arrangements, such as those Fiji chose for itself in 1997, which built flexibility, negotiation and consensus into political relationships. Fiji has had more than its fair share of prerogatives, exercised by communally based politicians. Perhaps now, in the wake of the 2006 elections, is a good time not so much for unilateral take-it-or-leave-it decision-making, but for a new style of politics based on greater give and take by both sides.

Notes

[1] The polls were conducted by Tebbutt Research, a private company based in Fiji, for *The Fiji Times*.

[2] 'House of Representatives By-Elections – 2004 – Returning Officers Report', *Fiji Government Gazette*, 4(11), 6 February 2004.

[3] See Field, M., Baba, T., & Nabobo-Baba, U. 2005. *A Speight of Violence, Inside Fiji's 2000 Coup*. Reed Publishing, where, pp.48–53; Keith-Reid, R. 1999. 'Chaudhry: the man in the hot seat', *Fiji Islands Business*, June.

[4] Beddoes had formerly been a loyal backer of long-serving Fijian Prime Minister Ratu Sir Kamisese Mara (1970–1987). His United Generals' Party had entered a coalition with Rabuka in 1999, and was part of the 'Moderates Forum' that gave its preference votes to the SDL rather than to the FLP at the 2001 election. It fared poorly at the 2001 polls, with Beddoes himself becoming the party's sole member in parliament. Prior to the 2006 election, Beddoes realigned the party with the FLP, ending a long association between general-voter-based parties and the mainstream Fijian leadership (see Yellow Bucket, 'The "Generals" – where to now?', this volume).

[5] 'Chaudhry defends Military Chief's Actions', *The Fiji Times*, 17 January 2006.

[6] FLP rally in the Suva Civic Centre covered by Sunayna Nandni, journalism student, USP.

[7] Radio debate, VitiFM, 3 May 2006.

[8] To appreciate just how poorly PANU performed, it is worth noting that the party received more votes from above-the-line first preference transfers from the FLP (1,565) than it obtained directly (1,264 above-the-line plus 59 below-the-line). (Data obtained from Master Tally Collection Sheet 0-39, Ba East Fijian, provided by Fiji Elections Office.) This outcome is invisible in the normally published results, which only show the totals obtained by each party at each stage of the count (in this case 2,888). In Fiji's elaborate voting system, parties are able to lodge preferences even where they do not stand candidates. These candidate-less party preference lists must place another party, with a candidate standing, as first preference. In this case, FLP first preference votes were directly transferred to PANU.

9 *The Fiji Times*, 8 July 2006, p.7.
10 Press Conference, Fiji Teachers Union conference room, 18 May 2006.
11 *Fiji Sun*, 23 May 2006.
12 Anonymous, personal communication to author by a Labour executive, 17 July 2006.
13 Personal communication to author for *Islands Business* cover story, June 2006.
14 FijiOne News, 15 June 2006.
15 Ratu Joni Madraiwiwi, Keynote address, Fiji Institute of Accountants Congress, Sheraton Fiji Resort, 23 June 2006.
16 FijiOne News, 24 June 2006.
17 *Oxford English Dictionary*, Oxford University Press, 1956 edition.

9

The failure of the moderates

The Yellow Bucket Team[1]

In the lead-up to the 2006 election, certain sections of Suva society and the media made much of the 'moderates' and the potential impact they would have at the polls. This was not a new phenomenon: exaggerated expectations of great gains for moderate parties were a feature of media reports and urban aspirations prior to the 2001 election. Similarly, prior to the 1999 election, many believed that the Soqosoqo ni Vakavulewa ni Taukei/National Federation Party/United Generals Party (SVT/NFP/UGP) coalition would fare well owing to its 'moderate' multiracial agenda. Each time, however, the 'moderates' have been rejected and not by a small margin.

First, let's examine this term 'moderate' and what it really means within the context of Fiji. In western politics, occupying the political centre tends to be the key to victory, leading parties to compete vigorously for the middle ground. For observers familiar with such settings, it therefore seems illogical that the political centre of Fiji's politics has proved such an electoral dead zone. The key difference is that the political wings of Fiji's politics are dominated not by the more conventional economic and social ideologies but by race.

A close examination of the actual economic policies of both major parties will find a pragmatic mixture of philosophies that in the final analysis turn out to be very similar. So, for example, while the Soqosoqo ni Duavata ni Lewenivanua (SDL) is assumed to be more on the right wing of the political spectrum, it is very strong on the kind of affirmative action policies traditionally associated with the left, while the FLP, despite portraying itself as worker-based and left of centre, vigorously promotes privatization.[2]

The reality of Fiji's politics is that you have a Fijian political right wing with, at its most extreme, aggressive nationalists who have in the past supported political figures like Sakeasi Butadroka and who were enthusiastic backers of the various coups and George Speight. At the extreme left, within the outer edges of the Indo-Fijian community, you will find figures with political views reminiscent of those expressed by Hindu nationalist politicians in India. Fueled by a fierce sense of grievance that finds its origin in the *girmit* (indenture) period, these views are rarely expressed openly, but provide a significant undercurrent to Indo-Fijian politics. Fiji's ideological spectrum, therefore, stretches between these two extremes, with, in the centre, a small group of educated élite promoting the cause of multi-racialism in its purest form.

The vision of a multiracial country working together in harmony represents a commonly expressed utopia for many in Fiji. Whether it be in school oratory contests, public debates or letters to the editors columns, you will find this dream described over and over again. Why then does it represent a political tar pit – one into which numerous politicians have seen their futures sink without a trace?

Dig a little deeper and you find that multiracialism in Fiji is viewed as a positive concept, but only if practiced on each race's terms. For example, you will find the view often expressed by Fijian voters that they welcome Indo-Fijians and other races, but political power must remain in the hands of the Fijians. Similarly, Indo-Fijians will talk warmly about Fijian friends and neighbours, but at the same time privately express extreme distrust as to their competence in running the country. Hence, the Indo-Fijian argument runs, there is a need for an aggressive, strong leader who will keep them (the Fijians) honest.

Multi-racialism as a political policy is, therefore, a charade in Fiji. Plenty play at it but very few really practice it – and this is why the so-called moderates have found it so difficult to dislodge the large Fijian- and Indo-Fijian-based parties (at present the SDL and FLP, respectively). These two parties typify what has been a successful strategy since independence – dominate a racial wing and from that position move to the centre when appropriate. This strategy is particularly useful as attitudes towards 'multiracialism on our terms' vary according to the political mood. In times of crisis, the support at the extremes hardens; during periods of calm and prosperity there is growth in the multiracial centre. It is, therefore, essential that a party have the flexibility to shift position to suit the prevailing mood. Getting it wrong, as the SVT and NFP found in 1999, is fatal.

This racial positioning is made all the more successful by Fiji's communal-based electoral system. With 23 Fijian communal seats and 19 Indo-Fijian seats, dominating one racial wing provides an essential political base. Moderate parties attempting to strike out from the centre have found this racial dominance of wings a huge barrier to achieving any form of electoral momentum.

The results of the 2006 election demonstrated this. While parties like the NFP and the new Alliance Party of Fiji (NAPF) tried to take a position in the centre, they were squeezed out by the FLP and the SDL, which both moved quite distinctly in their 2006 manifestos toward the multiracial centre. To quote the SDL manifesto:

> The SDL has a very large tent. It is not only for indigenous Fijians. It has room for everyone. Its membership has always been multiracial. Increasingly, the party has received support from non-Fijians, and expects to win more of their votes in this election.[3]

Similar views were expressed by the FLP in their manifesto – and yet minimal cross-racial voting was recorded. If anything, such voting declined in the 2006 election.

While it was always going to be a challenge to find room in the multiracial center of Fijian politics, both the NFP and the NAPF added to their political woes by making a number of strategic blunders.

The NFP, Fiji's oldest political party, entered the election without the most basic of political requirements, a recognizable leader. After several attempts to find a leader, they fought the election under the nominal control of Raman Pratap Singh, but it was widely recognized that the party was in fact being run by a committee of leaders featuring people like trade unionists Attar Singh and Pramod Rae. They were the public face of the NFP and, along with a number of senior advisors, determined strategies, leaving their party president to campaign for his Vanua Levu seat. The result amongst voters was total confusion. Potential supporters had little idea as to who the real leader of the party was, and, up against a powerful figure like Mahendra Chaudhry, they presented little competition. This confusion appeared an issue not only for voters; within the party itself there was considerable indecision over political direction and strategies to adopt.

In the lead-up to the election, the NFP viewed themselves as the king-makers. Recognizing that they would struggle to win a seat, they made much of holding the balance-of-power with what they hoped would be around 20 per cent of the Indian vote. With that kind of vote-share, NFP preferences would decide which of the two dominant parties would win power. Intense negotiations took place with both the SDL and the FLP about NFP preferences. While it was understood that the minor moderate parties would share early preferences, the real issue was whether the NFP would place SDL ahead of FLP or vice versa. It was assumed by many that ultimately the NFP would follow past practices and place the FLP last. In the SDL camp, Prime Minister Qarase handled negotiations personally, and, as the deadline for the filing of preferences approached, the SDL were confident they had NFP support – apparently in return for promises of Senate and, through the Senate, cabinet appointments. This, in the eyes of the SDL leadership, in addition to their own overwhelming Fijian support, would guarantee election victory for the SDL.

However, unexpectedly, the NFP ended up adopting a mixed approach to their preferences – switching the order of the FLP and SDL according to criteria based on the individual candidate in each seat, on the promotion of women candidates, and on making sure sugar-cane belt seats remained represented by an Indian party. This decision turned what the SDL thought would be a minimum 42-seat victory into a very tight election race.

At the same time, it won the NFP no favours from their bitter rivals, the FLP, who continued their very successful strategy from the past two elections of accusing the NFP of selling out to the SDL. This was ironic because a key factor in the NFP's decision to split preferences was to avoid just this accusation, but in taking this path they were caught in a classic no-win situation. The only way to avoid accusations of a racial sell-out by their opponents would have been to offer blanket support for the FLP, but this would have made participating in the election a rather pointless exercise.

In all this indecision, the NFP surrendered a politically advantageous position that appeared to be finally gaining some ground – that of being the Indo-Fijian party that could work with the Fijian community for the betterment of all. This position called for the abandonment of the past confrontational politics of the FLP (portrayed by some as 'boycott or high court'). While it didn't appear that this would enable the NFP to oust the FLP, it was at least a coherent and clear stand around which the NFP could have built a campaign.

It is hard to understand just what the NFP hoped to achieve with its approach to preferences. In addition to fears of an Indo-Fijian backlash, it could have been that the NFP feared giving all their preferences to the SDL and thereby delivering to them a two-thirds majority and the associated power to change the constitution. Whatever the logic, the reality was that the NFP destroyed whatever political influence they could have hoped to have had and denied themselves alliances with either of the two powerhouses, the SDL and the FLP.

In addition, along with their moderate counterparts – the NAPF, who adopted a similar strategy – they confused the electorate. With over 90 per cent of the electorate voting 'above-the-line' along party lines, the split preference approach left many unsure as to where their votes might eventually end up. Both the FLP and, particularly, the SDL exploited this situation. The SDL took out newspaper advertisements warning Fijian voters not to take the risk and instead to 'tick the dove [the symbol of the SDL] above the line'. This proved very effective and Fijian voters, already nervous about a repeat of 2000, decided to stick with what they knew and vote with either of the two major parties. Similarly, Indo-Fijian voters were reminded in election gatherings by the FLP not to take the risk of being sold out to the SDL.

The NFP's woes were shared by the 'new kids' on the political scene, the NAPF. The NAPF was created following the ousting of Ratu Epeli Ganilau as the chairman of the Bose Levu Vakaturaga (Great Council of Chiefs). In this role, he had impressed many educated urban observers with the innovative manner by which he attempted to transform this very traditional and previously rather ineffective body into one more relevant to the challenges facing the Fijian people of today. In the process he almost inevitably entered into conflict with the more conservative elements of the *vanua* and with the SDL government.

Much was expected of the NAPF, particularly within the Suva-based liberal élite, but Ratu Epeli never appeared very comfortable as a politician. He struggled to build a solid political base and relied heavily on the 'leftovers' of Fijian politics to stand as candidates. Many of these aging figures had previously been members of the SVT and the Fijian Association. It gave the party a very stale feel, when it desperately needed a younger, more dynamic image.[4]

To make this worse, the NAPF decided to link Ratu Epeli with the chiefly legacy of his father, Ratu Sir Penaia Ganilau, and a long line of respected chiefs, including former president Ratu Sir Kamisese Mara and earlier post-war leader Ratu Sir Lala Sukuna. The images of these figures of history featured prominently on NAPF advertising, reinforcing the very old feel of the party. The decision to try and give the party a chiefly image was a dangerous strategy. While it may have appealed to some within the General Voter category, to the critical Fijian electorate it did not relate to the Fiji of 2006 – and may even have appeared a little presumptuous.

The disastrous performance of the moderates speaks for itself. The NFP's share of Indo-Fijian votes dropped from 22.1 per cent to 14.4 per cent and, while they achieved a small increase in Fijian votes, this only amounted to 1.3 per cent. Altogether, the NFP won just 6.3 per cent of the total vote. The NAPF won 2.5 per cent of Fijian communal votes, 1.7 per cent of Indo-Fijian votes and, not surprisingly, 7.6 per cent of General votes. Together, however, this represented a mere 4 per cent of the total vote.

Despite brave words in the wake of the election, it is difficult to see how either of these parties will survive their crushing defeats. Tradition, and NFP's base in municipal councils and within a faction of the trade union movement, may sustain the NFP, but it is hard to see how they will achieve any level of national influence without a charismatic leader and a fundamental change in Indo-Fijian politics. The most likely fate of the NAPF is to follow parties like the Fijian Association, the VLV and SVT and slide away into obscurity, perhaps to re-emerge in another form in 2011.

What of the moderate multiracial political agenda? It is very hard in this current political environment to see an opportunity for a moderate party to emerge from the centre.

Continued political and economic stability will see both the SDL and FLP move more and more towards the middle ground of Fijian politics. This is already evident in the early days of the Qarase-led multiparty cabinet – and the longer this lasts the more attractive moderate multiracial policies will become to voters. However, this shift will come at the initiative of the two giants of Fiji politics, and most definitely on their terms.

Notes

[1] The 'Yellow Bucket' is a weekly column on Fiji politics and national affairs that can be found at <www.fijivillage.com>. Inspiration for the column is found, like many things in Fiji, around a yellow bucket of *yaqona* or kava – hence the name. Launched early in 2003, it has gained a reputation for providing astute observation of Fiji politics and its forecasts have proved remarkably accurate in recent years. Authorship of the column is credited to an editorial board that gathers regularly around a yellow bucket.

[2] Mahendra Chaudhry made such remarks on 'The Real Deal' talkback show, VitiFM/Radio Sargam, 3 May 2006; see also the references to 'public private partnerships to "weed out corrupt practices" in state owned industries' in the 2006 FLP Manifesto, 2006, <http://www.flp.org.fj/Fiji_Labour_Manifesto-final[2].pdf> (accessed 29 July 2006).

[3] SDL 2006 Manifesto, p.8, <http://www.sdlparty.com.fj/SDLManEngSum.pdf> (accessed 29 July 2006).

[4] Ratu Epeli even said that the party would finalize its list of candidates once the major parties had completed their pre-selection, so that the NAPF could pick up rejected candidates from the other parties. Certainly, beyond Ratu Epeli and one or two other figures the NAPF looked like a party of rejects.

10

The impact of the Reconciliation, Tolerance and Unity Bill on the 2006 election

Mosmi Bhim

'The re-election of the Soqosoqo Duavata ni Lewenivanua-led government hinges on the success of the Promotion of the Reconciliation, Tolerance and Unity Bill... If the Bill goes down, the government goes down with it.' So said Fiji's Attorney General Qoriniasi Bale, a key ally of the Prime Minister, at a public meeting on 15 June 2005.[1] That comment, a year prior to Fiji's May 2006 general election, indicated the great political importance attached by the government to legislation ostensibly aimed at bringing closure to five years of police investigations, settling differences between the victims and aggressors of the May 2000 coup, and establishing a framework for greater harmony between the country's 55 per cent indigenous Fijian and 40 per cent Indo-Fijian communities. Yet, from the time the Promotion of Reconciliation, Tolerance and Unity (RTU) Bill was first mooted, tensions between the Soqosoqo Duavata ni Lewenivanua (SDL) and the major Indo-Fijian party, the Fiji Labour Party (FLP), and between the government and the Republic of Fiji Military Forces (RFMF) were gravely inflamed by the proposed new legislation. Opponents saw the amnesty provisions in the Bill as a dangerous concession to Fijian nationalist opinion, and as potentially entailing the release from prison of 2000 coup leader, George Speight, and of prominent chiefs convicted for coup-related offences. Despite so explicitly pinning its electoral fortunes to the fate of the Bill, after months of great controversy, the government eventually chose to shelve the

Bill shortly before the 2006 election, declaring its intention instead to revisit the issues thereafter.

This chapter looks at why the government chose to introduce such controversial legislation in the run-up to the 2006 poll. It examines first the provisions of the Bill, and why, five years after the coup (rather than in its immediate aftermath), political difficulties arose that prompted resort to parliamentary legislation on the amnesty issue. In order to address that question, it is necessary to revisit the events of May–November 2000, and consider the coup-related offences committed at that time. The chapter then considers the positions of the government and other supporters, as well as the objections of opponents, including the FLP and the RFMF, and reviews the documentation arising out of the joint parliamentary select committee that was convened to deliberate on the proposed legislation. Finally, it considers why the RTU Bill was eventually deferred, prior to the 2006 election, and whether or not it nevertheless achieved important objectives for the SDL election campaign.

The provisions of the RTU Bill

The idea of a reconciliation Bill was first raised in August 2004, and the fully drafted Bill was introduced on the floor of parliament on 31 May 2005. The Bill provided for the establishment of a Reconciliation and Unity Commission with powers to conduct inquiries and to facilitate the granting of reparations, compensation and amnesty. The conduct of the inquiries, the Bill specified, would also take into account the traditional Fijian principles of restorative justice. Two committees were to be established – a Victims and Reparations Committee, responsible for granting reparations and compensation, and an Amnesty Committee, empowered not simply to release prisoners, but also to nullify the original convictions. Both of these committees were to have three members, who would deliberate on applications made and submit reports to the commission. In addition, a National Council for the Promotion of Reconciliation, Tolerance and Unity was to be established and entrusted with developing strategies for the promotion of greater understanding between the two major racial communities.

Of the 36 clauses contained in the RTU Bill, the longest was clause 21, titled 'Applications for Amnesty', which had 15 sub-clauses. It allowed those convicted of coup-related offences that were classified as 'politically motivated' and committed between 19 May 2000 and 15 March 2001 to apply for amnesty. 'Politically motivated' activities were to be distinguished from those of a 'criminal' nature, a proposal which generated obvious difficulties: 'treason', for example, is usually highly politically motivated but nevertheless usually also considered the most severe form of criminal activity against the state. The intended application of the Bill to the 2000 coup-related prisoners was explicit, and the four clauses relating to this indicated some urgency in securing the release of prisoners on the part of government. The four clauses were:

(2) In dealing with applications for amnesty, the Commission shall give priority to applications from persons in custody...

(6) If an applicant for amnesty is charged...or is standing trial...the Commission may request the court to postpone the criminal proceedings pending the consideration and disposal of the application for amnesty...

(12) Any person who has been granted amnesty...shall be released from prison forthwith on a warrant issued by the President...

(13) An amnesty granted by the President...shall have the effect of erasing the conviction.[2]

The final reference to 'erasing the conviction' provides further insight into the objective of the RTU Bill. The 1997 constitution potentially already provided the government with the means, via a Prerogative of Mercy Commission, to grant 'pardons' to chiefs and others imprisoned for coup or mutiny-related activities. Indeed, that Commission had been convened to commute a death sentence for George Speight to life imprisonment.[3] But amnesties, unlike pardons, wipe out the stain of the preceding conviction, a matter of no small importance for Fiji's status-oriented convicted chiefs, as shown in the next section.

Why was the RTU Bill introduced?

By 2005, the government had a number of good reasons for wanting to bring an end to the coup-related court cases. Fiji could not continue, forever, to thrash over the events of 2000. The Police Commissioner, Australian Andrew Hughes, would have liked to have finished the coup investigations before the 2006 elections.[4] In a statement to the media after introducing the RTU Bill in May 2005, Prime Minister Laisenia Qarase said the main purpose of the intended legislation was to bring closure to the turbulent era following the 2000 coup:

> It will enable us to more effectively concentrate on nation-building, strengthening our economy and improving living standards, especially for the poor…The long delays in completing investigations are evidence that our law enforcement authorities are having difficulty coping. This is an issue of great concern…The concept of restorative justice is not new to Fijians. It is built into their culture. The whole community becomes involved in finding solutions and imposing sanctions. This is reflected in various customary practices such as *veisorosorovi*[5] and *matanigasau*.[6]

Such appeals to traditional or customary ideals of reconciliation, however, were questioned by others, such as Citizens Constitutional Forum activist Jone Dakuvula, who suggested that Fijian rituals of *veisorosorovi* and *matanigasau* are customarily undertaken only after there has been prior agreement between the perpetrator and the victim. The offender cannot force the offended to accept *matanigasau*. Mr Dakuvula said the government's proposed Reconciliation and Unity Commission was not a genuine product of reconciliation because the victims had not been consulted.[7]

The Qarase government's Ministry of Multi-Ethnic Affairs and National Reconciliation and Unity, which sought to promote the ideals of Christian forgiveness, harmony and cooperation as a way forward for Fiji, came to play a central role in promoting support for the RTU Bill. The government declared 4–11 October 2004 as 'Reconciliation Week', to coincide with Fiji's independence day on 10 October. The Tui Cakau and Lands Minister Ratu Naiqama Lalabalavu led a *matanigasau* ceremony at Albert Park, Suva, at which 20 *tabua* (whale teeth) were presented to seek forgiveness from the parliamentarians held hostage during the 2000 coup. He was accompanied by Naitasiri chief Ratu Inoke Takiveikata, Bau chief Ratu Tanoa Cakobau and Ratu Inoke Seniloli, the younger brother of imprisoned Vice President Ratu Jope Seniloli.[8] It was an act of contrition viewed by many as hypocritical. Deposed Prime Minister Mahendra Chaudhry and the MPs held hostage in 2000 were not present to receive the *matanigasau*. Very few Indo-Fijians attended the event. Nevertheless, the themes of 'reconciliation' and 'forgiveness' struck a chord within predominantly Christian Fijian communities and seemed, for the government, to provide a means of mobilizing support for nation-building and perhaps also a means to marginalize critics in the FLP, who could thereby be accused of unwillingness to reconcile and forgive those who had, it was to be publicly acknowledged, done them such great injustice at the time of the May–July 2000 disturbances. This set the tone for the deliberations on the RTU Bill.

In order to fully appreciate the context of the RTU Bill, it is necessary to revisit the events surrounding the 19 May 2000 coup. On that day, George Speight had led a group of gunmen to seize control of Fiji's parliament, deposing the government of Fiji's first Indo-Fijian Prime Minister, Mahendra Chaudhry. The insurrection had coincided with a *taukei* march through Suva; some 15,000 people took to the streets of the city, greatly outnumbering police officers. A total of 167 shops were looted, 15 shops and five kiosks burnt down and 269 people arrested in the rampage, with total damage costs estimated at $30 million by then Police Commissioner Isikia Savua.[9] Around 7,500 people were to lose their jobs as a result of the 2000 coup.[10]

The day after the coup, inside parliament, Bau high chief Ratu Jope Seniloli swore in a rebel prime minister and cabinet – many of whom were later to be convicted for taking an illegal oath. For the next 56 days, members of parliament from the government side, including Prime Minister Mahendra Chaudhry, were held hostage inside the Veiuto complex. They were surrounded by a human shield of supporters, who drank grog, ate and sang in the grounds of the complex, where they also did their laundry and cooking.[11]

Military commander Frank Bainimarama was far away in Lebanon on the day of the coup, but cut short his trip upon hearing of events in Suva.[12] Speight and his group had hoped to trigger full backing from the RFMF, but, instead, the military encircled the complex, commencing a protracted siege. Soldiers were reluctant to move into parliament for fear the rebels might carry out their threat of injuring the hostages.[13]

Despite the loose cordon thrown around parliament, Speight and his followers were able to move in and out with comparative ease. A state of emergency was declared on 27 May 2000, but to little avail. That night, rebels marched through Suva and trashed the Fiji TV headquarters, threatening also to march on the President's residence.

Reportedly in response, on 29 May, the military commander asked the then president of Fiji, Tui Nayau Ratu Sir Kamisese Mara, to step aside. Bainimarama assumed executive authority, and issued a decree to abrogate the constitution. Thereafter, the army strengthened its presence around Suva and oversaw negotiations with the rebels. Daily curfews were imposed, lasting from sunset until sunrise. The city suffered power cuts over the 56-day siege, as a result of the sabotage of the Monasavu dam, the key hydro-electric power source for Viti Levu. Speight and the rebels also encouraged takeovers of police stations and the setting up of roadblocks in other parts of the country. Victimization of Indo-Fijian communities occurred in areas such as Muaniweni, Naitasiri, Dawasamu in northern Tailevu and Dreketi near Labasa, where farms were looted, Indo-Fijian villagers threatened and cattle killed. Fears that the coup might trigger a bloody split in the RFMF seemed realized after a mutiny at the Sukunaivalu Barracks at Labasa, on Fiji's second largest island Vanua Levu, in July 2000.

Eventually, top military officers' efforts to reach a settlement bore some success. Signed on 9 July 2000, the Muanikau Accord promised to address the political demands of the coup perpetrators and to give them an amnesty in exchange for the release of the hostage parliamentarians and the return of all weapons. The remaining hostages – including the deposed prime minister, Mahendra Chaudhry – were released by 13 July 2000.

Although the rebels vacated parliament, instead of disbanding they shifted to the Kalabu Fijian School on Suva's outskirts, and continued to destabilize the country. The military lost patience. George Speight, together with his lawyer Tevita Bukarau, his media advisor Josefa Nata and his personal bodyguard, known only as 'Cakau', were arrested on the night of 26 July 2000 at the Laqere Bridge, for failing to stop at a military checkpoint and for carrying illegal weapons in violation of the Muanikau Accord.[14] The next day, the army stormed the Kalabu school, in an operation which resulted in the death of one rebel and 32 casualties, and the arrest of key figures, such as the rebel strategist Colonel Ilisoni Ligairi and Josefa Savua, the brother of Police Commissioner Isikia Savua.[15] Altogether, 415 people were arrested. Others captured included Lieutenant Colonel Rusiate Korovusere, former Fiji Intelligence Services boss Colonel Metuisela Mua and Rewa MP Ratu Timoci Silatolu. As had been the case for Speight, amnesty provisions were deemed inapplicable because the rebels were carrying illegal weapons.

Four months later, the country appeared to be moving back to normality. But then, on 2 November 2000, a mutiny by rebel soldiers took place at the Queen Elizabeth Barracks in Nabua – not long before the date for a scheduled court hearing for George Speight. Commander Bainimarama narrowly escaped an attempt on his life. Mutinous soldiers from the Counter Revolutionary Warfare Unit (CRWU) killed three unarmed regular soldiers as the mutineers tried to take over the national operations centre. Five CRWU soldiers were later killed when loyalist forces recaptured the military camp.[16] The incident left a legacy of bitterness and tension within the army, and helps to explain officers' strong hostility to the RTU Bill.

Aside from wanting to bring an end to the long-drawn-out saga of coup-related court cases, by late 2004 the government had become greatly concerned about the growing legal threat to Fiji's customary chiefs. The initial arrests of the so-called 'civilian coup' leaders back in 2000, and then of the soldiers who had played a somewhat more secretive role, had left many of the country's traditional chiefs untouched, although some were widely known to have

Table 10.1   Police charges for offences committed during the 2000 civil unrest

Unlawful assembly	498
Mutiny	62
Treason[1]	24
Wrongful confinement	25
Arson	19
Robbery with violence	19
Incitement to mutiny	17
Damaging property	17
Shop-breaking and entering	15
Other offences	18
Total charges	714

Notes: [1] Includes taking an illegal oath.
Source: Police information provided for *Report of the Sector Standing Committee on Justice, Law and Order on the Promotion of Reconciliation, Tolerance and Unity Bill*, November/December 2005, p.53–54.

Table 10.2   Date of imprisonment, sentences and release dates for key leaders convicted as a result of disturbances between 19 May 2000 and 15 March 2001

	Date of imprisonment	Main offence(s)	Sentence	Date of release	Compulsory supervision order
Civilians					
George Speight	18 Feb 2002	Treason	Life	Still in prison	
Jim Speight	Feb 2002	Wrongful confinement	2 years	18 Feb 2004	
Colonel Ilisoni Ligairi	Feb 2002	Wrongful confinement	2 years	18 Feb 2004	
Josefa Nata	June 2003	Treason	Life	Still in prison	
Ratu Timoci Silatolu (former MP)	June 2003	Treason	Life	Still in prison	
Major Tevita Bukurau (former army lawyer)	May 2005	Unlawful assembly/ Firearms*	2.5 years	Still in prison	CSO from May 2006
Colonel Metuisela Mua (former FIS Director)	May 2005	Unlawful assembly/ Firearms*	2.5 years	Still in prison	
Iliesa Duvuloco (politician)	Feb 2002	Wrongful confinement	18 months	18 Feb 2003	
Viliame Savu (politician)	5 Aug 2004	Unlawful oath	12 months		CSO from Jan 2005
Peceli Rinakama	5 Aug 2004	Unlawful oath	3 years	Still in prison	
Viliame Volavola	5 Aug 2004	Unlawful oath	3 years	Still in prison	
Apisai Tora (politician)	Sept 2005	Unlawful assembly	8 months		CSO from 18 Nov 2005
Jioji Bakoso	May 2005	Unlawful assembly/ Firearms*	15 months	Still in prison	
Viliame Sausauwai	May 2005	Unlawful assembly/ Firearms*	2 years	Still in prison	
Eroni Lewaqai	May 2005	Unlawful assembly/ Firearms*	2 years	Still in prison	
Customary chiefs					
Ratu Jope Seniloli (VP)	5 Aug 2004	Unlawful oath	4 years		CSO from 25 Nov 2005

Name	Date	Offence	Sentence	Status	CSO
Ratu Naiqama Lalabalavu (MP)	4 April 2005	Unlawful assembly	8 months	October 2005	CSO from 14 Apr 2005
Ratu Inoke Takiveikata (Senator)	23 Nov 2004	Inciting mutiny	Life	Still in prison	
Ratu Josefa Dimuri (Senator)	4 April 2005	Unlawful assembly	8 months	October 2005	CSO from 14 April 2005
Ratu Rakuita Vakalalabure (MP)	5 Aug 2004	Unlawful oath	6 years	Still in prison	CSO from June 2006
Ratu Viliame Rovabokola	4 April 2005	Unlawful assembly	8 months	October 2005	CSO from 4 August 2005
Ratu Rokodewala Niumataiwalu	4 April 2005	Unlawful assembly	8 months	October 2005	CSO from 4 August 2005
Ratu Peni Waqa	..	Forceful entry into Dawasamu police post/ Wrongful confinement	12 months		1 year CSO from Sep 2000 at Dawasamu police post
Military personnel					
Captain Shane Stevens	14 Nov 2002	Mutiny (leader)	Life	Still in prison	
Josefa Savua	Feb 2002	Wrongful confinement	2 years	18 Feb 2004	
Maciu Navakasuasua	..	Wrongful confinement	..	..	
Sergeant Keni Naika	Aug 2006	Mutiny	6 years	Still in prison	
Corporal Lagilagi Vosabeci	Aug 2006	Mutiny	5 years	Still in prison	
Sergeant Viliame Tikotani	Aug 2006	Mutiny	4 years	Still in prison	
Corporal Filimone Raivalu	Aug 2006	Mutiny	4 years	Still in prison	
Sergeant Kalisito Vuki	Aug 2006	Mutiny	3 years	Still in prison	
Lance-Corporal Usaia Rokobigi	Aug 2006	Mutiny	3 years	Still in prison	
Private Jone Nawaqa	Aug 2006	Mutiny	3 years	Still in prison	
Private Ropate Nakau	Aug 2006	Mutiny	3 years	Still in prison	

Notes: 'Still in prison' is at time of writing (September 2006). Some prisoners were released early because they had been held for a long time pending conviction, and others had their terms reduced owing to good behaviour. Ratu Rakuita Vakalalabure's six-year jail term was overturned by the Supreme Court of Fiji on 15 June 2006. Ratu Rakuita is now serving four years' imprisonment (instead of six), commencing from April 6, 2004 (*Fiji Daily Post*, Friday, June 16, 2006, p.1) * Offence was 'Consorting with people carrying firearms', .. = Not available.

played a powerful behind-the-scenes role. By late 2004, however, the Director of Public Prosecutions Office had gathered sufficient evidence to launch such prosecutions. Vice President Ratu Jope Seniloli, along with Deputy Speaker of the House Ratu Rakuita Vakalalabure and three other chiefs were convicted on 5 August 2004 for taking an unlawful oath to be part of Speight's government on the day after the coup.[17] Ratu Seniloli was sentenced to four years imprisonment and Ratu Vakalalabure to six years.[18] On 23 November 2004, the *Turaga na Qaranivalu*, Ratu Inoke Takiveikata, the paramount chief of Naitasiri, was sentenced to life imprisonment for inciting mutiny in November 2000. In mitigation, Ratu Inoke, himself a former army officer, claimed that he had requested his backers to mount a non-violent takeover of the military camp, but this was not accepted by the presiding judge, Justice Anthony Gates.

Still more importantly, Minister of Lands and Tui Cakau Ratu Naiqama Lalabalavu was convicted for unlawful assembly during the takeover of the Sukanaivalu Barracks in Labasa between 4 July and 3 August 2000.[19] In his defence, Ratu Naiqama acknowledged that he had entered the Sukanaivalu Barracks at the height of disturbances, but claimed to have been fulfilling traditional leadership responsibilities. He said he had been traditionally invited – along with the three other chiefs – by Tui Labasa Ratu Joseva Ritova Qomate to go to the barracks to ensure nothing unlawful was done.[20] The three other Vanua Levu chiefs were Ratu Josefa Dimuri, Tui Nadogo Ratu Viliame Rovabokola and Tui Wailevu Ratu Rokodewala Niumataiwalu. All four, including Ratu Naiqama, were given eight month prison sentences; all four were admitted to Labasa hospital with alleged illnesses after serving one week of their sentences. Ratu Naiqama and Ratu Josefa were released within two weeks of their conviction on compulsory supervision orders to serve their sentences extra-murally.[21] Ratu Naiqama served, in total, only ten days of his sentence before being released to serve the rest by doing community work at the Sacred Heart Catholic Cathedral in Suva.[22] Six months later, in August 2005, Ratu Viliame and Ratu Rokodewala were also released on compulsory supervision orders.[23]

For Qarase, the arrest, conviction and imprisonment of such powerful customary chiefs posed a far-reaching challenge to the leadership within Fijian society:

Police enquiries have so far implicated more than 2,500 citizens. A characteristic of the year 2000 law-breaking was that probably the majority of those involved were motivated by Fijian customary belief, tradition and duty...there was a clash of values between the old and the new, between the traditional communal system and one founded on the rule of law and individual human rights. A significant section of Fijian opinion felt those charged and convicted had been acting in furtherance of their traditional functional responsibility...they were seen to be responding to the cultural concept of the *vanua* – the chiefs, the people and the land.... The nation moved into uncharted waters when high chiefs were found guilty of coup-connected offences and sent to prison .... (this had) associated implications for social stability.[24]

There were also important political reasons why the prosecution and imprisonment of such important political figures posed difficulties for the Qarase administration. In the wake of the August 2001 general election, Qarase's SDL had formed a coalition government with the Conservative Alliance–Matanitu Vanua (CAMV). The SDL had gained 32 MPs, while the CAMV had six. Of these six, Speight had been convicted – and, at a by-election, replaced by his brother, Samisoni Tikoinasau – and both Deputy Speaker Ratu Rakuita Vakalalabure and Ratu Naiqama had been given prison sentences.[25] At the time of his imprisonment, Ratu Naiqama was not only Minister of Lands: as Tui Cakau, he was also the paramount chief of Cakaudrove, and thus leader of Tovata, one of Fiji's three traditional confederacies. Perhaps most importantly of all, he was president of the CAMV. The imprisonment of such a senior figure in the government threatened to break up the SDL–CAMV coalition, which at least in theory might have resulted in an early election. In such circumstances, Fijians might have gone to the polls deeply split, with the consequence that the SDL might have lost.

That the threat of a split was at least plausible was indicated by the revelation that, shortly before the government's introduction of the RTU Bill, the CAMV had plans to introduce legislation of its own. CAMV MP Samisoni Tikoinasau indicated that CAMV parliamentarians intended to table a motion in parliament for the government to grant immunity to coup perpetrators.[26] This was not the first time that the CAMV had requested a pardon for imprisoned coup leaders. After Ratu Jope's conviction on 5 August 2004, Ratu Naiqama reiterated the CAMV stance that all those charged with coup-related offences should be pardoned, as after the 1987 coup.[27] Tikoinasau had demanded the

Great Council of Chiefs do something about Ratu Jope's conviction, and stated that the *matanigasau* performed in 2000 to seek forgiveness should have been given legal recognition. Tikoinasau also questioned why army commander Bainimarama had not been charged for abrogating the constitution and removing then president Ratu Mara.[28] But the new threat to put the issue before parliament left the Prime Minister in some potential difficulty. Any vote on such a motion would have left the SDL with the dilemma of either siding explicitly and emphatically with the coup convicts or lining up alongside the FLP in opposing the Bill. Both courses of action would have been deeply damaging for the government.

Qarase was intent on assuaging these potential frictions in his governing coalition, and on preserving 'Fijian unity'. Ratu Naiqama had resigned on 7 April 2005, and was replaced by Tikoinasau as Minister of Lands.[29] Earlier in the year, Cakaudrove East constituency MP Manasa Tuqia had been appointed deputy speaker, after Ratu Rakuita lost his West Cakaudrove parliamentary seat as a result of missing two parliamentary sittings due to his imprisonment.[30] That the SDL was being cautious in managing its relations with the CAMV was demonstrated by the SDL's decision to not field any candidates for the Cakaudrove West by-election in June 2005, resulting in an unopposed win by CAMV's Niko Nawaikula, a lawyer and former Native Lands Trust Board official.[31] Imprisoned CAMV chiefs were quickly welcomed back into the government upon their release. Ratu Josefa Dimuri returned as a senator and secretary general of the CAMV. Ratu Naiqama was appointed as the new Transport and Shipping Minister on 21 September 2005, after completing his prison term.[32] Unlike Speight and Vakalalabure, he did not lose his seat as a result of serving a prison term because the law insists on disqualification only if the sentence is more than 12 months.[33] He had been convicted for only eight months, and had had his prison term reduced to six months for good behaviour. Nevertheless, for Ratu Naiqama, the prison sentence was thought to have been harsh and unjust. After being released from prison, Ratu Naiqama reiterated in parliament that he and three other chiefs entered Sukanaivalu Barracks in July–August 2000 on the request of the police and military.

> As a traditional leader, I take slight that, at times, our traditional authority [has] been abused and exploited by the powers that be…During the 2000 crisis in Labasa, the late Tui Labasa

and I, amongst a few other Vanua Levu chiefs were approached, both by the Police and Military to intercede in the face-off between the soldiers at Sukanaivalu Barracks....had it not been for our positive contribution, Labasa would have been looted, burnt and soldiers would have been killed and probably maimed each other. Yet, when all was brought to normal, we were charged and convicted for offences against the Public Order Act. Here, Sir, is an example of abuse of our traditional authority .... For me as Prisoner Number LB32/05 at Vaturekuka is something I will live with for the rest of my life, without any regret or shame because...I know that what I did then was right.[34]

Despite the protestations to the contrary, the stain of being found guilty in such a way clearly was not regarded lightly in Fiji's status-oriented chiefly order.

There had also been political risks associated with the conviction of senior figures within the SDL itself. Ratu Inoke Takiveikata, for example, was the founding president of SDL, a government senator and, although by 2006 behind bars, remained the vice president of the governing party. SDL member for Lomaiviti, Simione Kaitani, was also dragged before the courts, although ultimately found not guilty; and new revelations suggested a threat to senior SDL ministers, such as Konisi Yabaki and Savenaca Draunidalo. Coup convict Maciu Navakasuasua had also named Ratu Epeli Kanaimawi (a senior figure in the Assembly of Christian Churches in Fiji), Pastor Poate Mata and then Methodist Church president Reverend Tomasi Kanailagi as supporters of the coup.[35] Army officer Viliame Seruvakula (at the time serving as an instructor with the New Zealand army) revealed being offered a bribe of $250,000 to support the 2000 takeover, and implicated still more senior figures in coup-related crimes. Although the seriousness of the offence for which Ratu Inoke Takiveikata had been convicted ruled out his early release, the evident sympathy of the Prime Minister for his imprisoned ally was shown by his regular private visits to Korovou prison to brief Ratu Inoke on 'the state of the SDL party and issues of political and national importance'.[36]

The opposition position

The RTU Bill generated strong opposition among Fiji's citizens, and from the leaders of neighbouring metropolitan powers. While the main supporters of the Bill were Fijian politicians, parties, provincial councils and related groups such as the Methodist Church and Fijian trade unions, those opposing the Bill were the disciplined forces, Indian religious groups, professional organizations, foreign governments and organizations, most civil society organizations, most of the non-Fijian political parties, and some of the Christian churches. Amongst the representatives of the Fiji Indian community, the Bill generated almost blanket condemnation, particularly from those who had been victims of the 2000 coup and held hostage at the parliamentary complex. Many of the country's European and part-European politicians opposed the Bill from a legal or human rights perspective, as did the bulk of non-Fijian lawyers.

Opposition leader Mahendra Chaudhry initially called on Prime Minister Qarase to resign because stakeholders, including political parties, religious bodies, and non-governmental organizations (NGOs) had not been fully consulted about the Bill's provisions. Chaudhry said the real purpose of the Bill was to free political prisoners and that this would mean legalizing terrorism.[37] The smaller, mainly Indo-Fijian backed National Federation Party (NFP) described the Bill as a catalyst for further political instability, and as likely to widen the racial divide and so derail economic recovery.[38] The leader of the United Peoples Party, Mick Beddoes, also claimed inadequate consultation.[39] Chaudhry later said he might support the Bill if it were substantially re-written to facilitate genuine reconciliation. Truth-telling, modelled on Bishop Desmond Tutu's activities in the South African Truth and Reconciliation Commission, needed to be a core component of the process, enabling perpetrators of coup-related crimes to divulge information about the events of May 2000 and the secretive backers of the coup.[40]

Overseas reactions were tempered by reluctance to interfere in Fiji's domestic affairs. Australian Minister for Foreign Affairs Alexander Downer said 'the army commander had no business in politics and should stick to his job – running the military'.[41] His New Zealand counterpart, Phil Goff, was more critical of the government, criticizing the idea that 'people who have overthrown a democratic government by force may be exempted from the category of criminals if it was done for political reasons'.[42] He urged Prime Minister Qarase to amend the controversial amnesty provisions. The US Ambassador to Fiji, David Lyon, expressed concern about the amnesty section saying that a coup culture had developed in Fiji since 1987 that was detrimental to Fiji's reputation and would have a negative impact on investment, tourism and the 2006 elections.[43] A

Tebbutt poll of 1,008 people found that 44 per cent of residents were against the Bill, 35 per cent were for it and 12 per cent did not care.[44]

Opposition was expressed by regional and international government bodies and NGOs. The European Union, local NGOs – such as the Citizens' Constitutional Forum, Women's Action for Change, the Ecumenical Centre for Research Education and Advocacy, and the Fiji Women's Rights Movement – protested against the Bill, saying it breached UN human rights conventions. The Fiji Cane Growers' Council and the National Farmers Union expressed opposition.[45] Fiji Public Service Association general gecretary Rajeshwar Singh claimed solid opposition by trade unions around the world.[46] The International Confederation of Free Trade Unions wrote to the Fiji Prime Minister expressing apprehension about the RTU Bill, and was particularly alarmed by the amnesty provision for coup perpetrators.[47]

The Fiji Police Force opposed the Bill on the grounds that the amnesty provision would interfere with the authority of the Police Commissioner to investigate offences and prosecute offenders. The military, as discussed in more detail in the next section, likewise opposed the Bill on security grounds, expressing anxiety that the amnesty provisions would legitimize terrorism.[48] The Fiji Law Society opposed the Bill on the grounds that some of its provisions were unconstitutional and that granting of amnesty would erode and have a harmful effect on the role of the judiciary. Such a law, it said, would retrospectively license terrorism, was a recipe for instability and would interfere with the powers of the Director of Public Prosecutions. The society warned against improper use of customary law and tradition for political gain; society president Graham Leung reminded the government that 'no culture, no religion and no government are above the law'. The International Commission of Jurists said the amnesty provision appeared incompatible with international law and insisted that it be amended so as not to violate Fiji's obligations under international human rights law. The Human Rights Institute of the International Bar Association expressed reservations that the Bill would be able to deliver the 'reconciliation' that it promised.[49]

The outcry amongst civil society organizations, political parties and international donors and diplomats came as a surprise to Qarase and Attorney General Qoriniasi Bale, who acknowledged the need for further consultation and declared an intention to consider substantial amendments to the Bill. The Prime Minister assured the public that, given the strength of the public reaction, the Bill would be reviewed: the report of the sector committee entrusted with examining the proposed legislation was to play a major role in determining the final draft. The government also promised to ensure that the final legislation met the requirements of the constitution and did not compromise the Office of the President.[50]

The military position

The RTU Bill exacerbated a previously existing rift between the government and the RFMF. The impasse between the military commander and the government had been ongoing since 2001. Frictions between the military and the government had forced the latter to change key position-holders in the Home Affairs Ministry two times – Home Affairs Minister Jonetani Cokanasiga was relegated to the back benches in December 2004 and replaced by Josefa Vosanibola; and Home Affairs CEO Jeremaia Waqanisau was transferred to an ambassador's post in China in January 2004. The commander also distrusted the new Home Affairs CEO, Dr Lesi Korovavala, and was later to hold him responsible for the stand-off between the military and the government in January 2006. The military then alleged that Korovavala and Prime Minister Qarase had encouraged Lieutenant Colonel Jone Baledrokadroka to incite a mutiny in that month.[51] The government had initially appeared reluctant to extend Bainimarama's contract in February 2004, but President Ratu Josefa Iloilo had decided to renew his term in office on 29 January 2004.[52]

For the RFMF, the RTU Bill was seen as a threat to its efforts to stabilize the security situation in the aftermath of the 2000 coup. RFMF commander Frank Bainimarama had faced a personal threat to his life during the November 2000 mutiny. He had purged senior commanders with suspect loyalties, often keeping them close to military headquarters at Berkeley Crescent in positions without major responsibility. Top commanders believed that the Bill would derail their efforts to bring to justice those responsible for the insurrections of May and November 2000.

The military conducted a succession of long-drawn-out trials from 2001. By April 2005, 159 sentences had been handed down: 58 soldiers had faced

court martial for their role in the 2000 parliamentary takeover, 63 were tried
for the takeover of the Sukanaivalu Barracks in Labasa, and the remainder were
convicted for their part in the bloody mutiny of November 2000 and other
coup-related offences.[53] The military refused to accept back into employment
any of the convicted soldiers. The RTU Bill was viewed as likely to reverse efforts
to bring those responsible for insurrection to justice. Even existing practices,
such as the release of coup convicts under compulsory supervision orders,
were strongly opposed by the commander. Bainimarama pointed out that the
government was not only allowing people tainted by coup allegations to go
free; they were 'even getting plush government jobs and diplomatic postings'.
This, he argued, was creating a generation of criminals with no respect for the
rule of law.[54]

Secondly, the formation of the Qarase government had, originally, been a
military initiative, and the commander felt that ministers owed some loyalty
to those who had put them into office. In the wake of the May 2000 upheaval,
Qarase had headed an 'interim administration', with former military commander
Ratu Epeli Nailatikau as deputy prime minister. It had not been intended as a
permanent fixture. Originally, these interim leaders were apolitical technocrats,
thrust into office to stabilize the political situation. That the government was
characterized by appeasement of the nationalists combined oddly with their
apparent support for the upholding of law. This was a contradiction expressed
in the regular refrain that the Prime Minister supported the coup goals, but not
its means. Comprised of realist politicians, the SDL realized that the support
of the nationalists was crucial if it were to win. Only in 2001, in the wake of
a court ruling rendering the government illegal, did Qarase reconstitute some
parts of the group, first as a 'caretaker' cabinet, and then as the core of the
new SDL party. In the process, the commander believed, the government had
lost sight of its original mandate and proved itself to be in thrall to nationalist
extremist demands.

The military's formal submission to the parliamentary select committee
entrusted with undertaking hearings on the proposed legislation stated:

> The Bill is ill conceived and is a recipe for internal conflict, unrest and violence. It is
> discriminatory and will breed ethno-nationalism… bring about despair, hopelessness and
> insecurity amongst the people as well as promote greater racial division. The majority of

the offences committed during the period were predominantly by the indigenous race (offender) against those of Indian descent (victim); it will allow for the pardoning of the indigenous offenders versus the interests of the victims, thereby breeding the ideology of ethno-nationalism that is detrimental to the safety and well being of our society.[55]

The conviction of Ratu Inoke Takiveikata for inciting and aiding the November 2000 mutiny in which the commander narrowly escaped assassination sheds some light on why Bainimarama had been against the SDL since its formation in 2001. As discussed above, Ratu Inoke had called, so he admitted in court, for a peaceful takeover of the military camp. He had nevertheless later become the founding president of SDL and, even after his conviction, remained on close terms with the Prime Minister. This implied that, since its commencement, the SDL had prominently featured people who would have liked to have seen the army commander removed. That the threats to the commander in November 2000 were not confined to history also seemed, whether rightly or wrongly, demonstrated by the alleged attempted mutiny by acting land forces commander Colonel Jone Baledrokadroka on 12 January 2006, which Bainimarama claimed had been orchestrated by the government.[56] Bainimarama refused to rule out overthrowing the government if the Bill were passed.[57]

Great Council of Chiefs' Senator Jim Ah Koy, businessman and former finance minister, echoed the commander's stance, explaining that 'his priority is national security and that is why he is coming out strong against the Bill'.[58] Despite years of vociferous denunciation of the government, the commander succeeded in retaining his position at the helm of the RFMF. Close connections with the Office of the President placed the commander in a unique position. As the President was the appointing authority, according to one interpretation, the commander – although normally subject to oversight from the Home Affairs Ministry – was ultimately under the control of the President. The military also insisted that its 'reserve powers' under the 1990 constitution had not been superseded by the 1997 constitution.[59] As a result, the commander believed he could securely speak out against the RTU Bill. Indeed, he vowed to continue doing so until the Bill was withdrawn.[60] Bainimarama stressed that the RFMF would not take part in any reconciliation on the grounds that this would interfere with the military's discipline and court martial processes.[61] In addition to opposing the RTU Bill, the army had reservations about the Qoliqoli Bill and the proposed Bill on the Fijian courts.[62] Nor was this oppositional activity confined to statements to the Fiji media. In the run-up to the 2006 election, the RFMF public relations team campaigned against the RTU Bill by distributing pamphlets[63] and visiting rural areas to warn people about the Bill's disadvantages.[64]

The government's reaction

When the RTU Bill was introduced into parliament on 31 May 2005, the Leader of the House requested the Standing Orders be suspended to allow the House to deal with its first reading. In the public gallery, as if in a show of strength, military personnel sat quietly, closely observing the progress of the Bill through parliament.[65] The Opposition Whip, the Hon. Krishna Datt, objected, saying the Bill contained certain provisions that were inconsistent and repugnant to the constitution of Fiji.[66] Instead of circulating the Bill to all 71 members of the Lower House 21 days before the next sitting of parliament, as required by law, the government had initially introduced it to the nine-member Parliamentary Business Committee, where it had a 56 per cent majority.[67] For Datt, the consultation had been inadequate. Datt pointed to the strength of opposition to the Bill around the country, emphasizing the concerns expressed by the president of the Fiji Law Society and the director of the Fiji Human Rights Commission. Nevertheless, the Speaker allowed the suspension of Standing Orders to allow the first reading of the Bill before the House.

The second reading, on 2 June, occurred at the Nasese police headquarters amid tight police security. Military observers turned up again in the public gallery to show their disapproval. The FLP members walked out of parliament in protest, with FLP deputy leader Poseci Bune hand-signalling an imminent RTU Bill-related electoral reversal of the positions of government and opposition as he departed the chamber with his colleagues. The sole remaining opposition MP voicing concern about the Bill inside the house was Ofa Duncan. Outside the makeshift and temporary parliament at Nasese, NGOs and concerned citizens protested against the Bill.[68] Many wore black in protest and lined the Nasese seawall holding placards.[69] At the same time, in an unusual mobilization, the SDL's Jale Baba organized busloads of rural Fijians to stage counter-

demonstrations in support of the Bill down near the Nasese seawall. After the
second reading, the Bill was referred to the Law and Justice Sector Committee,
entrusted to listen to submissions around the country. The Hon. Manasa Tugia,
CAMV MP from Cakaudrove East constituency, was appointed chairperson
of the committee by the government on 6 June 2005.[70]

The government reacted to criticisms inside and outside parliament by re-
emphasizing that the fundamental objective of the Bill was to promote, not
force, unity amongst the people of Fiji. 'It is to try and acknowledge that we
are made up of many different races, cultures, customs, languages, religions
and that we have been talking about the need for unity for decades and decades
now', insisted the Attorney General.[71] Qarase reiterated that there would be no
general amnesty, and that the Bill was not intended to free those who used the
coup for their own gain or other criminal intent. He said that the victims would
have a new opportunity to seek justice through compensation.[72] In comments
that echoed the concerns of many of the domestic critics, Qarase insisted that
one of the main reasons for the Bill was to find out exactly what motivated
people to concoct and support the coups of 1987 and 2000.[73] He said that
the government would embark on a wide-ranging consultation process and
that it would take into account objections to the Bill, and make the necessary
amendments. The Ministry of Multi-Ethnic Affairs and National Reconciliation
and Unity held three workshops, in Suva, Lautoka and Labasa, to inform the
Indian and minority communities about the Bill.[74]

In addition, the Prime Minister and Attorney General appeared before an
'open forum' at the University of the South Pacific's marine studies campus,
again promising amendments to the Bill, and facing down criticisms. The view
was expressed at the forum that pardoning criminals could dissipate the respect
for law among young Fijians and encourage criminality. Some urged that the
bitterly opposed Prime Minister and Leader of the Opposition set an example
to the country by reconciling with each other. Attorney General Bale insisted
the Bill would not entail a general amnesty for coup prisoners, arguing that
the statute of limitations had passed for conviction on treason charges. This
was inaccurate; the Bill was quite explicitly intended to apply retrospectively
to those already convicted of treason, subject to satisfying the other conditions
for amnesty.

The extra-parliamentary mobilization for and against the Bill continued as the Law and Justice Committee commenced its proceedings. The NGO Coalition on Human Rights launched a campaign encouraging people to wear yellow ribbons to show opposition to the Bill. Another NGO, the Citizens' Constitutional Forum, hung a giant yellow ribbon at the gate to their office and Bernadette Rounds Ganilau (interim Assistant Minister for Women in 2000–2001) unfurled and pinned up a giant yellow ribbon at the entrance to her home. In response, the SDL launched a rival campaign encouraging supporters of the Bill to wear blue ribbons. Blue ribbon committee advisor and Assistant Minister for Women (2005) Losena Salabula claimed that the majority of Fiji citizens, regardless of ethnic background, supported the Bill.[75] The blue ribbon campaign proved a potent means of gearing up the SDL party machinery, and particularly the SDL women's organizations, for the 2006 election.

The Joint Parliamentary Sector Committee

The Joint Parliamentary Sector Committee on Justice, Law and Order received 272 formal written and oral submissions. The strong demand for wide consultation resulted in many extensions of the original deadline for submissions.[76] The Bill was translated into Fijian and Hindi, and public hearings were held in the Central, Northern, Western and Eastern Divisions. Formal submissions were received from the disciplinary forces (police and military), political parties (SDL, FLP, NFP, National Alliance Party of Fiji (NAPF)), four trade unions, 21 religious organizations,[77] 20 Fijian organizations,[78] six NGOs, the Director of Public Prosecutions, the Fiji Human Rights Commission, the Fiji Law Society, the Fiji Women Lawyers Association, seven women's organizations, and from other professional groups. The Committee received 124 formal written and oral submissions, and another 148 submissions were presented orally during public hearings by individual groups and organisations.[79] Interestingly, the Muslim religious organizations did not make any submissions on the Bill, an absence that indicated some notable accommodation by some leaders with the SDL government. The FLP did not attend any of the meetings of the committee in the wake of their parliamentary walkout on 2 June.

In his report to parliament, presented on 1 December 2005, the committee chairperson, the Hon. Manasa Tugia, observed that villages and *tikinas* throughout the country supported the Bill. The report noted, however, that some of these views were expressed by people who had not actually read the Bill and were focused rather broadly on the need for reconciliation and unity.[80] Supporters of the Bill often saw such legislation as a vehicle by which to resolve the inter-ethnic tensions, put an end to conflict and upheavals in Fiji and promote genuine and lasting national unity. This, many said, could only be achieved through a biblically and spiritually based process of reconciliation, tolerance and understanding, and by use of the concept of restorative justice. Merely allowing normal judicial processes to take their course, it was argued, would not stop the kinds of events that occurred in 1987 and 2000 from recurring; the root causes of the problem, and the unresolved issues for both the indigenous and non-indigenous communities needed to be fully addressed.[81]

As part of the consultation process, deliberations concerning the Bill occurred in Fiji's 14 provinces. The Prime Minister and key cabinet members visited rural areas to encourage support for the Bill. Some NGOs sought to attend those meetings. The Lomaiviti Provincial Council was one which did not allow NGO representatives to speak at their one-day meeting in Levuka on 30 June 2005; Roko Tui Lomaiviti Ratu Filimoni Baleimua said only provincial council members were allowed to attend.[82] Kadavu was the first province to give approval to the Bill at a provincial council meeting on the island of Tavuki. Council Chairman Ratu Josateki Nawalowalo said the way forward for Fiji was to express support for the government's initiative. Initial reservations about the amnesty clause were allayed by Attorney General Bale.[83]

The Lau Provincial Council was the last of the 14 provinces to endorse the Bill.

Adi Koila Nailatikau, daughter of the late President Ratu Mara and a member of Fiji's Senate, condemned the RTU Bill saying 'reconciliation cannot eventuate...until the proper legal procedures have been followed'. Adi Koila said genuine forgiveness would not be forthcoming until the truth about who was involved and who funded the coup was known; she blamed the 2000 political events for contributing to her father's grief, leading to his death on 18 April 2004.[84] Adi Koila believed most members of the Lau Provincial Council – especially at the grass roots – did not understand the amnesty clause. The ex-minister and representative from Lakeba, Filipe Bole, opposed the Bill, saying the word 'truth' should also be included so that investigations would become meaningful and useful, and urging that the amnesty clause be refined.[85] But these two urban Lauans were unable to prevail on their island kinsfolk. The Lau Provincial Council decided to support the Bill, expressing a desire to move forward through the intended government-ordained process of reconciliation.

Following the endorsement by all 14 provincial councils, Fiji's Great Council of Chiefs – the Bose Levu Vakaturaga – convened, and endorsed the Bill on 28 July 2005; however, it urged the government to consider the concerns raised by the army and others.[86] The Bill was also endorsed by the Council of Rotuma, the Rabi Island Council, the Taukei Movement, the Fijian Dockworkers and Seafarers Union, the Methodist Church, the Assembly of Christian Churches in Fiji, the Fiji Institute of Research and Education, and the Fijian Teachers Union. It had the support of coup-related prisoners. Josefa Nata and Timoci Silatolu made submissions supporting the Bill. Oddly, both of these imprisoned coup-leaders sought to emphasize the importance of truth-telling, and struck a somewhat conciliatory tone. For Ratu Silatolu:

> The Bill will allay the fears of the RFMF; the fact that full disclosure is part of the amnesty provision…will enable everyone to tell the truth… The Bill will enable perpetrators to personally seek reconciliation through an arbiter otherwise the issue of 2000 will be used as a political tool when there is no closure… The concept of *veisorosorovi* or asking of forgiveness does not discount punishment; the seeking of forgiveness is still applicable.[87]

In his submission, Josefa Nata, who was also serving a life sentence for his part in the coup, stated:

> Drop the amnesty clause and make truth telling through a Truth Commission …the main focus of the Bill. The Commission should have an investigation adjunct to look into evidence that could not be verified through hearing.[88]

Those who opposed the Bill emphasized dangers associated with the amnesty provisions, and the likelihood that these would legitimize the type of Fijian extremism that had so damaged the country in 1987 and 2000.[89] The Group of Concerned (Fijian) Mothers circulated a petition rallying opposition to the Bill and attracted 25,706 signatures [as at 26 July 2005] of which 20,672 were Indians, 4,903 Fijians and 131 others.[90] The National Council of Women and the Fiji Association of Women Graduates protested that the Bill lacked provisions for gender equality. The Fiji Women's Rights Movement suggested that the Bill was biased in favour of ethnic Fijians and discriminated against non-indigenous Fijians because the majority of those eligible for amnesty would inevitably be indigenous Fijians.

In its final report, the Joint Parliamentary Sector Committee on Justice, Law and Order indicated concern that the draft Bill did not make clear what categories of crime would be considered as acts associated with 'political objectives'. The Committee rejected concerns about the constitutional implications of the Bill, about the possibility that entrenched powers of the judiciary might be usurped and about the likelihood of a post-passage legal challenge to the Bill. It stressed that there should be no interference with the courts' deliberations and that only afterwards should any RTU Bill-related considerations of restorative justice be entertained.[91]

After weighing up submissions and general public reactions, the committee recommended that the government 'slightly readjust the way in which the Bill is designed, whilst still maintaining the basic objective and the conceptual framework of the Bill'. In concession to the critics, the committee concluded:

> The Bill also needs to be consistent with the existing statutory powers of stakeholders, like the Police, DPP and the Fiji Human Rights Commission. The Bill must in no way be, or be seen as to compromise or to undermine, the integrity and independence of the judiciary and these other constitutional offices. Any adjustments to the Bill must comply with the law.[92]

The committee also suggested limiting the scope for reference to the Reconciliation and Unity Commission. Serious acts associated with the political and civil unrest, such as loss of life, grievous bodily harm, and offences against public order would, it was suggested, be referred to and processed by the courts. Amnesty should not be extended to those found guilty of murder, rape and other sexual offences. Where those given amnesty by the commission failed to obey any conditions set down, this would be regarded as an offence that could be prosecuted in court. The Bill did not intend, it was suggested, to provide any blanket amnesty to free persons already convicted for coup-related offences, neither did it aim to free those already charged or to be charged. As if to emphasize the likely limitations of such legislation in terms of practical impact, the committee pointed out that, in South Africa, of the 70,000 amnesty applications made to the Truth and Reconciliation Commission only 7,000 or 10 per cent were successful.[93]

These deliberations of the Joint Parliamentary Sector Committee on Justice, Law and Order largely escaped public attention, and the national debate remained starkly polarized despite the more cautious views expressed by the committee itself. The fairness of these deliberations and the sensible character of the conclusions surprised many, particularly given the chairmanship of CAMV parliamentarian, Manasa Tugia. That such measured advice came from a representative of the party representing the more militant wing of indigenous Fijian opinion perhaps eased the pressure on the government, and made the passage of the Bill less urgent for electoral purposes for the Qarase government.

The impact of the RTU Bill on the 2006 election

The election was held over the period 6–13 May 2006, eleven and half months after the Bill had first been introduced on the floor of the House. The intervening period had proved an era of controversy, an era of FLP boycott of parliament and military threat of insurrection. Yet the Bill had nevertheless played the politically useful role of enabling the SDL to rally Fijian support. Messages of 'forgiveness' and 'reconciliation' had played to perceptions of Christian moral righteousness about the RTU Bill. Indo-Fijian politicians also recognized something of the political role being played by the RTU Bill. FLP parliamentarian Ganesh Chand claimed in late 2005 that the Bill was part of a fear campaign politicians were running for the next year's general election – fear was being instilled in people over the RTU Bill, as well as the land and gay rights[94] issues.[95]

In the highly polarized election that was to ensue in May 2006, the RTU Bill proved, for the governing SDL, a vehicle for mobilizing Fijian support. The Labour Party's opposition – through boycotts and its refusal to enter into dialogue with the SDL – was portrayed as indicative of a hostile attitude towards the concerns of the *vanua*. Yet it was not so much the Labour Party's opposition that inflamed the Fijian voters as the military's implacable hostility to provisions that it felt would seriously undermine the rule of law. Fijians in many quarters appeared alarmed by the military's interference in the political process and by the RFMF's open condemnation of the Fijian-dominated government. The military's 'truth and justice' campaign thus received a hostile reception from many Fijians. Some provinces went so far as to tell the military that soldiers were not welcome in their village or province (see Ratuva, this volume).

Commander Bainimarama's criticisms of the Bill were used during election campaigns by both major political parties. The SDL portrayed the commander as supporting Mahendra Chaudhry's bid to return as prime minister, reviving longstanding Fijian fears about having an Indo-Fijian leader. Qarase emphasized on the campaign trail that Fiji was not ready for an Indo-Fijian prime minister and how important it was that Fijians ensure that the SDL win by giving them first preference votes. He portrayed the SDL as safeguarding Fijian interests through affirmative action programs, the Qoliqoli Bill, and the progress in converting crown land into native land. The Prime Minister capitalized on Chaudhry's support for Bainimarama's outbursts by claiming this indicated Labour Party support for an illegal takeover of the government by the military.[96]

For the FLP, the commander's outbursts were indicative of the military's firm intention to uphold the rule of law and protect the 1997 constitution. On the campaign trail, mention of Bainimarama's strong stance against the SDL government was used to allay fears that the re-election of a Labour government might lead, yet again, to a coup. The military, it was said, clearly intended to uphold the authority of the legitimately elected government. For the FLP, the RTU Bill also proved a means of rallying a broader-based oppositional coalition. Back in 2001, it had been left in a marginalized position, without the broad-based coalition it had relied upon to achieve power in 1999. The 'moderates forum' parties had favoured the SDL over the FLP, ensuring that the FLP could not win in the marginal open constituencies. The RTU Bill had so inflamed moderate opinion, particularly among the general voters but also among National Federation Party supporters, that the FLP stood a better chance of attracting moderate support than in 2006 than in 2001, although, as it turned out, the moderate parties proved unable to command a substantial share of the national vote.

The RTU Bill also proved important for the SDL's relationship with its coalition partner, the CAMV. In the years after the 2001 election, CAMV ministers had been drifting towards the larger and better-financed SDL. Without the intervention of the courts, Ratu Naiqama Lalabalavu and his colleagues would, in all probability (even without the RTU Bill), have contested the 2006 election as SDL candidates. The coup-related trials proved a millstone round the neck of this accommodation. They fuelled the objections of radicals at the grass roots of the party that the SDL had done little for the indigenous cause during its term in office. The RTU Bill thus played a potent ideological role: it convinced many of the CAMV rank-and-file that the SDL was sincere in its attempt to pardon the coup-related prisoners. It reassured key CAMV leaders that their interests and ideology would be looked after by the SDL and demonstrated that the two parties were basically on the same side. That SDL vice president Ratu Inoke Takiveikata remained in prison on mutiny-related charges also reassured the CAMV that harsh prison terms were not biased against their own party leaders.

In fact, the coup trials proved a double-edged sword for the CAMV; while they inflamed radical passions on the one hand, on the other they caused financial embarrassment for the party. The CAMV had an opening balance of over $36,000 on 26 May 2004; notably, this was boosted to over $50,000 by a $15,000 donation by the SDL in July 2004.[97] A little over $31,000 was spent on legal fees for party members from 8 July 2004 to 6 May 2005, including costs for the cases of Sports Minister Isireli Leweniqila, party trustee Metuisela Mua, and former MP Peceli Rinakama, and for the appeal for gaoled former deputy speaker Ratu Rakuita Vakalalabure.[98] As a result, the CAMV was cash-strapped, and had insufficient funds to contest the 2006 poll. Its leaders, in particular, urgently desired a cosy ride back into cabinet as part of the SDL. The RTU Bill placated the radical fringes, and promised something to the prisoner fraternity. This eased the inevitable transition. CAMV parliamentary leader Ratu Naiqama fended off opposition to CAMV's merger with SDL by insisting that the party had become impoverished because members had failed to contribute sufficiently. When the CAMV dissolved itself at its AGM on 17 February 2006, it had a closing balance of a little over $3,000. The merger with SDL took place that same night at a traditional ceremony held at Tamavua village, the birthplace of SDL.[99]

Conclusion

The RTU Bill was temporarily shelved in February 2006 because, so it was announced, the government did not have enough time to make the necessary amendments prior to the May 2006 election.[100] This was a strange decision given the electoral importance initially attached by SDL leaders to securing the passage of the Bill. SVT spokeswoman Ema Druavesi criticized the consultation exercise as a huge waste of taxpayers' money.[101] That was undoubtedly true, but from the SDL vantage point it seems reasonable to conclude that the Bill had achieved key objectives, even without passing into law. It had warded off the threat of a split in the governing coalition occasioned by the CAMV's announcement that it intended to table its own Bill in parliament for the release of prisoners. It had paved the way for a smooth liquidation of the CAMV, and for the Vanua Levu and Northern Tailevu ministers to contest under the SDL banner – a situation that provided the SDL with a crucial five extra seats at the 2006 election, giving the party an absolute majority in parliament.[102] Whether or not this was the original intention is questionable. More likely, political recognition that solid strategic advantages could be obtained even without passage of the Bill only became obvious in early 2006.

The SDL did not make a great play of the RTU Bill in the weeks immediately prior to the election. In its 32-page manifesto, 'reconciliation and unity' featured on the last page. SDL policy in this respect was described as based on internationally acclaimed principles of 'restorative justice' and it was made clear that the government intended to introduce 'amendments based on wide public consultation' and legislation that was 'consistent with the constitution'. Yet the nature of those amendments was, perhaps unsurprisingly, not made clear. Had big concessions to the opposition been announced, this might have generated disillusionment among the former rank-and-file in the CAMV. Had the government remained firm and insisted on passage of the draft Bill unchanged, it might have alienated moderate public support for the governing party and generated further instability in relations with the security forces. The tactically astute option was to shelve the Bill, and instead make vague public pronouncements about future intentions.

Nevertheless, over the longer run, the Bill had played a potent electoral role in inflaming racial emotions and polarizing voters during the year prior to the 2006 poll. The amnesty clause automatically drove the Indo-Fijian community against the Bill. Outright rejection by the Indo-Fijian political leaders of government proposals for reconciliation had been matched by an extraordinary mobilization of support for the Bill from the Methodist Church, provincial councils and the Great Council of Chiefs. Since this had become such a pivotal plank of government policy, it ultimately proved a powerful vehicle for consolidating support behind the SDL. Ethnic polarization, exacerbated by the controversy over the RTU Bill, was nurtured during the 2006 election campaign by use of the familiar 'us and them' rhetoric to incite racial fears. The oppositional stance of the military only contributed to that electoral polarization. Through mobilizing ethnic Fijian voters in this way, the SDL not only achieved its merger with the CAMV, but also secured an absolute majority in the post-election parliament, and left the FLP confined to its majority Indo-Fijian strongholds in the west and north of the country and unable to build strong alliances across the ethnic divide. For these reasons, the sentiments expressed by Attorney General Bale, as cited at the start of this chapter – that the electoral fortunes of the SDL and the fate of the RTU Bill were inextricably linked – proved accurate, even though the Bill was put into cold storage for the duration of the campaign. Whether or not the RTU Bill, which would potentially cost the country millions of dollars in compensation and would continue to exacerbate communal tensions, is useful or suitable given the new post-election multiparty cabinet setting is much more doubtful.

Notes

1 *The Fiji Times*, 16 June 2005, p.1.
2 Promotion of Reconciliation, Tolerance and Unity Bill, full text reproduced in *The Sunday Times*, 15 May 2005, under the title 'Unity – or more Division?'.
3 George Speight was convicted of treason and sentenced to death by hanging on 18 February 2002. However, the death penalty was commuted to a life sentence after a request by Attorney General Qoroniasi Bale to the Prerogative of Mercy Commission. As a result, Speight was still, at the time of the 2006 election, serving a life imprisonment term on the island of Nukulau, off Suva. The death penalty was abolished the day after the decision of the Prerogative of Mercy Commission.
4 Radio Fiji News, 1 May 2005 (Pacific Islands Report archives).
5 *Matanigasau*: a traditional Fijian ceremony to ask for forgiveness (*Macquarie Dictionary of English for the Fiji Islands*, 2006). *Veisorosorovi*: a ceremony that provides a means of

community peace-building and conflict resolution. It comes from the word *soro*, meaning to humble oneself, surrender or ask for forgiveness while admitting fault. *Veisorosorovi* is a reciprocal process and is more effective in addressing conflicts between groups (Ratuva, S. 2003. 'Reinventing the cultural wheel: reconceptualising restorative justice and peace building in ethnically divided Fiji', in S. Dinnen, A. Jowitt & T.N. Cain (eds). *A Kind of Mending: Restorative Justice in the Pacific Islands*, Pandanus Books, Canberra.

6   Hon. Qarase, Statement on Reconciliation and Justice, 5 May 2005, media briefing, 4 May 2005.
7   'Pardon Me: What is Fijian Reconciliation and Restorative Justice?', opinion article by Jone Dakuvula, 5 November 2005, <www.ccf.org.fj>.
8   *The Fiji Times*, 5 October 2004, p.1.
9   PINA *Nius Online*, 20 May 2000.
10 *Fiji Daily Post, Fiji Sun/PINA Nius Online*, 5 September 2000.
11 PINA *Nius Online*, 24 May 2000.
12 PINA *Nius Online*, 20 May 2000.
13 PINA *Nius Online*, 20 May 2000.
14 *Fiji Sun/Radio Fiji/Pacific Nius/Niuswire*, 27 July 2000.
15 *Fiji Sun/Radio Fiji/Pacific Nius/Niuswire*, 27 July 2000.
16 *Fiji Times/Fiji Sun/Pasifik Nius/* USP Journalism students, 7 November 2000.
17 *Fiji Sun*, 6 August 2004. Youth Minister Isireli Leweniqila was acquitted.
18 Fiji 1 News, 9 August 2004.
19 *The Fiji Times*, 26 August 2004.
20 *The Fiji Times*, 27 January 2005.
21 *The Fiji Times*, 11 April 2005.
22 Fijilive.com, 5 September 2005.
23 Fijilive.com, 10 August 2005.
24 Hon. L. Qarase, 'Summary of Remarks for New Reconciliation Legislation', 5 May 2005, <www.fiji.gov.fj>.
25 The six CAMV MPs who won seats at the 2001 election were George Speight, Isireli Leweniqila, Manasa Tugia, Ratu Naiqama Lalabalavu, Josateki Vula and Ratu Rakuita Vakalalabure. Apart from Josateki Vula, all CAMV MPs were charged for coup-related offences. Isireli Leweniqila was acquitted. Speight lost his seat after failing to attend consecutive sittings of the House because he was in prison, but his brother Samisoni Tikoinasau (CAMV) won the consequent by-election. Ratu Rakuita also lost his Cakaudrove seat after conviction, but this was taken by fellow CAMV member Niko Nawaikula in the resulting by-election.
26 Fijivillage.com, 30 June 2005.
27 *The Fiji Times*, 6 August 2004, p.3.
28 *The Fiji Times*, 6 August 2004, p.3.
29 Fijilive.com, 7 April 2005.
30 Fijilive.com, 7 April 2005.
31 *The Fiji Times*, 23 June 2005.
32 Fiji 1 News, 21 September 2005.
33 Fijilive.com, 5 September 2005.
34 Parliament of Fiji, Daily Hansard, 18 November 2005.
35 *Fiji Sun*, 30 August 2006.

36 *The Fiji Times*, 22 February 2006.
37 *The Fiji Times*, 16 June 2005.
38 Report of the Sector Standing Committee on Justice, Law and Order on the Promotion of Reconciliation, Tolerance and Unity Bill, November/December 2005, p. 27.
39 Fijivillage.com, 20 June 2005.
40 Fijilive.com, 2 August 2005.
41 *The Fiji Times*, 2 October 2005.
42 *The New Zealand Herald*, 10 June 2005, <www.nzherald.co.nz>.
43 Fijilive.com, 31 May 2005.
44 *The Fiji Times*, 21 June 2005.
45 Fijivillage.com, 28 June 2005.
46 Fijivillage.com, 27 June 2005.
47 Scoop, 24 June 2005, <www.scoop.co.nz>.
48 *The Fiji Times*, 31 May 2005.
49 The International Bar Association, 2 February 2006, <www.ibanet.org>.
50 Fijilive.com, 13 July 2005.
51 Fijilive.com, 30 January 2006.
52 *Fiji Sun*, 30 January 2004.
53 Fijilive.com, 14 April 2005.
54 Fijilive.com, 5 January 2005.
55 Report of the Sector Standing Committee on Justice, Law and Order on the Promotion of Reconciliation, Tolerance and Unity Bill, November/December 2005, p.44.
56 Fijilive.com, 30 Janury 2006.
57 Fijilive.com, 13 July 2005.
58 *The Fiji Times*, 2 October 2005.
59 Section 112 of the 1997 constitution, confirms that the '...Republic of Fiji Military Forces established by the Constitution of 1990 continues to exist', but the section also states that 'Parliament may make laws relating to the Republic of Fiji Military Forces', and that the exercise of military executive control by the commander is '...subject to the control of the Minister' (chapter 7, section 112, p.111, *Constitution (Amendment) Act 1997* of the Republic of Fiji Islands, 25 July 1997). Section 110 of the 1997 constitution makes it clear that the military and police are not to be regarded as government departments and therefore do not fall within the ambit of the Secretaries of Ministries (section 110, 1997 constitution of Fiji, p.110).
60 Fijivillage.com, 22 June 2005.
61 Fijivillage.com, 30 June 2005.
62 Fijilive.com, 17 January 2006.
63 Fijivillage.com, 20 June 2005.
64 Fijivillage.com, 30 June 2005.
65 *The Fiji Times*, 1 June 2005, p.1.
66 See Parliament of Fiji, Daily Hansard, 31 May 2005.
67 Fijilive.com, 16 May 2005.
68 Parliament had been re-located temporarily to allow repairs to the leaking roof of the normal chamber up at Veiuto.
69 *The Fiji Times*, 4 June 2005, p.7.

70 The previous chairperson had been Ratu Rakuita, but after his conviction in August 2004, the Parliament's secretary general, Mary Chapman, had revealed his replacement would have to be a CAMV MP (*The Fiji Times*, 25 August 2004, p.3).
71 'Bill will promote instead of Forcing Unity – Bale', Fiji Government Online, media release, 19 May 2005.
72 'No general amnesty – PM reiterates', Fiji Government Online, media release, 22 July 2005.
73 'Proposed bill would determine the reasons for coups – PM', Fiji Government Online, media release, 26 July 2005.
74 'Bill to be discussed at the Ministry's workshop in Labasa tomorrow', Fiji Government Online, media release, 14 July 2005.
75 Fijilive.com, 21 June 2005.
76 From 17 June 2005 to 31 July 2005 and then to 30 September 2005.
77 Including Christian and Hindu organizations, and the Fiji Kisan Sangh.
78 Including the Bose Levu Vakaturaga (Great Council of Chiefs), Rotuma and Rabi Councils, Viti Cauravou, provinces and villages and the Fijian Institute of Research and Education.
79 Report of the Sector Standing Committee on the RTU Bill, November/December 2005, p.16.
80 Hon. Tugia – Presentation of the Committee's Report on the RTU Bill (Bill No. 10 of 2005). 1 December 2005. The committee noted a Tebbutt Times Poll conducted in early June 2005 had been based on a sample of 1008 adults in Suva, Lami, Nausori, Nadi, Lautoka and Ba. Of these, 80 per cent had not read the Bill (p.43).
81 Report of the Sector Standing Committee on Justice, Law and Order on the Promotion of Reconciliation, Tolerance and Unity Bill, November/December 2005.
82 Fijivillage.com, 29 June 2006.
83 Fijilive.com, 27 June 2005.
84 *The Fiji Times*, 23 October 2004. The recent passing of Adi Koila's father, Ratu Mara, was followed by that of her mother, Roko Tui Dreketi Adi Lala Mara, a few months later.
85 *The Fiji Times*, 26 July 2005.
86 *The Fiji Times*, 29 July 2005.
87 Report of the Sector Standing Committee on the RTU Bill, Nov/Dec 2005, pp.183–84.
88 Report of the Sector Standing Committee on the RTU Bill, Nov/Dec 2005, p.182.
89 The following organizations largely opposed the Bill because of its amnesty provisions, its contravention of human and legal rights, and its protection of criminals which could breed terrorism, increase political instability and could lead to further coups: the Fiji Human Rights Commission, the Fiji Police Force, the Republic of the Fiji Military Forces, the Director of Public Prosecutions, the Fiji Law Society, the Fiji Labour Party, the National Federation Party, the National Alliance Party, the Roman Catholic Church, the Anglican Church, the Fiji Baptist Convention, the Seventh-Day Adventist Church, St Andrews Presbyterian Church, the Anglican Mission District, the Interfaith Search Fiji, Pasifika Communications, the Ecumenical Centre for Research, Education and Advocacy, the Fiji Trade Union Congress, the Pacific Concerns Resource Centre, the Fiji Institute of Accountants, the Fiji Women's Rights Movement, the Fiji Women's Crisis Centre, the Shree Sanatan Dharm Pratinidhi Sabha Fiji, the Kisan Sangh, and the Then India Sanmarga Ikya Sangam.

90 Report of the Sector Standing Committee on the RTU Bill, November/December 2005.
91 Report of the Sector Standing Committee on the RTU Bill, November/December 2005.
92 Report of the Sector Standing Committee on the RTU Bill, November/December 2005, p.27.
93 Report of the Sector Standing Committee on the RTU Bill, November/December 2005, p.31.
94 Politicians and Methodist Church factions had been organizing protests against gays as 'un-Christian'.
95 Fiji 1 News, 21 November 2005.
96 *The Fiji Times*, 17 January 2006.
97 Fijilive.com, 19 February 2006.
98 Fijilive.com, 19 February 2006.
99 Fijilive.com, 19 February 2006.
100 *Fiji Sun*, 9 February 2006.
101 *Fiji Sun*, 9 February 2006.
102 These five crucial seats are those of Isireli Leweniqila – Macuata Fijian Provincial; Niko Nawaikula – Cakaudrove West Fijian Provincial; Ratu Naiqama Lalabalavu – Cakaudrove East Fijian Provincial; Samisoni Tikoinasau – Tailevu North Fijian Provincial; and Ratu Josefa Dimuri – Bua/Macuata West Open.

11

Reflections on the economic and social policies of political parties at the 2006 general election

Biman Chand Prasad[1]

Political instability since 1987 has adversely affected Fiji's economic growth, which averaged less than 3 per cent over the period 1980–2006. Fiji's economic performance between 2001 and 2006, when the Soqosoqo Duavata ni Lewenivanua (SDL) government was in power, was even more modest. While the SDL government pursued policies that promoted private-sector-led growth, these largely failed as a result of continued perceptions of political volatility and the inability of political parties to agree on a solution to the impasse over land leases. In addition, over the two years prior to the 2006 poll, further political uncertainty arose from the disagreements between the government and the commander of the Republic of Fiji Military Forces.

Fiji's 2006 general election was the tenth since independence in 1970. During that 36-year period, the country experienced three coups and two changes of the constitution. Nevertheless, the formation of the Fiji Labour Party (FLP) in 1985 was seen by many as the beginning of a move towards more issue- and ideology-based, rather than race-based, political competition. However, the 2006 election appeared, at first sight, to produce a very ethnically polarized result: the two major parties, the SDL and the FLP, defeated moderate political parties trying to establish a position in the middle ground of Fiji's politics. Yet, on further examination – and in keeping with the median voter theory advanced by political scientists and political economists – both the SDL and FLP tried during the 2006 campaign to move their policies towards the political centre in order to capture floating voters, and gain votes at the expense of the other major party. In the process, they ended up with very similar policies on key issues and avoided advocating controversial and extreme positions.

The first section of this chapter provides an introduction to median voter theory, and the second section provides an extensive study of the positions of the major political parties with regard to economic policies, land, affirmative action, poverty and sugar industry reforms. The third section compares the manifestos of the two largest parties, the SDL and the FLP, at the 2006 and 2001 elections. The final section discusses the implications of the median voter-based analysis for the understanding of contemporary Fiji politics and the challenges facing the new multiparty government.

The political economy of party orientation towards the median voter

Political economy models assume that voters see governments as vehicles for maximizing the voters' self-interest. People want public goods to be provided to them in an efficient manner, and this influences voting patterns. However, it is not possible to always achieve unanimity when making decisions about the allocation of public goods and, hence, the majority vote rule is often the best way to arrive at political decisions.

While it is often argued that the median voter model is too simple to reflect real political settings, it does provide a useful way to analyze voter, candidate, and political party behaviour. The model has been accepted as the simplest possible model of majoritarian decision-making. Congleton goes further and argues that:

> ...the median voter's age, sex, income, information, ideology and expectations should all be systematically affecting public policy. To the extent that these predictions are largely borne out by empirical research, the median voter model can be regarded not only as a convenient method of discussing majoritarian politics and a fruitful engine of analysis, but also a fundamental property of democracy.[2]

The origins of the median voter model can be traced to the work of economist Hotelling[3], but more specifically to Black[4] and to Downs'[5] extension of the model to representative democracy. Downs postulated that a vote-maximizing politician or political party is likely to adopt the position of the median voter. The median voters' preferences are the middle of the distribution of different preferential positions. This can be explained more clearly using Figure 11.1.

Figure 11.1 shows a possible distribution of the preferences of voters. For this explanation we assume that there were only two major political parties standing in the 2006 election. Suppose that candidate X adopts the position of the median voter, and candidate Y adopts a position located to the right of X. Because X is the median voter, by definition, 50 percent of the voters lie to his or her left. Candidate X will be expected to win all these votes as well as some of the votes between X and Y. X must therefore receive the majority. The only way Y could outvote X is to move as close as possible to the position of the median voter. Therefore, in a two-party election, rational vote-maximizing candidates will try to move to the position of the median voter.

This model assumes that political parties with very different ideological positions will, for the purpose of winning elections, move towards the centre and

Figure 11.1   Median voter theory

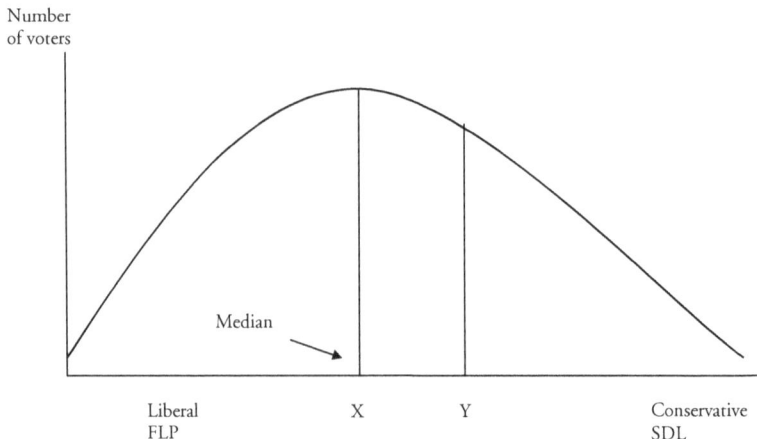

moderate their policies towards the centre-left or centre-right. The experiences of countries with two major political parties indicate that third parties with positions far away from the 'centre' do not fare well.

There are caveats to the median voter theory. First, outcomes may be affected by strong ideological positions and the leadership styles and personalities of candidates, rather than issues. Further, the fact that not everyone chooses to vote may influence outcomes, and, finally, there may be more than two parties. Despite these qualifications, the median voter theory offers a useful way of analyzing the behaviour of political parties and candidates. Empirical evidence also supports the claim that median voter theory can help explain the policies of political parties and candidates.[6]

Party policies at the 2006 election

This section provides an analysis of the main policies in the election manifestos of the major parties in the 2006 election. Some of the policies had the potential to create controversy and disagreement. However, many of the policies of the two major parties converged in the run-up to the 2006 poll. During the campaign, the differences in the manifestos of the SDL and the FLP were minimal. Both Prime Minister Qarase and Hon. Krishna Datt, Minister of Labour, conceded after the election that there was about 80 per cent convergence of the policies of the two parties.

The FLP was launched in 1985 on a strong socialist-oriented economic and social policy agenda. It was formed against the backdrop of deteriorating economic conditions in the early 1980s. In 1984, the Alliance government, led by Ratu Sir Kamisese Mara, had imposed a civil service wage freeze to curb the increasing government expenditure. However, within a short period of time the ideological position of the FLP came under scrutiny after it joined forces with the centre-right National Federation Party (NFP) to fight the 1987 election. After its formation in 1985, the Labour party had alleged that the NFP was supporting the wage freeze and that it was also looking after the interests of business. For political expediency and electoral gain, the FLP and NFP were quick to join hands to defeat the Alliance Party.

Many observers of Fiji's general elections have attributed results to voting on racial lines.[7] However, the median voter theory suggests that the voting patterns may also have been affected by differences in policies. The mainly ethnic Fijian political parties in office since independence in 1970 took a conservative approach to economic policy and emphasized affirmative action policies biased in favour of the indigenous Fijians. On the other hand, the mainly Indian political parties and their leaders historically had the support of the Indo-Fijian farmers, and many of their economic policies have derived from approaches to subsidies given to sugar farmers. The mainly Indo-Fijian political parties also had the support of the trade unions, and thus their economic policies reflected socialist approaches, such as more state involvement in the delivery of basic services. It can therefore be argued that voting in Fiji does not have an overwhelming racial overtone, but instead is embedded in the historical perception of economic policies propagated by Indo-Fijian and Fijian political leaders.

Perceptions of the economic policy agenda of Fijian and Indo-Fijian leaders have created fear about Fijian dispossession of land. This is one area where Indo-Fijian leaders have taken a conservative approach. In the late 1960s, the leader of the NFP, A.D. Patel, advocated the adoption of common roll voting. This was seen by Fijian leaders as an attempt to secure Indian control over government in order to legislate individual rights to land, in place of the prevailing communal ownership of the bulk of Fiji's land area. Some feared complete alienation of native land through ownership by non-Fijians. To maximize their share of the ethnic Fijian vote, Fijian politicians have often exploited this fear.

Economic policies

In the two-party systems that characterize many countries, differences in economic policies have narrowed significantly over the past 25 years. With the Thatcherism of the late 1970s and Reaganomics of the 1980s, and the broad acceptance of the Washington Consensus, many political parties in developing countries have closely followed the advice provided by international organizations such as the International Monetary Fund and the World Bank.[8] This is also true for Fiji. Both the major parties in the 2006 general election adopted centre-right economic policies. Both the SDL and the FLP recognized the increasing global economic integration and the need to adopt macroeconomic and microeconomic policies that support market-led growth. The FLP reversed earlier policy stances and supported privatization of public enterprises, including, to the surprise of many political commentators, the privatization of the water supply department. It also supported more competition in the telecommunications sector. The SDL took inspiration from the policies of the 1999–2000 Labour-led People's Coalition government and abolished value added tax (VAT) on essential food items. Its manifesto for the 2006 poll placed the emphasis on poverty reduction.

The FLP proposed a target of 6 per cent growth annually to cater for the 15,000 school-leavers entering the workforce every year. Recognizing that investor confidence and prudent governance is integral to the successful realization of this target, the FLP proposed to (i) develop special economic zones for industries; (ii) establish a venture capital fund to stimulate small-medium business; (iii) dismantle monopolies; (iv) keep bank charges/fees under surveillance; (v) invest in technical/vocational education; (vi) revitalize the sugar and garment industries; and (vii) promote rural development and sustainable development of natural resources.

The National Alliance Party (NAP) wanted to encourage more value added-focused manufacturing industries and the expansion of export capacity. Land for agricultural development was to be made available through negotiations with landowners. It also advocated greater government input into developing necessary infrastructure, and the promotion of non-discriminatory education and training systems for the country's work force needs.

The National Federation Party (NFP) proposed to provide a better business environment through targeting monopolies and putting in place policies to increase competition. It also proposed increasing government spending on infrastructure.

The SDL wanted a strengthening of ties with new trading partners (eg. China and India) to encourage additional investment and to expand the tourism industry. It proposed the establishment of a temporary seasonal worker scheme with Australia and New Zealand, to generate increased remittances.

The United Peoples Party (UPP) emphasized stability and investor confidence as key ingredients to improve the chances of success of policies aimed at achieving economic growth.

The setting out of broad economic policies in party manifestos is likely to continue. There is also likely to be more focus on reducing the size of the government and putting in place economic infrastructure to support market-led growth. The increasing emphasis on export promotion as one means of achieving higher rates of economic growth is also likely to be a major focus of future political party campaigns.

Land policies

The most sensitive issue for the parties in the run-up to the 2006 election was native land leases. The FLP was not concerned so much about the leasing of additional land, as about securing a land tenure system that provided long-term security for the tenants and was mutually beneficial to tenants and landowners. The FLP was also concerned about the vast tracts of protected land that were lying idle, and wanted to open these up for productive use. In its manifesto, the FLP avoided mention of the Agricultural Landlord and Tenants Act (ALTA) and the Native Lands Trust Act (NLTA). It obviously chose not to get into controversy over the ALTA and NLTA debate during the election.

The NAP and the NFP had similar land policies. They suggested the concept of a 'master lease' whereby the government would lease land from the Native Land Trust Board and sublease this to tenants. Both parties proposed that landowners be encouraged to be more proactive in allowing their land to be leased.[9]

In its 2006 election manifesto, the SDL party maintained its long-standing position that all native leases should be issued under the NLTA. The SDL government had introduced a proposal in November 2005 to provide 50-year leases for farmers and more income for landowners.[10] The proposal included the following:

- all agricultural leases to be issued under NLTA rather than ALTA (as per the wishes of the Great Council of Chiefs)
- on the consent of the landowners the lease duration to be 50 years
- if the landowners would not agree to 50-year leases, then shorter leases would be offered but they would not be shorter than 20 years
- leases would be renewable subject to the consent of the landowners
- decisions on the renewal of leases would be made two to four years before expiry of 50-year leases and three years before expiry for shorter-term leases

- rents under the new arrangement would be a flat 10 per cent of the Unimproved Capital Value (UCV) of the land
- the new leasing arrangements under NLTA would have fair and equitable arrangements for compensation, both for farmers and the landowners.

The Soqosoqo ni Vakavulewa ni Taukei (SVT) party, which fielded only one candidate, supported the overarching principles of NLTA and laid emphasis on the inclusion of landowners in the decision-making process as regards to the development of land for cultivation. The UPP did not share the view that landowners needed to give up more of their land for leasing to others. Instead, it argued that settlement of the land issue required a fair and just rental mechanism from which both landowners and tenants would benefit.

The FLP and SDL would need to work together to change the ALTA, because any amendments to, or replacement of, this legislation requires a two-thirds majority in parliament. However, the SDL and FLP have extreme positions on how to resolve the land lease impasse. During the 2001–2006 SDL government, the FLP maintained that ALTA should be retained, while the SDL wanted all native agricultural leases to be issued under NLTA. The formation of the multiparty government provides some hope for convergence towards the middle ground on this issue. The proposal for government to lease land from NLTB under a master lease under NLTA and sublease it to the tenants under a new arrangement may be the best option to resolve this long-standing issue.[11]

Affirmative action policies

The affirmative action policies of the previous SDL government were a contentious issue between the SDL and the FLP. Both held strong positions, in tune with the expectations of their respective ethnic voter bases. The FLP strongly rejected the blueprint for affirmative action because it was based on race rather than on needs or circumstances, and thus discriminated against minority communities.[12] The NAPF's position was more in tune with the FLP and NFP positions; it urged the need for affirmative action on the basis of needs rather than race. NAPF said that it would devise its own non-race-based affirmative action program. The NFP believed that there was a need for affirmative action policies as enshrined in the constitution (that is, irrespective of race), but that the policies should not create a 'handout culture' amongst recipients. They contended that affirmative action should be implemented to eradicate racial disparities in all sectors and not exacerbate them.

The SDL party had put forward the Blueprint for Affirmative Action in 2001, believing that affirmative action was both just and long overdue, and that it was in the national interest because it would achieve equality of opportunity and overcome the burden of poverty.[13] The UPP rejected the blueprint in its current form because government had failed to deliver on its promises. Assistance had not been given to those who genuinely deserved it and 75 per cent of assigned funds had been lost or wasted in administrative costs, red tape, and blockages. The blueprint needed to be seriously overhauled and the UPP proposed to establish a similar program for all citizens.

Poverty issues

In its election campaign, the FLP said that about half the population of Fiji lived below the poverty line or were at risk of being in poverty. The FLP urged a 'fair' wage rate (the lack of which was, in the party's view, one of the major causes of poverty), and provision of special health, housing, education, and affirmative action schemes for the poor. The FLP also proposed the introduction of a pension scheme for those over 60 years of age without income support; a national health insurance scheme for the poor; an increase in the social welfare budget; state housing allocations for the poor; control of prices of essential food items; and help to set up cottage industries and microfinance schemes for the poor.

The NAP offered four solutions to poverty: food banks for the destitute; education funds for the poor; more exemptions from VAT; and subsidies for landowners for the use of their land. The NFP proposed to place greater importance on microfinance schemes; attract greater investment; introduce tax-free zones in neglected areas; stop the rural–urban drift by resolving the land lease problems; provide affordable housing; and double the family and destitute allowances.

The SDL philosophy and strategy for poverty reduction was portrayed as one that would reduce poverty in all its forms. The party's benchmark was the 2002–2003 Household Income and Expenditure Survey (HIES), its analysis of which suggested that basic needs poverty affected 28 per cent of the population. However, this analysis has not been made public and other preliminary investigations have suggested that poverty may be at a much higher level.

The UPP described the level of poverty as alarming and offered three broad solutions: (i) employment creation, tax free incentives, and subsidies on freight cost for companies that set up business in economically depressed areas; (ii) a five-year program to reduce the number of squatter homes to 5,000, and to improve access to health and education; and (iii) the creation of 42,000 new jobs over five years through various schemes.

Sugar industry policies

In their proposal to revamp the sugar industry, the FLP emphasized the need for long-term land leases; maintaining cane incomes in the face of EU preferential tariff reductions; subsidies on farming inputs; crop rehabilitation/development; farming assistance for new indigenous Fijian farmers; a quality cane payment system;[14] reducing costs of harvesting and transportation; retaining and upgrading the rail transport system; retaining the Sugar Industry Master Award; and reassessing the planned industry restructure.

The NAP emphasized policies to encourage more people to take up cane farming and wanted institutional reform in the sugar industry. It concentrated on the land lease issue as the prerequisite for a revival of the industry, proposed to abolish the 3 per cent sugar export tax and emphasized the need to adopt policies to increase the income of farmers. The SDL's concerns were milling and farm efficiency and new economic opportunities for farmers via the Alternative Livelihoods Project. UPP pointed out that survival of the industry could be facilitated only if all the stakeholders were involved in negotiations to resolve issues. It supported the sale of government shares in the Fiji Sugar Corporation to landowners, farmers, millers, and Fiji citizens, thus giving ownership to the stakeholders, which in, turn would, create an environment of cooperation and support. At present, the government of Fiji is the major shareholder and the management of the FSC rests with the board of directors, appointed by the government.

2001 and 2006 manifestos of the two major parties compared

Analysis of some of the key pre-2006 election policies of the major political parties shows that they are broadly similar. In terms of economic policies, all recognized the need for higher rates of economic growth. All set out strategies for achieving economic growth, but most were broad statements of 'favoured direction' rather than detailed plans. Fiji's progress in the 10 years prior to 2006 had been held back by lack of consensus on major issues such as land, economic reform (including labour market reform) and civil service reform. The FLP, backed by unions, had a strong position on the mechanism for wages negotiation, and policies on corporatization and privatization. It had opposed privatization and reform of public enterprises in the past, but, in a striking reversal, it supported a much more pro-market reformist orientation in its public campaign in the 2006 election.

An examination of the manifestos of the FLP and SDL in 2001 and 2006 suggests that major political changes occurred over the intervening period. The 2001 manifestos had been formulated at a time when Fiji was a deeply fractured country, marked by political instability and economic difficulties. Businesses were making losses, industries were collapsing, the economy had ground to a halt and development projects were frozen. The consequent mass migration had resulted in a severe brain-drain, depriving the country of much-needed skilled labour. There was also an enormous level of uncertainty on all fronts propelled by ethnic tensions, and the general atmosphere was one of great mistrust between ethnic groups.

In its 2001 manifesto, the FLP reflected the objective of restoring the overthrown People's Coalition government. It applauded the successes of that government during 1999–2000 and took a highly confrontationist stance towards the newly formed SDL party. The SDL campaign in 2001 emphasized the centrality of affirmative action for indigenous Fijians, and advertisements in the newspapers played on the likely threat to indigenous interests (e.g. as regards land policies) if the Labour Party were to be returned to office. Both parties remained at loggerheads over key policies, and were firmly aligned with their prospective voters along racial lines. The FLP whipped up passion amongst the Indo-Fijians and the SDL sought to do the same with indigenous Fijians. Most minor parties aligned themselves with one or the other of the larger parties, save for the NFP, which carried on dauntlessly on its platform of multiracialism, tolerance and non-racial politics (even though they had been defeated when they joined hands with SVT for the 1999 election).

In summary, the 2001 manifestos of the two major parties had few similarities. The parties paid lip service to reconciliation, seeking instead to polarize the electorate. They were confident that their 'own people' would assist them to reach their goals of capturing the highest elected offices of the land.

Poor economic performance between 2001 and 2006, however, presented new challenges to both the SDL and the FLP. Both tried to take up positions normally associated with the other political party. The campaign rhetoric, however, continued to be couched in racial terms, even though the FLP tried to highlight the poverty issue as a major problem for indigenous Fijians.

For the 2006 election, the two parties paid greater attention to grievances of the people that they each perceived had been neglected in their 2001 manifestos. The FLP 2006 manifesto included policies that addressed the concerns of

Table 11.1   2001 election manifestos of SDL and FLP: similarities and differences on key issues

Issues	Similarities	Differences
Land	None	Starkly differing views held by the SDL and FLP. Each claimed that the other's policies were deeply damaging. SDL advocated NLTA whereas FLP advocated ALTA and the Lands Commission. The SDL took the position of the landowners and the FLP took the position of the tenants.
Poverty	None	The FLP blamed the SDL and poor 'Fijian leadership' for poverty in Fiji. The SDL advocated the imposition of VAT while the FLP bitterly opposed it.
Sugar	Both parties conceded that the industry was in dire straits. Both parties stances towards the sugar industry stemmed mainly from their policies on land tenure.	Conflicting views on the Sugar Cane Growers' Council, the Fiji Sugar Corporation, industry operations, milling efficiency etc. Compensation was also a contentious topic.
Economy	Both conceded that the economy was depressed and that some reform was necessary.	Policies were based on differing economic ideologies, centering on affirmative action (SDL-pro, FLP against).

indigenous landowners and the incoming, new indigenous farmers who had commenced working on land left idle by evicted tenants. The SDL, on the other hand, focused attention on the plight of Indo-Fijian evicted tenants and all those who had been affected by the land lease-related issues. Both parties concentrated on the electorate that they had previously chosen to disregard; that is, the FLP moved more towards indigenous Fijians and the SDL tried to gain the support of the Indo-Fijians. Both parties also diminished the blame-attribution game that so characterized their 2001 manifestos, when each held the other responsible for the economic woes of the country.

Table 11.2   2006 election manifestos of SDL and FLP: similarities and differences on key issues

Issues	Similarities	Differences
Land	Considerable: The FLP ceased the attack on SDL/NLTB and adopted a more consensual approach. The SDL tried to promote a mutually beneficial approach by paying more attention to the plight of tenants in the land crisis.	Marginal: The SDL shifted focus towards the farmers whilst the FLP shifted focus towards land-owners.
Poverty	Considerable: Both parties ceased to place the blame for poverty squarely on the other's shoulders. Both decided not to air their differences on the issue of VAT. There has been a concession that poverty is a big problem. The SDL also minimized rhetoric regarding Indians as the wealthier community.	Slight: The SDL believed that poverty was not what the FLP claimed it to be, but did concede to some of the FLP's arguments.
Sugar	Both parties maintained their 2001 stances, but in a more moderate manner. Both believed that the industry was facing an uncertain future unless sweeping reforms were initiated urgently.	Both parties focused attention on the pertinent issues in the industry rather then blaming its shortfalls on each other. They also re-aligned their positions, with FLP paying attention to the difficulties faced by incoming indigenous farmers and SDL paying attention to the plight of evicted tenants.
Economy	Considerable: Both parties sought to rejuvenate the economy, mainly targeting investors, private sector, IT, and remittances.	Marginal: Both parties addressed core problems and concentrated their manifestos on issues believed suitable for winning over floating voters.

Interestingly, both parties also sought to suppress focus on contentious issues, such as the debate on NLTA/ALTA, the Native Land Trust Board and the Promotion of Reconciliation, Tolerance and Unity Bill during the campaign. There was some discussion of these issues during the campaign, but it lacked the venom and vigour of the 2001 campaign. The parties embarked upon extensive public relations exercises, and utilized the mass media in bids to influence voters. In particular, floating voters or those outside each party's core support base were targeted. Both parties moved away from their usual left-wing and right-wing political positions towards seemingly more moderate, reasonable, and flexible platforms. This involved a removal of the focus on the more contentious issues and a greater emphasis on the national interest, particularly as regards key economic issues.

This show of amity in the 2006 manifestos could be mistaken for more deeply rooted shifts in the philosophical position of the two parties, rather than a campaign tactic. It might be assumed to be a highly congenial shift in Fiji's otherwise unstable sociopolitical climate (which is more normally characterized by deceit, suspicion, and racialism). Unfortunately, this goes too far, and gives too much credence to stylistic, rather than substantial, changes of approach. Fundamentally, the two parties remained staunchly attached to their racially based ideological foundations but made leeway – for campaign purposes – in certain areas, hoping that this would cast them in a good light, secure positive publicity, and lure voters to support them. If there was something more genuine in the campaign-related shifts from the more normal political styles, as one must hope, it will depend on the success of the multiparty cabinet to make this a reality.

Conclusion

Fiji's 2006 election results were similar to those normally found in two-party situations. Using the median voter theory it has been argued that, contrary to the popular perception that voting is always on a communal basis, perceptions about the respective economic and associated social policies have also determined voter behaviour. Historically, Indo-Fijian political leaders have taken a left-leaning approach to economic policies while indigenous Fijian leaders have taken a right to center-right position in terms of economic policies. However, in the 2006 election both the major political parties, the SDL and the FLP, sought to woo floating voters amongst the Indo-Fijians and Indigenous Fijians, respectively. In the process, they tried to move towards the centre of the political spectrum. Both tried to gain ground from the other in terms of their social and economic policies. As a result of this, the performance of the minor parties in the elections was not strong.

Fiji's economic performance during the period 2001–2006 was modest and, given the constraints on growth, neither a post-2006-election-style SDL government nor an FLP-style government, operating alone, would have been likely to improve economic performance substantially. As part of a multiparty cabinet, bringing both sides together, the prospects are considerably stronger. Land has been one of the most divisive issues for Fiji. From 2001 to 2006, both the SDL and the FLP took extreme positions on the land issue. While both parties continued to debate the issue, thousands of farmers were forced off their farms, severely affecting both tenants and landowners and ensuring that incomes of both groups declined.[15]

Past discussion of the reform agenda has been thwarted by myths, including claims that weak economic growth is attributable to the smallness of markets, that reform would reduce jobs, and that change would inevitably be too costly and too painful. Experiences of other small countries, such as Barbados in the Caribbean and Mauritius in the Indian Ocean, show that the greatest gains in efficiency, innovation and consumer welfare have come through promoting competition.

The economic policies of the SDL and FLP indicate that there are few fundamental differences between the two parties. Land and affirmative action policies could present some difficulties if the parties choose to take extreme positions. Finding the middle ground between ALTA and NLTA may present a way forward. Affirmative action policies may not present difficulties if the government develops them in accordance with the constitution, which provides for special state support based on the needs of individuals and families rather than on race.

Notes

[1]   I wish to thank Professor Ron Duncan, Dr Jon Fraenkel and Dr Paresh Narayan for their helpful comments, and Rajiv Naidu for research help.
[2]   Congleton, R.D. 2002. 'The Median Voter Model', *Encyclopedia of Public Choice*, Center for Study of Public Choice, George Mason University, p.1.

3   Hotelling, H. 1929. 'Stability in competition', *Economic Journal*, 39:41–57.
4   Black, D. 1948. 'On the rationale of group decision-making', *Journal of Political Economy*, 56:23–34.
5   Downs, A. 1957. *An Economic Theory of Democracy*, Harper Collins, New York.
6   See, for example, Poole, K.T. & Daniels, R.S. 1985. 'Ideology, party and voting in the US Congress, 1959–1980', *American Political Science Review*, 65:131–43; Stratmann, T. 1996. 'Instability of collective decisions? Testing for cyclic majorities', *Public Choice*, 88:15–28; Congleton, R.D. & Shughart, W.F. 1990. 'The growth of social security: electrical push or political pull', *Economic Inquiry*, 28:109–32; Holcombe, R. 1980. 'An empirical test of the median voter model', *Economic Inquiry*, 18:260–74; and Frey, B. 1994. 'The role of democracy in securing just and prosperous societies: Direct democracy: Politico-economic lessons from Swiss experience', *American Economic Review*, 84:38–42.
7   See, for example, Robertson, R. & Sutherland, W. 2001. *Government by the Gun: The Unfinished Business of Fiji's 2000 Coup*, Pluto Press, Sydney; Robertson, R.T. & Tamanisau, A. 1988. *Fiji-Shattered Coups*, Pluto Press, Sydney; Lal, B.V. 1988. *Power and Prejudice: The Making of the Fiji Crisis*, New Zealand Institute of International Affairs, Wellington; Lal, B.V. 1992. *Broken Waves: A History of Fiji Islands in the Twentieth Century*, University of Hawaii Press, Honolulu; and Norton, R. 1990. *Race and Politics in Fiji*, 2nd Ed, The University of Queensland Press, Brisbane.
8   Waeyenberge, E.V. 2006 'From Washington to post-Washington consensus: Illusions of development', in K.S. Jomo. & B. Fine (eds) *The New Development Economics: After the Washington Consensus*, Zed Books: London.
9   See, for example, Prasad, B.C. 2006. 'Resolving the agricultural land lease problem in Fiji: a way forward', *Pacific Economic Bulletin*, 21(2):177–93. Prasard argued that the government should lease the land from the Native Land Title Board (under the NLTA) and then sublease this to the tenants. This is likely to satisfy both the landowners and tenants. It could also remove the conflicts that often arise between the landowners and tenants. In addition, NLTB would be able to reduce the costs of lease rental collection as government would pay the rent directly to them. The NLTB could use its saved resources and time to promote land development for the benefit of the landowners.
10 *The Fiji Times*, 2 October 2005, p.16.
11 Prasad. 2006. 'Resolving the agricultural land lease problem in Fiji'.
12 For example, the minority Melanesian community of Solomon Islands' descendents and Rabi Islanders have missed out on affirmative action benefits because they fall into the minority group referred to as 'others'.
13 For more details on the debate on affirmative action policies see, for example, Reddy, M. & Prasad, B.C. 2002. *Affirmative Action Policies and Poverty Alleviation: A Case Study of Fiji Governments Farming Assistance Scheme*, <http://devnet.anu.edu.au/1660Reddy> (accessed 2 May 2005); Ratuva, S. 2002. 'Economic nationalism and communal consolidation: economic affirmative action in Fiji, 1987–2002', *Pacific Economic Bulletin*, 17:130–37; and Gounder, N. & Prasad, B.C. 2006. 'Affirmative action in Fiji: is it justified?', *Development Bulletin*, 70:60–64.
14 Quality cane payment refers to the method of paying canefarmers on the basis of the quality of cane they supply to the mill, taking into consideration the sugar content of the cane supplied by the farmers and the quality of sugar made.
15 Prasad. 2006. 'Resolving the agricultural land lease problem in Fiji'.

12

Broken promises: women and the 2006 Fiji election

Rae Nicholl

Prior to the 2006 election, the two major political parties specifically promised that there would be an increase in the number of female candidates. Yet, of the 338 candidates they selected, only 27 (8 per cent) were women.[1] This was a reduction of four compared with the 2001 election – and the same number that stood in 1999. How could there be so few women candidates when the parties had promised so much?

Promises to women began in 1993, when the Fiji government 'established a policy to increase women's membership of boards, committees and councils by 30 to 50 per cent within the following five years'.[2] This policy initiative was followed in 1995 by Fiji's ratification of the United Nations Convention on the Elimination of All Forms of Discrimination Against Women (CEDAW). Although countries cannot be forced to comply, article 7 of the convention requires signatory states to take 'all appropriate measures to eliminate discrimination against women in the political and public life of the country'. In particular, CEDAW refers to the right of women to vote and to stand for election; the right to participate in the formulation of government policy; and the right to participate in non-governmental organizations and associations concerned with the public and political life of the country.[3] The 1997 constitution also contains commitments to women, specifically in the Bill of Rights. The constitution guarantees that 'every person has the right to equality before the law' and that 'a person must not be unfairly discriminated against, directly or indirectly, on the ground of his or her actual or supposed personal characteristics or circumstances, including…gender'.[4] It is possible that the weight of expectation – engendered by government promises, CEDAW, and the constitution – led political parties to make some rash promises in the run-up to the 2006 election.

The promises began in September 2004, when the Fiji Labour Party (FLP) announced that it had decided to set aside a significant percentage of seats for women in the 2006 election. A large proportion of these would be safe seats, a party spokesman announced, adding that gender equality was one aspect of the FLP's broader commitment to human rights and social justice.[5] Eight months later, the National Alliance Party (NAP) announced that it would allocate 50 per cent of its seats to women in the next election.[6]

Hopes rose further when the Minister for Women, Social Welfare and Poverty Alleviation, Adi Asenaca Caucau, informed an International Women's Day celebration on 8 March 2006 that, after giving the subject much thought, she had undergone a 'change of mind'. After years of opposing quotas, she believed now that 'quotas are the way forward, enabling women to become candidates'. She claimed to be in the process of making a submission to cabinet asking for a 30 per cent quota, which would apply to the SDL party only and would contain a sunset clause. There was, she admitted, no strategy for placing women in winnable seats.[7]

Hopes were reinforced on the night before a huge rally in Suva on 17 March 2006, when Prime Minister Qarase told viewers of Fiji One's prime time television news that he was expecting to see a large number of female candidates running for his party, the Soqosoqo Duavata ni Lewenivanua (SDL).

Women MPs

For women, the results of the election were bitter sweet: bitter, because there had been a reduction in women candidate numbers, but sweet because a total of eight women won seats in the House of Representatives. This was an increase of three women compared with the 2001 election, but the same number as was elected at the 1999 election (Table 12.1).

In the 2006 election, the SDL won 36 seats, five (13.9 per cent) by women. The FLP won 31 seats, two of which went to women (6.5 per cent). The

UPP won two seats, with one going to a woman (50 per cent). The two new independent members were men.

The SDL consists mainly of indigenous Fijians, is both fiscally and socially conservative, and has close links to the Methodist Church of Fiji. While the party may appear to be an unpromising choice for career-minded women, it has attracted a number of female candidates. Historically, Fiji has had a number of influential women leaders. Importantly, they have – until recently – either been chiefs themselves or have come from chiefly families and enjoyed high status among the indigenous people. Voting for such women is culturally acceptable.

On the other hand, the FLP, which has a large Fiji Indian membership, does poorly in attracting women candidates. This is despite the party having had a woman president, Jokapeci Koroi, since 1991.[8] (Following the 2006 election, Koroi was nominated by the Leader of the Opposition to the Senate. She had previously served as a Senator and vice-president of the Senate during the period 1999–2000 when the FLP was in power.) Koroi is one of the FLP's Fijian members and, in general, women in the Fijian community are more likely to rise to prominence in their own right than women from the Fiji Indian community.[9] According to Chandra Reddy, Fiji Indian women remain in a subordinate position because they live within a culture that 'condemns women's assertiveness as disrespectful to those with traditional power'.[10] Such cultural norms may well inhibit women from seeking candidacies, but the paucity of female representatives in the FLP remains disappointing given the promises that the party had made to women in 2004.

The MPs forming the smallest party in the House were those elected to 'General' electorates, seats set aside for representatives of citizens who do not

Table 12.1   Fiji general elections: women candidates and members of
             parliament, 1999–2006

Year of election	Total number of seats	Number female candidates	Number women elected	Percentage women elected to parliament
1999	71	27	8	11.27
2001	71	31	5	7.04
2006	71	27	8	11.27

belong to the other ethnic groups (Fijian, Indian and Rotuman). In the 2006 election, the UPP attained the feminist goal of achieving equality between the sexes. While it is acknowledged that the party has only two members, one female and one male, from a symbolic viewpoint, attaining parity is a significant achievement.

Of the eight women elected, four were returning incumbents and four were new MPs. The four incumbents – Ro Teimumu Kepa, Adi Asenaca Caucau, Nanise Nagusuca and Losena Salabula – had been ministers or assistant ministers in the previous SDL administration and went into the campaign with the advantage of name recognition in the electorate.

Not all four new members were well known nationally, although two of the women were household names. Known throughout Fiji as the 'Hot Bread Queen', the new SDL member, Mere Samisoni, was contesting for the third time. She is a successful businesswoman – and founding owner of The Hot Bread Kitchen chain of bakeries. Bernadette Rounds Ganilau, the new MP for the UPP, had already achieved a high level of visibility through her broadcasting and other media work and her 'larger-than-life' personality. The other two new members represented the FLP. Adi Sivia Qoro was a former diplomat and women's development adviser at the Secretariat of the Pacific Community, and Monika Raghwan, who is considerably younger than the other women MPs, was an executive officer in a family business, Raghwan Construction, one of the largest construction companies in Fiji.

Two women did not return to parliament after the election. Marieta Rigamoto, the independent member for Rotuma, who had been the Minister for Information, Communications and Media Relations, retired from politics. Ofa Swann (Duncan), who had previously been a member of the New Labour Unity Party, chose to run as an independent, and lost her seat.

Cabinet appointments

By 24 May, the Prime Minister had selected his new cabinet. Ro Teimumu Kepa was reappointed Minister for Education, Youth and Sports, and the FLP's new MP, Adi Sivia Qoro, was elevated to cabinet to become the Minister for Commerce and Industry. In addition, the Prime Minister brought into cabinet a newly appointed woman senator, Adi Samanunu Cakobau, as Minister

Without Portfolio in the Prime Minister's Office. In a controversial move, a man, George Shiu Raj, was appointed the new Minister for Women, Social Welfare and Poverty Alleviation.

In a new departure, the Prime Minister also named a number of state ministers, including Adi Asenaca Caucau, who lost her position as Minister for Women, Social Welfare and Poverty Alleviation, and Losena Salabula. Adi Asenaca Caucau took on the position of Minister of State for Housing, while Losena Salabula, who had been an assistant minister in the previous administration, returned to a similar position as Minister of State for the Office of the Prime Minister. Nanise Nagusuca, who had been Assistant Minister, Culture and Heritage, was dropped from cabinet. Finally, subsequent to the UPP becoming the official opposition, Bernadette Rounds Ganilau became Deputy Leader of the Opposition.

The Senate

The term of the Senate, Fiji's non-elected second chamber, is the same as that of the House of Representatives and, as a consequence, new appointments are made after a general election. Six women (18.8 per cent) have been appointed to the Senate: Adi Samanunu Cakobau and Adi Lagamu Vuiyasawa (Prime Minister's nominees); Adi Koila Nailatikau and Adi Laufitu Malani (Great Council of Chiefs' nominees); and Jokapeci Koroi and Lavinia Padarath (Leader of the Opposition's nominees). As four women (12.5 per cent) of the 32 senators were appointed during the term of the 2001–2006 government, it is encouraging to see the increase in female presence in the Senate in the current government.

Party manifestos

While party leaders made rash promises to women in public forums, the policies relating to female representation, as set out in their manifestos, were more implicit than explicit. The first manifesto to be released came from the SDL, which held a huge rally in Suva on 17 March 2006 designed to showcase both the manifesto and the party's candidates. The glossy booklet, published in both Fijian and English, contained a section on women along with a raft of other policies. The manifesto told women that they were 'the pillars of the nation' and 'the backbone of our families' and that 'the government has always stressed the important part women play in the development of Fiji'. While acknowledging that 'more effort is required to increase the number of women MPs', the manifesto made no suggestions as to how this goal would be achieved.[11]

The FLP's manifesto conveyed similar sentiments regarding women's representation. It stressed that 'women are equal partners with men, and should play a full and active role in the political, economic, cultural and social life of Fiji'. Further, the party noted that 'there are still many barriers to women's full participation' and that women are 'not adequately represented in Parliament' although, as with the SDL, the party provided no initiatives as to how the problem of equitable female representation could be resolved.[12] The UPP gave no commitment to a quota system but indicated that it would include women parliamentarians in cabinet and the Senate and on select committees.[13]

The two largest losing parties also carried policies for women in their manifestos. As it had promised in May 2005, the NAP proved to be the only major political entity suggesting a quota for women candidates – but with a slight twist. It appeared to be encouraging other political parties 'to adopt a 50 per cent target for women candidates as part of their manifestos' but without committing themselves to a similar policy, although the party did promise to 'create an enabling environment for women, including young women, to seek and advance political careers'.[14] In this respect, the NAP policy had a resonance with the policy proposals not realized in the SDL manifesto, but mooted by the Minister for Women, Social Welfare and Poverty Alleviation, Adi Asenaca Caucau, when she had stressed the desirability of 'creating an enabling environment for women'.[15] The other big loser in the election, the National Federation Party, also promised to 'increase representation of women in Parliament and other private and public sector boards and institutions', but failed to give any indication of how this promise was to be effected.[16]

Women as voters

Election observers, especially those from Europe, were concerned about the heavy daily workload of women in Fiji, especially of those living a subsistence lifestyle in the rural areas and outer islands, where there is often no electricity or running water. They saw women, many of whom were elderly, with their backs bent double under huge loads of firewood, trudging along dusty roads. When the observers came into the villages, they found that it was the women who had set out fishing at midnight, who had cooked meals for all the visiting election officials, and who had then cleaned up afterwards before returning to their homes to carry on with their own household duties.[17]

These same village women, including many of the very elderly, voted in what appeared to be large numbers, but some were illiterate and needed assistance with filling out their ballot papers.[18] While observers could not see or hear if these women were being told how to vote by election officials, media reports suggested that family members, in particular, were grooming them to vote in a certain way. Journalist Verenaisi Raicola supported this suggestion in an article published in *The Fiji Times* on 9 May, which was part way through election week. Entitled 'Elderly unable to cast vote', Verenaisi Raicola told the story of a blind and deaf 83-year-old woman, Seni, from the remote island of Qoma in Tailevu. According to the reporter:

> Seini said her son had instructed her how to tick the Dove symbol above the line and that she knew that much was right because she had been reminded over and over again.[19]

The symbol of the dove represented the SDL party. A day after the story appeared in *The Fiji Times,* Shamima Ali, Executive Director of the Fiji Women's Crisis Centre, told the media that she had received complaints that women in rural areas were being pressured by their husbands and community leaders to vote in a certain manner.[20]

In anticipation of the 'grooming' problem, four of Fiji's women's organizations – fem'LINKpacific, Fiji Women's Rights Movement, Fiji Women's Crisis Centre and Women's Action for Change – combined to place full-page advertisements in the daily newspapers on at least two occasions during the voting period. Titled 'No-one sees who you vote for. No-one will ever know', the advertisement encouraged women to read the party manifestos; to remember what had been said in the campaigns; and to ask what politicians had done for the community. The advertisement ended by reminding women that 'this is your choice, your vote – yours alone'.[21]

Although it could be argued that the placement of the advertisements was mis-timed, to this reader it seemed clear that they were designed to alleviate the pressure to vote in a certain way that some women might be placed under by family members. However, the reaction to the advertisements by the Supervisor of Elections, Semesa Karavaki, was one of displeasure. According to Pacific Media Watch, the Supervisor confirmed that there would be a police investigation into what he described as 'the breach of Fiji's electoral laws that ban electioneering once polling has begun'.[22] At the time of writing, no police action against the women's organizations had begun.

As well as being voters, women played other roles in the election. The election cycle began with the registration of voters, a process carried out all over the country by teams of enumerators, people who travelled the length and breadth of Fiji to make sure every eligible citizen's name appeared on the electoral roll. Enumerators were expected to travel by foot and walk house-to-house, often over rough and mountainous terrain. In some cases, they were required to travel overnight and sleep in villages. Because of racial sensitivities, one problem that arose during the voter registration process was the suggestion that more Fijians than Fiji Indians were taking on the enumerator role. Some members of the Fiji Indian population were suspicious of Fijian enumerators who came to their houses and felt that their enrolment details might not be treated with sufficient diligence. Another concern was the shortage of female Fiji Indian enumerators, especially in rural areas where some older Fiji Indian women were reluctant to give their personal details to men. According to the Returning Officer, Northern Division, acquiring a racial – and gender – balance of enumerators was desirable, but it had proved difficult to maintain, and the necessity for enumerators to occasionally sleep away from home may have been a factor in the low recruitment of Fiji Indian women.[23]

Besides being employed as enumerators, many women worked during election week as polling clerks, joining teams of up to 18 members (including two police officers). The teams were all of mixed gender, but, on the whole, the polling clerks were women and the presiding officers were men, although there was a handful of women who took on the senior roles in the polling stations and vote counting centres. Many women voters, especially those with literacy or health problems, reported feeling more confident and comfortable if a woman assisted them. Providing more senior women in leadership roles at election time would be another step towards making the electoral process more female-friendly.

Action to increase women's participation and representation

The women's movement in Fiji has worked for decades to improve the profile of women in public life, and its various organizations have produced numerous documents and reports on the issue.[24] These publications have highlighted the many barriers to women's advancement, but, as yet, there have been no incremental increases in the number of women elected to the Fiji Parliament since eight women were elected in 1999. While disheartening, this stasis has not stopped women's organizations from taking action to improve the situation.

As previously discussed, four organizations jointly took out advertisements in the daily papers, reminding women that their vote was secret and that no one needed to know how they had cast their ballot. In addition to assisting with the advertisements, the fem'LINKpacific women's media organization broadcast interviews with women candidates and covered issues concerning the election.

One of the well-documented barriers preventing women from campaigning effectively is the lack of campaign finance.[25] The cost of running an effective campaign in Fiji can be considerable. Ofa Swann (Duncan) spent two terms in the House of Representatives (1999 and 2001) and was contesting her third election in 2006 as an independent candidate. She claimed that the estimated cost of her campaign was F$25,000 and that her main methods of fundraising would be hosting private parties and selling clothes.[26]

Political parties in many countries usually contribute a small amount to individual campaigns, sometimes through the production of advertisements featuring the party leader with the candidate, but large costs often remain to be absorbed by candidates. Women, generally, do not have the capacity to generate large sums of money, especially not in Fiji where wages and salaries are low. As well, women often are in no position to take out loans or mortgages. Feminists have understood this problem and, in some countries, financial assistance for women may come from organizations such as EMILY's list in the United States, which raises money for candidates who are members of the Democratic Party.[27]

In an effort to assist women candidates in Fiji with their heavy financial obligations, the Fiji Women's Rights Movement launched the Women In Politics (WIP) Appeal by donating F$1,000 to start the fundraising campaign. The appeal was designed to assist female candidates, irrespective of their political affiliation, and to mobilize women voters.[28] While the time frame for the appeal was short, it was successful, and, on the first day of election week, the Fiji Women's Rights Movement placed an advertisement in the press thanking all donors to the WIP Appeal and affirming that their 'generous donation was shared equally amongst all women candidates in the 2006 elections, irrespective of their political party affiliations'.[29] The movement also produced a leaflet that was inserted into the daily newspapers entitled 'Women Ask', which identified the 'strengths and strategies proposed by political parties to address the concerns of women'.[30]

Recruiting female candidates

One reason why political parties fail in their promises to field more female candidates is the shortage of willing and credible women. Unfortunately, attracting female candidates is problematic worldwide as capable women are not always interested in the prospect of a political career.[31] Women in Fiji are no different. Adi Asenaca Caucau noted that 'the SDL has as much trouble as any other party in attracting credible candidates even though there is strong grass roots support in the party'. In the bid to find candidates, the SDL had 'not only approached chiefly women, but other women as well'.[32]

If political parties really want to appear sympathetic to gender equality, they need to actively seek more women candidates and to allocate them safe seats, where they have a good chance of winning. Once women are selected, parties must acknowledge the barriers that they face. In particular, they must help women candidates raise the funds to cover the costs of campaigning.

The alternative vote and a quota system

Fiji uses the alternative vote electoral system to elect its members of parliament. Imported from Australia, the alternative vote replaced the first-past-the-post voting system and has been used since the 1999 election. The alternative vote is a majoritarian system very similar to first-past-the-post in that both systems are based on single-member electorates; the principal difference is that the alternative vote gives electors the choice of ranking candidates in order of preference. In any system with single-member electorates, there is a strong tendency to choose 'safe' candidates, who will not offend any citizens within the voting community. The result of this selection process tends to be a dull uniformity of middle-aged middle-class male candidates across all parties. The system does not assist those groups in society, such as women and ethnic minorities, who traditionally have been under-represented in parliament.[33]

The quickest way to bring diversity to parliament would be to abolish the alternative vote with its concomitant multiple communal rolls and introduce a proportional representation system, either the Mixed-Member Proportional system used in New Zealand or the list system used in South Africa. Both these voting systems have been successful in bringing a critical mass of women (usually considered to be 30 per cent) into parliament. For instance, in 2004, women won 32.8 per cent of the seats in South Africa's lower house, the National Assembly. In the following year, New Zealand women won 32.2 per cent of the seats in that country's House of Representatives.[34] A critical mass is considered important because there is an assumption, supported by the United Nations, that the greater the number of women in a legislature the more seriously women's social, economic, legal and cultural needs will be taken.[35]

One alternative to changing the electoral system could be the introduction of a quota system. Political parties need to be encouraged to consider this option seriously, to look at overseas models, and to consider ways in which they could institute a quota within their organizations. For example, South Africa's ruling party, the African National Congress, has enshrined a 30 per cent quota for women within its constitution.[36]

Another form of quota could be the use of reserved seats for women. Fijian constitutional lawyers could look at the New Zealand example of reserved seats for Maori, although the difficulty of introducing a new system that asked citizens to complete accurately a third ballot paper (there is already one ballot paper for the communal roll and another for the general roll) might prove a disincentive in pursuing this idea.

Conclusion

Attitudinal changes will be needed if women in Fiji are to forge ahead into leadership roles. Conservative views about women remain strong, as was evidenced by a recent letter to the editor in *The Fiji Times*. Under the heading

'Good leaders', the correspondent stated that: 'it is imperative to mention that we prefer a male president of Fiji. Women should be barred from holding the post'.[37] While feminists may not have been too surprised by the correspondent's misogynistic tendencies, they were dismayed and disappointed when the Assistant Minister for Culture and Heritage, Nanise Nagusuca, made several public statements that appeared to criticize the work of women's organizations. In one statement, she said:

> The traditional Fijian set-up does not make mention of the woman being superior or even on equal standing with men. A lot of Fijian women know that they should be subservient to their husbands and be good mothers to their children. They should see that the home is well looked after and that the life of the family members is comfortable. Women's rights is a western concept and shouldn't be adopted.[38]

The stagnation in women's political advancement in Fiji was apparent in the 2006 election. While the situation had improved over the 2001 result, women have yet to build on their 1999 success, when eight women were elected to parliament. Unless MPs and political parties decide on a critical review of the voting system and the consequent changes required to the constitution, or seriously consider introducing a quota system, women have little hope of increasing their parliamentary presence. If changes are not made, promises of increased representation for women will continue to be empty rhetoric and to be broken.

Notes

[1] Fiji Elections Office, <http://www.elections.gov.fj> (accessed 10 May 2006).

[2] Huffer, E. 'Review of Institutional Mechanisms, Policies, Legislation and Programmes in Support and Promotion of Gender Equality in the Republic of the Marshall Islands, Samoa and Fiji', Pacific Women's Bureau, Ninth Triennial Conference of Pacific Women, Nadi, Fiji, 2004, p.43.

[3] The Pacific Regional Human Rights Education Team. CEDAW: the Convention on the Elimination of all forms of Discrimination Against Women, Suva, 2001. Fiji ratified CEDAW on 27 August 1995.

[4] Section 38, (1) and (2) (a), Constitution of the Republic of the Fiji Islands, 27 July 1998, p.26.

[5] *Fiji Sun*, 21 September 2004, p.5.

[6] *Fiji Sun*, 6 May 2005, p.1.

[7] Speech given to the International Labour Organisation, Suva, 8 March 2006.

[8] Jokapeci Koroi, Remarks made to the Women and Leadership: 6th Triennial Conference

Report, The Fiji Association of Women Graduates, Parliament of Fiji Complex, Suva, 6 &
7 May 2000, p.20.

[9] United States Department of State, Fiji: Country Reports on Human Rights Practices -
1999. Released by the Bureau of Democracy, Human Rights and Labor, <http://www.state.
gov/g/drl/rls/hrrpt/1999/287.htm> (accessed 26 July 2006).

[10] Reddy, C. 2000. 'Women and politics in Fiji', in B.V. Lal (ed.) *Fiji Before the Storm: Elections
and the Politics of Development*, Asia Pacific Press, The Australian National University,
Canberra, pp.149–60.

[11] Soqosoqo Duavata ni Lewenivanua, 2006. *Beat Poverty. Raise prosperity. 2006 SDL Manifesto*,
Soqosoqo Duavata ni Lewenivanua, Suva, p.24.

[12] Fiji Labour Party, *Change the Future. Vote Labour. 2006 Election Manifesto*, Fiji Labour Party,
2006, p.24.

[13] Fiji Women's Rights Movement, *Women Ask – summary of a pre-election survey of all parties'
policies on concerns of women*, Fiji Women's Rights Movement, Suva, May 2006.

[14] National Alliance Party of Fiji, *Manifesto – 2006*, National Alliance Party of Fiji, 2006,
p.38.

[15] Speech given to the International Labour Organisation, Suva, 8 March 2006.

[16] National Federation Party, *2006 General Elections Manifesto – United Fiji*, National Federation
Party, Samabula, 2006, p.16.

[17] Personal discussions with election observers from the European Union, Commonwealth and
the Pacific Forum, Labasa, May 2006.

[18] Chandra, D. & Lewai, V. 2005. *Women and Men of Fiji Islands: Gender Statistics and Trends*,
Population Studies Programme, University of the South Pacific, Suva, p.18. Statistics show
that older rural women have the lowest levels of literacy, with Fiji Indian women being the
worst affected.

[19] Raicola, V. 'Elderly unable to cast vote', *The Fiji Times*, 9 May 2006, p.7.

[20] Fiji Gold FM, Report on comments made by Shamima Ali of the Fiji Women's Crisis Centre,
10 May 2006.

[21] 'Fem'LINKpacific, Fiji Women's Rights Movement, Fiji Women's Crisis Centre, and Women's
Action for Change', *The Fiji Times*, 6 May 2006, p.73 and *Fiji Sun*, 10 May 2006, p.13.

[22] Pacific Media Watch, 'Women activists cited over electoral adverts', <http://www.pmw.c2o.
org>, 10 May 2006.

[23] Interview with Officer in Charge of Postal Ballots – Northern Division, Labasa, 11 May
2006.

[24] Pacific Regional YWCA. 2000. *Pacific Regional Report on the Implementation of the Beijing
Platform for Action*, Suva, Fiji; Fiji Women's Rights Movement. 2002. *Exploring Women's
Employment Rights*, Suva, Fiji,; Fiji Association of Women Graduates. 2003. *Humanising
Globalisation: The Challenges for Pacific Women*, 7th Triennial Conference Report, Pacific
Harbour International Hotel, Deuba, Fiji Islands; Schoeffel, P. 2004. 'Pacific Platform for
Action on Women: An Evaluation of the Thirteen Critical Issues and the Status of Pacific
Women: 1994–2004', Pacific Women's Bureau, Ninth Triennial Conference of Pacific
Women, Nadi, Fiji; Pacific Regional Office of UNIFEM, 2005. *Developing a More Facilitating
Environment for Women's Political Participation in Fiji*, Suva, Fiji.

[25] Carroll, S.J. 1994. *Women as Candidates in American Politics,* second edition, Indiana
University Press, Bloomington, pp.49–51; Darcy, R., Welch, S. & Clark, J. 1994. *Women,*

Elections and Representation, second edition, revised, University of Nebraska Press, Lincoln, pp.71–73; Norris, P. & Lovenduski, J. 1995. *Political Recruitment: Gender, Race and Class in the British Parliament,* Cambridge University Press, Cambridge, pp.146–47.

26 Rina, S. 'Swann ready for her fight', *Fiji Sun,* 25 March 2006, p.2.

27 EMILY's list is an acronym for Early Money Is Like Yeast.

28 Virisila Buadromo, 'FWRM Kick Starts WIP Appeal', media release, Fiji Women's Rights Movement, 6 April 2006.

29 Fiji Women's Rights Movement, 'WIP Appeal – Funding Progress', *The Fiji Times,* 6 May 2006, p.44.

30 Fiji Women's Rights Movement, 'Women Ask', election pamphlet, May 2006.

31 Nicholl, R. 2001. The Woman Factor: Candidate Selection in the 1990s – New Zealand, Guam and South Africa, unpublished PhD thesis, Victoria University of Wellington, New Zealand.

32 Speech given to the International Labour Organisation, Suva, 8 March 2006.

33 Nicholl, R. 2006. 'Electing women to parliament: Fiji and the alternative vote electoral system, *Pacific Journalism Review,* 12(1):87–107.

34 Inter-Parliamentary Union, Geneva, <http://ipu.org/wnm-e/classif.htm> (accessed 20 May 2006).

35 United Nations Office at Vienna. 1992. *Women in Politics and Decision-Making in the Late Twentieth Century,* Martinus Nijhoff Publishers, Netherlands, p.107.

36 Constitution of the African National Congress as amended by and adopted by the 51st National Conference, December 2002. <http://www.anc.org.za/ancdocs/history/const/const2002.html> (accessed 23 June 2006).

37 *The Fiji Times,* 17 March 2006, p. 6.

38 Up Close and Personal Column, *Daily Post,* 29 April 2006. Nanise Nagusuca made similar remarks in a press statement released by the Ministry of Information on 6 December 2005 (Press release no 1614/10).

13

The media and the spectre of the 2000 coup

Michael Field

A green prison truck pulls into the crowded alleyway behind the old government buildings in downtown Suva. A handful of photographers and reporters try to catch a glimpse of a ghost riding in the back. George Speight. Almost exactly to the day six years before – 19 May 2000 – accompanied by special forces soldiers, he had charged on to the floor of parliament and seized Prime Minister Mahendra Chaudhry and his government. Although he now whiles away a pleasant, if dull, life on Nukulau as a convicted traitor, Speight's before-election appearance – such as it was – had nothing to do with the balloting. Rather, as a witness this time, Speight was part of the seemingly endless post-coup wash-up that Fiji and its interminable justice system just cannot throw.

A little earlier, and across the road, a mellow Sitiveni Rabuka had sat by a window at the Holiday Inn restaurant having breakfast. He too had been in court, although as a defendant, facing a charge of inciting mutiny in the Fiji military. In earlier times, conviction on such a charge would have led to a firing squad; these days it is life imprisonment – but Rabuka was calm. Having spent six weeks in India having knee replacement surgery, he was keen to talk about Mahatma Gandhi and India's political system. 'Minorities hold all the top positions in India', he says. 'The president is a Muslim, the Prime Minister and the military chief are both Sikhs and the head of the largest political party, Congress, is Italian.'

It could have been an odd conversation, given that, in 1986, Rabuka had seized power to overthrow the newly elected Indian-dominated government and was one of the founding prophets of *Taukei,* or indigenous rule. That it was not so unusual has much to do with the way in which post-independence Fijian political life, while obviously polarized, is still very much in the formative stages. History too is very compressed: the kind of events that elsewhere might have taken place over a century or more, in Fiji have occurred over the two decades since 1987. That Rabuka should become an advocate of Indian political processes is entirely natural in the context of Fiji. While racial and cultural divisions are mostly seismic in Fiji, with both sides well apart, refreshingly one also finds characters seemingly quite happy to live and partake of a multicultural Fiji.

At one level, it is kind of comforting: Fiji can get through these things. But at another, the whole air of uncertainty is distinctly destabilizing, and as Fiji moved into its elections in 2006, the whole sense of unfinished business created unease. Both Rabuka and Speight were, at the candidate and party level, an irrelevancy; but among voters and the media covering the election they were ghosts to be noticed. There was, though, another coup plotter, although he does not see himself that way: Republic of Fiji Military Forces head Commodore Voreqe Bainimarama. His view of himself as the nation's saviour, and his refusal to acknowledge that his behaviour in 2000 was unconstitutional, meant that the 2006 election had to be conducted with an eye to what the man with the guns was saying and doing. Any comfort anybody might have drawn from his statements on good order soon evaporated under the heat of his immoderate and erratic behaviour. It was hard to pick what he might do.

Rabuka's first coup, 14 May 1987, was in a pre-digital age (one of the last big Pacific events to be reported by a now forgotten machine – the telex) and one where the world media was content with the simple notion of a dashing lieutenant colonel saving his paradise nation from avaricious aliens. While the media were content with the glib, the regional politicians, not least Rabuka himself, found themselves in a cul-de-sac. International opinion, which was given to tolerating third world coups and disorder, was heading into a new globalization, and in 1991 this climaxed with the Harare Commonwealth

Declaration that was supposed to be the new benchmark for democracy. That host Robert Mugabe notoriously failed to honour the document is beside the point; Fiji, which actually cared about the Commonwealth despite being treated badly by it, faced the prospect of severe isolation, on the sports field in places like New Zealand, in the Commonwealth Games and in the wider social world that the Commonwealth organization provides across professions and interests. Isolation could only be avoided in the new post-Harare age with democracy for all citizens, not just the indigenous ones. To his credit, Rabuka recognized the problem he had created with his coup and began to move away from the *Taukei* nightmare. This led to what was, at least for the 2006 election, the seminal event: the drawing up of what became the 1997 constitution by a former speaker, the late Tomasi Vakatora, academic Brij Lal and former New Zealand Governor General Sir Paul Reeves. The last, an indigenous Maori, said soon after the report was tabled that the terms of reference the three had been given were 'amongst the more significant political statements Fiji had made in quite a long time'.

Rabuka, then prime minister, and the then opposition leader, Jai Ram Reddy, accepted many of the constitutional proposals, particularly the introduction of open seats and the new alternative voting system, and Reeves believed that what they came up with was the route away from communal politics.[1] Rabuka tabled the report in parliament on 10 September 1996 and on that day I wrote that it was 'a poignant way of bringing to an end the indigenous dream' that had ignited his coups nine years earlier. One line in the report got a lot of attention: '… trying to keep a predominantly Fijian Government in office in perpetuity may not be the best way of securing the paramountcy of Fijian interests'.

Then president Ratu Sir Kamisese Mara spoke to the joint session and, in a theme that has haunted Fijian politics since, he said traditional Fiji had a procedure for reconciliation. As in other Polynesian cultures, the business of saying sorry has always been deeply ingrained and much honoured, but the problem with the president's remarks was that he did not say who was meant to apologize to whom, and for what.

International media interest in Fiji's constitutional debate was limited mostly to how Rabuka would handle it – and, indeed, there was an element of surprise in his approach to the general election in 1999, the first under the new system and one in which the key players involved in the 1987 coup were active participants. Reddy and Rabuka were in an alliance around the new constitution, but the result suggested both Indian and indigenous voters were unimpressed by the coalition. In racially charged Fiji elections, such an artificial alliance was unacceptable to the majority, and the voters punished Rabuka and Reddy accordingly.

The scale of the Fiji Labour Party victory was a genuine international shock and the elevation of bruising trade unionist Mahendra Chaudhry to the top office quickly led to speculation on 'the next coup'. As argued in *Speight of Violence*[2], the Fiji media had a role in creating the environment that led to the 2000 Speight coup. The Rupert Murdoch-owned *Fiji Times*, then under particularly intellectually barren editorial leadership, engaged in unethical, unsourced and frequently wrong scandal-mongering about the Chaudhry government. Chaudhry was right at the time: 'Since taking office, my government has had occasion to be extremely disgusted by the antics of some elements in the media who have used the medium of the newspaper and television to further their own personal agendas to discredit the government'.

And so, as Chaudhry prepared to cut the first birthday cake for his government on 19 May 2000, Speight and his thugs were coming through the front door in a bid to seize power and kill off multiculturalism. For a time they succeeded, although the partial success of the subsequent 2001 election, and the real achievement of the 2006 election, suggest the people of Fiji are learning.

Naturally, the Speight coup – if that is what it was and many doubts still remain after successive treason trials – remains a defining political event for Fiji. But, within the context of the 2006 election, it was intriguing that the single most influential event was that which occurred 10 days after Speight charged into parliament – Commodore Bainimarama's declaration of martial law; an event which needs to be redefined now as a coup, and one eminently more successful than the hair-brained effort mounted by Speight. One casual piece of evidence for this occurred during the 2006 election: Speight was shipped over from Nukulau to appear as a witness in court and only the small overseas media corps thought it was worth staking out. But when the Commodore spoke, the nation was given to holding its breath.

During the afternoon and into the evening of 29 May 2000, a series of events occurred that climaxed with Ratu Sir Kamisese Mara stepping down as president and Commodore Bainimarama declaring martial law. The behaviour of those involved in this, which included Rabuka and the impotent Police Chief Isikia Savua, has – six years on – not been fully explained. On the face of it, the Commodore had staged a coup of his own and, while he was no more successful at resolving the hostage drama at parliament than Speight, he had all the trappings and advantages of power – including military power. His key action was something he did *not* do – restore Mr Chaudhry to power. This single absence of action has resulted in the Fiji we see today.

Quite early in the piece, the Commodore saw himself not only as the saviour of the nation, but also its grand director who would define its future according to a philosophy that was only accessible to his inner circle. It was a kind of military order that plays well on the poop deck. His 'order of battle' had him plucking an obscure senator and banker from Lau, Laisenia Qarase, and making him interim prime minister. It was never said explicitly, but was understood in those dark days of 2000, that Qarase was a caretaker, a stop-gap that would make long-term military rule of Fiji play well in the Commonwealth (Fiji is, ironically, one of the few ex-colonies that cares about that faded institution) and amongst the neighbours. The Commodore was not interested in a return to democracy, although he was to find out soon enough that in Wellington and Canberra that was all they were interested in.

Before the 'new military order' could be put in place, catastrophe struck, with a mutiny at the Queen Elizabeth Barracks on 2 November 2000. Eight men died, some tortured to death by loyal troops in what amounted to a bid to take out the Commodore, either dead or alive. At the time, the arrival on the scene of Rabuka, his uniform in the car and cell phone in his hand, was seen as little more than comedy and a media moment. He gave international radio interviews from the scene, gunfire crackling in the background. Only later did allegations arise that Rabuka was not the jester, but the organizer. These allegations were to splutter on for years, and at one point spoiled his chance of becoming Fiji's US ambassador. But he was not arrested until right in the middle of the 2006 election.

International pressure for a return to democracy saw Fiji go to the polls in 2001 and, to the chagrin of the Commodore, his stand-in appointee suddenly formed a rag-tag party, the Soqosoqo Duavata ni Lewenivanua (SDL), and top-polled in the ballot. To form a government though, Qarase was obliged to make an alliance with those the Commodore regarded as his enemy, the Conservative Alliance that had successfully run George Speight as a candidate. As Speight was serving life on Nukulau, he could not take his seat.

In understanding what happened in 2006, it's important to recognize the biggest failing of the 2001 election process: the failure to form a multi-party cabinet, as required by the constitution. This, and the debilitating process of court action over it, was to sap Fiji in more ways than people recognized at the time. In the increasingly tedious and legalistic action, Mahendra Chaudhry traded off most of the goodwill he had earned as a hostage. He went from martyr to international bore in short order.

It was the Promotion of Reconciliation, Tolerance and Unity Bill and the Commodore's extreme reaction to it that turned Qarase's first term in office into a see-sawing voyage of uncertainty. At several points, the Commodore, plainly awash in his belief that he was the nation's saviour, threatened to do it all again and remove the Prime Minister from office. The inability of Qarase to act against the Commodore, who enjoyed tacit, if limited, support from President Ratu Josefa Iloilo, prolonged Fiji's political pain. Rather than protect Fiji from the traitors and the coup-plotters, the battle between the two created a deep political malaise and consequently had an impact on the government's ability to carry the country forward.

Another burst of activity from the Commodore in early 2006, and claims that other senior officers were plotting against him, finally pushed the government to a slightly earlier than expected general election. All the ghosts of 2000 were conspiring again: Bainimarama, like some Superman in a phone booth, was again ready to save the nation. As was explored in *Speight of Violence*, the military mounted an advocacy program which looked, at best, suspiciously hostile toward SDL. The message it offered was implicit: out of the 2000 coup came disorder, chaos, death and, by the way, SDL and its supporters. That the Commodore had got things so wrong took a while to sink in, not least because most of the population was smart enough to recognize that, while the military had helped cause the problems, their prime minister had put an end to them. But several factors counted against Bainimarama, not least a palpable if poorly documented weariness in the wider community. National saviours are good in their place, but not as a substitute for democracy. Bainimarama was showing signs of homespun megalomania.

The country moved into its immensely complicated election system, under the less than adequate leadership of Election Supervisor Semesa Karavaki. In his defence, though, an outsider can readily recognize that Fiji's poorly resourced voting process is always going to be a mess and of no attraction at all to anybody with real skills. The 2001 election under then supervisor Walter Rigomoto was regarded much later as somewhat more successful; Rigomoto, though, was exhausted by it all and was not interested in taking his skills onto the next election. Whatever Karavaki learnt in the 2006 election will mostly be lost to the 2011 ballot; he, too, found the process thankless.

The media approached the election in a post-coup mode, although few involved in the day-to-day coverage had even reported the 2000 coup, such is the high turnover in the domestic Fiji media. The three dailies provided a mishmash of stories about problems around the country, but with no coherent wrap. It was all tree-counting without seeing the forest. Fiji TV, other than providing a platform for a somewhat confused leaders debate, was given to providing lots of numbers but no pattern. When it came to announcing results during the three days of counting, they were often reluctant to break into programs such as *Shortland Street*. The real talent in election coverage this time around was found in radio, which seemed to have acquired a maturity it had not had in the coup or the last election. Stations, such as the English language *Legend,* plainly went into the election well-briefed and ready to devote considerable resources to the business of election coverage. The international media was distinctly uninterested in what was going on, and only a handful of the journalists – mostly representing news agencies – turned up. Just one or two had been in Fiji for any other election, much less the coups. Radio New Zealand established the pattern of leaning heavily on Fiji Radio's *Legend,* its solitary correspondent reduced to taping *Legend.* Auckland-based Radio Tarana, an AM radio station targeted at the Indian community, weighed into the election coverage scene with a big team, including Riyaz Sayed-Khaiyum. Although he had been living in Auckland for two years, his long stint with Fiji TV's *Close Up* program – including one broadcast during the coup that had prompted Speight's gang to trash the television station – meant he retained strong local respect. The shame was that the effort was targeted at a largely irrelevant audience.

The 2000 coup kept breaking into the election campaign in a variety of ways, some of which had to do with the capacity of the Fiji and foreign media to keep re-spinning conspiracy yarns. It was easily done, in large part because of a very low institutional memory when it comes to matters Fijian. A small-time ex-soldier, Maciu Navakasuasua, who, like many others, served time in gaol for his role in the coup, demonstrated this particular failing. Sometime later he got some form of religion, moved to Australia and started making claims about what really happened in the coup. Most of it was recycled and had come out in the various trials earlier on, but the *Fiji Sun* and Australia's Graham Davis of Channel Nine acted as if it was all startling and new. It was particularly centred around claims that nationalist politician Iliesa Duvuloco had played a key role in the organization of the coup. Two years after his role had been revealed in court, it all popped up again. It had the extraordinary effect of giving Duvuloco, a five-times-failed politician, a kind of status and *mana* he was simply not entitled to. He had burnt the constitution on the steps of parliament when it was passed, and voters in election after election had steadfastly dismissed his brand of nationalism. This background was not provided by the media covering him and so, as a result of the media's fixation on short-term memory, he was elevated to some kind of anti-hero status. Happily, he managed to sink himself and his tiny Nationalist Vanua Tako Lavo Party with an appearance on Fiji TV's candidates' debate, chaired by Richard Naidu, when he seemed to lie in his chair almost flat, providing watchers with a view of his disproportionately bulky stomach. Voters were suitably unattracted.

Although the 2000 coup featured throughout the election campaign – largely as a result of the debate over the Promotion of Reconciliation, Tolerance and Unity Bill and the army's blundering efforts – during the calm week of voting the past was almost forgotten, until the Friday when, seemingly out of the blue, Rabuka was arrested on mutiny charges. That he was something of a relic was underscored by the way that his appearance in the Suva Magistrate's Court was almost casual; no additional security, no anxious supporters. He just strolled in to be greeted, mostly by journalists. An air of conspiracy seemed to hang around the timing, but Fiji Police Commissioner Andrew Hughes, on the afternoon after the court appearance, quickly dispelled the notion it was aimed at the election. The arrest timing, he said, had more to do with the fact that Rabuka had been in India having his knee caps replaced and had just come home. In the event, the arrest and court appearance proved merely to be a brief diversion in the election and had no obvious impact on its outcome. The High Court trial, still to come, might well prove much more threatening, potentially to the Commodore, whose distaste for Rabuka has been evident for a while. It has to be recalled that, on the night Bainimarama usurped power from Ratu Mara, Rabuka accompanied him. The Rabuka trial could well be a landmine yet to explode.

The protracted vote counting – a process no country the size of Fiji should willingly put itself through – was a dense affair, requiring observers to constantly run various equations through their heads. It got too much at times, even for people like Qarase who, at one point, told international media it was looking like he might lose. Only next day did he adopt a more positive demeanour and proclaim he had won. Chaudhry, as has always been his way, did not concede and nor did he offer congratulations. Fijian politicians are big on divisiveness.

Given the record, it was hardly surprising that much of the international media interest in the election was built around the possibility of a coup should Chaudhry return to power. It seemed to come as a genuine shock to discover that the one prospect of military action against an elected government would be against one led by Qarase. If one were to have taken place, it would most likely have occurred on 17 May, the day the Commodore re-emerged in one last desperate bid to produce an outcome he wanted. In a country given to action-packed days, that was one. Early that morning, Bainimarama was on Fiji Radio's *Legend* warning that the return of the SDL government did not 'auger well for the nation'.

Shortly after that comment, George Speight was briefly in Suva to appear in court and, as reporters waited, word came that Bainimarama would hold a press conference in his headquarters, just behind Government House. His body language and his demeanour throughout the press conference manifested agitation, confusion and anger. Asked repeatedly to rule out martial law or some kind of military action against the government, he preferred to play a dangerous game of claiming some higher duty to order and power. Bizarrely, he kept saying that elections and democracy were not a numbers game; and yet that is precisely what they were at that point. 'I prefer that the SDL don't come into government…. We are going to fight those bills if he brings them up again', the commander said. 'Take this message to the SDL party; we are going to fight them all the way.'

Bainimarama said that he hoped Qarase's government would provide the leadership the nation deserved, but added: 'the writing on the wall doesn't say that'. It was, though, a Parthian shot, as Qarase knew he had the numbers and an alliance ready to form government. The deals were sealed at a quickly called SDL caucus in a function room at JJs restaurant in downtown Suva. In the media huddle, Qarase was asked if he felt threatened by Bainimarama: 'I don't feel threatened by anybody, only God'.

By early afternoon he was at Government House being sworn in and, soon after, back at his less than grand office ready for the really big moment of the day. Without warning, and by way of surprise given the bitterness of 2001, Qarase popped out with a generous proposal for a multiparty cabinet – as required by the constitution.

And if Bainimarama, caught up in the last war he had fought, was not able to think ahead, Qarase spelled it out for him: 'He like everybody else should respect the parliamentary system and parliament is the supreme power of the land'. The comment was endorsed by the media. The *Fiji Sun* commented: 'He's gone too far this time. And the commander … now has to go the full distance. He has to quit'. *The Fiji Times* noted that the military head:

> …has become a danger and threat. That danger and threat have to be removed for the sake of the nation. And as his employer, it is the Government's task to do something about it quickly. No more pussyfooting around. The nation needs to move on.

It is too soon to believe that in the 2006 election the 'coup era' was buried. Too many of the participants are still around, but it is comforting to know that many of them are now in their 60s, and many younger people have moved beyond the crude, opportunistic use of indigenous causes for political gain. Indeed, the defining influences for many who will be leaders at a community level in Fiji are today being learned on the streets of Baghdad and on the bloody convoys hundreds of Fijians ride each day in Iraq.

The elder generation – both Indian and Fijian – have failed their country in unseemly grabs for power over the years. What is striking in Fiji, and indeed across the South Pacific, is the way in which politics excludes the young and the dynamic for the most part. Politics in Fiji is about the clique, the club and the corrupt. The ineptitude of much of the political leadership has always been the sub-text for Fiji's 'coup politics'. The same old names every time. But 2006 offers hints it might be different this time: new people have come in, some are of a different political mould, and the world has certainly changed from the day Rabuka walked into parliament and took over.

Qarase, who always seemed to be an incidental character in the political history of 1987 to 2001, has exhibited strong personal growth, and the 2006 election has made him stronger – although paradoxically his mandate is weaker. The controversial 'Reconciliation Bill' will, no doubt, finally see some legal light, but its biggest advocates have gone from parliament. A new order is slowly emerging. As Qarese said at his post-election press conference:

> This election outcome is consistent with what I've always said, that in promoting national reconciliation and unity in Fiji, it is not enough and, in fact, it is totally unrealistic to regard society in Fiji as nothing more than a collection of individuals with equal basic rights and freedoms. We have to recognize that we are a society of communities with differences in the way they look at their security and confidence in living in Fiji.
>
> The task before me and government in the next five years is to dedicate ourselves to the service of everyone in our nation, irrespective of their political loyalties, their ethnicities and cultures.

Notes

1   The joint parliamentary select committee, however, reversed the proposal for 45 open seats and 25 communal seats, settling instead on only 25 open seats and 46 communal seats. The original proposal to use the alternative vote in three-member constituencies was also dropped in favour of its use in 71 single-member constituencies.

2   Field, M., Baba T. & Nabobo-Baba, U. 2005. *Speight of Violence*. Reed Publishing, Auckland.

CASE STUDIES

14

From marginalization to mainstream? Rotuma and the 2006 election

Kylie Jayne Anderson[1]

The Rotuma Communal seat is one of the 'special' privileges conferred on the Rotuman people by the Fiji constitution. Elections in 1999 and 2001 saw the seat contested by two candidates in each election. Marieta Rigamoto won on both occasions and was made a Minister in the Fiji government; however, in 2006, she chose not to stand for the seat, which was contested by five candidates (all male). The increase in candidate numbers as well as the recent attention given to Rotuma and the community in general by prominent political parties in the campaign have links to broader political issues in Fiji. This chapter assesses the position of the Rotuman community in current Fiji politics and raises questions about effective representation for the Rotuman community in a Fiji parliament.

Politics in Fiji usually revolves around the 'major' players. Major political party manifestos tend to focus on the two majority communities, and media attention is ultimately focused on the major issues affecting the dominant populations of the country, often centralized in the capital or, at the least, the main islands of Viti Levu and Vanua Levu. For this reason, issues affecting outer islands and minority communities are often under-reported or pushed aside.

Fiji's population can be divided into a number of minority groups, although the defining of who actually constitutes a political minority in Fiji is problematic, with differing usages of the term minority and no international consensus.[2] It is from this context that the position of minority communities within the political arena of Fiji can begin to be understood. Within the framework of the Fiji electoral system – in which the majority of seats in the House of Representatives are decided by a communal roll system based on ethnic groupings – a minority community must, in electoral terms, be defined in terms of numbers and not power. As discussed elsewhere in this book, all eligible citizens in Fiji register on two electoral rolls – an open roll and a communal one. The four communal rolls are based on ethnic identification: 42 of the seats are allocated to 'Fijian' (23) and 'Indian' (19) citizens, and the remaining four to voters identifying as either 'Rotuman' or 'General' (those Fiji citizens who are 'registered otherwise than as Fijians, Indians or Rotumans'[3]). The very existence of communal seats, and the number of seats representing between 5 and 8 per cent of the population[4], has raised a number of questions about effective representation of minority communities in Fiji politics.

For the Rotuman community, questions relating to the representation of the community in the parliament of Fiji can, arguably, be linked to broader questions about the status of Rotuman people within the state. While much of the discussion is beyond the scope of this chapter, it is important to recognize that the debate exists. As a minority group, the Rotuman community is one of the more readily identifiable and recognized. With a population of approximately 10,000 throughout the Fiji Islands (a minority of approximately 2,000 living on the island of Rotuma itself) the Rotuman language, culture and traditions (which are distinct from others in Fiji) continue to be relatively strong, and deliberate attempts have been made by many members of the community to safeguard them.[5]

Arguments have been made previously about the status of Rotumans as a 'marginalized' minority within the Fiji population. While a number of notable Rotumans have been high achievers academically and professionally, the community is sometimes overlooked in broader political decision-making. Indeed, this political marginalization can be seen in a number of key government policy documents (including the '50/50 by 2020' affirmative action blueprint in which Rotumans are referred to as 'indigenous Fijians'); in generalizations about the economic and other status of the community (ensuring that social and economic reality for many members is not addressed); in the dismissal of the legitimate political concerns voiced by some members of the community; and in the way in which the island is treated as akin to other outer islands despite its 'special status' (the difficulty in delivering goods and services, the lack of development, the expense and difficulty in travel all indicative of the latter). It is these issues of the status of Rotuma within the Fiji Islands and effective representation (for the community as a whole and as individuals), which are arguably at the crux of many Rotuman political arguments.[6] Such arguments, however, are usually not aired by the media. Accordingly, contemporary Rotuman electoral politics tends to be characterized by an image of consensus.[7] The electoral contest may not be plagued by the dramatic tensions evident in mainland Fiji, but the changes in the status quo of election candidacy and campaigning in Rotuma for the 2006 election indicate that there is a need for further analysis of contemporary electoral politics in the community.

While past elections have seen few candidates and the absence of major political parties campaigning in the community, the 2006 election was different. What has changed? The characteristics of Fiji elections and the political arena in general have been altered somewhat by the events of the past decade. Increasing attempts to have democracy settled through the legal process is one example; the attempts of major parties to broaden their appeal beyond ethnic stratification is another. It is this second change which could be construed as contributing to the increasing political mainstreaming of the Rotuman community.

This chapter assesses the 2006 election results vis-à-vis past elections in 1999 and 2001. It reviews some of the key election issues for the Rotuman community and addresses some of the continued 'sticking points' relating to the status of Rotuma within Fiji.

Rotuma in the Fiji Constitution and electoral provisions

Annexed seven years after the colony of Fiji was created, Rotuma has occupied an uncertain position within the state, and moves towards independence have been mooted at various times (in the late 1970s, 1988 and 2000).[8] The 1988 and 2000 moves both led to arrests and court cases, with slightly varying outcomes.[9] The Rotumans are recognised simultaneously as indigenous, but different from, Fijians, and their 'uniqueness'[10] has been given emphasis at

Map 14.1   Rotuma

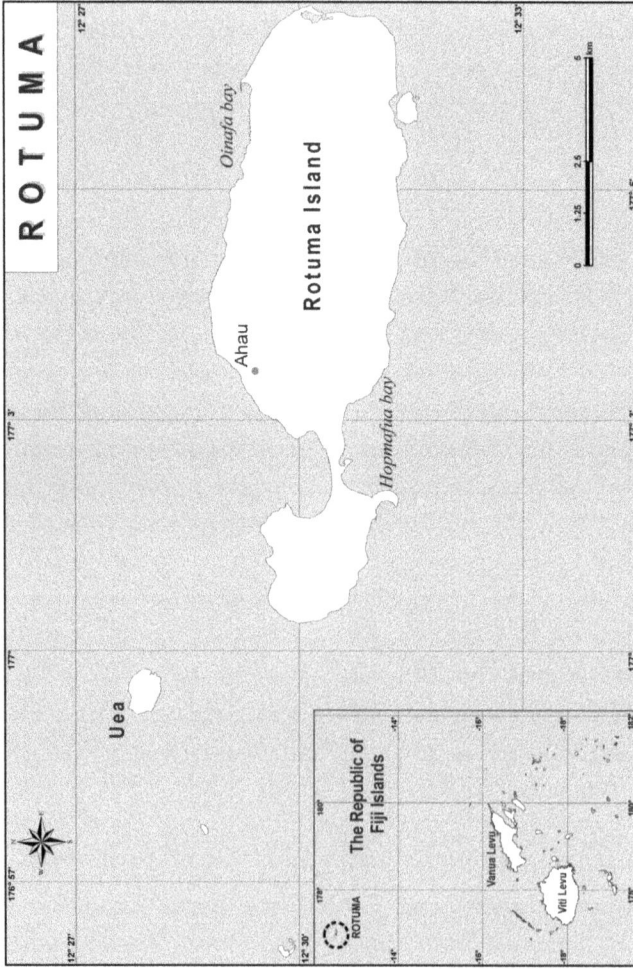

Source: Pacific Institute of Advanced Studies in Development and Governance (PIAS-DG) Mapping Database, University of the South Pacific, Suva.

multiple legal and policy echelons. Such recognition is exemplified by provisions within the constitution of Fiji, including the presence of a designated seat for the Rotuman community in the Senate, and the continued existence of the 'Rotuma Communal Roll', which not only serves as recognition of the community, but also entitles the Rotumans to one designated seat in the House of Representatives.[11] The inclusion of three Rotuman representatives in the Bose Levu Vakaturaga, the body responsible for appointing the Head of State, also indicates the importance of Rotuma as part of the broader political landscape in Fiji.

The population of Rotuman voters currently stands at 5,373. Of these, more than 4,000 live in parts of Fiji other than Rotuma.[12] Technically, Rotuman voters have more than one representative in parliament (as do all citizens in Fiji) by virtue of the dual roll system. Individual voters are required to vote in both the communal and open constituencies. Rotumans in Rotuma are, accordingly, represented at one level by the communal member and at another by the member for the Lau/Taveuni/Rotuma Open seat. Rotumans living in the rest of Fiji are also represented by their respective open roll members. The viability of the open seat as a source of representation for Rotumans has been challenged in the past. In 1999, president of the Rotuma Independent Movement Aleki Kafoa urged Rotuman voters to boycott the elections, arguing, 'We are now treated as sub-class citizens, we are told that we have two seats to contest but in reality we have only one that is the Rotuman Communal Constituency seat'.[13]

The question of representation in the open constituencies is valid when one realizes that, in most instances, the Rotuman voters make up less than 1 per cent of each constituency. Notable exceptions to this are in the Laucala Open and Suva City Open electorates – where Rotuman voters constitute 3.18 per cent and 4.61 per cent respectively – and in the Lau/Taveuni/Rotuma Open electorate, where Rotuman voters make up 7.65 per cent of voters (see Table 14.1).

The Rotuma Communal roll and seat in the House of Representatives has arguably been something of a mixed blessing for the community. While the communal seat secures some representation in the parliament, requests have been made that the number of seats reserved for Rotumans be increased:

> …to better represent the two communities [Rotumans living on Rotuma and Rotumans living elsewhere in Fiji] because of the difficulties of travel between Rotuma and Fiji and the wide distribution of Rotumans living outside the island of Rotuma.[14]

Table 14.1   Rotuman voters as a percentage of the open electorates in the 2006 election

Electorate	Total number of voters	Total number of Rotuman voters	Rotumans as a percentage of the electorate
Tailevu North/ Ovalau	17,893	58	0.32
Tailevu South/ Lomaiviti	21,620	35	0.16
Nausori/Naitasiri	19,977	253	1.27
Nasinu/Rewa	21,273	162	0.76
Cunningham	24,087	380	1.58
Laucala	19,774	629	3.18
Samabula/Tamavua	17,137	384	2.24
Suva City	15,206	701	4.61
Lami	17,815	253	1.42
Lomaivuna/Namosi/Kaduva	19,819	87	0.44
Ra	19,670	15	0.08
Tavua	15,996	198	1.24
Ba	20,759	38	0.18
Magodro	19,911	6	0.30
Lautoka City	19,084	249	1.30
Vuda	20,275	143	0.71
Nadi	23,658	248	1.05
Yasawa/Nawaka	20,002	15	0.07
Nadroga	18,590	47	0.25
Serua/Navosa	22,642	107	0.47
Bua/Macuata	17,925	7	0.04
Labasa	15,651	22	0.14
Macuata East	16,306	7	0.04
Cakaudrove West	17,717	36	0.20
Lau/Taveuni/ Rotuma	16,906	1,293	7.65

Source: Elections Office (2006), unpublished roll analysis.

Despite the specific definition in the Fiji Constitution of who can be classified as a 'Rotuman'[15] and, in the *Rotuma Act,* a specific definition of who is a member of the Rotuman Community,[16] there are differences in identification between those who live on the island and those who have 'migrated' or were born and raised outside of Rotuma.[17] This distinction in itself is complicated by the fact that the majority of constituents on the Rotuma Communal roll do not actually live on Rotuma. As already noted, more than 75 per cent of the constituency lives off the island. Of these, more than 2000, more than 43 per cent of the entire Rotuman constituency, live in electorates that could be considered part of the greater Suva area (Laucala, Cunningham, Suva City, Lami, Samabula/Tamavua). Adding the voting populations of Fiji's next two major urban centres – Lautoka and Nadi – to the equation shows that more than 50 per cent (2,844) of the Rotuma Communal constituency can be considered city- or urban-based. As a result, Rotumans living on the island of Rotuma are effectively minorities in both of their constituencies – making up only 7.65 per cent of the Lau/Taveuni/Rotuma Open constituency registered voters (combined with Rotumans living in Lau and Taveuni), and less than one-quarter of those in the Rotuma Communal constituency.

This urban–rural dichotomy is not only problematic in terms of effective representation of all Rotuman people included in this constituency. As this chapter demonstrates, election campaigning has also proven to be difficult, as many candidates seem to try to campaign 'to the island', rather than taking into account the wider Rotuman diaspora across the Fiji group. In terms of national government, there also seems to be some misunderstanding about the role of the elected Rotuma Communal member, with some politicians assuming that the member is the representative of the island alone and not of the broader Rotuman community.

Overview of past elections

In past elections, only two candidates have contested the Rotuma Communal constituency, although in 1999 Aleki Kafoa was also announced as an early candidate for the Party of National Unity (PANU)[18], but withdrew before the election.[19] The results of the 1999 and 2001 elections were close, and a relatively high number of invalid votes were cast. In 1999, independent candidate Marieta

Rigamoto won the Rotuma Communal seat by a margin of 30 votes, securing 50.38 per cent of the vote.[20] Of the 4,682 ballot papers counted, 688 (more than 14 per cent) were deemed to be invalid. Rigamoto entered the interim government in 2000, and was re-elected as Rotuma's Communal representative in the 2001 election (again as an independent). This was the second election in which Rigamoto was (ultimately) the sole candidate opposing a Lio 'On Famor Rotuma party candidate, Riamkau Tiu Livino, and once again winning by a slight majority. Again, invalid votes were quite substantial. Of the 4,255 counted, 493 (more than 11 per cent) were deemed to be invalid.

The 1999 election also gave rise to the beginnings of 'party politics' on Rotuma. The Lio 'On Famor Rotuma party was created that year to more effectively campaign for development on Rotuma and to represent the collective Rotuman people.[21] Candidate Kafoa Pene was reported as saying 'For too long Rotuma has been represented in Parliament by an independent candidate, which has denied us our democratic rights.'[22] The establishment of the party was intended to improve the representation of Rotuman interests, and a number of areas addressed in the Party's manifesto continue to be issues today.[23]

The 2006 election

2006 saw a record number of candidates contest the Rotuma Communal seat. Of the five, two stood as independents while the other three represented major parties within Fiji. Lio 'On Famor Rotuma did not field a candidate. Marieta Rigamoto decided not to stand, her time in office not having been without its difficulties,[24] including concern that her role as a government member prevented her from being a true representative of Rotuma. Her contribution to the 2006 Budget addressed Rotuman issues in passing, commenting that Rotuma was a province the public relations unit had not been able to visit.[25] An August 2005 response to the President's address in parliament mentioned the constituency as item 10 of 11 items, and thanked the government for its work on the island, without mention of the challenges it faces.[26] In contrast to 1999, all candidates fielded by major parties ran for the duration of the election. Sosefo Kafoa stood on behalf of the Soqosoqo Duavata ni Lewenivanua (SDL), Mua Ieli Taukave for the United Peoples Party (UPP), Sosefo Sikuri Inoke for the National Alliance Party of Fiji (NAPF), while Victor Fatiaki and former Fiji High Commissioner to Australia, Jioji Konousi Konrote, ran as independents. A record number of voters – 5,373 – registered and early predictions were that Konrote would win the seat.[27] In an interview with the *Fiji Daily Post* before the election, Konrote attributed the high number of candidates to a number of factors, including increased political awareness, and a sign '…that democracy is working well on the island'.[28] He also noted the dissatisfaction felt by many, acknowledging:

> …there are a lot of dissatisfied people on the island in terms of what the government could have done for the island. People feel let down in the areas of shipping and in terms of the little that has been done to create more income-generating activities on the island. Freight, for instance, is out of the question so people cannot export their crops and because of all this the rural to urban drift is now a major problem. The majority of the Rotuman people live off of the island.[29]

Campaigning for the election was conducted on multiple levels. Candidates used 'traditional' methods (party manifestos, interviews with the media, attendance at rallies, constituency visits) as well as more contemporary avenues, such as the Internet. The Noa'ia Mauri Rotuma website (www.rotuma.net), a long-standing virtual community for Rotumans around the world, invited all candidates to post their CVs and manifestos on the website. Only the two independent candidates (Fatiaki and Konrote) and the NAPF candidate (Inoke) chose to do so. While the manifestos of Konrote and Fatiaki were succinct (and included their CVs), Inoke chose not to post the official manifesto of the NAPF, but created his own manifesto of election promises tailored for the Rotuman electorate.

Inoke's choice of manifesto is an interesting one that can be seen to reflect the overlooking of Rotuma in the manifestos of the major parties. Of the three major parties fielding candidates for the Rotuma Communal constituency (NAPF, SDL and UPP), only the SDL party's manifesto included specific mention of the Rotuman community. The party's mission statement included the statement, 'Special assistance or affirmative action to reduce the economic gap between Fijians and Rotumans and other communities'.[30] In regards to 'values', the manifesto promised the party would continue to demonstrate 'Respect for the *Vanua* and the cultures and traditions of the indigenous Fijians and Rotumans', and 'Recognition of the paramountcy of indigenous Fijian and Rotuman interests, as proclaimed in the Constitution'.[31] It also referred to the affirmative action programs, but there were no specific promises made to the island or the community outside of those offered to the rest of the Fiji population. In contrast, the official manifesto for the NAPF (as opposed to the Inoke Rotuma version) made no specific mention of Rotuma or Rotumans.[32]

The overlooking of Rotuma by major parties, despite their fielding of candidates, reflects the ongoing marginalization of Rotuma within the political arena of Fiji. It could be argued that the key election issues for at least the past decade have remained the same. As with past elections, the predominant issues in the 2006 election for the Rotuma Communal constituency were linked to effective representation of the community collectively and development of the island itself. In relation to representation, both on and off the island, key concerns for some included the potentially conflicting role of the Rotuma Communal member as a representative of the community while also being a member of the government. Rotuma's legal and constitutional position in Fiji, infrastructure, education, the environment and health continued to be at the forefront of political discussion on (and off) the island. These issues were reflected in the manifestos tailored for the Rotuma Communal constituency and in all candidates' election campaigning.

Of the three 'Rotuma specific' manifestos, all raised the issue of Rotuma's constitutional and legal position within Fiji, although with varying emphasis. Fatiaki noted that the review of the Rotuman Lands Act needed to be 'pursued', while Konrote argued:

> As Rotumans, our sovereign rights as members of the Indigenous community are guaranteed in the Compact of our Constitution. In this regard we should appreciate and cherish with pride the old adage of 'Viti Kei Rotuma'.[33]

Later in the document, however, he stated:

> I am committed to engaging the Government of the day to ensure that the interests of our community and our special and unique status as an Indigenous ethnic group are protected at all times. In this regard I am equally committed to ensure that all amendments to existing statutes (Rotuma Act, Rotuma Lands Act etc) are done following wide consultations, but more importantly changes are effected with the full endorsement of the Chiefs and the people.[34]

The latter statement can be read as indicating that there has not been consensus in all of the discussions regarding these two Acts and proposed amendments. It was the manifesto of Inoke, however, which further highlighted the challenges faced by the community. Inoke's manifesto argued strongly in favour of change. In relation to the Rotuma Act he noted that:

> [T]he law worked well when we were a colony and the central government decided what was good for us. We have grown up as a people and as a nation and we don't need to be spoon-fed anymore.[35]

Inoke raised the issue of autonomy for the island, suggesting in an interview broadcast on the Australian Broadcasting Commission's Asia Pacific program that Rotuma could be governed in a similar way to Australia's Torres Strait Islands.[36] He also challenged the Rotuman Lands Act, arguing that the Act 'discriminates against women and children'[37] and 'goes against Rotuman traditional land rights'.[38]

The status of women within the community, and in general, was addressed by all three candidates who posted manifestos on the website (perhaps something of an irony given that, in contrast to in the past two elections, there was no female candidate contesting the seat). Inoke's observations relating to discrimination against women were specifically related to the Rotuman Lands Act, and Fatiaki's concerns about women were also linked to the review of the Act, the latter asking for 'the assurance that registration of all Rotuman land will be under both maternal and paternal lineages, and that women will not be disenfranchised from their traditional heritage'.[39] In contrast, Konrote did not link discrimination of women with any specific legislation, but concentrated on the employment sector, saying '…I believe that women are often discriminated against and are significantly under-represented at senior and middle-management levels in both the public and private sector.'[40]

Issues such as transport, infrastructure and development on Rotuma were key issues noted by all candidates in their manifestos and in other campaign aspects. Fatiaki's manifesto primarily concentrated on issues of sea transport, as well as infrastructure, such as roads, the Oinafa wharf, Rotuma's airport, electricity and water. Inoke wrote of the environment, investment and employment. Konrote addressed these issues as well as the need to improve the efficiency of shipping and air service. At a rally held in Suva before the election, Kafoa pledged to improve the shipping services to Rotuma (a long-standing issue) as well as deal with infrastructural issues such as roads and electricity.[41]

On the social welfare front, Fatiaki and Konrote both addressed the issues of health services and education. Fatiaki was more specific about these issues, outlining problems facing the Rotuma hospital and secondary school. Inoke wrote of youth and the reintroduction of sports and traditional activities. Interestingly, given the emphasis on religion and politics in Fiji, only Fatiaki emphasized religion as an issue for Rotuma (although Konrote's campaign symbol was the image of the island imposed over a Christian cross). His 'vision' (as stipulated in his manifesto) declared Rotumans to be 'a God fearing people with respect for tradition and culture, and for one another'.[42] Fatiaki later noted that he believed '… that Rotuma can only prosper and progress if all communities work together in Fear of God…', and advocated religious tolerance.[43] The other candidate's non-emphasis of religion may be due to the fact that, unlike mainland Fiji, where the population split between major faiths has been used as a source of political tension, the vast majority of Rotumans identify with the Christian faith. In the 1996 census, slightly more than 95 per cent identified as being of the Christian faith (various denominations, although the majority belong to either the Methodist or Catholic denominations), and less than 1 per cent identified with Fiji's other major faith, Hinduism.[44] While there have been difficulties in the past between congregations of the major Christian denominations, sectarianism has not caused overt or public political disputes in contemporary times.[45]

The decision of major parties to campaign in Rotuma was also a source of intrigue, and became a political issue in itself. Inoke traveled to Rotuma, launching the NAPF manifesto there and discussing the need to change two key laws – the Rotuma Act and the Rotuma Lands Act – to assist with the development of the island.[46] Neither Inoke's visit nor the campaigns of the other candidates caused as much controversy as the visit by UPP party leader, Mick Beddoes, with UPP candidate Taukave.

Beddoes was more vocal than the leaders of other major parties, and his statements and promises were reported more often than those of his party candidate, Taukave. Beddoes was critical of the SDL government's treatment of Rotuma during their five years of government, as was FLP's Mahendra Chaudhry, who accused the SDL of vote-buying.[47] Beddoes was scathing in his attacks; reportedly 'shocked' by his visit to the island, he apologized for not having visited in the past five years (while he was the representative of minority communities in parliament), saying:

...it is because I have always assumed that with the Rotuma Member of Parliament in Cabinet, all of the problems of Rotuma get resolved and acted upon on a continuous basis.[48]

He was reported as saying that it was time that the people of Rotuma:

Wake up to the lies and stop being used. What good have you realized from having a Cabinet Minister in the SDL Government over the past five years? It has been nothing more than a showpiece and after five years, they have nothing to show for it and certainly it has not benefited the people in any real and tangible way.[49]

While Qarase dismissed Chaudhry's comments, saying he should 'stop misleading the people and concentrate on the elections',[50] Beddoes' statements were taken more seriously and a press release was issued by the government. Branding Beddoes' comments as 'irresponsible politicking',[51] outgoing representative and Minister for Information, Communications and Media Relations Marieta Rigamoto's press release emphasized the contribution of the SDL government to the island and was contemptuous of Beddoes, stating:

In his fly-by-night visit for the first time in five years to the island, Mr Beddoes makes hollow promises of "immediate" developments for the island as a vote-catching gimmick for his candidate. And what's worse he has acted irresponsibly by closing his eyes to the visible contribution of the SDL towards the welfare of the people. [52]

Table 14.2   Outcomes in the Rotuma Communal constituency

		1st count	2nd count	3rd count
Sosefo Kafoa	SDL	526	531	
Mua Ieli Taukave	UPP	532	548	566
Sosefo Sikuri Inoke	NAPF	245		
Victor Fatiaki	Independent	1,149	1,348	1,361
Jioji Konousi Konrote	Independent	1,983	2,008	2,508
Informal		302		
Total votes		4,737		
Total registered		5,373		

Source: Fiji elections website, www.elections.gov.fj

2006 election results

Despite there being 5,373 registered voters, only 4,737 cast their ballots (an 88 per cent voter turnout).[53] There were fewer invalid ballots in this election (6 per cent) than in previous elections, perhaps a result of it being the third time that the system had been used or, alternatively, a sign that the election education campaign (conducted throughout the country prior to the elections) had been effective. The three major party representatives were excluded in successive rounds of voting. The NAPF's Inoke, securing 245 of the first preference votes, was the first to be eliminated from the contest (see Table 14.2). Most of his votes were transferred to Victor Fatiaki. The SDL's candidate, Kafoa, was the second to be eliminated, but the difference in votes between Kafoa and the UPP's candidate, Taukave, was minor. Kafoa secured 526 first preferences, Taukave 532. Distribution of Inoke's preferences saw Kafoa collect an additional five votes, ultimately gaining 531, while Taukave secured an additional sixteen. After the distribution of Kafoa's preferences, Taukave had won 566 votes, less than half of the votes given to either of the independent candidates.[54]

Konrote, the early favourite, led at every stage of the counting process. He secured 1,983 (41.86 per cent) of the first preference votes, his only real opposition being Fatiaki with 1,149 first preference votes (24.25 per cent). Distribution of preferences saw Konrote with 2,008 at the second round of counting and Fatiaki with 1,348. Ultimately, Konrote won the seat having secured 2,508 votes (52.94 per cent), although it is interesting to note that 500 of these were preferences from votes originally given to the SDL. Fatiaki was the runner up, gaining a total of 1,361 votes (28.73 per cent).[55]

Konrote's win could be attributed to a number of key differences between his campaign style and that of the other candidates. While all three of the Rotuma-specific manifestos made special note of tradition and culture, only Konrote's used the Rotuman language to any great extent (although two other candidates produced flyers using the Rotuman language).[56] Konrote's manifesto also addressed the issues of human rights, good governance, access and equity. His manifesto was less overtly political than those of the others, and his campaign style of 'not campaigning' stood in stark contrast to the style of UPP's Taukave. While Fatiaki and Inoke emphasized key issues on the island of

Rotuma and for the community as a whole, Konrote's recognized some of the broader and contemporary issues facing Rotumans living in the urban centres (the majority of the constituency).

Konrote decided to work with the government of the day and, with the SDL winning the majority of votes, was made Minister of State in the multiparty government. It remains to be seen what achievements he will make during his time in office, but his decisive win indicates that he has substantial support from the Rotuman people in general. With secret voting, it is virtually impossible to ascertain if Konrote's support is both on and off island. Many of the key issues facing the Rotuman community, in both Rotuma and in Fiji, need to be addressed and brought to the fore of politics in Fiji to prevent marginalization. The inclusion of Rotuma in the political campaigning of major parties indicates a change for the community, and the highlighting of a number of issues by re-elected Leader of the Opposition Mick Beddoes may be conducive to future positive developments.

Future pathways

Many of the political difficulties facing Rotuma have been related to a lack of development, the status of Rotuma in the Viti kei Rotuma (Fiji and Rotuma) relationship, challenges to effective leadership, and representation at the parliamentary level. On the matter of leadership, Howard and Rensel, who are amongst the leading authorities on political developments (and other aspects) of Rotuma, wrote in 1997:

> Leadership on Rotuma today is…in a state of crisis. The chiefs are at a great disadvantage. As members of the Rotuman Council they are supposed to formulate policies and guide the development of the island, but they are not well-equipped to do so. They lack the education and experience required to manage an expanding economy and to make informed choices concerning development opportunities. They are uncomfortable with bureaucratic procedures and with bureaucrats who control resources. Internally, they are perceived by most Rotumans as self-interested and ineffective, lacking in moral authority.[57]

And yet effective leadership cannot be considered a matter only for the chiefs, or the Council of Rotuma. In terms of national government and politics, leadership must be viewed at multiple levels. The chiefs have their role, as do all of the members of the Council of Rotuma. The Senator appointed by the

President of Fiji on the advice of the Council of Rotuma, Dr John Fatiaki, has his role to play, as indeed do the three members of the Bose Levu Vakaturaga. While it cannot be said that effective leadership or representation should be demonstrated by one person alone, in a democracy it is essential that the elected members of parliament also demonstrate their skills in this area. There is currently only one elected Rotuman member of parliament, Jioji Konrote, and the responsibility for effective representation of the Rotuman community in general in the House of Representatives is his. Konrote may be the member needed to lead the community and oversee some of the much-needed developments. His manifesto indicated an acute awareness of the constituency and his time in office (both military and diplomatic) has provided him with expertise that may be conducive to many of the changes needed and apparently desired by the community.

In response to a seemingly overt politicization of Rotuma and the community, the introduction of this chapter raised the question 'what has changed?'. In many regards, it is clear that little has changed in the past decade. The relationship between Rotuma and Fiji retains both benefits and disadvantages. The presence of the single communal seat remains unsatisfactory for some, transport to the island is still difficult and expensive, delivery of services and infrastructure to the island still problematic, and the generalizations made about the economic, professional and academic success of the community as a whole encourage a tendency to overlook those members of the community who are at a disadvantage. While it is true that individuals and communities must bear some responsibility, until the issues and concerns of all members of the Rotuman community, both urban and rural, island and other, are addressed and taken seriously by the government of Fiji, then it is likely that many of the political arguments related to the position of Rotuma in the Viti kei Rotuma relationship and the existence of one communal seat will continue.

In some regards, these issues are related to the broader political agenda of the current Fiji administration in the area of reconciliation and national unity. Rhetoric and brushing aside key issues will not serve anyone well in the long run. The concerns of all minority communities in Fiji must be addressed in the interest of national cohesiveness and stability. In terms of broader political arenas, democracies are now being judged not only on their successful representation of the majority of the population, but also on their ability to consider the concerns of minorities. Increasing concentration on the members of the minority communities in Fiji may augur well for the state's image internationally while also being conducive to more political harmony domestically.

Notes

1 The author is grateful for the Noa'ia Rotuma website, at <www.rotuma.net>, for its ongoing documentation of political issues and other concerns/events relating to Rotuma. Without this valuable resource, this chapter could not have been written. Thank you to Professor Stewart Firth and Dr Bruce Yeates for comments on an earlier draft of this chapter. Also appreciation and gratitude to those who read the draft, made comments and provided feedback but wish to remain anonymous. A final thank you to Liti Vasuturaga at the Fiji Election Office for supplying the 2006 roll analysis information.

2 Anderson, K. (nd)'The politics of identity and recognition: the status of protection and promotion of 'global minority' culture and language in Fiji', unpublished working paper.

3 *Constitution of the Republic of the Fiji Islands*, Part 2: 51(a) (iv).

4 Based on Fiji census statistics. The last census was conducted in 1996 and indicated that 42,000 belonged to neither the Fijian or Indian groups. Estimates made in 2005 by the Fiji Bureau of Statistics indicate that the number is closer to 66,560 (<http://www.statsfiji.gov.fj/>, accessed 15 June 2006).

5 Anderson, K. and Isimeli, F. (forthcoming). 'Protection and promotion of culture from the community level: a Suva Rotuma case study', *Fijian Studies: A Journal of Contemporary Fiji*.

6 The Noa'ia website noticeboard will provide the reader with an overview of some of the more critical issues and arguments. See also, Howard, A. and Rensel, J. 1997. 'Rotuma', in B. V. Lal and T. Vakatora (eds), *Fiji in Transition,* Vol. 1, Fiji Constitution Review Commission Research Papers. School of Social and Economic Development, University of the South Pacific, Suva (available online) <http://www.rotuma.net/os/howsel/28FijiConRpt.html>.

7 A useful overview of many of the mixed opinions is provided in Howard & Rensel. 1997. 'Rotuma'.

8 Prasad, J. 'Rotumans want out: Islanders seek Republican status', *Fiji Daily Post*, 27 January 2000, pp.1,4; Howard & Rensel. 1997. 'Rotuma'; State v Riogi [2001] FJHC 61; Haa0060j.2001s, 20 August 2001, (available online) < http://paclii.org.vu/fj/cases/FJHC/2001/61.html>; Tuwere, J.. 'Allow Rotuman Independence Debate, Fiji Court Rules', *The Fiji Times*, 30 March 2001.

9 Howard & Rensel. 1997. 'Rotuma'.

10 Irava, I. 1977. 'The emigration of Rotumans to Fiji', in C. Plant (ed.), *Rotuma: Split Island*, Institute of Pacific Studies, University of the South Pacific, Suva.

11 Information on Bose Levu Vakaturaga from Fiji Government website, page 'Fijian Culture & Tradition', <http://www.fiji.gov.fj/publish/history_culture.shtml>. Information on electoral and parliamentary provisions as per the *Constitution of the Republic of the Fiji Islands* (1998), chapter 6 'The Parliament', part 2 (section 51, 1 a and 4), part 3 (section 64, 1 d).

[12]   1996 Census.

[13]   'Govt sold our rights', *Fiji Daily Post*, 1 April 1999 (as reproduced on Noa'ia Rotuma website <http://www.hawaii.edu/oceanic/rotuma/os.NewsArchive/Archive1999/elections.html>).

[14]   Council of Rotuma. 2001. 'Submission by the Council of Rotuma to the Constitution Review Commission, Ahau, Rotuma', as reproduced on Noa'ia Mauri website, <http://www.hawaii. edu.oceanic/rotuma/os/Forum/Forum22.htm> (accessed 27 November 2001).

[15]   *Constitution of the Republic of the Fiji Islands*, chapter 6, part 2:55:5.

[16]   *Rotuma Act*, September 1927. In 1966, as a result of ordinance 37, the term 'Rotuman Community' referred to 'the indigenous inhabitants of Rotuma and also any Fijian resident on Rotuma'.

[17]   Howard, A.. & Rensel, J. 2001. 'Where has Rotuman culture gone? And what is it doing there?', *Noa'ia Rotuma* website, <http://www.hawaii.edu/oceanic/rotuma/os/howsel/33where. html>, (accessed 18 March 2002) (originally published in *Pacific Studies*, 24(1/2): 63–88).

[18]   'Candidate changes tune, joins race', *The Fiji Times*, 6 April 1999 (as reproduced on Noa'ia Rotuma website <http://www.hawaii.edu/oceanic/rotuma/os.NewsArchive/Archive1999/ elections.html>).

[19]   'Candidate wants boycott', *The Fiji Times*, 14 April 1999 (as reproduced on Noa'ia Rotuma website <http://www.hawaii.edu/oceanic/rotuma/os.NewsArchive/Archive1999/elections. html>).

[20]   'Elections 1999 Results by the Count', Fiji Elections website, < http://www.elections.gov. fj/results1999/constituencies/46.html>.

[21]   'Lio 'On Famor Rotuma's Plans', *Fiji Daily Post*, 25 April 1999 (as reproduced online < http://www.hawaii.edu/oceanic/rotuma/os/NewsArchive/Archive1999/elections.html>).

[22]   'Vote Pene, Rotuma', *Fiji Daily Post*, 14 April 1999 (as reproduced online < http://www. hawaii.edu/oceanic/rotuma/os/NewsArchive/Archive1999/elections.html>).

[23]   Lio 'On Famor Rotuma Party manifesto, as reproduced in *Fiji Daily Post*. See, 'Lio On Famor Rotuma's plans' *Fiji Daily Post*, 25 April 1999 (as reproduced on line <http://www.hawaii. edu.oceanic/rotuma/os/NewsArchive/Archive1999/elections.html>).

[24]   'Media Freedom in Fiji Vital to good Governance', *The Fiji Times*, 3 May 2006 (as reproduced on PIReprt <http://pidp.eastwestcenter.org/pireport/2006/May/05-04-ed2.htm>).

[25]   Rigamoto, M. 2005. 'Contribution on the 2006 Budget Address', 15 November, <http://www. fiji.gov.fj/publish/printer_5754.shtml>.

[26]   Rigamoto, M. 2005. 'Response to His Excellency's the President's Address in Parliament', 8 August 2005, <http://www.fiji.gov.fj/publish/page_5135.shtml>.

[27]   'Elections 2006', *Fiji Village*, <http://www.fijivillage.com/elections_2006/predictions. shtml>.

[28]   Movono, L. 'Konrote heeds Rotuma's call', *Fiji Daily Post*, 4 May 2006.

[29]   Movono. 2006. 'Konrote heeds Rotuma's call'.

[30]   SDL Manifesto, 2006.

[31]   SDL Manifesto, 2006.

[32]   NAPF Manifesto, 2006.

[33]   Konrote, J. 2006. *Election Platform/Constitution*, as reproduced on the Noaia Mauri Rotuma website

[34]   Konrote. 2006. *Election Platform/Constitution*.

[35] Sosefo, I. 2006. *My Manifesto and Vision for Rotuma*, as reproduced on the Noaia Mauri Rotuma website.
[36] ABC Asia Pacific, 2 May 2006.
[37] Sosefo. 2006. *My Manifesto and Vision for Rotuma*, p.6, 7
[38] Sosefo. 2006. *My Manifesto and Vision for Rotuma*, p.7
[39] Fatiaki, V. 2006. Manifesto, as reproduced on the Noaia Mauri Rotuma website
[40] Konrote. 2006. *Election Platform/Constitution.*
[41] 'Race for Rotuma seat intensifies', *The Fiji Times,* 30 April 2006.
[42] Fatiaki. 2006. Manifesto.
[43] Fatiaki. 2006. Manifesto.
[44] Ratuva, S. 2002. 'God's will in paradise: the politics of ethnicity and religion in Fiji', *Development Bulletin*, 59, October (cites Fiji Bureau of Statistics 1996, unpublished figures for religious affiliation, Fiji National Census, Fiji Bureau of Statistics, Suva).
[45] 'Difficulties' may be a bit of a misleading term, given that there was a veritable war between the two in the late 19th century. Howard, J. & Kjellgren, E. 1995. 'Martyrs, progress and political ambition: reexamining Rotuma's "religious wars"', <http://www.hawaii.edu/oceanic/rotuma/os/howsel/22religiouswars.html> (originally published in *Journal of Pacific History*, 39:131–152).
[46] 'Change laws on Rotuma: Sosefo', *The Fiji Times,* 25 April 2006.
[47] 'Call for State funds probe', *The Fiji Times,* 11 April 2006; 'FLP alleges vote buying by SDL', Fijivillage.com, 10 April 2006.
[48] Rina, S. ' Rotuma trip shock Beddoes', *Fiji Sun*, 3 April 2006.
[49] Rina. 2006. ' Rotuma trip shock Beddoes'.
[50] 'FLP alleges vote buying' Fijivillage.com, 10 April 2006, <http://www.fijivillage.com/cgi-bin/artman/exec/view.cgi?archive=50&num=28675>.
[51] Fiji government, 'UPP Leader's statement on Rotuma "IRRESPONSIBLE" – Minister', media release, 4 April 2006, (<http://www.fiji.gov.fj/publish/page_6511.shtml>.
[52] 'UPP Leader's statement on Rotuma "IRRESPONSIBLE"'.
[53] Elections Office. 2006. 'Election Results by the Count', Elections 2006 Fiji Islands website, <http://www.elections.gov.fj/results2006/constituencies/46.html>.
[54] Fiji Times election results, <http://www.fijitimes.com.fj/fijielections/seat.aspx?seatno=46>.
[55] *The Fiji Times*, Election results, <http://www.fijitimes.com.fj/fijielections/seat.aspx?seatno=46>.
[56] Senator John Fatiaki, pers. comm. to editors, 28 October 2006.
[57] Howard & Rensel. 1997. 'Rotuma'.

15

Tailevu North: five years down the line

Anare Tuitoga

Tailevu North sprang to prominence in the 2001 election as the constituency from where the incarcerated coup leader, George Speight, was elected as an MP for the Conservative Alliance–Matanitu Vanua (CAMV). He survived only a short time as an MP, before being dismissed for missing three consecutive sittings of parliament. Yet his legacy lived on. Speight's brother became MP for Tailevu North after a by-election in 2002. In the run-up to the 2006 polls, sympathies remained strong for the imprisoned coup leader and his family. The people of the Wainibuka region, as shown in this chapter, are *bati* (warriors) to the powerful chiefs of Bau Island, and thus traditionally obliged to follow the Bau chiefs' backing of the more militant fringe of Fiji politics. The dissolution of the CAMV helped to draw the politics of this disadvantaged province back into the mainstream of Fiji politics, but Tailevu North remains a dissident province in Fiji's political firmament.

Background

Fiji is traditionally divided into three confederacies or *matanitu*: Kubuna, Burebasaga and Tovata. Kubuna is the leading *matanitu* and, within it, Tailevu is the principal province. The five *vanua* of Bau, Nakelo, Sawakasa, Verata and Wainibuka make up the province of Tailevu. The Tailevu North Constituency consists of the *vanua* of Sawakasa, Verata and Wainibuka. Within these three *vanua* are 22 *tikina makawa*. (*Tikina* is loosely translated as 'district' and was a colonial concept, which was introduced into the traditional Fijian structure to help ease administration by the colonial administrators. A *tikina makawa* is loosely translated as an old district.) Within these *tikina makawa* there are a total of 78 villages. Within the *vanua* of Sawakasa are the following *tikina makawa*: Dawasamu, Namena, Nailega, Namalata and Sawakasa, whilst Verata consists of Tai, Tai Vugalei, Verata and Vugalei. Naloto, Nasautoka, Nayavu and Wailevu make up the *vanua* of Wainibuka.

Data on candidates for the Tailevu North Fiji Provincial Communal constituency

As in 2001, 71 seats were contested in the 2006 elections. In total, there were 17 Fijian provincial constituencies. Tailevu North Fijian Provincial was contested by Laisiasa Cabenalevu of the Fiji Labour Party (FLP), Samisoni Tikoinasau of the Soqosoqo Duavata ni Lewenivanua (SDL) party, and Iliesa Duvuloco of the Nationalist Vanua Tako Lavo Party (NVTLP).[1] There were 9,682 voters listed. But there were only 8,687 ballot papers counted. Of these, 923 were invalid; thus, there were only 7,764 valid ballot papers. To gain a majority the successful candidate needed to secure 3,883 votes. At the end of counting, Cabenalevu secured 312 votes (4.02 per cent), Tikoinasau obtained 6,281 (80.9 per cent) and Duvuloco 1,171 (15.08 per cent). Duvuloco had also contested this seat in 1999, then gaining 1,814 votes, but losing out to Savenaca Tikoinavo, Tikoinasau's father.

In 2006, Tikoinasau was declared the elected member for the Tailevu North Fijian Provincial Communal constituency.

Success of the SDL party and its candidate

Much of Tikoinasau's success in 2006 may be attributed to the fact that he was the SDL candidate. Across the country, support for the SDL in Fijian communal constituencies was overwhelming. It secured 44.59 per cent of the national total and a total of 36 seats. The party had been founded in 2001 by the then caretaker prime minister, Laisenia Qarase, and absorbed most of the Christian Democratic Alliance and other conservative groupings. It had the informal endorsement of the Great Council of Chiefs and was seen to be a successor to the Alliance Party. The SDL has campaigned on a platform of economic and social advancement of the indigenous Fijians along with the development of other ethnic groups. It promoted Fijian interests and advocated that Fiji be governed by indigenous Fijians. This appealed to the indigenous voters everywhere, but especially in Tailevu North. One of the reasons why Fijians in Tailevu supported George Speight's civilian takeover in May 2000 was their wish to see the government remain in the hands of indigenous Fijian leaders. The voters of Tailevu North, we can safely say, are not ready to accept a non-Fijian as prime minister. They are not interested in a moderate manifesto, such as that of the National Alliance Party of Fiji, with its call for multiracial government. As far as these voters are concerned, people of other ethnic groups are *vulagi* and should not rule in their place.[2] As elsewhere, voters in Tailevu were advised by the SDL to tick above-the-line, and to cast their ballot along party lines rather than for an individual. The campaign speeches that were made, advised them to place their ticks next to the symbol of the dove above the line.

Yet there were local reasons, too, that explain Tikoinasau's victory.

First, there were family ties. Tailevu North was won in 1999 by Savenaca Tokainavo, Tikoinasau's father, and in 2001 by George Speight, Tikoinasau's brother. The Speight name was well known in the Tailevu North area, and the prestige accumulated by the gaoled coup leader had some bearing on Tikoinasau's re-election – although unlike in 2002, when he was an unknown person, it was not the only factor. More important than his brother in attracting support to him was his father, Sam Speight Snr, who has served extensively in the region in his capacity as the general manager of the Rewa Dairy Company. Speight Snr was also a director of the Dritabua Dairy Farm, which is owned by the people of Naloto.

Second, Tikoinasau was the sitting member for the constituency and a minister in the Qarase government, factors which he said counted in his favour. During his four years as a sitting MP, he had been able to make a name for himself. He campaigned effectively, visiting the villages in his constituency, and using the same successful campaign team he had used in the 2002 by-election. Part of his build-up for the 2006 election included setting up a constitution office in Korovou so that he would be accessible to his voters. Korovou is the municipality of the Tailevu North constituency.

Map 15.1   The *Tikina Makawa* of Tailevu North Fijian Communal

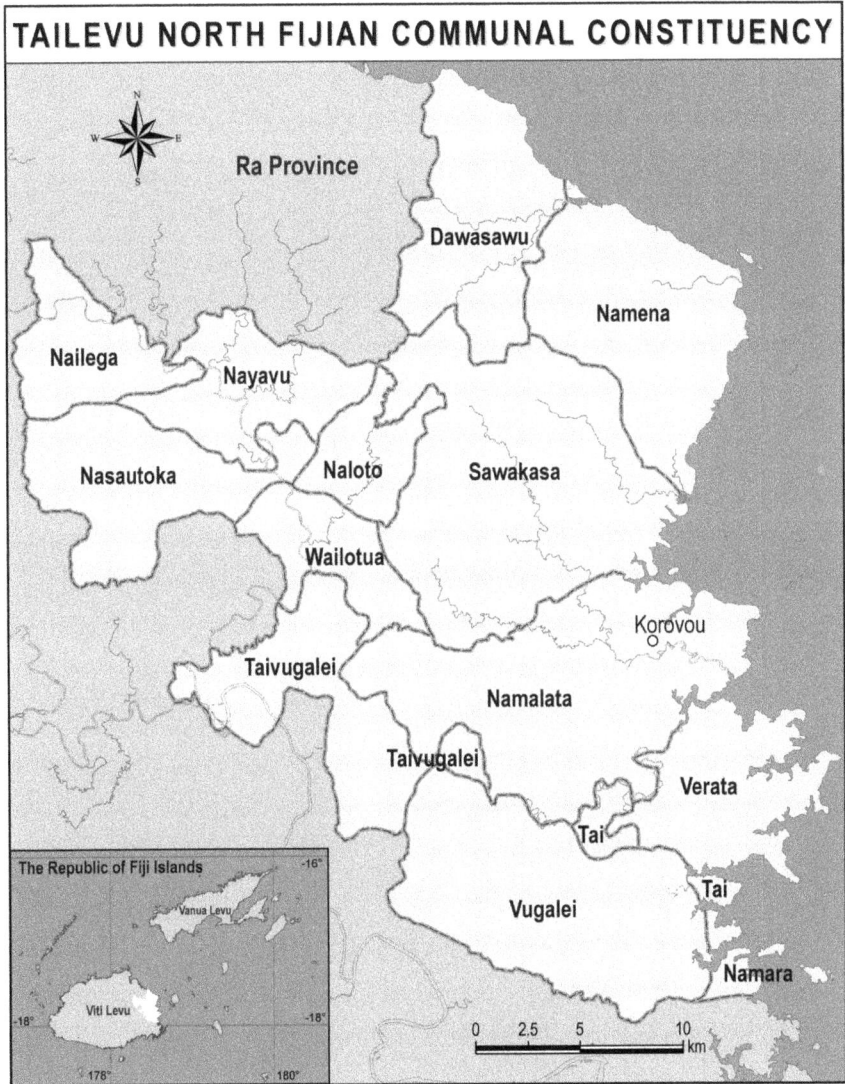

TAILEVU NORTH FIJIAN COMMUNAL CONSTITUENCY

Ra Province

Dawasawu

Namena

Nailega

Nayavu

Nasautoka   Naloto   Sawakasa

Wailotua

Korovou

Taivugalei

Namalata

Taivugalei

Verata

Tai

The Republic of Fiji Islands

Vanua Levu

Tai

Vugalei

Viti Levu

Namara

0   2.5   5   10 km

Source: Pacific Institute of Advanced Studies in Development and Governance (PIAS-DG) Mapping Database, University of the South Pacific, Suva.

Third, there were traditional loyalties and obligations. Tikoinasau claimed that the traditional links between the *tikina* of Wainibuka and those of Verata and Sawakasa contributed to his victory. These *tikina* belong to the *vanua* of Waimaro. In Fijian history, before Bau became powerful in Tailevu, Verata was the dominant *tikina*. The people of Tailevu North are militant people. They justified their participation in the events of 2000 by stating that they are traditional *bati* to the Vunivalu na Tui Kaba of Bau.[3] Many of the people of the *tikina makawa* of Namena and Dawasamu can trace their roots back to the province of Ra, the war cry of which is '*ma'e na ma'e*' – which loosely translates as 'they are prepared to die for what they are fighting for'. So, the people of this constituency rallied behind the SDL and Samisoni Tikoinasau, it is argued, because they believed that doing so was a fulfillment of their duty as traditional warriors fighting to retain power in the hands of indigenous Fijian leaders. While traditional loyalties clearly played their part in 2006, Tikoinasau's interpretation may need to be qualified in the light of further research, given the traditional hostility shown by Verata towards Bau, which can be traced to Verata's defeat as a great chiefdom in the 19th century, and which could still be seen in Verata's failure to support George Speight in 2000.

The coalition of the CAMV and the SDL

The coalition of the CAMV and the SDL was particularly important for Tikoinasau's electoral victory. A majority of the voters of Tailevu North had been strong supporters of the CAMV. The CAMV had been established in late 2000 and early 2001 in opposition to the direction being taken by the Soqosoqo ni Vakavulewa ni Taukei (SVT) under the leadership of Ratu Inoke Kubuabola as the leader of the opposition in parliament. Those initially involved in establishing the CAMV included SVT MPs Ratu Naiqama Lalabalavu, Ratu Rakuita Vakalalabure and Sireli Leweniqila and, later, Senator Ratu Josefa Dimuri. Lalabalavu noted that there was a lot of disagreement amongst the SVT parliamentarians about the manner in which parliamentary leader Ratu Inoke Kubuabola was behaving.[4] He was making decisions without fully consulting the other members. The SVT constitution stated that the parliamentary caucus would meet and make a decision on any issue that was to be dealt with. However, Kubuabola had gone ahead and advised Government

House that he was available for the position of prime minister. This took place after the 1999 election.

At an emergency SVT management board meeting there was a head-on disagreement, and the group decided to form their own party to represent Vanua Levu. Lalabalavu, in his position as Tui Cakau, had visited the Tui Macuata and Tui Bua to solicit their support, and the chiefs of Vanua Levu unanimously agreed with the setting up of the CAMV and to disassociate themselves from the SVT. The result was a gradual decline in support for the SVT in Vanua Levu. At the official launch of the CAMV in June 2001, Ratu Epenisa Cakobau was appointed the president, while Ratu Naiqama Lalabalavu of Tovata and Ro Alivereti Tuisawau of Burebasaga became the two vice presidents. What this meant was that the apex of the party was represented by the leading chiefly clans of the three confederacies to which all Fijian chiefs belong. And where the chiefs went so did their subjects.

Tailevu North's inclusion in the CAMV was by default rather than by design. The leaders of the CAMV had registered the party in Labasa, the main urban centre in the north, but during one of their management meetings in Suva they received a delegation from Tailevu North requesting membership of the CAMV party. The delegation took this step because they could not form a party of their own, but, nevertheless, wanted to sever ties with the SVT. Many resented the clampdown by the military in their area that had followed the arrest of Speight and his supporters in 2000, and some still harboured rebellious sentiments. By joining the CAMV they hoped they could get George Speight set free, and revive his cause. Lalabalavu argues that the CAMV was set up primarily as a political party with its own manifesto rather than as a rebel party.[5] Yet, it was widely seen as a party for the militants, and attracted followers on this basis.

When it was established, the CAMV sought to fight for the paramountcy of Fijian interests and advocated that the governing of Fiji remain in the hands of Fijians and their chiefs; in other words, that the offices of president and prime minister be reserved for indigenous Fijians. They also wanted the return and preservation of Fijian land and *qoliqoli*.[6] This was to correct previous wrongs by way of legal processes. CAMV also sought the academic and economic development of Fijians. This appealed to the people of Tailevu North, many of whom mistakenly thought that by joining the CAMV their nationalistic ambitions would be fulfilled and their petition for George Speight's release would be successful.

The Cakobau family, moreover, supported the CAMV. Lalabalavu, again in his capacity of Tui Cakau, had paid a visit to the family of the Vunivalu of Bau. Lalabalavu explained that he came to the family of the Vunivalu as a *vasu* – a descendant of the female line.[7] As is common in Fijian culture, the *vasu* is held with high regard and, being aware of this, the members of the Vunivalu's family joined forces with the Tui Cakau and the CAMV. As previously noted, the people of Tailevu North are *bati* to the Vunivalu, so wherever the Vunivalu and his family go his warriors follow, as it is their traditional responsibility to guard and protect the Vunivalu and the members of his family.

In the 2001 election, it was too late for the SDL and CAMV to coalesce, as the two parties had already been registered separately. So, it was decided that they would contest the elections separately and then form a coalition in parliament. The CAMV won six seats in 2001. The FLP tried to woo support from the CAMV in an effort to form a government after the 2001 polls, despite the party being associated with the instigators of a coup against Mahendra Chaudhry's government. Lalabalavu claims that there was an offer from the leader of the FLP to make him prime minister and Rakuita Vakalalabure the deputy prime minister.[8] There was also the promise of amnesty. But the CAMV joined with the SDL instead.

In preparation for the 2006 election, at its annual general election meeting in February 2006, the party voted to dissolve itself and merge with its coalition partner, the SDL, to form the Fijian United Party. It is alleged that Ratu Tanoa Cakobau, as part of the merger, wrote a letter requesting that the six CAMV parliamentarians be endorsed unopposed as SDL candidates. But Cakobau said that certain portions of the letter were not authentic. Lalabalavu clarified that the CAMV had not set any conditions prior to the merger.[9]

There was some dissent surrounding the deregistration of the party. Some rebels claimed to have been railroaded into liquidating their cherished party, and that this entailed an abandonment of the ideals for which they had fought hard during 2000. Lalabalavu claimed that those within the party who opposed this decision did so because of self-interest. He had explained at the final CAMV meeting that Fiji President Ratu Josefa Iloilo had been informed of the decision, as had the chiefs of Vanua Levu, Naitasiri and Tailevu, the areas where the party had most support. Others condemned the merger. Some thought the decision unwise as it would polarize Fiji's ethnic communities, while the military saw it as betrayal of the trust that it had invested in Qarase and the SDL when appointing him prime minister in 2000.

Constraints

Two key constraints hindered full participation in the 2006 poll. One was the high number of invalid votes. Of the 3,883 votes cast, 923 were invalid, a similar number to that in the 1999 election, when 958 votes were invalid. It seems that some voters are still not familiar with the voting system, while others may have deliberately invalidated their ballot papers because the person or party of their personal choice was not represented.

Proper voter education is needed to reduce the number of invalid votes. The current 'alternative vote' system, first used in 1999, is relatively new. Before that, Fiji had used the first-past-the-post, simple majority system inherited from the United Kingdom. The new system requires that the voters are well educated in order to vote correctly. It is not enough to have officials from the Elections Office visit the voters to conduct training a few months before the election. This should be on-going, so that the voters understand the system thoroughly, and the number of invalid votes is reduced.

A second constraint arose from the logistics of setting up eight polling stations daily. This consumed a lot of the time and effort of the different candidates. There were instances when Tikoinasau, for example, had set up his sheds at the polling stations in the early hours of the morning. Then, when he came the next day, the shed had been usurped by members of other parties. Setting up polling stations in Tailevu North is not easy, as most of the roads are a challenge to the travelling public.

Conclusion

The 2006 election saw the voters of Tailevu North expressing the same sentiments as in 2000 and 2001. They were not ready to accept Mahendra Chaudhry as prime minister in 2000, and six years later were still not ready to accept a non-indigenous prime minister. The traditional links between the people of this constituency are important, and any politician who disregards this is jeopardizing his or her chances of getting voted into parliament. In addition to traditional links, the service that a candidate has provided to the people is taken into account. Tikoinasau's father had served previously in this constituency and this augured well for Tikoinasau as he sought election for a second term in parliament. The support he received was overwhelming.

Is there hope that the voters of Tailevu North will entertain moderate sentiments in future elections? Perhaps. But in order to accept moderate policies, education is necessary. This would take a long time. It must not be forgotten that these are a people who value their traditional links and are proud to go to battle on behalf of their chief as his warriors. To get them to change their mindset would be to alter the social and traditional fabric of their lives.

Notes

1   The NVTLP was founded in the late 1990s by a merger of Sakeasi Butadroka's Fijian Nationalist Party and Duvuloco's Vanua Tako Lavo Party, and champions Fijian ethnic nationalism. Both leaders strongly opposed the adoption of the current constitution. Duvuloco calls it a betrayal of the Fijian people. The NVTLP campaigned on a platform of 'Fiji for the Fijians and that their rights at all times should be preserved'.
2   *Vulagi* is a word used normally to refer to visitors. So those of other ethnic groups are still viewed as visitors though they have lived in Fiji for a long time.
3   Vunivalu na Tui Kaba is the title of the paramount chief of the Kubuna Confederacy.
4   Personal communication, Ratu Naiqama Lalabalavu, 2006.
5   Personal communication, Ratu Naiqama Lalabalavu, 2006.
6   *Iqoliqoli* is the traditional fishing grounds for a clan/tribe or *yavusa,* especially for those living in coastal areas.
7   Personal communication, Ratu Naiqama Lalabalavu, 2006.
8   Personal communication, Ratu Naiqama Lalabalavu, 2006.
9   Personal communication, Ratu Naiqama Lalabalavu, 2006.

16

Bose ni Vanua[1] and democratic politics in Rewa

Baro Saumaki

The most intense intra-Fijian struggle of the 2006 election occurred in Rewa, historically a dissident province in Fiji's highly diversified political firmament. The contest was between independent candidate Ro Filipe Tuisawau and his aunt, Soqosoqo Duavata ni Lewenivanua (SDL) Education Minister Ro Teimumu Kepa. This was potentially a contest that defied party lines and threatened outcomes that diverged from broader national trends. The history of chiefly leadership in the province was important: following the death of Ro Lady Lala Mara, the wife of former president Ratu Sir Kamisese Mara, her sister, Ro Teimumu Kepa, had succeeded to the highest title in Rewa. That succession had been contested by Ro Filipe Tuisawau, whose father had previously been a challenger for the Roko Tui Dreketi title. The 2006 electoral contest, between the same two contestants, was initially one for the SDL nomination. After losing that, Ro Filipe stood as an independent, and was widely expected to do well within Rewa. Yet, Ro Teimumu easily won, Ro Filipe pulling up well short of the share of the vote required to force a second count – an outcome that showed just how strong party loyalties were at the 2006 election.

The Rewa contest provides an intriguing study of how traditional Fijian leadership is shaping in the 21st century. Rewa people are debating the importance of chiefs and the legitimacy of current chiefly political practice. This case study focuses on the two main issues at the forefront of Fijian leadership today: the duality of traditional and democratic leadership, and the ethical challenges of public leadership that appear to take advantage of traditional means to satisfy democratic ends. In Fiji, there exists a duality of values, a duality of laws and a duality of leadership authority. Traditional values, modes of authority, and custom law exist alongside democratic values, modern legal law and political authority. Fijians recognize their chief as the person who occupies the traditional leadership office; however, they cannot easily and appropriately blend traditional systems of authority with the democratic system. Nayacakalou argued that '…a traditional Fijian leader as distinct from various types of modern leaders is the person who occupies the customary office of chief of the group and thus the chief's jurisdiction covers all matters '*vakavanua*' (matters of the land) and he has a definite right to make decision on behalf of the group'.[2]

Owing to Tongan intervention, Rewa lost the protracted pre-cession wars that ended in Bau chief Ratu Seru Cakobau assuming ascendancy over the Fiji islands. With a land area of just 272 square kilometres (the smallest of Fiji's provinces), the province of Rewa includes the capital city of Suva and is made up of two parts – one including part of Suva's hinterland to the west, and the other a non-contiguous area to the east, separated from the rest of Rewa by Naitasiri Province. At the 1996 census, the province (including Suva) had a population of 101,547, making it Fiji's third most populous province. Without Suva City proper, as indicated by the data shown in Table 16.1, the population is 11,634, of which slightly over 36 per cent live in the core Rewa River delta *tikinas*, 32.8 per cent in Fijian villages linked to Rewa within Suva City, a little under 20 per cent in the territory known as 'Rewa' *tikina* to the west of Suva and 10.6 per cent on Beqa (in the *tikinas* of Sawau and Raviravi).[3]

Map 16.1 shows the Rewa Fiji Provincial Communal constituency, which excludes those areas of Rewa Province that are covered by Suva's urban constituencies (although the wider provincial boundary, is also shown by the dotted line). Some villages within Suva are, for administrative purposes, counted as part of Rewa Province and entitled to vote on the Rewa Fijian communal roll. Both Ro Teimumu and Ro Filipe, for example, campaigned in the four villages of Navukavu (Waiqanake) and in other villages along the highway from Lami westwards, although these are officially part of the South West Fiji Urban Communal constituency. Rewa ballot boxes were also present at many

polling stations throughout the capital city. The 'Rewa connection' of many
of the villages shown as part of Rewa *tikina* to Suva's west is a post-cession
administrative innovation. Pre-cession, some of these villages were more closely
linked with Naitasiri Province.[4]

For both socioeconomic and traditional reasons, Rewa is a powerful province.
It is not only the hinterland of the national capital, but also the heart of the
Burebasaga, one of three traditional chiefly confederacies. In population
terms, Burebasaga is the largest of the confederacies represented at Fiji's Great
Council of Chiefs.[5] It covers the southeastern part of the island of Viti Levu,
stretching around the south coast to the extreme west of Viti Levu. It consists
of the provinces of Rewa, Nadroga, Namosi, Serua, Beqa and Kadavu Island off
the coast of Suva, and parts of Ba. At the zenith of its power, in 1817, Rewa's
territories extended through the river tribal areas as far inland as Naitasiri, 40
miles from the mouth of the river.[6] Lomanikoro (in Rewa *tikina*) is the capital of
this confederacy. The Roko Tui Dreketi is the paramount chief of the province
and of the Burebasaga Confederacy. This title is considered to be the second
most senior to Bau in Fiji's House of Chiefs. The dynasty holding the title is

Table 16.1   Selected features of Rewa Province, 2004–2005

Tikina	Population	Households	Land area (acres)
Rewa	2,429	453	3,130
Noco	1,409	296	2,129
Burebasaga	617	132	1,173
Vutia	344	80	739
Toga	946	183	3,318
Dreketi	848	185	1,316
Suva	3,812	645	32,787
Sawau	636	153	4,466
Raviravi	593	147	4,344
Total	11,634	2,274	53,405

Note: This table shows the results of a survey conducted by the Rewa Provincial Council during 2004–5.
The population figures do not include those away from their villages at the time of the survey.
Source: Rewa Province website, www.rewapc.com/prov_profile.aspx

Map 16.1 The *Tikina Makawa* of Rewa Fijian Communal

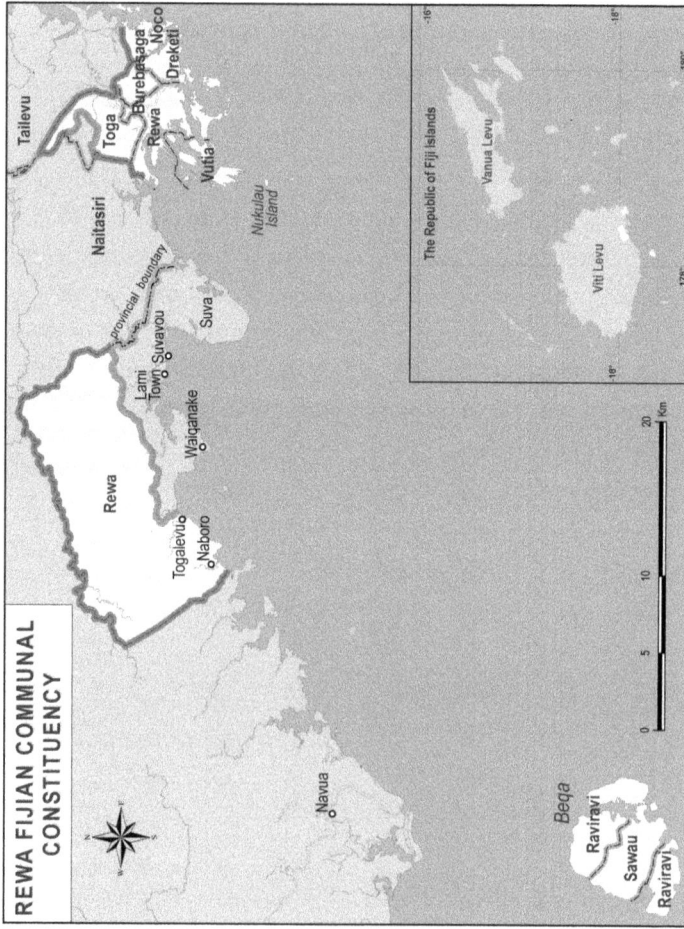

Source: Pacific Institute of Advanced Studies in Development and Governance (PIAS-DG) Mapping Database, University of the South Pacific, Suva.

the Tuisawau family. Unlike some chiefly titles in other parts of the Fiji group, this one is not reserved for males. The present Roko Tui Dreketi is, as previously mentioned, a woman: Ro Teimumu Vuikaba Tuisawau-Kepa, who was also the Minister for Education in the 2001–2006 Qarase government.[7]

Rewa is governed by a provincial council.[8] The position of chair of the council was vacant at the time of the 2006 poll, and the council had decided not to fill it until the constitution was changed to allow parliamentarians to hold national and provincial office simultaneously: this would allow their paramount chief, Ro Teimumu Kepa, to assume the position. In the interim, Pita Tagicakiverata from Vutia, was the acting chairman.

Historically in Rewa, the democratic process through the ballot box has indirectly been used as a means of bolstering the traditional legitimation of authority. This continued to be the case in 2006, when the two prominent chiefs from the ruling chiefly household both vied for endorsement as the SDL candidate. Ro Filipe was a popular choice because of his previous involvement with the people as a former president of the provincial rugby union. Ro Teimumu's decision to stand was based on the claim that traditional stature should also acquire a political expression by way of a ministerial portfolio. She argued that 'if you're not in Cabinet even if you're not in the house of reps there's no assistance in Rewa, I cannot see any other way we will be able to help our province'.[9]

Before the primary election, SDL received two petitions from the *vanua* representatives supporting Ro Filipe. SDL officials advised Ro Filipe not to stand, but to await the following election. They were worried that Ro Teimumu might be defeated in the primary election. Ro Teimumu's supporters argued that leaders of the various traditional houses (*liuliu ni veibure vakaturaga*) in Rewa were effectively the SDL branch representatives, and were the rightful people to cast votes in the primary election rather than the ordinary leaders in the villages.[10] On the day of the primary election, the *vanua* of Rewa held a meeting in Lomanikoro. During the meeting, despite a motion from the Vunivalu, Ro Jone Mataitini, urging the meeting not to discuss any political issues, the Roko Tui Dreketi's spokesperson told *tikina* representatives that Ro Teimumu would be their representative.[11] The move to consolidate support behind Ro Teimumu was obviously backed by the SDL campaign team, which emphasized that 'A vote for Ro Teimumu is a vote for the Vanua of Burebasaga', and that the SDL would not endorse any second party or shadow independent candidates. Voters were to be urged to tick 'the dove above the line'; by doing so they would endorse the party's preferred candidate, Ro Teimumu.[12]

Ro Filipe Tuisawau demurred and, to reinforce his case, initiated a debate that provides some insight into the nature of political institutions in the province. He argued that 'the vanua and the chiefly system has been used many times to manipulate Fijians for political gain and this has confused them into not accepting democratic values'.[13] This comment followed Ro Teimumu's call for the 'Bose ni Vanua', a meeting reserved only for traditional purposes, to discuss pre-selection of the province's candidate for parliament. Ro Filipe suggested that democratic party politics should be based only on the choices exercised by individual voters, and that the Bose ni Vanua was a meeting only for the hereditary chiefs. Ro Filipe argued:

> ...the two essentially are in conflict and when you hold a meeting to discuss political issues, you are undermining the integrity of the Bose ni Vanua, because they make the decision but then the people will have an individual vote later which might contradict the decision they make. It undermines the whole basis of the Bose ni Vanua, and really they shouldn't be discussing political issues.[14]

To probe more deeply into the background of this pre-election dispute, we need to revisit the earlier, succession-related differences that emerged between provincial factions following the passing away of the late Roko Tui Dreketi, Ro Lady Lala Mara, in July 2004. For many people in Rewa, the ballot box was another way of resolving customary contests for chiefly leadership.

There is an age-old succession struggle within the Tuisawau clan, the current holders of the Roko Tui Dreketi title. In the previous generation, it was between Ro Lady Lala Mara (1931–2004) and her half brother, Ro Mosese Tuisawau (1926–2000). With their passing, the saga appears to be continuing between Ro Teimumu and her nephew, Ro Filipe Tuisawau (Ro Mosese's son). The origins of the dispute involved questions about the legitimate inheritance of the title. Ro George Tuisawau had four children, the oldest, Ro Aporosa Rageci Tuisawau, Ro Mosese, Ro Lala and the youngest, Ro Teimumu. Ro Lala and Ro Teimumu's mother, Adi Asenaca Vosailagi, was from the chiefly Ka Levu clan of Nadroga.[15] Ro Lala's marriage, on 9 September 1950, to Ratu Mara was considered a dynastic marriage, as it united two powerful feudal families. Ratu Mara was later to become the Tui Lau and Tui Nayau (the traditional ruler of the Lau Islands), and Fiji's long-serving post-independence prime minister. Ro Lala inherited the title of Roko Tui Dreketi from her father.

The dispute between the ruling families of Rewa can be traced back to the 19th century. In 1821–22, dissension among the members of the ruling family – a result of the system of polygamy among the high chiefs and of intermarriage among the chiefly families – split Rewa into hostile factions.[16] Jealousies and intrigue between the children of one father with different mothers led to intervention by interested kingdoms and, occasionally, to war. Derrick argued that the tale of the disintegration of the Roko Tui Dreketi family was intimately connected to the 19th century downfall of Rewa.[17] The fate of the Tuisawau dynasty (1936 – to the present) has echoed some of those earlier difficulties. While Ro George Tuisawau, who reigned for 25 years (1936–1961), was revered by the people of Rewa, Ro Lala was not as popular amongst her people. During the 2000 coup, for example, one account has suggested that Ro Lady Lala Mara's half-brother, Ro Mosese Tuisawau:

> ...rode the tide of popular opposition to the Mara dynasty, with the aim of having himself installed as Roko Tui Dreketi. Flyers circulated in and around Suva pointed to years of top-level chiefly appropriation of rent incomes derived from the Fijian Hotel, dredged up controversies about the relocation of the peoples of Suvavou (the traditional landowners of Suva) and made allegations about the spiriting away of port clearance fees and hurricane relief funds.[18]

Rewa province has produced some of Fiji's most influential political leaders, including Semesa Sikivou, Tomasi Vakatora, Berenado Vunibobo and Sakeasi Butadroka. Sikivou graduated from New Zealand's Auckland University, and went on to become the first Fijian to acquire a postgraduate degree from the London School of Economics. He served as a member of the Legislative Council in the 1960s, and in January 1963 was one of the eight who signed the Wakaya Letter, which affirmed the principles of Fijian paramountcy. When Fiji gained its independence from the United Kingdom in 1970, he was appointed Fiji's first Ambassador to the United Nations, serving until 1976. He re-entered politics in the 1980s, and served as Minister for Foreign Affairs. Sikivou was offered a knighthood by Queen Elizabeth II, but declined it, saying that it was his honour to serve her without remuneration.

In the first post-independence election, Rewa became an Alliance Party stronghold, with Sakeasi Butadroka taking the then Rewa/Serua/Namosi Fijian Communal seat in 1972, with 91.2 per cent of the vote. Butadroka was a politician noted for his strident ethnic nationalism, but his first falling out with Alliance Prime Minister Ratu Mara had more to do with grievances about the government's failure to assist Fijian development (and, in particular, his Rewa Provincial Council Bus Company). Butadroka was expelled from the Alliance Party in 1973, after he assisted an opposing candidate in a by-election for the Suva East Fijian National seat.[19] In October 1975, he introduced a parliamentary motion calling for a resolution to repatriate Indians back to India, and for their travelling expenses and compensation for their properties in Fiji to be met by the British government. Butadroka founded the Fijian Nationalist Party, which took 25 per cent of the Fijian vote in the general election held in April 1977. Although the party won only one parliamentary seat, its votes were mostly at the expense of the Alliance. This allowed the opposition National Federation Party to win 26 seats to the Alliance's 24, precipitating a constitutional crisis. Rewa was where Butadroka's Nationalist Party received its strongest showing in the country.

Butadroka lost the September 1977 election, when he secured 40.2 per cent of the vote in comparison with new Alliance candidate Tomasi Vakatora's 59.8 per cent. Vakatora had trained as a teacher at Nasinu Teachers Training College and briefly attended Ruskin College, Oxford, and the London School of Economics. He became the Permanent Secretary and Commissioner of Labour in 1969, one of the very few locals to attain such distinction at that time. Prior to his retirement from the civil service, he was Permanent Secretary of Works and Tourism. After a brief stint in the Senate he unsuccessfully contested a seat in the House of Representatives as Alliance candidate for Rewa in April 1977. However, after success at the September poll, he served in a range of ministries before being appointed Speaker of the House from 1982–1987. In the wake of the coups, he served in Ratu Mara's interim administration, becoming Deputy Prime Minister and Minister of Finance and Economic Development in 1992. Vakatora held the Rewa Communal seat from September 1977 until the elections in 1992, when Butadroka and Ro Mosese Tuisawau won the two Rewa seats (Vakatora did not stand). Vakatora's greatest achievement was as a

Table 16.2   Election results for Rewa Fijian communal constituency, 1972–2001

Year	Winner	Party	Votes won	Total valid votes cast	Votes won/Total valid votes cast (per cent)
1972	Sakeasi Butadroka	Alliance	6,263	6,868	91.2
1977 (Apr)	Sakeasi Butadroka	Nationalist	4,640	8,684	53.4
1977 (Sept)	Tomasi R Vakatora	Alliance	5,231	8,743	59.8
1982	Tomasi R Vakatora	Alliance	7,492	11, 164	63.3
1987	Tomasi R Vakatora	Alliance	6,002	10, 826	55.4
1992	Ro Mosese Tuisawau	Nationalist	2,288	7,498	30.5
	Sakiasi Butadroka	Nationalist	2,269	7,498	30.3
1994	Berenado Vunibobo	SVT	1,955	7,122	27.5
	Atunaisa B Druavesi	SVT	1,790	7,122	25.1
1999	Timoci Q Silatolu	FAP	3,100	5,193	20.5
2001	Teimumu V Kepa	SDL	2,636	5,133	51.4

Notes: Results shown cover the Rewa/Serua/Namosi Fijian Communal seat from 1972–1987, the two-member Rewa Fijian provincial seat in 1992 and 1994, and the single member Rewa Fijian Communal seat in 1999 and 2001.
SVT = Soqosoqo ni Vakavulewa ni Taukei; FAP = Fijian Association Party; SDL = Soqosoqo Duavata ni Lewenivanua

member of the 1995–96 three-person Fiji Constitution Review Commission, headed by Sir Paul Reeves. Election results over the period 1972–2001 are shown in Table 16.2.

In the wake of the 1987 coup, a new (1990) constitution was promulgated; it gave Rewa two seats in parliament. Butadroka had been one of the leaders of the 1987 Taukei Movement, whose agitation formed the backdrop to the two military coups of 1987 that deposed the elected government and severed Fiji's ties to the British monarchy. Otherwise, however, he operated largely on the political fringes, although he secured one of the Rewa seats in 1992. He strongly opposed the adoption of the 1997 constitution, which reversed most of the provisions institutionalizing ethnic Fijian supremacy in the 1990 constitution. When parliament passed the new constitution, Butadroka publicly burned a copy. In 1999, he merged his party, now called the Nationalist United Front Party (NUFP), with Iliesa Duvuloco's Vanua Tako Lavo Party to form the Nationalist Vanua Tako Lavo Party. The party obtained one seat at the 1999 poll, although

Butadroka himself was not elected. The Soqosoqo ni Vakavulewa ni Taukei (SVT) emerged as the dominant ethnic Fijian party of the early 1990s, and Berenado Vunibobo and Atunaisa Druavesi took the Rewa seats for this party in 1994. The switch in political allegiances from Nationalist to SVT between 1992 and 1994 was indicative of the long-run volatility of Rewa politics.

Nationalist sentiments brewed beneath the surface during the late 1990s. The Rewa seat was taken in 1999 by Ratu Timoci Silatolu, who was a member of the Fijian Association Party (FAP). Led by Navosa politician and high chief Adi Kuini Speed, the FAP entered the People's Coalition government with the Labour Party. Adi Kuini became deputy prime minister, while Ratu Silatolu remained on the backbenches. When George Speight burst into Fiji's parliament on 19 May 2000, the one politician who immediately joined the insurgents was Timoci Silatolu. He was also, at one point, announced as the Speight group's favoured choice for the prime ministership. Ratu Timoci pleaded 'not guilty' to charges associated with his role during the 2000 coup, and, as a result, received a much stiffer sentence than many of the other coup-instigators.

In the 2001 election, Ro Teimumu Kepa, for the first time, took the Rewa seat. Rewa had played an important role in the formation of the SDL prior to the 2001 poll, particularly as a result of the backing of Tui Noco, Ratu Josaia Rayawa[20], who later became a government nominee ito the Senate. Ro Teimumu had entered the interim cabinet formed by Laisenia Qarase in July 2000 as Minister for Women, Culture, and Social Welfare.[21] In the August 2001 election, she secured a 51.5 per cent majority, defeating the incarcerated Silatolu, who stood alongside George Speight for the newly formed Conservative Alliance–Matanitu Vanua and obtained 34.4 per cent of the vote. Another 10

Table 16.3   The 2006 election result in Rewa

Candidate	Political party	Votes won	Votes won/votes cast (per cent)
Ro Teimumu Kepa	SDL	3,401	56.4
Ro Filipe Tuisawau	Independent	2,371	39.3
Taniela R. Senikuta	FLP	167	2.8
Viliame V. Raile	Independent	95	1.6
Total		6,034	100.0

per cent of the Rewa vote in 2001 was taken by the SVT, which at that time still had a dwindling following in the province. Ro Epeli Mataitini, a member of the family of the Vunivalu of Rewa, had been SVT president, and fought a losing battle to sustain the SVT vote in the new millennium.

In 2006, the contest was a race between Ro Teimumu Kepa (who won 56.4 per cent of the vote) and Ro Filipe Tuisawau (39.3 per cent). The other parties jointly obtained only 4.4 per cent of the vote. The SVT did not stand. The results (see Table 16.3) suggest that Ro Filipe had considerable backing (despite lacking the official SDL nomination), and may pose a threat to Ro Teimumu in future elections. While Ro Filipe had strong support in some districts within the Rewa delta region, Ro Teimumu had overwhelming support in districts along the coast westward from Suva, on Beqa Island and in the Rewa villages within the Suva urban constituencies. The SDL's affirmative action policies assisted the coastal districts, where electricity, telephones and piped water had been connected through the villages. The perception amongst these voters was that, should they vote for Ro Filipe, they might be excluded from further assistance. The SDL campaign team had a strategic development plan used to court support in Rewa and other provinces around Fiji. Although election-related hostility between aunt and nephew was marked, it is notable that both put the Fiji Labour Party last on their list of preferences.

In Fiji, chiefly power remains firmly embedded in indigenous social and political tradition. As shown in Rewa in the 2006 poll, chiefs are able to use their traditional position to gain political mileage. The political endorsement of Ro Teimumu, and her achievements as Minister of Education, also legitimized her traditional position as the Roko Tui Dreketi. However, a growing younger, urbanized and educated generation is emerging, who are probably the vanguard of a new style of legitimate national leadership. They are not necessarily of chiefly status, but some are younger chiefs who have a measure of support in the provincial districts. The prevailing duality of political systems means that there is occasional conflict between traditional and democratic criteria for leadership. Good governance principles are essentially principles that promote democracy. Fijian chiefs face an ethical challenge arising from the dual legal and cultural systems and dual modes of authority, and some people argue that chiefs should concentrate solely on their traditional roles and keep out of politics. When they do decide to participate in national politics, they need to ensure there are transparent democratic processes of selection and ensure that their political positions are based on meritocracy.

Notes

1 'State council' or 'traditional district meeting'.
2 Nayacakalou, R. 1975. *Leadership in Fiji*, Melbourne, Oxford University Press in association with the University of the South Pacific, Melbourne, p.31.
3 Uncertainty about the figures arises from the fact that both the area to the west of Suva and one of the *tikinas* in the delta to the east of Suva are known as 'Rewa' *tikina*. Both are included in the data provided in Table 16.1.
4 Personal communication (with editors), Sakiusa Tuisolia, Chief Executive Officer of Airports Fiji, 4 June 2006.
5 The Great Council of Chiefs comprises representatives from Fiji's 14 provinces and the Council of Rotuma, as well as representatives nominated by the Minister of Fijian Affairs and the President, Vice President and Prime Minister, as well as former prime minister Sitiveni Rabuka who was made a 'life member' after the 1987 coup.
6 Derrick, R.A. 1946. *A History of Fiji*, Government Press, Suva, p.56.
7 Ro Teimumu Kepa succeeded her late sister, Ro Lady Lala Mara, Fiji's former First Lady, in 2004. Hence, the last two holders of the title have been women.
8 The provinces have direct input into national affairs through the Great Council of Chiefs and the Senate. The Great Council of Chiefs advises the government on indigenous affairs and also functions as an electoral college to elect the President and Vice President; 42 of the 55 members of the Great Council are chosen by the provincial councils, three from each province. In addition, 14 of the 32 members of the Senate, the upper house of the Fijian Parliament, are chosen by the provincial councils (one Senator each) and confirmed by the Great Council of Chiefs.
9 Fiji TV 1 National News, 22 March 2006.
10 These are supposedly the districts' men's, women's and youth leaders.
11 *The Fiji Times*, 24 March 2006. The Vunivalu title is the second highest in Rewa, and is held by the Mataitini family, who, like the family of the Roko Tui Dreketi, are from Lomanikoro village.
12 Fiji ballot papers have an 'above-the-line' section allowing voters to endorse party preferences (as opposed to ranking candidates themselves 'below-the-line').
13 *The Fiji Times*, 4 April 2006.
14 www.fijivillage.com, accessed 22 March 2006.
15 The Ka Levu title is that of the paramount chiefs of Nadroga, in western Viti Levu.
16 Derrick, 1946. *A History of Fiij*, p.56.
17 Derrick, 1946. *A History of Fiji*, p.57.
18 Fraenkel, J. 2000. 'The Clash of Dynasties and Rise of Demagogues; Fiji's Tauri Vakaukauwa of May 2000', *Journal of Pacific History* 35(3):302.
19 We are indebted to Robert Norton for clarification of this point.
20 Ratu Josaia Rayawa had previously been president of the now-defunct Christian Democratic Alliance (VLV), which won three seats in the 1999 election.
21 'Fiji Interim Cabinet Named', *Fijilive*, 28 July 2000.

17

Whatever happened to Western separatism?

Apolosi Bose and Jon Fraenkel

Political parties hostile to the dominance of the eastern chiefly élite in national politics have regularly emerged in western Viti Levu.[1] Most have emphasized the economic centrality of the west as the source of most of the country's sugar, gold, timber and tourism earnings.[2] Twice since independence, prime ministers from the west have been deposed by coups (Dr Timoci Bavadra in 1987 and Mahendra Chaudhry in 2000), fuelling western perceptions of regional injustice. The Party of National Unity (PANU) gained four seats at the 1999 poll and became part of the short-lived Labour-led People's Coalition until the coup of 19 May 2000. At the election of 2001, the emergence of a new rival western-based party, the Bai Kei Viti (BKV), split the western Fijian vote and enabled the governing Soqosoqo Duavata ni Lewenivanua (SDL) to take all the western Fijian communal constituencies. PANU hoped to avoid a repeat of that outcome. Yet, in 2006, the SDL again took all of the western Fijian communal seats. This chapter looks at the background to the SDL's triumph in the west, and at the shifting politics in Ba Province.

Ba Province extends around the north-western side of Viti Levu, and includes Nadi town, Lautoka city, Ba and Tavua (see Map 17.1). It covers a region of fertile cane fields, from where sugar is transported to the Lautoka and Rarawai sugar mills. It also includes the Nadi international airport, the main gateway for tourist arrivals into the country and a key crossroads for trans-Pacific air transport. To the north, Ba Province includes the scattered islands

Map 17.1   The *Tikina Makawa* of Ba Province

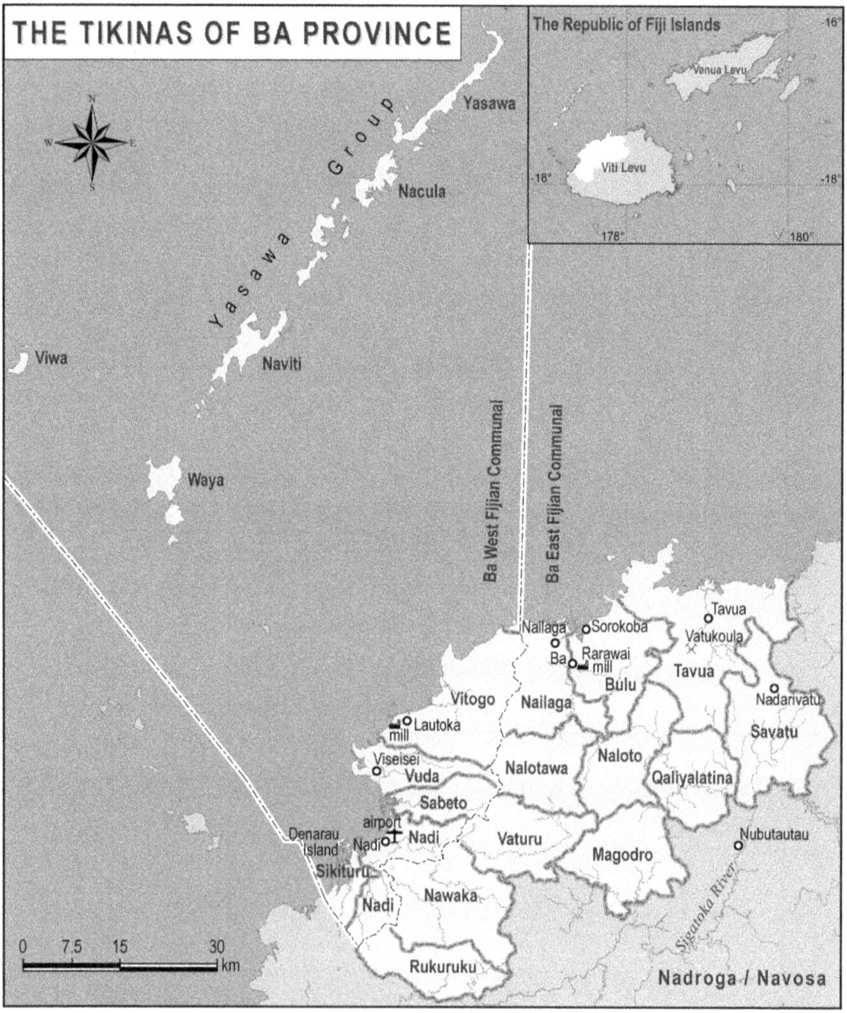

Source: Pacific Institute of Advanced Studies in Development and Governance (PIAS-DG) Mapping Database, University of the South Pacific, Suva.

of the Yasawas, a major destination for tourists. Close to Nadi, the island of Denarau features a major golf course, a high-end residential development and several internationally renowned hotels, which are regularly used as venues for international conferences. In addition, the province has rich forestry resources (particularly pine and indigenous hardwoods), mostly in the interior *tikinas* of Savatu, Qaliyalatina and Naloto. The country's only operating goldmine is at Vatukoula in Tavua. Ba Province is easily the richest province in terms of natural resources in Fiji, as well as being the country's biggest foreign exchange earner.

Political power, however, has been traditionally concentrated in Fiji's east. Leading 19th century chiefs, such as Ratu Seru Cakobau and Enele Ma'afu were, respectively, from Bau Island, off Viti Levu's eastern coast, and the Lau group, further east towards Tonga. Their 20th century successors, Ratu Sir Lala Sukuna and Ratu Sir Kamisese Mara, were also from the eastern islands. The country's great Fijian confederacies (*matanitu*), which play an important role in the decision-making of the Bose Levu Vakaturaga (BLV – Great Council of Chiefs), are Kubuna, Burebasaga and Tovata, all of which are centred on the eastern part of Fiji. The western part of Viti Levu is nominally divided between Burebasaga, at the helm of which stand the Rewa chiefs, and Kubuna, the confederacy centred on Bau Island, off the eastern coast of Viti Levu. This partitioning of the west reflected, first, the establishment of larger chiefdoms in the east during the late 18th and early 19th centuries, and the greater fractiousness of tribes in the west. Second, it reflected the colonial development of a neo-traditional order, which brought the west under the provincial controls of the Fijian administration. Aspirations for a separate western confederacy, the Yasayasa Vaka Ra, have at times proved politically significant, but this has never formally materialized or been accepted by the Great Council of Chiefs.

The political marginalization of the west resulted in a long history of dissent and revolt.[3] Warfare from around 1867 was between coastal and interior groups, and was triggered by land sales and European settlement.[4] Clashes at the upper reaches of the Ba and Sigatoka rivers were the most difficult to subdue. In 1873, European officers acting for the Cakobau government (1871–74) led around 160 trained native troops and a larger number of auxiliaries through Magodro to seize the mountain stronghold of Nubutautau, taking around a thousand prisoners, many of whom were forcibly relocated away from their interior villages.[5] After cession, British Governor Arthur Gordon led a military campaign to suppress uprisings in the Ba interior in 1876 (known locally as the *Valu ni Lotu* – the 'Church War').[6] The 1892 separation of Colo North[7] from Colo West and Colo East, with a new headquarters at Nadarivatu, was in part intended to 'lessen dangerous combines' and isolate the 'Tuka' movement of Navosavakadua.[8] In all the interior provinces, including Colo West and Colo East as well as Colo North, villagers were, after the advent of colonial rule, without single rulers, and as a result fell under the control of European district administrators.[9] Hostility to the new order also festered on the grounds that Ba and Nadi chiefs had not been represented amongst those who had signed the Deed of Cession in 1874. Indeed, 300,000 acres of land in the interior *tikina* of Magodro had been formally appropriated in the schedule attached to the Deed, although the appropriation was later rejected by the colonial administration.[10] In 1945, Colo North, like the other inland provinces, was incorporated into the coastal provinces.[11]

Dissident movements also emerged in 20th century western Viti Levu, sometimes as echoes of the 'Tuka' movement.[12] Apolosi R. Nawai, from Narewa in Nadi, commenced the Viti Kabani (Fiji Company) in 1912–13 with the objective of challenging colonial control over commerce, starting a movement that spread eastwards to Tailevu and Rewa.[13] In the post-colonial period, Fijian political leaders in Ba have sometimes aligned themselves along provincial or regional, rather than ethnic, lines, and found common cause with local Indo-Fijian leaders.[14] For many left-wing intellectuals, the predominantly Indian support base of the Fiji Labour Party (FLP) could potentially be extended by alliances with Fijians in the west.[15] Labour's Dr Timoci Bavadra, from Viseisei village, briefly became prime minister in 1987 before being dislodged by a military coup in May. For many in the west, the overthrow of that government was yet another attempt by Fiji's eastern rulers to retain power and authority.

The population of Ba, as recorded at the 1996 census, was 212,197, making this easily the most populous province in the country. The majority of the population is Fiji Indians (63.9 per cent). Ethnic Fijians have just over half that share (32.9 per cent).[16] As a result, the major Indian party, the FLP, has been able to win all seven of the Ba-located open constituencies at the elections of 1999, 2001 and 2006.[17] Including also communal constituencies,

Ba Province controls just over a quarter (18) of the seats in the 71-member parliament. Western-based Fijian parties have, in earlier years, been centred on provinces other than Ba. The 1960s Fijian National Party and the 1980s Western United Front, for example, had their strongholds in the neighbouring Nadroga province. Since the 1990s, however, emergent western parties, such as the All National Congress (ANC) and PANU, have been Ba-based, and relied critically on the sponsorship of the Ba Provincial Council.

The Ba Provincial Council brings together the region's 21 *tikinas*, each of which has a chiefly representative and a *tikina* representative (the total membership is 42). Politics on the council are influenced by the fact that there is no single ascendant paramount chief, unlike provinces in most other parts of the Fiji group.[18] The *tikina* of Vuda has occasionally claimed pre-eminence. Its chiefs have assumed leading positions in national affairs. In the early post-independence years, Tui Vuda Ratu Sir Josaia Tavaiqia was a minister in successive Alliance governments (1977–87) and in the post-1987 coup Military and Civilian Council. He became vice president from 1993 until he passed away in 1997. The Vuda title and the vice presidency then passed to Ratu Josefa Iloilo, who acceded to the presidency in 2000. Vuda's claims are also strengthened by the Fijian legend that the first people to arrive in Fiji disembarked at Vuda Point, where a popular resort called 'First Landing' now exists. When the British royal family visits Fiji, they regularly visit Vuda. Yet, this claim to pre-eminence can rest uncomfortably in neighbouring *tikinas*, such as Vitogo, Nadi and Sabeto. Tavua's leading chief, Ratu Ovini Bokini, is fond of saying in some Provincial Council Meetings that, in Ba Province: '*xo da na momo ni Ba dei tautauvata, xei tixai tla xei cecere tatla qa tixai tla xei te momo sewa*' ('We, the chiefs in Ba, are equal in rank'). This type of appeal to an egalitarian distribution of authority amongst western leaders is sometimes used by the current chairman of the Ba Provincial Council to quell any push for pre-eminence.[19]

The chiefs of the coastal *tikinas* are the most wealthy and powerful within the province. They are recipients of large agricultural and commercial rents from the Native Land Trust Board (NLTB), and have access to capital. Some, like the Tui Nawaka and the Saunaka chiefs, have provided residential plots for resettlement on the outskirts of Nadi, where displaced Indians have established hundreds of new homes without obtaining NLTB leases (via '*vakavanua*' arrangements).[20] The interior chiefs tend to be less prominent, despite their important role in political campaigning. Their *tikinas* are nowadays sparsely populated, and some villages are so remote that people do not understand the Bau dialect, the lingua franca across most parts of the Fiji group. They are considerably poorer than their coastal counterparts, owing to the hilly terrain and the paucity of access roads to regions such as Vaturu, Nalotawa and Naloto. During provincial council meetings, *tikina* representatives from the interior of the province often lament the lack of access to markets, and the difficulties of bringing sugar cane to the Lautoka or Rarawai mills. Interior peoples remain predominantly subsistence-oriented, although cash incomes are secured by migrating to cut cane in the coastal districts or by sales of inland produce in urban markets.

The five *tikinas* of the Yasawas also have a less central influence in the affairs of the Ba Provincial Council than do the Viti Levu coastal chiefs. The islands do not have the land resources of the mainland peoples. Their main sources of income are fish, yams, and subsistence agriculture, as well as, increasingly, tourism. The Yasawa group has, historically, done well in winning national scholarships. Prominent officials, such as the CEO in the Ministry of Agriculture, the Commissioner Northern and the Commissioner Eastern and the country's Catholic Archbishop, come from the group. Yet, the islands themselves remain under-developed. There is only one secondary school in the Yasawas, there are difficulties with the water supply and, although every island has a health centre, there is no hospital. Linkages between the Yasawas and Ba are sometimes contested. Questions have been raised at the council about the size of the Yasawa contribution to the *tikina* levies, and there have been occasional calls to re-establish the five island *tikinas* as a separate province.[21] There have also been separatist commercial aspirations; an islander initiative in the early 1990s was the Asayawa Holding Company Limited, established before Ba Provincial Holdings Company Limited (BPHCL). The former was shelved in 1994, in response to appeals for a more unified provincial company. Ba Holdings, the commercial arm of the Ba Provincial Council, was registered in 1995.[22] By 2006, BPHCL had interests in shipping, property, hardware and a satellite television company (Pacific Broadcasting Services), and ran the Ba Province Secondary School on behalf of the council.

Animosities between rival chiefs in Ba Province, often centering on land disputes, exert a critical influence over local political alignments. The dispute between the Tui Ba (Bulu) and the Tui Ba (Nailaga) blew up in the 1860s and centres on rival claims to lands on the border between these neighbouring regions.[23] In the early colonial days, the headquarters of the provincial administration was at Vitogo village, until it was brought to Lautoka. Many Vitogo people believed that this was at the instigation of the Viseisei chiefs (of Vuda), and that Viseisei peoples had also otherwise been favoured under colonial rule. When Viseisei's Ratu Tevita Moemeodonu took control of BPHCL in the wake of the 2006 election, amongst those who stormed the Rogorogoivuda building in opposition to the takeover, people from the *vanua* of Vitogo (or those who had blood ties to Vitogo) figured prominently. Many had been workers at the company under the previous administration, and had been sacked by Ratu Moemoedonu. Claims by the people of Sabeto to ownership of the land around Nadi airport have been vigorously contested by the Saunaka people (from within the Nadi *tikina*), some of whom benefit greatly from rental incomes from land and commercial interests at Nadi Airport. Whatever the characteristic political frictions of the day, some of the Saunaka chiefs will tend to be on one side, and some of the people of Sabeto on the other side.

Fissions are as common within as between *tikinas*. The Sabeto peoples once lived in fortified villages up in the range separating Nadi and Lautoka, until the Cakobau government troops forced them to burn their villages and move down to the coast.[24] Apisai Tora, a veteran trade unionist and instigator of PANU, is the head of one of the *yavusas* within Sabeto, but had major differences with the Tui Sabeto, who was a supporter of Rabuka's 1992–99 Soqosoqo ni Vakavulewa ni Taukei (SVT) administrations and later of Qarase's SDL governments. Tavua's Ratu Ovini Bokini had been a cabinet minister in the SVT government, but was sacked in the mid-1990s after he was charged with several offences relating to official bribery, including complicity in the National Bank of Fiji fraud case.[25] This also contributed to the diminishing respect he commanded within the anyway large and fractious Tavua area. Saunaka landowners have also fallen out over the Westfield City development near the airport. A long-running dispute over the Tui Nadi title stems from an incident many decades ago when the title was rightfully to have passed to a small child, but was instead given to the uncle from a collateral *i-tokatoka* (sub-clan). Today, the title includes rights to earnings from the Denarau development, believed to amount to more than a million Fiji dollars a year. The Native Lands Commission clearly established the genuine title-holder, but local political allegiances were more uncertain. While the dispute remains unresolved, royalties and rental incomes are frozen, and held by the NLTB on behalf of the rightful owner. The heads of the two rival *i-tokatoka* invariably support different parties, in the hope of using modern political triumphs to settle these deeper disputes. The continued fractiousness of the sub-clans arising from support for rival candidates for the Nadi title often spills into backing for different political parties or candidates.

Intra-Fijian conflicts are also reinforced by chiefly linkages with the big Indian companies that operate in Ba Province, which themselves have internecine squabbles that at times curiously resemble those among Fijian landowners. Top Gujarati executives are sometimes humorously called 'Guja-ratus', appending the Fijian honorific 'ratu'. These companies have benefited from the affirmative action programs of the post-1987 coup era, cashing in by way of joint ventures with nouveau riche Fijians. Many of them originated from Ba town.[26]

Saunaka landowners have a joint venture with Motibhai Co. Ltd., responsible for the Prouds duty-free store at Nadi Airport. Executive chairman Mahendra Motibhai Patel is close to the Qarase government, and doubles as the chairman of Post Fiji. Motibhai Co. Ltd also had close relations with the Mara and Rabuka governments, which for many years enabled the company to secure important commercial concessions. The Tappoo Group of Companies is the other major duty-free chain at Nadi Airport, although it has been less favoured by Fijian governments. Rumours circulating within the business community alleged that Tappoo had given $50,000 to the FLP for the 2001 election campaign.

Business rivalries amongst leading Gujarati firms are often sparked or reinforced by expansion into each other's traditional areas. The wholesale distributor and flour manufacturing firm, Punjas, is opposed to Tappoo because of the latter's diversification from retail of luxury goods into foodstuffs and spices, traditionally the specialities of Punjas. Closest to the BPHCL is the hardware retail giant Vinod Patel; the two have a joint venture called Bavin Ltd. Vinod Patel managing director is Bachubhai Patel, another close associate of Prime Minister Qarase. Company chair Vinod Patel was mayor of Ba town and then stood successfully for the National Federation Party (NFP) in 1992 and 1994. Because of their stiff competition in the hardware market, R.C. Manubhai, yet another Ba-originated firm, is a great rival to Vinod Patel, and the two often engage in behind-the-scenes backbiting ('*kuch kuch*').

For many, but not all, of these Indian business leaders, the Chaudhry government's socialist policies and the threat of tax probes encouraged alliances with the Fijian opposition. Chaudhry himself, and the Fiji Military Forces' Lieutenant-Colonel Viliame Seruvakula, went so far as to allege that some Indian business leaders had been involved in backing the coup in May 2000.[27] Yet, Chaudhry also had friends in high business circles, which were in part a legacy of the alliance he forged with President Ratu Mara at the time of his 1999 election victory – such friends included, for example, Mahendra Patel, RC Manubhai and other non-Gujarati figures such as Rajendra Prasad.[28] Most of the big Gujarati firms played it safe in 2006 by giving tacit support to both sides. There were also claims that the FLP was proactively seeking the support of Gujarati businessmen in the lead-up to the 2006 general election. When the FLP launched its campaign for the 2006 election in Ba, Vinod Patel, despite his long association with the NFP, was one of the chief guests.

Although links with the Indian companies have grown in commercial importance over recent decades, the dynamics of western Viti Levu-based indigenous party formation have centred primarily on rivalries amongst the Fijians themselves.

Prior to the 1999 general election, with the support of the Ba Provincial Council, a group of prominent western politicians who were dissatisfied with the Rabuka-led SVT government, formed PANU. The SVT had convincingly won all three communal seats in Ba Province during the 1994 election.[29] In 1995, Prime Minister Rabuka had embarked on a constitutional review in cooperation with NFP leader Jai Ram Reddy. When PANU was formed, a major element of its case against the SVT was that it had 'sold out the Fijians' by passing the 1997 Constitutional Amendment Act.[30] Ba politicians believed that, by establishing a new party, they might emerge victorious in the province's 18 seats, thus effectively controlling 25 per cent of the House of Representatives. Sabeto chief Apisai Tora played an important role in the party's formation, and became the PANU general secretary.[31] Another major player was Ratu Sairusi Nagagavoka, the Tui Ba (Bulu) and one of the largest landowners in the province. The Vice President and Tui Vuda, Ratu Josefa Iloilo, was appointed patron of the party.[32] The SVT strongly challenged this appointment, arguing that, as stipulated in the constitution, the Office of the President is a 'Symbol of Unity of the Nation', and should not therefore be identified with any political party. As a result, Ratu Josefa Iloilo resigned from PANU.

In the lead-up to the 1999 elections, PANU at first courted a coalition arrangement with the SVT, but eventually signed a memorandum of understanding with the FLP. This was an odd coalition as the Labour Party had been critical of the NFP's close relationship with the Rabuka-led SVT Government, labelling it a 'sell out'. Parties from different ends of the political spectrum were rallying together against those which had reached a cooperative arrangement at the centre of Fiji politics. Cracks soon appeared in the marriage between the FLP and PANU. Part of the agreement between the two had been to avoid fielding parallel candidates in certain constituencies. After the FLP stood Pradhman Raniga against Apisai Tora for the Nadi Open constituency, antagonism emerged between the Sabeto politician and Mahendra Chaudhry. A year after the election, Tora was one of the leaders of the revived *taukei* movement of ethnic nationalist Fijians that marched through the streets of Suva while George Speight seized control of Fiji's parliament.

Tora's newfound antipathy to Chaudhry and the FLP after the May 1999 election led to a realignment within the board of the BPHCL. At the time,

Table 17.1   Western Fijian parties' shares of the first preference Fijian communal vote in target constituencies, 1999–2006 (per cent)

	1999	2001		2006
	PANU	PANU	BKV	PANU
Ba East Fijian Communal	52.5	25.3	19.8	31.6
Ba West Fijian Communal	49.2	14.8	36.2	7.8
Northwest Urban Fijian Communal	43.1	3.9	13.1	–
Ra Fijian Communal	31.7	11.3	6.4	–
Total Fijian Communal	9.6	2.9	4.7	2.0
Total Open constituencies	3.9	0.8	1.3	0.5

Notes: PANU = Party of National Unity; BKV = Bai Kei Viti.
Source: Basic data from the database of the Pacific Institute for Advanced Studies in Development and Governance, University of the South Pacific, Suva.

the company was run by SVT minister Isimeli Bose. Tora had previously been highly critical of the running of the company. Together with PANU president Ratu Sairusi Nagagavoka, he had filed a writ in the High Court against the company and Bose. Yet, in the wake of the election-related fall-out with Chaudhry, Tora's relationship with the BPHCL management improved, while his relationship with Ratu Sairusi soured. The Bulu chief remained loyal to Mahendra Chaudhry. In one of the BPHCL debates in the wake of the 1999 general election, he described Chaudhry as 'Kai Ba', adding that this was the first time that Bulu had a direct line to a prime minister.

PANU obtained four Fijian communal seats at the 1999 election. In addition to the two Ba seats, Eloni Goneyali took the Ra Fijian seat and Akanisi Koroitamana took the Northwest Fijian urban seat. The two Ba MPs entered the People's Coalition cabinet. Meli Bogileka, from Yasawa Island, served as the Minister for Civil Aviation; Ponipate Lesavua, a native of Nawaka Village in Nadi and a former policeman, became Minister for Youth and Sports. Like the FLP, PANU was assisted by advisors from the Australian Labor Party at the 1999 polls.

Land issues were always going to be difficult for the new Labour-led government, and were of particular importance for the NLTB rent-dependent chiefs in this sugar-rich province. Prior to the polls, Ba landowners had issued a report rejecting renewal of land leases under the 1976 Agricultural Landlord and Tenants Act.[33] Prime Minister Chaudhry, who also led the National Farmers Union, hoped for renewal of that legislation, and, failing that, needed land for resettlement of evicted Indian farmers. He sought to purchase land in the Qara region from close ally Ratu Sairusi Nagagavoka. The Tui Ba (Nailaga), Adi Senimili Cagilaba, challenged the sale, claiming the land belonged to her. The Ministry of Agriculture found in her favour. This renewed the long-running dispute between the Nailaga and Bulu chiefs, with Adi Cagilaba emerging as a vociferous critic of the Chandhry government.[34] While in office, Chaudhry built a substantial *bure* for Ratu Sairusi at Sorokoba, clearly hoping to thereby cement that politically important alliance.

When PANU ministers toured the west seeking to forestall the threat posed by the revived *taukei* movement to the Chaudhry government, the two chiefs who opposed them were Tui Sabeto Ratu Kailova Mataitoga and Marama Tui Ba (Nailaga) Adi Senimili Cagilaba.[35]

The 2000 coup further exacerbated frictions amongst the Fijian chiefs in Ba Province, in ways that remained evident at the 2001 polls. Ratu Sairusi and the PANU ministers continued to support deposed Prime Minister Chaudhry, and threatened the formation of a breakaway state in western Viti Levu. A two-day meeting of western chiefs at the Mocambo Hotel that ended on 8 June 2000 appeared to have opted for the more moderate course of establishing a new confederacy. The day after the end of the Mocambo meeting, a delegation of western chiefs and politicians, including Vice President Ratu Josefa Iloilo, visited Speight's stronghold in parliament. *Taukei* leader Apisai Tora hugged Speight in a ceremony of mutual reconciliation that included Nadroga chief Ratu Osea Gavidi. Speight had held the chairs of both Fiji Pine and the Fiji Hardwood Corporation, but he had been sacked by the People's Coalition government. Ratu Gavidi also had interests in timber exports.[36] From that point onwards, Speight and his group forged a new alliance with western chiefs, calling on the military to pass a decree appointing Tui Vuda Ratu Josefa Iloilo president.[37] This was a call that later drew Sabeto landowners to set up one of the many roadblocks around Viti Levu in early July 2000, a disturbance for which Apisai Tora was later convicted.

Tora entered the post-coup interim cabinet, and became Minister of Agriculture. Instead of joining the SDL in July 2001, however, he formed a new western Viti Levu-based party, the Bai Kei Viti, to challenge PANU in the latter's core Fijian communal constituencies (Ba West, Ba East, Ra and Northwest Fijian Urban). Both of these parties put the other as last preference, ensuring a mutual destruction of the two contending western-based parties. In both of the Ba Fijian communal constituencies, the SDL candidate leapfrogged from second place at the first count to win on the basis of transfers from one or other of the western parties.[38]

In the polarized post-coup circumstances, PANU's alliance with the FLP government took its toll. Ponipate Lesavua's first preference vote in Ba East fell from 52.5 per cent in 1999 to 25.3 per cent in 2001, while Meli Bogileka's vote in Ba West plummeted from 49.2 per cent in 1999 to 13.5 per cent in 2001. The Qarase government's triumph at the 2001 polls proved a disaster for both Ba-based parties. Ba Province no longer had any representation in the post-election SDL cabinet, although the SDL victor in Ba West, Tomasi Sauqaqa, became Assistant Minister for Health. Tora received a seat in the Senate as one of the Prime Minister's nominees; PANU's Ponipate Lesavua received an FLP seat in the Senate; and the Tui Nawaka, Ratu Apisai Naevo, was one of the Great Council of Chiefs' nominees to the Senate. Tavua chief Ratu Ovini Bokini also became chairman of the Great Council of Chiefs in July 2004. Although these were powerful positions, Ba politicians were no longer in core positions in government. In Ratu Mara's cabinets, there had always been ministers from Ba Province, and politicians from the west had also been strongly represented in the cabinets of Rabuka and Chaudhry.

Both PANU and the BKV were merely electoral vehicles, whose survival rested in part on the blessing and financial sponsorship of the Ba Provincial Council. In the wake of the 2001 election, Meli Bogileka broke away from PANU and formed a new People's National Party (PNP). In October 2004, efforts were made through the Ba Provincial Council to merge the BKV and PANU under the new PNP banner, but these met with resistance. Both PANU and the BKV had received loans from the Ba Provincial Council for their election campaigns, which had not been repaid. The PNP's latest request, backed by some who had also figured as executives in the BKV and PANU, was seen as use of a party front as a cash-raising mechanism. Some walked out of the meeting, not wanting to hear the PNP presentation. Ratu Ovini Bokini announced that the council would

Table 17.2   Election results in Ba Fiji Provincial Communal constituencies in 2006

	Party	Votes	Per cent
Ba East Fijian Provincial			
Paulo Ralulu	SDL	5,528	60.4
Apimeleki Nabaro	NFP	732	8.0
Ponipate Lesavua	PANU	2,888	31.6
Informal		1,067	10.4
Total registered		11,836	
Ba West Fijian Provincial			
Pauliasi Namua	NFP	257	2.2
Ratu Meli Q Saukuru	SDL	9,211	80.0
Taniela Wai	FLP	1,156	10.0
Meli Bogileka	PANU	883	7.7
Informal		1,143	9.0
Total registered		15,348	

remain apolitical, and that people had a right to choose whatever political party they wanted.[39] In the midst of the multiparty cabinet disputes in the law courts, which kept the polarization witnessed at the 2001 poll to the forefront of Fiji politics, PANU announced its own liquidation. Bogileka's PNP joined the 'Grand Coalition of Fijian Parties', spearheaded by former speaker Tomasi Vakatora.[40] By contrast, Ponipate Lesavua, because he was an FLP nominee to the Senate, inevitably retained stronger links with the FLP leader.

Shortly before the 2006 poll, PANU was revived, again bringing together Ponipate Lesavua and Meli Bogileki as party leaders.[41] Apisai Tora had retired from active politics, an event which also brought an end to the Bai Kei Viti, his brainchild for the 2001 election. PANU emerged again as a close ally of the FLP, with these two parties exchanging second preference votes.

Unlike in 2001, the SDL was able to take both of the Ba Fijian communal seats at the first count in 2006. In Ba West, Ratu Meli Saukuru, whose traditional title is the Taukei Navo, secured 9,211 votes, while PANU's Meli Bogileka obtained only 883 votes. Ratu Meli, *yavusa* head from the village of Dratabu in Nadi, acquired prominence owing to his achievements within the Methodist Church and as a businessman. He is a lay preacher and former vice president of the Methodist Church. He rose to prominence through the successful organization of the Methodist conference in Nadi in 2005, when he was chosen to head the church's investment company. He later accepted instead the SDL nomination in response to entreaties from within the church. Bogileka's support would have come from his home island of Yasawa, and perhaps also Vuda, but the Tui Sabeto was behind the SDL. The SDL must have also secured the bulk of the Nadi and Vitogo vote.[42] Here, as throughout Fiji, the backing of the Methodist Church exerted a powerful influence on Fijian voting patterns.

In Ba East, the SDL faced a sterner challenge, but Paulo Ralulu, from Natunuku (Bulu Tikina), nevertheless easily won with 60 per cent of the first preference vote, defeating PANU's Ponipate Lesavua, who managed only 31.6 per cent of the vote.[43] PANU would have received support from Ratu Sairusi Nagagavoka's area, including the village of Sorokoba and parts of the surrounding Bulu *tikina,* and perhaps from dissident areas in Tavua and from parts of Lesavua's home region of Nawaka. But even in his home region of Nawaka, the pro-SDL influence of the Tui Nawaka must have lost Lesavua votes.

He also would have had negligible support in Nailaga, where retired nurse Adi Laite Kotoiwasa had succeeded her sister as Tui Ba (Nailaga), and staunchly backed the SDL. The Tui Tavua was behind the SDL, although that was a mixed blessing. In the Tavua by-election of January 2004, the SDL had fielded Ratu Ovini's son, Inoke Bokini. He was a human resources manager at Emperor Gold Mines at Vatukoula, a position that earned him some unpopularity amongst the Emperor employees and their family members that was reflected in the by-election outcome. He obtained only 28 per cent of the vote in a 45 per cent indigenous Fijian constituency.[44] Ratu Ovini Bokini is nevertheless an important linkage for the SDL in the province. His mother is from the island of Bau, giving him *vasu* relations with that politically important island, and his wife is from the Prime Minister's island of Vanuabalavu in the Lau group.

Support for Labour and its allies had once been strong in interior *tikinas* like Magodro, where, in the 1980s, left-wing University of the South Pacific lecturer Simione Durutalo rallied many villagers in opposition to the SVT party supported by his father, the Tui Magodro.[45] Durutalo's support had come largely from his mother's people, descended from the earlier *taukei* inhabitants who were related to the nearby Navosa peoples, whereas his father's family came from a line of conquering chiefs, related to the Tui Tavua and the Tui Ba (Nailaga).[46] By the time of the 2006 election, both father and son had passed away, and the father's elder son had assumed the title. Most in Bukuya, the key Magodro village and *tikina* government station, backed the SDL in 2006, as did those in the surrounding villages. The former remoteness of the interior *tikinas* has been diminished by links with resettled interior peoples in coastal districts, which act as conduits for intermittent migration and, by and large, for the consolidation of support behind mainstream Fijian political parties.

The SDL's second triumph in western Viti Levu in 2006 signaled a watershed in Ba provincial politics.[47] Not for the first time, the objective of a distinct western Fijian alliance with the big Indian-backed parties had been frustrated. As Nicholas Thomas found in 1990, internal divisions amongst western political leaders and cultural connections with other parts of the Fiji group mean that 'the thesis of a persistent east-west divide cannot be sustained in any strong form'.[48] Sixteen years later, new factors influenced political organization in the west. In particular, the development of the tourism industry and affirmative action programs had encouraged the emergence of a growing western indigenous élite, with strong connections with Gujarati big business. On balance, these ventures have tended to exacerbate, rather than soothe, rivalries among the coastal chiefs, which now play a greater political role than do dissident movements from the interior. That so much of the country's economic activity and foreign exchange earnings stem from the west probably enhances the potential for the emergence of western Viti Levu-based political organizations. Whether these will prove any more successful than their predecessors or whether the SDL will consolidate support in the west by giving this part of the country a greater stake in cabinet, remains to be seen.

Notes

[1]   The Western Democratic Party and Fijian National Party in the 1960s, the 1980s Western United Front, the early 1990s All-National Congress and the later 1990s Party of National Unity.

[2]   This chapter focuses on the post-1999 experience. For accounts of the earlier parties, see Alley, R.M. 1973. The Development of Political Parties in Fiji, PhD thesis, Victoria University of Wellington, Wellington; Norton, R. 1990. *Race and Politics in Fiji*, University of Queensland Press, Brisbane, 2nd edition, p.110; Lal, B.V. 1983. 'The Fiji general election of 1982; the tidal wave that never came', *Journal of Pacific History*, 18(1–2):139–44; Durutalo, A. 2006. 'Fiji: party politics in the post-independence period', in R. Rich, L. Hambly & M. Morgan (eds) *Political Parties in the Pacific Islands*, Pandanus Books, Canberra, pp.165–83.

[3]   Drawing on oral evidence, Durutalo suggests that efforts by Bau chiefs to subjugate the interior peoples in western Viti Levu commenced as early as 1815–20 (Durutalo, S. 1985. Internal colonialism and unequal regional development : the case of western Viti Levu, M.A. thesis, University of the South Pacific, Suva, p.87. See also Sahlins, M. 2004. *Apologies to Thucydides; Understanding History as Culture and Vice Versa*, University of Chicago Press, Chicago & London, pp.50–52).

[4]   Tanner, A. 1996. 'Colo Navosa local history and the construction of the region in the western interior of Vitilevu, Fiji', *Oceania*, 66(3):231–2.

[5]   Derrick, A. 1946. *History of Fiji*, Government Press, Fiji, [1974 reprint].

[6]   Routledge, D. 1985. *Matanitu, The Struggle for Power in Early Fiji*, Institute of Pacific Studies, University of the South Pacific, Suva, pp.154, 176.

[7]   Colo North or Colo Nadarivatu included the Tavua, Qaliyalatina and Savatu *tikinas* in present-day Ba Province (see Brewster, A.B. 1922. *The Hill Tribes of Fiji*, Seeley, Service & Co Ltd, pp.284–5; *Fiji Royal Gazette*, 57, 19 December 1892).

[8]   Kaplan, M. 1990. 'Meaning, agency and colonial history: Navosavakadua and the *Tuka* movement in Fiji', *American Ethnologist*, 17(1):3–22; Tanner, 'Colo Navosa', p.245. The internal quote comes from the government agriculturalist W.L. Parham, cited in Tanner, 'Colo Navosa', p.246. The *Tuka* rebellions, led by Navosavakadua, spread across many parts of the Tavua-Rakiraki coast, as well as inland, and to many parts of Colo North (Robert Nicole, pers. comm. September 2006).

[9] MacNaught, T. 1982. *The Fijian Colonial Experience: A Study of the Neo Traditional Order under British Colonial Rule prior to World War II*, Pacific Research Monograph, 7, ANU, Canberra, p.4.

[10] Derrick, *History of Fiji*, p.218n; Scarr, 1984. *Fiji: A Short History*, George Allen & Unwin, Sydney & London, p.75.

[11] *Royal Fiji Gazette*, 10, 20 February 1945. Three tikinas in Colo North, Tavua, Qaliyalatina and Savatu, became part of Ba Province. In addition, Naloto and Magodro were separated from Colo West to become part of the new Ba province, while the rest of Colo West joined Nadroga/Navosa.

[12] Kaplan, M. 1995. *Neither Cargo nor Cult: Ritual Politics and the Colonial Imagination in Fiji*, Duke University Press, p.120.

[13] MacNaught. *The Fijian Colonial Experience*, p.78.

[14] The Western Democratic Party joined forces with the Fijian National Party to form the National Democratic Party ahead of the 1966 polls, and together these joined A.D. Patel's Federation Party in 1967–68 to form the National Federation Party (Robert Norton, pers. comm. September 2006).

[15] Durutalo, S. 1985. Internal colonialism and unequal regional development: the case of western Viti Levu, Fiji, MA thesis, University of the South Pacific, Suva; Robertson, R. & Tamanisau, A. 1988. *Fiji: Shattered Coups*, Pluto Press, Sydney, p.17; but see Thomas, N. 1990. 'Regional politics, ethnicity and custom in Fiji', *The Contemporary Pacific*, 2(1).

[16] Parliament of Fiji, Bureau of Statistics, *1996 Fiji Census of Population and Housing*, General tables, Parliamentary Paper No. 43 of 1998, table 31.

[17] Ba, Tavua, Magodro, Yasawa/Nawaka, Nadi, Vuda, Lautoka City.

[18] Routledge, *Matanitu*, p.154; Derrick, *History of Fiji*, p.9n.

[19] Personal communication with Tikina Council representatives, Lautoka, August, 2006. Thanks to Paul Geraghty for assistance in conveying this in the Tavua dialect.

[20] The going rate usually entails start-up payments of F$500 and ongoing rentals of F$150 per annum for quarter acre sites.

[21] Tikina representatives from Yasawas, Lautoka, pers. comm. August, 2006.

[22] The late Tui Vuda Ratu Sir Josaia Tavaiqia had asked the Yasawans who were responsible for the establishment of Asayawa Holdings to concentrate first on a provincial company, hence the incorporation of BPHCL.

[23] For the respective locations of Bulu and Nailaga, see Map 17.1. According to Adi Senimili Cagilaba, Tui Ba (Nailaga), the Bulu chiefs had historically used the title Tui Momo, but Ratu Sairusi's grandfather had obtained the Tui Ba title during Ratu Sukuna's years at the helm of the Fijian administration (*The Fiji Times* 4 January 2000; see Routledge. *Matanitu*, p.154; Scarr. Fiji: *A Short History*, p.62).

[24] Routledge. *Matanitu*, pp.154, 176.

[25] Pacific Media Watch/Pasifik Nius/Niuswire, 14 January 1999; PacNews 11 November 1997.

[26] See Keith-Reid, R. 1992. 'The little town that's big in millionaires', *Islands Business Pacific*, 18(2); 'Giving Ba a fair go', *The Review*, April 1994.

[27] *The Fiji Times* 24 April 2001; *Fiji Daily Post*, 20 June 2001.

[28] We are indebted to Biman Prasad for highlighting this point.

[29] Under the 1990 constitution, a block voting system was used in some Fijian communal constituencies, whereby eligible citizens had three votes for three MPs. In the case of larger provinces, like Ba, there were three such seats.

[30] Despite this, the Ba Provincial Council was one of the few Fijian provinces to support the 1997 constitution.

[31] Apisai Tora had previously opposed Rabuka's selection by the Great Council of Chiefs as SVT leader, and he founded the All-National Congress to oppose the SVT at the 1992 and 1994 polls.

[32] Ratu Josefa Iloilo grew up on Taveuni, and does not speak the Vuda dialect. This made his chairmanship of the Ba Provincial Council difficult, and made it easier for Apisai Tora to engineer the formation of PANU in 1998–99.

[33] See the report of the findings in Parliament of Fiji, Parliamentary Paper No 4. of 1998, ALTA Task Force, Final Report, volume 2, pp.50–64.

[34] Both Adi Senimili and Ratu Sairusi, as well as Ratu Kaliova Mataitoga, were Ba Provincial Council nominees on the Great Council of Chiefs. That they voted in different ways on issues such as the controversy over the renewal of the Agricultural Landlords and Tenants Act was, according to Adi Senimili, embarrassing for the *Yasana* of Ba (Personal communication between Apolosi Bose and Adi Senimili Cagilaba in 2002 at the Elixir Motel, Suva).

[35] *Fiji Daily Post*, 19 April 2000.

[36] See Wise, M. 'Unravelling a Web of Intrigue', *The Fiji Times*, 11 June 2000; Wilkinson, M. 'Mahogany Row', *Sydney Morning Herald*, 27 May 2000.

[37] See Speight's nine-point proposal, published in *The Fiji Times*, 15 June 2000; see Fraenkel, J. 2000. 'The clash of dynasties and the rise of demagogues; Fiji's Tauri Vakaukauwa of May 2000', *Journal of Pacific History* 3(3).

[38] In Ba East, the SDL's Epeli Seavula won at the fourth count with the margin of victory provided by BKV preferences. In Ba West, the SDL's Tomasi Sauqaqa won at the sixth count on the basis of PANU preferences.

[39] Ba Provincial Council meeting, 26 October 2004; see also the reiteration of the stance by Roko Tui Ba Viliame Burenivalu in March 2006 (*The Fiji Times,* 3 March 2006).

[40] 'Five Fijian parties United', *The Fiji Times*, 15 August 2005.

[41] *Fiji Sun*, 5 March 2006.

[42] Local-level results, at the village or polling station-level are impossible to establish under Fiji's new vote-counting system, since all ballots are cast into a 'common bin' before being counted.

[43] In both constituencies, the FLP in fact received more first preference votes than PANU. This was only obvious in Ba West, where the FLP's Taniela Wai obtained 10 per cent. What the official figures do not show, however, is that more than half of Lesavua's votes were above-the-line votes for the FLP. Since the FLP had no candidate, and since the FLP had listed Lesavua as their first preference, these 1,565 votes were transferred directly to Lesavua (data obtained from Master Tally Collection Sheet 0-39, Ba East Fijian, provided by Fiji Elections Office).

[44] House of Representatives By-Elections, 2004, Returning Officers Report, Constituency of Tavua, 17 January 2004, *Fiji Government Gazette*, 6 February 2004.

[45] Under the SVT government, a mini-hydroelectric power station had been built near to Bukuya, supplying power to the village, and later developments – including the government's promised increase in family welfare payments – consolidated support behind the SDL.

[46] Alumita Durutalo, pers. comm. 5 October 2006.

[47] After failing to secure an FLP Senate nomination, PANU announced the end of its coalition with the FLP. Adi Ma Lutuciri, from the chiefly family of Saunaka village, was made vice president of the SDL at the party's post-election annual general meeting in September 2006.

[48] Thomas, N. 1990. 'Regional politics, ethnicity and custom in Fiji', *The Contemporary Pacific*, 2(1):42.

18

The 'Generals' – where to now?

The Yellow Bucket Team[1]

The 2006 election resulted in fundamental change for the General voter[2] community in Fiji. For the first time, the 'Generals' party, the United Peoples Party (UPP) – with two of the three general communal seats – found itself forming the opposition. This was not entirely unfamiliar territory for party leader Mick Beddoes, as he had played the role of leader of the opposition for the opening period of the previous parliamentary session. However, on that occasion he was a party of one (albeit with support from New Labour Unity Party (NLUP) member Ofa Swann), the remaining general communal representatives – NLUP/ Independent Ken Zinck and the Soqosoqo ni Duavata ni Lewenivanua's (SDL's) David Christopher – having joined the government.

The 'Generals' as opposition represents a huge shift from the traditions of General voter politics. It gave rise to spirited debate in the letters to the editor columns[3] about the betrayal of indigenous Fijians by their *vasu* (part-European) relatives, is the cause of some concern, particularly amongst the older members of the part-European community.

The UPP is the latest in a succession of General voter parties that trace their origins back to the General Electors Association (GEA) established pre-independence. Led by figures like Charles Stinson, Doug Brown, Bill Clarke and Ted Beddoes, it stood in partnership with Ratu Sir Kamisese Mara's Fijian Association as part of the Alliance Party, and some of its members occupied prominent cabinet positions. Mick Beddoes himself, as a young and enthusiastic party organizer, played a role in those early elections, and often fondly reminisces about those post-independence days. Sitting now in opposition, having fought an election in coalition with the Indo-Fijian-dominated FLP, those Alliance days of power must seem a long way off.

But first, who are the Generals? The answer is complex, as they represent a mixture of all the 'others' – that is, anyone who can't be classified as Fijian, Indian or Rotuman. While most in this community fall under the very broad category of part-European, or *kai loma,* they share the title with Europeans (usually more recently settled in Fiji), Chinese, Banabans, Koreans, Melanesian descendants of Solomon Island 'blackbird indentured labourers', Samoan and Tongan communities and other smaller communities. To add to the confusion, Fiji's various constitutions have added to and subtracted from the communal roll. Pre-1987, the Rotumans were 'Generals'. Under the 1990 constitution, they were given their own seat (although many Rotumans remain unsure where to register!). Similarly, the Melanesian community was formerly regarded as Fijian, but then moved to the General roll.

As a result, the Generals are notoriously difficult to typecast. Attitudes and voting behaviour can vary dramatically within an individual community. To complicate matters further, the three General communal electorates are quite distinct in their make-up and require individual analysis. It also appears that the number of voters on the General communal roll is in decline, possibly due to migration, but also to official confusion about the exact racial origin of a person. Such factors have led to potential Generals being registered on the Fijian roll – sometimes by request, but often as a result of mistakes by registration officials.

In recent years, in contrast to the early success of the GEA and, in the early 1990s, the General Voters Party (GVP), unifying the 'Generals' has proved difficult. There have been numerous splits – a history of which could be a chapter on its own – resulting finally in the formation of the United Generals Party (subsequently, the UPP) under Mick Beddoes' leadership. This last name change was part of an ambitious attempt to capture the middle ground of Fiji politics.

Up until the mid-1990s, General politics, beyond internal personal rivalries, shared a common philosophy. With tiny numbers, the only way the Generals could play a significant role in politics was to unite and align themselves with the dominant Fijian party of the time. However, despite all the talk of *vasu*, equally important was a belief that it was vital to stand independent and separate from the Fijians and Fijian politics. This fierce *kai loma* sense of racial/cultural pride has its roots in colonial segregation, and it contrasts with views held, for example, by the Banaban, Melanesian or other communities, which appear more comfortable voting with a Fijian party like the SDL. This drive to stand apart from the Fijians surfaced with the rise of Sitiveni Rabuka and the rise of Fijian nationalism.

Analysis of General politics has to take into account the varied views of the individual communities that make up this electorate. To make it even more complex, each of these communities tend to live in geographic pockets around the country – resulting in the three General communal constituencies having quite different dynamics.

Suva City General Communal is the smallest of the constituencies: its registered roll of just 3,515 for the 2006 election was down by 598, or 14.5 per cent, on 2001. Traditionally, the Chinese vote played a key role in this seat, but in the 1997 constitution, the number of General communal seats was reduced from five to three, and Nasinu was included in the Suva City General Communal constituency. This extension, combined with the political apathy of the local Chinese and a general decline in the legal Chinese population, has meant Chinese influence has declined. Nowadays, the constituency is much more varied in its make-up. While still dominated by part-European voters, the electorate has become much more westernized and liberal in its thinking, and has a recent history of being driven by individual qualities rather than by party politics. For example, Suva City General Communal and Suva City Open were the only seats where New Labour Unity Party candidates were successful in the 2001 general election.

The part-European voters of the Suva City General Communal electorate, described by one Fijian nationalist as the 'Eurocentrics', are particularly disturbed by the rise of Fijian nationalism, and of all the electorates Suva City General Communal appears most attracted to the politics of 'moderation' or multiracialism. A number of the more liberal churches, in particular the Catholic Church, have helped promote the moderate philosophy in this electorate. They campaigned vigorously against the perceived erosion of human rights by the nationalists in the Methodist and evangelical churches. Religion reflects much of the difference between the *kai loma* community and their Fijian cousins. The vast majority of *kai loma* are Catholics, Anglicans or members of the more liberal Methodist congregations, like the Wesley Butt Street church in Suva. The Promotion of Reconciliation Tolerance and Unity Bill enraged them, confirming concerns and doubts that they had about the SDL government and, despite SDL's attempts to diffuse the issue, possibly contributing to the first count victory of the UPP's Bernadette Rounds Ganilau.

The resounding defeat of incumbent independent candidate and Minister of Labour Ken Zinck came as a surprise to many observers. It was a comprehensive victory on the first count for Rounds Ganilau who, as a prominent broadcaster, social worker and everyone's favorite mistress of ceremonies, swept to victory despite UPP's coalition with the Labour (FLP) party (more on this later). She was impressive on the campaign trail and, married to Ratu Sir Penaia Ganilau's son, is a reminder of those reassuring times when the four great chiefs, led by Ratu Sir Kamisese Mara, ruled, and Fijian nationalism had yet to surface.

Ken Zinck's strong ties with the SDL, plus his very public and enthusiastic social life (Zinck consistently displayed himself live on local television, ukulele in hand, leading the cheer squad at most of Fiji's international sevens tournaments), was a bit much, particularly for the older section of the electorate. That, combined with strong female support for Rounds Ganilau and respect for the efforts of her leader, delivered the seat to the UPP.

The Western/Central General Communal electorate is the largest in terms of geographic area. It extends from the Tamavua River, including parts of upper Tamavua on the outskirts to Suva, across the western division to Ra. It encompasses a number of quite separate communities, including a large Melanesian group in Delainavesi, and quite separate *kai loma* clans in Lami, Sigatoka, Nadi, Lautoka, Vatukoula and areas stretching to the Tailevu provincial boundary.

Kai loma politics isn't easy to read or understand; it is almost impossible for those born outside the culture to comprehend. The great families operate like mini-dynasties, often controlled by matriarchs who guide the activities of family members from birth to marriage and through all the trials and tribulations of life. Loyalties are fierce and outsiders regarded with deep suspicion. While most clans have connections into the Fijian community, these are typically stronger in the more northern rural communities.

Mick Beddoes is a master at playing *kai loma* family politics. He understands the various genealogical connections that tie these clans back to their various home bases. He worked hard and publicly as a constituency representative, holding regular constituency meetings – usually at the homes of key figures within the community – not only in his own constituency but across the country. His linkage with Labour disturbed some, but he overcame this with his energy, prominence and the strong stand he took against the Fijian nationalist element. Interestingly, however, the SDL did close the gap in this seat by presenting a strong Melanesian candidate. But the candidate was unknown outside his own community and appears not to have won much support beyond the Solomon Islanders.

Finally, there is the North Eastern General Communal constituency that covers Vanua Levu and Taveuni, down to Ovalau, through Tailevu, skirting Suva and stretching down to Kadavu. This was once dominated by Savusavu *kai loma* politicians like Ted Beddoes and Leo Smith, but the inclusion of the Banabans and Kioa islanders in the electorate changed this constituency dramatically – as was seen in 2001 when Banaban David Christopher won for the SDL.

Like the Viti Levu *kai loma*, northern clans' loyalties are strongly held – but, in contrast, they have greater empathy with the Fijian community. It is in these more rural communities that you see the real *vasu* relationship in action. Stories of fair-skinned, part-Europeans riding down from the hills and communicating solely in Fijian are common and reflect a key difference between the northern clans and their Viti Levu cousins. They love their politics, are notorious 'bush lawyers', and fierce rivalries often spring up within the community. However, the reality is that, as long as the Banaban/Kioa vote is united, the *kai loma* of the north have little chance of winning the northern seat. (Another factor in this constituency is the changes that tourism is bringing to Savusavu; many of the old freehold plantations are being sold to foreigners, reducing the power and influence of the old families.)

The Banaban vote is also heavily influenced by the views of the paramount chief, the Tui Cakau Ratu Naiqama Lalabalavu. However, in 2006, the Banaban vote partially split, with two alternative candidates challenging Christopher for the seat and, fatally for Christopher, giving preferences to candidates outside the Banaban/Kioa communities – in particular to the independent, Robin Irwin. Despite holding a good lead on the first count, the SDL incumbent failed to cross the 50 per cent threshold, handing the seat on preferences to Irwin. Irwin is an interesting character; a long time European Savusavu resident, he is a former vet and property developer. By standing and tirelessly campaigning in the last few elections, he built a solid support base; successfully negotiating preference support gave him victory. The UPP failed badly in this constituency, reflecting the very different attitudes held by northerners.

So where to now for the Generals and, more specifically, the UPP? Mick Beddoes has long dreamed of creating a political party capable of grabbing the middle multiracial ground of Fiji politics. He first attempted this in the 1990s with the formation of the All National Congress in partnership with the mercurial Apisai Tora. Its collapse led him to help form the United General Party. His spell as leader of the opposition during the court battles that took place after the 2001 election encouraged him to try again, and he adjusted the name of his party with the promise that they would contest all 71 seats in 2006.

As it turned out, he was only able to field 10 candidates and – squeezed between the FLP and the SDL, both of which moderated their position for the 2006 elections, and facing competition from the National Alliance and the NFP – he failed dismally to win support outside his core General base.

Six months before the general election, Beddoes made a coalition deal with the FLP. It seemed to many observers almost suicidal to commit so early to one of the major players, particularly to the FLP, whose leader, Mahendra Chaudhry, was not particularly popular amongst General voters.

If a week is a long time in politics, six months is an eternity – and so it proved for the UPP. In committing so completely to the FLP, Beddoes relinquished the one key bargaining chip he could bring to Fiji's political table – two of the three General voter's seats. In such a close-fought election this was valuable currency, as independents Robin Irwin and Jioji Konrote found out.

With only two seats – well short of the eight required to demand a position in cabinet – and committed to supporting Chaudhry, who didn't have the numbers to win power anyway, the UPP was the only party shut out of government. This leaves the UPP and the 'Generals' in a difficult position. However, if the FLP were to return to the opposition benches, the UPP would be consigned to a parliamentary 'no man's land' – a far cry from the Generals glory days when figures like Stinson, Clarke, Brown, Falvey, Ted Beddoes and, more recently, Leo Smith and David Pickering held positions of real power.

Demographics will determine the future of Fiji politics. With a rapidly growing Fijian population and declining numbers of Indo-Fijians and others, the UPP and the General voters are in real danger of finding themselves irrelevant in Fiji politics. For the moment it seems unlikely that the UPP can win more than two or three seats. Their only hope is to return to the centre of Fiji politics, where they can hold the balance of power and ensure that the Generals win back their place at the political table.

Notes

[1]   The 'yellow bucket' is a weekly column on Fiji politics and national affairs that can be found on fijivillage.com. Inspiration for the column is found, like many things in Fiji, around a yellow bucket of *yaqona* or kava hence the name. Launched early in 2003, it has gained a reputation for providing astute observation of Fiji politics and its forecasts have proved remarkably accurate in recent years. Authorship of the column is credited to an editorial board that gathers regularly around the yellow bucket.

[2]   General voters are those other than Fijian, Indian or Rotuman voters. Colloquially they are often referred to as 'the generals'. Three of the 46 communal seats in the Fiji parliament are reserved for general voters. Their seats represent the constituencies of Suva City General Communal, North Eastern General Communal and Western/Central General Communal.

[3]   See, for example, 'The Curse of the Kai Loma Vote', *Fiji Daily Post*, 24 February 2006.

19

Elections and nation-building: the long road since 1970

Robbie Robertson

In Fiji it is communalism that has most given distinctive shape to politics and *vice versa*. When Fiji became independent in 1970, its freshly negotiated constitution endorsed a communal basis for voting. This was not surprising given that colonialism had divided the country ethnically, with each community isolated from the other geographically, economically, educationally and socially.[1] Industrial and political forms of organization – often closely related – also assumed ethnic characteristics. Indo-Fijian cane-farmer organizations easily transformed into political parties, the most notable being the Federation Party (formed in 1963) and the shorter-lived Indian Alliance (formed in 1966). Fijian organizations similarly derived in part from the chiefly-led and *vanua*-structured Fijian Association, which, after 1956, lobbied for Fijian interests.

However, social change would always sorely test such neat ethnic demarcations. Indeed, these early political developments can easily be read as attempts to deal with social change: for Fijians the gradual breakdown of communal lifestyles; for Indo-Fijians the need to correct the perceived injustices of colonial practice. But long before colonialism ended, the limitations of communalism had become obvious for those who wished to see them. As urbanization gathered pace and employment patterns changed, new multiracial unions began to form and make their presence felt, the most notable example being the 1959 Fiji oil workers' strike in Suva.

Although the impact of colonial pressures diminished in the 1950s and 1960s, the illogic of communalism continued to affect the operation of political parties. As an independent country, Fiji's prosperity would be tied closely to cooperation between its communities. After all, Fijians would rely on income derived from sugar – then the country's greatest annual source of wealth – to fund the programs that they envisaged would lift Fijian economic performance. Antagonizing Indo-Fijians – the main producers of sugar – could hardly help their cause. Both communities might appear to have had separate goals, but neither could achieve them without the other's support. The zero-sum attitudes fostered during colonialism had the potential to seriously erode nation-building efforts; certainly they hindered the evolution of at least one aspect of nation-building – national identity.

Interdependence was the new reality and, as the country neared independence, it was reflected in political manoeuvrings: in 1968 the largely Indo-Fijian Federation Party joined forces with the small Fijian National Democrats party, based in the west of Viti Levu, to become the National Federation Party (NFP); and the Fijian Association became the dominant component of the Alliance Party (established in 1966), which itself was made up of the Indian Alliance and the General Electors Association (GEA). (The GEA represented citizens who were neither Fijian nor Indo-Fijian.) The Alliance was more successful than the NFP, capturing 84 per cent of the Fijian vote in 1972, as well as, between 1972 and 1987, 16–24 per cent of the Indo-Fijian vote and nearly 90 per cent of the General vote. In fact, it owed much of its success to this wide appeal, especially among the General voters population, which effectively held the balance of power.

Even the 1970 constitution represented accommodation between the communities. Indo-Fijians had wanted a simple one person/one vote system in single electorates, but accepted the Fijian wish for a communal-based constitution on the understanding that a degree of cross-voting would prepare Fiji for a less communal-based electoral system in the future. That future is yet to arrive, not so much because communalism itself is entrenched, but because the political parties, themselves communal, appear resistant to change. This outcome was not necessarily apparent to the framers of the 1970 constitution, who declared that the Lower House would be made up of 22 representatives of the Fijian community, 22 representatives of the Indo-Fijian community and 8 members representing the remaining voters. Twenty-seven of the 52 seats were communal seats; that is, members of each community voted for their own communal representative, thereby producing 12 Fijian, 12 Indo-Fijian and three General members. In the remaining 25 General Communal constituencies, everyone had three additional votes to elect a suitable Fijian, Indo-Fijian and General elector representative; resulting in 10 Fijian, 10 Indo-Fijian and five General elector representatives, respectively.

This constitutional form of post-colonial accommodation – promoted politically as multiracialism – had two principal weaknesses. First, despite the appearance of multiracial political groupings, the two main parties each remained dominated by a different community. No amount of cross-voting could disguise the constitution's emphasis on communal identification as the basis for political activity. This effectively made intra-communal divisions more politically damaging than inter-communal rivalry because the former threatened the party itself. Second, it held communities hostage to the fortunes of their political parties. To succeed, parties had to demand communal unity. Issues of leadership or governance always took second place. Not surprisingly, the zero-sum logic of political competition soon superseded the cooperative ideal fostered by the post-colonial ideology of multiracialism. Party survival demanded it. Communal unity always came first. Thus, the ideology of multiracialism and the cooperative nation-building it underpinned were undermined by the very structures it promoted.

The weaknesses discussed above are the ones that have most shaped Fiji's politics since independence in 1970, with the coups of 1987 and 2000 being extreme manifestations of the same features, in that they represented extra-legal means for the Fijian governing élite to overcome the effects of communal disunity. However, such reactions failed to acknowledge that the cause of communal disunity did not lie in inter-communal rivalry. The political system only gave that appearance.

Community disunity has largely resulted from two factors. The first has to do with popular expectations that independence would deliver development. In part, as in any country, development would be affected by the quality and organizing skills of the country's leaders. It would also be affected by the strategies for development they pursued, and by the nature of the regional and global environment they confronted. All influenced the access to and availability of resources for meaningful development.

During the 1970s and 1980s, the external environment did provide new opportunities, which Fiji's leaders tapped into. The opportunities were in new timber, clothing and light manufacturing activities, and in the expansion of tourism and sugar production. Clothing and sugar, however, were dependent on preferential access to markets and, in the long term, these industries would suffer both from the global trend towards free trade and from the failure of political leaders to use preferences as the basis for economic diversification. But development would also be frustrated by the growing disjuncture between, first, rural and urban development and, second, state nationalist rhetoric and transnational economic linkages. In the 1970s, the former was the greatest test of communal unity for the Alliance; in the 1980s, the latter. In many respects, it was development that most affected the 1990s. However, the push towards external alliances strengthened, and the local impact of these alliances was offset in part by the suspension of democracy (between 1987 and 1992) and in part by the introduction of the 1990 constitution, which consolidated Fijian political dominance. These offsetting factors did not of themselves address the key development issues facing the country, but they did highlight and make more obvious the key importance of leadership and governance as ingredients of development, thus providing new scope for division within all communal blocs.

The first three decades of independence demonstrated the fundamental weaknesses of communalism as the basis for political organization. Unity in both main communities depended on maintaining the status quo, yet the goal of communal leadership was development, which – whether successful or not – held the potential to destabilize the status quo as a result of the social change it effected. Over time, education alone created tensions; it either further raised expectations or helped expose the failures of leadership. Urbanization had a similar impact, but, in addition, it undermined communal distinctiveness, as more and more people from different communities lived together, worked together and schooled together. These were not rapid processes of change, although urbanization was more rapid in and after the 1990s because of the failure of rural development plans, the negative impact of the coups and poor leadership on economic growth. But the political impact of urbanization tended to be delayed because, initially, it brought together people with little experience of multiracial living, who sought to maintain their communal distinctiveness by way of urban settlements and social/religious associations. At least in the short term, urbanization created as many obstacles to multiracial accommodation as it resolved.

Accordingly, social change – although consistent throughout the first three decades of independence – was neither rapid nor necessarily politically destabilizing. Nonetheless, communal disunity could dramatically change party fortunes, as the Alliance Party first discovered in April 1977 when the dissident Fijian Nationalist Party, riding on the back of rural dissatisfaction with the pace of development, managed to secure 24 per cent of the Fijian vote and destroy the Alliance's majority. Only intra-communal (Muslim–Hindu) rivalries prevented the NFP from claiming a narrow victory and, in the subsequent September poll, the Alliance learned the value of raising the spectre of Indo-Fijian political dominance to offset indigenous Fijian divisions. This hardening of racial polarization increasingly came with notions of Fijian paramountcy – the idea that, as the original indigenous people of Fiji, Fijians possessed an inherent right to political rule. Indeed, by the same logic, they alone were permitted to use the national name to describe themselves. 'Indians' – for some, even use of the descriptor Indo-Fijian became contentious – were portrayed variously as foreigners or as guests ungrateful for the hospitality already given them by Fijians. Although, by the 1980s, transnational corporations, many of them in association with Fijian investment companies, clearly dominated the Fiji economy, Indo-Fijians monopolized very visible sectors, such as cane farming, transport and retail. This enabled Fijian nationalists to characterize their struggle as one against both Indo-Fijian political and Indo-Fijian economic domination. While Fijian nationalists saw their purpose as healing intra-communal division, such political campaigning carried immense dangers for stability and national development.

In many respects, the NFP never recovered from the ruptures of 1977 – although it did manage to give the appearance of recovery in the 1982 election, when it regained much of the ground it had previously lost. It was assisted by a new coalition with a small western Fijian party (the Western United Front, or WUF) that won two seats on the strength of western Viti Levu dissatisfaction with the Alliance's handling of its pine resources. However, economic recession and conflict with trade unions shifted the focus of politics in the 1980s and left the still divided, business-oriented NFP increasingly marginalized. The vacuum was filled in 1985 by a Fiji Trade Union Congress-sponsored Fiji Labour Party (FLP), a multiracial alternative to both the Alliance and NFP, which declared that the handling of issues rather than race should be the crucial determinant of fitness for office. As a worker-based party, it wished to focus on economic and social issues that all communities faced in common, and which it felt the two main parties neglected because of their concentration on communalism. However, in late 1986, in a major change in tactics, the FLP formed a coalition with the NFP. In the following April 1987 election, as a result of increased Fijian support in four Suva open constituencies, where Labour's issues-based strategy had most appeal, this coalition narrowly defeated the Alliance government.

Labour's sudden victory demonstrated the impact social change could have on political outcomes, especially in open seats where margins were potentially tighter. For those who lost, it also demonstrated the inability of communalism as established under the 1970 constitution to maintain Fijian paramountcy. Consequently, in May 1987, the losers re-seized power through a military coup and introduced a completely new dimension to Fiji politics that survives to this day. For, once invited in, the military demonstrated great reluctance to return to the barracks. Although the Governor General, Ratu Sir Penaia Ganilau, succeeded in taking charge of the regime which came to power after the coup, he was powerless to control the military. Indeed, when he and former Alliance prime minister Ratu Sir Kamisese Mara sought to head off economic collapse by seeking accommodation with the ousted FLP, they were deposed in a second coup in September 1987. This time, the army imposed a military government on the country and, in order to forestall legal challenges, declared Fiji a republic. Military commander Sitiveni Rabuka did permit both chiefs to return to their respective positions as president and prime minister at the end of 1987, but, for the next five years, relations between the interim government and the military were strained. Indeed, once a new constitution was promulgated in 1990, Rabuka, to prevent any possibility of future Indo-

Fijian political rule, moved swiftly to seize control of, first, the new political process – gaining leadership of a new Fijian establishment party (the Soqosoqo ni Vakavulewa ni Taukei or SVT) – and then, in 1992, the prime ministership. The SVT signaled the demise of multiracialism. Despite its shortcomings, the Alliance had at least symbolized a coalition of communities. The SVT made no such pretence; it was defiantly a Fijian-only party constructed on the basis of Fijian paramountcy.

The military's role as guardian of national security was enshrined in the new constitution. In addition, the new constitution specifically bestowed immunity from prosecution on all people who had engaged in the coups of 1987. It also strengthened communalism as a bulwark against social change, reserving all senior political and constitutional posts for Fijians, increasing the role of the Great Council of Chiefs, doing away with open seats and the cross-voting they entailed, provincializing Fijian electorates, and penalizing all communities deemed disloyal in 1987, including those of western and urban Fijians. It produced a 70-member lower house made up of 37 Fijians, 27 Indo-Fijians, five General Electors, and one Rotuman. Indo-Fijians no longer enjoyed equality with Fijians, and General Electors lost their once influential balance of power role. Urban Fijians, proportionately entitled to 13 seats, received only five, while provincial seats were disproportionately weighted to favour the eastern provinces of the chiefly establishment.

Ironically, this remaking of communalism failed to achieve one of its main objectives – Fijian reunification. Shorn of its raison d'être – the potential threat of Indo-Fijian dominance – the new Fijian governing party was never able to emulate the Alliance's command of Fijian support. In 1992, it gained 66 per cent of the Fijian vote, well short of the Alliance's 84 per cent in 1972. What the constitution did do, however, was to create a form of political apartheid in which each election resembled two separate elections, one Fijian and one Indo-Fijian, with the former representing a struggle between the governing party and dissident individuals and provinces, and the latter a struggle between two supposedly ideologically opposed (but, in reality, simply differently led in terms of style) parties for the hearts and minds of Indo-Fijians. While the former took government as its prize, the latter had to settle for opposition leadership.

This system ended abruptly with the introduction in 1997 of another new constitution. The SVT's monopolization of power had not prevented political drift and economic decline; if anything, it had contributed to the malaise. Sham democracies that prevent the turnover of government, such as that created by the 1990 constitution, rarely provide a check on the exercise of political power. Perhaps sensing this, Rabuka sought to reinvent himself by forming a partnership across the communal divide with the NFP in order to reduce the most obvious obstacle to national development. But such a partnership represented a (largely unstated) recognition that 1987 had been a mistake and that the country needed to revert to the principles of multiracialism espoused in 1970. However, little was done to prepare Fijians for this transformation in political rhetoric. Rabuka refused to concede explicitly that 1987 had been a mistake, and planned *vanua* consultations on the new changes were never completed.

Nonetheless, the new constitution was promulgated. It introduced a new Lower House of 71 members derived from 46 communal and 25 open seats. Twenty-three of the communal seats were reserved for Fijians, 19 for Indo-Fijians, one for Rotumans and three for General electors. The constitution also foreshadowed Rabuka's planned partnership, by mandating that any party that received more than 10 per cent of the seats (that is, eight seats or more) had the right to share proportionately in cabinet posts. It also introduced a new system of voting – the alternative vote system – that was promoted as more likely to produce multiracial accommodation than the older first-past–the-post system. In practice, however, it didn't; it was to prove every bit as non-accommodating of minority views as its predecessor (see Fraenkel, this volume). Finally, although progressive compared with its predecessors (especially with respect to human rights), the new constitution's electoral provisions still produced large disparities in electorate sizes (particularly among Fijian communal constituencies) and still under-represented urban Fijians.

Nevertheless, the first election under the 1997 constitution, in May 1999, did produce a significantly different result, although more for political than electoral reasons. Uncertainty over the power-sharing provisions of the constitution and widespread dissatisfaction with SVT rule saw the latter's share of Fijian votes plummet to 38 per cent. The SVT's proposed partner, the NFP, suffered a worse fate, winning no seats at all. From this election, a new People's Coalition government emerged, dominated by a now strongly Indo-Fijian FLP, but partnered with very substantial dissident Fijian parties that, together, had garnered about 60 per cent of the Fijian vote.[2] For this reason, perhaps, the FLP did not feel obliged to honour the constitution's power-sharing commitment; when the SVT imposed conditions on its involvement in a multiparty cabinet, the FLP rejected them and excluded the SVT from cabinet.

As in 1987, the upset victory was short-lived. On 19 May 2000, Fijian nationalists and a rebel military unit (originally established by Rabuka to protect his 1987 'revolution') staged a coup that, although ultimately unsuccessful for the coup-leaders, enabled the Fijian establishment to reassert itself and conduct – in 2001 – fresh elections, with a new all-Fijian party (the Soqosoqo Duavata ni Lewenivanua or SDL) that carried none of the baggage of its predecessor. Like the Alliance in the September 1977 election, the SDL employed nationalist rhetoric to heal Fijian divisions and to minimize the impact of another new Fijian party, the Conservative Alliance–Matanitu Vanua (CAMV), which was allied to the 2000 coup plotters. The tactic succeeded, and the new establishment party, the SDL, won 70 per cent of the Fijian vote (if the 20 per cent share of its eventual partner – the CAMV – is included). The FLP similarly consolidated its hold on Indo-Fijian support at the expense of the NFP, with the FLP winning 75 per cent of the Indo-Fijian vote.[3] The result reflected the uncertainties created by the 1999 election and, more particularly, the 2000 coup, and the failure of the alternative vote system to give space to minority voices.

Such polarization also effectively meant that these uncertainties could not be easily resolved. Only inter-communal cooperation could have that impact, and, in the wake of 2000, with each party boxed in with their respective community, there was little possibility of cooperation. Thus, differences over land rentals, which had simmered all through the late 1990s, remained unresolved because of political obstinacy. The SDL went to the polls in 2001 on a platform of affirmative action for Fijians. The FLP opposed this as a form of racial discrimination, and, although differences between the parties were not great, rhetoric alone made a meeting of minds impossible. The SDL refused to entertain power-sharing with the FLP as the constitution mandated, just as the FLP had refused power-sharing with the SVT in 1999. However, unlike the SVT, the FLP rigorously pursued the matter through the courts until 2005, when it finally accepted a role as opposition party. Despite the basic legality of its position, its court action served to reduce possibilities for cooperation further.

In 2005, the SDL introduced a controversial Promotion of Reconciliation, Tolerance and Unity Bill, which Labour dismissed as an attempt to heal divisions within the Fijian community over post-coup investigations and prosecutions. The matter might have remained as yet another symbol of intercommunal division but for the military's defiant stand against the Bill. As a largely Fijian institution, the Republic of Fiji Military Forces had traditionally supported ruling Fijian parties. However, the 2000 coup revealed serious divisions within the military that were dramatically exacerbated in November of that year when the military unit responsible for the 2000 debacle suddenly mutinied. This second failed initiative hardened the military leadership against reconciliation and, during early 2006, its troops were displayed around the capital as a sign of its displeasure with the government, a move that was eerily reminiscent of its behaviour towards the interim government between 1988 and 1992. Prior to the 2006 election, its leadership even hinted at the possibility of a coup if its views were ignored. [See Ratuva, this volume.]

The unconstitutional role of the military was not the only issue of debate after 2000. Increasingly, the rapid decline in the Indo-Fijian population gained greater public recognition.[4] Indeed, nearly one-quarter of the Indo-Fijian population had left Fiji in the two decades after 1987, and that decline had electoral implications, particularly in open seats. In effect, it meant that, in time, Indo-Fijians as a bloc were unlikely ever again to achieve political power in their own right, as they had in 1999. Instead, they would have to return to their roots, and devote more attention to developing a multiracial constituency. This was always one of the goals of power-sharing, and perhaps one reason why, at the conclusion of the 2006 election, both parties saw advantages in the practice that they had previously neglected. Certainly, it provided an opportunity to reduce political heat and effect a more cooperative environment in which to address the many unresolved issues that affected all communities alike.

Whether such power-sharing accommodation will extend to the joint development of Bills to resolve these issues remains to be seen, but at the very least it suggests that, with political will and responsible leadership, a way can be found to overcome the inherent dangers communalism has always inflicted on the nation, and to create the necessary political trust on which to build a more responsive political system for the future. This has been the one undeniable lesson of Fiji's long road since 1970, a lesson Fiji has constantly been forced to confront after each occasion of communal polarization. Then, as now, the behaviour of political parties and their leaders have most determined the success or otherwise of multiracialism, and with it the development prospects of the country.

Notes

[1] From the end of World War II until quite recently, Fijians and Indo-Fijians constituted approximately the same demographic proportion of the community.

[2] The Party of National Unity (PANU) was a Ba-based party with four seats. The Fijian Association Party (FAP), founded in opposition to Rabuka in 1994, won 10 seats. These two parties were in coalition with Labour on the eve of the election. Not so, the Veitokani ni Lewenivanua Vakarisito (VLV), which had been set up as an unofficial Methodist party in opposition to the new constitution, and which demanded both the return of the 1987 'Sunday Ban' and that Fiji be declared a Christian state. Its three members promptly joined the People's Coalition after the election.

[3] This communal polarization behind two large parties would be repeated in 2006, with both parties gaining around 81 per cent of their respective communal votes.

[4] The Indo-Fijian population has fallen rapidly since 1987 and by 2006 is assumed to make up only 37 per cent of Fiji's total population.

20

Indigenous title disputes: what they meant for the 2006 election

Morgan Tuimaleali'ifano

The 2006 poll produced a mixed score-card for Fiji's customary chiefs. On the one hand, finding a place for Fiji's ruling dynasties at the centre of government remained a central concern for the re-elected Qarase government, not only because Fiji's Bose Levu Vakaturaga (Great Council of Chiefs) holds the critical swing votes in the Senate, but also because the newly elected prime minister felt obliged to bring top title-holders from all three of the country's confederacies into the post-election multiparty cabinet in order to guarantee ethnic Fijian support. On the other hand, as is shown in this chapter, chiefs have fared increasingly poorly at the last three elections, indicating a profound social transformation. What is the role of chiefly titles in determining success or failure at modern elections? Are there discernible trends in the performance of customary leaders at the polls?

This chapter explores the influence of chiefly rivalries on modern-day Fiji politics, particularly the performance of chiefs as traditional indigenous leaders at the 1999, 2001 and 2006 polls, and how these influenced the post-election formation of governments.

After more than a century of colonial structures, the hereditary chiefly hierarchy continues to exercise a major influence on the majority of indigenous Fijians and other citizens of Fiji. The colonially instituted Bose Levu Vakaturaga is the highest indigenous political body, comprising representatives of Fiji's hereditary hierarchy. Approximately 7,170 *yavusa* (tribal) and *mataqali* (clan) titleholders are represented in this body.[1] In concert with the Native Land Trust Board, it controls 89–90 per cent of the land (this figure has increased with the return of Schedule A and B Crown lands). Of the 7,170 tribal and clan titles, 25 per cent remain vacant, not through lack of interest, but because of strongly contested clan views that, in former times, could only have been resolved by warfare. At the time of the 2006 election, these title vacancies included some of the highest in the land – for example, the Tui Kaba na Vunivalu of Bau and titular head of Kubuna (vacant since 1989), Na Ratu mai Verata and head of pre-contact Fiji (since 2001), Tui Nadi (covering the Nadi airport), Tui Ba of Nailaga and Tui Navitilevu of Rakiraki (the latter two covering the western cane belt), and the Tui Nayau and the concurrent title of Sau ni Vanua ko Lau, of the Lau group of islands. A successor to the late Roko Tui Dreketi title-holder was installed in early 2005, but the political ramifications of this appointment for the *vanua* and *lotu* (itself an important issue in the electoral contest in Rewa) appear unclear at this stage. These long-standing succession issues are embedded in indigenous Fijian society and frame Fiji's political history; they inform, fuel and shape local perspectives and national disputes.

Customary chiefs in Fiji do not necessarily win at the polls, but social ranking in local hierarchies can prove highly significant to the outcome of the elections. From the 1970s to the 1980s, politics was dominated by the Ratus, particularly the big four, Ratu Sir George Cakobau, Ratu Sir Edward Cakobau, Ratu Sir Kamisese Mara and Ratu Sir Penaia Ganilau. With the exception of Ratu Edward, all held *vanua* and *matanitu* titles. Ratu George held the Tui Kaba na Vunivalu titles of Kubuna, Ratu Penaia the Tui Cakau title of Tovata, Ratu Mara held the Tui Nayau and most senior title of Lau while his wife, Ro Lady Lala Mara, held the Roko Tui Dreketi title and paramountcy of the confederacy of Burebasaga.

In the 2006 election, leader of the National Alliance Party Ratu Epeli Ganilau, was the son of a former Tui Cakau and former president. Ratu Epeli was a candidate for the Tui Cakau title and is married to the daughter of former president Ratu Sir Kamisese Mara, but his party gained not a single seat. In contrast, his rival and successor to the Tui Cakau title, Ratu Naiqama Lalabalavu, who had formed the Conservative Alliance–Matanitu Vanua (CAMV) prior to the 2001 election, was elected and formed a coalition government with Lauan

Prime Minister Qarase's Soqosoqo ni Duavata ni Lewenivanua (SDL) party. As the paramount titleholder of Tovata in the pre-Tui Lau Ma'afu period, an area which covers Qarase's constituency, Lalabalavu was immediately elevated to cabinet and appointed to the all-important land portfolio. During his term in office, he was charged and convicted for inciting a mutiny during the 2000 unrest in the Northern Division. After serving his sentence extramurally at the Nadera Catholic parish, he was reinstated to cabinet though not to the same portfolio. During the lead-up to the 2006 election, Lalabalavu disbanded the CAMV, joined the ruling SDL and was elected under the SDL ticket. In terms of traditional Fijian polities, Lalabalavu's membership of the SDL has considerably strengthened its position in northern Fiji.

Included among the SDL's senior party members are well-placed chiefs. As well as Ratu Naiqama (the Tui Cakau), they include Ratu Suliano Matanitobua (the Tui Namosi) and Ro Teimumu Kepa (recently appointed Roko Tui Dreketi). The Tui Cakau and Roko Tui Dreketi titles are the paramount positions in two of Fiji's three confederacies. The third confederacy, which was unrepresented at the parliamentary level, is Kubuna. The close association among the three ruling families made the absence of a direct representative of the Bau conspicuous in the parliament. This was redressed by nominations to the Senate. Soon after the 2006 election, the Prime Minister decided to appoint a member of the Vunivalu family to cabinet through the Senate. She is Adi Samanunu Cakobau-Talakuli, eldest daughter of the late Vunivalu, and one of the most eligible contenders for her father's title. In this way, it would appear, Qarase has galvanized Fijian support while forming a multiparty cabinet with the Fiji Labour Party (FLP).

How did customary chiefs fare as political candidates in the 2006 elections? From Table 20.1 it can be seen that the number of chiefs standing as political candidates increased by eight between 1999 and 2001, but decreased by 20 in 2006. The number of chiefs elected fell (by five) between 2001 and 1999, but increased (by four) between 2001 and 2006. However, while these figures show a declining number of chiefly candidates between 1999 and 2006, the decline is compensated for by the number of chiefs holding high titles among the elected candidates. In other words, chiefs vested with high titles, such as Tui Cakau and Roko Tui Dreketi, continued to be returned, while the

Table 20.1   Performance of chiefly candidates in parliamentary elections

Election year	No. of candidates standing in 48 constituencies (23+25)	No. of candidates known as customary chiefs	No. of chiefly candidates expressed as per cent of total candidates	No. of elected chiefly candidates	No. of elected chiefly candidates expressed as per cent of total candidates
1999	240	30	12.5	12	5
2001	256	38	15	7	3
2006	247	18	7	11	4

number of electorally successful chiefs with lesser *vanua* titles (or none at all) fell. The reason for the declining number of chiefs in national politics is not because of lack of Fijians' interest in their chiefs, but because of the intense competition among rival candidates for chiefly titles. Many of the title disputes are under investigation by the Native Lands and Fisheries Commission, and decisions on others are undergoing judicial review. Because of the intensity of competition, rival candidates and supporters have agreed to disagree, postpone an appointment and continue the discussion until a consensus has been reached. This was confirmed by a leading member of the *mataqali* Tui Kaba and former speaker of the House, Ratu Epeli Nailatikau: when asked whether the *mataqali* was losing interest in the leading title of Kubuna, he was adamant that there was no loss of interest. 'On the contrary', he said. 'as soon as the election and the Methodist conference are over, we will meet to settle it. It is largely an internal family dispute'.[2]

Limitations in identifying who is and who is not a chief

While some chiefs indicate their *vanua* status by prefacing their candidacy with the *ratu/adi/bulou/ro* style of address, many do not. Many enter the election without chiefly style, but, once they enter parliament, a chiefly style suddenly appears, conferred either by themselves or by someone else. In theory, it should be possible to identify a Fijian chief by the style of address used during the election campaign: *ratu* for men, *adi* and *bulou* for women and *ro* in Rewa for either gender. But identifying who is and who is not a chief at elections is a complicated matter. In this regard, two kinds of chiefs are distinguished: one who inherits a chiefly style by birth, and the other who is a chief by birth and by appointment and installation to one of various offices within the *vanua*. Normally accompanied by ceremony, such offices include *na turaga na mataqali, yavusa, tikina, vanua* or a *matanitu*. Another term signifying a chief is apparent in kin relationship. Between equals, relations are usually conducted on a first-name basis, but between unequals, or those acknowledged as lower position or younger, use of *ratu/adi/bulou/ro* styles of address often punctuates the conversation. Identifying election candidates who are chiefly is particularly difficult in Fijian elections because, unlike Samoa or Tonga, Fiji has electoral regulations that do not distinguish between chiefs and non-chiefs.

Was there a discernible pattern in the number of chiefly candidates and elected chiefly candidates over these past three elections? The following analysis focuses on candidates whose chiefly rank is clearly established.

Chiefs in the 1999 election

In 1999, there were 30 candidates of known chiefly rank out of the 240 candidates from the 48 constituencies in which Fijians can stand (23 Fijian and 25 Open). Of these, 12, or 5 per cent of the 240 candidates, were elected. Among the casualty list were important chiefs of *vanua* and *yavusa/mataqali*, and siblings of *vanua* and *matanitu* chiefs. One *vanua* chief who lost was Ratu Tevita Bolobolo, holder of Na Tuvitilevu title and paramountcy of Ra. His defeat was doubly humiliating because he is a paramount titleholder. Moreover, his defeat was at the hands of Fiji-Indian candidates. In the first count, Ratu Bolobolo lost out to the Fiji Labour Party (FLP) candidate Sanjeet Chand Maharaj, and, when the count went to preferences, he lost to independent candidate George Shiu Raj. Another paramount titleholder who failed to secure a seat was the Na Ka Levu of Nadroga. Contesting the Nadroga Open constituency, Ratu Sakiusa Makutu polled the largest number of votes on the first count. However, he failed to secure a simple majority and, when the count went to preferences, he was beaten by the FLP candidate, a chief of lower rank, Ratu Mosese Volavola. Other casualties included: the children of Fiji's former Governor General and Vunivalu of Bau, Adi Litia Cakobau (Tailevu North/Ovalau Open) and Ratu Epenisa Cakobau (Tailevu South/Lomaiviti Open); the son of a former president and Tui Cakau, Ratu Epeli Gavidi Ganilau; the sister of former president and Tui Nayau, Adi Senimili Tuivanuavou (Lau/Taveuni/Rotuma); and Ratu Kamisese Mara's brother-in-law, Ratu Tu'uakitau Cokanauto (Tailevu North/Ovalau Open).[3]

Of the twelve winning chiefly candidates, nine were in government and three in the Opposition. In government were: Koila Nailatikau-Mara (Veitokani ni Lewenivanua Vakarisito); Esira Rabuno (Fijian Association Party (FAP)); Isimeli Jale Cokanasiga; Isireli Vuibau (FLP); Tu'uakitau Cokanauto (FAP); Tevita Moemoedonu (FLP); Mosese Volavola (FLP); Kuini Vuikaba-Speed (FAP); and Ema Tagicakibau (FAP). In opposition were Kinijoji Maivalili, Inoke Kubuabola, and Naiqama Tawake Lalabalavu.

The opposition had higher-ranking chiefs than the government. One was the head of a *matanitu*, Tovata, and the other two were leading members of leading clans of the leading province within Tovata. Ratu Inoke Kubuabola is a member of the important 'Ai Sokula clan, and Ratu Kinijioji Maivalili is the heir apparent to the Tui Wailevu and Vunivalu titles of Wailevu; both have close ties to the 'Ai Sokula. The Tovata number was strengthened when another Cakaudrove chief from Natewa entered parliament. Former prime minister Sitiveni Rabuka resigned from his Cakaudrove West Open seat, and was replaced by Ratu Rakuita Vakalalabure, contender for the Vunivalu of Natewa title.

While the government side had nine *ratus* and *adis*, and represented all three *matanitus* (Kubuna, Tovata and Burebasaga), they were clearly not of the same ranking. Adi Koila Nailatikau Mara's mother and father covered both Burebasaga and Tovata, and her husband, the former Fiji Military Forces commander, former ambassador to the United Kingdom, roving ambassador to the Pacific region, and former Speaker of the House, covered Kubuna. Adi Kuini Speed was Tui Noikoro, a *vanua* chief in Navosa. Because Navosa had been marginalized due to its resistance to colonial authority, it did not have the same clout as other *vanuas*. Ratu Tu'uakitau Cokanauto is from the Tui Kaba and king-making clan of the Vunivalu of Bau, but he was not from the dominant household, the Mataiwelagi. Similarly, Ratu Tevita Moemoedonu and Ratu Mosese Volavola were not holders of *vanua* titles, and so did not have the same standing as the others within the *vanua* and *matanitu*.

In terms of the Fijian hierarchy's support for the Labour coalition government, only Adi Lady Lala Mara, as the Roko Tui Dreketi, could be counted upon. Her daughter and a collateral cousin (who was also her brother-in-law) were members of the FLP coalition government. The other paramount chief, Tui Cakau, was in opposition, and the leading siblings of the other *matanitu*, Kubuna, from the competing sides of the Mataiwelagi household, each failed to secure a seat.

Chiefs in the 2001 election

In 2001, 38 candidates of known chiefly rank were amongst the 256 candidates that stood in the 48 constituencies (up from 30 candidates in 1999). Out of 38, only seven, or 3 per cent of the total number of candidates, won – considerably down from 1999. The successful chiefly candidates were:

- Ratu Suliano Matanitobua (SDL)
- Ro Teimumu Vuikaba Tuisawau Kepa (SDL)
- Ratu Jone Yavala Kubuabola (SDL)
- Adi Asenaca Caucau (SDL)
- Ratu Naiqama Tawake Lalabalavu (CAMV)
- Ratu Rakuita Saurara Vakalalabure (CAMV)
- Ratu Savenaca Draunidalo (independent – and heir apparent to the Tui Moala title).

The only survivor from the 1999 election was Ratu Lalabalavu, who was then in the opposition; once the two parties joined in coalition, he was given the lands portfolio. Unlike the 1999 election, the 2001 'casualty list' did not include a high number of significant *vanua* or *yavusa* chiefs, or their siblings. The losses included two *vanua* chiefs: Ratu Kinijioji Maivalili, heir apparent to the Tui Wailevu title; and Ratu Aisea Katonivere, the then heir apparent to the Tui Macuata title. The other losses include chiefs of secondary ranking, such as Bauans like Ratu Tu'uakitau Cokanauto, Adi Finau Tabakaucoro and Ratu Timoci Tavanavanua, Rewans like Ro Alipate Doviverata Mataitini, and Cakaudrovens like Ratu Aisake Kubuabola and Adi Ema Tagicakibau, the latter four contesting in constituencies outside areas of their chiefly standing. In doing so, it was commonly observed, many chiefs did not style themselves as *ratus/adis*.

Of the seven chiefly candidates who were elected, four were from SDL, two were CAMV and one was an independent. None belonged to the FLP. The two CAMV chiefs and the independent chief joined the SDL-led coalition government, two in cabinet and one as Deputy Speaker. As for the opposition, the only support they could count on from chiefs came from those in the Great Council of Chiefs and the Senate. But they were very few, the notable one being the Tui Ba-i-Bulu, Ratu Sairusi Nagagavoka, who wielded considerable influence over his Party of National Unity from inside the Great Council of Chiefs.

Chiefs in the 2006 election

In 2006, the total number of candidates that stood for the 48 constituencies was 247. The number of candidates of known chiefly rank that stood for election dropped from 38 in 2001 to just 18. Of those 18, only 11, or just 4 per cent of all the candidates in the 48 constituencies, were elected.

The 11 chiefly candidates that were elected, all SDL members, were Ratu Isikeli Tasere, Ratu Suliano Matanitobua, Ro Teimumu Kepa-Tuisawau, Ratu Meli Saukuru, Ratu Naiqama Lalabalavu, Ratu Jone Y Kubuabola, Ratu Jone Waqairatu, Adi Asenaca Caucau-Filipe, Ratu Josefa Dimuri, Ratu Osea Vakalalabure and Ratu Savenaca Draunidalo.

Candidates of chiefly rank were not conspicuous among the FLP's newly elected Fijian MPs. After the election, a new female member with an impressive majority from the Yasawa Nawaka Open constituency, Adi Sivia Qoro, appeared in the FLP line-up for the multiparty cabinet and was given the commerce portfolio. Adi Sivia is from Naviti island in the Yasawas. Her mother, Adi Titilia, is Tui Marou and she herself is *vasu* to Marou village on Naviti, where she grew up.[4] Overall, though, the overwhelming Fijian support in parliament firmly lies with the SDL government.

How representative is the SDL government of Fijian confederacies? Two *vanua/matanitu* titleholders are included, those of Burebasaga and Tovata through Ro Teimumu Kepa-Tuisawau and Ratu Lalabalavu, respectively. The only other *vanua* chief who stood and was elected was Ratu Suliano Matanitobua, the Tui Namosi, and representing the *vanua* of Serua and Namosi. Nadroga/Navosa is represented through Ratu Isikelu Tasere, Nadi-Ba-Tavua through Ratu Meli Saukuru. In addition to the Tui Cakau, the representation of Tovata is strengthened by Ratu Savenaca Draunidalo (Tui Moala of Yasayasa Moala), Ratu Josefa Dimuri of Bua/Macuata, and Natewan chief Ratu Osea Vakalalabure, and non-resident Cakaudrove chiefs, such as the powerful finance minister, Ratu Jone Yavala Kubuabola. A potential Tovata ally was Ratu Jone Waqairatu, a Lauan from Yaroi in Yasayasa Moala, who stood and was elected to the Tamavua/Laucala Communal constituency.[5] (Ratu Draunidalo is an example of an urbane category of chiefs who consistently spurn being styled a *ratu*; on every occasion that I have met him his outstretched hand has always been accompanied by just '*Bula, Save*'.)

The sole elected chiefly representative from Kubuna was Adi Asenaca Caucau-Filipe. The scarcity of Kubuna's presence in the Lower House and the conspicuous absence of a Cakobau descendant was addressed by a Senate appointment. After the 2001 election, the failure of any of Ratu George Cakobau's children (Adi Litia, Ratu Jioji and Ratu Tanoa Visawaqa) in elections was compensated for by the appointment of three Cakobaus at different times to Senate. In the 2006 election, none of the children contested and, in order to maintain a balance of representation at the parliamentary level, Prime Minister Qarase appointed the former ambassador to Malaysia, Adi Samanunu Cakobau-Talakuli, to cabinet as Minister of State through the Senate. With her appointment to cabinet, the SDL/FLP multiparty cabinet has representation from all of Fiji's 19th century confederacies.

While the number of chiefly and successful candidates has decreased, those elected constitute a strong representation of Fijian *vanua* interests and hierarchy. In other words, while the overall number has decreased, the 'quality' of representation at the highest level has remained constant – an indication of the tenacity of the indigenous hold to nineteenth century governance structure.

Conclusion

In contemporary politics, succession struggles over *vanua* chiefly titles continue to plague current indigenous leadership. One striking theme from recent elections has been the consequence of the absence of leadership from Kubuna, particularly the *mataqali* of Tui Kaba. 'Because of the longstanding vacancy [in Kubuna], …you cannot expect *mana* to flow down to the minor chiefs when there is no one holding that powerful position.'[6] Vacant since 1989, the title of Vunivalu of Bau has generated a long-standing power struggle within the *mataqali* Tui Kaba, centred on the Mataiwelagi household, Ratu George Cakobau's household. Failure to resolve this indigenous issue has, I suggest, contributed to the events which brought Fiji to its knees in 2000. The consequences include pitting close siblings against each other in the 1999 election (consider the Tailevu North/Ovalau Open contest between Litia Cakobau of Mataiwelagi and collateral cousin Tu'uakitau Cokanauto of Naisogolaca). The split resulted in a victory for FLP candidate Ratu Isireli Vuibau, who did not command the same level of status within indigenous leadership. When the 2001 and 2006 elections were held, not a single member of the *mataqali* Tui Kaba stood, reflecting the unresolved leadership struggle. The Mataiwelagi family squabble within the Tui Kaba is just the tip of a growing iceberg. Figures released by the Native Land and Fisheries Commission in 2004 show the increasing number of vacant *vanua/yavusa/tikina/mataqali* titles. Such vacancies result in power vacuums all over Fiji at the local level.[7] If the local leadership issues are not addressed, the Great Council of Chiefs and its associate arms, as a conglomerate institution of indigenous authority, risks becoming a refuge for unelected customary chiefs. The Council has already been labelled an anachronism by some observers, including Fijians. The all-too-familiar pattern that emerges is the use of both the Council and the Senate as havens for failed politicians of chiefly rank.

General elections provide an important indicator of the state of health of Fiji's chiefly institution. It has been a long-standing assumption that titled candidates such as chiefs have better chances of getting into parliament. The outcome of the past three elections disproves this. Titleholders who rely solely on ancestry are unlikely to fare well in politics. Higher levels of education and professional experience in the modern globalized world and selective church engagement are increasingly more important. Political aspirants of hereditary stock may display their titles in preference to qualification and experience, but most voters will judge them by their performance. This is a trend that is likely to continue, in line with contemporary politics in Samoa and Tonga.

Notes

[1] Lewa, S. 'Confusion over chiefly titles', *The Fiji Times,* 26 October 2004.
[2] Ratu Epeli Nailatikau, pers. comm., 30 April 2006.
[3] Ratu Tu'uakitau later won the Tailevu North/Ovalau seat after the court overturned the earlier result because of an error in the way preferences were summed.
[4] Apolosi Bose and Jon Fraenkel, pers. comm. 18 August 2006.
[5] Adi Ema Tagicakibau, pers. comm. July 2006.
[6] Ratu Sakiusa Matuku in *The Fiji Times,* 6 September 2004.
[7] Lewa, S. 'Confusion over chiefly titles', *The Fiji Times,* 26 October 2004.

21

Bipolar realignment under the alternative vote system: an analysis of the 2006 electoral data

Jon Fraenkel

Fiji's third election under the alternative vote (AV) system showed some startling developments, including a shift towards robust, single, rival political parties representing, on the one hand, the indigenous Fijians and, on the other, the Indians.

This trend needs to be viewed over the longer term. At the first election after the introduction of the AV system, held in May 1999, two multi-ethnic coalitions emerged, and entered into deals with each other over the exchange of preference votes. The resulting government, led by the country's first Indian prime minister, was overthrown in a coup a year later. At the second AV-using election, held in August 2001, a Moderates Forum emerged, bringing together several centrist parties, but this was badly defeated at the 2001 poll. Moderate Forum preferences went mostly to one or other of the more radical, mainly ethnically based, political parties. At the 2006 election, there was no sign of 1999's cross-ethnic alliances, nor was there any repeat of 2001's Moderates Forum. Instead, anticipating that the contest would be a two-horse race between the Fiji Labour Party (FLP) and Laisenia Qarase's Soqosoqo Duavata ni Lewenivanua (SDL), moderate parties prior to the poll sought to make deals with the more ethnically based parties.

This strategic realignment towards a two-party system over the three elections merits some investigation. The AV system was originally introduced as part of the 1997 constitution, and had been aimed at encouraging the formation of multi-ethnic governments. By requiring voters to rank candidates, it was hoped that moderate parties would fare well. It was also thought that political parties might moderate policies to appeal to floating voters across the ethnic divide. Party arrangements over the exchange of preference votes would, it was hoped, generate strong inter-ethnic coalitions.[1] In practice, however, the major strategic advantages accrued to the big parties, whether or not they were moderate. Many votes were transferred between Fijian-based and Indian-based parties, but such preference transfers tended to undermine, rather than reinforce, the centrist coalitions that emerged in 1999 and 2001. The shift back to a two-party system in 2006 undermined the claims that had been made for preferential voting as a tool for promoting multi-ethnic government. It had been assumed that the system would generate multiparty constellations, and necessarily so. Only with multiple parties would outcomes be decided on preferences, allowing the AV system to work in the way it was supposed to.[2] Even with multiple parties, in 1999 and 2001, those claims had proved inaccurate; and with only two large parties in 2006, even the basic premise was absent.

Seats and votes

Figure 21.1 examines party shares of votes secured and seats won at the 2006 election. Together, the two largest parties received 84 per cent of all votes, and 94.4 per cent of seats. In other words, both major parties secured a modest seat bonus; their shares in seats were above their shares in the vote. The SDL took out all 23 Fijian communal seats, while the FLP obtained all 19 Indian communal seats. And the SDL secured 13 of the 25 open seats, while the FLP won the other 12.

This bipolarization of Fiji's politics was, at least to some degree, a response to the electoral experience in 1999 and 2001. In 1999, the Fijians had been split, enabling the mainly Indian-backed FLP to secure a landslide victory. In 2001, the long-standing split in the Indian vote between the FLP and National Federation Party (NFP), and centrist parties ranking the FLP in last position, were sufficient to hand the predominantly indigenous Fijian-backed SDL the largest number of seats.

In 2006, the Indian parties settled their differences and exchanged preferences with each other, while the ethnic Fijian parties formed a 'Grand Coalition'

spearheaded by former Constitutional Review Commissioner Tomasi Vakatora.[3]
The middle ground in Fiji's politics had so diminished that centrist preferences
decided fewer outcomes in 2006 than they did in 1999 or 2001, although
some contests were so close that even these small shares of votes delivered the
margin of victory.

Of the registered voters, 53 per cent were ethnic Fijian and 43 per cent were
Indian, reflecting an ongoing shift in the demographic balance towards the
indigenous community.[4] The 2006 Indian turnout (88.7 per cent) was slightly
above that of the indigenous Fijian community (87 per cent), but the share of
invalid ballots was slightly higher among Indians (9.4 per cent) than among
indigenous Fijians (8.7 per cent). In the General communal constituencies,
both turnout and invalid voting were lower than average (83.9 and 6.8 per
cent respectively). Turnout was notably lower than average in the Fijian urban
communal constituencies, and in many of the urban open constituencies.
Nevertheless, at 87.7 per cent, the overall average turnout was well up on 2001
levels (79.1 per cent).

Figure 21.1   Seats and votes won by parties, 2006

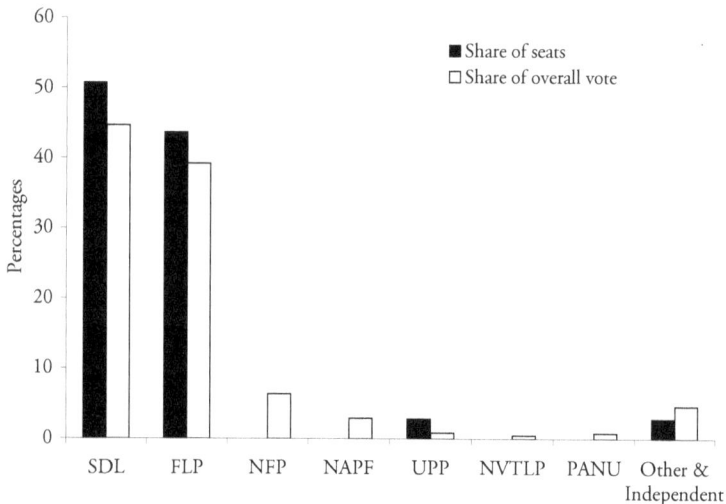

A total of 1,778,900 ballot papers, including 120,000 for postal votes, were produced, although there were only 479,693 registered voters. Each eligible voter has two votes and thus needs two ballot papers, bringing the required total ballot papers to 959,386. Additional ballot papers were required because, under the new compulsory voting system, voters may cast their ballots in any polling station within their communal constituency, so where they may choose to vote is uncertain. Even bearing in mind that need for additional ballot papers, however, that nearly twice as many ballot papers were in circulation as were required generated problems of administration.[5] Since fines for failing to vote were not implemented in 1999, 2001 or 2006, the heavy administrative cost of shifting away from designated polling stations may, for the future, not be worth paying.

All three elections under the AV system have produced a high degree of invalid voting – 9 per cent in 1999, 12 per cent in 2001 and 9 per cent again in 2006, despite the widespread introduction in 2006 of 'ushers', who shepherded citizens into the polling booths and assisted even able, literate voters.

A collision of landslides

In 2006, in the Indian communal constituencies, the FLP repeated its previous achievement of securing a clean sweep of all 19 seats. In 1999 and 2001, the FLP had secured, respectively, 66 and 75 per cent of the Indian communal vote. In 2006, the party obtained an average share of 81 per cent of Indian votes, again with little variation across the country (see Figure 21.2). Claims of a likely Muslim rebellion or North/South Indian schisms denting the FLP vote proved false, as they had in 1999 and 2001. So, too, did the notion, repeating the 1970's illusions of Ratu Mara's Alliance Party, that the ruling SDL might make substantial advances in the Indian communal constituencies, or even gain three Indian seats. Imraz Iqbal, former Fiji TV personality and SDL deputy campaign manager, who featured prominently in SDL TV propaganda, obtained only 222 votes in Nasinu, a seat easily taken by veteran FLP frontbencher Krishna Datt. Overall, the SDL obtained only 2 per cent of the Indian vote, indicating a negligible level of Indian support for the governing party.

The National Federation Party (NFP), under the leadership of Jai Ram Reddy, had been the largest of the Indian parties in the 1990s. But it slumped to 32 per cent of the Indian communal vote in 1999, and on down to 22 per cent in 2001. The NFP's Sugar Cane Growers' Association had long been fighting a losing battle with Mahendra Chaudhry's National Farmers' Union for the hearts and minds of the cane farmers. In the 1990s, the NFP's strength had been in some of the urban areas, but out-migration by middle class professionals led to an erosion of the party's support base. Continuing changes in the party leadership, and association with prominent Gujarati businessmen, lost the party support amongst the descendents of indentured labourers.[6] The NFP also suffered from being left without seats in 1999 and 2001, and thus lacked candidates with extensive parliamentary experience. It had increasingly to make appeals to past glories. In 2006, the party gained only 14.6 per cent of the Indian vote, despite having strategically given strong preferences to the FLP in the hope of avoiding electoral annihilation. As in 1999 and 2001, the NFP was left with no seats in parliament. As a result, the FLP consolidated its claim to be the majority Indian party, leaving the NFP reliant on its base in the municipal councils and among older unionised cane farmers if leaders opt for some kind of nocturnal survival.

The ruling SDL was able to mirror the FLP's performance in the Indian constituencies, taking out all 23 of the Fijian communal seats at the first count. Back in 2001, Qarase's party had faced more powerful rivals, both to the west and in the east. Then, the SDL was troubled by those provincial schisms that frequently prevent Fijian parties from sustaining homogeneous ethnic support. Localized *vanua* ties, and rivalries based on the struggle over hereditary titles, often underpin contests between indigenous candidates in a way that differs markedly from the more ideologically based differences that define Indian politics.

Yet, in 2006, the SDL secured close to 80 per cent of the Fijian vote, well up on the 50 per cent it had received in 2001 (see Figure 21.3), and, again unlike 2001, its vote share was reasonably steady across the country. Only in Rewa and Ba East Fijian Communal constituencies did SDL candidates face strong opposition. In Rewa, Ro Teimumu Kepa saw off the challenge from her nephew, Ro Filipe Tuisawau, who stood as an independent after having been unsuccessful in securing the official SDL nomination (see Saumaki, this volume). In Ba East Fijian Communal, the threatened re-emergence of a Western Viti Levu-based

Figure 21.2   Major party vote-shares in the 19 Indian constituencies, 2001 and 2006

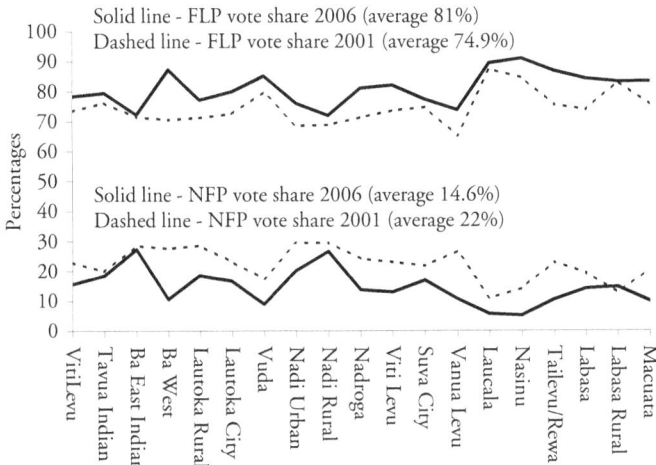

Solid line - FLP vote share 2006 (average 81%)
Dashed line - FLP vote share 2001 (average 74.9%)

Solid line - NFP vote share 2006 (average 14.6%)
Dashed line - NFP vote share 2001 (average 22%)

Figure 21.3   SDL vote share in the 23 Fijian communal constituencies, 2001 and 2006

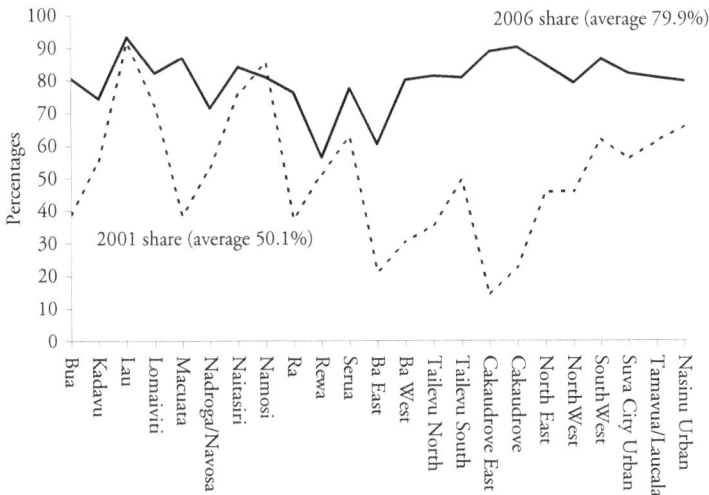

2006 share (average 79.9%)

2001 share (average 50.1%)

Fijian party was thwarted, despite the vanishing act by the 2001 SDL front party in the west, the Bai Kei Viti (see Bose and Fraenkel, this volume). On Kadavu, Jim Ah Koy, the sitting member during the Rabuka years and a major financier of development projects on the island, stood as an independent, but failed to stop the SDL's Konisi Yabaki retaining the seat with 74.4 per cent of the vote. Even relative newcomers to politics, as long as they stood on an SDL ticket, were able to defeat sitting members or veteran politicians.

The Fijian Nationalist Party performed poorly at the 2006 election. It had commanded 25 per cent of the indigenous vote at the polls in April 1977, and remained a small, but significant, force through the 1990s. Under the leadership of Sakeasi Butadroka, the party had been the standard-bearer of the Fijian extremist cause, even at one point calling for the expulsion of the country's Indian population. The renamed Nationalist Vanua Lavo Tako Party (NVTLP) managed 9.1 per cent of the vote in 1999, but thereafter it faded. After the 2000 coup, the emergence of the Conservative Alliance–Matanitu Vanua (CAMV) party, led by Cakaudrove chief Ratu Naiqama Lalabalavu and counting imprisoned failed coup leader George Speight as one of its MPs, resulted in an eclipse of the NVTLP. It obtained only 1.4 per cent of the vote in 2001. The liquidation of the CAMV shortly before the 2006 poll, and the movement of most of its MPs into the SDL, might have left space for the older Fijian Nationalist Party to re-emerge. Yet, the NVTLP obtained only 1.1 per cent of the indigenous Fijian vote in 2006. Party leader Iliesa Duvuloco mustered 15 per cent of the vote in Tailevu North Fiji Provincial Communal, well below what was required to dislodge SDL sitting member Samisoni Tikoinasau, brother of the still imprisoned George Speight. NVTLP president Viliame Savu, recently released from prison for his part in the May 2000 coup, secured only 57 votes in Lami Open. The key characteristic influence over policy-formulation under the SDL's first administration – looking over its shoulder at the threat from Fijian extremists – will not necessarily characterize its second administration.

There was no sign of the military's 'truth and justice' campaign having a major impact on the indigenous Fijian vote. In the weeks leading up to the election, army commander Frank Bainimarama made increasingly vociferous denunciations of the SDL government. The natural beneficiary of that campaign would have been the newly formed (or reformed) National Alliance Party of Fiji (NAPF), led by former military commander Ratu Epeli Ganilau. Like the New Labour Unity Party back in 2001, the NAPF was the focus of greatly exaggerated expectations before the poll. Yet, Ratu Epeli's party secured only 2.2 per cent of the Fijian communal vote, and a similar share of the Indian communal vote. Ratu Epeli himself obtained only 14.6 per cent of the vote in the Suva City Open constituency, and the party's other major leader, Filipe Bole, a former minister in the Rabuka-led governments of the 1990s, managed only 7.2 per cent in Samabula/Tamavua Open. The failure of newly emerging moderate and multi-ethnic parties to make an impact at the 2006 poll was, at least in part, a product of a longer-run polarization. But it also reflects the fact that more centrist approaches, when they do emerge in Fiji politics, tend to come from within the mainstream ethnically based parties, rather than springing up afresh on un-nurtured ground.

The FLP's vote share in the Fijian communal constituencies was 6.3 per cent, above its totals in 1999 (1.9 per cent) and in 2001 (2.3 per cent). This was partly because the increasingly well-oiled FLP party machine was able to stand a larger number of candidates in the Fijian communal constituencies. Only four FLP candidates stood in the Fijian communal constituencies in 1999; this rose to six in 2001, and to 15 in 2006. On average, they obtained 10.2 per cent of Fijian votes in 1999, 7.3 per cent in the fraught post-coup circumstances of the 2001 elections and 8.6 per cent in 2006. At the 2006 election, unlike those in 1999 and 2001, even the NFP stood candidates in the Fijian communal constituencies, hoping that some Fijian communal voters would simultaneously mark ballots in favour of the NFP in the more winnable open constituencies.

The strength of party affiliations in determining vote shares was evident even in the general communal constituencies – where those other than the ethnic Fijians, Indians and Rotumans vote. Sitting member in the Suva City General seat, Kenneth Zinck – who crossed the floor to join the Qarase government after the 2001 poll, but who rejected the offer of an SDL ticket for the 2006 poll – obtained only third position behind the SDL's Aca Lord. The major political parties fought more fiercely for the General Voter and Rotuman constituencies than at previous elections. Nevertheless, it was only in these that independents or smaller parties stood any chance. The Suva City General seat was taken by Bernadette Rounds Ganilau, a popular former radio show host and member of the United Peoples Party (UPP). Mick Beddoes, the UPP leader, narrowly won in the Western/Central General Communal constituency, and the third and final General communal seat was taken by an independent, Robin Irwin, whose anti-Labour economic philosophy led him to align himself with the SDL. The UPP had entered a pre-election coalition with Mahendra Chaudhry's FLP, signalling a major turnaround for the historically Fijian-allied General voter parties.

The battle for the open seats

Because all the Fijian and Indian communal seats were divided between the two major parties, the ultimate election outcome was inevitably decided in the 25 open constituencies, as had been the case in 1999 and 2001. Yet, this time around, the fracturing of the Fijian vote witnessed in 1999 was no longer in evidence, rendering impossible a repetition of one of the critical elements in the FLP success at that previous election. On the Indian side, the long-standing two-party FLP/NFP divide no longer had the same potential influence as in 2001, when NFP's across-the-board ranking of the FLP as last preference gave the SDL several crucial marginal open constituencies. In the run up to the 2006 poll, the NFP entered negotiations with the SDL and was offered seats in the Senate as the price for favouring the governing party. Yet, shortly before the deadline for party preferences to be lodged with the Elections Office, the party mended its fraught relationship with FLP leader Mahendra Chaudhry. The two parties signed a memorandum of understanding in which the NFP promised the FLP superior preferences to the SDL in seven of the ten potentially marginal open constituencies.[7] SDL leaders and newspaper editorials fumed at the NFP betrayal, calling the party '*liu muri*' (figuratively translating to 'lowly and untrustworthy'[8]), but the governing party nevertheless gained two seats thanks to NFP preferences. The NFP strategy had been to avoid giving 'blanket preferences' to either of the major parties, in the hope that, in that way, with one or two seats, it might hold the balance of power.

The outcomes of the 2006 poll in the all-important open constituencies were strongly determined by ethnically based voting patterns. In Figure 21.4, constituencies are ordered from right to left in accordance with the ratio of Indians to ethnic Fijians in electorates. The black columns show the ethnic Fijian share of registered voters in the 25 open constituencies, and the grey columns show the Indian shares. Constituencies towards the right are those in the densely Indian populated sugar cane districts of western Viti Levu and northern Vanua Levu. Constituencies towards the left are mostly those outer island constituencies where ethnic Fijians form the overwhelming majority of the population. Those towards the centre of the chart are mainly in the urban and peri-urban areas around the capital, Suva, where Indians and ethnic Fijians each form close to 50 per cent of the electorates, although recent demographic changes have ensured that some of the western Viti Levu constituencies are now also much closer to having equal numbers of ethnic Fijians and Indians.

The dashed horizontal line in Figure 21.4, at the 50 per cent mark, shows the share of the vote required to secure victory under Fiji's AV system. The grey sloping line shows a projected FLP 80 per cent of the Indian vote, and indicates the seats that the FLP could be expected to take at the first count (from Vuda rightwards to Ba – those electorates where the grey 80 per cent line is above the horizontal 50 per cent threshold). The black sloping line shows a projected SDL 80 per cent of the Fijian vote, and those seats which the SDL could be expected to take at the first count (Bua/Macuata leftwards to Tailevu North/Ovalau). In the middle of the chart are the marginal open seats, where most results were always likely to depend on transfers of preference votes (Yasawa/Nawaka through to Suva City).

As Figure 21.5 indicates, results corresponded fairly closely with the model shown in Figure 21.4. Figure 21.5 shows the 25 open constituencies, again ordered from right to left in accordance with the ratio of Indians to Fijians among registered voters. The block at the base of each column shows the ultimate victor's first preference votes, and additional blocks above the base block show transferred preference votes that were required to take the victor over the 50 per cent threshold (shown by the horizontal line). Owing to ethnically based voting, all the seats to the right of the chart were taken by the FLP at the first count, and all those to the left of the chart were taken by the SDL. The only constituency towards the left of the chart that went beyond the first count was Serua/Navosa Open, a large, highly dispersed and mountainous constituency

Figure 21.4   Ethnic composition of open constituencies

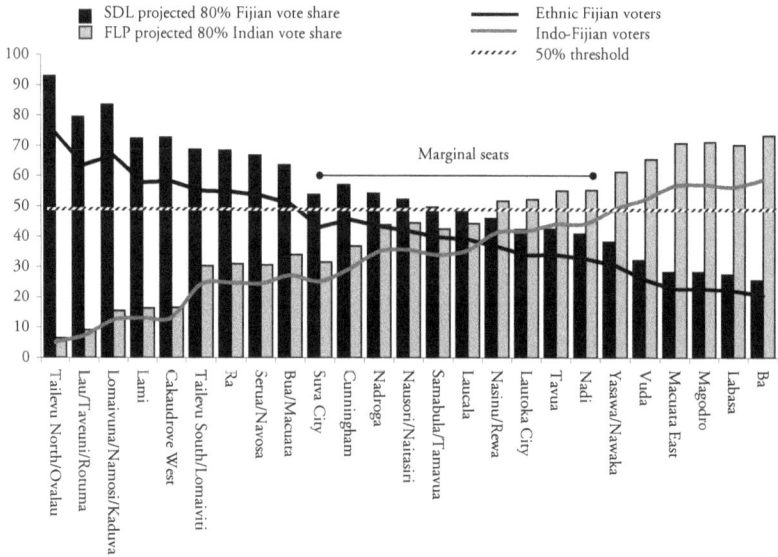

Figure 21.5   Winners' majorities in the 25 open constituencies, 2006

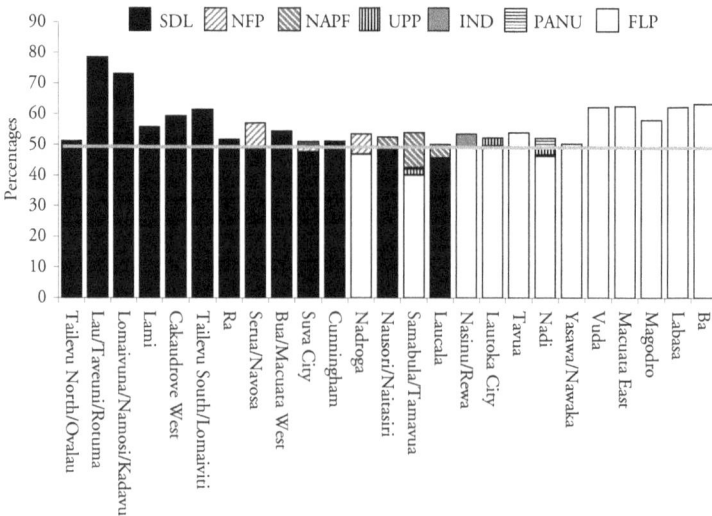

on the southwestern side of Viti Levu. This was a contest complicated by the fact that the sitting member, Pio Wong, had been de-selected by the SDL in favour of newcomer Jone Navakamocea, a civil servant previously employed in the Prime Minister's office. Navakamocea eventually won, at the 7th count, and only then because the NFP ranked the SDL (6th) above the FLP (7th) in its preferences. Negative ranking, and victory for the penultimate placed party, featured in 2006 – as it had done in 1999 and 2001, even though the number of seats decided on preferences was considerably lower than at those previous elections.

In both 1999 and 2001, 18 open constituencies were decided by transfer of preference votes. This time around, only nine were decided in this way. The middle ground of Fiji's politics was much smaller than it had been in 1999 and 2001, due to the decline in the NFP's Indian vote and the weak performance of Ratu Epeli Ganilau's NAPF. It was in those constituencies shown towards the centre of Figure 21.4, where Fijians and Indians approach parity in electorates, that results were so close that minor party preferences decided outcomes. These close-to-parity open constituencies are mostly located in the Suva-Nausori corridor, where urban drift by evicted Indian tenant farmers had spawned SDL fears that the FLP might do well.[9] Yet, Fijians as well as Indians had moved towards the towns, and continued overseas migration countered the Indian influx. Outcomes thus remained highly uncertain in these parts of southeast Viti Levu. The SDL tactic of fielding FLP renegades Tupeni Baba and John Ali in marginal urban open constituencies like Samabula/Tamavua Open and Nasinu/Rewa Open backfired. More effective was standing women candidates in the marginals, a tactic that gave victory to the SDL's Losena Salabula in Laucala Open and the FLP's Monica Raghwan in Samabula/Tamavua Open. Fielding popular Indian former Naitasiri rugby team manager Rajesh Singh in Cunningham also proved effective, and gave the SDL at the first count what might otherwise have been a marginal seat.

Ethnically based voting in Fiji has for long meant backing political parties because their policies are deemed to favour one or other ethnic group, not backing particular candidates because they are indigenous Fijian or Indian. Ethnic Fijians had no qualms voting for Indian candidates like George Shui Raj in Ra or Rajesh Singh in Cunningham, because they were members of the pro-indigenous SDL party. Indians were unperturbed about voting for ethnic Fijians like Poseci Bune in the Labasa Open constituency or for Sivia Qoro in Yasawa/Nawaka Open, because they stood for the solidly Indian-backed FLP. Racial politics in Fiji has long been much more sophisticated than the mere exercise of voter prejudice based on skin colour, culture, religion or language.

Overlaying the strongly ethnic dimension to Fiji's politics was a regional divide. FLP candidates performed more strongly in western Viti Levu, taking out marginal open seats like Nadi Open, Tavua Open and Lautoka City Open, while Nadroga Open in the west, a seat secured by the SDL in 2001, this time fell to the FLP.

Remarkable was that, for the first time, below-the-line voting made a major difference in highly marginal open constituencies. Across the country as a whole, the vast majority of voters – as in 1999 and 2001 – ticked their ballot papers above-the-line. In so doing, they endorsed their first choice party's list of preferences that had earlier been lodged with the Elections Office. Yet, in all three elections, around 5–8 per cent of voters chose to rank candidates 'below-the-line'. In most elections, the big blocks of above-the-line votes commanded by the parties make the overwhelming difference – a feature strongly condemned by even some of the greatest enthusiasts for Fiji's AV system. But in this election, results were so close in the 10 marginal open constituencies that in some cases, below-the-line votes decided outcomes. This was not the result of voters marking ballots below-the-line to any greater extent than previously. For example, in Laucala Open, where marking the ballot paper in this way decided the outcome in favour of the SDL's Losena Salabula, who won by only 11 votes, only 3.5 per cent of ballots were cast below-the-line.[10]

Discussion

Party strategizing under the AV system in 1999, 2001 and 2006 illustrates the danger inherent in the use of majoritarian voting systems in bipolar societies. Under Fiji's previous first-past-the-post system, monolithic ethnically based parties also emerged. Then, as with AV after 1997, communal seats tended to give each party a number of 'safe' seats and contests were decided in the common roll or 'national' open constituencies where the two ethnic groups approached parity.[11] In these, minor splits in the vote on either side, or slight variations in turnout, could decide outcomes one way or the other. Parties sought to sustain homogeneous ethnic backing from their own group, while hoping for – or actively fomenting – splits amongst parties representing the other group.[12] Such splinter parties were more common among Fijians than among Indians (owing to the greater importance of provincial or hierarchical ties for Fijians), encouraging a repeated emphasis on 'Fijian unity' in the run up to general elections.

The new AV system potentially lessened the danger of party splintering, in the sense that it allowed like-minded parties to field separate candidates but exchange second preferences. This, after all, had been the rationale behind the original introduction of the system in Australia in 1918.[13] In Fiji, however, the split format (above-the-line and below-the-line) ballot paper, and the fact that around 95 per cent of voters tended to tick above-the-line, gave political parties extraordinary control over preference votes. Parties tend to strategize more than voters.[14] Where they are battling for the support of specific sections of the electorate, they will often do everything possible to destroy close rivals. The FLP, for example, put the NFP as last preference in 1999 because they were fighting for pre-eminence in the Indian electorates, and the NFP reciprocated in 2001. Fijian splinter parties put Rabuka's SVT as last preference in 1999. In 2001, the two western Viti Levu parties (the Bai Kei Viti and Party of National Unity) each put the other as last preference, ensuring their mutual destruction and the victory of the SDL in the west.

As a result of this tactical usage of preferences, the type of party strategizing witnessed under the 1970 constitution applied also under the new electoral system, but with increased potency. Fomenting splits in the *other* camp no longer simply made possible plurality victories. It also created the potential for actually acquiring the splinter votes of breakaway parties. The pressures for 'ethnic unity' were thus just as acute, if not more so, under the new system.

In ethnically bipolar circumstances, all single-member district-based systems tend to encourage the types of strategic dynamics witnessed in Fiji in 1970–87 and 1999–2006. In contrast, multi-member district-based proportional systems diminish the electoral incentive for 'ethnic unity'. Party shares of the vote determine party shares of seats, although there are various different ways of accomplishing this.[15] There may still be some pressure to avoid the emergence of small splinter parties if, as is commonly the case, there is a threshold below which small parties do not acquire seats. Otherwise, there are fewer disincentives to the emergence of multiple parties. If ethnicity remains the crucial issue, nothing stops different political parties aligning along racial lines within parliament. No electoral system can abolish ethnically based voting. Guyana, for example, uses list proportional representation, but has two robust ethnic parties representing the Indo- and Afro-Guyanese. What proportional systems *can do* is take the electoral system-driven heat out of contests, and allow politics to shift in new and unexpected directions.

Notes

[1] For some debate over these issues, relating to Fiji's 1999 and 2001 elections, see Fraenkel, J. & Grofman, B. 2006. 'Does the alternative vote foster moderation in ethnically divided societies? The case of Fiji', *Comparative Political Studies*, 39(5):623–52; and the response by Donald Horowitz in the same journal ('Strategy takes a holiday', pp.652–62) and the rejoinder by Fraenkel & Grofman ('The failure of the alternative vote as a tool for ethnic moderation in Fiji' (pp.663–66).

[2] Horowitz, D.L. 1991. *A Democratic South Africa? Constitutional Engineering in a Divided Society*, University of California Press, Berkeley, p.191; Horowitz, D.L. 1997. 'Encouraging electoral accommodation in divided societies', in BV. Lal & P. Larmour (eds) *Electoral Systems in Divided Societies: The Fiji Constitutional Review*, ANU, Canberra; but see Lijphart, A., 1991. 'The alternative vote: A realistic alternative for South Africa?', *Politikon*, 18(2):95.

[3] Appeals for 'Fijian unity' are common at general elections, while explicit calls for 'Indian unity' are less frequent. Yet, at the 2006 polls, these were much more frequent and explicit than in either1999 or 2001 (see, for example, the reports of an FLP rally at the Gujarati Grounds in Ba in the *Fiji Sun*, 12 February 2006).

[4] In 2001, 51 per cent of registered voters were indigenous Fijian, and 44.6 per cent were Indo-Fijian. Population projections using the 1986 and 1996 Censuses of Population and more recent migration data would suggest a still wider discrepancy (56 per cent as compared with 39.1 per cent respectively for 2006), but these changes affect primarily the younger population (below the voting age of 21 years), and only with a lag will they come to influence the voter registration data.

[5] European Union Election Observation Mission, Fiji 2006, 'Final report', September 2006, section 5.5, p.9.

[6] Gujarati migrants mostly arrived in Fiji as 'free' settlers, and many established profitable businesses which monopolise the retail sector in particular. Indian political parties seeking a mass appeal therefore steer clear of too close an association with Gujarati leaders. Part of the difficulty the NFP had in finding a strong party leader in 2006, for example, was the reluctance of senior party members to accept a Gujarati in the position.

[7] The open constituencies of Nadroga, Nausori/Naitasiri, Samabula/Tamavua, Tavua, Nadi, Lautoka, and Suva City. In return, the FLP agreed 'to rank the NFP above the SDL in its list of preferences for all Indian Communal, Fijian Communal and Open constituencies contested by the NFP' ('Agreement between the National Federation Party and the Fiji Labour Party', 18 April 2006, copy obtained from NFP offices).

[8] *The Fiji Times*, 22 April 2006.

[9] Results in municipal council elections, for example in Nasinu, had encouraged such fears (see 'Fiji Labour Party secures municipal majority', Fijilive.com, 23 October 2005). However, turnout in municipal council elections tends to be so low that they offer little reliable evidence on which to predict general election results.

[10] Data obtained from the O-39 completed by the Count Team Leader at the Suva Grammar School.

[11] The difference was that, under the 1970 constitution, communal seats were combined with 'cross-voting' or 'national' seats, where the ethnicity of the candidate was specified, but all eligible citizens voted together. Citizens had four votes, one in a communal constituency, where they were separated by race, and another three in common roll constituencies where they were required to vote for 'Fijian', 'Indian' and 'general' candidates. That system was often confusingly interpreted in its own narrowly racial terms, but is better appreciated if viewed in terms of party outcomes. In practice, seats where Fijians formed a majority tended to fall to the Alliance Party and those where Indians formed a majority tended to fall to the National Federation Party (or, in 1987, the NFP/FLP coalition).

[12] For example, in April 1977, the NFP went so far as to pay the deposits for candidates contesting for the extremist Fijian Nationalist Party in the hope of thereby splitting the Fijian vote.

[13] Graham, B.D. 1962. 'The choice of voting methods in federal politics, 1902–1918', *Australian Journal of Politics and History*, 8:164–82.

[14] Cox, G. 1997. *Making Votes Count: Strategic Coordination in the World's Electoral Systems*. University of Cambridge Press, Cambridge.

[15] There are three types of PR system that merit consideration for Fiji.
1. List system proportional representation, as used in New Caledonia, South Africa or Guyana, either treats the entire country as a single constituency or divides up the country into several constituencies. Within each constituency, the party share of votes is used to allocate seats.
2. The single transferable vote system, as used in Ireland and Malta, is an elaborate preferential voting system used in multi-member constituencies. It resembles AV, but in addition to redistributing the votes of eliminates candidates at successive stages in the count, it also involves the redistribution of surplus votes from victorious candidates who cross the threshold.
3. Mixed member systems, as in New Zealand and Germany, usually combine single-member districts that elect a part of the parliament with 'list' members who 'top up' party seat shares to arrive at something close to overall votes/seats proportionality (for further details, see International IDEA, *Electoral System Design: The New International IDEA Handbook*, International IDEA, 2005).

22

Fiji's electoral boundaries and malapportionment

Kesaia Seniloli

It has been claimed that demographic distribution and the drawing of constituency boundaries together had significant impacts on the outcomes of Fiji's 1999, 2001 and 2006 elections. In part, this was due to constitutionally entrenched provisions by which Fiji's parliament mainly comprises members from 'communal' constituencies – currently 23 for the ethnic Fijians, 19 for the Fiji Indians, three for the General voters and one for the island of Rotuma – and a number (since 1997, 25) of open constituencies, with the boundaries drawn in such a way that 'voters should comprise a good proportion of members of different ethnic communities'.[1] The Constituency Boundaries Commission (CBC) could do little about the constitutionally entrenched provisions. Nevertheless, many commentators felt that the 25 open constituencies were insufficiently heterogeneous. Furthermore, prior to the 2006 poll, many political parties claimed that substantial population movements over the period 1998 to 2006 necessitated some redrawing of the open constituency boundaries. The aim of this chapter is twofold. First, it outlines the process of electoral boundary demarcation for the 1999 election. Second, it explains the implications of the use of the 1998 boundaries in the 2006 election. It concludes with some reflections about the future.

Delimitation of constituencies in Fiji, under the Constitution (Amendment) Act 1997, was an enormous undertaking in terms of time and resources. Delimiting was complicated because four different sets of boundaries had to be drawn – one set each for urban Fijian, General voter, ethnic Indian and the open constituencies. In addition, three provinces each had to be divided into two constituencies. The determination of the electoral boundaries by the CBC in 1998 was final and could not be challenged through the courts; it was intended to serve for the 1999 elections. However, these same electoral boundaries were also used in the elections of 2001 and 2006.

Accurately delimited electoral boundaries ensure geographic representation for areas that may otherwise be neglected, and may improve the accountability of representatives to their voters.

The legal framework (structure and rules)

The distribution of seats in Fiji's House of Representatives is determined, as follows, by section 52 of the 1997 constitution:

(2) In determining the boundaries of the constituencies for the election of members to the communal seats to be filled in accordance with subparagraph (51)(1a)(i), the Constituency Boundaries Commission:

(a) must ensure that the boundaries for 17 of the constituencies are in accordance with the provincial boundaries prescribed under the Fijian Affairs Act and that, subject to paragraph (b):

(i) the provinces of Ba, Tailevu and Cakaudrove comprise 2 constituencies each; and

(ii) the other provinces comprise 1 constituency each;

(b) must ensure that the remaining 6 constituencies comprise predominantly urban or peri-urban areas in which the number of voters is, as far as reasonably practicable, the same; and

(c) subject to paragraphs (a) and (b), must give due consideration, in relation to each proposed constituency, to:

(i) the physical features of the proposed constituency;

(ii) the boundaries of existing recognized traditional areas; and

(iii) means of communication and travel within the proposed constituency.

(3) In determining the boundaries of the other constituencies, the Constituency Boundaries Commission:

(a) must try to ensure that the number of voters in each communal seat (other than a communal seat referred to in subsection (2)) is, as far as reasonably practicable, the same;

(b) must try to ensure that the number of voters in each open seat is, as far as reasonably practicable, the same; and

(c) subject to paragraph (a) or (b), must give due consideration, in relation to each proposed constituency, to:

(i) the physical features of the proposed constituency;

(ii) the boundaries of existing administrative and recognised traditional areas;

(iii) means of communication and travel within the proposed constituency; and

(iv) if the proposed constituency relates to an open seat – the principle that the voters should comprise a good proportion of members of different ethnic communities.

(4) In this section:

communal seat means a seat to be filled in accordance with paragraph 51 (1)(a);

open seat means a seat to be filled in accordance with paragraph 51 (1)(b).

Delimitation of new electoral constituencies for the 1999 election

The CBC, charged with drawing up the boundaries for the 1999 election, was appointed for a term of 12 months. Different Ministries cooperated in this undertaking, as did the cartography section of the Ministry of Lands, the Public Service Commission, Government Printing and the Bureau of Statistics. The process involved a number of steps, including data collection, delimiting of constituencies and the evaluation of the boundaries before they were finalized.

Data collection involved obtaining the census population data and maps from the Bureau of Statistics. The Bureau provided the CBC with provisional results of the 1996 census covering the population aged 20 years and over. Maps, needed to identify physical features, administrative boundaries, urban boundaries and enumeration areas (EAs), and to ensure that contiguous geographic population entities were allocated to constituencies, were provided by the Ministry of Lands.

While collecting all the data needed for delimitation, the CBC invited the public (political parties, provincial councils etc), through the press and radio, in English, Fijian and Hindi, to make submissions on prospective constituency boundaries. The original period for submissions (31 January to 1 February) was extended to 16 February because no submissions were received during the initial period. Still, very few submissions were received by the new deadline. Residents of urban villages were also consulted about whether they wanted to be included alongside the urban Fijians or within the provincial communal constituencies.

Problems with the database

The data provided by the Bureau of Statistics were only the provisional data from the 1996 population census. Furthermore, at the time, no registration of voters had taken place. The Electoral Commission was waiting for the CBC to complete its work before commencing registration. Hence, there was no voter registration roll to use. Even when registration of voters began, not all eligible voters registered for the elections, despite the legal requirement for compulsory voting. In addition, the detailed local maps were in some instances dated or unavailable.

Delimitation

The Fijian urban, Indian and General communal constituencies

The CBC determined the boundaries of the six Fijian urban communal constituencies, the three General communal constituencies and the 19 Indian communal constituencies, as dictated by the constitutional requirement to 'ensure that the number of voters in each communal seat is, as far as reasonably practicable, the same'. Each ethnic communal constituency followed the principle that 'all voters should cast a vote of equal weight'. For example, an urban Fijian communal voter was supposed to cast a vote equal in weight to that of another urban Fijian communal voter and an Indian communal voter in any one constituency was supposed to cast a vote of equal weight to that of an Indian communal voter in any other constituency. The ideal average of voters in the six Fijian urban communal constituencies was 12,173; the Indian urban communal average was 9,621; while that for the three General communal constituencies was 6,036. All the Fijian urban communal constituencies were within the (+/-)10 per cent tolerance levels; all the General communal constituencies were within the (+/-) 15 per cent tolerance levels and all the Indian urban communal constituencies were within the (+/-) 20 per cent tolerance levels (Tables 22.1, 22.2 and 22.3). In these constituencies, the geographical size did not matter. However, the CBC tried to ensure that, as much as possible, the electoral boundaries coincided with communities of interest.

Table 22.1   Fijian Urban Communal constituencies, 1998

Number of people 21 years of age and over (provisional 1996 population census results) = 72,776
Number of constituencies = 6
Average number of people per constituency = 12,129
Maximum and minimum number of electors per Fijian Urban Communal constituency

Tolerance level	10 per cent (1,213)	15 per cent (1,819)
Maximum number of voters	13,342	13,948
Minimum number of voters	10,196	10,310

Note: All 6 constituencies were within the 10 per cent tolerance level.

Table 22.2   General Communal constituencies, 1998

Number of people 21 years of age and over (provisional 1996 population census results) = 18,108
Number of constituencies = 3
Average number of people per constituency = 6,036
Maximum and minimum number of electors per General Communal constituency

Tolerance level	10 per cent (604)	15 per cent (905)
Maximum number of voters	6,640	6,941
Minimum number of voters	5,432	5,134

Note: Only 1 of 3 constituencies – North Eastern General Communal constituency – was outside the 10 per cent tolerance level; all were within the 15 per cent tolerance level.

Table 22.3   Indian Communal constituencies, 1998

Number of people 21 years and over (provisional 1996 population census results) = 182,799
Number of constituencies = 19
Average number of people per constituency = 9,621
Maximum and minimum number of electors per Indian Communal constituency

Tolerance level	10 per cent (962)	15 per cent (1,443)	20 per cent (1,924)
Maximum number of voters	10,583	11,064	11,545
Minimum number of voters	8,659	8,178	9,697

Note: 15 constituencies were within the 10 per cent tolerance level; 4 of 19 constituencies – Viti Levu East Maritime, Tavua, Labasa and Bua/Macuata West Indian Communal constituencies – were outside the 10 per cent tolerance level; only 1 of 19 constituencies – Bua/Macuata West – was outside the 20 per cent tolerance level.

The open constituencies

Section 52(3)(b), (c)(i-iv) of the Constitution (Amendment) Act 1997 stipulates that the CBC must ensure that the number of voters in each seat is, as far as is practicable, the same, and section 52 (3) (c) requires it to give due consideration in relation to each proposed constituency to:

i.   the physical features of the proposed constituency
ii.   the boundaries of existing administrative and recognized traditional areas
iii. the means of communication and travel within the proposed constituency and
iv.   the principle that voters should comprise a good proportion of members of different ethnic groups.

Delimitation of the open constituencies was quite a difficult undertaking because the constitution required them to have parity of numbers as well as a good proportion of different ethnic groups. In the real world, of course, people do not settle in a place for the purpose of fulfilling the requirements for drawing up the ideal constituency. Ethnic Indians tend to concentrate in western Viti Levu, northern Vanua Levu and urban areas. The outer islands, the interior of the two main islands and the urban areas are largely populated by ethnic Fijians. The CBC considered dividing the two main islands into strips or into oblong-shaped constituencies, but was restricted by other considerations as stipulated in the constitution, such as respect for administrative boundaries, geographic criteria and community of interest. Electorates were also to be contiguous geographic areas.

The CBC attempted to have parity of numbers of voters in every open seat so that all voters would cast a vote of equal weight. This resulted in the number of voters in all but one constituency falling within the 10 per cent tolerance level (Table 22.4).

Delimitation of the open constituencies resulted in ten of them being dominated by Fijians and ten by Indians. The remaining five had close to parity of numbers in the two major ethnic groups. The current situation of dominance of most open seats by a particular ethnic group will not change, because of the demographic situation. However, many commentators, including political parties, want the number of open constituencies to be increased to 45, as recommended by the Reeves Commission.

Table 22.4   Open constituencies, 1998

Number of people 21 years of age and over (provisional 1996 population census results) = 403,625
Number of constituencies = 25
Average number of people per constituency = 16,145
Maximum and minimum number of electors per Open constituency

Tolerance level	10 per cent (1,615)	15 per cent (2,422)
Maximum number of voters	17,760	18,567
Minimum number of voters	14,530	13,723

Note: Only 1 of 25 constituencies – Cakaudrove West Open constituency – was outside the 10 per cent tolerance level.

After the electoral boundaries were delimited, the public was again invited to make submissions to the CBC regarding the proposed boundaries. Many comments suggested minor additions to or contractions of the constituencies. These were considered before the final determination of Fiji's electoral boundaries. There were no objections. Many political parties, including the Soqosoqo ni Vakatulewa ni Taukei (SVT) and the National Federation Party (NFP), major parties at the time, were very happy with the proposed boundaries.

However, some academics were critical of the determination of the electoral boundaries.[2] They wanted more of the ethnically mixed open constituencies. They had hailed the adoption of the AV system in Fiji, believing it to be the most appropriate system. They and the architects of the constitution believed that the AV system would promote cooperation across ethnic lines. They were particularly critical of the large number of open constituencies created by the CBC determination of the electoral boundaries that did not have a good proportion of different ethnic groups. The effective operation of AV as a tool for promoting ethnic accommodation depended on these constituencies having near parity of numbers in relation to the two major ethnic groups in Fiji.

The past three elections have shown that even the ethnically mixed open constituencies did not bring about cross-ethnic vote trading or genuine inter-ethnic cooperation. Coalitions were created purely for electoral advantage, rather than on the basis of genuine shared goals and values. Most parties tried to win seats on the first count. Moderates, who the electoral engineers assumed were going to be successful, were obliterated. The AV system had the opposite to its anticipated effect – it resulted in limited representation of some of the moderate parties and increased ethnic polarization. If moderation and inter-ethnic cooperation are to be achieved, we need to rethink our electoral system.

The case for redistribution in 2006

Redistribution is the process of altering electoral boundaries to accommodate changes and movements in population. In 2005, the Bureau of Statistics acknowledged that there had been much internal movement of people in Fiji since the previous census in 1996, but admitted that there was no way of obtaining accurate and detailed data on current population distribution because there had been no more recent census. Redistribution can be controversial, especially in Open constituencies with near parity of different ethnic populations, because those who are included in or excluded from an electoral constituency can determine the election outcome. In other words, there is the potential for gerrymandering. Redistribution is important to political parties because it can affect their support base.

The decision to change the boundaries must be taken well before a general election to ensure transparency, particularly when there has been considerable internal movement of population. A number of politicians called for the review and change in boundaries for the 2006 election.[3] The members of the CBC were appointed in early 2005, a year before the general election, to review the electoral boundaries and to determine whether or not to alter them.[4]

The electoral boundaries: to alter or not to alter

Database

The 1996 census figures were the only official figures available to the CBC in 2005, so the CBC could not ascertain the shifts in Fiji's population since 1996. They therefore commissioned the Bureau of Statistics to undertake a survey of urban and peri-urban constituencies to assess populations. The Bureau surveyed 13 Open constituencies to compare the data with the 1996 census data. The survey started in April 2005 and took seven months to complete. The CBC was able to establish that there had been population growth in a number of constituencies and declines in others. The constituencies that had significant gains were Nadi Open, Cunningham Open, Nausori/Naitasiri Open and Nasinu/Rewa Open, while losses were recorded in Labasa Open, Suva City Open and Vuda Open. Survey results also established that the ethnic proportions remained stable despite the changes in total population of the constituencies.

The survey was, however, a futile exercise, because the CBC could not get data for the areas not surveyed in order to make meaningful 'redistricting' possible. They were, however, satisfied with the unchanging ethnic distribution within the constituencies surveyed and, as a result, made no attempt to increase the number of heterogeneous open constituencies.

As mentioned earlier, the CBC sought public comment on the proposed boundaries in January and February 2006. Almost all groups that made submissions wanted to maintain the current boundaries because current population data were not available to review. In addition, the Electoral Commission was using the 1998 electoral boundaries in its voter registration program and it would have been a mammoth task to reallocate people within new boundaries, especially in the time available. As a result, the CBC determined that there should be no change to the existing constituency boundaries for the 2006 election.

Table 22.5　　Fijian Urban Communal constituencies, 2006

Number of people 21 years of age and over (Number of registered voters – Elections Office) = 95,582
Number of constituencies = 6
Average number of people per constituency = 15,930
Maximum and minimum number of electors per Fijian Communal constituency

Tolerance level	10 per cent (1,593)	15 per cent (2,390)
Maximum number of voters	17,523	18,320
Minimum number of voters	14,330	13,540

Note: 4 of 6 constituencies were within the 10 per cent tolerance level; 5 of 6 constituencies were within the 15 per cent tolerance level; 1 constituency – Suva City Fiji Urban Communal – was outside the 20 per cent tolerance level.

Malapportionment

Malapportionment refers to the discrepancy between the shares of parliamentary seats and the shares of population by constituencies. It applies when a set of boundaries in each of the ethnic reserved seats (Fijian Urban Communal constituencies, the General Communal, and the Indian Communal) and in the Open constituencies have unequal numbers of voters. In other words, malapportionment refers to uneven distribution within each type of constituency, not to that constitutionally entrenched inequality in the value of votes between the different types of constituency. Malapportionment violates the principle that all voters should cast a vote of equal weight and can occur if constituencies are not redrawn to accommodate population movements. Malapportionment was seen in the 2006 election in the Indian Communal constituencies and the Open constituencies, where a number of constituencies lie outside the 20 per cent tolerance level (Tables 22.5, 22.6, 22.7 and 22.8).

The future

If elections in Fiji are to be egalitarian, there is a need to redraw the electoral boundaries to reflect population shift in the past decade. Redistribution must be undertaken two or three years before an election to ensure transparency. The constitution stipulates that redistribution must be done after each census. However, there are other factors that are important in redistribution, such as the proportion of constituencies that experience significant change in population proportions, and whether or not there are marked departures from any proposed and accepted prescribed levels.

Redistribution in future will depend on Fiji's changing population composition. Bureau of Statistics' projections for 2006 show Fijians as making up 54.7 per cent of the population, ethnic Indians 38.1 per cent and others 7.2 per cent. In addition, Bakker's (forthcoming)[5] analysis of Fijian and Indian fertility shows that Fijian fertility decline is slow compared with that of Indians. The Indian fertility decline is resulting in a below replacement level of fertility. The impact of this will be reflected in the ethnic distribution of the population in future, and of course on the delimitation of electoral boundaries.

Table 22.6   General Communal constituencies, 2006

Number of people 21 years of age and over (Number of registered voters – Elections Office) = 13,820
Number of constituencies = 3
Average number of people per constituency = 4,607
Maximum and minimum number of electors per General Communal constituency

Tolerance level	10 per cent (461)	15 per cent (691)
Maximum number of voters	5,068	5,298
Minimum number of voters	4,146	3,916

Note: 1of 3 constituencies was within the 10 per cent tolerance level; 1 constituency – Western/Central General Communal – was outside the 15 per cent tolerance level.

Table 22.7   Indian Communal constituencies, 2006

Number of people 21 years of age and over (Number of registered voters – Elections Office) = 204,477
Number of constituencies = 19
Average number of people per constituency = 10,762
Maximum and minimum number of electors per Indian Communal constituency

Tolerance level	10 per cent (1,076)	15 per cent (1,614)	20 per cent (2,152)
Maximum number of voters	11,838	12,376	12,914
Minimum number of voters	9,686	9,148	8,610

Note: 7 of 19 constituencies were within the 10 per cent tolerance level; 8 constituencies were within the 15 per cent tolerance level; 9 constituencies were within the 20 per cent tolerance level; 10 Indian communal constituencies – Viti Levu East Maritime, Tavua, Ba East, Nadi Urban, Viti Levu South/Kadavu, Vanua Levu West, Laucala, Nasinu, Labasa Rural and Macuata East/Cakaudrove – were outside the 20 per cent tolerance level.

Table 22.8   Open constituencies, 2006

Number of people 21 years of age and over (Number of registered voters – Elections Office) = 479,693
Number of constituencies = 25
Average number of people per constituency = 19,188
Maximum and minimum number of electors per Open constituency

Tolerance level	10 per cent (1,919)	15 per cent (2,878)	20 per cent (3,837)
Maximum number of voters	21,106	22,065	23,024
Minimum number of voters	17,268	16,309	15,350

Note: 15 of 25 constituencies were within the 10 per cent tolerance level; another 4 constituencies were within the 15 per cent tolerance level; another 3 – were within the 20 per cent tolerance level; three constituencies – Cunningham Open, Nadi Open and Suva City Open – were outside the 20 per cent tolerance level.

Notes

[1] Constitution of the Republic of the Fiji Islands 1998, S52(3)

[2] Reilly, B. 2001. 'Evaluating the effect of the electoral system in post-coup Fiji', Pacific Economic Bulletin, 16(1):142–49.

[3] According to Section 53 of the 1997 constitution:

(1) The Constituency Boundaries Commission must, in the year following each official census, and may, at other times, review the boundaries of constituencies and determine whether or not the boundaries should, be changed to give effect to the requirements or subsections 52 (2) and (3).

(2) The Parliament may make laws relating to reviews conducted by the Commission under subsection (1), including law requiring the Commission to give notice of proposed redistributions and to hear objections before making a determination.

(3) Upon the making of a determination on a redistribution, the Commission must report its findings to the House of Representatives, together with; (a) a summary of any objections made to it; and (b) the reasons for its determination.

(4) Subject to the jurisdiction of a court to entertain an application for judicial review, a determination of the Commission is final.

[4] The Fiji Times 24/4/06.<http://www.fijitimes.com/fijielections/no-change-in-boundaries. aspx>.

[5] Bakker, M. 2006. 'Recommendations to the Government Statistician (and Census Commissioner) concerning the inclusion of retrospective questions on the 2007 Census Questionnaire'.

23

The role of the Assembly of Christian Churches in Fiji in the 2006 elections[1]

Lynda Newland

Towards the end of the polling week of the 2006 election, the Assembly of Christian Churches in Fiji (ACCF) ran a full-page advertisement in the *Fiji Times*. On the right side of the page was a Christian cross, below which the Fiji flag flew over a map of Fiji. The text on the left side of the page ran:

> THE ASSEMBLY OF CHRISTIAN CHURCHES IN FIJI (ACCF) IS REQUESTING CHURCHES
> that we all please go ✓
> and vote during this election!
> Note: PARLIAMENT IS THE SUPREME LAW MAKING BODY OF THIS NATION.
> It is God's Will that the Laws of this Land are based on the Laws of God!
> IT IS THEREFORE THE DUTY OF ALL CITIZENS OF THIS NATION TO ELECT A GOD-FEARING & PROVEN PRIME MINISTER[2]
> whose party will make righteous laws
>
> Prov 29:2
> When the righteous are in authority the people rejoice:
> But when a wicked man rules, the people groan. NKJV[3]
> GOD IS WITH US
> when we build our nation according to His ways!
> BUT NATION BUILDING WITHOUT GOD IS A REWARDLESS LABOUR!
> Ps127:1
> Unless the LORD builds the house, they labour in vain who build it;
> Unless the LORD guards the city, the watchman stays awake in vain NKJV
> In nation building, Fiji must be ruled

By the laws of God given at
Mt Sinai and at Calvary.
Building with the practice of compromising Christian and non-Christian values
as already reflected in the Constitution[4]
is misleading the nation to stand on false foundation
which is demonic and distasterous [sic] in nature.
THIS WILL SURELY BRING CURSES UPON THE NATION:
  Droughts and famines!   Earthquakes and tsunamis![5]
  Poverty and slavery!   Diseases and Deaths!

(Amos 4: 7–11)

Healthy Nation Building should be founded on God's Law
which reflects the higher and eternal values of the Kingdom of God
  LOVE   JUSTICE   PEACE
  RECONCILIATION   UNITY
WE THEREFORE HAVE NO OPTION BUT TO VOTE FOR THAT LEADER WHO
CHERISHES AND LIVES BY GOD'S LAWS
Only then would we be assured of Peace and Prosperity

(Ezekiel 34: 22–31)[6]

Putting aside questions of the legality of this kind of advertisements during the election – when political advertising is banned – the advertisement raises questions about the style of governance proposed for Fiji. It is indicative not of the views of a small fundamentalist section of the community, but of major and influential Christian churches, including the Methodist Church, the Assemblies of God (AOG), the Christian Mission Fellowship (CMF), the Church of God (COC), and a host of other Pentecostal churches, all of which form the membership of the ACCF.[7] For people living in Fiji, its message was clear: vote for Laisenia Qarase and the SDL (*Soqosoqo Duavata ni Lewenivanua*) or face spiritual and material disaster. Moreover, it was a clear call to mobilize Fijians to participate in the election in order to achieve a Christian state in which Fijians would hold paramountcy. The advertisement relied heavily on established cultural structures and values in calling the Methodist and Pentecostal churches to respond to issues within the Fijian community.[8] In this chapter, I explore the common ideological framework of the member churches of the ACCF in relation to the political sphere; and the way it informed the religious rhetoric of the 2006 election.

To understand the underlying logic of these churches, it is necessary to understand how Christianity has become central to Fijian identity and the values it implies for Fijians. Methodism first came to Fiji through the Wesleyan Methodist Missionary Society in 1835.[9] The conversion of Cakobau, a paramount chief, was pivotal for the missionaries, as large numbers of conversions followed. Called *lotu* (religion), Methodism became appropriated to such an extent that it has become viewed as one of the three pillars of Fijian society and culture, of which the other two pillars are the *vanua* (land and community) and *matanitu* (chiefly system).[10] The introduction of Catholicism, Anglicanism, Presbyterianism, Seventh-Day Adventism and, later, Hinduism, Sikhism, and Islam, brought by the indentured labourers, meant that religion in Fiji quickly became pluralistic, but the majority of indigenous Fijians have remained Methodist. Current figures suggest that 93 per cent of the Methodist Church members are Fijian.[11]

If the Methodist Church has remained the largest Christian church – with 36.3 per cent of the total population of Fiji – it has, since the 1960s, also played an increasingly important political role. Before then, indigenous Fijians were tied to their villages, and obliged to provide services for the chiefs under the Fijian Regulations. With the abolition of the regulations in the mid-1960s, the strength of the rural chiefly order was eroded, with the result that many Fijians migrated to urban areas. During this process, the Methodist Church also became progressively more influential in the political sphere.[12]

To begin with, many politicians and political agitators have been trained as pastors in the Methodist Church, and, therefore, their politics are informed by a combination of Fijian cultural values, the specific type of Methodism that arrived with the missionaries, and by more recent contact with the Middle East. For instance, in the 1970s, Sakeasi Butadroka, the founder of the Fijian Nationalist Party and a politician who was vocal in fighting for Fijian paramountcy, was a Methodist lay preacher.[13] While he and his party advocated the deporting of Indo-Fijians back to India, Fijian soldiers returning from peacekeeping in the Middle East brought back reports about Israel. According to Garrett, this revived the Methodist emphasis on Sabbatarianism, the Old Testament notion that the seventh day should be a day of rest, in conjunction with Fijian ideas of *tabu,* where holiness is associated with prohibition. The ideas that the descendants of the indentured labourers should return to India with their idolatrous religions and that Sunday should be an enforced day of rest became central themes for the increasingly political rhetoric of the *taukei*.[14]

Then, in 1987, coup leader Sitiveni Rabuka claimed he was 'Moses of the Chosen People' and that Christianity should be the official religion of Fiji – at the expense of the Indo-Fijians who were represented as heathens who threatened to overtake Fijian land.[15] Aligned closely with the Methodist Church, Rabuka invited people such as his kinsman and Methodist minister, Raikivi, to serve as a minister in the interim government.[16] Further, while Rabuka was filmed preaching his politics in his role as pastor for the Methodist Church, Indo-Fijians were harassed and beaten in disturbances on the streets of Suva.[17] Meanwhile, the general secretary of the Methodist Church and supporter of Rabuka, Reverend Manasa Lasaro, was central in influencing the military's decision to impose the Sunday Decree, which prohibited all work on Sundays. In response to the interim government's attempt to lessen the impact of the decree, roadblocks were set up at 70 places around Suva. At the same time, a split was deepening between rival factions in the Methodist Church, with the consequence that the president of the church, Rev. Josateki Koroi, who opposed Rabuka, was ousted in favour of Reverend Ratu Isireli Caucau.[18]

Looking back at that period, Lasaro explained that he would still 'like to see that Sunday is kept a special day in this country'.[19] For him, keeping Sunday as a day of rest is a sign that moral values are kept and maintained. The 1980s were about Fijians finding a voice:

> We don't want to be pushed around by any other country, no matter who it is: the colonial government or other foreign countries which are very active in this region, particularly New Zealand and Australia and of course India… Even now the feelings are still strong… What Rabuka did [the 1987 coup] sort of opened the door to indigenous Fijians. Now, with the present government [under SDL], we have seen affirmative action and since then we find a lot of Fijians going into commercial activities, a lot of Fijians have gone to higher educational institutions, a lot of Fijians have started asking questions about their own destiny as a people…

Here, Lasaro combines the politics of maintaining indigenous identity in the face of the forces of globalization with the religious and moral expression of keeping Sunday as a day of rest. Although Lasaro seemed to be arguing that it was not so much the Indo-Fijian community that was to blame for the threats to indigenous identity, but foreign governments, in an interview conducted a few days before, he had noted:

> Fijian interests are not exclusive to Fijians. Traditionally, Fijians are a very caring community. They will inconvenience themselves to accommodate the needs of their guests and friends. But the impact of economic and social changes has changed this dramatically in terms of property ownership; Fijians feel that sooner or later they will – what they hold so dear to them will be taken away by somebody else, whether he's European, Indian or anybody else for that matter.[20]

The perception of Fijians as the authentic landowners and Indo-Fijians as guests strongly resonates with the view that the ACCF has placed at the centre of its ethos. However, it differs in that Lasaro's emphasis remains on a fear that Fijian land and, by association, their culture, will be taken away from them by foreigners. By contrast, the ACCF emphasises the importance of Fijian unity, in accordance with God's plan.

Despite the visibility of Methodist Church leaders in politics, the church's dominance has not remained uncontested by those Fijians who converted to other denominations. While Pentecostal and evangelical churches had been entering Fiji since the Assemblies of God was first established in 1926, their numbers burgeoned after independence in 1970[21] and most of their converts have been Fijian Methodists. In the villages, such churches were perceived as threatening the chief and the chiefly system,[22] and, before 1987, they had to be registered. Now, however, they are free to establish themselves, despite periodic calls from the Methodist Church for their numbers to be limited. Thus, the post-election coup led to Methodist leaders undertaking a different strategy and spearheading the unification of many of these churches with the Methodist Church under the umbrella organisation, the ACCF.[23]

The 2000 coup demonstrated that sentiments from 1987 remained strong in parts of the Fijian community, despite much of the community rejecting the arguments of George Speight, or no longer viewing a coup as an acceptable way to achieve Fijian ethno-nationalist objectives. This became clear when the actions of Christian leaders differed during and after the coup. For example, Rev. Ratu Epeli Kanaimawi, head of the Worldwide Church of God and a chief of Cakaudrove, led the Great Council of Chiefs into a meeting of mediation with Speight.[24] Meanwhile, Reverend Kurulo, head of the Christian Mission

Fellowship, wrote to Speight to demand the release of the hostages, and called prayer meetings. Speight then asked Kurulo for a reconciliation meeting to be held at parliament, at which a group of pastors spoke with him and visited the hostages.[25] While the timing of Kurulo's visit is not clear, it was reported that leaders from the Methodist Church, All Nations, and Apostles Gospel Outreach Fellowship International (AGOFI) participated in a 'Festival of Praise' at the parliamentary complex.[26]

Churches such as the Seventh-Day Adventists,[27] the AOG, Fiji, the CMF, the United Pentecostal Church International of Fiji, and the Anglican Church denounced the coup in advertisements in the *The Fiji Times* and the *Daily Post*.[28] The president of the Methodist Church, Reverend Tomasi Kanailagi, also took out a full-page advertisement which said that, while Speight's terrorist activities could not be supported, the Methodist Church supported the interim government, because all of Speight's objectives had been met,[29] a view often reiterated during the coup.[30]

As a result of feelings that 'the Fijian people were very much fragmented', leaders from the AOG made a traditional approach to Rev. Kanailagi and asked him to call a meeting of churches, the consequence of which was the formation of the ACCF.[31] Pastor Tamani, an influential leader in the CMF, noted that, 'we wanted to prove to the Great Council of Chiefs that these small churches, we can work together. The problem is not in the church. The problem is in leadership'.[32] In this way, the member churches of the newly established ACCF shared the vision of uniting the indigenous Fijian community into a political force through the unity of churches as part of God's plan. If the Methodist and Pentecostal God is the spiritual pinnacle of the ACCF, the administrative organization is chaired by a leading member of the Methodist Church: in 2006, that member is Reverend Waqairatu, the Methodist Church's assistant general secretary.

In the view of ACCF leaders, the wounds between Fijians must be healed before any healing of the nation can be undertaken.[33] Such a view is predicated on the continuing theme that Fijians as the indigenous landowning people should have privileges over and above other Fiji citizens, particularly Indo-Fijians, who are viewed as guests. This was echoed in an interview with Rev. Matalomani, Coordinator for the ACCF:

Forget about the Indians. It's amongst the Fijians and, if the Fijians are unhappy, the Indians will be in trouble too because we will not give up our land. When the Fijians are satisfied that their land, their right to belonging comes back to them, we are a giving people, we are an accommodating race, and it is only the differences in the political field that are blowing out the racial differences.[34]

This view is typical in that it continues to promote the idea that Fijian landownership is threatened by changes in the law, despite the fact that, by 1992, 87 per cent of the land in Fiji has been categorized as Native Land[35], and despite the protection of Fijian land in the constitution. In contrast to Rabuka and Lasaro, people like Reverend Matalomani no longer consider Indo-Fijians an imminent threat. Rather, they view Fijians as having suffered primarily from colonization, when laws robbed Fijians of land that was rightfully theirs, and they consider, therefore, that such laws need to be revisited.[36] However, once again, the threat to Fijian unity is seen to come from outside.

The ACCF's vision statement is that ACCF members must strive to make Fiji 'God's Treasured Possession', as a nation that honours and glorifies God. Further elaborated into four principles, the mission statement notes that all flocks must unite, members should live God's way of love, leadership should be God-fearing, and Fiji should be reconciled for peace and prosperity. Reverend Kanaimawi (the acting chairman at the time of interview) further explained that the last principle is drawn from Corinthians II:5, which describes God's reconciliation to humanity through Christ.[37] The principle also resonates with concerns regarding the reconciliation of Fijian communities (*vanua*) after the 2000 coup, and echoes the Fijian notion of the good chief, who, by virtue of his wisdom, bestows peace and prosperity upon the village, thus revealing a conjunction between ideas about chiefliness and *lotu*.

In advocating that members strive for a nation that honours and glorifies God, the vision statement implicitly endorses the notion of a Christian state, where all laws are based on Christian teachings as interpreted by the member churches of the ACCF. While this is the same stance that Rabuka held in 1987,[38] many accept that, if Fiji were to become a Christian state, those who are not Christian should be tolerated, providing they conducted themselves according to Christian law.[39] The notion of the exclusively Christian state has periodically emerged since the 1987 coups, and it reappeared in March 2006 in an ACCF project aimed at healing the land, which then became a call to make each province in Fiji Christian.

'Healing the land' is the core project of the Evangelical Fellowship, recently renamed the Covenant Evangelical Church and a member of the ACCF. Under the project, a team visits the provinces to reconcile chiefs and all the Christian denominations in the villages, and to eradicate social ills. Reverend Kanaimawi, who was acting chairman of the ACCF in 2005, described them as:

> very skilled in healing the land. They go out to the village and get all the villagers, irrespective of what church they are, look at their problems, do a spiritual mapping, map out where the devil has been influential – whether it's a killing field in one place or it's where they worshipped demons in the past – and then they cleanse those out. Then the people repent for what they have done and ask God to come in and the whole village just transforms itself.[40]

Critics have noted that 'healing the land' includes exorcising gods of other religions (including Hinduism) from the land, and supporting the political rhetoric of the SDL; a counter to the army's truth and justice exercise.[41]   Only two months before the 2006 election, Ratu Soqosoqo, an influential member of the ACCF and Kadavu chief, was reported as saying that, 'If we cannot make Fiji a Christian country then we chiefs should make our territories and everyone in it Christians'.[42]

While the provinces experience a particular kind of Christian revival, Fijian allegiance to the increasing diversity of emerging Pentecostal/evangelical churches is not, according to Kanaimawi, considered a threat to the established churches, but rather 'a link for us to some greater things that God is preparing'.[43] This statement demonstrates the ACCF's strategy of incorporation and cooperation between churches as much as it does the theological importance of the return of Jesus to harvest souls at the 'End-Times', in which most of the member churches believe. Indeed, as almost all these churches except the Methodist Church are Pentecostal/evangelical, with roots in the US Pentecostal movement, their theology is based on the idea of being born again with the entry of the Holy Spirit and the conviction that the End-Times, when Christians will be saved and havoc wreaked upon the earth and unbelievers, are near.[44] The extent to which most member churches are theologically similar enables the ACCF to draw upon and coordinate the different strengths of the churches in different activities. For instance, the CMF has ACCF support in inviting international evangelists to Fiji, and the Covenant Evangelical Church conducts ceremonies to heal the land in the provinces on the ACCF's behalf.[45]

Under the previous government, the ACCF worked closely with government and was perceived as a think-tank for the Prime Minister. ACCF leaders justified this as furthering the project of reconciliation among Fijians, which is criticized by those arguing for ethnic equality.[46] Certainly, the Prime Minister is known for his devout Methodism, and his comments before the election showed his commitment to ACCF principles. He argued the need for a Fijian prime minister and for the notion that Fiji was a nation of communities rather than a nation of individuals, where communal needs (and particularly those of Fijians) needed to be respected over and above the individualism that he perceived in human rights, saying:

> Now for the Fijian people, we need to be acutely aware that democracy in terms of every individual being equal in their basic rights and freedom is quite different from the value systems that provide the basis for traditional Fijian society.[47]

According to Qarase, the fact that Fijians were both numerically 'the majority community' and the landowners meant that the Fijian people should be consulted first over national issues. If this suggests a belief in Fijian paramountcy, the SDL manifesto openly expresses the values behind their objectives as:

1) The ideals and principles of the Christian faith
2) Respect for the Vanua and the cultures and traditions of the indigenous Fijians and Rotumans
3) Respect for the cultures, traditions and religious beliefs of other communities in Fiji
4) Recognition for the paramountcy of indigenous Fijian and Rotuman interests, as proclaimed in the Constitution
5) Respect for legal authority and law and order
6) Respect for human and group rights
7) Honesty in public life and general standards of conduct, which reflect our fundamental beliefs.[48]

With Christianity at the apex of SDL values, SDL uses the symbol of the dove to represent their commitment to Christianity, but, for Fijians, this is clearly a reference to a Christianity embedded in the particular brand of Fijian cultural values propagated by the ACCF. Reflecting ACCF concerns, points

1, 2, and 4 all show that the SDL give priority to indigenous Christian Fijians and Rotumans and their communities over other citizens and individual rights in Fiji.[49] Likewise, point 6 suggests that group rights should be considered as much as human rights, which are often perceived by ACCF members as individualistic and therefore foreign.[50] In addition, if the SDL shares its ideology with the ACCF, their allegiance is also displayed openly in political events. For example, religious leaders from the Methodist Church and the AOG led the prayers at the launch of the SDL manifesto at a rally in Suva.[51]

As the turn-out in the elections steadied, the ACCF advertisement discussed earlier, appeared in *The Fiji Times*, a clear call to indigenous Fijians to vote in support of Qarase and the SDL, and a sign of ACCF's continued participation in the political sphere. Many ACCF principles appeared in this advertisement, with particular emphasis on mobilizing members to vote for God-fearing leadership in order that they may live by Christian laws, especially in response to the constitution's tolerance of homosexuality.[52] The latter became publicized in a local case in which an Australian tourist and a local were sentenced to two years' prison for homosexuality. The High Court over-rode the sentence by referring to the constitution, which effectively legalizes private consensual homosexual relationships. In response, the Methodist Church publicized its rejection of homosexuality as a civil right by organizing a protest march in Nausori, with the intention of organizing further marches around the country, a move supported by the AOG.[53] Reverend Waqairatu was further reported as saying that homosexuality could only be eradicated if everyone was converted to Christianity or other religions.[54] In support, the ACCF leadership sent a letter to the government, arguing against 'all sexual perversions that somewhat has [sic] been encouraged by the so-called 'sexual orientation' clause in the Constitution Section 38 (2) (a)'.[55] Commonly viewed as foreign, this clause is perceived as threatening the morality of the Fijian community and disengaging them from God's blessings.[56]

Thus, the ACCF's concerns about Fiji legislation relate specifically to existing laws about land, reconciliation between Fijians, and sexual morality, as instances of the need to correct the relationship of indigenous Fijians to each other and to God. In the leadership's view, when the relationship with God is correct, all else will fall into place (a concept I have heard many times when

interviewing ACCF leaders). Notwithstanding this view, the advertisement
in the election showed that the ACCF leaders were also aware that Christians
belonging to ACCF churches needed to be mobilized to vote for the correct
political leader. Given their close relationship and shared vision with Qarase
and the SDL, the ACCF leaders were faced with a potential problem over and
above that of ensuring that a Fijian prime minister was elected: the problem
being that, if Fijians were not mobilized into voting and the Indo-Fijian Fiji
Labour Party (FLP) were to win, the political influence of the ACCF would
likely cease altogether.

After the election, Qarase thanked God for his victory, saying, 'I would like
to acknowledge the hand of God for the victory. I believe God has a plan for
Fiji and the SDL is part of that plan for Fiji'.[57] Elsewhere, he is reported as
thanking 'the Christian churches and people for their prayers and members
of the Great Council of Chiefs for their support', saying that he believed, 'it
is the Lord's choice that allowed his party to remain in power for another
term'.[58] The swearing-in was opened with Methodist prayers. Many of Qarase's
ministers are Methodists, including Josefa Vosanibola, Ratu Meli Saukuru,
Misaele Weleilakeba, and Jone Waqairatu; the last of whom is also the brother
of Reverend Waqairatu, assistant general secretary of the Methodist Church
and chairman of the ACCF.[59]

Therefore, it might have been a surprise for the ACCF leadership that, despite
Qarase's belief in the need for a Fijian government to promote Fijian interests
and his preference for the FLP to stay in opposition,[60] he offered the opposition
seats in the cabinet.[61] As the offer was perhaps a tactical manoeuvre, Qarase
was himself a little surprised that the FLP accepted.[62] For his part, Kanaimawi
noted that a multiparty cabinet would not work, but that it was 'worth giving
it a try'.[63] Given the oppositional aspirations of the two parties, whereby the
SDL wishes to promote Christian and Fijian interests, while the FLP seeks to
promote Indo-Fijians as citizens with equal political rights, the move towards
a multiparty cabinet is indeed ambitious.

The rhetoric of the ACCF's advertisement thus draws from culturally
accepted ideas about how to bring God's blessings to Fiji, which are circulating
in many of the Christian Fijian communities. According to these ideas, if

people in Fiji do not recognise the need for God's leadership, the End-Times will bring retribution to all. A multiparty cabinet, therefore, brings with it the ambivalence and tensions of a compromise, which, in the final judgement, is not in the interests of the ACCF.

Notes

[1]   Research in this paper draws on the results of research conducted since 2001. The first period was funded by the School of Social and Economic Development (SSED) at the University of the South Pacific (USP), with the help of a research assistant, Akanise Tarabe. In 2003–2004, I was further funded by the School of Social Sciences and the Centre for Asia Pacific Social Transformation Studies (CAPSTRANS) at the University of Newcastle, and transcriptions were paid for by SSED, USP, in 2005. These interviews appear here for the first time. In the same year, subsequent material was gathered during research for the Pacific Theological College (PTC) and the Ecumenical Centre for Research, Education and Advocacy (ECREA), which is available in Newland, 2006, and Newland, forthcoming. This paper has benefited from the comments of Robert Norton, and the contributions/comments of Jon Fraenkel, Steve Ratuva, Jone Dakuvula, Kevin Barr, Manfred Ernst, and Jonathan Prasad.

[2]   Fijian Laisenia Qarase, head of the SDL (*Soqosoqo Duavata ni Lewenivanua*) party, was a staunch Methodist and previous Prime Minister, whereas Indo-Fijian Mahendra Chaudhry, head of the Fiji Labour Party (FLP), had been deposed in the 2000 coup.

[3]   New King James Version.

[4]   This refers most particularly to the Constitution's tolerance of homosexuality.

[5]   The reference to tsunamis had particular currency, given the tsunami warning issued in Suva in the early hours of 4 May 2006.

[6]   *The Fiji Times*, 10 May 2006, p.22. The same advertisement appeared in *Fiji Daily Post* and the *Fiji Sun* immediately prior to the elections (6 May 2006 and 7 May 2006, respectively). Rev. Akuila Yabaki, head of the Citizens Constitutional Forum (CCF), subsequently complained about them to the police and the Supervisor of Elections (pers.comm. Jone Dakuvula, 20 June 2006).

[7]   Current members are listed as: the Apostles Gospel Outreach Fellowship International (AGOFI); Assemblies of God, Fiji (AOG); Christian Mission Fellowship (CMF); Christian Outreach Centre (COC); Church of God of Fiji (COG); Covenant Evangelical Church (CEC), [formerly the Evangelical Fellowship]; Grace Baptist Church; Advanced Breakthrough Ministry (ABC); Jesus Power Church; the Methodist Church in Fiji and Rotuma; the Methodist Davuilevu Theological College; New Life Centre; Pentecostal Churches of Fiji; Rescue Mission Fellowship; the Redeemed Christian Church of God (RCCG), the Worldwide Church of God in Fiji and Tonga; the Fiji Brethren Assemblies Partnership (Gospel Churches); the Family Life Ministry; the New Methodist Church; Fiji Baptist Convention; the Prison Chaplancy; Impact World Tour/YWAM; Prison Fellowship; Global Sports Ministries; Summit Ministries (World Views); Teach us to Pray (ministry); and Assemble Communication (ACCF, 2005). Churches that strongly diverge from these views and which remain outside the ACCF include the Roman Catholic Church, the Anglican and Presbyterian churches, the Salvation Army, the Seventh-day Adventists, the Latter-day Saints and the Jehovah's Witnesses.

8 In this way, this paper reflects Carrithers' argument that there is a need for anthropologists to study rhetoric as a form of persuasion which draws from cultural structures to respond imaginatively to historical events (Carrithers, M. 2005. 'Why Anthropologists Should Study Rhetoric', *Journal of the Royal Anthropological Institute*, 11(3):577–583).

9 Thornley, A. 1996. 'The Legacy of Siloam: Tahitian Missionaries in Fiji' in Munro, D. & Thornley, A. (eds) *The Covenant Makers: Islander Missionaries in the Pacific*, Pacific Theological College and IPS Publications, Suva.

10 There are various terms for this triple-aspected feature of Fijian culture. Tuwere describes it as 'the Trinitarian solemnity' (Tuwere, I.S. 2002. *Vanua: Towards a Fijian Theology of Place*, IPS Publications, Suva and College of St John the Evangelist, Auckland). Both Niukula and Tuwere have written books as Methodist theologians, exploring the connections between Methodism and Fijian culture; Niukula, P. n.d. 'The triple aspect of Fijian society: the Three Pillars', Christian Writing Project, Suva.

11 For more details see, Newland, L. 2006. 'Fiji' in Ernst, M. (ed.) 2006. *Globalization and the Re-Shaping of Christianity in the Pacific Islands*, Pacific Theological College, Suva.

12 Given that the Methodist Church is so strongly related to Fijian culture, one of its contradictions has been its Indian Division, which, in 1996, had nearly 5,500 members (Fiji Islands Bureau of Statistics, 1996). Many Indo-Fijians left the Church after the 2000 coup, however, and up to 3,000 have since migrated and formed Methodist Indo-Fijian communities in Canada, the USA, New Zealand and Australia (Newland, 2006).

13 Garrett, J. 1990. 'Uncertain sequel: The social and religious scene in Fiji since the coups', *The Contemporary Pacific*, 2(1):87–111; Norton, R. 1990. *Race and Politics in Fiji*, St. Lucia, Qld, University of Queensland Press, Qld.

14 Garrett, J. 1997. *Where Nets Were Cast: Christianity in Oceania since World War II*, Institute of Pacific Studies, USP and World Council of Churches, Suva.

15 Ratuva, S. 1999. 'Ethnic Politics, Communalism and Affirmative Action in Fiji: A Critical and Comparative Study', Unpublished PhD Thesis, University of Sussex, England; Norton, R. 1990. *Race and Politics in Fiji*.

16 Garrett, J. 1997. *Where Nets Were Cast.*

17 Wolmsley, C. (producer) 1987. *Paradise in Peril* (film), Martin Young (Reporter), BBC.

18 Halapua, W. 2003. *Tradition, Lotu, and Militarism in Fiji*, Fiji Institute of Applied Studies, Nadi; Ryle, J. 2001. 'My God, my land: interwoven paths of Christianity and tradition in Fiji'. Unpublished thesis, University of London; Ratuva, S. 1999. 'Ethnic Politics, Communalism and Affirmative Action in Fiji'; Ernst, M. 1994. *Winds of Change: Rapidly Growing Religious Groups in the Pacific Islands*, Pacific Conference of Churches, Suva; Garrett, J. 1997. *Where Nets Were Cast;* Garrett, J. 1990. 'Uncertain sequel'.

19 Interview with M. Lasaro, Education Officer, Methodist Church, 11 February 2004.

20 Interview with M. Lasaro, Education Officer, Methodist Church, 5 February 2004.

21 Ernst, M. 1994. *Winds of Change.*

22 Newland, L. 2004. 'Turning the Spirits into Witchcraft: Pentecostalism in Fijian Villages', *Oceania* 75(1):1–18.

23 However, the Methodist Church continues to call for a limit to new churches (e.g. *The Fiji Times*, 13 August 2006, p.1).

24 Fraenkel, J. 2000. 'The Clash of Dynasties and the Rise of Demagogues: Fiji's Tauir Vakaukauwa of May 2000', *Journal of Pacific History*, 35(3):1–17.

[25] Newland, L. 2006. 'Fiji' in Ernst, M. (ed.) 2006. *Globalization and the Re-Shaping of Christianity*

[26] Kikau, R. 2000. 'Christians gather for service', *The Fiji Times* 29 May, p.3.

[27] In a post-coup meeting, the Seventh-day Adventists changed their president and now maintain a radical disinterest in politics. However, Speight and his former mentor, Jim Ah Koy, were both Seventh-day Adventists, and many of the villages that obeyed Speight's call from Parliament House in July 2000 for an 'uprising of the *vanua*' were Seventh-day Adventist villages. Speight and the brother of the former President of the Seventh-day Adventists (among others) were subsequently imprisoned (personal communication, Jon Fraenkel, Jone Dakuvula, August, 2006).

[28] For example, *The Fiji Times,* 8 June 2000, 10 June 2000, 17 June 2000.

[29] *The Fiji Times,* 17 June 2000, p.44.

[30] Field, M., Baba, T. and Nabobo-Baba, U. 2005. *Speight of Violence: Inside Fiji's 2000 Coup.* Reed Books, Auckland.

[31] 3 February 2004 Interview with Reverend Waqairatu, Assistant General Secretary of the Methodist Church who has recently become the Chairman of the ACCF, also described the formation of the ACCF in 2001 as a 'response to the fragmentation of indigenous communities by political parties' (Newland, L. 2006. 'Fiji').

[32] Interview with Rev. Tamani, Education Officer, Christian Mission Fellowship, 12 February 2004.

[33] It should be noted that the Roman Catholic Church has taken quite a different stance and has been involved in reconciliation meetings between Fijians and Indo-Fijians across the country.

[34] Newland, L. (forthcoming) Social Justice in Fiji: Christian Perspectives, ECREA, Suva.

[35] Coalition of Human Rights. 2005. 'Submission to CERD' in Ghand, G. (ed.) *The CERD Papers: Papers on Racial Discrimination Volume 1*, Fiji Institute of Applied Studies, Lautokoa; Halapua, W. 2003. *Tradition, Lotu, and Militarism in Fiji.*

[36] History suggests a more complex picture. One of the examples Reverend Matalomani used in his discussion with me was in the allocation of land to another landless family unit who were also Fijian over 50 years ago (Newland, forthcoming). A revisiting of such laws may well mean making that family unit's descendants landless.

[37] Newland, L. 2006. 'Fiji'.

[38] Ernst, M. 1994. *Winds of Change.*

[39] Kanaimawi cited in Newland , L. 2006. 'Fiji'.

[40] Cited in Newland, L. 2006. 'Fiji'.

[41] Kevin Barr, personal communication, 3 July 2006. The Evangelical Fellowship has been healing the land since at least 2003, when they travelled with Qarase, ACCF heads, representatives of the Great Council of Chiefs, and other officials, to Nabutautau Village, where Rev. Thomas Baker had been murdered 136 years before (Harvest Times. 2003. *Healing the Land* (24):20–22). Since then, 'healing the land' has become a major emphasis of the ACCF and was particularly visible prior to the elections.

[42] Fijilive.com, 21 May 2006 'Provinces want a Christian State'

[43] Newland, L. 2006. 'Fiji'.

[44] There are, nonetheless, theological tensions, as Methodist leaders feel uneasy about Pentecostal/Evangelical ideas of receiving the Holy Spirit and speaking in tongues, although

some Methodist congregations have absorbed the concept of being born again. There are also other differences between Pentecostal/Evangelical groups. For instance, as the New Life Centre is multiracial in composition, it does not accept ideas they deem discriminatory (Newland 2006).

45   Newland, L. 2006. 'Fiji'.
46   Newland, L. 2006. 'Fiji'.
47   Singh, M. 'PM must be Fijian: Qarase', *The Fiji Times* 4 May 2006, p.3.
48   Soqosoqo Duavata ni Lewenivanua (SDL). 2006. 'Beat Poverty, Raise Prosperity', SDL Manifesto, www.sdlparty.com.fj – accessed 23 June 2006.
49   While point 3 may seem to counter-balance point 2, respect for the indigenous community is prioritised over and above and separately from respect for other communities. In other words, some cultures are given more validity than others.
50   Newland, L. 2006. 'Fiji'.
51   Personal communication, Steve Ratuva, July 2006.
52   The ACCF was also actively involved in the legal justifications for the Promotion of Reconciliation, Tolerance, and Unity Bill (Newland 2006).
53   Newland (forthcoming).
54   *The Fiji Times,* 3 September 2005.
55   Letter to Director of Prosecutions from Kanaimawi Gavadi Kacimaiwai, 22 April 2005.
56   Just after the elections, similar arguments were made about the film, *The Da Vinci Code*, which provoked the Methodist Church to march in Suva. See, for instance, Fijilive.com, 4 June 2006.
57   *Herald Sun,* 17 May 2006 'Qarase claims victory in Fiji vote'.
58   *The Fiji Times,* 2 June 2006
59   Soqosoqo Duavata ni Lewenivanua (SDL). 2006. 'Beat Poverty, Raise Prosperity', SDL Manifesto, www.sdlparty.com.fj – accessed 23 June 2006.
60   *Herald Sun*, 17 May 2006.
61   While in the constitution, this had never been attempted before.
62   *The Fiji Times*, 21 May 2006.
63   *The Fiji Times,* 20 May 2006.

24

The role of Hindu and Muslim organizations during the 2006 election

Jonathon Prasad[1]

On the walls of many Fiji Indian households, next to pictures of Hindu deities, hangs the photograph of Mahendra Chaudhry. Routinely garlanded whenever *pujas* (religious ceremonies) are performed, the image depicts a leader often cast in the role of saviour, deity and martyr. Transcending the realm of politics and entering into mythology, Chaudhry evokes the role of King Rama in the Ramcaritmanas, a popular Sanatan religious text; a good, just ruler banished from his kingdom and forced to wander in the wilderness enduring numerous trials at the hands of *raksas* (demons) until he is permitted to return home and take up his rightful place on the throne. The tragedy of Labour's rise and fall between 1999 and 2001, and the righteousness of its cause at the 2006 poll seemed to mimic Hindu mythology. On the campaign trail, Fiji Labour Party (FLP) candidates appealed to the symbolism of Hinduism, weaving marigold garlands normally used for prayer and laying these at the feet of elders whilst touching their feet as a traditional sign of respect.

The relationship of Hindu and Muslim symbolism to the politics of Fiji needs to be seen in the broader context of the relations between the migrant-descended and indigenous Fijian communities. Nearly all ethnic Fijians are Christian, whereas the Fiji Indian population is approximately 76.7 per cent Hindu, 15.9 per cent Muslim and 6.1 per cent Christian.[2] The Christian churches in Fiji, in particular the Methodist Church, have often been associated with a virulent brand of Fijian nationalism, including calls for the country to become a 'Christian state'.[3] The governing Soqosoqo Duavata ni Lewenivanua (SDL) party's manifesto explicitly paid homage to 'the ideals and principles of the Christian faith'.[4] As with minority religious groups elsewhere in the world, Hindu and Muslim religious leaders have, unsurprisingly, responded by emphasizing the importance of secular politics, the importance of distance between faith and state, and their own lack of strong ties to any of the major political parties. In addition, the collectively felt pressures on the Indian community in the wake of the coups of 1987 and 2000 have emphasized the need for a common front, and diminished political articulation of internal cultural difference. As a result, the influence of religious organizations and symbolism on the Indian community has become more subtle, nuanced and indirect – on balance, lessening in favour of a greater engagement with educational advancement.

The way in which Indian religious organizations influence the political process has changed over the past two decades along with the culture of politics in Fiji. Previously, charismatic political leaders linked to religious organizations could count on the support of the leadership of those organizations and, in turn, the votes of their members. Voting was based on religious affiliation as much as on political persuasion. The events of 1987 did much to alter the political landscape, with religious groups becoming increasingly self-conscious of their activities and public profile. This led them to adapt their strategy and sphere of influence to a more focused approach, targeting education as a specific policy issue, as it is an area in which they have a vested interest.

This is not to say that communal voting is no longer relevant for both Indo-Fijians and Fijians; it is still very much a part of the political culture of Fiji. Both groups continue to vote for those parties that have the highest levels of communal appeal. Party policies and political manifestos rarely receive close scrutiny from the electorate. As a result, ethnic block voting, with its emphasis on ethnic allegiances, is commonplace, and religious persuasion acquires political salience. This chapter aims to assess the extent to which Indo-Fijian religious organizations continue to influence the electoral process, and the way in which this is achieved. In order to understand the culture of Indo-Fijian politics, we need to begin by understanding the origins of intra-communal divisions, which continue to shape political realities.

The myth of the Indian 'community'

To the gaze of the outside world, Fiji begins with the Fijians and ends with the Indians: two neatly packaged identities that need little explanation and can be interpreted without difficulty. These two truncated forms of grand traditions are regarded as unproblematic and immediately accessible. The international media chose to adopt this interpretation in order to portray the coups of 1987 and 2000. However, such a view fails to take account of the degree of fragmentation that exists within both communities. In the case of the Fijians, challenges to the idea of group homogeneity are based upon regional power struggles, which have led to a fragile political unity during elections.[5] This is highlighted by the elections of April 1977, 1987 and 1999, when divisions within the community led to defeat for each of the parties presumed to have majority ethnic Fijian support. In order to avoid a repeat of this during the 2006 election, and in part also because of the large number of parties (20) contesting in Fijian communal seats, calls were made for Fijian unity.

A number of divisions exist within the Indian community; these developed historically as a result of the indenture process and, later, during the post-indenture period. They generated distinct regional and linguistic identities, which would later crystallize around new religious organizations and lead to the formalization of deep hostilities. Beneath the umbrella term 'Indian' are a number of religious groups – Hindus, Muslims and Sikhs – each claiming a distinct cultural heritage and identity on which they continue to draw. Further sources of differentiation resulted from the various regions from which they originally came – particularly the divisions between northern and southern Indians, which in turn led to linguistic divisions.[6] The arrival of free Indians – mainly Punjabis and Gujaratis who paid their own fares to Fiji in order to provide services for the indentured labourers – led to strained relationships between the two groups, as the later-arriving free Indians prospered to a greater degree than did the former indentured labourers.[7]

During the indenture period, these differences were irrelevant, due to the shared experience of living through *narak,* or hell, as the labourers referred to it. This provided them with a shared identity based upon the suffering they endured[8], and was further strengthened by the concept of the *jahazi bhai* ('ship brothers'). Ship brothers were the fictive kin who had travelled together from India and worked together on the plantations. Their relationships were based upon common experience, and cut across religious, regional and caste differences, with groups co-existing and sharing in one another's culture and religious functions. Such was the extent of interaction between the two groups that an early mosque was built at Nausori with funds largely contributed by Hindus prior to 1920.[9] However, such generosity was short-lived; during the post-indenture period of the 1920s and 1930s, differences became apparent when various religious groups began organized programs of building schools, temples and mosques.[10] Indians formed groups to advance these objectives – often with the guidance of missionaries brought from India. It was these missionaries from outside the colony who highlighted the differences between groups and led to the formation of oppositional identities.

Romila Tharpar convincingly argues that Hinduism is an 'invented modern tradition' from which an ancient identity was constructed during the 19th century. By drawing together a number of local traditions[11], political support was mobilized for Indian independence.[12] As a modern construct, the term Hinduism remains a contested category. In the absence of a clear definition of what Hinduism was, two major streams emerged – Sanatan Dharm[13] (the Eternal Tradition) and Arya Samaj, both of which vied for authenticity in India and, subsequently, Fiji.[14] The Sanatanis are regarded as orthodox; they emphasize the importance of the Epic tradition of the Mahabharata and Ramcaritmanas. Integral to the faith are deity worship and ritual performances. Its devotees regard it as the most accessible form of Hinduism due to its emphasis on *bhakti* (devotional) forms of worship. In Fiji, the Shree Sanatan Dharm Pratinidhi Sabha (SDS) has the largest following of any of the Indian religious organizations. It was established in 1928 to improve literacy and education among Indians, but also to provide a countervailing voice to the reformist Arya Pratinidhi Sabha (APS/Fiji).[15]

The Aryas dominated the political scene in Fiji in the period immediately after indenture, establishing a central body in 1917.[16] In contrast to the Sanatanis, the Aryas adhere only to the Vedic tradition. They reject the Epics and what they regard as the superfluous rituals attached to them. Bitter debates erupted between the two groups during the late 1920s and early 1930s.[17] These controversies were largely instigated by several preachers, and played out variously in public debates and the media, which focused on child marriage, widow remarriage, and the sexual conduct of prophets and gods. Several controversial published works critical (often obscenely so) of religious leaders from the Sanatan, Arya and Muslim faiths were imported.[18] The Aryas were scornful of the Sanatan corpus of the Epic tradition, especially the Ramcaritmanas, which led to heated debates between the two groups. These debates tore the Indian community apart at the time, and left it weakened when negotiating with the colonial government and sugar companies. Whilst the divisions are still evident today, they are not as pronounced as they were in the 1930s and 1940s, and tend to be focused on fundamental differences in religious practice. Politically, this has led to divisions between the groups during the post-independence era. Most notably, the APS/Fiji originally supported Ratu Mara's Alliance Party, but subsequently shifted support to the FLP; most of its members, it is believed, then shifted to the SDL party in 2006. By contrast, the leadership of the SDS has consistently supported the National Federation Party (NFP).

Further divisions within the Hindu community arose between those originating from northern India and those from the south (the latter arriving in Fiji as indentured labourers later than the former). Those of south Indian origin, despite being Sanatan Hindus, bore the brunt of what may be termed 'black-racism' as a result of them generally having a darker skin tone than north Indians. Culturally and historically, they were perceived as different from the other migrant communities.[19] Forming only a quarter of the Indian population, they were victimized as a minority group. In some instances, Indian community schools in western Viti Levu refused to admit south Indian children. This demonstrated a belief widely held by south Indian families that, as a socially isolated and economically marginalized group, they counted for little in the social and political agenda of the Fiji Indian leadership.[20]

Reaction to exclusion and disadvantage led to the formation of the TISI Sangam in 1926. Through the preservation and promotion of south Indian culture, that organization sought to protect people of south Indian origin from prejudice, while at the same time providing an educational base for the south Indian community. Despite being closely identified with the Sanatan religious tradition, the TISI Sangam considers itself a cultural organization, open to members of various religious backgrounds as long as they are able to trace their ancestral roots to south India. However, the idea of a unified south Indian group was short-lived as divisions began to appear within the Sangam. Telugu-speaking Indians originating from Andhra Pradesh felt that their interests were not being represented. A prominent leader from Andhra Pradesh, Alipaty Tataiya, accused the executive members of the TISI Sangam of deliberately recruiting unqualified people to executive posts within the TISI Sangam in order to ensure that they would receive no opposition in the promotion of the Tamil community and culture.[21] Future leader of the NFP A.D. Patel was at the time legal advisor to the TISI Sangam executive, and a target for Telugu criticism.[22] This led Tataiya, who was one of the founders of the TISI Sangam, to found a separate organization, the Andhra Sangam (AS), in 1941, to protect the interests of the Telegu-speaking community. This mirrored events in India, where active agitation would eventually lead to the creation of the state of Andhra Pradesh in 1953. As a result, the Andhra Sangam sustained a long-run hostility towards A.D. Patel and the NFP. While these hostilities are no longer as pronounced, they still continue to influence the pattern of support for political parties. In recent elections, the leadership of the TISI Sangam has continued to support the NFP, while the leadership of the Andhra Sangam has supported the FLP.[23]

Another minority group in Fiji, the Muslims, began to assert their communal identity during the 1920s, partly as a result of increased religious and political tensions in India. The Fiji Muslim League (FML) was formed in 1926, and was to serve as a central coordinating body that would try to realize the ambitions of Muslims to hold office.[24] It also made possible a unified Muslim voice against the activities of the Arya Samaj in Fiji – and especially against its preacher, Sri Krishna. Sri Krishna preached that the Muslims and Indian Christians were against progress, a claim that generated considerable anxiety on the part of the Muslim community.[25] Since the 1920s, the FML has resisted Muslim incorporation into the Indian communal rolls, agitating for separate representation based upon distinct Muslim religious and cultural identity and history. The rift between the Aryas and FML was reinforced by the experience of Hindus and Muslims during the partition of the Indian subcontinent during independence. Following Fiji's independence in 1970, the call for separate Muslim representation found considerable support from sections of the indigenous Fijian élite, who saw it as a means of decentralizing the Indian community's numerical strength. In the aftermath of the 1987 coup, the leadership of the FML gave its support to the Great Council of Chiefs' proposal for Fijian dominance in Parliament, in the hope that it would lead to them receiving separate political representation.[26] Lal suggests that this effectively provided support for the Nationalist Taukei Movement.[27] A section of the Muslim community was instrumental in helping to establish the Alliance Party[28] and maintained strong relationships with it – and later the SDL party – after independence; however, they are pragmatic when it comes to securing their goal of separate representation, and backed the FLP in 1999.

A significant cleavage, which continues to influence the culture of politics in Fiji, is the division between those who arrived as free Indians (Gujaratis and Punjabis) and those descended from indentured labourers. The free Indians were more successful in maintaining a distinct identity in the post-indenture period, partly because their ties to their homeland and their freedom to return whenever they chose meant that family ties were maintained – with two-way trade, in remittances from Fiji, and in merchandise from India, being established. Cultural and linguistic traditions were also maintained and renewed through visits 'home' for marriage etc. Most Gujaratis chose not to wed Fiji Indians, but to return to India to marry within their caste. Caste remained important for Gujaratis, as most immigrants from the same caste were related, which in business meant that they joined together to fight against non-Gujarati competition. This sense of group loyalty was an aid to their business success, but also led to resentment from other, less successful, groups. Several Gujarati families continue to enjoy considerable business success: Vinod Patel, Tappoo and R.C Manubhai being prime examples.[29] A further source of differentiation is that Gujaratis, as Hindus, have tended to align themselves with the APS/Fiji; this places them in a minority compared with the majority Sanatani community.

Gujarati merchants were instrumental in establishing and funding the NFP in 1960.[30] It is claimed that they were also able to control the political loyalties of their indebted farmer customers.[31] Nevertheless, consciousness of potential resentment due to business success and the threat that this might jeopardize the intended aim of the party to represent cane growers, led those early Gujarati leaders to quickly relinquish control. Divisions within the NFP in 1977 (outlined in further detail below) led many in the Gujarati community to move to the Alliance for the 1982 election, a liaison encouraged by close links established and maintained by way of joint ventures with Fijian élites, and by the Alliance Party's promise of 'business as usual'.[32] The promise of a stable economy has subsequently proved to be an important influence over Gujarati political loyalties, and in 2006 it is widely believed that they placed significant support behind the SDL.

Divisions within the Indian community continue to persist, although in new shapes and forms. It has been suggested that a group of Indian businessmen funded the 2000 coup against Chaudhry's government owing to fears that the FLP's pledge to root out corruption would damage their business interests. Mahendra Chaudhry made similar claims on the FLP website, stating that several Indian businessmen had 'actively assisted the rebel elements in Labasa with food and cash'[33], in the hope of thereby dispelling the myth that the coup was racially motivated. Despite Chaudhry's claims, no Indian businessmen have been charged in relation to the 2000 coup.

Voter alignment in the past

Despite occasionally severe divisions, the Indian community has, at times, aligned itself with political parties during elections. An early example of religious divisions influencing voting patterns occurred during the 1929 election for the Legislative Council. This was the first time that Indians were permitted to elect members, albeit on a communal franchise. In the eastern constituency, two candidates stood, one, Khalid Sahim, was a Muslim, the other, James Maharaj, was a former Arya Samaji who had converted to Christianity. Out of the 83 valid voting papers, 63 had voted for Maharaj, and 20 for Sahim. It was claimed by the FML that, having become tools of the Arya Samaj, the Hindus had voted en bloc by 'herd instinct', as the other two winning candidates were also Arya Samajis.[34] Later, the divisions between the Arya Samaj and the Muslim community would heal, enabling them to form alliances. During the 1951 Legislative Council election, the FML supported a political leader strongly linked to the Arya Samaj. A request was made of the Muslims in the rural constituency of Namboulima to vote for this candidate, which they duly did.[35] This alliance is still in evidence today. During the 2006 election it was widely believed that the leadership of the FML and APS/Fiji supported the SDL, the reasons for which are examined below.

The events surrounding the April 1977 election provide a telling example of the role played by religion in politics. The outcome was an unexpected, but narrow, victory for the NFP and defeat for Ratu Mara's Alliance Party, by 26 seats to 24. Yet, in the wake of the poll, the Governor General exercised his power of discretion to return the Alliance Party to power under the leadership of Ratu Mara, rather than handing the reins to the leader of the NFP, Siddiq Koya. His reasoning for this was that the country had failed to provide a clear mandate and that Mara was the person best able to command the support of the majority of members of parliament. Internal divisions within the NFP before the election led to speculation that it was members of Koya's own party that had informed the Governor General that they would be unwilling to work with Koya. It was suggested by Koya some years later that his Hindu colleagues withheld their support for him, as they did not want a Muslim prime minister.[36] Mara's government was later toppled by an NFP-led vote of no confidence, which led to fresh elections being held in September 1977.

In that election, both sides exploited religious divisions. The NFP was divided into two factions – known as the 'flowers' and the 'doves'. The flowers, led by K.C. Ramrakha and Irene Jai Narayan, were widely regarded as a Hindu party, whilst Koya led the doves, commonly believed to be a Muslim party.[37] The campaign was characterized by the manipulation of religious symbols for political gain. Hindus were urged to vote for the flower, which is commonly used in practices of Hindu religious worship, whilst advertisements for public meetings organized by Irene Jai Narayan of the flower faction featured a caricature of her with her hands clasped together as in prayer; flanking the corners of the advertisement the clasped hands were reproduced and enlarged.[38] The language used during the election was also designed to manipulate religious sentiment – Koya was described by Ramrakha as a 'high priest who was trying to set up a rival temple',[39] an allusion to the NFP as a strongly religious and sacred body. The divided NFP subsequently lost the election, with the Alliance Party being returned to office with a stronger majority. Koya claimed that the loss was because the leaders of the flower faction had 'sown the seeds of discord in the Indian community, setting Hindus against Muslims'.[40]

Hafizud Dean Khan and the FML

Claims that religious organizations continue to influence the political process are strongly denied by both parties and religious organizations alike. After the death of former SDL Minister for Information, Ahmed Ali, in 2005, the SDL party appointed the FML president, Hafizud Dean Khan, as his successor to the Senate. He maintained a high-profile relationship with Qarase, which led many commentators to predict that the 2006 election would see significant increases in the Muslim vote for the SDL at the expense of the FLP. When the election candidates were announced, it was revealed that the SDL would be fielding Muslim candidates in nine out of the 21 Indian communal constituencies, and in four out of the seven open seats in which it had placed Indian candidates. This was disproportionate to the size of the Muslim community, and indicates a strategic attempt to swing votes away from the FLP. Whilst the FML did not make any public statements in support of the SDL, nor ask their members to vote for the party, it was believed that the close relationship that developed between Hafizud Dean Khan and Qarase indicated some measure of political support.[41]

Traditionally, some leaders of the FML have pragmatically supported those parties that went on to form the government. Because of their pragmatism, they maintained a strong relationship with the Alliance party. In previous years, all parties tried to court the support of the Muslim community.[42] However, in the 2006 election, Muslim candidates did not win any of the Indian communal seats. While the leadership of religious groups, like the FML, may maintain high profile relationships with political leaders, it does not follow that the rank and file membership will follow. During the 2001 election, the leaders of several religious organizations contested seats. D.S. Naidu, president of the TISI Sangam, stood for the NFP in his home constituency – Nadi Urban Indian Communal – in which is located the iconic Sri Subramaniyam temple. Yet, the NFP vote fell by 0.5 per cent in the constituency compared with the 1999 result. This pattern was repeated in the Nadi Rural Indian Communal constituency, in which Surendra Kumar, president of the SDS, stood in 2006.

Again, he stood for the NFP in his home constituency, but failed to win the seat, delivering a 4.5 per cent drop in the NFP vote compared with the previous election. The secretary of the AS, Immanuel Manu,[43] also stood for the NFP in Nadroga in 2006, but secured only 5.2 per cent of the vote at the first count and lost to the FLP candidate.[44]

Similarly, when religious leaders stand down, it seems to have little impact on electoral outcomes. APS/Fiji leader Kamlesh Arya vacated his Laucala Indian Communal seat just before the 2006 election. He had won the seat in 2001, with a 9.5 per cent increase on the previous election. In 2006, a new candidate contested the seat for the FLP, winning by a margin similar to that of his predecessor. This suggests that the votes cast in 2001 were for the FLP, rather than for Kamlesh Arya, as president of the APS/Fiji.

The FLP and the Chaudhry effect

It seems likely that rank and file members of most Hindu and Muslim religious organizations voted for the FLP in the Indian Communal constituencies in 2006. Prior to the election, Chaudhry suffered considerable setbacks when several high-profile MPs announced that they would not be re-contesting their seats. Some suggested that this was the end of his career. Yet, Chaudhry remained a strong and popular leader with the Indian electorate, with support cutting across religious and cultural boundaries. Results in the Indian Communal constituencies at the 2006 election show that, out of a total of 165,398 valid votes, the FLP won 134,022 (81%), whilst the NFP polled 23,263 (14%) and the National Alliance and SDL parties had a combined Indian Communal vote of 7,000 (4.2%).[45] The FLP's vote was also reasonably steady across the country, suggesting that variation in religious affiliation had little impact.[46]

Divisions within religious organizations also called into question the political credibility of the organizations. Both the AS and TISI Sangam, in unrelated incidents, had suffered from internal problems, which led to a loss of confidence in their leaders and attempts to replace them. With both of the south Indian groups in disarray, it seems unlikely that they would have appeared credible advocates for one or other of the major parties in the eyes of their members during the election. The electoral influence of the SDS is also open to question. With a claimed membership in excess of 200,000 people, academic Ganesh

Chand suggests that the SDS is too big an organization to be able to influence voting preferences at grassroots level.[47]

The real source of influence rests with the individual *Ramayan mandalis* (local congregations), located throughout Fiji. The purpose of these organizations is to encourage the reading of religious texts in a group setting; however, due to their relatively small size, these localized units are also better equipped to encourage informal political debate. While, officially, candidates are not permitted to use the *mandali* as a political platform, many candidates and people close to them are members of them and able to informally circulate their political message. Hock points out that the SDS as a national organization grew out of the *mandali* system.[48] However, a number of sources suggest that few of the *mandalis* have regular formal contact with the SDS executive, and so are free from any executive influence.

Candidates have also used religious events for political gain. The 2006 election fell during three religious festivals – Ram Naumi (Hindu), Easter (Christian) and The Prophet Mohammed's Birthday (Muslim). Each was used as a platform by election candidates to address potential voters. Lek Ram Vayeshnoi, who stood for the FLP in the Nadroga Indian Communal constituency, attended a religious event at a private house at which he gave a speech on good governance. For Vayeshnoi, 'religious functions are one of the few places where young and old are together – as such this is why religion is used as a weapon to get votes'.[49]

A number of factors contributed to Mahendra Chaudhry's success in attracting Indian votes in 2006, including compulsory voting and increased voter awareness of issues arising from comprehensive media coverage.[50] Disputes between the army and the governing SDL also appeared to make another coup a less likely accompaniment to a 1999-style FLP victory. What of the role of religious convictions? Chaudhry's close ties to India and his well-documented religious beliefs mean that he is seen as a leader reflecting Indian values, as well as one with a strong record of defending Indian interests. As mentioned above, Chaudhry is often venerated with quasi-religious respect, with his photo adorning the walls alongside a pantheon of gods, and his strident condemnation of injustice echoing lingering popular bitterness about the experience of indenture and the coups of 1987 and 2000. The comparisons with Rama's banishment continues the popular theme of suffering within the Indian community, and places Chauhdry as the inheritor of a tradition that extends from the indentured labourers to the present.

1987: A time for change

The changing relationship between Indian religious organizations and the political scene can be seen by the response to the coups of 1987 and 2000. Writing three years after the 1987 coup, John Garrett talked of the silence of the Indian community, which had previously been vocal and assertive through the NFP. He found instead a 'silent citizenship' alternating with occasional non-violent protests. These protests were mobilized through trade unions rather than religious groups, and it was the unions which increasingly voiced Indian political concerns.[51] There were no explicit statements from religious groups condemning the coups, partly due to the internal divisions within both the Hindu and Muslim communities.

There were other, more problematic, reasons for Indian silence. The ever-present threat of targeted violence against those speaking out is highlighted by the case of Chandrika Prasad, who filed a lawsuit in which he claimed that the interim government installed in 2000 was illegal. He won his case, bringing into question the legitimacy of the interim government. On the day his victory was announced, another farmer with the same name was seriously assaulted in what is believed to have been a case of mistaken identity. In the wake of the coups, Fiji Indians '…had few public forums within the country where they felt safe to voice their grievances'.[52] Indian places of worship were attacked, adding to the sense of a community under siege.[53] During the 2006 election campaign, a temple in Waila Nausori was broken into, which led Chaudhry to propose an intelligence network for the police to curb attacks on places of worship.[54]

The falling Indian population after 1987, owing to significant numbers leaving for overseas, further heightened the sense of insecurity. In 1986, the Indians had been the majority population, with 347,445 people (48.6%) compared with the Fijian population of 330,441 (46.2%).[55] In the months after the 1987 coup, large numbers of well-educated professionals fled the country, settling in Australia, New Zealand and America; this was repeated after the 2000 coup.[56] Perhaps 80,000 or 90,000 Indians have left the country since

1987, around 20–25 per cent of the 1987 population of Indians. Numbers have continued to fall, and the current population is 316,093 compared with a Fijian population of 463,432.[57]

In the aftermath of the 1987 coup and subsequent political upheavals, Indian religious organizations began to distance themselves from the political process. The desire to separate religion and politics is understandable given Rabuka's post-coup rhetoric, in which he claimed, for example, his role as coup leader to be a mission ordained by God, and referred repeatedly to both Hindus and Muslims as heathens.[58] Rabuka also famously declared that he wanted to turn Fiji into a Christian state:

> Those that do not choose to become Christians can continue to live here but they will probably find it a difficult place to live in, for we may not have Hindu religious occasions celebrated as such, and their holy days may not be holy days from now on.[59]

These sentiments were echoed in the Assembly of Christian Churches in Fiji's 2006 election advertisement, which called for Fiji to be ruled by the laws of God (see Newland, this volume). Against this backdrop, Hindu and Muslim religious organizations have chosen to remain quiet, in order to avoid becoming a visible target for attack. They have moved their attentions to forcing the education agenda as a way of maintaining their influence over the political process. It is an area in which they have a long-standing interest.

Education: for the future or for security?

Education had always been a priority for Fiji's Indian community, particularly after the end of indenture. After 1987, it took on an added urgency in that it offered a degree of security. An Indian student at the University of the South Pacific commented to me, '…they can take away my land and my home, but they can't take away my degree…with my degree I can escape and start a new life if things become difficult'.[60] This sentiment is widely held by Indian families from across the various communities.

In a country in which few Indians own land[61], education is regarded as the most important thing the Indian community can provide for their children: it offers security through financial independence. With this in mind, most Indian religious organizations have established a range of educational institution[62], with most of them either having expanded into the tertiary education market, or having plans to do so in future. While these schools are owned and run by the various religious groups, they rely heavily on government support and funding to provide teachers' pay, grants and loans for building repairs, scholarships, academic accreditation and curriculum planning. It is because they provide funding and are involved in the day-to-day running of schools, that most religious groups wish themselves to be seen as politically neutral, as to align oneself with a particular political party could jeopardise future sources of funding.

However, education is not the exclusive concern of the Indian community. A Tebbutt poll in *The Fiji Times* indicated that 41 per cent of ethnic Fijians identified it as their most significant concern during the 2006 election.[63] As education has broad appeal, it is a safe issue around which religious organizations can influence the political agenda. During the election, the president of the SDS, Surendra Kumar, requested the newly elected government to allocate approximately F$50,000 to registered religious groups, in order to alleviate the financial hardships that forced children to leave school:

> I urge the government to help poor children in all levels of education…religious groups are the best means by which they can support poor children…the government and religious groups should work in partnership to provide scholarships to children in primary and secondary schools. We can curb social problems by making families feel they are wanted.[64]

In this way the political agenda shifts to social policy, with poverty alleviation and crime and disorder entering the debate. The continuing struggle to secure funding lies at the heart of the political debate around education, with parties conscious that this is a significant vote-winning issue. Mindful of this, the then Minister for Multi-Ethnic Affairs, George Shiu Raj, stated that his ministry would provide more than 8,000 scholarships over the next parliamentary session if the SDL were re-elected, this being an increase of 2,400 on the previous parliamentary session, when 5,600 scholarships were distributed.[65]

Further promises were made to help religious groups establish nursing schools for students unable to secure a place at the Fiji School of Nursing. With an eye to wider policy issues, Shiu Raj stated that:

> The setting up of nursing schools would ease the lives of many families when their children graduated and started working…If 1,000 nurses graduated each year from the schools, the problem of poverty would be solved. The graduates could work locally or migrate to countries that needed their skills…foreign earnings would increase because they would send money back home to their families.[66]

The government saw the expansion into tertiary education and the sending of nurses overseas as a way of increasing national wealth and reducing unemployment.

The official reason for the founding of the University of Fiji[67] was that it would have a Fiji focus, something that the University of the South Pacific was unable to do as it serviced the educational needs of 12 Pacific nations. The decision was prompted by the need to provide a home for Indian students who perceive themselves to have been marginalized under the affirmative action schemes of successive governments since 1987. During his June 2005 speech to open the AD Patel Centenary Carnival in Ba, Professor Rajesh Chandra, the Vice-Chancellor of the University of Fiji stated:

> In a very real sense, the Indian community had been searching for some time for a way to expand the provision of higher education in Fiji, and to avoid its dependence on the government-controlled University of the South Pacific. Despite having access to the University and the obvious benefits of the USP to Fiji, people in Fiji had been feeling that their access was being limited by quotas or threats of quotas, and that people in the Western Division and those in the Northern Division did not have good access to higher education in the way that the residents of Suva and surrounding areas had…[T]he University is fulfilling the dreams that AD Patel, Pandit Vishnu Deo, and other leaders had, and the dreams that the Indo-Fijian community had to ensure that it had good access to high quality higher education.[68]

The founding of the University of Fiji may be seen as a politically motivated decision, but its establishment was dogged by problems. The Minister for Education, Ro Teimumu Kepa, tried to prevent the name 'University of Fiji' being used, whilst it was unclear as to whether or not government funding and accreditation would be forthcoming. At the start of the 2006 election campaign, the two people most closely identified with the establishment of the university – Ganesh Chand and Kamlesh Arya, both FLP MPs – announced that they would not be re-contesting their seats at the forthcoming election. A week prior to this announcement, both Arya and Chand had been with SDL

THE ROLE OF HINDU AND MUSLIM ORGANIZATIONS

leader and Prime Minister Qarase at a high profile dedication function at the University of Fiji. The FLP leaders were absent from the event, with no reason given for their absence. Arya claims that the FLP had been invited, and that he hand-delivered an invitation to Chaudhry. In addition to this he had 'personally cajoled several of them [FLP members] to come but they were not there'.[69] In the weeks prior to the dedication ceremony, Arya had publicly criticized Chaudhry.[70] At the same time, Qarase strengthened the relationship between the SDL and Arya Samaj by saying at the dedication, as quoted in *The Fiji Times*: 'The SDL coalition and the motivating spirits behind the new university had a shared belief in the high importance of education'.[71] In making such a statement, Qarase was able to plant in the public mind the idea that the two organizations had a shared vision for Fiji, and touched on an issue of importance to Indian voters – that of education. At the same time, the motivating spirits, Arya and Chand, were two former FLP members who had left the party due to disagreements with its leadership.

The public perception of these events was well illustrated by a letter titled 'Bad Leader' printed in *The Fiji Times* during the election campaign. In it, the author accused the SDL of orchestrating Mr Arya's public condemnation, and departure from the FLP, and said that Mr Arya willingly went along with it for personal gain. It was alleged that it was done in order to secure the victory of the SDL party, which, in turn, would provide government grants for the University of Fiji.[72] Whether this is true or not, it represents a suspicion that was around at the time. It is unclear whether or not this was deliberate political positioning by the Prime Minister in order to win votes; however, as with Hafizud Dean Khan and the FML, this did not translate to rank and file votes migrating to the SDL Party.[73]

Conclusion

The way in which religious organizations influence the political process has altered over time. In the post-indenture period, divisions between religious groups resurfaced, and led to the establishment of a number of religious and quasi-religious groups dedicated to the protection and promotion of education and culture. Through the post-war years, the leadership of these groups was able to influence voting patterns and provide religious blocks of support to a particular candidate or party. After 1987, there was a movement away from this style of direct support for political parties. Increased political sophistication in the electorate, with information drawn from a number of sources, means that religious organizations are no longer such a powerful source of opinion during election campaigns. While religious leaders may align themselves with particular parties, it does not follow that rank and file members will follow their lead – as the cases of D.S. Naidu and the TISI Sangam, Surendra Kumar and the SDS, and Immanuel Manu and the AS demonstrate. Whilst the leaders of religious bodies may have political ambitions, their members do not necessarily share these. As a result, organizations that were once vocal backers of political parties are now more circumspect when making political statements, tending to focus only on those issues that the public expects them to speak on – such as education policy, temple desecration and the Promotion of Reconciliation, Tolerance and Unity Bill.[74] They have, however, found that, through their focus on education and its expansion, wider issues of social policy can be debated, and the political agenda shaped. The 2006 election resulted in a multiparty cabinet – with individuals from various ideological persuasions coming together for the national benefit. Similarly, while divisions between the different Indian religious groups persist, and are essential in sustaining Indian identity, the movement towards the expansion of higher education can be seen as these groups working together for a common cause. However, the question remains whether this is for the national benefit or for the betterment of a specific community.

Notes

1   This paper deals with the following organizations: The Fiji Muslim League (FML), The Arya Pratinidhi Sabha of Fiji (APS/Fiji), The Shree Sanatan Dharam Pratinidhi Sabha (SDS), The Dakshina Andhra Sangam (AS) and Then India Sanmarga Ikya (TISI) Sangam. Thanks to Jon Fraenkel, Linda Newland, Robert Norton and Biman Prasad for comments on an earlier draft of this paper; however, any errors or omissions remain the responsibility of the author.

2   Fiji Bureau of Statistics. 1996. <http://www.spc.int/prism/country/fj/stats/cens&surveys/Popu_census.htm – accessed 2/6/2006. These statistics, whilst the most up-to-date official statistics on religion issued by the Fiji Bureau of Statistics (1996), are subject to query. Newland highlights that the figures fail to reflect the rise of new religious groups, such as the International Society of Krishna Consciousness (ISKCON), nor do they accurately reflect the true membership of organizations. As an example, the official statistics for the Sai Baba movement are recorded as 60 members, whereas the organization claims a membership of 2,000. Similarly the statistics do not take account of those organizations that are not deemed

to be religious organizations but rather ethical bodies. Newland, L. 2006. 'Fiji' in Ernst, Manfred (ed.) 2006. *Globalization and the Re-shaping of Christianity in the Pacific Islands.* Pacific Theological College, Suva.

[3] See Newland, this volume.

[4] SDL Manifesto 2006:3.

[5] Durutalo, A. 2000. 'Elections and the Dilemma of Indigenous Fijian Political Unity' in Lal, B.V. (ed.) 2000. *Fiji Before the Storm: Elections and the Politics of Development,* Asia Pacific Press, The Australian National University, Canberrra. pp.73–93; Norton, R. 1990. *Race and Politics in Fiji* (2nd edition), University of Queensland Press, Queensland. pp.49–50.

[6] Lal, B.V. 1983. 'Girmitiyas: The Origins of the Fiji Indians', *Journal of Pacific History,* Canberra. pp.43–67.

[7] Lal, B.V. 1992. *Broken Waves: A History of the Fiji Islands in the Twentieth Century.* Pacific Islands Monograph Series. No 11. University of Hawaii Press, Honolulu. pp.77.

[8] For further details of this period see Naidu, V. 2004. *The Violence of Indenture in Fiji.* Fiji Institute of Applied Studies, Lautoka; and Prasad, R. 2004. *Tears in Paradise,* Glade Publishers, Auckland.

[9] Gillion, K.L. 1977. *The Fiji Indians: Challenge to European Dominance 1920–1946.* Australian National University Press, Canberra. pp.150.

[10] Ali, A. 1977. 'The emergence of Muslim separatism in Fiji'. *Plural Societies,* 8(1):57–69; Norton, R. 1990. *Race and Politics in Fiji,* pp.50.

[11] This idea is given further credibility by others. See, for example, Singer, M. 1972. *When a Great Tradition Modernizes; An Anthropological Approach to Indian Civilization,* Pall Mall, London, and M.N. Srinivas. 1976. *The Remembered Village,* Oxford University Press, Delhi.

[12] Tharpar, R. 1989. 'Imagined Religious Communities? Ancient History and the Modern Search for a Hindu identity', *Modern Asian Studies,* 23(2):228.

[13] A number of groups subscribe to the Sanatan Dharm philosophy; however, further divisions have led to the formation of additional groups in Fiji. These include the SDS, the AS and TISI Sangam.

[14] Kelly, J. 1991. *A Politics of Virtue: Hinduism, Sexuality and Counter-Colonial Discourse in Fiji,*University of Chicago Press, Chicago and London, pp.126–39, 206–18.

[15] A comprehensive overview of the SDS and APS/Fiji can be found in Hock, K. 'Non Christian Religions in Fiji' in Ernst (ed.) 2006, *Globalization,* pp.390–439.

[16] Kelly, J. 1991. *A Politics of Virtue,* pp.128.

[17] Detailed treatment of these events is provided by Kelly. 991. *A Politics of Virtue;* and Gillion. 1977. *The Fiji Indians,* pp.108–11.

[18] Kelly, J. 1991. *A Politics of Virtue,* p.208.

[19] See Mayer, A. 1961. *Peasants in the Pacific.* Routledge and Kegan Paul; London, pp.144–149.

[20] Lal, B.V. 1997. 'A vision for change: A D Patel and the politics of Fiji', *History of Development Studies* 6. National Centre for Development Studies, The Australian National University, Canberra, p.51.[21] Krishna, A. 1973. 'History of the Andhra Sangam in Fiji' (unpublished SE300 thesis) University of the South Pacific, Suva, p.31; Fiji Girmit Council. 2004. Girmits Greatest Gift. Commemorative publication to celebrate the 125th Anniversary of the first arrival of Indians in Fiji. Unknown publisher.

[22] When the TISI Sangam was registered as a company in 1937, Patel became its general manager (Gillion 1977:111).

[23] Interview with Vinod Naidu, National President of the Dakshina Andhra Sangam, 13 March 2006.

[24] Ali, A. 1977. 'The Emergence of Muslim Separatism in Fiji', p. 60.

[25] Ali, A. 1977. 'The Emergence of Muslim Separatism in Fiji', p. 61.

[26] *The Fiji Times*, 10 August 1987, p.1.

[27] Lal, B.V. 1992. *Broken Waves*, p.286.

[28] Norton, R. 1990. *Race and Politics in Fiji*, p.86.

[29] Gillion, K L. 1962. *Fiji's Indian Migrants: A History to the End of Indenture in 1920*, Oxford University Press, Melbourne and New York, p.135.

[30] The TISI Sangam and Ramkrishna Mission also had a significant role in its foundation.

[31] Norton, R. 1990. *Race and Politics in Fiji*, p. 78.

[32] Lal, B.V. 1986. *Politics in Fiji*. Allen and Unwin, Sydney.

[33] 'Labour slams Labasa businessmen' http://www.flp.org.fj/N030123.htm – accessed 10 July 2006

[34] Ali, A. 1977. 'The Emergence of Muslim Separatism in Fiji', p.62.

[35] Mayer, A. 1961. *Peasants in the Pacific*, pp.148–49.

[36] Lal, B.V. 1992. *Broken Waves*, p.240.

[37] Despite the commonly held belief that the Doves were a Muslim party – a view perpetuated by the 'Flowers', Koya also had the support from significant sections of the South Indian community (Biman Prasad – Pers. Comm 8/8/2006).

[38] *The Fiji Times* 6 August 1977, p.3

[39] *The Fiji Times,* 12 August 1977, p.1.

[40] *The Fiji Times*, 30 September 1977, p.4.

[41] Interview with the 2006 SDL campaign team (Sivoki Matenamia – Manager, Political Awareness; Angve Davetawalu – Operations Manager, Nausori Cluster; Mosese Vosavogo Manager IT Services and Communications; and Viliame Sotia – Manager Research Media) 9/6/2006.

[42] At approximately 8 per cent of the population they are regarded as a significant support base.

[43] That Manu stood for the NFP while the leadership of the AS gave their support to the FLP demonstrates that religious organizations are no longer dogmatic in their support of political parties.

[44] Comprehensive statistics for the 2001 elections are available at http://psephos.adam-carr. net/countries/f/fiji20013.txt

[45] This contrasts with the elections of 1999 when, out of 165,886 votes cast, 108,743 went to the FLP and 53,071 to the NFP. In 2001, 145,428 votes were cast, of which 108,459 went to the FLP and 32,142 to the NFP. Progressively, the FLP have been the beneficiaries of approximately 30,000 NFP votes, which may have come either from members of the TISI Sangam, or from the SDS. See http://psephos.adam-carr.net/countries/f/fiji20013.txt

[46] A member of the public at the first Fiji Institute of Applied Studies (FIAS) public debate on the 2006 election (Waterfront Hotel, Lautoka, 15 May 2006) commented that most of the candidates on the voting slips were unknown and that the electorate voted for Chaudhry rather than the individual candidates.

47 In rural areas, power and influence operate at a grassroots level. Ganesh Chand suggests that the 'gang sirdar' – the head of the cane-cutting gang in cane-farming areas – is able to influence voting outcomes. His role is to decide the order in which cane cutting is to take place. Cane, which is cut later in the season, is drier, earning less for the farmer. If the gang sirdar were to support a particular candidate, it is likely a majority of farmers would go along with his decision in order to win his favour (Chand, interviewed 15/06/2006).

48 Hock. K. 2006. 'Non Christian Religions in Fiji', p.393.

49 Unpublished election report by Sunayna Nandni, student journalist at the University of the South Pacific, see also her report 'Campaigning a Family Affair for Vayeshnoi' http://www. usp.ac.fj/journ/wansolnews/2006/elections2006/april/wansol1205061.html. Accessed 10 June 2006.

50 A number of letters to *The Fiji Times* during and after the election campaign commented on how useful Fiji TV's 'Question Time' series was, while the output from radio and print media has been commended as the most comprehensive of any election. See, for example, the letters page in *The Fiji Times*, 2 May 2006, p.10 'Question Time' and 5 May 2006, p.11 'Thanks Fiji One'.

51 Garrett, J. 1990. 'Uncertain Sequel: The Social and Religious Scene in Fiji Since the Coups'. *The Contemporary Pacific*, 2(1):87–111.

52 Trnka, S. 2002. 'God Only Listens to Those who Sweat. Violence, The Body and Community in Sanatan Hindu dialogues of the May 2000 coup'. Unpublished PhD Thesis. Princeton University, p.373.

53 In 1989, a group of youths attacked a Hindu temple, stating that it was their religious duty to do so. Since then the vandalism and desecration of Indian places of worship have become common. During 2005, an average of one attack a month was reported (http://www. hinduamericanfoundation.org/pdf/hhr_2005_html/fijiislands.htm).

54 *The Fiji Times*, 3 April 2006, p.4.

55 Bureau of Statistics. 1986. Statistical News. No. 27, p.1.

56 Voigt-Graf, C. 2002. The Construction of Transnational Spaces: Travelling Between India and Australia'. Unpublished PhD Thesis, University of Sydney, Sydney.

57 Fiji Island Bureau of Statistics estimates at 31 December 2005 http://www.spc.int/prism/ country/fj/stats/, accessed 25 July 2006.

58 Dean, E. & Ritova, S. 1988. *Rabuka: No Other Way*. Doubleday, Moorebank. p.121.

59 Dean, E. & Ritova, S. *Rabuka: No Other Way*. p.121.

60 Conversation with an anonymous student at USP, 23 May 2006.

61 This is evidenced by expiring Indian farm leases and the significant increase in squatter settlements, for example along the Suva–Nausori corridor.

62 Each of the religious groups maintains a number of primary, secondary and tertiary institutions. The FML has 22 primary schools, six colleges and two junior secondary schools. The TISI Sangam has 21 primary schools, 55 secondary schools, one nursing school and one technical vocational school, and plans to establish a multi-sited technical university. The AS has six primary schools and 22 colleges. SDS has a large number of primary and secondary schools. At the time of writing, this number was unconfirmed. The APS/Fiji has 11 primary schools, eight secondary schools, eight colleges and training centres and one university.

63 *The Fiji Times*, 15 March 2006, p.2.

64 *The Fiji Times*, 17 May 2006, p.17.

65 *The Fiji Times,* 15 May 2006, p.10.

66 *The Fiji Times,* 4 March 2006, p.13.

67 The decision to establish the University of Fiji was a joint decision between the APS/Fiji (as funding body) and academic Ganesh Chand. At the time, both Chand and the president of the APS/Fiji, Kamlesh Arya, were FLP members of parliament. The council of the University of Fiji includes a number of stakeholders drawn from post-primary education as well as prominent business leaders and renowned intellectuals. Several Indian religious organizations are also part of the council, including Arya Pratinidhi Sabha, Shri Sanatan Dharm of Fiji, FML, Gujarat Education Society, Sikh Education Society, the Andhra Sangam, the TISI Sangam, the Kabir Path Sabha. http://www.unifiji.ac.fj/about_us.htm, accessed 15 July 2006.

68 http://www.unifiji.ac.fj/speech_chandra_adpatel2005.htm accessed 15 July 2006.

69 Interview with Kamlesh Arya, 7 July 2006.

70 Dr Arya expressed concerns about his leadership, referring to Chaudhry as having 'lost the plot' and stating that he would have to be replaced in order for the FLP to win the election. 'Bad Blood spills from Cracked Walls'. *Fiji Sun,* 11 March 2006, p.7.

71 *The Fiji Times,* 6 March 2006, p.3.

72 *The Fiji Times,* 13 March 2006, p.6.

73 Overall the SDL party polled approximately 3 per cent of votes in Indian Communal constituencies.

74 The SDS, TISI Sangham and Kisan Sangh entered submissions to the Sector Standing Committee on Justice, Law and Order in relation to the Promotion of Reconciliation, Tolerance and Unity Bill, 2005. All agreed that the bill would increase the potential for future coups to occur and lead to increased instability. See: http://www.parliament.gov.fj/

25

Fiji's system of elections and government: where to from here?

Laisenia Qarase

Since my party's victory in the May 2006 general election, I have concentrated my attention on the formation of the multiparty cabinet with the Fiji Labour Party (FLP), and on laying the groundwork to ensure the success of this new approach to the governance of Fiji.

I am committed to ensuring that the multiparty cabinet with Labour will successfully take us through the next five years. This is not only because it is a requirement of the 1997 constitution. More importantly, it is because I believe it provides our country with an exceptional opportunity to start a new era of cooperation between our major communities through a multi-ethnic form of government.

Since the 2006 election, suggestions have been made about the appropriateness for Fiji of a system of proportional representation, as opposed to the current alternative vote system provided under the 1997 constitution. Proponents of proportional voting consider it to be more democratic and fair in ensuring a direct correlation between votes for, and seats won by, a political party campaigning on a national scale. As 'purists' in the application of democracy, they believe that an electoral system based on proportional representation more accurately reflects the wishes of the voters. Furthermore, they assert that, in a multi-ethnic society, proportional representation helps to mitigate the effects of racial political polarization.

This chapter posits that the people of Fiji would be best served in exercising their democratic rights, both to elect their members of parliament and to elect a strong and effective government, by an electoral arrangement that promotes a political party system dominated by two parties, even though those parties are mainly ethnically based. I argue that this would be more appropriate than a system that would tend to encourage the proliferation of small political parties within each of our ethnic communities. Experience has shown that such proliferation in the Fijian polity is a recipe for instability.

I am, therefore, suggesting that we keep the election method established under the 1997 constitution and allow it to operate in a few more elections before we consider any major changes. This does not exclude adjustments recommended by the Electoral Commission to improve the operations of the current system.

The challenge in a political party system dominated by two major and ethnic-based parties is to devise a form of multi-ethnic government, which, in the words of section 6 (h) of Fiji's constitution, would take 'full account…of the interests of all communities' in our multi-ethnic and multicultural society. Section 99 (4) also provides that the composition of cabinet should, as far as possible, fairly represent the parties represented in the House of Representatives.

Background

Ever since the first national election in post-independence Fiji, that of 1972, different political parties or coalitions of parties have been elected to form the government: the Alliance Party in 1972, in the second election of 1977, and in 1982; the National Federation Party (NFP) in the first election of 1977; the FLP/NFP coalition in 1987; the Soqosoqo ni Vakavulewa ni Taukei (SVT) in 1992, and again in 1994; the FLP-led People's Coalition in 1999; the Soqosoqo Duavata ni Lewenivanua (SDL)/Conservative Alliance–Matanitu Vanua (CAMV) coalition in 2001; and the SDL on its own in 2006.

In all these elections, the most prominent and consistent feature is the ethnic base of the political parties, and racial voting behaviour.

The Alliance Party was proud that it was multiracial, having three components (the Fijian Association, the Indian Alliance and the General

Electors Association). However, in the main, it was essentially a Fijian party, and it was the indigenous vote that determined its success or failure at elections.

Most of the other parties have also claimed to be multiracial. Indeed, in their respective constitutions, they have opened membership to all citizens, irrespective of race and cultural background. But in their membership and in voter support at elections, the FLP and NFP have always overwhelmingly drawn support from the Indian community. The SDL, the CAMV, the SVT, and others like the Fijian Association Party, the Veitokani ni Lewenivanua Party (VLV), and PANU, have been supported, in the main, by Fijians.

In addition, one important development in elections under the 1997 constitution is the emergence of what is essentially a dual-dominant political party polity: the SDL largely supported by Fijians, and the FLP by members of the Indian community. This trend toward two dominant parties has been reinforced by a better understanding by the voters of the above-the-line and below-the-line methods for choice of preferences. The overall result in the 2006 election was that the SDL received approximately 81 per cent of all votes in the Fijian communal constituencies, and the FLP 81 per cent of all votes in the Indian communal constituencies.[1]

In terms of voting behaviour, Fijians essentially vote for the 'Fijian' party they consider would best secure the interests of their community. Indians, for their part, support the 'Indian' party which, in their view, would best safeguard their interests as a community. The two communities see their security ultimately in winning control of parliament and government in elections. Voters shift or move their votes within their community. There is little movement of votes across communities. Fijian votes for the FLP in the 2006 election in the Fijian communal seats were only 6 per cent. Indian votes for the SDL in the Indian communal constituencies were even less, at 2 per cent.[2]

Indians switched largely to the FLP from the NFP in the 1999 election. The NFP's share of the Indian vote fell from 32 per cent in 1999 to 22 per cent at the 2001 election. The New Labour Unity Party, led by Dr Tupeni Baba, broke away from the main Fiji Labour Party. But its low Indian vote (3 per cent in 2001) showed that Indian voters still preferred NFP, when judged against this newer multiracial party. More importantly, they favoured a single political party to articulate communal interests. The consolidation of Indian support around the FLP continued at the 2006 election, when the FLP received 82 per cent of Indian votes and the NFP share dropped to 14 per cent.[3]

On the Fijian side, Fijian votes crossed over from the SVT to the VLV and the Fijian Association parties in the 1999 election. In the 2001 election, Fijian votes shifted from these two political parties to the SDL and the CAMV. In the 2006 election, Fijian votes moved overwhelmingly to the SDL from all other parties within the Fijian community. As a direct result, there was a 60 per cent increase in overall voter support for the SDL.[4]

Where to from here?

Given our experience and the trends from past elections, the question that arises is, where do we go from here? A combination of continuing ethnic-based support for particular political parties; the racial vote by individual voters preferring the party and candidates closely identified with, and supported by, their ethnic community; and the continuation of the above-the-line choice of preferences under the current alternative vote system, will tend to consolidate the dominance of the two political parties – the SDL and the FLP. This, in my view, will be further reinforced if the current SDL/FLP multiparty cabinet continues successfully to run government until the next general election in 2011, and to resolve the country's main national issues. These include the renewal of agricultural leases on native land, promoting sustained high growth in the economy, and devoting more resources to alleviating and eradicating poverty amongst Fiji's poor and the low-income sections of our society.

The known advantage of the proportional representation system over first-past-the-post and alternative voting is that it reduces the discrepancy between votes cast for a party and seats won by that party. This ensures that a party's representation in parliament directly reflects the level of support it received. But this advantage is undermined if it leads to a proliferation of small political parties. This makes it harder for any single party to win a clear or outright majority in general elections. The New Zealand example is relevant.

From past trends, the introduction of a system of proportional representation is unlikely to draw, to any significant extent, Indian voter support away from the FLP and the NFP, or lead to the formation of a third 'Indian' party. There is, however, a real probability that it would exacerbate the problem of political fragmentation within the Fijian community, and take Fiji back to the kind of political situation that led to the defeat of the Alliance government in 1977, and of the SVT government in 1999. It would make it harder in future elections for a single 'Fijian' political party to win with a clear majority in the House of Representatives. Without a 'Fijian' party winning with an outright majority, Fiji could see a repeat of what followed the 1999 general election. That election produced a coalition government led by a 'non-Fijian' party, despite the Fijian numerical majority. The reason for this was the fragmentation of Fijian votes caused by numerous parties competing for Fijian support. And this could happen again, even though the Fijians have an increasing Fijian political advantage, stemming from the growing Fijian population.

Voting results in the open seats in the 2006 election confirm the mobility of Fijian votes among several 'Fijian' parties, and the stability of Indian votes with the two 'Indian' parties, the FLP and the NFP. Amongst Fijian voters, 65 per cent voted for the SDL; 35 per cent voted for other parties, with the majority of these votes going to other 'Fijian' parties. Amongst Indian voters, 80 per cent voted for Labour. With only a 2 per cent vote for the SDL in the Indian communal constituencies, it was clear that the majority of the remaining 20 per cent of Indian votes in open constituencies went to the NFP and minor 'Fijian' parties.[5]

In assessing the suitability for Fiji of the proportional voting system, the following comments by researchers who have thoroughly studied it are relevant:

> Various Western European countries use proportional electoral systems. More often than not, they bring about coalition or minority governments because no party wins an overall majority.[6]

> Proportional representation, where it has been tried, has not noticeably improved the standards of public life. In Belgium, it has tended to eliminate independence. In Switzerland, it has so multiplied the tiny groups that no coherent opinion has been able to emerge. That always implies weak government, and weak government ultimately means an irresponsible government.[7]

Whilst variations can be made to the proportional representation system to lessen its tendency to encourage a proliferation of political parties, its application in New Zealand is illustrative of the unclear electoral outcomes it can produce. There, it has led to a succession of coalition governments, with weakened authority for the prime minister.

When no party wins an outright majority, a coalition of convenience becomes necessary for the formation of a government. In Fiji, this kind of result would make it almost impossible for a prime minister to create the kind of multiparty cabinet envisaged in section 99 of the constitution.

An illogical consequence could be a cabinet in which the prime minister's own party was in a minority. I doubt whether this was envisaged by the architects of the constitution, because section 98 appears to assume that the person to be appointed prime minister will have a parliamentary majority.

Clearly, what Fiji needs is an electoral system that delivers:

- the democratic right of the voters to elect their members of parliament and their government
- a government with a clear majority in the House and strong constitutional authority for the prime minister to lead decisively
- an effective opposition in parliament
- constitutional support for the prime minister to form a multi-ethnic cabinet to promote intercommunity accommodation and cooperation.

The Electoral Commission has proposed an amendment to the Electoral Act to simplify the ballot paper in relation to the above-the-line and below-the-line option for voters. Specifically, the amendment is to restore the discretionary powers of Returning Officers during the counting process, to assess and declare the voting intention of a voter.

The Commonwealth Observer Mission has also recommended improvements to the counting and reporting system. It has called for a review to refine, streamline and simplify the process for future elections. The mission believes that this could be done without any loss of transparency or damage to the overall integrity of elections.

The process of developing an electronic voter roll, constantly updated and improved, will be ongoing, as will be the strengthening of the Elections Office to take on full responsibility for municipal elections as well as national elections.

However, other than the above, there are several aspects of the electoral system that could usefully be considered in public discussions.

The first is whether or not, in the long run, the present system of mixed communal and open constituencies should be changed to make all 71 seats in the House of Representatives open and non-racial. There have been many suggestions that communal representation perpetuates racial polarization and should, therefore, be abolished. The 1996 Reeves Report[8] commented on this and recommended that the majority of seats should be through open constituencies. This issue is something the Indian and minority communities, in particular, will have to think carefully about, because of the continuing decrease in their population numbers. Recent reports on population trends have indicated that the annual birth rate of the Indian community has fallen to such an extent that, even without emigration, the number of Indians in Fiji will continue to decline. Fijians, on the other hand, have continued to increase to the extent that they now comprise more than 54 per cent of Fiji's total population. Assuming that the Indian community regards its assured communal representation as vitally important to its political future and security, the question that arises is whether or not that community will, in the light of population changes, now opt to reverse its earlier historical preference for the 'common roll', or one-person-one-vote in open and non-racial constituencies, and insist instead on retaining its communal seats.

It should be noted that our constitution actually allows our three main communities – the Fijians, the Indians and the General electors – to retain their communal seats. There are 23 for Fijians, 19 for Indians and three for the General electors. This right of communal representation is entrenched. The numbers cannot be changed without the express consent of the respective community representatives in the House. Ironically, Fijians, who have always been averse to the earlier demands of Indian political leaders for a 'common roll', will, as their numbers continue to increase, see political advantage in moving toward an all open and non-racial constituency system.

If communal seats are to be retained, an aspect that is worth considering is whether or not we should reintroduce the cross-voting system established under the 1970 constitution. This would be one way of opening up and further democratizing voting for communal representatives. It would also confer a political advantage to those candidates who could muster support from all communities.

An issue for the Constituency Boundaries Commission to consider following the population census scheduled for 2007 is the desirability of closely aligning, as far as possible, the constituency boundaries of communal seats to the geographical boundaries of the 14 Fijian provinces and Rotuma. Already, the government's development administration and the geographical boundaries of all Rural District Advisory Councils are being harmonized with the Fijian provincial boundaries. Such a move would encourage all members of parliament from the same 'province' to support each other, across the parties to which they individually belong, in serving the people.

Those who have shown a keen interest in the continuing development and improvement in Fiji's electoral system would greatly assist our ongoing efforts to promote unity if they would also closely examine the persistence of ethnic voting. Why, precisely, do Fijians vote mainly for Fijian candidates, or for parties they consider to be predominantly 'Fijian' in their membership and policies? And, *vice versa*, why, precisely, do Indians vote largely for candidates who are from their community, or for a party they consider to be 'Indian' in its membership and policies? If this continues in the long term to be an entrenched feature of voting in Fiji, what can be done to ameliorate its negative impact on race relations and intercommunal cooperation in Fiji?

On the promotion of intercommunity cooperation through the formation of a multiparty cabinet, I acknowledge that the provisions under section 99 of Fiji's constitution reflect a sincere attempt to promote political power-sharing and mutual accommodation between the country's major political parties and the ethnic communities they represent. The intention was to move our country away from the identification of government and opposition with particular ethnic groups. With decision-making by majority in the House of Representatives and the convention of the opposition vigorously projecting itself as the alternative government, the adversarial nature of the government/ opposition relationship in parliament only served to widen and embitter intercommunal relations in Fiji.

However, the question that arises now, and on which I would encourage research and welcome ideas, is whether or not there is a better alternative to the current approach of an enforced multiparty cabinet under Fiji's constitution. Whilst the SDL/FLP multiparty cabinet is working well and is a credit to the commitment of all ministers from both political parties, there have also been attendant difficulties and uncertainties. For example, are the backbencher members of the entitled party in the multiparty cabinet strictly bound to support the government's legislative and other proposals in the House in exactly the same way as are those from the prime minister's party? Then there is the role of the opposition. A government can only be fully responsible and accountable to the people if there is also an effective opposition. In the current House of Representatives, how can the opposition play this role effectively when it is made up of only two out of the 71 members!

The Compact chapter of the constitution, in section 6 (g), lays down the guiding principle for the formation of a government following a general election. A government has to have majority support among the members of the House of Representatives. This majority support can come from the winning political party, or a pre-election coalition of parties. But the constitution goes further. It says, '… if it is necessary or desirable to form a coalition government from competing parties, [that] depends on their willingness to come together to form or support a Government'.

I believe that constitutionally encouraging the prime minister to form a multi-ethnic government, through a voluntary coalition of willing political parties, is a far better approach to political power-sharing and intercommunal accommodation in Fiji than that currently provided under the provisions of section 99.

Conclusion

In a multi-ethnic and multicultural country like Fiji, where communities have been kept apart by communal concerns and interests, it is imperative to have an electoral system that produces clear and unequivocal results. The experience of other countries indicates that proportional representation does not do this. It is crucially important to have a prime minister appointed under section 98 of the constitution whose party, or pre-election coalition of parties, has an outright majority in the House of Representatives. A clear popular mandate and strong constitutional authority would enable the prime minister to form what would essentially be a voluntary coalition of parties represented in the House, and willing to join in a multi-ethnic government. Such a government should represent, as widely as possible, our different communities, and govern Fiji in the best interests of all.

Such a government would also be strong because it would be led by a prime minister with a clear mandate. What will bring it together, and sustain it, is an abiding conviction from all of Fiji's communities that this voluntary form of inclusive government offers the best way forward for our country.

Although communal representation may not be 'politically correct', and may also not be in keeping with the universal principles of democracy, in Fiji's situation the Indians and other minority communities may prefer its continuation and retention. Their support for the multiparty cabinet of the SDL and the FLP has clearly indicated that they regard their equitable representation in parliament and participation in cabinet as being important in assuring them of their place in our multi-ethnic and multicultural society. The retention of their communal representation would be a matter for consideration by the members of these communities themselves. For the Fijians, it would be an act of altruism and goodwill, and a demonstration of our caring concern, to respect their wishes – and, in any case, Fiji's constitution entrenches communal representation.

Notes

[1] Office of the Supervisor of Elections.
[2] Office of the Supervisor of Elections.
[3] Analysis of 2001 and 2006 election results in the Prime Minister's Office.
[4] Analysis of 2001 and 2006 election results in the Prime Minister's Office.
[5] Office of the Supervisor of Elections.
[6] S.A. de Smith. 1973. *Constitutional and Administrative Law*, 2nd Edition, Penguin Education. p.251.
[7] Harold H. Laski. 1973. *A Grammar of Politics*, Third Impression. George Allen & Gawin Ltd, London. pp.317–18.
[8] Fiji Constitutional Review Commission 1996 (Reeves Commission). *The Fiji Islands: Towards a United Future*, Government Printer, Suva.

26

Tainted elections

Mahendra Chaudhry

It's a bald question, but one that's surely unavoidable after the combined experiences of 2001 and 2006: is it possible ever to hold free and fair elections in Fiji anymore?

Since 2001, a culture of vote-buying, poll-rigging and manipulation has seeped into our electoral process and threatens to destroy the very foundations of our democratic traditions and undermine the integrity of our elections.

The exact nature and extent of the behind-the-scenes manipulation to engineer the results of the 2006 polls are not fully known, but enough credible evidence is available to cast serious doubts on the integrity of the 2006 election. Likewise the 2001 general election. Certainly, no critical observer could give them a clean bill of health, and one notices that even the European Union (EU) observer mission in its final report has this time fallen short of declaring the elections free and fair. Indeed, the numerous concerns it has raised and the recommendations it has made, on the conduct of the 2006 and future polls is tantamount to saying, in diplomatic language, that the 2006 election was seriously flawed.

A local observer, Father David Arms, is not so constrained in his criticism of the racial bias and other malpractices he observed during the 2006 poll – to the point where he has refused to declare the elections free and fair.   His final observations are worth noting for anyone interested in an honest review of the 2006 poll. He concluded that the ethnic imbalance among those conducting the elections was 'a serious blotch on the integrity of the whole electoral process'. Father Arms further noted:

> On the basis particularly of the ethnic bias which was so pervasive in the 2006 elections, I cannot possibly give a verdict that they were 'free and fair'.

The elections of 2006 were so administratively biased that the overall results were undoubtedly influenced thereby.

Many of Father Arms' observations and concerns are similar to those held by the Fiji Labour Party (FLP), and are contained in our fairly comprehensive report to the EU observer mission and the Electoral Commission. I am of the opinion that much of the mess and malpractice that characterized the 2006 poll, deliberate or otherwise, could have been avoided had the Electoral Commission paid heed to a lengthy report I sent to the chairman of the Commission as early as 5 May 2005 highlighting the main problems that marred the 2001 election and urging him to ensure they were not repeated.

The 2001 general election

As a precursor to the 2006 poll, the 2001 election set the trend for what should have been expected. For the first time in Fiji's electoral history, there was massive vote-buying in the lead-up to the 2001 general election by the Laisenia Qarase-led interim administration – as evidenced by the $30 million agricultural scam, currently before the courts. No other government before this had ever been tainted by such a blatant vote-buying exercise.

The FLP has consistently held that the 2001 general election was not free and fair – marred by vote-buying/bribery, defective electoral rolls, official bias and systematic vote-rigging. As a result, the FLP was deprived of victory in at least six marginal Open constituencies, which altered the results in favour of the Soqosoqo ni Duavata ni Lewenivanua (SDL).

A detailed report highlighting cases relating to vote-rigging, tampering with ballot papers and ballot boxes was submitted to the then Supervisor of Elections, Walter Rigamoto, but he failed to investigate any of these, or to treat the matter with the seriousness it deserved. His failure to do so meant that similar malpractices and electoral fraud were again practised in the 2006 election.

The 2006 election

The conduct of the 2006 poll was deeply flawed right from the beginning – starting with the voter registration exercise. I must also comment critically on the fact that the Supervisor of Elections, Semesa Karavaki, was on study leave until January 2006 – just four months before the May election. In his absence, Tomasi Tui was sent from the Prime Minister's office as Deputy Supervisor – the whole process was controlled from the Prime Minister's office. Tui was subsequently promoted to be Commissioner Eastern.

Flawed voter registration

To begin with, house-to-house voter registration was confined to a mere two weeks, 12–23 September 2005 – clearly not enough time to compile an entirely new electoral roll. Requests by political parties to have the house-to-house registration period extended were not granted.

Furthermore, the process was highly politicized and lacked transparency; enumerators were hand-picked by staff of the Elections Office and District Offices – often friends and family of officials. Voter registration teams were headed by persons who were politically affiliated and not impartial. A case in point is that of Prem Singh, a National Federation Party (NFP) candidate for the Nadi Open constituency, who was assigned registration and voter education activities by virtue of his being an advisory councillor. Subsequently, irregularities in the registration of voters in the Nadi Open constituency were noticed – some 1,400 voters in localities known to be FLP strongholds were found registered in the adjacent rural constituency of Yasawa/Nawaka Open. Unfortunately for him, the displacement of these voters was picked up by FLP branch representatives, and the matter rectified.

There was also gross ethnic imbalance in the recruitment of enumerators. Out of a total of 4,284 enumerators, only 407 were Indians; 155 were from other minority communities, while the rest, 3,722, were indigenous Fijians. This would clearly have created communication problems for Indians in rural areas, and for the elderly, many of whom cannot speak English. And, no doubt, such biased recruitment was responsible for much of the mess in the voter registration process, as well as for the very high number of invalid votes in the 2006 election compared with the 2001 election.

Parliamentary questions from the FLP asking for details on enumerators for each constituency were rejected by the Prime Minister, who made the ludicrous claim that such information was of a confidential nature. His refusal to provide the information underscored the lack of transparency in the process, and further fuelled suspicion that something was afoot.

In the past, school teachers, civil servants and political parties conducted the registration of voters. Why was this convention not followed in the 2006 election?

The FLP-conducted surveys of the registration process found the following major flaws/discrepancies:

- Many Indian households in rural and urban areas were not visited by enumerators – leaving large segments of Indian voters unregistered. In Labasa, for instance, just a three-day survey by the FLP in March 2006 uncovered 805 voters who had not been registered. Likewise, significant numbers of voters in Korovuto, Nawaicoba and Meigunya in Nadi were not registered.
- Hundreds of voters were either not given registration slips to show they had registered or were given blank slips – they were told slips were not necessary.
- People living in the same house were registered to vote in different constituencies – a subtle way of disenfranchising voters, as they would not be aware that their names were actually on the rolls of adjacent constituencies. They would simply assume that their names were missing from electoral rolls. Such attempts to disenfranchise voters would have made a crucial difference in closely fought Open constituencies, particularly those in the Central Division.
- For some reason, registration was not carried out on weekends when most people can be found at home. Enumerators did not make call-back visits.
- Faulty registration slips – numerous cases of names incorrectly entered, blanks left for constituencies or slips tagged 'to be decided' – rendered the entire registration invalid.
- Married women were deliberately asked to register under their maiden names – again this would have disenfranchised the voter.

- Hundreds of bizarre cases were noted of people listed in wrong constituencies that were not even borderline cases. The following cases recorded in the Ba, Lautoka and Nadi districts serve as illustration:
- 1,300–1,500 voters in the settlements of Nalovo and Uciwai, well within the boundary of the Nadi Rural Indian Communal constituency, were registered in the Nadroga Indian Communal constituency
- over 1,000 residents from Sariyawa, Savusavu, Waica and Momi were registered in the Nadroga Indian Communal constituency instead of Nadi Rural Indian constituency
- over 1,000 voters from the Nadroga Indian Communal constituency were wrongly listed in the Nadi Rural Indian Communal constituency
- 1,321 voters were wrongly listed in the Ba West Indian Communal constituency instead of the Ba East Indian Communal constituency
- 373 voters from the Ba Open constituency were listed in the Magodro Open constituency
- about 600 voters residing in Meigunya and Votualevu in the Nadi Urban Indian constituency were registered instead in the Nadi Rural Indian constituency
- 1,900 residents, mostly Fijians, from the Magodro Open constituency were listed in the Vuda Open constituency
- Indian and General voters were also found registered in Fijian Communal constituencies
- Some 2,000 voters from the Vuda Indian Communal constituency were registered elsewhere, particularly the Lautoka Rural Indian constituency.

Such high numbers of discrepancies, irregularities and anomalies are clear evidence of a calculated and orchestrated move to disenfranchise Indian voters. They were too numerous to be merely accidental omissions or errors.

These irregularities/anomalies were regularly brought to the attention of the Supervisor of Elections and the Electoral Commission as they surfaced. In most cases, however, they remained uncorrected by polling day, often despite assurances that they would be addressed. In the case of the 1,321 voters from the Ba East Indian Communal constituency wrongly listed in the Ba West Indian Communal constituency, although the Elections Office agreed to rectify a significant number of these, during polling week it was discovered that no such rectification had indeed been made.

Observer missions have been unanimous in their criticism of flaws in the registration process that saw scores, if not hundreds, of voters turn up at the polling stations only to be told their names could not be found on the electoral rolls. These people were effectively disenfranchised. And, as I have mentioned earlier, in closely fought open seats, such malpractices made a difference to the final result.

The EU observer mission noted that in a fifth of all polling stations visited, a number of voters were denied their right to vote. Names were misspelled, constituencies were wrongly allocated, and eligible voters were not registered. Some registered in the Communal constituencies, but not in the Open constituencies, should have been allowed to vote but were not.

Vote-buying

Blatant vote-buying/bribery by the SDL continued to be a feature of the 2006 general election, although not to the same extent perhaps as in the agricultural scam prior to the 2001 poll, when fishing boats, brush cutters, cooking utensils and money were blatantly handed out.

Soon after it had announced the dates for the 2006 general election, the SDL began giving out money for education, ostensibly earmarked for the poor. The point is that in the past five years since its inception, the SDL had not once spared a thought for these struggling students from poor families, at least to public knowledge. In another unprecedented move, Indian religious organizations and women's groups this time received money, pots and pans etc. Just two days before polling began, TV showed footage of an Indian man overwhelmed by the generosity of the Prime Minister who had gifted a brush cutter to him after his was stolen. Such altruistic gestures from the PM had been unheard of in the previous five years!

SDL's campaign director Jale Baba openly boasted that the party had spent $7.5 million for the 2006 election campaign. Where did the money go? And, more interestingly, where did such a large amount of cash come from? Was it corrupt money? The campaign could not have cost so much. It is well known that money was handed out to chiefs in the Ba Province, even during polling week. Buying votes in any form is a criminal act under the Electoral Act.

Failure to comply with the Electoral Act

Considering all the errors, irregularities, anomalies and omissions that surfaced during the registration process, it was important that the final electoral rolls be published in time to allow thorough scrutiny. Sections 22 and 23 of the Electoral Act provide a mandatory period of 42 days for objections to be lodged in regard to incorrect entries in the electoral rolls and their settlement by the Elections Office.

This important requirement was not met. Provisional rolls carrying only registrations made up until 31 December 2005 were released to political parties on 17 February 2006. The public was given a mere two working weeks to scrutinize the rolls, from Thursday 23 February to 13 March 2006. The main roll closed on 24 March. All registration after this was to go in a supplementary roll, with registration finally closing on 4 April – a week after the writ of election was issued. The so-called main roll, clearly a misnomer, was released to political parties in batches from 29 March onwards, and thereafter opened for public scrutiny.

Our major concern, however, is that the final main roll, which included the provisional and supplementary rolls, was not released until 27 April – and then only for 33 (less than half the) constituencies. Another 35 rolls were released on 29 April, a week before polling started. And the final three came out on 2 May. These were for the Nasinu/Rewa Open, the Magodro Open and the Nadi Open constituencies – giving barely three days for voters to scrutinize the rolls. Clearly the Supervisor of Elections and the Electoral Commission had failed to meet their obligations under the Electoral Act as far as publication of the electoral rolls was concerned. They had also failed to update the electoral rolls each year, as required by the Act.

Furthermore, the Supervisor of Elections failed to comply with the requirement of the Act to gazette the names of candidates standing for each constituency, following their nominations. He also failed to meet the requirement to gazette all polling stations, and dates for the opening and closure of each station, as required under the Electoral Act. Had this been done, a lot of the confusion, and, in at least two instances, unscheduled polling without the knowledge of most political parties and candidates (except for the SDL), would have been avoided. Dates for polling at various stations kept changing right into polling week. It was not until after polling, when the count was nearing its end at the Veiuto Centre, that a gazette notice was issued listing schedules for polling stations; it was backdated to comply with the Act. The Electoral Commission must be held equally guilty for this omission. Indeed, they rendered themselves culpable by advising that all preparations for the proper conduct of the election would be completed before polling began.

It is clear that the Office of the Supervisor of Elections was just not ready for the rushed national poll beginning on 6 May 2006. The Supervisor of Elections failed in his duty to inform the Prime Minister of this fact when he was asked if he would be ready in time for early elections.

Both the Supervisor of Elections and the Electoral Commission must accept full responsibility for the incompetence, the inefficiencies, the delays and the shambles that characterized the 2006 poll. Having given the nation, and the Prime Minister, over-confident assurances that the electoral machinery would be ready for the rushed poll, they must now accept the blame for seriously compromising the integrity of the 2006 general election.

Indian voters misled by the Elections Office

Indian voters were told in advertisements placed by the Elections Office that they could continue to register until 8 July 2006, well after elections were over, when advertisements in Fijian and English gave the correct date of 4 April 2006.

How-to-vote TV commercials placed by the Elections Office informed Indian voters they could vote by ticking either above or below the line, when to tick below the line rendered the vote invalid. In contrast, the Fijian and English versions of the advertisements gave the correct information. Despite repeated complaints by the FLP, the incorrect Hindi advertisement was not removed until I personally called up the chairman of the Electoral Commission, Graham Leung, after 8 pm on Friday 5 May, the eve of the polls, to complain. He then ordered television officials to remove it.

Excessive printing of ballot papers

The FLP has reliable information that excessive ballot papers were printed for a number of constituencies. We believe that these were used to stuff ballot boxes in certain crucial constituencies, as in 2001. Candidates, for instance, are baffled by the very high number of ballots cast in the Nasinu/Nausori

Communal constituencies – numbers which belie the low voter turn-out experienced – and by the lack of correlation between Communal votes and those cast for the open seats.

Polling

The first day of polling was an utter shambles, as everyone knows. This is despite assurances by the Supervisor of Elections through the media that his Office was 'ready to roll' come 7 am Saturday 6 May. The truth is that ballot papers were not ready at most of the polling stations scheduled to open at 7 am on 6 May. A number of polling stations did not open until well into the afternoon – the polling station at Kalabo opened at 1.30 pm, that at Colo-I-Suva at 12 noon – but the loss in polling time was never made up.

The problem with unavailability of ballot papers plagued various stations throughout the week. It caused unnecessary frustration to voters who had to queue for hours on end, and in some cases walk away without voting because the polling station had either not received the ballot papers or had run out of them. Here again, there was a noticeable racial and political bias that could not be ignored. It was pretty obvious that, while polling for the indigenous Fijian streams at almost all polling stations went on unhindered, it was the Indian constituencies and those for other minorities that were affected.

Senior Labour executive and candidate for the Nasinu Indian Communal seat, Krishna Datt, reckoned that much of the 'mess' was deliberate. 'It is designed to frustrate the process and disenfranchise Indian voters', he said. The Leader of the United Peoples Party, Mick Beddoes, expressed similar sentiments in his report:

> The scale of the disruptions and level of unpreparedness is far too extensive for it to be a simple matter of mass incompetence on the part of the Electoral Commission and the Supervisor of Elections and his officials.

The fact that the Fijian voters, ballot boxes and ballot papers were in adequate supply and in a state of preparedness and [that] they were voting in many cases for up to 4–5 hours before the first General or Indian ballot papers and boxes arrived, adds greater suspicion about the intent of electoral officials.[1]

The large numbers of voters who turned up to vote with registration slips, but found their names missing from voter rolls, reflected the earlier deliberate mess-up in the voter registration process. Had the Electoral Commission accepted my request made in May 2005 that registration forms be made accountable documents, this problem would have been avoided. As the problem began to surface with consistent regularity at polling stations, a request was made to the Electoral Commission that voters with registration slips whose names were not on electoral rolls be allowed to vote. This is the Commission's response:

> If a person's name does not appear on the electoral rolls, that person is not a registered voter and, therefore, not entitled to vote.

This response was both disappointing and unexpected, because the voter was being deprived of his or her democratic right to vote, not through any fault of his or her own, but because of a mess-up by the Elections Office, of which the Commission had been kept fully informed. It also failed to appreciate that voting is compulsory in Fiji, and a denial of a person's right to vote is tantamount to disenfranchising the voter.

The American Ambassador, Larry Dinger, clearly concerned at the high number of voters being turned away because of missing names, pointed out that:

> In my country, problems like this of missing names are catered for when a provisional roll is created so that the person can vote and his vote counted.[2]

In some cases where the presiding officer did allow such people to vote, these votes were kept separate, but in the end not included in the final count.

In tightly contested marginal seats, such as the Laucala Open, which was lost by the Labour Party by a mere 11 votes, missing names become crucial.

Nasinu polling

At least 200,000 people live in the Suva/Nausori corridor – most of them travel to Suva to work. Due to the very heavy traffic congestion during peak hours, workers generally leave home well before 7 am to get to the city by reporting time at 8 am. Likewise, in the evenings, with a 5 pm knock-off on week-days, they do not get home until 6 pm or after. Despite these considerations, all polling stations in the heavily populated Nasinu region were scheduled to close at 5 pm. This is contrary to past practice. Even though the Commissioner Central said presiding officers had the discretion to stay open late, almost all polling stations closed promptly at 5 pm, discouraging voters from queuing to vote. In the rare cases where polling stations did stay open, they conveniently found that they had run out of ballot papers. The FLP made several written as well as verbal requests to election officials to accommodate voters who turned up after 5 pm, but to no avail.

The impression thus created, was that every effort was being made to frustrate voting rather than facilitate it. As far as the FLP is concerned, this was an orchestrated plan to frustrate Labour supporters from voting in these crucial seats – it must be noted that constituencies in the Nasinu area have large numbers of low-paid workers and squatters who traditionally vote Labour.

One must also note that polling stations on a number of occasions did not open at 7 am as scheduled, but several hours later. To cite a few examples:

- On 6 May, the Training and Productive Authority of Fiji polling station opened at 11.30 am instead of 7 am – hundreds of voters who had turned up early to vote went away frustrated
- On 6 and 8 May, Nepani polling station opened at 9 am instead of 7 am – a number of FLP supporters went away without voting; it closed at 5 pm sharp
- At Rishikul Primary School, on 10 May, polling started one and a half hours late but finished promptly at 5 pm
- At Wailoku, polling finished at 3 pm even though voters were lined up to vote
- At the Assemblies of God Primary School polling station in Suva on 6 May, polling began late in the morning but ended sharply at 5 pm. It was noticed that, while Fijian voters were allowed in to vote after 5 pm, Indians were refused entry.

Unscheduled polling

As mentioned earlier, the Elections Office kept making last-minute changes to polling schedules that were not gazetted as required under the Electoral Act. Once polling programs had been finalized and publicized, they should not have been changed. If changes were absolutely necessary due to unforeseen circumstances, then it was the responsibility of the election officials to ensure that all candidates and political parties were notified of the change, in writing.

The most bizarre case was the incident at the Rishikul Nadera Primary School on Thursday 11 May. Polling at the primary school in Reba Circle was not scheduled to take place until Friday 12 May. For some inexplicable reason, the Elections Office decided to move polling there forward to Thursday 11 May without notifying all political parties or candidates. Mystifyingly, only the SDL was aware of the changed polling schedule at this station and were there to kick it off. Others heard about it closer to noon. Several serious concerns arise:

- Why was a last minute switch necessary?
- Why were other candidates and political parties not informed of the switch, but SDL was?
- How could election officials allow ballot boxes to be opened in the morning without other candidates or their agents being present?

Clearly, there was mischief afoot. Inquiries by the Labour candidate, Vijay Nair, disclosed that the directive to hold polling one day ahead of schedule was issued by the District Officer's office in Suva. This incident is a clear case of collusion between election officials and the SDL. It becomes even more significant considering that Nair lost this seat by a mere 11 votes. Surprisingly, none of the observer missions made note of this incident. Labour's request that voting that took place at this particular station on Thursday 11 be disallowed was ignored by the Electoral Commission.

Such malpractices added to the general air of suspicion regarding the impartiality of the Electoral Office. The fact that a serious incident of this nature can be treated so casually by those in authority bodes ill for future elections in Fiji.

Ballot boxes and the count

There were numerous mishaps with ballot boxes that should never have been tolerated. Boxes breaking up, as occurred in 2006, is something unheard of in Fiji's electoral experience. Ballot boxes were not properly sealed – a point noted even by observer missions. The EU mission recommended that in future plastic boxes be used to ensure greater security. The law requires ballot boxes to be properly sealed leaving no room for tampering with ballot papers. By failing to ensure this, the Elections Office breached section 86 (1) (a) of the Electoral Act.

There were concerns about ballot boxes being left unguarded for hours at polling stations before they were transported to the count centre. One such instance occurred on Tuesday 9 May at the Naivitavaya Church Hall polling station for the Laucala Open constituency. The ballot boxes were left unattended for three hours until 9 pm, while the presiding officer went to drink grog at the SDL shed. It wasn't until a complaint was lodged with the Elections Office that the boxes were finally taken to the Flagstaff operations centre. The entire incident was repeated the following day. This case is particularly significant because ballot papers for Box No. C404L from this polling station could not be reconciled at the count. According to the presiding officer, the total number of ballot papers issued was 1,200; yet total votes cast were only 463 – what happened to the balance of 737 ballot papers?

From this same polling station, five ballot boxes were placed aside following queries from FLP agents because papers could not be reconciled. However, a little later, the count team-leader said he had spoken to the presiding officer, who said he had made a mistake in stating the number of ballot papers issued. They then brought back the boxes put aside to include them in the count. Surprisingly, however, only four not five boxes were brought back. What happened to the fifth box? There was an absolute lack of transparency in dealing with this complaint. And how could the presiding officer have made such a huge mistake in stating the total number of ballot papers issued? Was he grossly incompetent or just plain dishonest?

Another questionable incident concerned Box No. C579 from the Vatuwaqa Church Hall polling station. Here the total votes cast were 12; total ballot papers issued were also 12. Yet, the actual count revealed 21 ballot papers in the box. Where did the extra ballot papers come from?

The FLP candidate for the Nausori/Naitasiri Open constituency maintains that 15 extra ballot boxes were introduced at the count for her constituency. The manner in which the count officials and the Returning Officer dealt with this complaint again lacked transparency and smacked of political bias.

Count for the Laucala Open constituency

By the morning of Wednesday 17 May, it became obvious that the election, so closely fought, now hinged on the marginal open seats in the Suva/Nasinu/

Nausori corridor. The Nausori/Naitasiri Open constituency, stuffed with 15 extra boxes, emerged a winner for the SDL.

The Samabula/Tamavua Open seat was wrested by Labour after a tough count battle, during which the bias of election officials towards the SDL became very obvious.

The Suva Open went to the SDL in another close battle, but it was confidently expected that Labour would win the two Nasinu Open constituencies – the Laucala Open and the Nasinu/Rewa Open – in view of the very high polling (90%) for the corresponding Indian communal seats in these constituencies.

Labour had good preferences and too high a lead in the Nasinu/Rewa Open constituency for games to be played there. The Laucala Open constituency thus became crucial if the SDL were to win the election. Despite the very close run, it should be noted that Mr Qarase had already hailed victory for the SDL. He therefore had to win Laucala Open by hook or by crook.

As the first count drew to a close on Wednesday, there was confusion. It seemed the SDL had asked for a recount, and polling agents were waiting for a decision while count officials left the room to confer. However, as everyone waited for the final outcome, suddenly, the count team began sealing up the ballot papers even though an official announcement declaring the winner had not been made. Just then, the Labour team at the count centre was informed via a phone call that the radios were announcing an SDL victory for the seat by 17 votes.

I was en route to Suva from the west when I received this stunning news. I immediately called the chairman of the Electoral Commission, Mr Graham Leung, and informed him that we wanted an immediate recount and that no papers should leave the room in the meanwhile. It was as well that Mr Leung came down because the Commissioner Central was obviously hell-bent on packing up the ballot papers and having them removed from the room. Mr Leung put a halt to this, and the Commissioner had no choice but to allow a recount. In the recount stage, a serious breach of procedure took place. The count team refused to recheck the validity of votes earlier declared valid. The fact that, despite all this, the difference in votes was reduced from 17 to 11 was significant. Had the team rechecked the validity of the 'valid' votes, it is possible that the result may have been overturned altogether.

Independent observer Father Arms, who was present at this stage, says in his report that he had noted at least two invalid ballot papers put into the valid votes box. He makes the following observation:

> The last seat won that gave the SDL an absolute majority of seats, was won only on the mis-conducted recount ….where the difference between the SDL and the FLP was only 11 votes. Had the FLP won that seat (which they might have under fairer circumstances or if the recount had been conducted properly) it is possible they would have been able to form a government…
>
> If there had not been the mistakes that worked against the Indo-Fijians and if the electoral administration had been properly balanced ethnically, another seat or two might have gone the way of the FLP.
>
> Add to this the unacceptably high percentage of invalid votes, and it becomes clear that Fiji has a few important, but quite manageable, things to do in order to ensure free and fair elections.[3]

Transporting and security of ballot boxes

There were other questionable and untoward happenings. For instance, why were private security companies with very close links with the SDL used in the Central Division to transport boxes to the count centre and to guard boxes? Trucks belonging to Global Risks, owned by Sakiusa Raivoce, a known SDL supporter and brother-in-law to Ratu Jone Kubuabola, were used to transport ballot boxes. Sunia Cama's (security/bailiff) men, dubbed the 'box boys', provided 24-hour security at the Veiuto count centre, sleeping on the premises. It was not their job under the Electoral Act. Why could not the police provide this security? Sunia Cama is a former professional boxer with known extremist nationalist sympathies and a relative of Jale Baba, SDL's campaign director. Win Gate Marketing Company Ltd was also used to transport boxes. The company has close association with Jale Baba in the carting of mahogany logs from Tailevu North to the mills.

The Electoral Act requires transportation of ballot boxes to be carried out by trustworthy companies. The above are too closely associated with the SDL to be classified trustworthy or impartial.

I have attempted to highlight a few of the more glaring and questionable practices and acts, and examples of non-compliance with electoral laws, that compromised the integrity of the 2006 poll. The trend emerged in 2001. Fiji has held eight general elections since independence. Apart from minor concerns and hiccups, the integrity of the first six elections was beyond suspicion. High standards and professionalism were generally the hallmarks of our electoral machinery.

The manipulation, rigging and deliberate disenfranchisement that characterized the 2001 and 2006 general elections should be a concern to all citizens who believe in the integrity of the democratic process. What went wrong occurred with too much regularity to be simply brushed off as incompetence or oversight. As Shakespeare's Hamlet would say, there was clearly 'a method to the madness'.

The neutrality of the civil service and the police is now a serious issue. In 2006, there was a palpable, pervasive aura of pro-SDL sentiment among both the police and count officials, certainly in the Central Division count centre. This could stem from the fact that there was gross racial imbalance in the recruitment of count officials, and in the police presence on the premises.

Indeed, when the count seemed to go against the SDL, those present could sense the palpable hostility through the body language, and even in the actions, of officials and police. At times, the situation bordered on being dangerous for FLP supporters. A clear demonstration of such bias was the spontaneous manner in which Fijian count officials burst out singing as SDL emerged 'victorious'.

Unless timely action is taken to weed out these malpractices, they will become a cancer that will completely destroy the integrity of our electoral machinery.

Conclusion

The reports of all observer groups must be thoroughly studied, and their recommendations implemented. The final report of the EU observer mission, for instance, makes comprehensive recommendations to improve the system and ensure greater security.

Major concerns are the registration and preparation of the electoral rolls and the conduct of postal ballots. Since 2001, there has been an alarming increase in the number of postal ballots despite the considerable increase in polling stations to facilitate voting in remote areas. For instance, there were some 20,000 postal ballots in 2006 – an unbelievably high number. Furthermore, postal ballots were being allowed even after polling proper started, and late postal ballots were included in the count well after the legal deadline of Monday 15 May. The process clearly lacked transparency.

Postal ballots can be a vehicle for vote-rigging, and must be brought under control. The EU observer mission report is highly critical of the manner in which postal voting was conducted and reports as follows:

> The vulnerability of the postal voting exercise to errors or fraud (impersonation) was increased with the provision to allow postal voting in person to continue during the official ordinary polling days and the fact that postal ballot boxes were not sealed overnight… Party agents were not present throughout the postal polling process and in any case would not have been allowed to stay at the premises overnight.

It is obvious that Fiji can no longer rely on the neutrality of the civil service to conduct future elections. An independent body must be created to conduct elections in order to restore the credibility of the process. Ethnic parity in the appointment of elections officials, both in the Elections Office and at the polling and counting stages, must be paramount.

All observer group reports have emphasised the need for Fiji to move away from the current emphasis on communal voting, and to encourage more cross-racial voting. This entails a move away from having a majority of Communal constituencies to having more Open constituencies. This is something that the FLP fought vigorously for during negotiations on the 1997 Constitution. Our call was not heeded then. It is now obvious to a wider group of observers and political pundits that, unless constitutional reforms take place to embrace more Open constituencies as opposed to Communal constituencies, national politics will continue to be dominated by ethnic rather than national considerations.

In this respect, I wish to deny the observation made by the EU in its report that the two major political parties, namely the SDL and the FLP, staged a highly ethnic political campaign rather than concentrating on issues of national concern. The FLP at no stage played racial politics in its 2006 election campaign, and this can be clearly gauged from our election manifesto as well as from advertisements placed in the newspapers and on television. If anything, there was an attempt to woo indigenous Fijian votes. Indeed, our entire 2006 election campaign focused on national issues. I call on observer groups to be fair in compiling their reports.

The SDL stole the 2001 and 2006 general elections. It used, at a conservative guess, over \$40 million of taxpayers' money under the guise of agricultural programs, to buy votes. The Office of the Supervisor of Elections, senior electoral officers and divisional commissioners facilitated an SDL victory.

Notes

[1] Letter to Chairman of Electoral Commission, 8 May 2006 (unpublished).
[2] *Daily Post*, 9 May 2006.
[3] 'Report of Fr David Arms; Observer to the 2006 Fiji General Elections, circulated 18 September 2006, unpublished, p.1.

27

A view from the Electoral Commission

Graham Leung

Whatever one's views about the success or otherwise of Fiji's 2006 general election, there seems to be a consensus that there is a need for a wide-ranging, thorough and critical examination of Fiji's voting laws, not least of the country's 'alternative vote system'.

Clearly, the Electoral Commission has a role to play in spearheading discussions aimed at developing bipartisan support for electoral reform. Some of the issues that emerged from the 2006 election are by no means new; they have been raised in the past by various observers. However, between general elections, very little appears to have been done to promote debate on the country's electoral laws and system. It is evident that, unless there is a concerted effort to address these issues, they will arise time and again.

While section 56 of Fiji's 1997 constitution makes casting a vote in general elections compulsory, there has never been any attempt to ascertain whether or not every registered voter does indeed cast a ballot. The anecdotal evidence suggests that many people did not cast a ballot in any of the 1999, 2001 and 2006 general elections. Despite this, there is little evidence of people who did not do so being prosecuted. While there are competing arguments for the retention of section 56 of the constitution, there is much to be said for discarding a law that is not being enforced and that is difficult to enforce; laws that cannot be enforced bring the legal system into disrepute and may even encourage non-compliance. On the other hand, a compelling argument can also be mounted that not casting a ballot is as much an expression of the democratic choice of a voter, as is casting one. Whatever the arguments, it seems to me that the law on 'compulsory voting' in Fiji needs revisiting to determine whether or not it has succeeded in meeting the objective of its architects.

Under the electoral regulations of the 1970s and 1980s, and again under the Electoral Decree of 1992, the Returning Officer had the discretion to allow a vote which might otherwise have been discarded as invalid, where the voter's intention was clear. In the Electoral Act 1998, this provision was removed. While the number of invalid votes fell in the 2006 general election – down to 8.7 per cent compared with 11.8 per cent in the 2001 election – many commentators have observed that this figure is still too high and must be reduced even further. Although precise figures are not available, information gleaned from election officials at the count centre suggests that the format of the ballot paper may create confusion in the minds of the voters. In many instances votes were declared 'invalid' because the voter had ticked above and below the line. Arguably in some cases, the voters' intention was obvious. But the current law is quite clear, a voter cannot tick both above *and* below the line. Given this situation, there appears to be a strong argument for the restoration of the discretionary power of the Returning Officer.

Fears that giving the Returning Officer the power to validate votes is giving the officer too much power, could be misplaced as there are checks and balances. First, there must be a 'finding' that the voter's intention is clear. Furthermore, the presence of party agents at the count increases the level of transparency and ensures that only valid votes are counted. The restoration of the discretionary power would ensure that the highest number of valid votes are counted, and reduce the number of voters that are inadvertently disenfranchised.

Sections 130 and 131 of the Electoral Act deal respectively with bribery and undue influence of voters. Section 131 makes it an offence for any person to hinder or interfere with the free exercise or performance by any other person of any political right or duty. Since voting was first introduced in Fiji, party sheds, banners and the serving of *kava* have been accepted and indeed encouraged by political parties as part of the overall election process – even though many political parties often complain about the expense associated with erecting and staffing the sheds. It is difficult to ignore the reality that, despite voters visiting the sheds to obtain assistance, the process often influences the way in which they vote. This influence can take various forms – ranging from voters being given how-to-vote cards to more subtle means of coercion and influence. Electoral laws neither expressly permit nor prohibit the sheds. There is only the caveat that they be no closer than 50 metres from the polling station. Given the need to improve the ethical environment under which polling is conducted so that elections are 'freer and fairer', parliament should, in consultation with relevant stakeholders, give serious consideration to the banning of party sheds. Voters should proceed directly to election officials to obtain their registration details and ballot papers. While no reliable evidence is available, the possibility of some voters being inadvertently misled or improperly advised on how to cast accurate votes cannot be ruled out. Banning party sheds, while perhaps making the atmosphere of elections less 'carnival-like', is likely to increase the ability of voters to cast their votes independently.

Section 164 of the Electoral Act empowers the Electoral Commission to make regulations prescribing 'all matters required or permitted' by the Electoral Act or 'necessary or convenient to be prescribed for carrying out or giving effect' to the Act to be prescribed. Presently, there are regulations on only a limited range of issues. In the past, the Electoral Commission has used its regulation-making powers sparingly, if at all. I would suggest that it is timely for the Electoral Commission to consider taking a more robust attitude with regard to the exercise of its statutory powers in this regard. Under section 164(2) of the Electoral Act, there is clearly enormous potential for the Electoral Commission to introduce wide-ranging measures aimed at improving the transparency and conduct of general elections. These regulations would have the force of law and bring about greater uniformity and accountability in election administration, thus assisting the Supervisor of Elections and his/her staff.

Many useful, if not altogether new, recommendations have emerged from the various missions that were present in Fiji to observe the 2006 general election. The Electoral Commission hopes to complete a comprehensive review of the general election before the end of 2006. The expectation is that it should then be in a good position to develop a strategy for the conduct of future elections in Fiji. This strategy is likely to have, as a high priority, the establishment of a State Elections Office.

28

Multiparty cabinet and power-sharing: lessons from elsewhere[1]

Jon Fraenkel

The ultimate outcome of Fiji's 2006 election was paradoxical. In some respects, it was the most polarized election in Fiji's history.[2] The two major parties, each with unanimous support from their respective ethnic communities, were able to divide up all the Fijian and Indian communal seats, as well as all the open seats.[3] Yet, in the aftermath of the election, the formation of a multiparty cabinet represented a historically unprecedented effort at power-sharing between the leaders of Fiji's two major communities.

The idea that some kind of coming-together in cabinet of leaders representing Fiji's different ethnic communities might provide some means of getting beyond Fiji's communalist impasse was not new. It had been raised during Ratu Sir Kamisese Mara's period as prime minister in the late 1970s, but never got off the ground. It was entrenched in the 1997 constitution by the then prime minister, Sitiveni Rabuka, and by then opposition leader Jai Ram Reddy, but they lost the 1999 election.[4] A multiparty cabinet was formed after the 1999 election, but it did not include the party with the largest share of the indigenous vote (Rabuka's Soqosoqo ni Vakavulewa ni Taukei (SVT), which won 38 per cent of the Fijian vote in 1999). Instead, the Fiji Labour Party (FLP) obtained an absolute majority (with 37 of the 71 seats) and, although it formed a coalition with several smaller Fijian parties, the emergence of splits within these Fijian allied parties generated difficulties for the multiparty cabinet even before the coup of 19 May 2000.

Such splitting is always a difficulty with multiparty cabinets; the minority party or parties run the risk of being seen as powerless within cabinet and lose popular support. None of the indigenous Fijian politicians who participated in the 1999 cabinet proved able to secure re-election in majority Fijian electorates in either 2001 or 2006. The key challenge for the post-2006 election multiparty cabinet was to achieve real influence for the minority party, and enable its leaders to sustain popular Fiji Indian backing for their participation in cabinet.

Fiji is not alone in looking to power-sharing as the answer to long-standing political polarization, but the country does have some uniquely favourable circumstances that might make it possible to avoid the type of difficulties experienced elsewhere.

Many of the world's experiments in power-sharing – for example, those in Africa – have occurred in post-civil war circumstances. The protagonists have armies stationed in different parts of the country, and the power-sharing arrangements often attempt to bring these together. So great is the bitterness between former combatants that these arrangements are often used to gain strategic advantage – and regularly fall apart.[5] Fiji is fortunate not to have this experience of civil warfare and violence; polarization has been largely political, while relationships at the grass roots level have remained reasonably amicable. As incoming FLP cabinet minister Krishna Datt put it shortly after the 2006 poll, political leaders have at times behaved like burlesque American wrestlers feigning fights with each other, instead of seeking cooperative ways to manage the affairs of state.[6]

The best-known modern power-sharing experiment was that adopted as part of the South African 1994 constitution by Nelson Mandela and F.W. de Klerk, and this influenced the design of Fiji's own institutions. The ability of those leaders to transcend ethnic politics, and establish for that country a more accommodative style of politics made a decisive difference, not just for that country, but more broadly for the southern part of Africa.[7] Yet, in other respects, South Africa is a poor model for Fiji. There, arrangements were inevitably temporary, and were aimed at reassuring the white minority during the transition away from apartheid. F.W. de Klerk's National Party pulled out of the cabinet in 1996, and, in the same year, a new permanent constitution abandoned the multiparty cabinet provisions. Power-sharing, of a sort, continued, but it was no longer mandatory. Fiji's situation is very different; here, the two populations are much closer in size than those of Africans and whites in South Africa and, owing to this, the multiparty cabinet provisions are potentially longer-term, rather than temporary, arrangements.

Northern Ireland has also pursued an experiment in power-sharing, as part of the 1998 Anglo-Irish Good Friday Agreement, but ongoing tensions between Loyalists and Republicans have delayed the implementation of the power-sharing rules. There, it is pressure from the British and Irish governments that has provided the critical encouragement to power-sharing, whereas in Fiji the incentives are largely domestic. In many ways, this is a great, and insufficiently recognized, advantage: for Fiji, the desire to make these arrangements work is not driven primarily by overseas links (important though those may be in the future if managed sensitively). Rather, Fiji's more astute politicians have recognized the advantages that can potentially be secured by having a government that rules by consensus and draws on the reservoirs of talent in both communities.

Neighbouring New Caledonia also has a multiparty cabinet experiment, although one that has not received the international attention it deserves. Back in the mid-1980s, that territory was close to a civil war between mainly Kanak-backed, pro-independence groups and the mainly settler-backed government. The 1988 Matignon Accord provided an initial agreement centred on devolution of powers to the three provinces (something, incidentally, never tried in Fiji for various reasons). A decade later, the 1998 Noumea Accord provided for a power-sharing territorial executive, coupled with steady transfer of powers from Paris to Noumea. The result has been a transformation of the New Caledonian political scene, with Kanak leaders participating in cabinet and a reconfiguration of political alliances on both sides.[8]

There are many other international experiences with power-sharing; some more successful, others less successful. Switzerland, for example, has nearly a century of experience with a Federal Council, which brings together representatives of the German-, French- and Italian-speaking minorities. Several of the other continental European states – including Austria and Belgium – also have experience with power-sharing institutions. There are also some notorious failures – Cyprus in the 1960s or Lebanon in the 1970s, for example. In the Lebanese case, external factors played an important role in the breakdown of the post-war national pact, even if the inflexibility of domestic arrangements – and in particular the 6:5 ratio of parliamentarians in favour of Christians over Muslims – also generated difficulties. Nevertheless, when former adversaries finally sought to end the civil war that had so ravaged the country from the mid-1970s to the 1990s, they almost inevitably reverted to a new power-sharing agreement (the 1989 Ta'if Accord), although one that entailed a shift to parity between Christian and Muslim MPs, a stronger role for the Muslim prime minister and a less powerful role for the Maronite Christian president. Similarly, in Bosnia and Iraq, the settlement of severe conflict critically depends on some commitment to the sharing of power in cabinet.

Surveying the global power-sharing experience suggests that, while the provisions adopted in different parts of the world differ markedly, there are some important common features that help to explain the success or failure of accords. What lessons can be learned from the international experience?

An effective voice for minority representatives

Power-sharing cabinets need to provide an effective voice for those politicians representing the minority community (or smaller party or parties). There is always a danger that the majority community's leaders will view the multiparty cabinet as a vehicle for rubber-stamping their own program, and deny minority leaders an effective voice, so that the latter come to be seen as unrepresentative 'Uncle Tom'-type figures. This is sometimes dealt with by having a minority veto, although such provisions run the risk of generating gridlock and immobilism. Effective multiparty cabinets enable parties to bring their own policies and perspectives into cabinet, and to establish some kind of balance between different interests through negotiation. In New Caledonia, this has also been much debated, with discussion centring on the meaning of the Noumea Accord's provisions for 'collegiality' in cabinet. The success or failure of Fiji's 2006 experiment will depend on the minority party being able to demonstrate greater influence in determining policy than was the case for the smaller parties in the 1999–2000 cabinet.

Multi*party* cabinets, where both parties have strong support from the peoples they represent, have the advantage over multi-*ethnic* cabinets in that they bring a more genuinely representative mix into cabinet. Under Ratu Mara's Alliance

Party governments in the 1970s and 1980s, there were repeated efforts to create multi-*ethnic* governments, but these never received majority support from the Indian community. Those who crossed over to join Ratu Mara's cabinets tended, as a result, to lose their seats at the following election, or to be seen as unrepresentative leaders. Muslim cabinet minister Ahmed Ali, for example, was the Indian member for the Lau constituency, where the electorate was overwhelmingly Fijian. He once described trying to forge links with the Indian community as being like trying to build a house by putting the roof on first.[9] Where, instead, the undisputed leaders of the Indian community join the cabinet there is the potential for a more genuine type of accommodation.

The need for real accomplishments

Power-sharing governments need to show genuine accomplishments. One of the weaknesses of the Rabuka–Reddy Accord back in 1996 was that the two subsequent years did little to demonstrate to the electorate the advantages of the new cooperative arrangements. Inertia set in. 1997, for example, was also the year when thousands of Agricultural Landlord and Tenant Act (ALTA) leases began expiring, resulting in severe hardship for the Fiji Indian rural communities. Almost ten years later, in 2006, the ALTA expiry issue remains unresolved. Partly as a result of this failure to deliver concrete achievements connected with sharing power, both Rabuka's SVT and Reddy's National Federation Party proved unable to hold the support of their respective communities at the 1999 poll, and the consequence was a rocky ride for the new constitution.

In the wake of the formation of the 2006 power-sharing executive, some suggested that potentially controversial legislation should be shelved or abandoned, and that discussion of some of the thorny issues should be deferred. Such delay would have the potential to quickly exhaust the new power-sharing government's post-election honeymoon. Without real accomplishments on ethnically sensitive issues, two or three years down the line, criticism of ministers enjoying perks and Pajeros would inevitably feature in the media reports, and/or government backbenchers would become more restive. Ethnic out-bidders would find themselves getting a wider hearing, putting pressure on their more moderate colleagues in cabinet.

Timing is also important for other reasons. Power-sharing arrangements, like coalition governments more generally, frequently break down beyond the middle of a parliamentary term, ahead of impending general elections, as political parties seek to re-galvanize support among core electorates. At that stage, minority parties in cabinet often look for potent issues around which to make a break from cabinet, hoping that electorates will punish the governing party for any breakdown in coalition arrangements.

An approach more likely to cement power-sharing arrangements is to demonstrate to the public real gains to people's living standards, that arise out of the new cooperation in cabinet. Fiji's economic growth and investment levels have been seriously diminished by political instability and civil strife. As a result, there exists scope for substantial gains should that epoch in Fiji's history now be closed. Even prior to the 2006 election, some politicians were collaborating together in the government select committees on land and sugar issues, and aiming to arrive at real solutions to these pressing questions. The land-leasing question, in particular, is an issue that is susceptible to some accommodative resolution (although *not*, as some propose, by creating an additional tier of state bureaucracy to deal with leasing).

The Promotion of Reconciliation, Tolerance and Unity (RTU) Bill is another issue that could either break up the multiparty cabinet or, if handled sensibly and sensitively, show real gains for cooperation in cabinet. The government's desire to draw a line under the experience of the 2000 coup, and to open a new chapter in Fiji's history was understandable. It has been the amnesty provisions of the RTU Bill that generated the most concern, on the grounds that they might facilitate the release of those convicted for involvement in the 19 May 2000 coup or the 2 November 2000 mutiny at the army's Queen Elizabeth Barracks. There is a possibility for compromise here too; a thoughtful amendment to the Bill could address the concerns of the minority community that the arrests and convictions after 2000 should stand out as an emphatic warning against any return to Fiji's cycle of coups, but still put in place machinery that assists the country in shifting beyond the fraught experience of the 2000 coup.

Visionary leaders and change in political parties

Power-sharing arrangements need the engagement of visionary leaders, and political parties often need to change substantially to make these work effectively. Power-sharing arrangements depend on the ability of political leaders to transform the parties they represent. Mandela's role in changing the African National Congress away from the politics of confrontation, and de Klerk's similar role in relation to the National Party were crucial in ensuring the success of the transition in South Africa. Conversely, Ian Paisley and other Loyalist leaders' resistance to the implementation of the 1998 Anglo-Irish Good Friday Agreement have proved an obstacle to the constructive continuation of the peace process in Northern Ireland. The sudden death of political leaders who provide the critical inspiration behind power-sharing accords (as in New Caledonia or Sudan[10]), inevitably entails a bumpy ride for the new arrangements. If the leader of one of the cooperating parties stands outside the multiparty cabinet, its chances of success are, inevitably, slim. The post-2006 election power struggle in the FLP was an almost inevitable result of party leader Mahendra Chaudhry's decision to remain outside the cabinet. In South Africa or Northern Ireland, the FLP leader would have been entitled to a vice presidency or deputy chief minister position, an arrangement that is probably the logical counterpart of effective power-sharing arrangements where these involve two large communities.

As they adjust to sharing power after a period of bitter antagonism, both majority and minority party leaders inevitably face difficulties in managing internal party affairs. The majority party leader is potentially threatened by government backbenchers eager for portfolios should power-sharing arrangements fall apart. The minority party leader may face charges of 'selling out' his or her community. In Fiji's post-2006 case, the FLP leader stayed outside the cabinet and FLP ministers were subjected to disciplinary charges for breaching party policy. The alternative of a breakaway faction separating from the FLP was, perhaps fortunately in this context, legally discounted by constitutional provisions against party-hopping.[11] FLP ministers seeking to align themselves outside the party would have to face by-elections in their constituencies; this would potentially require them to cross the difficult hurdle of over-turning the strong support for the FLP shown at the 2006 polls in

Indian electorates. Differences are inevitable under Fiji's multiparty cabinet arrangements, and are best dealt with by thoughtful and flexible negotiation within political parties as much as within cabinet.

Government and opposition

Power-sharing arrangements entail a reconfiguration of the 'opposition' and other constitutional arrangements. Internationally, power-sharing arrangements are normally associated with a shift away from the Westminster-style government opposition model. Normally, there is no leader of the opposition. Instead, backbenchers – whichever political party they are associated with – serve as the check on government policy, as with the *Bereichsopposition* during the time of the Austrian grand coalition.[12] Fiji's constitution remains ambiguous in this respect because the multiparty cabinet provisions were added later, superimposed after the assembly of a Westminster-based framework. This has resulted in all sorts of anomalies. For example, the constitution provides for a proportional distribution of the senate nominees from the leader of the opposition, but not those from the prime minister. The precise interpretation of the cabinet proportionality provisions in section 99 (5) of the constitution was an issue of continual litigation in the Court of Appeal and Supreme Court after the 2001 poll, with the decision of September 2004 placing judges in the position of being effectively law-makers rather than interpreters of the law.[13] Not having a limit on cabinet size was also unfortunate, because the requirement to retain dual majorities inevitably imparts an inflationary impetus to cabinet formation (New Caledonia, it should be noted, does have an 11-member limit on cabinet size).[14] Rules about 'cabinet confidentiality' and 'collective responsibility' also reflect the Westminster tradition, rather than the more flexible type of arrangements normally found in power-sharing executives.

Affirmative action programs

Affirmative action programs often accompany power-sharing provisions, but these work best if they relate to distribution of gains arising from a higher rate of economic growth, and if they are oriented towards all disadvantaged groups rather than one or the other ethnic group. In many countries that have looked to power-sharing rules to find a route away from political polarization, improving the position of disadvantaged communities has been important. Even where the differences are small, as between the Catholics and Protestants in Northern Ireland, improvements in living standards for the more disadvantaged community can make a big difference (improving prosperity in largely Catholic Southern Ireland had significant knock-on effects for Northern Ireland's Catholics). In New Caledonia, the Matignon and Noumea Accords have been accompanied by heavy French expenditures aimed at *rééquilibrage* ('re-balancing') to improve the position of the Kanaks. As in Fiji, those provisions often stimulate criticism that more is being done to foster the emergence of an indigenous élite than to improve general living standards. Nevertheless, those affirmative action policies have proved important in changing the orientation of the political leadership on both sides in New Caledonia, and are intimately connected with the success of the power-sharing accords.

In Fiji, discussions of relative indigenous disadvantage often occur in a time warp. It is as if nothing has changed since the time of the Spate (1959) and Burns (1960) reports, when around 90 per cent of indigenous Fijians still lived in rural villages, when there were few Fijian professionals, and when Fijians scarcely participated in the formal sectors of the economy (other than in the civil service, on the docks and in the gold mines).[15] Yet, this position has changed vastly, and not primarily due to affirmative action programs. Even before the unravelling of the Fijian Regulations in the mid-1960s, many ethnic Fijians had moved towards the towns. In the 1970s and 1980s, Fijian participation in formal sector employment grew strongly. Nevertheless, household income and expenditure surveys in 1977 and the early 1990s showed Fijians, on average, to be worse off than Fiji Indians.[16] A big part of the reason had to do with poverty in Fijian rural villages, although there was also evidence of urban poverty. Those studies found that, although Fijians were on average worse off than Fiji Indians, income inequality was more severe amongst Fiji Indians. So the lowest 20 per cent of Indian income-earners were somewhat worse off than their Fijian counterparts.

Fears are often expressed that affirmative action programs, particularly those aimed at encouraging indigenous businesses, are disproportionately aimed at élites. But there are alternative ways of handling such policies that earn greater legitimacy. Notably, the once heavily criticised Malaysian model of affirmative action is now much more internationally favoured, to a large degree because it became increasingly growth-oriented – rather than simply aimed at dividing up a diminishing or stagnant pie – and because it became aimed at all disadvantaged groups rather than favouring only one of the country's ethnic groups. Politicians in Fiji tend to feign a division on principle in relation to affirmative action; the Labour Party, when in power, accepted the need for programs that were aimed at tackling indigenous disadvantage. So, the issue is how to establish some degree of consensus around policies that have the effect of improving the situation of Fijians without being viewed as excessively ethnically slanted.

This list of important lessons from the international experience is not exhaustive; there are many others that merit consideration. But the list highlights some of the core issues that will need to be addressed, preferably through negotiation and compromise rather than through excessive resort to the law courts. If this is accomplished, ten years down the road, it might be Fiji that becomes the model to which other countries look, rather than Fiji looking to other countries to find examples of how to make power-sharing work effectively.

Notes

1   This chapter provides a modified and extended version of a keynote address to the Ministry of Multi-Ethnic Affairs, National Reconciliation & Unity Seminar on 'National Identity and Multi-Culturalism', Holiday Inn, 19 July 2006. It is included as a time-specific chapter, addressing the issues of the day, and steers clear of avoiding any prediction as regards the likely survival or failure of the post-2006 multiparty cabinet arrangements.

2   Meaning by this not that the conduct of the election was any more venomous than previously, but rather that there were fewer splinter parties representing each group. In all other post-independence elections, minority parties were able to get a seat or two, either in Fijian or 'national' (1972–87) or 'open' (1999–2006) constituencies.

3   The only space for other parties or independents was in the General or Rotuman constituencies.

4   'In establishing the cabinet, the prime minister must invite all parties whose membership in the House of Representatives comprises at least 10 per cent of the total membership of the House to be represented in proportion to their numbers in the House' [Fiji Government, 1997 Constitution, S.99(5)].

5   Spears, I.S. 2002. 'Africa: The Limits of Power-Sharing', *Journal of Democracy*, 13(3).

6   Parliament of Fiji, Parliamentary Debates, Daily Hansard, 8 June 2006; http://www.parliament.gov.fj/hansard

7   Koelble, T. & Reynolds, A. 1996. 'Power-sharing democracy in the new South Africa', *Politics and Society*, 24(3):221–36.

8   Maclellan, N. 2005. 'From Eloi to Europe: interactions with the ballot box in New Caledonia', *Commonwealth & Comparative Politics*, 43(3):394–417.

9   Ali, A. 1997. 'The Fiji general election of 1977', *Journal of Pacific History*, 12(4):195.

10   FLNKS leader Jean-Marie Tjibaou was assassinated on 4 May 1989, shortly after the Matignon Accord had been signed. Sudan Peoples' Liberation Movement leader John Garang died in a helicopter crash in July 2005, only months after becoming vice president in a power-sharing deal ('The death of John Garang', *Economist*, 4 August 2005).

11   'The place of a member of the House of Representatives becomes vacant if the member…

(g) resigns from the political party for which he or she was a candidate at the time he or she was elected to the House of Representatives;

(h) is expelled from the political party for which he or she was a candidate at the time he or she was last elected to the House of Representatives and:

    (i)   the political party is registered

    (ii)   the expulsion was in accordance with the rules of the party relating to party discipline; and

    (iii)   the expulsion did not relate to action taken by the member in his or her capacity as a member of a parliamentary committee' [Constitution of the Republic of the Fiji Islands, 1997, S 71. (1)].

12   Personal communication, Arend Lijphart, 1 June 2006; Lijphart, A. 1977. *Democracy in Plural Societies: A Comparative Exploration*, Yale University Press, p.48.

13   On the history of these decisions, see the multiparty cabinet time-line produced as an appendix to this volume.

14   By requirement to maintain dual majorities, I mean that Fiji governments have, potentially, to be formed twice. Initially, the onus is on a potential prime minister to persuade the president that he or she can command the support of a majority in the House. The president offers the premiership to the 'member of the House of Representatives who, in the President's opinion, can form a government that has the confidence of the house' (1997 constitution S. 98). Where a coalition is required, this is likely to be accompanied by inter-party agreements about the distribution of ministerial portfolios. Once appointed, the prime minister must reform his or her government in accordance with the 10 per cent entitlement provision, often incorporating parties from the opposite end of the political spectrum.

15   Only 11 per cent of Fijians were recorded as resident in the urban areas at the 1956 census (Colony of Fiji, *Report on the Census of Population, 1956*, Legislative Council of Fiji, Council Paper No 1 of 1958, Government Press, Suva, 1958).

16   See Stavenuiter, S. 1983. *Income Distribution in Fiji*, ILO, Suva; UNDP *Fiji Poverty Report*, 1996; Ahlburg, D.A. 1996. 'Income Distribution and Poverty in Fiji', UNDP, Suva.

29

Women and minority interests in Fiji's alternative electoral system

Suliana Siwatibau[1]

The 2006 election

Candidates from ten different political parties and some 69 independent candidates contested the 2006 national election. Amongst the 336 candidates were some 32 women, three of whom were standing as independents. The large number of parties and independent candidates could be an indication of the people's growing discontent with the policies of the two major parties and of their increasing confidence in political participation.

Table 29.1 shows how the different parties performed. The National Alliance Party (NAP) is of interest as it is a new party contesting elections for the first time. It fielded the third largest number of candidates and also the highest number of women candidates. Both the NAP and the United Peoples Party (UPP) made special efforts to field more women. The UPP, a small party, had 30 per cent women candidates and a gender-balanced winning team. The two major parties – the Soqosoqo Duavata ni Lewenivanua (SDL) and the Fiji Labour Party (FLP) – had poor representation of women candidates at 6 per cent and 12 per cent respectively.

Women's performance

Of the eight winning women, five stood on SDL tickets, two stood for the FLP and one for UPP. By definition, all gained the required majority of at least 50

Table 29.1   Summary of party performance, 2006

Party	Total number of candidates	Number of women candidates	Women as proportion of total (per cent)	Seats won by party	Seats won by women	Proportion of women representatives (per cent)
SDL	79	5	6	36	5	13.9
FLP	59	7	12	31	2	6.5
NAP	51	8	16	-	-	
NFP	44	4	9	-	-	
NVTLP	11	2	18	-	-	
UPP	10	3	30	2	1	50.0
PANU	9	-	-	-	-	
Party of Truth	2	-	-	-	-	
Justice & Freedom	1	-	-	-	-	
Social Liberty	1	-	-	-	-	
Independents (+COIN)	69	3	4	2	-	-
Total	336	32	9.5	71	8	11.3

Notes: SDL = Soqosoqo Duavata ni Lewenivanua; FLP = Fiji Labour Party; NAPF = National Alliance Party of Fiji; NFP = Mational Federation Party; NVTLP = Nationalist Vanua Tako Lavo Party; UPP = United Peoples Party; PANU = Party of National Unity; COIN = Coalition of Independent Nationals
Source: *The Fiji Times*, 19 May 2006.

per cent +1 of the valid votes cast. Of the other women candidates, 17 gained less than 10 per cent of the vote in their various constituencies and seven gained over 10 per cent, with the highest of these garnering 47.5 per cent of the votes in her constituency.

The communal seats were contested by 17 women and the open seats by 15 women. The percentage of candidates who emerged victorious in the Open constituencies was almost double that in the Communal constituencies (Table 29.2).

Did the voters favour women or men? According to at least four women candidates, some women supported them simply because they were women even though they did not specifically campaign solely on gender issues. One of the successful candidates publicly thanked her two main women campaign managers who helped her visit voters door-to-door and for their dedication during the campaign. Another candidate, though unsuccessful, acknowledged the support of women's groups in her constituency. This support enabled her to develop a network that has been maintained since the election and is still used to assist and empower women.

Promoting fairer representation

Despite government rhetoric, women's representation in parliament has remained below the minimum 30 per cent target set. This is due to such reasons as:

- difficulties in adapting very strong traditional cultures and attitudes that see women's status as subordinate to that of men
- continuing male influence over the way women in their families vote
- difficulties of those with little education (often women) comprehending the alternative vote (AV) system
- women being hesitant to nominate for election
- political parties making little concerted effort to encourage women as candidates
- the high cost of election campaigns combined with the relatively poor financial status of women
- the fact that the AV electoral system works against women and minority groups.

While the first two reasons are difficult, long-term problems, the rest would be relatively easy to address given political will. For example, the AV system, which tends to favour large parties over small ones, could be replaced by a system of proportional representation in which smaller parties were represented in parliament in proportion to their popular support; women could be encouraged by government and political parties to stand as candidates; public funding

Table 29.2   Women's performance in communal and open seats

Constituency	Number of women candidates	Women winners	Percentage winning
Communal	17	3	17.6
Open	15	5	33.3

Source: Analysis of figures extracted from *The Fiji Times* 19 May 2006.

could be used to defray the costs of election campaigns; and Fiji could give consideration to a quota system for gender representation in parliament.

Studies of democracies worldwide show the critical role of a country's electoral system in determining the extent of meaningful democracy achieved and in shaping the long-term political landscape.[2] One of the important features of democracy is its capacity to represent the range of interests and concerns of the populace in decision-making bodies. This requires that small parties representing special interest groups are able to sit in the elected legislative bodies alongside major parties that represent majority interest groups; and that marginalized groups, such as women and youth, are fairly represented.

The smaller parties: the National Alliance Party of Fiji (NAPF) and the National Federation Party (NFP)

The manifesto of the indigenous Fijian-led NAPF addresses the SDL's blueprint policies by promising to eliminate racial and discriminatory policies and to provide services based on need rather than race. It promises to eliminate corruption in government, and to promote good governance and multiculturalism. It also promises to encourage political parties to set a 50 per cent target for women candidates in elections. The manifesto of the Indo-Fijian-led NFP promises to enhance genuine multi-ethnic cooperation and power-sharing and to promote respect for the *vanua*, cultural diversity and ethnic differences. Achieving an ethnic balance in the diplomatic and civil service that would address the current apparent bias towards indigenous Fijians was also an important election promise.

These two parties, with their message of multiculturalism, appealed to small groups within the electorate – and yet neither won a seat, despite having garnered sufficient votes to warrant representation. As mentioned above, meaningful democracy requires such minority parties to be represented in national parliament; an outcome that is less likely to be achieved under Fiji's AV system than it would be under proportional representation (PR).

Table 29.3 shows the percentage of national votes that each party won and the number of seats gained in the 2006 election. It also shows the number of seats each party would have gained had the votes been counted under a full PR system rather than an AV system. The calculations are

Table 29.3   Party representation in 2006 under AV and PR systems

	SDL	FLP	NAP	NFP	NVTL	UPP	PANU	PT	JF	SL	IND
Votes won (per cent)	45.0	41.8	3.4	6.9	0.5	0.8	0.9	<0.1	<0.1	<0.1	0.7
Seats under AV	36	31	-	-	-	2	-	-	-	-	2
Seats under PR	32	30	2	5	-	1	1	-	-	-	-

based on the assumption of a PR system that treats the whole country as a single constituency, and no minimum vote threshold for representation in the parliament. In practice, most countries that use the PR system have limited PR systems with sub-national constituencies rather than a single national one. The single national constituency of a full PR system, however, is the closest to fair representation of the electorate; it is used in the Netherlands.

As the election was run on an AV system with single member representation, the comparison in Table 29.3 is only an indication of what would have resulted. Note that under a PR system, three other parties – the NAP, the NFP and the Party of National Unity (PANU) – would have gained seats in parliament. The UPP's share of seats would have been reduced to one.

In Fiji we need to ensure small minority groups have a say in parliament, and so some Communal constituencies may be necessary. At the same time, small groups sometimes have to compromise vital interests in order to survive. For example, the UPP adopted much of its major partner's policies when it joined with the FLP to form the New People's Coalition. It did not have an independent policy on land and so missed the opportunity to formally address a pressing concern of its migrant Pacific islander communities, some members of whom have been in Fiji for generations but lack rights to land (UPP Manifesto).[3]

A possible way forward

Fiji has been independent for over 30 years; it has had time to get used to elections and has had experience with two kinds of plurality majority electoral systems. Furthermore, it has achieved high literacy rates for both women and men and a highly educated female workforce. Yet despite these positive factors women continue to lag far behind men in positions of responsibility, including participation in national parliament.

Given the experience of other countries and democracies, it is clear that Fiji's plurality majority electoral system will not encourage either rapid increase of women's participation in parliament or the inclusion of minority interests in national decision-making bodies. A review of the Electoral Act, including a review of the electoral system is needed if a more meaningful democracy involving greater representation of women and minority groups is to be achieved. Such a review should seriously consider changing Fiji's elections system to a PR system with fewer communal and more open constituencies. It could also consider the other issues that limit the participation of women and minority groups, including campaign financing, and the issue of making party lists more gender-balanced.

Notes

[1] The author gratefully acknowledges the help of three strong women politicians, Hon. Bernadette Ganilau, Mrs Priscilla Singh and Mrs Fane Vosaniveibuli, who willingly agreed to be interviewed during the preparation of this paper. Any misinterpretations of their parties' policies are entirely those of the author.

[2] Reilly, B. & Reynolds, A. 1999. *Electoral Systems and Conflict in Divided Societies*, National Academies Press, Washington, DC. Available online at http://www.nap.edu.

[3] The issue is, however, being addressed by the women's wing of the party (personal communication, Hon. B. R. Ganilau, 6 July 2006).

30

The case for reform of the electoral system in Fiji

Rev. David G. Arms

Since the time the alternative vote (AV) was first proposed for Fiji in the Reeves Commission's report of 1996, there have been those (such as myself) who opposed it, regarding it as unsuitable to Fiji's political circumstances. Ever since the first elections using AV were held in 1999, there have been calls for reform. A lot of the suggestions being made have to do with improving the AV system as currently designed for Fiji. However, there has also been a consistent call for complete abandonment of the AV system. Between 1999 and 2001 there was a strong push by some for a return to the first-past-the-post (FPP) system, which Fiji had used previously.[1] Use of FPP would certainly remove the complexities of the present AV system, but it would do nothing at all to overcome AV's other deficiencies. What has been consistently advocated for this purpose is a form of proportional representation (PR). In this chapter, I discuss briefly some of the main arguments for switching to PR,[2] dwelling at a bit more length on the question of ethnic cross-voting. Needless to say, in arguing for reform, all three elections held under AV must be put under scrutiny, not just that of 2006.

The main argument for PR, in my view, is one of fairness. In 1999, the coalition led by the Fiji Labour Party (FLP) received a total of 336,868 first preferences, the coalition led by the Soqosoqo Vakavulewa ni Taukei (SVT), a total of 255,690 first preferences. Respectively, they held 46.8 and 35.5 per cent of the first preferences of the whole electorate. Yet when it came to seat allocation under AV, the FLP-led coalition received 52 seats, more than five times as many as the STV-led coalition, which received only 10! While it is true that AV is intended to take into account more than just first preferences, the disproportion it provided in this case can in no way be interpreted as reflecting the wishes of the people, which is what an electoral system is supposed to do. The results were grossly unfair, and were certainly a contributing factor to the coup of 2000. A PR system on the other hand would have divided up the seats much more fairly (see Tables 30.1 and 30.2).

Although the above example of unfairness is perhaps the most striking, there are other clear examples of unfairness in all three elections held under AV (1999, 2001, and 2006). Take, for instance, the National Federation Party (NFP), which is mainly an Indo-Fijian-backed party. In 1999 it received a total of 104,676 first preferences, in 2001 a total of 63,915 first preferences, and in 2006 a total of 49,116. This represents about a third, a quarter, and a seventh respectively of the Indo-Fijian vote. Yet the NFP received no seats at all in any of the three elections. How can this be in any way construed as fair?

Another argument for PR is that AV has failed in the very purpose for which it was adopted. The main reason given by the Reeves Commission for adoption of AV was to promote multi-ethnic government.[3] AV has done nothing of the kind – indeed it has done the very opposite. In 1999, the FLP-led coalition was indeed multi-ethnic and became the government; but every Indo-Fijian in parliament was in the government (except for George Shiu Raj), leaving the opposition benches to be filled by the other ethnic groups (and George Shiu Raj). This was hardly what was envisaged. What made things worse in practice, was that many of the indigenous Fijian members of the government were not happy with developments. Their support slipped away, clearly making the Lower House ethnically divided. In 2001, this division was even more apparent – the government was basically one of indigenous Fijians (and George Shiu Raj), with the other ethnic groups in opposition (with a couple of non-Indo-Fijian MPs, however, opting to join the government).

In 2006, the situation has become worse, with almost everyone alleging that the voting has taken place along ethnic lines – indigenous Fijians voting mainly for the SDL, and Indo-Fijians for the FLP. Indeed, instead of promoting multi-ethnic government parties, as the Reeves Commission had intended,[4] it

Table 30.1   1999 election: parties, first preferences and seats

Party	1st Prefs	%	AV	FPP	PR
Fijian communal constituencies:					
23 seats, total valid votes 179,216					
FAP	32,032	17.87	9	4	4
FLP	3,352	1.87	-	-	-
NVTL	16,352	9.12	1	1	2
PANU	17,149	9.57	4	4	2
SVT	68,114	38.01	5	11	10
VLV	34,758	19.40	3	2	5
Indep	5,645	3.15	1	1	-
Others	1,814	1.01	-	-	-
Indian communal constituencies:					
19 seats, total valid votes 165,841					
FAP	955	0.58	-	-	-
FLP	108,735	65.57	19	19	13
NFP	53,076	32.00	-	-	6
PANU	153	0.09	-	-	-
Indep	1,015	0.61	-	-	-
Other	1,907	1.15	-	-	-
General communal constituencies:					
3 seats, total valid votes 11,013					
FAP	1,057	9.60	-	-	-
GVP	3,367	30.57	2	-	1
UGP	5,412	49.14	1	3	2
Indep	20	0.18	-	-	-
Other	1,157	10.51	-	-	-
Rotuman communal constituency:					
1 seat, total valid votes 3,994					
Indep	2,012	50.38	1	1	1
Other	1,982	49.62	-	-	-
Open constituencies:					
25 seats, total valid votes 359,491					
FAP	38,863	10.81	2	2	3
FLP	119,563	33.26	18	15	8
NFP	51,600	14.35	-	-	4
NVTL	15,234	4.24	-	-	1
PANU	14,009	3.90	-	-	1
SVT	72,726	20.23	3	7	5
UGP	4,732	1.32	1	1	-
VLV	35,314	9.82	-	-	3
Indep	5,323	1.48	1	-	-
Other	2,127	0.59	-	-	-

has provided a situation in which each communal group has its own communal party: the SDL for indigenous Fijians, the FLP for Indo-Fijians, the UPP for the Generals, and an Independent for the Rotumans. Only Robin Irwin, for the Generals, forms an exception! Any multi-ethnic government that eventuates will be due to the multiparty cabinet provisions of the constitution (which were not a part of the Reeves report); it will not derive from the AV system. On the other hand, a PR system, while not forcing a multi-ethnic government, presents good opportunities for voluntary coalition formation – and such coalitions are likely to cross ethnic lines.

A further argument for PR is that it promotes the role of women in politics. Of the 15 nations with the highest percentage of women MPs in the Lower House, 14 use PR electoral systems. This speaks for itself. While there are now eight women MPs in the Lower House (which constitutes an improvement over 2001, but is only the same as in 1999), this is far below what is desirable. Women comprise 50 per cent of the population. While parity may not be a practical option, the nation would profit greatly from having women's direct input in governance. PR, not AV, is a practical way of facilitating this. Not only does the system itself give women a better chance of succeeding, but it is easier in PR systems to legislate increased representation for women. For instance, under a list or mixed-member proportional system,

Table 30.2   1999 election: parties, preferences and seats – overall view

Party	1st Prefs	%	AV	FPP	Com/ Open PR	71-Open PR
All constituencies:						
71 seats, total valid votes 719,555						
FAP	71,952	10.00	11	6	7	8
FLP	231,650	32.19	37	34	21	24
GVP	3,367	0.47	2	-	1	-
NFP	104,676	14.55	-	-	10	11
NVTL	31,586	4.39	1	1	3	3
PANU	32,266	4.48	4	4	3	3
SVT	140,840	19.57	8	18	15	14
UGP	10,144	1.41	2	4	2	1
VLV	70,072	9.74	3	2	8	7
Indep	14,015	1.95	3	2	1	-
Other	8,987	1.25	-	-	-	-

legislation could require that at least one in every four candidates on a party's list be a woman.

Another supporting argument for changing to PR at this time, is that of simplicity. PR systems can of course be complex. But there are PR systems that are quite simple – just one tick, or at most two, on an easy-to-understand ballot paper. The complexity of the AV system is itself a serious issue in Fiji. But is seems pointless to tamper with the system in order to make it simpler when AV is deficient on other grounds, as indicated above and also below. It would surely be more efficient to adopt a suitable and simple PR system that simultaneously solves those other deficiencies of AV.

Another aspect of PR is that it would have a moderating effect on communalism. This matter is clearly related to the larger topic of multi-ethnic government. As indicated earlier, the 2006 election is generally looked upon as being very much an ethnic tussle: the SDL supported mainly by indigenous Fijians versus the FLP supported mainly by Indo-Fijians. But AV has exaggerated this bipolar division. And it has also deprived of representation a more accommodating middle ground.

Contrary to public perception, in 2006, more indigenous Fijians voted for the so-called Indo-Fijian parties (FLP and NFP) in the Fijian communal seats than ever before – 7.26 per cent of them in fact (see Table 30.5). This compares with 2.8 per cent in 2001 (see Table 30.3) and a measly 1.87 per cent in 1999 (see Table 30.1). This outcome is in spite of the fact that most of the voters would have known that the party they were voting for had no chance of winning the seat. Had there been a real chance of such a vote affecting the outcome (which there would have been under List PR, for example), it is probable that the percentages would have been higher. If List PR had been in operation, the FLP would have picked up two seats from indigenous Fijian votes in 2006, perhaps one seat in 2001, but none in 1999.

There are similarly Indo-Fijian voters in Indo-Fijian communal seats voting for parties viewed as primarily indigenous Fijian. Their numbers were miniscule in 1999 and 2001 because such parties figured it was a waste of time and money trying to compete against the major Indo-Fijian parties. In most Indo-Fijian constituencies therefore, there was no primarily indigenous Fijian party that could be voted for. But the SDL gave it a real try in 2006, and, though their

Table 30.3   2001 election: parties, first preferences and seats

Party	1st Prefs	%	AV	FPP	PR
Fijian communal constituencies:					
23 seats, total valid votes 166 775					
BKV	7,826	4.69	-	1	1
CAMV	33,776	20.25	5	5	5
FAP	3,528	2.12	-	-	-
FLP	3,857	2.31	-	-	1
NFP	817	0.49	-	-	-
NLUP	6,666	4.00	-	-	1
NVTL	2,738	1.64	-	-	-
PANU	4,900	2.94	-	1	1
SDL	83,506	50.07	18	16	12
SVT	14,331	8.59	-	-	2
Indep	4,085	2.45	-	-	-
Other	745	0.45	-	-	-
Indian communal constituencies:					
19 seats, total votes 145,431					
FAP	8	0.01	-	-	-
FLP	108,459	74.58	19	19	15
NFP	32,143	22.10	-	-	4
NLUP	3,731	2.56	-	-	-
SDL	149	0.10	-	-	-
Indep	565	0.39	-	-	-
Other	376	0.26	-	-	-
General communal constituencies:					
3 seats, total valid votes 10 045					
CAMV	325	3.23	-	-	-
FAP	314	3.13	-	-	-
GVP	1,904	18.95	-	-	1
NLUP	993	9.89	1	1	-
SDL	2,477	24.66	1	1	1
SVT	252	2.51	-	-	-
UGP	3,260	32.45	1	1	1
Indep	520	5.18	-	-	-
Rotuman communal constituency:					
1 seat, total valid votes 3,772					
Indep	1,969	52.20	1	1	1
Other	1,803	47.80	-	-	-

Table 30.3 continued

Party	1st Prefs	%	AV	FPP	PR
Open constituencies:					
25 seats, total valid votes 310,765					
BKV	3,750	1.21	-	-	-
CAMV	30,313	9.76	1	2	2
FAP	4,296	1.38	-	-	-
FLP	106,412	34.24	8	13	9
NFP	30,955	9.96	1	-	3
NLUP	17,099	5.50	1	-	1
NVTL	944	0.30	-	-	-
PANU	2,188	0.70	-	-	-
SDL	83,095	26.74	13	9	7
SVT	20,560	6.62	-	-	2
Indep	10,099	3.25	1	1	1
Other	1,054	0.34	-	-	-

Table 30.4   2001 election: parties, preferences and seats – overall view

Party	1st Prefs	%	AV	FPP	Com/ Open PR	71-Open PR
All constituencies:						
71 seats, total valid votes 636,788						
BKV	11,576	1.82	-	1	1	1
CAMV	64,414	10.12	6	7	7	7
FAP	8,146	1.28	-	-	-	1
FLP	218,728	34.35	27	32	25	25
GVP	1,904	0.30	-	-	1	-
NFP	63,915	10.04	1	-	7	7
NLUP	28,489	4.47	2	1	2	3
NVTL	3,682	0.58	-	-	-	-
PANU	7,088	1.11	-	1	1	1
SDL	169,227	26.57	32	26	20	20
SVT	35,143	5.52	-	-	4	4
UGP	3,260	0.51	1	1	1	-
Indep	17,238	2.71	2	2	2	2
Other	3978	0.62	-	-	-	-

Table 30.5   2006 elections: parties, first preferences and seats

Party	1st Prefs	%	AV	FPP	PR
Fijian communal constituencies:					
23 seats, total valid votes 203,176					
FLP	12,865	6.33	-	-	2
PANU	4,127	2.03	-	-	-
NAP	5,050	2.49	-	-	1
NFP	1,883	0.93	-	-	-
NVTL	2,203	1.08	-	-	-
SDL	163,799	80.62	23	23	20
UPP	115	0.06	-	-	-
Indep	13,106	6.45	-	-	-
Other	28	0.01	-	-	-
Indian communal constituencies:					
19 seats, total valid votes 165,082					
FLP	134,002	81.17	19	19	16
PANU	-	0.00	-	-	-
NAP	3,170	1.92	-	-	-
NFP	23,263	14.09	-	-	3
NVTL	-	0.00	-	-	-
SDL	4,260	2.58	-	-	-
UPP	-	0.00	-	-	-
Indep	349	0.21	-	-	-
Other	38	0.03	-	-	-
General communal constituencies:					
3 seats, total valid votes 10,809					
FLP	383	3.54	-	-	-
PANU	-	0.00	-	-	-
NAP	776	7.18	-	-	-
NFP	60	0.56	-	-	-
NVTL	-	0.00	-	-	-
SDL	3,874	35.84	-	1	1
UPP	4,220	39.04	2	2	2
Indep	1,496	13.84	1	-	-
Other					
Rotuman communal constituency:					
1 seat, total valid votes 4,435					
NAP	245	5.52	-	-	-
SDL	526	11.86	-	-	-
UPP	532	12.00	-	-	-
Indep	3,132	70.62	1	1	1

Table 30.5 continued

Party	1st Prefs	%	AV	FPP	PR
Open constituencies:					
75 seats, total valid votes 387,407					
FLP	156,913	40.52	12	11	11
PANU	2,099	0.55	-	-	-
NAP	13,363	3.46	-	-	1
NFP	23,910	6.18	-	-	2
NVTL	1,454	0.39	-	-	-
SDL	70,952	44.14	13	14	11
UPP	1,615	0.43	-	-	-
Indep	16,618	4.30	-	-	-
Other	483	0.03	-	-	-

success came nowhere near their pre-election hype, it was impressive enough. At their first effort, the SDL were able to pick up 2.58 per cent of the Indo-Fijian vote. This would not have won them a seat under List PR, but it would have come pretty close. What's more, this percentage was obtained even though the SDL would not generally have been considered benign towards Indo-Fijians in its five-year term of government, only going after their vote late in the day.

We see then that there is a certain amount of ethnic cross-voting. There could, in fact, be quite a lot of such cross-voting in the open seats, but since voting is done in secret, any estimate of the percentage of cross-voting in open seats would be largely guesswork. In the communal seats, however, even though cross-voting may be on a small scale, it has significantly increased in 2006. The big problem is that AV is not rewarding these votes in any way, whereas List PR would do so. AV is in fact misrepresenting Fiji's voters, and misleading them into believing that Fiji has become more polarized, whereas the truth is the opposite. The tragedy is that the continued use of AV is highly likely to bring about and intensify this polarization. Why would parties like the SDL and FLP continue to spend money and make efforts to draw cross-ethnic votes in the communal seats when AV makes such efforts futile? What is said here about communal seats will also apply to many open seats. As about 20 of these 25 seats are ethnically lop-sided, and it is predictable which party will win, there may soon be a tendency by the party of the other ethnic group not to contest them, for such effort will also be seen as futile. This is why an immediate change to PR becomes so important. Fiji needs to build on what willingness there is to vote across ethnic boundaries, not discourage it.

Unfortunately, AV discourages other smaller parties too, some of which occupy the middle ground between the two giants. The NFP and NAP (National Alliance Party) are excellent examples. Though they drew 49,116 first preferences (as mentioned earlier) and 22,604 first preferences, respectively, in 2006 (see Table 30.6), they received no reward, whereas under PR they would have (the reward would have been five seats for the NFP and two seats for the NAP). Why keep the AV system, which wipes out such minority viewpoints? Such parties, though small, have a valuable contribution to make. Who can deny the value of the United Generals Party (UGP) – now the United Peoples Party (UPP) – in parliament, for example? Though the party had a solitary representative in the last parliament, it wielded substantial and constructive influence. But notice again AV's abhorrently haphazard nature. While we may rue the failure of the NFP and NAP to win any seats, even with their large number of first preferences, the UPP with only 6,482 first preferences in 2006 managed to win two! What a ridiculous perversion of justice!

To cut out certain minorities in this way is against Fiji's own cultural norms. Fiji prides itself on its respect for minorities – except, it would appear, when they are political parties. Rotumans receive a place in the Senate and their own Lower House seat; the Generals are very well catered for with three seats; provinces such as Serua and Namosi receive separate Fijian communal seats even though

Table 30.6   2006 elections: parties, preferences and seats – overall view

Party	1st Prefs	%	AV	FPP	Com/ Open PR	71-Open PR
All constituencies:						
71 seats, total valid votes 770,909						
FLP	304,163	39.46	31	30	29	29
PANU	6,226	0.81	-	-	-	1
NAP	22,604	2.93	-	-	2	2
NFP	49,116	6.37	-	-	5	5
NVTL	3,657	0.47	-	-	-	-
SDL	343,411	44.55	36	38	32	33
UPP	6,482	0.84	2	2	2	1
Indep	34,701	4.50	2	1	1	-
Other	549	0.07	-	-	-	-

their population is far smaller than many other provinces; proportionality is required for deciding seats in the multiparty cabinet; proportionality is also required in deciding which opposition members will be appointed to the Senate. There seems to be in all these cases a genuine concern for inclusiveness. Such an attitude is necessary also toward political parties.

PR would provide this inclusiveness, as well as the fairness spoken of earlier. At the same time, it would not exaggerate the importance of such parties. By being proportional it gives all groups their due. It may be thought that, while AV and FPP may tend to push politics too much into a two-party struggle, PR would multiply parties excessively and thus make governance too difficult. Experience in other countries, however, does not bear this out. There may indeed be a need for more comprehensive dialogue, but surely that is often what is best for a country. It is, in fact, precisely what is being called for in Fiji's current multiparty cabinet situation.

However, can we realistically expect the two major parties, the SDL and the FLP, to opt for a change to PR when it would clearly weaken their overall power? To get them to do so will certainly be a challenge, but it should be attempted for the good of the country. Hopefully, the leadership of these two parties, especially in a multiparty cabinet context, will have enough statesmanship to give this consideration due priority.

Self-interest, however, would also indicate that these parties consider PR.[5] As Fiji's demographics change with the emigration of Indo-Fijians, the FLP's main power-base is shrinking. PR would ensure that it would retain fair representation no matter what happens in regard to population ratios in the future. On the other hand, the SDL needs to consider that, as fear of Indo-Fijian leadership subsides in the indigenous community, more internal differences (especially, perhaps, regional ones) are likely to emerge within that community, as has happened before (in the first 1977 election with Sakeasi Butadroka, and in the 1994 election with Josefata Kamikamica). If splits occur in indigenous Fijian politics, it is important that the resulting factions be represented fairly, otherwise the injustice of the 1999 election towards the SVT-led coalition could be repeated for the SDL and/or the dissident factions.

While PR cannot be expected to solve all of Fiji's political difficulties, it would help the country enormously in the various ways suggested here.

Table 30.7 Seats won in the 1999, 2001 and 2006 elections as counted by the AV, FPP and PR systems

1999

	FAP	FLP	GVP	NFP	NVTL	PANU	SVT	UGP	VLV	Indep	Others
AV	11	37	2	–	1	4	8	2	3	3	–
FPP	6	34	–	–	1	4	18	4	2	2	–
Com/Open PR	7	21	1	10	3	3	15	2	8	1	–
71-Open PR	8	24	–	11	3	3	14	1	7	–	–

2001

	BKV	CAMV	FAP	FLP	GVP	NFP	NLUP	NVTL	PANU	SDL	SVT	UGP	Indep	Others
AV	–	6	–	27	–	1	2	–	–	32	–	1	2	–
FPP	1	7	–	32	–	–	1	–	1	26	–	1	2	–
Com/Open PR	1	7	–	25	1	7	2	–	1	20	4	1	2	–
71-Open PR	1	7	1	25	–	7	3	–	1	20	4	–	2	–

2006

	FLP	PANU	NAP	NFP	NVTL	SDL	UPP	Indep	Others
AV	31	–	–	–	–	36	2	2	–
FPP	30	–	–	–	–	38	2	1	–
Com/Open PR	29	–	2	5	–	32	2	1	–
71-Open PR	29	1	2	5	–	33	1	–	–

A note on the electoral data

Tables 30.1, 30.3 and 30.5 deal respectively with the elections of 1999, 2001 and 2006. Each table provides the abbreviated names of the political parties, the number of first preferences each party received, the percentage of the ethnic (or joint) group vote that figure represents, the actual number of seats won by each party under the AV system, the number of seats each party would have won if the votes had been counted under Fiji's former FPP system, and the number of seats each party would have won if the allocation was proportional to the number of first preferences each party received. This latter way of allocating seats is one method of what is called proportional representation (PR).[6]

Tables 30.2, 30.4 and 30.6 summarize Tables 30.1, 30.3 and 30.5, respectively, adding together the first preferences and seats for all the different constituency types. These three tables have two PR columns, not just one. The first of these (titled Communal/Open PR) summarizes the PR seats allotted in Tables 30.1, 30.3 and 30.5. In those tables, PR was applied separately within the respective group of constituencies, Communal and Open. PR could be applied in this way, and would indeed work quite well if communal seats were retained. In point of fact, however, it becomes unnecessary to retain communal seats when PR is used, for PR itself provides fair ethnic representation between the various ethnic groups, if this is what the voters themselves want (that is, if they vote along ethnic lines).

The second PR column (titled 71-Open PR) calculates the proportions as if all 71 seats were open seats. It uses the totals of each party's first preferences, Communal and Open, to determine how the 71 seats might have divided out proportionally. There is an inherent weakness in calculating the proportions in this way, however, in that independent candidates and some parties (e.g. the UGP/UPP) will have run in one half of the system (say, the Communal) but not in the other. Similarly, some voters may have been constrained in their voting by the number of parties running in their constituency. Nevertheless, it gives us a rough idea as to how PR results might look. One could, of course, calculate how the 71 seats might have divided up on the basis of the 25 open seats alone, but this would have the same weakness as that described above.

Table 30.7 provides an overall view of the seat division under AV, FPP, Communal/Open PR and 71-Open PR for all three elections.

What I would particularly like the reader to consider in these seven tables, is the very different seat allocations provided by the three different voting systems. Election results are supposed to reflect 'the will of the people', but clearly that will is interpreted by the voting system used. Surely we should look for a system that reflects that will most accurately. The tables illustrate how the AV and FPP systems provide us with gross inequities in representation. In contrast, a PR system would respect the various opinions in our midst and contribute to a greater degree of collaboration (rather than winner-takes-all). Such working together is what the multiparty cabinet provisions of the constitution are trying to encourage. For large and small groups alike, PR provides genuine and fair representation. The Lower House, after all, is supposed to be a house of representatives.

Notes

[1]   Interest in a return to FPP waned after 2001, probably for reasons given in footnote 5.

[2]   There are three main forms of PR: a list system; a mixed-member proportional system; and a single transferable vote system. Any of these would be fine for Fiji provided they are suitably adapted for Fiji's circumstances. I have elsewhere made concrete suggestions in this regard (see Arms, D.G. 2006. 'Concrete options for proportional representation in Fiji', in *Reviewing Fiji's Electoral System*, proceedings of workshop hosted by the Citizens' Constitutional Forum, 9–10 February, Printhouse, Suva, pp.9–119; and Arms, D.G. 2006. 'The failure of the alternative vote system and the case for proportional representation in Fiji' in *Journal of Pacific Studies*).

[3]   Fiji Constitution Review Commission. 1996. *The Fiji Islands: Towards a United Future*, Parliament of Fiji Parliamentary Paper 34, Government Printer, Suva, p.310.

[4]   Reeves Commission 1996, p.315–17.

[5]   Unfortunately, self-interest is all too often the over-riding factor – a self-interest which is frequently misguided. The indigenous Fijian leadership was in favour of changing back to FPP from AV in the period 1999–2001. The SVT would certainly have done much better under FPP in 1999 (see Table 30.2). However, if FPP had been used in 2001, the FLP would have won, not the SDL (see Table 30.4). There was, thus, little talk of a change back to FPP after 2001. Ironically, had the SDL implemented such a change, the party would have won by a large absolute majority in 2006 (see Table 30.6) rather than by an extremely narrow one.

[6]   The Sainte Laguë method has been used for the proportional allocation of seats.

31

An election retrospective

Ratu Joni Madraiwiwi

The 2006 election confirmed the polarization in the country that has been extant for much of our voting history. The process has tended to ebb and flow at critical periods, with little sign of any sustained development towards integration. The inability of political parties promoting multiracialism and multiculturalism to make inroads was unsurprising. Six years after the events of 2000, divisions remain. Our respective communities continue to find security and support among their kind, and their attitudes are, in turn, reinforced by an electoral system that is ethnically based.

The campaign itself was remarkable for its relative lack of invective, insult and ill will. There were certainly some isolated personal attacks on individual politicians that reflected little credit on the critics. However, by and large, it was open and freewheeling and 'negative' incidents were limited. Radio, television and 'the dailies' provided full coverage and were accessible to the people. The barrage of criticisms leveled at the Electoral Commission and the Supervisor of Elections had some substance, but the problem was largely systemic: the consequence of successive governments since independence leaving those offices in hibernation between elections. The lesson learned is not to allow this to happen in future. The authorities need to ensure that the offices are fully resourced and in a constant state of readiness. There was some defensiveness about the election observers. I take the view that the measure of comfort and assurance they provided the electorate was a sufficient riposte to any criticism. Credit is due the Prime Minister for inviting them.

The election outcome was influenced by several significant factors. I have already mentioned the existing ethnic divisions. The fraught relationship between the Soqosoqo ni Duavata ni Lewenivanua (SDL) government and the military, further compounded by the military's campaign for truth and justice in the villages, only served to strengthen support for the SDL. This strengthening was significant in the light of Indo-Fijian emigration coupled with higher Fijian birthrates, neither of which have been given sufficient attention. Next year's census should remedy the situation. What it will reveal, I would respectfully suggest, is the increasing difficulty the Fiji Labour Party (FLP) will face in future elections unless it broadens its Fijian base.

The SDL, and the Prime Minister in particular, were impressive in being able to hold the Fijian electorate together. The calls for unity appear to have been largely heeded. However, differences based on provincial, *vanua* and other rivalries remain, and will need to be dealt with sensitively and expeditiously if they are to be kept in check. The potential for disunity remains because, as the proportion of Fijians in the population increases, real and imagined grievances are fueled and respective groups feel emboldened to assert their claims. Fijian national leaders have to be more direct in telling their own people about restraint and forbearance. The Pandora's box of ever-increasing expectations in the context of unrealistic time frames is a threat to all of us.

Yet, I do not despair: there is a paradox in these election results that fuels my optimism. The ethnic slant of the voting patterns did not preclude a deep-seated desire across our communities for more cooperative governance. Having cast their ballots, the electorate wanted the political parties to work together more closely. In over a century of multiculturalism, much of it with little or any engagement, we have learned to live with each other. We are still learning, sometimes painfully. Part of that lesson is working with each other and engaging in a limited fashion. We prefer our own leaders, but we expect them to build the bridges that we are reluctant to construct ourselves.

As for the National Federation Party, it has failed in a second general election to secure any seats. While I do not predict its demise, it will not make any headway as long as Mr Chaudhry remains leader of the FLP. He is the undisputed political leader of the Indo-Fijian community. His standing was reinforced following the events of May 2000. By his courage while being held hostage in Parliament, he upheld the *izzat,* or honour, of his people. They have not forgotten and they are grateful. Ironically, it is that status as well as his articulation of Indo-Fijian fears and concerns that make him a bogeyman to many Fijians. He is, of course, not one, but rather, a relentless and articulate advocate of the causes in which he believes.

The issues in the election included the Promotion of Reconciliation, Tolerance and Unity Bill, resolution of the land tenure issue, economic management, poverty and the plethora of squatter settlements, as well as the relationship between the government and the military. As is the nature of such debates, there was an ethnic hue to the positions people took. For example, if one was Fijian, one tended to favour the expiring leases being brought under the Native Land Trust Act rather than the Agricultural Landlord and Tenant Act. At the same time, since May 2000, Indo-Fijians see the military as a necessary check on the more nationalist inclinations of the government. The Promotion of Reconciliation, Tolerance and Unity Bill created much disquiet in the community because of its implications. Overall, the support that opposition parties might otherwise have gained from Fijian votes was more than offset by support for the SDL government on the basis of continuing stability.

A pleasing aspect of the new House of Representatives is the eight female members. However, these women represent only a little over ten per cent of the House. There is ample scope for more women representatives. While the FLP adopted a quota system (of sorts) for women candidates at its annual conference in Lautoka in 2004, no political party has been bold enough to implement the initiative. Women have generally had to struggle against heavy odds for endorsement. The arguments about a level playing field are spurious because there is none. Having said that, one must acknowledge the relative success of the SDL government in having five women members of parliament.

In the last few days before the general election commenced on 6 May 2006, advertisements appeared that implied support for the SDL government on the basis of its Christian orientation. Such sentiments had also been expressed from the pulpits in many churches across the nation. Those initiatives were unfortunate and have no place in a multicultural, multireligious society like ours. They influence impressionable minds and thereby encourage bigotry and arrogance. It is sufficient that Christians are enjoined to vote to allow God's will be done. He of course moves in His own unfathomable manner and may use anyone to effect His will. As for the response of Indo-Fijian religious organizations, while more subtle than their Christian counterparts, some could not divorce themselves from the demands of politics, while others remained apolitical.

The electoral system still remains too complicated for people to understand. However, there is little prospect of change. The major parties appear to be comfortable with the status quo, but that should not be an obstacle to continuing debate and discussion. I do not apologize for favouring a form of proportional representation. It is important that the support for political parties in our community be reflected in that proportion in parliament. Otherwise, certain sections of the electorate are not properly represented. The requirement for a partly pre-determined ethnic composition of the House should also be reviewed with a view to its gradual removal over time. I believe this may happen slowly, as the proportion of Fijians in the population increases significantly, and this scenario provides them with a measure of security.

In the context of the minority General Voter population, the realignment of the United General Party with the FLP generated much soul-searching within these communities. While there were those who feared the consequences of alienation from traditional allies, others were convinced it was time to seek an alternative to the 'step-daughterly' treatment received hitherto. The strategy appears to have worked. Whether it will improve the position of minorities, in terms of the equal opportunities to which they are entitled, is an open question. There are those on the Fijian side of politics who take the view that as 'the generals' have cut loose from their usual moorings, they should be held to account. Politics is not a forgiving pastime here or elsewhere.

It would be easy to feel some disquiet about the continuing ethnic division in our community as revealed in recent voting patterns. I accept such division as largely the result of our history. Yet it also camouflages the accommodations we have made with each other in the years we have lived together. It does not fully reflect the extent of our engagement, although this is still too limited for this author's liking. The strength of this engagement lies in the ordinary people of this country. Twice, almost a decade and a half apart, we have had two significant political upheavals. Our resilience is due in large part to the people and to their hope of a better future for their children, whatever their ethnicity. It is this vision that links all of us. We need to expand the vision to narrow the distances between us and draw us more closely together. For all these reasons and more, the general election of May 2006, with all its imperfections, was a cause for celebration.

EPILOGUE

Understanding Fiji's political paradox

Robert Norton

The wide-ranging contributions to this volume on Fiji's 2006 general election and its aftermath reflect some continuities in the country's political history since the late colonial period. The land issue was central in the minds of Indo-Fijian farmers in the 1960s, when political party competition began, for many leases were being lost to the Fijian reserves. Indo-Fijians were at that time offered a choice between leaders who pushed strongly for radical constitutional changes and those who promised security and progress by working with conservative Fijian leaders. Perhaps in the formation of the post-2006 election multiparty cabinet we see a potential for that choice to emerge again as it did in the 1999 election. But the demographic trend, contrasting so starkly with the Indo-Fijian majority at the time of independence, is likely to discourage radicalism in Indo-Fijian leadership and strengthen the emphasis on cultivating Fijian allies.

Another continuity is the importance of chiefly influence and chiefly rivalries. Although the leading Fijian chiefs have, since 1987, been displaced at the helm of government by commoners or people of modest traditional rank, it is clear from the chapters by Tuimaleali'ifano, Tuitoga, and Saumaki,[1] how strong chiefly influence and rivalry continue to be – particularly at the local level, and even in areas such as Rewa that have long been subject to strong urban economic and cultural influences. It should be noted, however, that, contrary to popular assumption today, commoner representation among members of parliament has been strengthening since the late 1960s when, in fact, nearly

half the then twelve Fijians elected by popular vote to the colonial legislature
were commoners. After the extension of adult franchise to Fijians in 1963, the
Great Council of Chiefs' nominated representation was reduced to only two of
the six Fijian members of the Legislative Council, and further weakened in 1966
to just two out of fourteen Fijian members. Since 1970, Fiji's constitution, in
contrast to those of Tonga and Samoa, has not given chiefs (nobles in Tonga)
any privileged representation in the main legislative assembly. The extent to
which Fijians of chiefly rank have enjoyed influence in electoral politics has
been due to traditional loyalties and to the significance acquired by leading
chiefs as perceived bastions of Fijian identity and strength in the context of
ethnic conflict – not to legal prerogative.

Bose and Fraenkel's inquiry into the fate of 'western separatism' addresses a
dimension of politics that has long interested political analysts[2]: western Viti
Levu as a regional seed-bed for the growth of radical challenge to the political
establishment – among both Fijians and Indo-Fijians – with the potential to
nurture political alliances. The 'National' in the National Federation Party
(NFP) derives from the National Democratic Party in western Viti Levu that
Apisai Tora and Isikeli Nadalo merged with A.D. Patel's Federation Party in
1968. Many western Fijians had resented the colonial government's privileging
of southeastern Viti Levu and the eastern islands by way of support for education
and development and recruitment to government jobs. Tora's earlier Western
Democratic Party and Nadalo's Fijian National Party were born from those
grievances, while the Federation Party simultaneously grew from the Indo-Fijian
farmers' industrial struggles with the Colonial Sugar Refining Company.

Western Fijian dissent has waxed and waned, moderated partly by countervailing
relationships between local chiefs and eastern political leaders, and by the greater
force of ethnic consciousness. From the early 1970s, Ratu Mara strengthened his
support in the west through his influence in the Western Tuis (chiefs) Association
– which he helped establish – by directing development projects to the region,
and by increasing westerner representation in parliament and cabinet. The
leading western chief, Tui Vuda, was eventually recruited to government, along
with others – including even Apisai Tora himself, once feared by the commercial
and political establishment. When, in 1987, a new government was formed
with a west Viti Levu Fijian (Timoci Bavadra) at last at the helm, Tora led street

marches in protest against it. Fijian nationalism, originating in southeast Viti Levu, became a far greater problem for Mara than dissent in the west. Political observers and aspirants alike have long tended to overestimate the potential for militant regionalism to weigh heavily in Fijian politics.

Laisenia Qarase's endeavour to become a national leader has been frustrated by the demands of Fijian extremists. The problem of Fijian ethno-nationalism has a long history. In his political planning for self-government, Ratu Mara argued patiently with younger Fijian colleagues in the leadership of the Fijian Association – soon to be the major body in the Alliance Party – to dissuade them from their initial vision of a 'Fiji for the Fijians'. If not for the untimely death in 1964 of the staunchest Fijian nationalist of that time, Ravuama Vunivalu, Mara's task would have been even more difficult. Soon after Mara and NFP president Siddiq Koya led Fiji to independence, Mara faced a far more daunting challenge from Sakeasi Butadroka and the Fijian Nationalist Party (FNP) that dashed his hope to strengthen Indo-Fijian representation in government. Just as Mara had his problem with the 'young Turks' in the Fijian Association, and later with the FNP, Rabuka was bedevilled by the 'Taukeists' and reactionary Methodists when, in the mid-1990s, he reinvented himself politically to embark on the project of constitutional reform. Qarase may have succeeded in taming Fijian ethno-nationalism for the moment, but it is likely to continue to haunt him. All three leaders have also been constrained by the political need to placate provincial or *vanua* rivalries and grievances. These are likely to be intensified by the strengthening nexus between political power and access to material benefits of various kinds.

What is perhaps most remarkable about the 2006 election is the way its outcome repeats a pattern of dialogue and conciliation that had followed phases of crisis on the eve of Fiji's independence – and that emerged again several years after Rabuka's coups. Labour Party leader Krishna Datt is surely to Laisenia Qarase, what Jai Ram Reddy was to Sitiveni Rabuka, and Siddiq Koya to Ratu Mara: a partner in projects of political reform aimed at bridging the ethnic political divide. The strong accord that quickly grew between Mara and Koya following the death of A.D. Patel late in 1969, was a triumph over an ethnic polarization that came close to widespread violence following the NFP victory in by-elections forced by that party's boycott of the colonial parliament.[3] The understanding that grew between Reddy and Rabuka in the late 1990s seemed a strong echo of that historic pact, and the conciliatory potential now appears yet again in Qarase's relationship with Datt.

This brings me to Ratu Joni Madraiwiwi's observation about 'the paradox' of the recent elections: such a strong ethnic polarization, yet followed by a promising start to collaboration in a multiparty cabinet.[4] This outcome directs attention to the question of the nature of ethnic difference and conflict in Fiji, the paradox that such electoral polarity is not necessarily a measure of the intractability of conflict.

After the many elections and much experimentation with multi-ethnic political organization since parties first competed for power in 1966, the ethnic divide persists in the political arena as starkly as ever, confounding the visions of proponents of grand theoretical narratives about inevitable directions of political change driven by forces of modernity. When the question of Fiji's political development first loomed large in academic debate, following Rabuka's coups, Marxist and liberal democratic analysts agreed that ethnic identities and conflicts must surely fade in the political arena under the increasing weight of cross-cutting interests evident in the market economy. The major obstacles to dispelling the allegedly false consciousness of race or ethnicity, it was confidently claimed, were the vested interests and manipulative rhetoric of the powerful (especially Fijian chiefs).

Generalizing paradigms, fashioned from western experience and ideals, have tended to impede the understanding of Fiji's complexities and paradoxes, obscuring more than they illuminate. Insufficient attention has been given to discerning the social and political dynamics of the society in its particularity. How might we understand Fiji in terms of its distinctive features and history? In these respects it is helpful to inquire into how Fiji differs from other small-scale post-colonial societies such as Trinidad and Guyana in the Caribbean, where ethnic identities also continue to dominate political alignments despite the strong presence of cross-cutting interests of social class. How might an inductive understanding of these national histories offer inspiration for theorizing about the nature of ethnic conflicts? To stress the significance of the ethnic divide in such societies is not at all to deny the importance of the cross-cutting interests and values associated with occupation, social class, consumerism, and shared citizenship. Rather, it is to recognize the special problems that ethnic differences and conflicts pose for the design of political institutions that might allow effective expression of common interests. It is a question of what institutional arrangements would best constrain and contain the ethnic concerns and tensions, what form of democratic government would best suit a society like Fiji? The paradoxical outcome of the 2006 election suggests support for this perspective. It dramatized the compatibility of strong expression of ethnic group allegiances in the electoral arena with prospects for dialogue and compromise in the executive and parliament on issues concerning interests shared across the ethnic divide (such as urban poverty, educational and health service needs, and rural development), as well as on issues which, while largely placing the major ethnic groups in opposition, are nonetheless negotiable (such as land-leasing and affirmative action for Fijians). I will return to the question of dialogue and negotiation later.

An important point to make in connection with the paradox Ratu Joni Madraiwiwi highlights concerns the extent to which, as Fraenkel observes, the generally agreeable mood of everyday inter-ethnic relations tends to be insulated from ethnic conflict at the political level.[5] There have, of course, been times when political tensions flood into these relations to the point of abuse and violence, and we cannot ignore the longstanding mutually denigrating stereotypes. Yet, what perhaps most distinguishes Fiji from many other countries with deep ethnic divisions, is the degree to which cooperation and friendliness in everyday relations has resisted corrosion by political conflict.

I recall illustrative vignettes from my field research: Ratu Mara's political lieutenant, David Toganivalu, campaigning in the villages to strengthen the Fijian Association against the Federation Party in 1966 – with dire warnings about threats to political privilege and land – and then relaxing at clubs in Suva to share drinks and play snooker with Indo-Fijian friends; Isimeli Bose, principal author of the controversial Soqosoqo ni Vakavulewa ni Taukei submission to the Constitutional Review Commission in 1995 – with its unrelenting discourse on justifications for Fijian resentments against Indo-Fijians – explaining that treatise to me as we sat alone in the board room of Vinod Patel Co (hardware suppliers to the Ba Provincial Council), and then our affable encounter with the Patel men as we left; my old teacher friend Narayan Govind, staunch NFP and later FLP man, recounting friendly street chats with Sakeasi Butadroka, who had moved in parliament that Indo-Fijians be deported to India ('Buta is not really a bad man you know…').

Literature on life in Trinidad and Guyana, and observations by Indo-Fijians who have visited these countries, suggest that routine inter-ethnic relations there (between people of East Indian and African descent) are more often marred by antipathy than is the case in Fiji, despite a greater convergence in similar occupations and lifestyles, which many intellectuals and politicians long hoped would encourage social and political integration. There seems to be a greater conjunction of ethnically polarized political relations with the mood of everyday social relations, the long-standing competition and antipathy in everyday life influencing the tensions of the political arena more than the reverse.[6]

Yet, it is also very significant that in Guyana and Trinidad political power has, in recent years, been transferred from one ethnically based party to another without incurring major violence, and certainly not coups d'état.[7] This further highlights the need to inquire into the distinctive features of Fiji: a place where, in everyday life, ethnic relations tend, for the most part, to be harmonious despite the marked cultural, social and economic differences, and where political polarization does not preclude friendly dialogue and compromise, but where transfer of political power has not been tolerated. A place where, as Firth and Fraenkel remark, democracy seems to work only so far as it keeps the indigenous Fijians in political control.[8]

To understand the paradox of the 2006 Fiji election we must consider it in relation to some aspects of the bifurcated nature of Fiji society, economy, and polity as these were shaped by colonial policy and practice. The term *bifurcated* highlights Fiji's contrast with Trinidad and Guyana which, for all their ethnic tensions, are best described as *unitary* societies in respect to an essentially shared, if highly competitive, engagement in common institutions, most importantly the economy and political system in which there has been no institutional privileging of ethnic groups.[9] The old term *plural society*, applicable in some respects to all these countries, glosses over this important difference.

The most obvious contrast with Fiji is that indigenous Amerindian populations are very small (almost non existent in Trinidad), and have hardly figured at all in national politics, let alone enjoyed special rights. There is no constitutional differentiation of ethnic group rights – as there is in Fiji – and no history of a compulsory separation in space, such as was rigidly maintained for most Fijians by the colonial administration. There is no ethnic difference in prerogatives of land ownership. Cultural differences are slighter than in Fiji, a fact belied by the apparently stronger ethnic antipathies; the most significant cultural differences are in religion and in family and marriage customs. The Hindi language has not been as strongly preserved as it has in Fiji, and the vast majority of descendants of the African slaves speak only English. Over the last four decades, however, there have been 'movements' of rediscovery and reassertion of cultural difference among both the Indian and African populations, and these movements have been associated with political rivalry. By their oppositional energy, the cultural revivalist efforts have more strongly influenced ethnic tensions in Trinidad and Guyana, than the deeper, but taken-for-granted and routinely lived, cultural differences have contributed to ethnic tension in Fiji.

A major aspect of the bifurcation of Fiji was the structure of the capitalist economy in which, for a very long time, the great majority of indigenous Fijians were only marginal participants. Their predominantly subsistence village-based lifestyle, forcibly maintained by colonial laws, produced an enduring sense of economic weakness in the wider society, and yet at the same time facilitated the supply of much of the best arable land for relatively cheap leasing by Indo-Fijian farmers. Compulsory village living for most indigenous Fijians minimized their dependence on rent income and, therefore, indirectly subsidized Colonial Sugar Refining Company profits by keeping down the price the company needed to pay to the Indo-Fijian tenant farmers for their sugar cane. Of course, the confinement of most Fijians to their villages also supported the CSR Co.'s project of developing a highly skilled Indo-Fijian labour force, wholly committed by financial necessity to the industry. By the mid 1930s the CSR Co. was firmly opposed to a strong Fijian participation in cane farming, viewing that prospect as a threat to the efficiency it had developed through the Indo-Fijian small farmer system.[10]

Associated with this highly unbalanced yet complementary ethnic divide in the economy was the privileged status of Fijians – through their leading chiefs – in the colonial state, and the strengthening of the Fijian conviction – in the transition to independence – of their entitlement to political pre-eminence.[11] Ethnic Fijian convictions about who they are in modern Fiji, their sense of worth and strength in the wider society, became inextricably tied in with their leaders' power in the state, just as, for Indo-Fijians, strength and social status came to be identified especially with individual ability and success in the capitalist economy, whether as farmers, businessmen, or independent professionals.

Yet it is a mistake to understand this bifurcation simply as the source of conflict. We need to recognize the distinctive modes of inter-ethnic 'getting along', of accommodation through dialogue, negotiation, and conciliation, which the bifurcated structure of Fiji has encouraged over many decades of intermittent impasses and crises. Bridging difference has long been a central value in public social and political life. At the level of social interaction, there has been a remarkable ease of sociability, facilitated by the relative absence of the kind of status rivalry and economic competition that have contributed to ethnic enmity in Trinidad and Guyana. Indeed, it might be argued that inter-ethnic sociability in Fiji has in a way been facilitated and encouraged by the reality of deeper cultural and social differences. The value of 'the races coming together' is affirmed in a variety of social contexts, from social and sports clubs to community service groups, local government councils, and town festivals. Regularly bridging difference, getting happily together despite persisting divides in much of routine social life, became a shared value that began to emerge in the last two decades of the colonial era.[12]

At the national political level, as at the local social level, there has evolved a culture of interaction. There are the long-standing major issues about which there has repeatedly been dialogue and conciliation, not just acrimonious dispute. Indeed, the great issues of land and the constitution have enabled and encouraged the objectification of ethnic conflict as a shared problem for dialogue and conciliation. The domain of national political relations has been regulated over a long period of time, especially by consultative institutions such as the Great Council of Chiefs and by negotiable issues. After successful deliberation on highly contentious matters, with phases of tension and mutual recrimination, there comes a sense of shared achievement and a celebration of what binds the opponents after all. The energizing context for such moments is partly the very depth of the divide itself, and its distinctive character of different and conflicting domains of interest about which there can be negotiation and accommodation.

Political conflict associated with the ethnic divide in Fiji has tended to have this characteristic of negotiability, and in this respect sometimes bears comparison with enduring conflicts in industrial relations. The most notable instances include: the agreements on reform of the terms of land leasing that led to the passage of the Agricultural Landlord and Tenant Ordinance in 1966, at the height of political party conflict, and of the Agricultural Landlord and Tenant Act in 1976 (also amidst political tension); the quite remarkable negotiation of agreements for constitutional reform in 1969–70 and in 1996–97 after phases of severe ethnic tension; and, most recently, the agreement on the multiparty cabinet after several years of argument and court cases following the traumas of 2000.

Biman Prasad's chapter is especially interesting for its focus on the significance of issues on which political parties seem to be converging, and on each party's rhetorical efforts to attract support from across the ethnic divide.[13] However, Prasad is perhaps mistaken in drawing a stark contrast between 'race-based' and 'issue- and ideology-based' political competition. The ethnic or race divide has itself long been partly determined by issues; ethnic support for political parties, as Fraenkel notes, has not been simply a matter of ethnic sentiments and prejudices.[14] A study of issues in Fiji politics must include the examination of issues on which the major parties are strongly opposed but which are open to compromising dialogue. These issues, like those of increasing agreement that Prasad focuses on, have tended to be 'masked' by ethnic polarization.

The question of the special interests of the indigenous Fijians has itself long been an issue open to dialogue and agreement, with a lineage going back to the famous debate in the colonial parliament in 1946 on 'safeguarding the Fijian race' (often referred to as the 'Deed of Cession' debate). This debate, after an acrimonious start, concluded in a relaxed mood of accord, with all agreeing on the principle of at least a protective paramountcy of Fijian interests.[15] In the late 1960s, the NFP campaigned as the party committed to defending not just the rights of Indo-Fijians but also the interests of the *Taukei* (Fijians) against alleged oppression and exploitation by an alliance of European capitalists, Fijian chiefs, and colonial officials. The NFP was indeed the first political party to declare that it wanted to make the needs and concerns of the *Taukei* a national issue, and it was the NFP leaders who, in the dialogue that led to independence, proposed giving the Great Council of Chiefs veto power in the Senate.

The importance of negotiable issues is a favourable condition for the new multiparty cabinet. Provincial and *vanua* pressures influencing Qarase in the allocation of resources and appointments are likely to compromise his will to indulge requests and proposals from his FLP cabinet colleagues, and may threaten to undermine the collaboration – the fate of Ratu Mara's attempt to increase Indo-Fijian participation in his Alliance Party government during the 1970s and 1980s. But if Qarase wishes to strengthen the new collaboration, perhaps with a view to encouraging political re-alignments and building Indo-Fijian electoral support, he must make these concessions and allow the FLP cabinet ministers to share in decision-making about the delivery of patronage in the constituencies, as well as in the making of policy.

Of course, Fijian disaffection with Qarase's government might itself favour new inter-ethnic alliances. Durutalo suggests that, while the SDL has succeeded for the present in unifying Fijians by way of an ideological 'orthodoxy' centring on the theme of the unity of *vanua* (Fijian community and its land), *lotu* (church) and *matanitu* (the state), in the longer term imbalances in SDL policies 'may be seen as offering solutions to some groups of indigenous Fijians only'.[16] While such imbalance might provoke destabilizing rivalries among Fijian political leaders, it might also offer opportunities for an Indo-Fijian-based political party to cultivate new Fijian allies, a strategy that the demographic trend toward an increasing Fijian majority will surely encourage.

The 2006 election is the first in which the army actively sought to influence voters, conducting an 'educational' campaign to explain the officers' opposition to the SDL government's proposed Promotion of Reconciliation, Tolerance and Unity Bill. In considering the question of the army's involvement in Fiji's political life, there is an interesting comparison to be made with the Great Council of Chiefs. In the course of crisis and constitutional change over the last two decades, both institutions have become powerful actors in the political arena. Both are viewed by most indigenous Fijians as bastions of protection for their ethnic interests, and both have played a part in the assertion of Fijian demands for political paramountcy. Yet both have also supported political stability and a multi-ethnic constitution by helping to constrain Fijian ethno-nationalism.

The contrasting figures of Sitiveni Rabuka and Voreqe Bainimarama as commanders dramatically illustrate these different possible directions of military action in the political arena: Rabuka, once the charismatic champion of indigenous hegemony who threw out Fiji's independence constitution, and Bainimarama, resolutely maintaining his stance of professional responsibility not to side with Fijian ethno-nationalists but to defend the 1997 constitution against them.

Past Fijian political leaders, including Ratu Sukuna, Ratu Mara, Ratu Penaia Ganilau, Ratu Edward Cakobau, and Rabuka himself, were crucially important in their capacities to persuade members of the Great Council of Chiefs, typically very conservative and ethnocentric, to agree to various reforms in the national interest in respect to land and the constitution. But the uncertainty of such influence and guidance was dramatized by the divisions that emerged in this forum during the coup crisis of May 2000. Like the Council of Chiefs, the military has become an institution with political power, whose contribution to the political process, whether in support of an excluding ethno-nationalism (or perhaps provincialism) or of building an equitable multi-ethnic society, is likely to continue to be contingent on the will and persuasive authority of particular leaders.

Postscript

> The armed forces have three massive political advantages over civilian organisations: a marked superiority in organisation, a highly emotionalised and symbolic status, and a monopoly of arms. They form a prestigious corporation or Order, enjoying overwhelming superiority in the means of applying force. The wonder, therefore, is not why this rebels against its civilian masters, but why it ever obeys them.[17]

Rabuka's coups in 1987, efficiently executed by a powerful army in support of Fijian ethno-nationalist demands, created the spectre of recurring military interventions. I wrote at the time that 'it seems most improbable that the army might cease to be a crucial factor in Fiji's political life in the foreseeable future'.[18] The ethno-nationalism that provoked Rabuka's two coups has remained a chronic source of crisis or impasse in Fiji's democratic political system, and was the major factor driving Speight's coup in 2000 and Bainimarama's interventions in 2000 and 2006.

Yet what is most interesting about the four military interventions in Fiji is the shift from actions strongly embedded in ethnic sentiments and objectives, to actions claimed by the army leaders to fulfil their responsibility to ensure the good governance of the nation by combating that same ethno-nationalism. The military has become a political force in its own right, attempting to manage the intractable problems of ethnic conflict that have long marred democratic government in Fiji.

Bainimarama's imposition of martial law soon after the 'Speight coup' in May 2000, was widely welcomed in Fiji as rescuing the country from a prospect of growing violence. A striking feature of the popular responses to Bainimarama's coup in December 2006 has been the frequent supportive remarks by Indo-Fijians – the declaration that 'we Indians are happy about this coup' is commonly heard. The commander had become well known for his stand against Fijian ethno-nationalists and support of non-discriminatory government. Moreover, an immediately felt consequence of this coup, with its ongoing deployment of armed soldiers at street checkpoints, was a reduction in violent robberies of Indo-Fijian and Chinese businesses and homes by young Fijian men. In one well-publicized incident, a group of Indo-Fijian town councillors presented soldiers with packed meals to thank them for their presence.

This latest coup is nonetheless an expression of ethnic Fijian power and identity, and, for the soldiers, a legitimate form of communal Fijian action. Yet, paradoxically, it is an expression of Fijian strength that conceivably might have potential to help resolve the longstanding dilemma of how to reconcile the Fijian conviction of entitlement to state power with the multi-ethnic reality of the society and economy. This dilemma is a legacy of the bifurcation of Fiji created by colonial rule, and discussed earlier in this chapter.

During the three decades before independence, colonial officials had encouraged the strengthening of the Fijian position in two arms of the state: the Fijian Administration and the Royal Fiji Military Forces, which were linked by several chiefs who had served with authority in both. In the 1960s, this strengthened Fijian position in the colonial state led the British officials, who were preparing Fiji for self-government, to abandon an initial plan to introduce a common franchise to replace ethnic voting and representation. The Fijian political leaders' vehement opposition to the proposal raised fears of the possibility of violent upheaval, especially in the event of disaffection in the predominantly Fijian army.

The Fijian Administration, in close relationship with the Great Council of Chiefs, supported a political élite of high-ranking chiefs who were able to preserve their dominance of Fijian leadership after the advent of party politics and the Fijian franchise in the 1960s, in the context of ethnic tension. Their lieutenants in the Fijian Association campaigned in the villages to persuade popular acceptance of the multi-ethnic Alliance Party as the means by which Fijians could secure political power (the Fijian Association was the dominant body in the Alliance).

However, it was in the electoral arena that the ability of these leaders to accommodate the interests of non-Fijian groups, especially the Indo-Fijians, was eventually weakened by the emergence of the Fijian Nationalist Party. This extremist pressure, together with rapid economic and social changes that were transforming Fijian needs and expectations, began to erode the strength of the paramount chiefs in political leadership several years after independence.

By contrast, the Fijian-dominated army steadily strengthened during the early post-colonial decades, in size and weaponry, and in the sophistication and experience of its personnel. Major ingredients for this strengthening have been service with UN peace-keeping forces in the Middle East and elsewhere, and the interventions in Fiji's political arena. The military has sometimes been led by high-ranking chiefs, and it has strong affinities with traditional Fijian society and the colonial Fijian Administration in respect to its hierarchical structure and communal values. But the army has also long been a domain in which commoner Fijians have been able to achieve status and career advancement, or at least economic security, and thus many indigenous Fijian families have army ties. In the popular view, soldiering is a mark of Fijian achievement and strength. Like the administrative bureaucracies concerned with Fijian affairs, the army developed as a Fijian institutional domain counter-balancing Indo-Fijian strength in the world of business and professions. Although the army is open to recruits from any ethnic background, it continues to be an overwhelmingly indigenous Fijian body.

As mentioned, attempts by Fijians, chiefly and non-chiefly, to become national political leaders attending to the interests of Indo-Fijians and others, have repeatedly been frustrated by the challenges from Fijian extremists. By contrast, Fijian extremism has helped to strengthen the army as a political force by providing a springboard for the seizure of political power – initially in support of ethno-nationalist demands, but recently in opposition to them.

Rabuka deposed a government which most Fijians rejected as illegitimate, but that most Indo-Fijians supported. Twenty years later, Bainimarama threw out a government most Fijians supported, and that most Indo-Fijians opposed as discriminatory and corrupt, an embodiment of Fijian power oppressive to them. This contrast between the coups of 1987 and 2006 is a measure of the growth of the military as an independent political force, with corporate beliefs in its possession of special responsibilities and rights which surpass the authority of elected governments that are broken or compromised by Fijian ethno-nationalist groups.

The army now conceives itself to be the most important part of the state, as much in the protection of domestic order and governance as in matters of external defence. This claim is backed by invoking a now much-debated clause in Fiji's current constitution which, the army insists, implicitly preserves the following provision in the previous constitution established by Rabuka in 1990: 'It shall be the overall responsibility of the Republic of Fiji Military Forces to ensure at all times the security, defence and well-being of Fiji and its peoples'.[19]

The army's conviction about its political prerogative is vividly conveyed in a 'message' from the commander to his men published in the RFMF newsletter just before the 2006 election:

> I can assure you, my loyal soldiers, that whatever government comes into power will not be a threat to our existence because the military in Fiji is strongly intertwined and embedded on the firm belief that without the RFMF there is no spine to our democracy or sovereignty. Politicians have a somewhat distorted perception of why we exist. We are the final guarantor of security in this country. For without a dedicated, loyal and strong military there can be no security or stability. And national sustenance and the successful generation of economic wealth can only be achieved if you have a military dedicated to its call of duty and one that champions truth and justice.[20]

The crises of 2000 were the crucible for this transformation of the army's corporate mission. In particular, these events largely explain the great weight of the personal motivations and iron resolve of the commander in the long lead-up to the 2006 coup.

Bainimarama, scarcely 15 months into his post after appointment from the navy over the heads of several eligible military officers, returned to Suva from an overseas trip in May 2000 to experience threats on his life and to find his forces in danger of a catastrophic split. After holding his men together and taking control of the country under martial law, he faced renewed threats to his life and his army from an attempted mutiny. These traumatic events compelled an obsessive personal mission to strengthen the RFMF as a force to combat the threat of Fijian ethno-nationalism which Bainimarama viewed as continuing to dominate and corrupt the government he had put in place and that was returned to power in the elections of 2001 and 2006. Bainimarama initiated a program of indoctrinating his officers and troops on their duty to become guardians of good governance for the nation. Officers who were not sympathetic to his vision resigned or were expelled.

The project of preparing the military for an on-going political role has precedent in a plan drafted by Rabuka and his officers in 1989 to institute a lengthy period of army rule, in support of objectives of advancing indigenous Fijians in the economy. Severe measures were then proposed, including suppression of trade unions and 'neutralization' of political leaders deposed by Rabuka's first coup.[21] The plan was abandoned after its rejection by the president Ratu Penaia Ganilau and the prime minister Ratu Mara. Bainimarama is pursuing a very different agenda, initially against the resistance of the Great Council of Chiefs, and after pushing aside the vice-president, Ratu Joni Madraiwiwi, one of Fiji's highest-ranking chiefs and a former High Court judge and unbending defender of constitutional government.

This latest coup d'état presents the paradox of the army as the strongest embodiment of indigenous Fijian power supporting a project ostensibly aimed at transforming governance to serve the needs of the multi-ethnic nation, especially by eliminating discriminatory policies and practices. How to counter the tendency for ethnic interests and conflicts to dominate political life has been Fiji's major problem since the advent of party politics 40 years ago. Perhaps an entrenchment of ethnic Fijian power through an enduring overseer role for the military in the domains of political competition and government could have the potential to encourage more flexibility for inter-ethnic cooperation, given that the issue of securing Fijian pre-eminence in the state would then have been removed from the arena of political struggle.

However, the major political reality in Fiji now is the fact of military-backed rule, whatever its proclaimed agenda. Military power, directly or indirectly exercised, contains its own imperatives and tendencies that inevitably encourage resort to the organization's special capacity to dominate the populace by use or threat of physical force. At the time of writing, the army is more preoccupied with displaying this coercive power than with making credible attempts to pursue its proclaimed mission to 'clean-up' alleged corruption and malpractice of the deposed government. Rhetoric about this national-reform purpose of the coup is being used to justify intimidation of people who strongly voice their opposition to the takeover. They are denigrated as threats to the army's work for the well-being of the nation. Some have been assaulted or bullied after being taken from their homes or work places to the barracks.

Will an army leadership that attempts a guardian role for the nation and encourages inter-ethnic cooperation in government remain committed to this mission over the long term? Several trends might work against the project. Military officers might develop vested interests in strengthening their control in various domains of government. There is the possibility, perhaps related to such a trend, that politically destabilizing rivalries will emerge within the army leadership, along old *vanua* or provincial lines. There remains, too, the possibility of a return to an ethnocentric exercise of power under changed leadership and in response to popular indigenous Fijian discontents.

February 2007

Notes

[1] Saumaki, B. 2007. 'Bose ni Vanua and democratic politics in Rewa', this volume; Tuimaleali'ifano, M. 2007. 'Indigenous title disputes: what they meant for the 2006 polls', this volume; Tuitoga, A. 2007. 'Tailevu North: five years down the line', this volume.

[2] Bose, A. & Fraenkel, J. 2007. 'Whatever happened to western separatism?', this volume. The regional factor in Fiji politics was originally analysed in Norton, R. 1977. *Race and Politics in Fiji*, University of Queensland Press, St Lucia, 1st edn.

[3] Norton, R. 2004. 'Seldom a transition with such aplomb: From confrontation to conciliation on Fiji's path to independence', *Journal of Pacific History*, 39(2):163–84, pp.176–84.

[4] Madraiwiwi, Ratu Joni. 2007. 'An election retrospective', this volume.

[5] Fraenkel, J. 2006. 'Polarization and power-sharing: the paradox of Fiji's 2006 election'. Address to the Ministry of Multi-Ethnic Affairs, National Reconciliation and Unity seminar on National Identity and Multiculturalism, 19 July, Suva.

[6] Ethnic antipathies in Guyana and Trinidad were historically influenced by a social status rivalry carried on in terms of values and norms of life-style and conduct imposed by the British colonial rulers. The Afro-Guyanese and Afro-Trinidadians were particularly imbued with these values, having lost most of their ancestral culture under slavery and having been pressured to

acquiesce in Anglo cultural hegemony in their quest for economic and social progress after emancipation. This acquiescence produced the deep tensions of what some writers have termed 'double consciousness', graphically characterized by Franz Fanon's phrase 'black skin white masks'. The Africans' endeavour to conform with the colonizers' cultural values and norms was constantly rebutted in social relations and in their own minds by the colonizers' racism. This chronic insecurity of identity and status sharpened their antagonistic rivalry with the East Indians who were more socially and psychologically secure in their retention of far more of their ancestral cultures and eventually rivalled the Africans for advancement in the urban middleclass. In Fiji there is competition in the economy, and some mutual antipathy. But this is not really comparable with the kind of social rivalries and antipathies that developed under the very different colonial experience in the Caribbean. Colonial policies protected and valorized many aspects of indigenous Fijian culture and society and encouraged a strong preservation of Indian cultures. Under these conditions, ethnic relations in Fiji developed without the corrosive edge of status insecurities produced by a colonial cultural hegemony of the kind that became characteristic in the Caribbean societies. The contrast is perceptively analysed by Chandra Jayawardena, in his 1980 paper 'Culture and Ethnicity in Guyana and Fiji', *Man* 15:430–50; for Guyana see also Williams, B. 1991. *Stains on My Name, War in My Veins: Guyana and the politics of cultural struggle*, Duke University Press, Durham.

[7] Meighoo, K. 2003. *Politics in a Half Made Society: Trinidad and Tobago 1925–2000*, Ian Randle Publishers, Kingston, pp.183–277.

[8] Firth, S. & Fraenkel, J. 2007. 'Introduction: Changing calculus and shifting visions', this volume.

[9] Jayawardena. 1980. 'Culture and ethnicity in Guyana and Fiji'; Karran, K. (ed.) 2000. *Race and Ethnicity in Guyana*, Offerings Publication, Demerara; Ryan, S. 1972. *Race and Nationalism in Trinidad and Tobago*, University of Toronto Press, Toronto.

[10] Norton, R. 1999. 'Chiefs for the nation: Containing ethno-nationalism and bridging the ethnic divide in Fiji', *Pacific Studies*, 22(1):21–50, pp.34, 38–39.

[11] Norton, R. 2002. Accommodating indigenous privilege: Britain's dilemma in decolonising Fiji', *Journal of Pacific History*, 37(2):133–56, pp.135–37.

[12] Norton, R. 1990. *Race and Politics in Fiji* (2nd edition). University of Queensland Press, St Lucia, pp.54–58; Bossen, C. 2000. 'Festival mania, tourism, and nation-building in Fiji: the case of the Hibiscus Festival', *The Contemporary Pacific*, 12(1):123–54.

[13] Prasad, B. 2007. 'Reflections on the economic and social policies of political parties', this volume.

[14] Fraenkel, J. 2007. 'Bipolar realignment under the alternative vote system: an analysis of the 2006 electoral data', this volume.

[15] Norton, R. 1990. *Race and Politics in Fiji* pp.55–56.

[16] Durutalo, A. 2007. 'Defending the inheritance: The SDL and the 2006 election', this volume.

[17] Samuel Finer 1976 *The Man on Horseback: The Role of the Military in Politics*, 2nd edn, Penguin, London, p.5.

[18] Norton *Race and Politics in Fiji* 1990 p.152.

[19] Constitution of Fiji, 1990, Clause 94 (3).

[20] *Mataivalu* No.11, March–April 2006, p.2.

[21] Callick, R. 'Fijian army at the ready to assume control', (Australian) *Financial Review*, 25 September 1989, pp.1, 10.

ADDENDUM

The Fiji coup of December 2006: who, what, where and why?

Jon Fraenkel

The Fiji military's 'clean-up' coup reached a climax on 5 December 2006. Although President Ratu Josefa Iloilo rubber-stamped the takeover that morning[1], he was swayed by Vice President Ratu Joni Madraiwiwi to disassociate himself from it in the afternoon. The official statement from Government House said that the Republic of Fiji Military Forces (RFMF) had acted 'contrary to the wishes of their Commander in Chief', but conveyed the President's intention to remain in office only to preserve some semblance of continuity.[2] That was not to be. Because the Prime Minister had declined to resign and the President equivocated, the illegality of the takeover had become inevitable. At 6 pm on Tuesday 5 December, military commander Frank Bainimarama declared that: '…the President has been prevented by some, including the Vice President, from exercising his constitutional prerogative to dismiss the Prime Minister in exceptional circumstances. As Commander of the RFMF, I, under the legal doctrine of necessity will step into the shoes of the President given that he has been blocked from exercising his constitutional powers'.[3]

This was a coup that, unlike that in 2000, was reasonably quickly and straightforwardly logistically consolidated, but nevertheless remained highly politically precarious. There was none of the mayhem of 2000, no trashing of Suva's business district, no curfews, no more than the usual power and water cuts. In the days before the coup, in 'exercises' announced beforehand to the national media, illumination flares were fired into the night sky above Suva

Harbour and close to Nukulau Island, and soldiers fanned out across Suva. This was a show of strength aimed at ratcheting up the tension and convincing the somewhat incredulous political classes that the military meant business. Off the reefs of Kadavu, a Black Hawk helicopter crashed in to the sea while attempting to land on one of three Australian warships that were standing by if needed to evacuate nationals. Fijians said it had been taken down by the shark god, *Dakuwaqa*. Newly arrived Australian security personnel attached to the High Commission were, Fiji's military command declared, to be treated as 'mercenaries'[4], and the army top brass condemned the anticipated use of the Biketawa Declaration as a justification for invading Fiji.[5] In the event, both Australian warships and security forces departed, and, from Canberra, Prime Minister John Howard declined to commit troops, publicly – if ill-advisedly – reporting that he had been asked to do so three times by Qarase, but did not want to risk Australian lives.[6]

When the coup itself started, it was not a surgical strike, but rather a slow, methodical, and seemingly irresistible takeover of state power. On 4 December, weapons were seized from the police armouries at Nasinu and Nasova in Suva and from smaller weapons' stores in Nadi, Lautoka and Labasa to prevent any potential threat to the RFMF's monopoly on the use of armed force. The next morning, Prime Minister Laisenia Qarase was summoned to Government House, to be confronted, he anticipated, with the options of capitulation or humiliating resignation.[7] His vehicle was stopped at the gates, where soldiers insisted that he walk the remaining distance. Qarase refused, and returned to his Richards Road residence, declaring that 'under no circumstances will I resign or advise Ratu Josefa [Iloilo] to dissolve parliament'.[8] In the glare of the international media, soldiers tried to raid Qarase's home, eventually succeeding in whisking away the Prime Minister's two official vehicles, thereby stripping him of the remaining trappings of statehood. He left, the next day, for his home island of Vanuabalavu. Parliament was not sitting on the day of the coup, depriving the 2006 takeover of those critical focal points of the 2000 and 1987 coups. But the Senate, which was in session, was shut down, and soldiers raided the Prime Minister's office, carting away papers and computer hard drives to be used as evidence in the intended clean-up campaign. Confirming the impression of preparedness for a prime ministerial resignation rather than a seizure of power, military personnel that day roamed the offices of the Government printer and the Parliamentary Library seeking copies of Rabuka's 1987 coup decrees to use as models for the inauguration of the new order.[9]

The 2006 military takeover had been an event so regularly threatened that many doubted that it would ever eventuate, not least because the commander himself had for several years repeatedly and emphatically publicly denied that he was intending a coup. The Police Commissioner, Australian Andrew Hughes, had also regularly reassured the nation that there would not be a coup, based on private guarantees from the commander. Repeated spats with the government had encouraged the perception that the commander's antics were mere brinkmanship, designed to influence rather than control the political agenda. There were other good reasons why so many ruled out a military takeover. Previous coups had had quite different dynamics, or at least so it appeared. In both 1987 and 2000, coups had occurred in the wake of election victories by predominantly Indian-backed political parties. Each had overthrown reformist governments that were associated with the left of the political spectrum and identified with the politics of the sugar cane belts. Each time, takeovers had been carried out in the name of upholding 'indigenous paramountcy', extending the reach of a notion formally embedded only as a 'protective principle' in the 1997 constitution. Both previous coups had the backing of the bulk of the ethnic Fijian establishment, as indicated by the endorsement of the Bose Levu Vakaturaga (Great Council of Chiefs (GCC)) and the Methodist Church. Both had brought into office governments committed to 'affirmative action' aimed at uplifting the position of the indigenous community. Both post-coup governments had ultimately pulled back from the abyss of ethno-nationalism and veered towards a more moderate and internationally acceptable style of politics.

The December events turned Fiji politics upside down. Key coup victims of 1987 and 2000 emerged as defenders, enthusiasts and beneficiaries of the military takeover, while, overnight, the coup backers of 2000 became democrats and supporters of the rule of law. The Director of the Fiji Human Rights Commission, an assortment of Catholic social justice advocates, much of the business community and probably the majority of left-leaning civil society activists supported the coup.[10] Vociferous opponents of previous illegal regimes, such as the widely respected Justice Anthony Gates, took positions in the new order, as did several well-travelled participants on the Pacific's 'good governance' workshop circuit. Deposed 1999–2000 prime minister Mahendra Chaudhry became interim Finance Minister, as well as acquiring a host of other important portfolios, including sugar industry restructuring. The reaction from the bulk of the Fiji Indian community to the 2006 coup was astonishing; the group that had such a strong sense of its own victimhood, due to the 1987 and 2000 coups and the much earlier experience of *girmitya* (indentured labour), was strongly in favour of the clean-up coup.[11]

That remarkable reorientation in Fiji politics had been brewing, behind the scenes, for a considerable time. In January 2006, FLP president Jokapeci Koroi astounded Fiji TV viewers by pronouncing support for a military takeover, seeing in this the potential for a fulfilment of the agenda of the deposed 1999–2000 People's Coalition government. RFMF antagonism to the Qarase government – a government that it had originally, in July 2000, put into office – became apparent in the wake of Justice Gates' November 2000 decision to restore the 1997 constitution. After the government appealed, the higher courts upheld that decision (in the Chandrika Prasad Case), but left space for the then 'interim' administration to transform itself into a caretaker government, pending fresh elections in August 2001. In response to those judgments, the RFMF had wanted a restoration of the former parliament, and the formation of a 'government of national unity'.[12] Instead, Qarase's newly formed Soqosoqo Duavata ni Lewenivanua (SDL) used the advantages of incumbency and, in particular, a generous agricultural assistance scheme, to procure indigenous electoral support in rural Fiji. Its detractors alleged that this was what won the 2001 election. In the wake of its victory, the SDL formed a coalition with the 2000 coup-supporting Conservative Alliance–Matanitu Vanua party, much to the dismay of the RFMF. The new government exerted pressure on the President's Office to drop charges against the November 2000 mutineers and to ease sentences for prominent coup leaders or allied chiefs (or release them under 'compulsory supervision orders') and, in mid-2005, threatened to enact a controversial Promotion of Reconciliation, Tolerance and Unity (RTU) Bill that might have provided an amnesty to those still incarcerated as a result of their involvement in the coup of May and the associated mutiny of November

2000. The RFMF vigorously opposed other pieces of intended SDL legislation as well, such as the Qoliqoli Bill and the Indigenous Claims Tribunal Bill, and strongly resisted proposals in a 2005 government-commissioned review to downsize the RFMF.

Alarm bells first started ringing when, in December 2003, RFMF commander Frank Bainimarama told soldiers dining at the officers' mess at the Queen Elizabeth Barracks (QEB) that he intended to take over the running of the government if his contract was not renewed. In the three following years, the outspoken commander was to engage in a series of high profile spats with the Qarase administration, each commencing with RFMF criticisms of government policy or personnel and vague threats of one type or another, and ending with various half-hearted reconciliatory statements, coupled with assurances that there would not be a coup d'état. Each spat served, internally, as a loyalty testing instrument for the purging and restructuring of the RFMF. As a result, over the five years after the 2000 coup, virtually the entire senior, often Sandhurst-educated, command had been dismissed, sent on leave or resigned. And still that cathartic transition continued. In January 2006, freshly appointed land forces commander Lt. Col. Jone Baledrokadroka, a close fellow-Marist-educated friend and ally of Bainimarama, warned that he had received orders which he deemed potentially treasonous, sparking a potentially violent showdown with the RFMF commander. Baledrokadroka was sent on leave pending a court martial.

There were robust attempts at peace-making. Vice President Ratu Joni Madraiwiwi, who as Roko Tui Bau was high chief to the Tailevu-born commander, sought to mediate between Bainimarama and Qarase, and wholeheartedly backed the multiparty cabinet formed after the 2006 election. When the commander publicly attacked the government yet again in September, the Vice President endorsed the government's long-running efforts to seek a Supreme Court ruling as regards the military's constitutional position.[13] While the commander was out of the country in October, the President sought to remove him from office, and appoint instead Lt. Col. Meli Saubulinayau. But the takeover was badly mishandled, and other senior officers again rallied behind the commander and threatened a coup should the President issue such directions. The order was consequently withdrawn. Soon, Saubulinayau too was removed from his position and placed under investigation. After each destabilizing crisis, the commander purged disloyal officers, or moved them to positions without responsibility at Strategic Headquarters at Berkley Crescent. By December 2006, the senior RFMF ranks were exclusively staffed by rapidly promoted and extremely junior officers who owed their position to the commander.

Before departing to inspect Fiji's Middle East troops in October, Bainimarama announced a three week deadline for the Qarase government to comply with RFMF demands or resign. While he was away, heavily armed soldiers raided the Suva wharf to secure the release of a consignment of imported RFMF weaponry and ammunition being held by the customs authorities on instructions from police chief Andrew Hughes, who had insisted on clear military assurances that they would not be used for a coup. Hughes had also commenced investigations aimed at laying charges against the commander for 'sedition', entailing a hugely controversial raid on the President's Office seeking incriminating evidence. Many alleged that the sedition charges were the trigger for the December 2006 coup. According to this view, further appeasement was the preferable course, and without that personal threat to the commander there would have been no coup. In fact, the point of no return had been reached earlier, at the time of the botched attempt to replace Bainimarama by Saubulinayau. After that, insiders knew that the so-called 'impasse' or 'stand-off' that had so destabilized Fiji politics was likely to be resolved by a military coup, and not by the government successfully asserting its authority.[14] By November, it was widely known in local diplomatic circles that there was going to be a military takeover, and that nothing short of utter capitulation, resignation by Qarase or installation of a puppet government could avert it.

Commodore Bainimarama returned from his trip to the Middle East on 4 November, only to depart again for New Zealand to attend his granddaughter's first Holy Communion. While he was there, the New Zealand government facilitated crisis talks between the commander and Qarase, who flew down for the purpose. At these, Fiji's Prime Minister conceded to all the main RFMF demands, agreeing to suspend action on controversial legislation, to take into account RFMF views when considering whether or not to renew Hughes' contract, and even to accept advice from the Director of Public Prosecutions or Solicitor General, were it offered, to publicly drop charges against Bainimarama.[15] Yet, as soon as Bainimarama returned to Fiji, he declared that Qarase was 'lying' about the Wellington deal, that the bills should be withdrawn not stalled, and that nothing could stop the intended clean-up campaign.[16] The deadline had fallen due, but now the commander said there would be no action until the school holidays and then, in a farcical climax to the pre-coup phoney war, put off the ousting of Qarase to attend the scheduled Ratu Sukuna Bowl rugby contest between the army and the police.

This time, the coup that had hovered finally happened: Bainimarama, having himself rendered the government incapable of acting, claimed its incapacity as justification for the takeover. The illegality of his action was nevertheless clear. The 1997 constitution does not permit the president to dismiss a prime minister unless he has lost the confidence of the majority in parliament, and a dissolution is only possible on the advice of a legally appointed prime minister.[17] With President Ratu Josefa Iloilo in place, it was probable that RFMF lawyers would suggest that certain 'reserve powers' existed (on the Kerr/Whitlam model[18]) and that Ratu Josefa was acting under the 'doctrine of necessity' to speedily restore constitutional rule in Fiji. Without the President in place, the 'doctrine of necessity' was irrelevant; it was an unsuitable line of defence for a usurper, as the commander clearly was, and 'necessity' could scarcely be invoked to tackle an RFMF-provoked crisis.[19] The more plausible line of legal defence was to suggest that a 'glorious revolution' had occurred (using Kelsen's theory of revolutionary legality) and established a new constitutional order. But, for that, the commander needed to abrogate Fiji's 1997 constitution, which he steadfastly refused to do through December–February, presumably because of the rift this might create with Ratu Josefa Iloilo and other conditional pro-constitution allies. Even with a formal abrogation of the constitution, the 2001 Chandrika Prasad case had left many in Fiji very familiar with the required tests of 'the doctrine of effectiveness', namely 'acquiescence'. That perhaps helps to explain the recurrent post-coup cycles of beatings and intimidation at the QEB in Nabua directed against outspoken critics, lawyers, women's rights activists, and SDL party officials, if not the considerable number of ordinary civilians picked up from the check-points, the police stations or from their homes for various allegedly criminal activities.

In the weeks before the coup, international opinion and local diplomats had rallied behind the Qarase government. At a meeting of the Pacific Islands Forum, held in Nadi in October, Qarase was fêted by Helen Clarke and John Howard, and served as their ally in controversies with other members of the Melanesian Spearhead Group.[20] Australia, New Zealand, the USA, the European Union, Britain and the United Nations made clear their disapproval of the commander's intended coup, and threatened sanctions. On 28 November, the American Ambassador, and the Australian and British High Commissioners, had visited the QEB during Bainimarama's absence, urging a stand down of forces and change in the command structure. On the eve of his retirement, the UN's Kofi Annan threatened to withdraw Fiji peacekeepers serving with the UN, something potentially far more damaging to the RFMF than the Australian and New Zealand severing of bilateral military ties. Australian Minister for Foreign Affairs Alexander Downer urged people in Fiji to rise up against the new military order, prompting those sympathetic to Bainimarama to talk of double-standards given the more muted responses to the 1987 and 2000 coups.[21] In fact, once the initial outrage had abated, there was no great difference in the overseas reaction as compared with previous Fiji coups. The hard-pressed UN was never likely to deprive itself of an urgently needed supply of peacekeepers for Iraq. Although there were targeted travel bans, Australia and New Zealand ultimately did not impose trade sanctions, concerned as they were of the consequences for antipodean expatriates and businesses in Fiji.

In his new role as self-proclaimed 'President', Commodore Bainimarama temporarily appointed the army physician, Dr Jona Senilagakali, as prime minister, and announced the commencement of his clean-up campaign. On the day after the coup, a nervous-looking Bainimarama declared a state of emergency and promised stern repression against any who dared to incite popular resistance. Yet, on the following days, the commander dropped his severe green military fatigues for florid *bula* shirts at his daily press conferences, and announced a series of populist measures designed to bolster support for the takeover. The deposed government's previously announced imposition of an increase in VAT was to be reversed. The board of the Fiji National Provident Fund (FNPF) was to be purged, with the suggestion that its excessive take-up of government debt would be halted and the associated monopolies in the Fiji telecommunications market abolished. Costly prison facilities on the offshore island of Nukulau were to be dismantled, enabling the island to become, once again, a popular weekend picnic resort. 2000 coup leader, George Speight, was transported from there to the Naboro Maximum Security Prison, and other still-imprisoned 2000 'coup convicts' were spread out amongst prison facilities elsewhere on Viti Levu.

Ministers were given a month to vacate their government quarters. Vice President Ratu Joni Madraiwiwi was given only hours to leave his official residence, in a petulant response to his refusal to support the military takeover. A new broom swept through the commanding heights of the state apparatus. Military officers took over key positions in the civil security institutions; Colonel Ioane Naivalurua became Commissioner of Prisons, naval commander Viliame Naupoto took over as Director of Immigration, and Col. Jim Koroi became Commissioner of Police. A succession of government CEOs, including the key advisor in the Prime Minister's Office, Jioji Kotobalavu, and the Chairman of the Public Service Commission, Stuart Huggett, were sacked, as were the Solicitor General, the Supervisor of Elections and the Parliamentary Secretary. The boards and chief executives of state-owned enterprises – including Fiji Pine, Fiji Post, the FNPF, Airports Fiji, Air Terminal Services, the Civil Aviation Authority of Fiji, Ports Corporation and Ports Terminal Ltd, the Fiji Electricity Authority and the Sugar Cane Growers' Council – were all purged. Those targeted were usually officials identified with the Qarase government or known opponents of the new regime, but dismissals were invariably accompanied by allegations of corruption, mismanagement and abuse of office. On Radio Fiji One, military spokesmen initiated daily attacks in the Fijian language on such opponents, making accusations of grave misdemeanours that were not repeated on the station's English language programs.[22]

The coup had been justified by claims of military knowledge of deep-seated corruption under the Qarase government. If such there was, the military was well placed to know. In addition to 3,500 or so paid RFMF personnel, some 20–25,000 Fijians had passed through the military since independence, many serving on overseas peace-keeping missions. Perhaps 5,000 were no longer alive, but the remainder were all, at least in theory, military reservists. As a result, the RFMF had former officers positioned throughout Fiji's key institutions; in the police force, at the airport and customs authorities, in the Lands Transport Authority, on the Native Lands Trust Board, and through all the ministries and state-owned enterprises. Such prying eyes, where sympathetic, should have been able to discern multiple incidents of small- and large-scale fraud. Yet, in the wake of the coup, the military set about primarily seeking evidence, rather than exposing already known scandals. Often, what proof there was, was far from robust. The RFMF dismissed Fijian Affairs Board CEO Adi Litia Qionibaravi, claiming that she had 'used money from the Fijian Affairs Board to buy herself a vehicle' and to 'renovate a private house at Ma'afu Street', based on information from the two Indian carpenters contracted to do the work.[23] Like ousted Airports Fiji Ltd Chief Executive Sakiusa Tuisolia, she responded by taking out paid advertisements in the Fiji newspapers denying the RFMF allegations. The military was publicly soliciting informers to assist the proposed 'national audit', and large volumes of papers and computer hard drives were being stored away as evidence for the 'forensic accountants' that Bainimarama wanted to bring to Fiji. Australia and the UK refused his requests for such assistance, not wanting to have anything to do with efforts to discredit the ousted Qarase government.

In one sense, corruption under the deposed government was well known; especially in the government tendering process, in the immigration department, in the Native Land Trust Board, in the affirmative action programs and at the interface between foreign investors and government. Reports from the Auditor-General's Office, down the years, had highlighted hundreds of irregularities, not only under Qarase's administration but also under those of his predecessors.[24] The Public Accounts Committee, when it had functioned, had also documented incidents of gross mismanagement of public funds, although it had a poor record of initiating prosecutions. The courts had heard evidence of significant abuses of public office under the Ministry of Agriculture's Agricultural Assistance Scheme, and had convicted former permanent secretary Peniasi Kunatuba for his role in what became widely known as the 'agricultural scam'. But the RFMF too had been subjected to scrutiny, in particular for busting spending limits and failing to obey repeated court judgements requiring an audit of its regimental funds.[25] The democratic process had been far from perfect in encouraging enquiries, or securing convictions against public officials for corruption. The Qarase government had failed to pass pressing anti-corruption legislation, but it was far from clear that a coup could rectify those weaknesses, and prove midwife to the emergence of a cleaner social order. Unleashing an accusatory culture, and putting judgement into the hands of those who were not experts, also elevated the position of those with axes to grind on the mill of the clean-up campaign. Detailed scrutiny was always likely to pick up some evidence of government corruption, as it always had done in the past, but would this be sufficient to justify, retrospectively, the December coup?

Evidently aware of the small pickings in the early days of the anti-corruption crusade, the commander promised extraordinary revelations on January 1, so as to see in the New Year 'on a truth and transparency note'. Spokesman Neumi Leweni applauded a junior officer's initiative in mounting 'Operation Free Fiji' to expose major fraud among senior SDL officials and provide evidence of ballot-rigging at the 2006 election and of kickbacks for ministerial favours.[26] The RFMF, it turned out, had recruited notorious Australian conman Peter Foster to solicit the information. Foster had, before the coup, been hunted down and unceremoniously arrested by the Fiji police for using a forged Queensland police report to obtain a work permit. More disturbingly, he had published black propaganda on the internet seeking to depict the Champagne Beach resort in the Yasawas as a 'heavenly haven for homosexuals' in the hope that this would bring down the wrath of conservative landowners upon the promoters.[27] The motive, apparently, was that he had previously secured a US$580,000 loan from the Bank of the Federated States of Micronesia to develop his own resort in the Yasawas, and thus urgently needed somehow to secure the termination of his rivals' lease.[28]

Foster had been released on bail by the Fiji court, but ordered to stay under police guard at the luxury Suva hotel, JJ's on the Park. From there, he was taken into RFMF custody and wired to gather evidence of corruption and election-rigging from senior SDL officials – evidence which the RFMF spokesman initially described as 'irrefutable proof' of ballot-rigging.[29] The resulting heavily spliced tapes were aired on Fiji TV on 2 January; Navitalai Naisoro, a key SDL strategist was shown purportedly admitting involvement in ballot-rigging in May 2006, but his claims lacked plausibility and, before long, the RFMF had abandoned its plans to release any more of the footage obtained by Foster.[30] In early January, having already breached bail apparently with RFMF collusion, Foster evaded his military minders and escaped Fiji aboard a vessel bound for Vanuatu.[31] 'Democracy is corrupt', Foster had told the *Fiji Daily Post* in early January at the time when he extolled the virtues of the military's coup, but now he claimed that it was military corruption that was halting the further public disclosure of his revelations.[32] The junior officer previously acclaimed for his initiative in mounting 'Operation Free Fiji', was subsequently, allegedly, badly beaten up by RFMF soldiers for his role in the Foster escape.[33]

According to the plan initially laid out by 'President' Bainimarama, the Great Council of Chiefs was to meet to 'reappoint' President Ratu Josefa Iloilo, and in so doing demonstrate acquiescence in the military takeover.[34] With a similar objective, the commander insisted that he would only attend the GCC meeting if invited as 'President', rather than as 'commander'. But the chiefs delayed and demurred, with Chairman Ratu Ovini Bokini cancelling the scheduled Levuka meeting, and taking refuge in Tavua, where the traditional bodyguards of the Tui Tavua set up roadblocks, reportedly to halt an expected RFMF assault. Reports filtered out that the 'warriors of the 14 provinces' were preparing an uprising and assassination of the commander, and soldiers were sent out into the provinces to pre-empt that threat, although the military denied harassing the GCC chairman. When the GCC eventually met at the FMF Dome in Suva on 20–22 December, Ratu Ovini lamented that never before had the GCC been so 'ridiculed and suppressed'. The chiefs had refused RFMF entreaties to invite the commander as 'President' but instead requested his presence as military commander. Bainimarama consequently refused to attend. Qarase, although invited, was also absent, stranded on his home island of Vanuabalavu owing to military insistence that no plane or vessel carry him to the capital.

At the meeting, Fiji's three confederacies[35] were at odds as to how to react to the ousting of the Qarase government; Burebasaga and Kubuna were united in refusing to endorse Bainimarama's request, but Tovata was divided. One member of the Lau (Tovata) delegation, Ratu Tevita Uluilakeba, who was the son of former president, Ratu Mara and who had recently been promoted commander of the all-important Third Fiji Infantry Regiment (3FIR), insisted that the council be 'realistic' and acknowledge that the military held executive authority. That language of 'realism' was also embraced by other members of the family of Ratu Mara, echoing the former president's post-1987 coup epithet about accepting positions in an illegal interim administration; 'when my house is on fire how can I stand and watch?'. The GCC disagreed, and stood instead, temporarily, on principle; it resolved to uphold the 1997 constitution, suggesting that the President and Vice President remain in office and the army return to barracks. The GCC did, however, recognise that the Qarase government had been 'rendered ineffective and incapable of discharging its constitutional responsibilities', recommending that 'since there is no other alternative in this crisis, the GCC has regretfully advised the Prime Minister Laisenia Qarase to tender his resignation to the President'.[36] Under the GCC plan, a Privy Council would have been established to advise the President, including representatives from the military, the SDL and the FLP, which would choose a prime minister and establish membership of a 'Government of National Unity', paving the way for fresh elections fifteen months later.

Many expected greater Fijian resistance to the military takeover. Australian Minister for Foreign Affairs Alexander Downer and ex-police chief Andrew Hughes anticipated civil unrest; so too did the RFMF itself. The rationale for constant beatings and harassment up at the QEB and the continuation of the emergency decree was, after all, that the security threat remained real. Labour leader Mahendra Chaudhry insisted that there were 'elements out there who would not hesitate to create disorder should there be any slackness on the part of the law enforcement authorities'.[37] These fears were, perhaps, exaggerated. Fijians were scared. Back in 2000, there had been enduring resistance to the RFMF in some parts of the country, such as Wainibuka (in Tailevu) and Wailevu as well as other parts of Vanua Levu. But Fijians in these areas had been brutally repressed, and they feared a repeat of the military onslaught.[38] The 2000 protests had, in most cases, been orchestrated by prominent chiefs, many of whom had been beaten up and imprisoned in the aftermath. Calls from chiefs in Namosi and Cakaudrove for their soldiers to stand down were countered by rival RFMF provincial contingents visiting villages to solicit communal support.[39] Although 80 per cent of Fijians had backed the Qarase government in May, popular enthusiasm was hardly such as to spark an uprising in its support. And Qarase's flight to Mavana removed the short-lived focal point of post-coup resistance in Suva. Within Fijian society, there exists a tradition of submission to forceful and violent overlords, but silence, culturally, is not acquiescence. In time, indigenous Fijian resistance to the interim government might grow. The Methodist Church is by no means reconciled to the new order, and nor are the Bau and Cakaudrove chiefs. The government – short of money – will impose public spending cuts that are likely to stir resentment in the indigenous Fijian community, especially as Mahendra Chaudhry will be the minister implementing them.

The greater immediate potential for resistance, or for some kind of counter-coup, came from within the army itself. Repeated internal incidents of opposition to Bainimarama over 2000–2006 had shown this to be a real possibility. The poor turnout of reservists called into the army camps shortly before the coup also indicated some lack of enthusiasm for the coup. At the May 2006 election, the bulk of rank-and-file soldiers probably backed the SDL, as did ethnic Fijians more generally. But, as we have seen, Bainimarama had also cemented a dependable command structure, and subjected this to repeated loyalty tests. Amongst the rank-and-file, loyalism held its attractions. Not least, the RFMF offered reasonable salaries to otherwise unemployed Fijians, as well as the possibility of lucrative participation in overseas peacekeeping missions. Internally, the RFMF provided a highly structured life experience for soldiers, like a spiritless carbon copy of the long lost village order. The army was *the vanua* for many Fijians, and this coherence provided potential reservoirs of support for the senior command. Active mobilization, keeping soldiers on their toes, was also used to galvanize the rank-and-file; the threat of foreign intervention before the coup, for example, was used to rally soldiers in 'defence of the nation'.

The most vociferous opposition to the coup came from civil society activists, but these too were divided. People were urged to wear black on Thursdays, and citizens were implored to wear blue ribbons and attend silent prayer vigils to support 'peace and democracy, the rule of law and active non-violence'.[40] A 'democracy shrine' established by businesswoman Laisa Digitaki, consisting of a house in the Suva suburb of Lami sporting a large banner saying 'Yes to Democracy, No to guns', was repeatedly raided by the military. Outspoken May 2006 SDL candidate, and former TV presenter, Imraz Iqbal had his business burnt to the ground. Digitaki responded to allegations that their protests were against the law by insisting on the illegality of the emergency regulations, and pointing out that 'their interim Prime Minister himself has publicly admitted that the military takeover is illegal'.[41] On Christmas eve, Digitaki, Iqbal and Fiji Women's Rights Movement coordinator Virisila Buadromo were amongst a group taken up to the QEB, threatened and manhandled, and then frog-marched up Mead Road with soldiers behind them shouting '*toso! toso!*' (move! move!). Local music celebrity, *Vude* Queen Laisa Vulakoro was among the many protestors taken up to the camp after she penned critical letters comparing the commander to Idi Amin.[42] One by one, the critics were effectively silenced, usually after a single visit to the camps. Fiji Human Rights Commission Director Shaista Shameem said many of the protestors were 'not genuine pro-democracy activists', prompting fellow commissioner, Shameema Ali, to denounce the Director and suggest that the organization had lost credibility. [43] Many NGOs remained silent, or, as in the case of the local branch of Transparency International, expressed their support for the military's anti-corruption objectives.[44] Those that resisted were isolated, largely because of the muted grassroots Fijian reaction.

To convey the GCC resolutions to the Commodore, Paul Manueli, 1974–79 RFMF commander and finance minister under Rabuka, was sent up to the barracks; he was followed by a broader delegation, comprising chiefs from the three confederacies. On the TV news, military spokesman Neumi Leweni said, 'why should we meet them when they don't recognise us as the executive authority?' By this point, the Mara dynasty had publicly identified itself with the coup, as Ratu Tevita Uluilakeba made clear at the GCC meeting. His sister, former Senator Adi Koila Mara, had also strongly supported the clean-up campaign on Radio New Zealand.[45] So too had a politician widely alleged to be Mara's illegitimate son, Poseci Bune, and Mara's son-in-law, Ratu Epeli Ganilau, Bainimarama's predecessor as military commander, was clearly positioning himself for a top position in the new government. Ganilau's National Alliance Party of Fiji (NAPF) had obtained less than three per cent of the national vote at the May 2006 election, but his party members emerged at the forefront of those insisting that Fiji accept the 'reality' of the situation, and acquiesce in the new order. NAPF spokesman Kini Rarubi said of the GCC plan 'their resolution is nothing more than a wish list and they should take it to the Santa

Claus'.[46] The commander concurred with this disdain for the chiefs' resolutions; 'I am of the view that the GCC in their last meeting embroiled themselves too much into the legality of our actions'.[47] He refused to allow any further chiefs' meetings unless these were instigated by the RFMF.

Now cut adrift from all the traditional bastions of state power in Fiji, the RFMF turned inwards for its Christmas festivities, with internal ceremony acquiring added importance now that the commander had transformed himself into the pivotal figure in Fiji politics. At the QEB, an increasingly busy hive of activity, church services became a means for cementing an inevitably fragile coherence. 'We must clean ourselves', the army's Reverend Major Josefa Tikonatabua told close to 700 soldiers attending the Rabuka Hall Christmas church service at the QEB, 'although you have been spat upon and sworn at by your own people because of the uniform you wear, you must remain strong'.[48] These were sentiments echoed by the commander, whose rhetoric regularly featured the objective of a disciplinarian transcendence of Fijian primitivism; 'we the Fijians are too selfish', he told soldiers at the Rabuka Hall, emphasizing the importance of the family, of sharing and of multi-ethnic harmony, as against the 'teachings of some chiefs, church leaders and politicians who have now been sacked'.[49] In another Rabuka Hall church service several days later, the commander – evidently concerned by allegations about RFMF abuses at the checkpoints – again emphasized that 'the clean-up starts from within us', and Reverend Tikonatabua appealed to soldiers to pray three times a day, at 4 am, noon and 4 pm. The assembled throng attending the Sunday service was told that senior commanders intended to embark on a month-long spiritual fast and that the rank and file should likewise deny themselves something, such as tobacco, *yaqona* or alcohol.[50]

Many of the commander's statements about the Qarase government had, down the years, echoed the Fiji Labour Party's attacks on government corruption, mismanagement and inefficiency. But there were also not-so-subtle differences. George Speight's coup was seen by the commander as a 'cry of the land', and the contemporary pleas of Nadroga landowners, as well as evidence of a spurt in land transactions in the two weeks immediately following the coup, led the commander to temporarily ban all land sales, claiming that native title was being converted to Crown land and then sold as freehold.[51] Returning

Crown lands to native owners was used to bolster popular Fijian support for the coup, but capital gains tax policies on land sales also threatened to ruin the already troubled half-completed Momi Bay development in western Viti Levu.[52] The neighbouring Natadola development, financed by the displaced old guard at the FNPF, also found itself in trouble. Many fortunes were endangered by the new order, including that of Ballu Khan, whose Pacific Connex joint venture with the Native Land Trust Board was placed under investigation. The cancellation of the affirmative action programs threatened to halt the post-1987 gravy train, which had catapulted a generation of educated Fijians into the propertied élite.

Authoritarian rule was directed at Fijian and Indian alike, and several Indians reported severe bashings at the hands of the RFMF. But most Fiji Indians welcomed the checkpoints, and extolled the virtues of a government that had, at least temporarily, substantially improved the law and order situation. Fijians were mostly opposed, and they felt the brunt of military repression. One Tailevu villager, Nimilote Verebasaga, was taken into custody by the RFMF in the wake of a village land dispute. Up at the barracks, he was allegedly beaten to death in such a gruesome way that his clothes had to be changed before the body was returned to his distraught kinsfolk.[53] Many others were subjected to intimidation and harassment at the QEB barracks, including politicians, civil society activists and outspoken lawyers. Usually, they were forced into humiliating 'exercises', such as running round the army grounds or crawling through muddy ditches, in what were evidently RFMF externalizations of its internal disciplinary procedures.

Immediately after the coup, FLP leader Mahendra Chaudhry remained unusually silent; then he suggested a speedy return to democracy but notably did not call for the restoration of the elected Qarase government. Three weeks after the coup, with Fiji well embalmed in the softening rhetoric of 'accepting realities', 'coming to terms with what has happened' and the need to 'move the nation forward', the Labour leader ventured an explicit endorsement of the Bainimarama takeover. 'Last year's coup was warranted', said Chaudhry in his New Year message; 'One cannot forget that the current constitutional crisis had its roots in a growing discontent and frustration with six years of bad governance, characterised by pervasive corruption, ethno-nationalism and defiance of the rule of law'.[54] The May 2006 election, like that of August 2001, had been rigged, said the FLP leader, dismissing the 'rhetoric about the takeover of a democratically-elected Government'.[55]

In these statements, Chaudhry was clearly positioning himself for an extraordinary transition from steadfast upholder of the rule of law to participant in an illegal administration, from RFMF victim to ally of the latest military insurrection and from principled democrat to coup apologist. He had not been prepared to enter Qarase's post-May election multiparty cabinet, and had successfully undermined, out-manoeuvred and disciplined the 'gang of five' FLP supporters of power-sharing. Of these, Krishna Datt, Poseci Bune and Atu Emberson-Bain were expelled from the party. At the first crucial test, the 2007 budget vote, the multiparty cabinet had all but fallen apart. Now the FLP leader was poised to enter a new form of power-sharing arrangement, no longer inspired by sophisticated constitutional engineering theories, but rather by a Bonapartist transcendence of ethnic divisions and a blunt and remorseless shift onto the path of authoritarian modernization.

With the GCC now cut out of the loop, Bainimarama chose to directly 'reappoint' the President, Ratu Josefa Iloilo, as the precursor to setting up an interim government. The event was to prove yet another extraordinary spectacle – despite the absence of the foreign dignitaries, ambassadors, and high commissioners usually in attendance on such occasions. After detailing 21 reasons why the RFMF takeover had been justified, the commander explained that 'extra-constitutional steps' had been 'necessary to preserve the Constitution', insisting that legal precedents existed for his use of 'reserve powers' and had not been over-turned, and thus remained 'binding and valid law'.[56] Ostensibly to facilitate an inquiry into the activities of the judiciary at the time of the 2000 coup, Chief Justice Daniel Fatiaki and Chief Magistrate Naomi Matanitobua had been sent on leave a day before the presidential handover. Justice Anthony Gates was soon made acting Chief Justice.[57] The independence of the judiciary, which had been damaged but not broken by the events of 29 May 2000, was now to be more thoroughly compromised by senior judges' assumption of positions under the auspices of an illegal regime.[58]

On 4 January, the re-appointed President addressed the nation for the first time since the December coup.

Good citizens of our beloved Fiji Islands. I know that the events of the past few weeks have been trying on all of us. In particular in early December we were at cross roads at which hard and decisive decisions needed to be made. I was, as has been noted by the Commander of the Republic of the Fiji Military Forces, unable to fully perform my duties as I was prevented from doing so. I do not wish to elaborate further on this point but I can state that they were predominantly cultural. In any case given the circumstances I would have done exactly what the Commander of the RFMF, Commodore Josaia Voreqe Bainimarama did since it was necessary to do so at that time. These actions were also valid in law. Therefore, I fully endorse the actions of the Commander of the RFMF and the RFMF in acting in the interest of the nation and most importantly in upholding the Constitution.[59]

For the President to so blatantly endorse such an illegal act was extraordinary, and flatly contradicted the Government House statement of 5 December, when he had refused to 'condone' or 'support' the military takeover. The unelaborated 'cultural reasons' referred to the advice of Vice President Ratu Joni Madraiwiwi, who, as Roko Tui Bau, might in traditional terms be seen as the higher-ranking of the two chiefs. But Ratu Joni had been dismissed from his position, and the President's military speech-writers were no longer constrained in their efforts to rubber-stamp the new order. Nonetheless, the President's statement sent shock waves through the Fijian community, not least through the Methodist Church, which suggested that the President be 'medically boarded, and if necessary, retired with dignity and respect'.[60]

The day after he had relinquished the Presidency, Commodore Bainimarama was sworn in as prime minister, replacing the rather ineffective Dr Jona Senilagakali. Esala Teleni, who had shot up through the ranks to become deputy commander after the coup, became acting commander of the RFMF, although Bainimarama retained the substantive position. The interim cabinet was then announced, an occasion for those civilian politicians sympathetic to the coup to emerge into the public glare. The Fiji newspapers had, prior to Christmas, published novel adverts soliciting applications from the general public for positions in the interim cabinet, with the job description requiring clean criminal records and a declaration that applicants would not stand in the next election. A slimmed-down cabinet of 16 members was announced, replacing Qarase's bloated 36-member collection of ministers and 'state ministers', with the commander claiming to thereby save $2m annually. Former parliamentary speaker Ratu Epeli Nailatikau emerged from a behind-the-scenes role liaising with the Commonwealth and bilateral partners, to become Foreign Minister. Several politicians associated with the NAPF, and some former RFMF officers with civil service experience, acquired portfolios. The popular Bernadette Rounds Ganilau amazed the chattering classes of Suva by taking up the post of interim Minister for Labour, Industrial Relations, Productivity, Tourism and Environment, while the sole other MP in her United Peoples Party was being hauled into barracks in western Viti Levu to face military questioning for his critical public statements about the coup. The president of Fiji's Chamber of Commerce, Taito Waradi, became Minister of Commerce, and Ratu Epeli Ganilau belatedly took up the Fijian Affairs portfolio. Lawyer Aiyez Sayed-Khaiyum became interim Attorney General, surrendering a $150,000 per annum position at the Colonial Bank. Frustrating Labour warnings about 'opportunists', Poseci Bune, the former 'hard man' in the deposed 1999–2000 government became interim Minister for Public Service Reform. Bune had only recently been expelled from the FLP, but had previously established for himself a chameleonic reputation for traversing all manner of political divides.

In what he admitted was 'a strange twist of destiny', Mahendra Chaudhry became interim Minister of Finance, as well as interim Minister for National Planning, Public Enterprise and the Sugar Industry. Lekh Ram Vayeshnoi, who had formerly been Chaudhry's Trojan horse in Qarase's multiparty cabinet, took up the Minister of Youth and Sports portfolio and promptly sacked the entire board of the Sports Council. The only other surviving cabinet member was the SDL's Jonetani Navakamocea, who explained that he had spent close to $30,000 on the May election campaign and did not want to lose out – rather oddly, given the clean-up mandate that was intended to define the new order.[61]

Realism soon took its toll. With an interim government in place, domestic critics were presented with the conundrum of whether to continue to insist on the seemingly impossible restoration of the Qarase government or to instead call for the interim government to settle on a roadmap for the restoration of democracy. That ambivalence between pragmatism and strict legality, which always figures in the aftermath of coups, led to a wave of more nuanced domestic accommodation with the new order amongst the non-enthusiasts – those with no hope of places either in the new order nor, any longer, in the resurrection of the old. The formerly stalwartly pro-government *Fiji Daily Post*, managed by Qarase's cousin Mesake Koroi, now concluded that the SDL had 'failed in its duty' because 'a coup happened on their watch' owing to its non-inclusion of 'the military leadership in its deliberations on national security'.[62] Also, internationally, key bilateral and multilateral agencies had by January abandoned much hope of restoration of the elected government. Even ousted Prime Minister Qarase was, by the time the Pacific Islands Forum Eminent Persons Group visited him in late January on his home island, primarily taking issue about the timetable for the next election.[63]

Efforts were made to 'normalize' the political situation, to rubber-stamp the decrees of the previous month, and earnestly pursue the anti-corruption program. Following the President's statement, a wide-ranging immunity decree was passed, although the legality of this (and of all the other decrees) remained to be tested. Chaudhry was to re-design the 2007 budget, and somehow fill the F$70m gap left by the dropping of the previous government's proposed VAT increase, avoid the impending economic collapse anticipated to result in a F$190m revenue shortfall (including an undisclosed sum to cover the military's giant blow out of its budget during December) and, he hoped, persuade the European Union to continue to provide F$350m to assist sugar restructuring after the inevitable end of sugar price subsidies. Poseci Bune announced the sacking of all government CEOs, and a reversion to the former system of lower paid 'permanent secretaries', as well as a reduction in the retirement age from 60 to 55, opposition to which earned general secretary of the Fiji Public Service Association Rajeshwar Singh a visit to the QEB. With the new government installed, Ratu Ovini Bokini announced the support of the GCC for the decisions of the President, albeit without the chiefs being allowed to meet to ratify this shift in stance. The Methodist Church, whose leaders had formerly been outspoken in their criticism of the new order, and then been temporarily silenced, again challenged the new regime in a statement sent to the Pacific Islands Forum's Eminent Persons Group.[64]

December 5 signalled an extraordinary inversion of Fiji's earlier political trajectory. Ethno-nationalist coups had been countered by what Catholic social justice advocates called a 'multi-culturalist coup'.[65] Some fellow travellers denied that it was a coup at all. The RFMF had transformed itself from *the* guarantor of indigenous Fijian paramountcy into its nemesis. The FLP had cartwheeled from victim to victor in the illegal overthrow of elected governments, and the despised language of the 2000 coup ('I agree with the goals, but not the means') had become the favoured retort of those seeking accommodations with the new order. It was an event justified, like previous coups, by claims that perhaps Fiji was not yet ready for democracy, nor for institutions that had been carefully nurtured over hundreds of years in Europe and North America.[66] Precisely because the longer-run character of the RFMF program remained so obscure, all manner of local reformists, erstwhile optimists and vigorous enemies of Qarase sought to impress on this seemingly blank sheet their own pet projects and vague aspirations. In the early weeks, the commander evidently cherished such valuable reservoirs of legitimacy; even to the point of organising a tea party for selected representatives of the civil society organizations. As the economic downturn set in, this honeymoon era was inevitably displaced by the harsher realities of consolidating the military takeover.

The December 2006 coup signalled the collapse of the mid-1990s 'constitutional engineering' project. At the core of that effort to address the post-1987 coup crisis and to put in place institutional supports to promote 'multi-ethnic government' was a hybrid mixture of two political science perspectives; the Horowitz approach to electoral system design meshed together with the Lijphartian recommendation of top-level power-sharing among élites.[67] Fiji's Constitutional Review Commission had embraced the alternative vote system as a means of promoting moderation, encouraging cross-ethnic alliances around the exchange of preferential votes, and fostering stable 'coalitions of conviction'.[68] But the 1999, 2001 and 2006 elections had provided negligible support for such expectations and, particularly in 2001 and 2006, produced highly ethnically polarised results.[69] The Lijphartian power-sharing provisions, which entitled all parties with over 10 per cent of seats in parliament to cabinet portfolios, had remained untested, at least until 2006.[70] In the wake of the 2006 election, Qarase formed a government that, for the first time, brought together in cabinet parliamentarians from the two largest political parties, one representing the ethnic Fijians and the other the Fiji Indians. Nine FLP members had entered cabinet, and had received substantial portfolios, like Labour, Health and the Environment. But, as we saw above, FLP leader Mahendra Chaudhry had refused to enter cabinet, a decision that was always likely to entail a death sentence for the new arrangements. Even before the swearing in of the new cabinet, it had become clear that this would spark a power struggle within the

FLP. Given the constitutional penalties for floor-crossing,[71] FLP disciplinary measures against the moderate supporters of power-sharing had the potential to bust apart the multiparty cabinet. The most senior FLP enthusiast for power-sharing, Krishna Datt, had his effigy burnt at a meeting of the Nasinu FLP in one event among several that indicated the absence of strong Fiji Indian support within the FLP for power-sharing. Still deeper divisions were always likely when controversial SDL legislation, such as the RTU Bill, the Qoliqoli Bill and the Indigenous Claims Tribunal Bill, were put to the parliamentary vote. Would FLP cabinet ministers adhere to the Westminster rules of 'collective responsibility' codified in the 1997 constitution? Or would they follow the FLP party line, as also required by the 1997 constitution?

In the event, the multiparty cabinet collapsed at the first hurdle. FLP ministers were confronted by ultimatums both from Qarase and Chaudhry to, respectively, support and oppose the 2007 budget. Four backed the FLP line and voted against the budget, while five conveniently absented themselves. In a last ditch effort to save his crumbling cabinet, Qarase relented from dismissing the four anti-budget ministers, but Chaudhry showed little sign of wishing to make any peace with his rebel ministers, although he smartly embraced those other FLP members who sought reconciliation.[72] Would there have been a coup in December had the multiparty cabinet been working smoothly and constructively? That seems unlikely, and, had there not been a military coup, the political ramifications of the collapse of power-sharing might well have been more severe for the FLP leader. Internationally, the break-up of coalition governments is frequently accompanied by efforts by antagonistic parties to make each other appear as the 'spoilers'. In this sense, Bainimarama's coup saved Chaudhry from appearing as the destroyer of an arrangement that had been so warmly welcomed by Fiji's citizens in May 2006.

The fact that the break-up of the power-sharing cabinet, an aspect of the December events that received insufficient attention both at home and abroad, and the 2006 coup happened simultaneously was not a coincidence. After the May 2006 election, Bainimarama had publicly and enthusiastically supported the new arrangements.[73] Outspoken hostility to the Qarase government had, albeit temporarily, been silenced. Only in September, as politicians battled over the issue of 'ground rules' for the new cabinet arrangements, did the commander again resume his public challenges to the Qarase regime. Given the lack of any groundswell of FLP support for the moderate position, the refusal of Mahendra Chaudhry to enter cabinet and the timidity of Qarase in re-orienting his government's policies and personnel to bolster the new accord, the fate of the multiparty cabinet had been sealed by early December 2006. In its place, although the majority Fijian-backed party was excluded, a different grouping of Fijian and Indian leaders was to come together in a new kind of embrace, but this time in violation of the constitution, of democracy and of fashionable theories of institutional design.

That broader structural explanation for the December 2006 coup needs to be combined with more specific accounts of institutional galvanization, repulsion and attraction. How significant were the 'shadowy backers' of the 2006 coup, which Police Commissioner Andrew Hughes claimed to have under investigation prior to the coup? Did the 2006 coup primarily reflect the revenge of the Mara dynasty, long shut out of the corridors of power and altogether eclipsed by the death of Ratu Mara himself? Alternatively, was the coup driven, at least ideologically, by Mahendra Chaudhry in a thinly-veiled effort to capture power on the back of a military coup? Or was Commodore Bainimarama correct when, responding to allegations of hidden backers, he said 'it starts from within us'.[74] It was, after all, the RFMF that had internally re-made and steeled itself through protracted power struggles with the Qarase government. Others had only seized upon the opportunities presented by the showdown, even if they encouraged and took succour from it. In the process, the RFMF had acquired the ideological colours of those most bitter opponents of Qarase's government, following the principle of 'my enemy's enemy is my friend'. But if it was Qarase, as incumbent, who precipitated such an unholy alliance among his adversaries, what was to happen once these lost the focus of their coming together and featured as fellow ministers in cabinet?

Last but not least, what of the role of personal factors? The threat to the commander's life in November 2000 encouraged a relentless pursuit of those responsible, and ensured a breakdown of relations with the very government he had once put into power. Charges of sedition against the commander and the longer-running controversies about the killing of Counter Revolutionary Warfare Unit soldiers during the November 2000 mutiny generated some personal incentive to overturn the legal order. The role of the individual in Fiji's modern history should not be lightly dismissed. For military leaders, personal loyalty can prove to be everything, particularly when their political interventions do not express the broader social uprisings. Loyalty pledges and psychological tests had – for many years – proved a regular feature at Strategic Headquarters at Berkley Crescent and at the QEB. Would there have been a coup in December 2006 if Bainimarama had accepted a diplomatic posting to Wellington in 2003, as he nearly did? Was it possible that a stronger response from the Office of the President might have dislodged the commander back in 2003 or 2004? Would history have taken the same course if Bainimarama's contract as commander had not been renewed in 2004, or if he had become commander of the United Nations in Kuwait Observer Mission, a job he applied for and for the purposes of which he was promoted, temporarily, to Rear Admiral?[75] As the military leader responsible for appointing the Qarase government back in July 2000, the commander always held a unique position, and he never accepted the subordination of the RFMF to the government.

Fiji's May 2006 election was thoroughly eclipsed by the December coup, but the issues it raised may continue to haunt Fiji politics. How can the country overcome ethnically based voting patterns and, if it cannot do so, does power-sharing among political élites provide the only effective answer?[76] If Fiji follows the pattern of past post-coup settlements, there will be a reversion to constitutional democracy. Several factors are likely to delay that process. In particular, a new population census will entail a redrawing of constituency boundaries, possibly accompanied by electoral system changes. Anticipation of the post-electoral configuration of a future parliament may also prove a deterrent to holding elections for some time – especially if concerns remain about the weakness of support for the interim government amongst ethnic Fijians. Will those Fijian politicians who have rallied to the RFMF cause settle easily for a part as bit players if the Fiji Indian vote delivers the bulk of support for the next government? And, even if alliances change much more dramatically, will it prove possible to get the military out of Fiji's political life when elected politicians are returned to the national stage? These are questions Fiji must inevitably wrestle with over the years ahead.

February 2007

Notes

1   *Fijilive*, 5 December 2006.
2   Government House Statement, 5 December 2006.
3   Press Statement from Government House, 6 December 2006.
4   *The Australian*, 7 November 2006; *Sydney Morning Herald*, 6 November 2006.
5   The Pacific Islands Forum's Biketawa Declaration allows regional intervention in a member country after an invitation from the government concerned.
6   Essentially the same non-interventionist policy could, more diplomatically, have been defended by saying that it would not help the situation in Fiji if the government became dependent on outside military support for its survival and that this was an élite power struggle that had to be, ultimately, resolved internally, preferably without bloodshed. Qarase was later threatened with treason charges for, allegedly, making such requests for foreign intervention.
7   Address to the Nation by the Hon. Laisenia Qarase, 5 December 2006.
8   *The Fiji Times*, 6 December 2006.
9   *The Fiji Times*, 6 December 2006.
10 Shaista Shameem, Director, Fiji Human Rights Commission, 'The Assumption of Executive Authority on December 5th by Commodore J.V. Bainimarama, Commander of the Republic of Fiji Military Forces: Legal, Constitutional and Human Rights Issues', 3 January 2007, http://www.humanrights.org.fj. For a critique, penned anonymously by senior lawyers also, ironically, under the FHRC logo, see 'A Response to the Fiji Human Rights Commission Director's report on the Assumption of Executive Authority by Commodore J.V. Bainimarama, Commander of the Republic of Fiji Military Forces', available online on the Intelligentsiya website, http://intelligentsiya.blogspot.com.
11 There were, of course, exceptions, but to a considerably lesser degree than there were Fijian critics of either the 1987 or 2000 coups.
12 In January 2001, a military delegation to Government House including Commodore Bainimarama, Colonel Ratu George Kadalevu, Ilaia Kacisolomone and Lesi Korovavala, told the President that it would uphold Anthony Gates' November 2000 ruling restoring the 1997 constitution if it was upheld in the Court of Appeal and support the formation of 'Government of National Unity' (Margaret Wise, 'Fiji Army Stands Firm, Law and Order Top Priority List', *The Fiji Times*, 24 January 2001; see also Dakuvula, J., 'The Fiji Military Forces Vs The Elected Government of Fiji; A Case Study of Conflict', Citizens Constitutional Forum, 19 January 2004).
13 Senior military personnel held the view that the 1997 constitution had not displaced the earlier 1990 constitution provisions, granting that 'it shall be the overall responsibility of the Republic of Fiji Military Forces to ensure at all times the security, defence and well being of Fiji and its peoples' [Republic of the Fiji Islands, 1990 Constitution, S94(3)]. The Qarase government had, even before the May 2006 election, wanted to put this matter before the courts.
14 In early November, for example, Lesi Korovavala, Chief Executive Officer in the Ministry of Home Affairs was suspended from duty by Home Affairs Minister, Josefa Vosanibola, for failing to turn up to three consecutive meetings of the National Security Council, which Korovavala chaired (Radio New Zealand International, 9 November 2006). Korovavala,

himself a former military man, clearly saw the writing on the wall for the Qarase government, and made himself scarce.

[15] 'Meeting between Prime Minister Qarase and Commodore Bainimarama', Government House, Wellington, November 29 2006; Points of Agreement & Next Steps', http://img. scoop.co.nz/media/pdfs/0612/WellingtonMinutes.pdf

[16] *Fiji Sun*, 1 December 2006.

[17] 1997 Constitution of Fiji, Sections 99 (1), 109 (1) & (2).

[18] Appealing for international support, the commander made reference to Governor Kerr's dismissal of Australian Prime Minister Gough Whitlam in 1975 (see 'Coup leader invokes Whitlam sacking', *Sydney Morning Herald*, 6 December 2006).

[19] Mahmud, T. 1994. 'Jurisprudence of Successful Treason: Coup d'État and Common Law', *Cornell International Law Journal*, 49, pp.49–140.

[20] That, in turn, ensured lukewarm support from other Melanesian leaders for Qarase after the coup, a schism manipulated by officials in the Fiji Ministry of Foreign Affairs to secure international recognition for the post-coup government.

[21] Graham Davis 'An island enigma', *The Fiji Times*, 11 December 2006.

[22] The program ran on weekday mornings, and was hosted by former Fiji Broadcasting Corporation Ltd (FBCL) radio personality Sitiveni Raturala, who had been fired by FBCL in early 2006 for running an interview in which the commander fiercely attacked the Qarase government.

[23] *The Fiji Times*, 23 December 2006.

[24] See http://www.oag.gov.fj/reports.html.

[25] Commander, Republic of Fiji Military Forces V Auditor General, Court of Appeal of Fiji, 26 August 2003; Commander, Republic of Fiji Military Forces V Auditor General, Supreme Court of Fiji, 17 September 2004.

[26] *The Fiji Times*, 29 December 2006.

[27] 'Fijian Police seek Foster over Resort Claims', *Sydney Morning Herald*, 12 October 2006.

[28] Radio New Zealand, 3 October 2006; *Pacific Magazine*, 15 January 2007.

[29] *Fiji Sun*, 24 December 2006.

[30] To rig elections merely in the way claimed, by stuffing extra ballots into the boxes, was implausible, at least without also altering the reconciliation forms that tally ballots issued with the numbers emptied out of the boxes at the counting centres. More suspicious was the long-standing failure to release the 0-39 forms that provide detailed evidence as regards the counting and transfer of preference votes in the marginal urban open constituencies along the all-important Suva–Nausori corridor, despite strong pre-election assurances from the Chair of the Electoral Commission that this would be done.

[31] In Vanuatu, he was again arrested, and eventually deported to Australia, where he was arrested for a third time, now on charges related to securing the Bank of the Federated States of Micronesia loan.

[32] *Daily Post*, 2 January 2007; *The Australian*, 19 January 2007.

[33] *The Fiji Times*, 15 January 2007.

[34] The GCC, after all, was the constitutional appointing authority for the President and Vice President.

[35] Fiji's three chiefly confederacies, Kubuna, Burebasaga and Tovata, have nowadays become the basis for the organization of GCC meetings, which regularly break up into smaller confederacy-based groupings before reaching decisions as a whole.

36 *Fiji Sun,* 23 December 2006.
37 *The Fiji Times,* 28 December 2006.
38 See *The Fiji Times,* 23 September 2000, and letters to *The Fiji Times* on 25 September and 30 September 2000. See also 'Pacific People Building Peace', Update No. 12, email circular, 20 December 2006.
39 *The Fiji Times,* 7 December 2006; *Fiji Post,* 9 December 2006; *Fiji Sun,* 9 December 2006.
40 *The Fiji Times,* 15 December 2006.
41 *Fiji Sun,* 9 December 2006.
42 *The Fiji Times,* 24 December 2006. A subsequent letter to the newspapers stated '[Lt. Col.] Driti should know that as long as he walks this earth, the people of Yacata in Cakaudrove will always despise him and his bullies for what they did to Laisa Vulakoro' (*The Fiji Times,* 6 January 2007).
43 *Fiji Sun* 31 December 2006; *Fiji Sun* 27 December 2006.
44 'If the military is cleaning up corruption, then we are more or less with them on that, and support their campaign' (Hari Pal Singh, Chairman Transparency International (Fiji), *The Fiji Times,* 28 December 2006).
45 Radio New Zealand, 7 December 2006.
46 *Daily Post,* 24 December 2006.
47 *The Fiji Times,* 28 December 2006.
48 *Daily Post,* 23 December 2006.
49 *Fiji Sun,* 24 December 2006.
50 *The Fiji Times,* 8 January 2007.
51 Only 5 per cent of Fiji's total land area is freehold, while 87 per cent is native land, which cannot be bought and sold. The residual 8 per cent is crown land, which the Qarase government, following a policy also embraced under previous governments, had been gradually reverting to native owners.
52 'Attitude "Caused Resort Loss"', *The Fiji Times,* 15 February 2007. The responsibility of the Fiji Islands Revenue and Customs Authority (FIRCA) for the resort's difficulties was subsequently rejected in an advertisement paid for by FIRCA (*The Fiji Times,* 23 January 2007).
53 *Fiji Sun,* 7 January 2007.
54 *Fiji Sun,* 1 January 2007.
55 *The Fiji Times,* 3 January 2007.
56 Commander of the RFMF's Handover Speech, 4 January 2007, http://www.fiji.gov.fj/publish/page_8136.shtml . The commander's reference was to the judgement of M.D. Scott, in Yabaki v President of the Republic of the Fiji Islands, 11 July 2001, available at http://www.paclii.org.
57 Justice Gates was the former Lautoka High Court judge who had initially upheld the 1997 constitution in November 2000, a decision which was appealed by the government leading to the February–March 2001 case held before the Court of Appeal (mentioned above). Justice Gates had, down the years, vehemently criticized former Chief Justice Timoci Tuivaga, as well as the new Chief Justice Fatiaki, and Justice Scott's judicial complicity in the attempted 2000 illegal abrogation of the 1997 constitution. Since it was the military itself that had purported to abrogate that constitution back in 2000, it was strange that these judges should now suffer such a fate. Realizing that he had departed with too little protest, the 'suspended'

Chief Justice later turned up at his chambers on 18 January, claiming to be back at work and holding an impromptu TV press conference before being escorted away by senior police officers.

58 Interim Attorney-General Aiyez Sayed-Khaiyum later claimed to have constitutionally convened a meeting of the Judicial Services Commission (JSC) to appoint Justice Gates as Acting Chief Justice, and to have appointed as JSC chair Justice Nazrat Shameem (the sister of FHRC Director Shaista Shameem). But both the Shameem and Gates appointments were found to be unconstitutional by the University of Cambridge's James Crawford S.C. in 'Opinion. Re: Judicial Services Commission of Fiji – recommendation for Appointment of Acting Chief Justice', 20 February 2007, published on the Intelligentsiya website, http://intelligentsiya.blogspot.com/.

59 H.E the President Ratu Josefa Iloilovatu Uluivuda's speech after Commander of the Republic of the Fiji Military Force, Commodore Voreqe Bainimarama handed back Authority 5 January 2007, http://www.fiji.gov.fj/publish/page_8194.shtml accessed 6 February 2007.

60 Methodist Church in Fiji, 'Here we stand', reprinted in the *Fiji Daily Post*, 3 February 2007.

61 For a broader survey of SDL campaign expenditures, countering some of the wilder speculations, see Verenaisi Raicola 'It's money down the drain', *The Fiji Times*, 1 February 2007.

62 *Fiji Daily Post*, 7 February 2007.

63 *The Fiji Times*, 1 February 2007.

64 Methodist Church, 'Here We Stand', reprinted *Daily Post*, 3 February 2007. Several church leaders were taken into military custody after the issuing of this statement, which was consequently said in the media to have been 'withdrawn', although Methodist Church President Ratabacaca insisted that the RFMF and church had 'agreed to differ'. Later reports suggested that the report had in fact been approved by the Methodist Church Standing Committee (see letter, Rev T.K. Waqairawai, Deputy General Secretary, on behalf of the Church Media Committee, *The Fiji Times*, 26 February 2007).

65 Paulo Baleinakoro-Dawa, Father Kevin Barr and Semiti Qalowasa, 'Time of Uncertainty, Opportunity', *The Fiji Times*, 19 December 2006.

66 See the comments of Commerce Minister Taito Waradi before his appointment in *The Fiji Times*, 29 December 2006, and those of Catholic Archbishop Petero Mataca in *The Fiji Times*, 23 January 2007.

67 Horowitz, D.L. 1991. *A Democratic South Africa? Constitutional Engineering in a Divided Society*, University of California Press, Berkeley; Horowitz, D.L. 1997. 'Encouraging Electoral Accommodation in Divided Societies', in Lal, B.V. & P. Larmour (eds) *Electoral Systems in Divided Societies: The Fiji Constitutional Review*, ANU, Canberra; Lijphart, A. 1985. *Power-Sharing in South Africa*, Policy Papers in International Affairs, 24, Institute of International Studies, University of California, Berkeley; Lijphart, A. 1991. 'The Power Sharing Approach', in Montville, J. (ed.) *Conflict and Peacemaking in Multiethnic Societies*, Lexington Press, Lexington, Massachussets,.

68 Constitutional Review Commission. 1996. *The Fiji Islands: Towards a United Future*, P. Reeves, T. Vakatora & B.V. Lal (eds), Suva: Parliamentary Paper 34, pp. 309–10, 312, 316, 317.

⁶⁹ See Fraenkel, J. & B. Grofman. 2006. 'Does the Alternative Vote Foster Moderation in Ethnically Divided Societies? The Case of Fiji', *Comparative Political Studies*, 39(5):623–51.

⁷⁰ In 1999, the FLP had formed a power-sharing cabinet, but this had been beyond what was constitutionally required owing to concerns about the security situation and it had not included the party that obtained the largest share of indigenous Fijian votes. In any case, it had lasted only a year, and none of the Fijian politicians who had participated had secured re-election from their own community in 2001. (The one exception, Poseci Bune, had abandoned his Fijian communal seat and stood, in 2001, instead for the FLP in the 70 per cent Indian Labasa Open constituency. He was elected on the basis of Indian votes). After the 2001 poll, the Qarase government had avoided assembling a multiparty cabinet, at first by repeated delaying tactics, and then by compliance with the letter but not the spirit of the law, although Labour in any case rejected the 2004 offer of cabinet participation and shifted into opposition.

⁷¹ 'The place of a member of the House of Representatives becomes vacant if the member: …(g) resigns from the political party for which he or she was a candidate at the time he or she was last elected to the House of Representatives; (h) is expelled from the political party for which he or she was a candidate at the time he or she was last elected to the House of Representatives and: (i) the political party is a registered party; (ii) the expulsion was in accordance with rules of the party relating to party discipline; and (iii) the expulsion did not relate to action taken by the member in his or her capacity as a member of a parliamentary committee' [1997 Fiji Constitution, 71.-(1)].

⁷² Only two of the FLP ministers were expelled, Krishna Datt and Poseci Bune.

⁷³ In one post-election issue of the RFMF newsletter, the commander applauded 'the evolution of this great and new concept of power sharing at the executive level of government' and reiterated earlier calls for 'total support to the Multi-party cabinet from each and every member of the Republic of Fiji Military Forces' (*Mataivalu News*, July/August 2006, p.3; see also 'Fiji Military Pledges Support for Government', *The Fiji Times*, 28 July 2006.

⁷⁴ Fiji TV *Viti Nikua,* 3 December 2006.

⁷⁵ Keith-Reid, R., 'Frankly Speaking', *Islands Business*, June 2003; *Fiji Daily Post*, 13 December 2003.

⁷⁶ The 'paradox' of the 2006 election, that voters were strongly polarized on ethnic lines in May 2006 but then also strongly supportive of post-election power-sharing, is perhaps not as odd as it at first sight appears. Why, many liberals asked, if they endorsed power-sharing, did voters not support those moderate politicians who were most committed to making multiparty cabinet work? The answer is obvious: power-sharing cabinets do not supersede the antagonisms they are intended to resolve. They provide means for negotiating them. Putting the more obstinate representatives of one's own ethnic group into office may seem a better negotiating strategy than sending into cabinet the more conciliatory, or less hard-line, politicians.

Appendix 1: Multiparty government in Fiji: a timeline, 1997–2006

Piccolo Willoughby

25 July 1997	The Constitution (Amendment) Act 1997 ('the Constitution') is passed by Parliament. Section 99 calls for executive power to be shared between the governing political party or coalition and other major parties in Parliament. This is achieved by requiring the Prime Minister to invite all parties holding at least 10% of the total membership of the House of Representatives (8 or more seats, if all 71 seats are occupied) to be represented in the Cabinet. The overall size of Cabinet is left to the Prime Minister, but parties accepting the invitation to be represented must be offered Cabinet seats in proportion to their numbers in the House. The Prime Minister may also invite minor parties that do not fulfil the 10% requirement (such as a coalition partner) to be represented in his or her Cabinet, but if this is done then the representatives of those parties are deemed to be representatives of the Prime Minister's party for the purpose of calculating the number of Cabinet seats that must be offered to parties that fulfil the 10% requirement. Section 64 of the Constitution then uses the formula from section 99 to determine the entitlement of parties holding seats in the House of Representatives to nominate Senators. 8 out of the total of 32 Senators are to be appointed on the advice of the Leader of the Opposition from among nominations made by the leaders of parties holding at least 10% of the total membership of the House of Representatives (that is, parties entitled to be offered Cabinet seats under section 99). The Leader of the Opposition must ensure that these 8 Senators comprise such number nominated by each entitled party as is proportionate to the size of their membership in the House.
27 July 1998	The Constitution comes into force.
26 January 1999	Meeting in retreat at Korolevu, leaders of the Soqosoqo ni Vakavulewa ni Taukei (SVT), the National Federation Party, the Fiji Labour Party (FLP), the General Voters Party, the Fijian Association Party (FAP) and the General Electors Party sign a declaration setting out various 'principles, conventions and practices' that they consider appropriate in the implementation of the new Constitution as it relates to the establishment and functioning of a multiparty Cabinet. This becomes known as the 'Korolevu Declaration'.
8–15 May 1999	National elections are held to elect 71 members of the House of Representatives in accordance with the new Constitution. The President is later advised of the results as follows: The FLP wins 37 seats. The FAP wins 10 seats. The SVT wins 8 seats. The Party of National Unity wins 4 seats. The Christian Democratic Unity Party, the United General Party and the Nationalist Vanua Tako Lavo win 2 seats each. The remaining 5 seats are won by independents. The High Court, sitting as the Court of Disputed Returns, later revokes the election of one of the Nationalist Vanua Tako Lavo candidates and declares a FAP candidate to be the winner of that seat.
19 May 1999	The President appoints the Leader of the FLP, Mahendra Chaudhry, as Prime Minister. Mr Chaudhry writes to the Leader of the SVT, Sitiveni Rabuka, inviting the SVT to be represented in a multiparty Cabinet in accordance with section 99 of the Constitution.

20 May 1999	Mr Rabuka replies to Mr Chaudhry's letter with a list of conditions on which the SVT would be willing to accept the invitation to join a multiparty Cabinet. The conditions include that Mr Rabuka be made Deputy Prime Minister and Minister for Fijian Affairs, that 3 other portfolios be allocated to named SVT members, that 3 of the 9 Senators to be appointed by the Prime Minister be nominated by the SVT, and that all ambassadors, high commissioners, and board members of statutory and state-owned enterprises appointed by the SVT be allowed to complete their terms of office. Mr Chaudhry replies to Mr Rabuka's letter, rejecting these conditions.
21 May 1999	The President, acting on Mr Chaudhry's advice, appoints 18 Ministers and 5 Assistant Ministers. None are from the SVT. The President summons Parliament to meet on 14 June 1999.
24 May 1999	The President appoints the Deputy Leader of the SVT, Ratu Inoke Kubuabola, as Leader of the Opposition.
7–11 June 1999	Correspondence is exchanged between Ratu Inoke and the President regarding the 8 Senators to be appointed on the advice of the Leader of the Opposition under section 64 of the Constitution. There are conflicting interpretations of the formula for calculating the number of Senate seats that must be offered to each political party holding at least 10% of the total membership of the House of Representatives.
12 June 1999	The President writes to Ratu Inoke and Mr Chaudhry, advising that he intends to ask Cabinet to advise him to refer the question of how many Senate seats must be offered to each party under section 64 to the Supreme Court for an advisory opinion.
15 June 1999	Mr Chaudhry replies to the President that Cabinet has agreed to advise him to make a reference to the Supreme Court regarding the interpretation of section 64. The President formally opens the new Parliamentary session at a joint sitting of both Houses.
16 June 1999	Ratu Inoke commences legal action in the High Court to contest the opening of Parliament before all disputes concerning the elections have been resolved and all Senators appointed.
21 June 1999	The Speaker of the House of Representatives declares the seat of SVT Leader, Sitiveni Rabuka, vacant following his resignation and election as Chairman of the Bose Levu Vakaturaga (Great Council of Chiefs).
24 June 1999	A Presidential reference is filed in the Supreme Court concerning the interpretation of section 64.
6 July 1999	Ratu Inoke commences legal action in the High Court to contest the exclusion of the SVT from Cabinet.
24 August 1999	The President's reference to the Supreme Court is enlarged to include issues raised in Ratu Inoke's legal actions.
3 September 1999	The Supreme Court delivers its opinion on the enlarged President's reference (President of the Republic of Fiji Islands v Kubuabola (Tuivaga P, Lord Cooke, Mason, Brennan and Toohey JJ, Miscellaneous Case No. 1 of 1999)). It holds that power sharing is a 'central purpose' of the 1997 Constitution. Sections 64 and 99 of the Constitution modify the traditional Westminster pattern so that political power is 'divided among a number of groups, persons and parties' and 'the share of each is in some way limited'. Under section 64, the Prime Minister is entitled to nominate 9 Senators only. The Prime Minister's party is not entitled to be offered additional Senate seats from among the 8 to be filled on the advice of the Leader of the Opposition. However, parties in coalition with the Prime Minister's party are not to be regarded as members of the Prime Minister's party for the purposes of sections 64 and 99. Accordingly, if such parties hold at least 10% of the total membership of the House of Representatives, they will have a separate

entitlement to be offered seats in the Senate and in Cabinet. The time for calculating the number of Senators that each party is entitled to nominate is the date when the Leader of the Opposition advises the President of the nominations. This has not yet occurred at the date of the Court's judgment. There is one vacancy in the House of Representatives, leaving a total membership of 70. Besides the FLP, only the FAP (with 11 seats) and the SVT (with 7) hold at least 10% of this total. As a result, of the 8 Senators to be appointed on the advice of the Leader of the Opposition, the Court rules that 5 must be offered to the FAP and 3 to the SVT. Since the President must summon Parliament to meet no later than 30 days after the last day of polling in national elections (section 68 of the Constitution), this cannot be dependent on the receipt of advice from the Leader of the Opposition on Senate appointments. Accordingly, the Parliamentary session may begin before all Senate seats are filled.

In relation to section 99, the Court holds that the Prime Minister may only withdraw his or her invitation to other parties to join the Cabinet after a reasonable time has passed for accepting or rejecting it. The Court rules that Sitiveni Rabuka's response of 20 May 1999 to Mahendra Chaudhry's invitation to the SVT included conditions that Mr Chaudhry was not bound to accept. Mr Rabuka's conditional acceptance of the invitation therefore amounted to a rejection.

27 August – 1 September 2001

Following the May 2000 coup and the ruling of the Court of Appeal on 1 March 2001 that the 1997 Constitution remains in force, national elections are held to elect a new House of Representatives.

The results are as follows: The Soqosoqo Duavata ni Lewenivanua (SDL) wins 32 seats. The FLP wins 27 seats. The Conservative Alliance/Matanitu Vanua (CAMV) wins 6 seats. The New Labour Unity Party (NLUP) wins 2 seats. The National Federation Party (NFP) and the United General Party (UGP) win 1 seat each and the remaining 2 seats are won by independents. The High Court, sitting as the Court of Disputed Returns, later revokes the election of the NFP candidate and declares a FLP candidate to be the winner of that seat.

10 September 2001

The President appoints the Leader of the SDL, Laisenia Qarase, as Prime Minister. Mr Qarase writes to the Leader of the FLP, Mahendra Chaudhry, inviting the FLP to join in a multiparty Cabinet in accordance with section 99 of the Constitution. The letter states that the policies of Mr Qarase's Cabinet would 'be based fundamentally on the policy manifesto of the [SDL]' and that 'it is simply inconceivable that we should allow a situation where we become the minority group in [Cabinet]'. Mr Chaudhry replies that the FLP accepts the invitation but its participation 'in Cabinet and in government' would be in accordance with the Korolevu Declaration, and that 'Cabinet decision making…should be on a consensus seeking basis' and 'consensus seeking mechanisms in Cabinet should include the formulation of a broadly acceptable policy framework'.

12 September 2001

Mr Qarase replies to Mr Chaudhry's letter, stating that the conditions on which the FLP purported to accept his invitation to join Cabinet are unacceptable.

18 September 2001

The President, acting on Mr Qarase's advice, appoints Ministers from the SDL, the CAMV and the NLUP. An independent and a Senator are also appointed to be Ministers. The FLP is excluded.

25 September 2001

Mr Chaudhry commences legal action in the High Court claiming that the FLP is entitled to be represented in Mr Qarase's Cabinet.

2 October 2001	The President formally opens the new Parliamentary session at a joint sitting of both Houses.
19 October 2001	Acting on the advice of the Leader of the Opposition, Prem Singh, the President appoints 4 FLP nominees and 1 each from the CAMV, NFP, NLUP and UGP as Senators. This is done despite a difference of opinion between Mr Singh and Mr Chaudhry as to the FLP's entitlement to be offered seats in the Senate. Mr Chaudhry has earlier declined the President's offer to appoint him as Leader of the Opposition.
29 November 2001	The High Court poses a series of legal questions arising from Mr Chaudhry's claim that the FLP is entitled to be represented in Cabinet, in the form of a Case Stated for decision by the Court of Appeal.
15 February 2002	The Court of Appeal decides the Case Stated (Chaudhry v Qarase (Eichelbaum, Ward, Handley, Smellie and Keith JJA, Miscellaneous No. 1/2001)).
	It holds that section 99 of the Constitution does not enable the Prime Minister to impose any conditions on the offer of Cabinet seats to parties holding at least 10% of the total membership of the House of Representatives. The invitation to join Cabinet must be unconditional. The Court rules that Mr Qarase's letter to Mr Chaudhry of 10 September 2001 did contain an invitation in accordance with section 99, and the inclusion of information as to how he intended the affairs of Cabinet to be conducted did not amount to a condition. Mr Chaudhry's response of the same day accepted this invitation, and the inclusion of information concerning how the FLP would participate likewise did not amount to a condition. Accordingly, while Mr Qarase retains a discretion as to the overall size of Cabinet, he is required to advise the President to appoint a Cabinet in which the FLP is represented in proportion to its numbers in the House of Representatives. In selecting members of the FLP to become Ministers, Mr Qarase must consult Mr Chaudhry. The Court concludes that, in failing to appoint any FLP Ministers, Mr Qarase has breached, and is presently in breach, of a constitutional duty.
15 March 2002	The Supreme Court decides a Presidential reference dated 6 February 2002, concerning the appointment of Senators under section 64 of the Constitution (In the matter of section 123 of the Constitution Amendment Act 1997 (Tuivaga P, Tikaram, Eichelbaum, Amet and Sapolu JJ, Miscellaneous Case No. 1 of 2002S)).
	The issue in dispute is the distribution of the 8 Senate appointments made on the advice of the Leader of the Opposition. The Court holds that only parties holding at least 10% of the total membership of the House of Representatives, other than the Prime Minister's party, are entitled to nominate Senators to fill these 8 seats. Nominations are made by the leaders of entitled parties, but the nominees need not be members of those parties. It is clear from the Supreme Court's opinion on the 1999 Kubuabola reference that each entitled party must be offered that number of Senate seats from among the 8 which bears the same proportion to the total as the number of seats in the House of Representatives held by that party bears to the total number of seats in the House held by all entitled parties. This may be expressed mathematically as:

SEP   8
———— = —————
HREP   HRAEP

where 'SEP' means Senate seats that must be offered to each entitled party, 'HREP' means seats in the House of Representatives held by |

that entitled party and 'HRAEP' means the total number of seats in the House held by all entitled parties. Following the 2001 national elections, only one party, namely the FLP, is entitled to be offered Senate seats from among the 8 to be appointed on the advice of the Leader of the Opposition. Upholding its earlier opinion, the Court rules that, where there is only one entitled party, that party must be offered all 8 Senate seats. Accordingly, the FLP is entitled to nominate 8 Senators. In addition, the Court suggests that the President should decline to act on advice which he or she considers is not in accordance with the Constitution. The President may obtain independent legal advice on such matters.

24 April 2002 The High Court makes a declaration giving effect to the Court of Appeal's decision on 15 February 2002 in the Case Stated.

24 May 2002 The Court of Appeal dismisses an appeal by Mr Qarase against the High Court's declaration, but grants leave for an appeal to the Supreme Court.

18 July 2003 The Supreme Court decides Mr Qarase's appeal (Qarase v Chaudhry (Fatiaki P, Spigelman, Gault, Mason and French JJ, Civil Appeal No. CBV 0004 of 2002S)).

It holds that section 99 requires the Prime Minister to establish a multiparty Cabinet. This represents a modification of the traditional Westminster model, and may require some corresponding modification of Cabinet conventions. However, multiparty Cabinet can be achieved consistently with other requirements of the Constitution, including collective responsibility of the Cabinet to Parliament (section 102 of the Constitution) and the doctrine of Cabinet solidarity, which collective responsibility implies. 'It is not to be expected, at this early stage of the implementation of the 1997 Constitution, that there will be settled conventions to cover all contingencies or difficulties'. Likewise, a multiparty Cabinet is not to be rejected as unworkable only because it may be more difficult to manage than a Cabinet whose members belong to the same party or a coalition that has worked out some consensus before its formation. There will no doubt need to be negotiations as to which members of parties other than the Prime Minister's own will be appointed as Ministers, and which portfolios will be allocated to them. While the Prime Minister retains the authority to decide these questions, he or she must conduct the negotiations in good faith. It may even be necessary for such negotiations to take place during the formation of coalitions, before the Prime Minister is appointed. The Court also holds that 'the obligation to establish a multiparty Cabinet carries with it an obligation to maintain a multiparty Cabinet. This latter obligation may arise in connection with ministerial resignations, by-elections or changes in the size of the Cabinet.' Accordingly, the appeal is dismissed and Mr Qarase is ordered to pay Mr Chaudhry's costs.

9 July 2004 After unsuccessful negotiations between Mr Qarase and Mr Chaudhry concerning the number of Cabinet seats that should be offered to the FLP, the Supreme Court decides a Presidential reference on the question (In the matter of section 123 of the Constitution Amendment Act 1997 (Fatiaki P, Gault, Mason, French and Weinberg JJ, Miscellaneous Case No. 1 of 2003)).

Upholding its opinions on the 1999 and 2002 references, the Court holds that parties entitled to be offered Cabinet seats under section 99 of the Constitution are to be identified by dividing the number of seats in the House of Representatives which each party holds by the total membership of the House. If the result is equal to or greater than 10% then the party in question is entitled to be offered Cabinet seats.

While the Prime Minister is free to choose the overall size of his or her Cabinet, entitled parties must be offered proportionate representation in it. The Court holds that each entitled party must be offered a number of Cabinet seats which bears the same proportion to the number to be held by the Prime Minister's party as the number of seats in the House of Representatives held by the entitled party bears to the number of seats in the House held by the Prime Minister's party. This may be expressed mathematically as:

CEP   =CPM

HREP   HRPM

where 'CEP' means Cabinet seats that must be offered to each entitled party; 'HREP' means seats in the House of Representatives held by that entitled party; 'CPM' means Cabinet seats to be held by the Prime Minister's party and 'HRPM' means seats in the House of Representatives held by the Prime Minister's party. So, for example, in the present case, the SDL holds 32 seats in the House of Representatives and the FLP holds 28. The number of Cabinet seats to be offered to the FLP must therefore be equal to 28/32 or seven-eighths of the number to be held by the SDL. If the Prime Minister chooses to invite a coalition partner that does not hold at least 10% of the total membership of the House of Representatives to join the Cabinet, then any seats to be held by that non-entitled party will be counted as being held by the Prime Minister's party. The proportion of Cabinet seats to which all parties are entitled must be re-calculated from time to time as the composition of the House of Representatives changes.

However, section 99 is silent on the appointment as Cabinet Ministers of members of the House of Representatives who are independent of any political party or of Senators who are not members of a party represented in the House. The Court holds (with Gault J dissenting on this point) that the Prime Minister may appoint such independents or Senators to the Cabinet at his or her discretion, and any seats filled by them will not be counted in calculating the number of seats that must be offered to entitled parties. Accordingly, Cabinet seats to be held by such independents or Senators will be in addition to the entitlement of the Prime Minister's party under section 99.

24 November 2004   After further negotiations with Mr Qarase concerning which FLP members would be appointed as Ministers and which portfolios would be allocated to them, Mr Chaudhry announces in Parliament that the FLP has decided to reject Mr Qarase's offer to join his Cabinet and that it will instead assume the Opposition benches.

6–13 May 2006   National elections are held to elect a new House of Representatives.

The results are as follows: The SDL wins 36 seats. The FLP wins 31 seats. The United Peoples Party (UPP – formerly the United General Party) wins 2 seats. The remaining 2 seats are won by independents.

18 May 2006   The President appoints the Leader of the SDL, Laisenia Qarase, as Prime Minister. Mr Qarase writes to the Leader of the FLP, Mahendra Chaudhry, inviting the FLP to join in a multiparty Cabinet in accordance with section 99 of the Constitution. According to a press release the following day, the letter identifies 7 portfolios to be allocated to the FLP, should it accept the invitation, and asks Mr Chaudhry to nominate 12 FLP members as candidates from among whom Mr Qarase may choose the 7 Ministers.

19 May 2006   Mr Qarase reveals in a press conference that he is contemplating a multiparty Cabinet consisting of 10 members of his own SDL, 7

| | members of the FLP, 2 independents and a small number of Senators who are not members of any political party represented in the House of Representatives. Mr Chaudhry meets with Mr Qarase, and reportedly accepts 'in principle' his offer to join the FLP to join the Cabinet, while at the same time seeking certain clarifications. Several days of negotiations follow, during which Mr Qarase increases the number of Cabinet seats he is willing to allocate to the FLP from 7 to 9, Mr Chaudhry announces that the FLP will join the Cabinet, but he personally will remain outside it, and the FLP provides Mr Qarase with a list of its nominees. |

| 23 May 2006 | The President, acting on Mr Qarase's advice, appoints as Ministers: 10 SDL members (besides Mr Qarase himself); 1 independent; and 3 of Mr Qarase's nominees to the Senate. The FLP nominees to the Cabinet do not attend the swearing-in ceremony. This follows an emergency meeting of the FLP caucus the night before at which the members are reportedly unable to accept last-minute changes made by Mr Qarase to the Cabinet portfolios allocated to their nominees. After the swearing-in ceremony, Mr Chaudhry tells the media that he doubts the legality of appointing as Ministers nominees to the Senate who have not yet been appointed as Senators. He also alleges that the 3 Senate nominees are not independent, but aligned with the SDL. Later the same day, the FLP announces that it has accepted the changes made by Mr Qarase to the portfolios allocated to its nominees. |

| 24 May 2006 | The President, acting on Mr Qarase's advice, appoints 9 FLP members as Ministers. For the first time in Fiji's history, a multiparty Cabinet is formed that includes all the major political parties of the day. The total number of Cabinet Ministers is 24. |

Looming questions include:

- whether Mr Chaudhry is eligible for appointment as Leader of the Opposition now that members of his party have joined the Cabinet;
- how the FLP will apply its party rules and discipline to the 9 members who, as members of Mr Qarase's Cabinet, are also bound by the doctrine of Cabinet solidarity; and
- what 'ground rules' can be agreed between the SDL and the FLP to guide the functioning of the Cabinet.

| 22 November 2006 | In the absence of ground rules agreed between the two parties represented in Cabinet, 4 of the 9 FLP Ministers vote against the SDL's proposed national budget for 2007 in the House of Representatives. The other 5 FLP Ministers are absent when the vote is called. Due to the SDL's majority, the budget is passed anyway. Previously, Mr Qarase has demanded unanimous support for the budget from all of his Ministers, while Mr Chaudhry has demanded that FLP Ministers vote along party lines, and therefore oppose the budget. After the vote, Mr Qarase threatens to dismiss the 4 Ministers who broke Cabinet solidarity, but he later offers to refrain from doing so if Mr Chaudhry agrees not to discipline the 5 FLP Ministers who absented themselves. |

| 28 November 2006 | The FLP expels 2 of its representatives in the Cabinet (along with 3 other party members) after a disciplinary hearing by its national council. The expulsions are the result of a dispute between the FLP's management board and Mr Chaudhry over the selection of nominees to the Senate. |

| 5 December 2006 | The Commander of the Republic of Fiji Military Forces, Commodore Voreqe (Frank) Bainimarama, leads a military takeover, announcing that he has assumed the executive authority of the State and removed Mr Qarase and all members of the multiparty Cabinet from office. |

Appendix 2: 2006 election results

	Party				Totals Counts					
		1st	2nd	3rd	4th	5th	6th	7th	8th	

1. Bua Fijian Provincial

	Party	1st
Selaima Kalounivit Veisamasama	Ind.	684
Etonia Bose	Ind.	207
Vula Josateki	Ind.	146
Mitieli Bulanauca	SDL	4,321
Informal		887
Total votes		6,245
Total valid		5,358
Turnout (per cent)		92.5
Total registered		6,749

2. Kadavu Fijian Provincial

	Party	1st
Konisi Tabu Yabaki	SDL	3,766
Semesa Matanawa	FLP	45
Rupeni Drodroveivau Koroi	Ind.	57
James Michael Ah Koy	Ind.	1,191
Informal		417
Total votes		5,476
Total valid		5,059
Turnout (per cent)		89.9
Total registered		6,089

3. Lau Fijian Provincial

	Party	1st
Laisenia Qarase	SDL	4,896
Viliame Cavubati	NAPF	350
Informal		697
Total votes		5,943
Total valid		5,246
Turnout (per cent)		89.9
Total registered		6,612

4. Lomaiviti Fijian Provincial

	Party	1st
Filise Baleinakoro	NVTLP	136
Simione Kaitani	SDL	5,109
Jone Kauvesi	Ind.	920
Iliesa Tora	Ind.	44
Informal		696
Total votes		6,905
Total valid		6,209
Turnout (per cent)		90.3
Total registered		7,650

	Party		Totals Counts							
		1st	2nd	3rd	4th	5th	6th	7th	8th	

5. Macuata Fijian Provincial

Wasasala Samuela	NFP	215	
Savenaca Lario Damudamu	Ind.	103	
Samuela Nakete	FLP	459	
Isireli Lewaniqila	SDL	7,075	
Erami Biaunisala	Ind.	295	
Informal		809	
Total votes		8,956	
Total valid		8,147	
Turnout (per cent)		91.2	
Total registered		9,823	

6. Nadroga/Navosa Fijian Provincial

Sakiusa Timoci Manumanunivalu	NVTLP	172	
Veniana Gonewai	FLP	2,527	
Ratu Isikeli Tasere	SDL	10,624	
Peniasi Kunatuba	Ind.	1,167	
Inoke Kadralevu	PANU	356	
Informal		1,857	
Total votes		16,704	
Total valid		14,847	
Turnout (per cent)		87.7	
Total registered		19,044	

7. Naitasiri Fijian Provincial

Ilaitia Bulidiri Tuisese	SDL	8,455	
Maika Moroca	FLP	424	
Jope Gonevulavula	NVTLP	353	
Kavekini Navuso	NAPF	404	
Manoa Laqere Naitala	Ind.	413	
Informal		825	
Total votes		10,874	
Total valid		10,049	
Turnout (per cent)		90.1	
Total registered		12,067	

8. Namosi Fijian Provincial

Ratu Suliano Matanitobua	SDL	2,481	
Waisea N Batilekaleka	NVTLP	178	
Koleta Marama Sivivatu	FLP	125	
Informal		282	
Total votes		3,066	
Total valid		2,784	
Turnout (per cent)		91.8	
Total registered		3,340	

	Party	Totals Counts							
		1st	2nd	3rd	4th	5th	6th	7th	8th
9. Ra Fijian Provincial									
Mosese Ramuria	NAPF	225							
Tevita Tabalailai	Ind.	734							
Timoci Naco	FLP	1,048							
Tomasi Vuetilavoni	SDL	6,456							
Informal		1,127							
Total votes		9,590							
Total valid		8,463							
Turnout (per cent)		88.1							
Total registered		10,880							
10. Rewa Fijian Provincial									
Viliame Raile	Ind.	95							
Ro Teimumu Kepa Tuisawau	SDL	3,401							
Filipe Q Tuisawau	Ind.	2,371							
Taniela Robonu Senikuta	FLP	167							
Informal		639							
Total votes		6,673							
Total valid		6,034							
Turnout (per cent)		90.9							
Total registered		7,341							
11. Serua Fijian Provincial									
Ananaiasa Qio Vucago	Ind.	232							
Pio Kameli Tabaiwalu	SDL	2,792							
Sakeasi Lomalagi	Ind.	431							
Levani Tonitonivanua	NVTLP	147							
Informal		510							
Total votes		4,112							
Total valid		3,602							
Turnout (per cent)		91.9							
Total registered		4,473							
12. Ba East Fijian Provincial									
Paulo Ralulu	SDL	5,528							
Apimeleki Nabaro	NFP	732							
Ponipate Lesavua	PANU	2,888							
Informal		1,067							
Total votes		10,215							
Total valid		9,148							
Turnout (per cent)		86.3							
Total registered		11,836							

	Party	Totals Counts							
		1st	2nd	3rd	4th	5th	6th	7th	8th

13. Ba West Fijian Provincial

Pauliasi Namua	NFP	257
Ratu Meli Q Saukuru	SDL	9,211
Taniela Wai	FLP	1,156
Meli Bogileka	PANU	883
Informal		1,143
Total votes		12,650
Total valid		11,507
Turnout (per cent)		82.4
Total registered		15,348

14. Tailevu North Fijian Provincial

Laisiasa Cabenalevu	FLP	278
Samisoni Tikoinasau	SDL	6,281
Iliesa Duvuloco	NVTLP	1,171
Informal		923
Total votes		8,653
Total valid		7,730
Turnout (per cent)		89.4
Total registered		9,682

15. Tailevu South Fijian Provincial

Irami Ului Matairavula	SDL	6,722
Akuila Wailevu Raikoti	Ind.	59
Saukelea Erini	NAPF	493
Levani V Tuinabua	Ind.	1,046
Informal		1,069
Total votes		9,389
Total valid		8,320
Turnout (per cent)		91.1
Total registered		10,303

16. Cakaudrove East Fijian Provincial

Vilimone Vosarogo	Ind.	287
Lutuvakula Melania	NAPF	480
Ratu Naiqama Lalabalavu	SDL	6,120
Informal		752
Total votes		7,639
Total valid		6,887
Turnout (per cent)		100.7 (sic)
Total registered		7,588

	Party	Totals Counts							
		1st	2nd	3rd	4th	5th	6th	7th	8th

17. Cakaudrove West Fijian Provincial

Vaniqi Manasa Ramasirai	Ind.	607	
Niko Nawaikula	SDL	7,674	
Vosawale Josua	NFP	236	
Informal		1,103	
Total votes		9,620	
Total valid		8,517	
Turnout (per cent)		82.8	
Total registered		11,616	

18. North East Fijian Urban Communal

Nanise Vunisere Kasami Nagusuca	SDL	11,548	
Manasa Tugia	Ind.	353	
Sainiana Rokovucago	FLP	1,357	
Saimoni Raikuna	NAPF	338	
Bogivitu Lotawa	Ind.	61	
Informal		906	
Total votes		14,563	
Total valid		13,657	
Turnout (per cent)		84.9	
Total registered		17,156	

19. North West Fijian Urban Communal

Lemeki V Vuetaki	NAPF	283	
Joji Natadra Banuve	SDL	11,620	
Ravuama Rainima Nanovu	Ind.	477	
Mosese Tukikaukamea	Ind.	31	
Vuli Salusalu Mahe	UPP	115	
Ratu Maikeli Lalabalavu	NFP	158	
Akanisi Koroitamana	FLP	2,017	
Informal		849	
Total votes		15,550	
Total valid		14,701	
Turnout (per cent)		82.4	
Total registered		18,864	

20. South West Fijian Urban Communal

Viliame Katia	FLP	817	
Jone Yavala Kubuabola	SDL	10,123	
Silikiwai Emosi	NAPF	470	
Seveci Naisilisili	Ind.	305	
Informal		803	
Total votes		12,518	
Total valid		11,715	
Turnout (per cent)		82.9	
Total registered		15,093	

	Party		Totals Counts							
		1st	2nd	3rd	4th	5th	6th	7th	8th	

21. Suva City Fijian Urban Communal

Peni Vulaca Secake Volavola	SDL	880	
Josaia Waqabaca	FLP	675	
Apete Naitini	NAPF	760	
Mataiasi Ragigia	SDL	7,205	
Semi Uluivuya	NVTLP	46	
Akuila Bale	Ind.	142	
Miriama Rayawa Cama	NFP	157	
Informal		570	
Total votes		10,435	
Total valid		9865	
Turnout (per cent)		82.1	
Total registered		12,707	

22. Tamavua/Laucala Fijian Urban Communal

Netani Sukanaivalu	NAPF	788	
Laisiasa Corerega	NFP	128	
Ratu Jone Waqairatu	SDL	10,880	
Jone Tubuto	FLP	970	
Kaumaitotoya U.K.M.S	POT	28	
Basilio D Kalokalodromu	Ind.	18	
Informal		679	
Total votes		13,491	
Total valid		12,812	
Turnout (per cent)		84.0	
Total registered		16,068	

23. Nasinu Fijian Urban Communal

Joji Uluinakauvadra	NAPF	459	
Inoke Luveni	SDL	10,631	
Emasi Qovu	Ind.	630	
Vilikesa Ravia	FLP	800	
Informal		837	
Total votes		13,357	
Total valid		12,520	
Turnout (per cent)		79.8	
Total registered		15,694	

	Party	Totals Counts							
		1st	2nd	3rd	4th	5th	6th	7th	8th
24. Suva City General Communal									
Aca Lord	SDL	702							
Daniel Robert Johns	NFP	60							
Rounds Ganilau									
Lavenia Bernadette	UPP	1,458							
Kenneth Zinck	Ind.	510							
Informal		166							
Total votes		2,896							
Total valid		2,730							
Turnout (per cent)		82.2							
Total registered		3,523							
25. North Eastern General Communal									
Harry Arthur Robinson	UPP	528	545	561	941				
Nawaia Touakin	Ind.	357	361						
Rebo Terubea	FLP	383	391	423					
David Christopher	SDL	1,467	1,478	1,511	1,547	1,639			
Rocky Percival Billings	NAPF	289							
Irwin Robin	Ind.	629	873	1,158	1,165	2,014			
Informal		389							
Total votes		4,042							
Total valid		3,653							
Turnout (per cent)		86.0							
Total registered		4,702							
26. Western/Central General Communal									
Millis Malcolm Beddoes	UPP	2,234							
Noel Iupasi Tofinga	NAPF	453							
Anaseini Tuineau Henry	NAPF	34							
Vula Tawake Shaw	SDL	54							
Pateresio Nunu Polania	SDL	1,651							
Informal		231							
Total votes		4,657							
Total valid		4,426							
Turnout (per cent)		83.2							
Total registered		5,595							
27. Vitilevu East/Maritime Indian Communal									
Sanjeet Chand Maharaj	FLP	4,744							
Bhima Sami	NFP	946							
Jayant Prasad Maharaj	Ind.	200							
Akmal Ellyas Ali	SDL	162							
Informal		569							
Total votes		6,621							
Total valid		6,052							
Turnout (per cent)		91.2							
Total registered		7,256							

	Party		Totals Counts							
		1st	2nd	3rd	4th	5th	6th	7th	8th	

28. Tavua Indian Communal

Anand Babla	FLP	5,707	
Suresh Chandra	NFP	1,329	
Mohammed Janif Khan	SDL	144	
Informal		732	
Total votes		7,912	
Total valid		7180	
Turnout (per cent)		92.7	
Total registered		8,536	

29. Ba East Indian Communal

Jain Kumar	FLP	4,956	
Praveen Bala	NFP	1,874	
Nirbhay Chand	SDL	34	
Informal		668	
Total votes		7,532	
Total valid		6,864	
Turnout (per cent)		91.8	
Total registered		8,203	

30. Ba West Indian Communal

Madan Sen	SDL	180	
Farouk Janeman	NFP	870	
Narendra Kumar Padarath	FLP	7,229	
Informal		876	
Total votes		9,155	
Total valid		8,279	
Turnout (per cent)		79.3	
Total registered		11,538	

31. Lautoka Rural Indian Communal

Mohammed Shameem	SDL	252	
Deo Kumar	NAPF	125	
Udit Narayan	FLP	6,832	
Naren Prasad	NFP	1,643	
Informal		989	
Total votes		9,841	
Total valid		8,852	
Turnout (per cent)		87.9	
Total registered		11,200	

	Party		Totals Counts							
		1st	2nd	3rd	4th	5th	6th	7th	8th	

32. Lautoka City Indian Communal

Jai Gawander	FLP	7,629
Rosemary Satanji	NAPF	172
Rakesh Kumar	NFP	1,590
Azizul Dean	SDL	158
Informal		1,085
Total votes		10,634
Total valid		9,549
Turnout (per cent)		86.4
Total registered		12,308

33. Vuda Indian Communal

Vyas Deo Sharma	FLP	7,131
Rajendra Singh	NFP	748
Abdul Afizu Rahiman	SDL	330
Arbin Prakash Narayan	Ind.	14
Sanel Prasad	NAPF	155
Informal		861
Total votes		9,239
Total valid		8,378
Turnout (per cent)		87.8
Total registered		10,526

34. Nadi Urban Indian Communal

Gunasagaran Gounder	FLP	8,108
Sushila Rameshwar	NFP	2,151
Mohammed Zarib	SDL	266
Kamlesh Prasad	Ind.	120
Sanmogam Naidu Sanu	Ind.	15
Informal		793
Total votes		11,453
Total valid		10,660
Turnout (per cent)		87.6
Total registered		13,081

35. Nadi Rural Indian Communal

Perumal Mupnar	FLP	6,825
Karna Waddi Raju	NFP	2,528
Armogam Sami	SDL	138
Informal		903
Total votes		10,394
Total valid		9,491
Turnout (per cent)		90.6
Total registered		11,467

	Party		Totals Counts							
		1st	2nd	3rd	4th	5th	6th	7th	8th	

36. Nadroga Indian Communal

Lekh Ram Vayeshnoi	FLP	7,219
Parma Nand	NFP	1,215
Ashok Kumar	SDL	474
Informal		1,452
Total votes		10,360
Total valid		8,908
Turnout (per cent)		92.2
Total registered		11,240

37. Viti Levu South/Kadavu Indian Communal

Pravin Narayan	NAPF	143
Chaitanya Lakshman	FLP	5,575
Bimal Singh	SDL	205
Bimal Bimlesh Prasad	NFP	877
Informal		786
Total votes		7,586
Total valid		6,800
Turnout (per cent)		90.2
Total registered		8,407

38. Suva City Indian Communal

Gyani Nand	FLP	7,660
Shiu Ram	COIN	20
Chandra Kant Umaria	NFP	1,675
Mohammed Salamat Ali	SDL	147
Dildar Shah	NAPF	405
Informal		711
Total votes		10,618
Total valid		9,907
Turnout (per cent)		84.5
Total registered		12,568

39. Vanua Levu West Indian Communal

Suresh Chand	NAPF	33
Bijay Prasad	SDL	48
Suvinay Kumar Basawaiya	NFP	708
Surendra Lal	FLP	4,886
Charan Jeath Singh	NAPF	950
Informal		568
Total votes		7,193
Total valid		6,625
Turnout (per cent)		92.8
Total registered		7,755

	Party		Totals Counts							
		1st	2nd	3rd	4th	5th	6th	7th	8th

40. Luacala Indian Communal

Dewan Chand	FLP	13,133
Praveen Chand	NAPF	504
Indar Singh	SDL	203
Sundresan Goundar	NFP	828
Roshan Dildar Shah	JFP	18
Informal		1,257
Total votes		15,943
Total valid		14,686
Turnout (per cent)		85.7
Total registered		18,610

41. Nasinu Indian Communal

Hari Prasad Sharma	SDL	5
Mohammed Khalim	NFP	615
Krishna Datt	FLP	10,940
Fatima Bano Shad	NAPF	28
Imraz Iqbal Ali	SDL	226
Liaquat Khan	NAPF	222
Informal		1,291
Total votes		13,327
Total valid		12,036
Turnout (per cent)		90.1
Total registered		14,789

42. Tailevu/Rewa indian Communal

Ragho Nand	FLP	8,058
Anay Sumeshwar Yadav	NFP	967
Mohammed Tazim	NAPF	144
Nilesh Chand Maharaj	SDL	126
Informal		1,230
Total votes		10,525
Total valid		9,295
Turnout (per cent)		90.4
Total registered		11,641

43. Labasa Indian Communal

Jaiwant Kris Arulappan	NFP	1,137
Subrail T Goundar	SDL	147
Kamlesh Reddy	FLP	6,813
Informal		889
Total votes		8,986
Total valid		8,097
Turnout (per cent)		87.7
Total registered		10,248

Party		Totals Counts							
		1st	2nd	3rd	4th	5th	6th	7th	8th

44. Labasa Rural Indian Communal

Mohammed Tahir	FLP	5,279							
Satya Deo	NAPF	139							
Mohammed Rafiq	NFP	930							
Informal		664							
Total votes		7,012							
Total valid		6,348							
Turnout (per cent)		94.6							
Total registered		7,416							

45. Macuata East/Cakaudrove Indian Communal

Vijay Chand	FLP	5,298							
Kamal Kumar Raj	NFP	632							
James Venkat Sami	NAPF	350							
Chitra Singh	SDL	81							
Informal		754							
Total votes		7,115							
Total valid		6,361							
Turnout (per cent)		92.5							
Total registered		7,688							

46. Rotuma Communal

Sosefo Kafoa	SDL	526	531						
Mua Ieli Taukave	UPP	532	548	566					
Sosefo Sikuri Inoke	NAPF	245							
Victor Fatiaki	Ind.	1,149	1,348	1,361					
Jioji Konousi Konrote	Ind.	1,983	2,008	2,508					
Informal		302							
Total votes		4,737							
Total valid		4,435							
Turnout (per cent)		88.2							
Total registered		5,373							

47. Tailevu North/Ovalau Open

Isoa Gonenicolo Tamani	Ind.	1,585							
Tomasi Tokalauvere	FLP	1,769							
Aisake Bukavesi	NVTLP	849							
Josefa Dulakiverata	Ind.	2,800							
Josefa Vosanibola	SDL	7,342							
Informal		1,633							
Total votes		15,978							
Total valid		14,345							
Turnout (per cent)		89.3							
Total registered		17,893							

	Party	Totals Counts							
		1st	2nd	3rd	4th	5th	6th	7th	8th
48. Tailevu South/Lomaiviti Open									
Adi Asenaca Caucau	SDL	10,400							
Aisea Naikawakawa	FLP	5,736							
Wailevu Jone Tovehi	Ind.	793							
Informal		2,597							
Total votes		19,526							
Total valid		16,929							
Turnout (per cent)		90.3							
Total registered		21,620							
49. Nausori/Naitasiri Open									
Asaeli Masilaca	SDL	7,723	7,804	7,811	8,298				
Peter Anuresh Chand	NFP	485	485						
Josaia Gucake	NAPF	584	587	1051					
Lavenia Wainiqolo Padarath	FLP	6,935	6,937	6,951	7,515				
Lasarusa Sovea Ben Zion	Ind.	86							
Informal		1,473							
Total votes		17,286							
Total valid		15,813							
Turnout (per cent)		86.5							
Total registered		19,977							
50. Nasinu/Rewa Open									
Indar Deo	NAPF	748	760						
John Ali	SDL	5,188	5,199	5,225	6,764	8,179			
Azim Hussein	FLP	8,611	8,625	8,663	8,688	9,436			
Priscilla Singh	NFP	563							
Seru Serevi	Ind.	845	1,362	2,035	2,181				
Pita C Tagicakiverata	SDL	1,664	1,672	1,692					
Informal		1,572							
Total votes		19,191							
Total valid		17,619							
Turnout (per cent)		90.2							
Total registered		21,273							
		8,809							
51. Cunningham Open									
Aminiasi Delana	Ind.	536							
Leoni Tuisowaqa	NAPF	659							
Ramesio Rogovakalali	FLP	7,492							
Rajesh Singh	SDL	9,831							
Joketani Delai	SLMP	49							
Peni Vatubai	NAPF	225							
Manuel Lui Arisais (Snr)	NFP	428							
Informal		1,344							
Total votes		20,564							
Total valid		19,220							
Turnout (per cent)		85.4							
Total registered		24,087							

	Party	Totals Counts							
		1st	2nd	3rd	4th	5th	6th	7th	8th
52. Laucala Open									
Vijay Krishna Nair	FLP	6,985	6,985	6,986	7,015	7,845			
Keshwan Nadan	NFP	638	638	638					
Salabula Losena	SDL	7,138	7,140	7,161	7,171	7,856			
Manunivavalagi Dalituicama Korovulavula	NAPF	874	875	916	1,515				
Nimilote Jitoko Fifita	POT	23							
Viliame Civoniceva	Ind.	43	63						
Informal		973							
Total votes		16,674							
Total valid		15,701							
Turnout (per cent)		84.3							
Total registered		19,774							
53. Samabula/Tamavua Open									
Baba Tupeni L	SDL	5,939	6,000	6,011	6,021	6,118			
Pramod Rae	NFP	666	668	671					
Pita Kewa Nacuva	SDL	92							
Monica Raghwan	FLP	5,332	5,341	5,599	5,656	7,162			
Filipe Bole	NAPF	961	979	999	1,603				
Monoa Dobui	UPP	290	292						
Informal		947							
Total votes		14,227							
Total valid		13,280							
Turnout (per cent)		83.0							
Total registered		17,137							
54. Suva City Open									
Ofa M.P. Swann	Ind.	341	345						
Misaele Weleilakeba	SDL	5,705	5,707	5,746	5,963	6,135			
Tom Ricketts	FLP	3,261	3,475	3,493	3,524	5,903			
Attar Singh	NFP	745	746	965					
Tikotikoca Inoke Seru	UPP	223							
Epeli Gavidi Ganilau	NAPF	1,763	1,765	1,834	2,551				
Informal		813							
Total votes		12,851							
Total valid		12,038							
Turnout (per cent)		84.5							
Total registered		15,206							

	Party		Totals Counts							
		1st	2nd	3rd	4th	5th	6th	7th	8th	

55. Lami Open

	Party	1st
Eroni Ratuwalesi	Ind.	36
Esaroma Ledua	Ind.	1,474
Filimoni Lacanivalu	FLP	2,260
Mere Tuisalalo Samisoni	SDL	7,664
Benjamin Wainiqolo Padarath	NAPF	681
Viliame Savu	NVTLP	57
Jasper Singh	Ind.	1,087
Vilikesa Rauca	NAPF	168
Lionel Danford	UPP	303
Informal		1,083
Total votes		14,813
Total valid		13,730
Turnout (per cent)		83.1
Total registered		17,815

56. Lomaivuna/Namosi/Kadavu Open

	Party	1st
Ted Young	SDL	11,817
Mitieli Baleivanualala	FLP	2,972
Peter Asiga Lee	Ind.	1,395
Informal		1,632
Total votes		17,816
Total valid		16,184
Turnout (per cent)		89.9
Total registered		19,819

57. Ra Open

	Party	1st
Epineri Vocevuka	FLP	4,870
George Shiu Raj	SDL	10,172
Vurewa Aporosa	NAPF	968
Informal		1,587
Total votes		17,597
Total valid		16,010
Turnout (per cent)		89.5
Total registered		19,670

58. Tavua Open

	Party	1st
Damodar	FLP	7,231
Narendra Reddy	NFP	1,723
Semi Leiene	SDL	4,069
Savenaca Tuwai	PANU	303
Koroinasau Ratu Semi	NAPF	92
Informal		1,145
Total votes		14,563
Total valid		13,418
Turnout (per cent)		91.0
Total registered		15,996

	Party	Totals Counts							
		1st	2nd	3rd	4th	5th	6th	7th	8th
59. Ba Open									
Ram Lajendra	NFP	2,981							
John Nacamavuto Dunn	NAPF	139							
Jale O Baba	SDL	60							
Mahendra Pal Chaudhary	FLP	10,709							
Ralulu Rusila	NAPF	16							
Savenaca Nabeka	PANU	283							
Faiaaz Ali	SDL	2,737							
Informal		1,422							
Total votes		18,347							
Total valid		16,925							
Turnout (per cent)		88.4							
Total registered		20,759							
60. Magodro Open									
Vijay Lal	NAPF	731							
Josese Drikalu Botitu	SDL	3,761							
Davendra Naidu	NFP	2,023							
Gyan Singh	FLP	9,000							
Informal		1,973							
Total votes		17,488							
Total valid		15,515							
Turnout (per cent)		87.8							
Total registered		19,911							
61. Lautoka City Open									
Isimeli Savutini Bose	Ind.	351	351	353					
Daniel Urai	FLP	7,420	7,424	7,429	7,448	7,839			
Josefata Niumataiwalu	Ind.	88	89						
Alexander David O'connor	UPP	402	402	406	410				
Jone Saumaimuri Bouwalu	SDL	5,222	5,278	5,356	5,380	5,390			
Sailesh Chandar Naidu	NFP	1,450	1,451	1,451	1,757	1,766			
Bijesh Chand	Ind.	62							
Informal		1,244							
Total votes		16,239							
Total valid		14,995							
Turnout (per cent)		85.1							
Total registered		19,084							

	Party	Totals Counts							
		1st	2nd	3rd	4th	5th	6th	7th	8th
62. Vuda Open									
Mahammed Yusuf	SDL	4,435							
Felix Anthony	FLP	9,745							
Narend Kumar aka Bissun Datt	NFP	1,267							
Viliame Rakuli	PANU	177							
Aca Tuigaloa Saukuru	Ind.	54							
Informal		1,623							
Total votes		17,301							
Total valid		15,678							
Turnout (per cent)		85.3							
Total registered		20,275							
63. Nadi Open									
Arvind Deo Singh	SVT	237	237	238	238	238			
Amjad Ali	FLP	8,630	8,631	8,691	8,691	8,694	8,695	9,060	9,069
Prem Singh	NFP	2,645	2,645	2,645	2,645	2,652	2,653	2,664	2,669
Williams Josephine Raikuna	UPP	389	389	390	390	393	394		
Shyam Sundaram	SDL	5,432	5,486	5,487	5,575	5,584	5,818	5,829	6,215
Qoro Ratu Vero Naovuka	Ind.	65	65						
Rajendra Kumar	Ind.	56							
Kamenieli Nawaqavonovono	PANU	476	476	476	476	622	622	624	633
Joseva Samudunatua Vatunitu	Ind.	168	169	171	178				
Ratu Jeremaia Lewaravu	Ind.	392	392	392	393	403	404	409	
Pravin Jamieson	Ind.	96	96	96					
Informal		1,356							
Total votes		19,942							
Total valid		18,586							
Turnout (per cent)		84.3							
Total registered		23,658							
64. Yasawa/Nawaka Open									
Sivia Qoro	FLP	7,858							
Bal Subramani	NFP	2,772							
Saimoni Naivalu	SDL	4,163							
Mataiasi N Saukuru	PANU	769							
Dewa Nand	Ind.	60							
Informal		1,752							
Total votes		17,374							
Total valid		15,622							
Turnout (per cent)		86.9							
Total registered		20,002							

	Party	Totals Counts							
		1st	2nd	3rd	4th	5th	6th	7th	8th
65. Nadroga Open									
Ali Mohammed Jamal	NAPF	260	369						
Mesulame Rakuro	FLP	6,959	6,960	6,973	7,939				
Immanuel Manu	NFP	770	770	1012					
Viliame Navoka	SDL	6,734	6,739	6,853	6,899				
Vilisite Qera	NVTLP	115							
Informal		1,856							
Total votes		16,694							
Total valid		14,838	14,838	14,838	14,838				
Turnout (per cent)		89.8							
Total registered		18,590							
66. Serua/Navosa Open									
Atunaisa Lacabuka Rasoki	NDP	123	196						
Anisi Dau Bati	Ind.	81							
Jona Rokowai	NVTLP	433	434	621	623				
Pio Iowane Wong	Ind.	1,005	1,008	1,009	1,016	1,022			
Peniasi Lavava Dakua	FLP	6,318	6,319	6,319	6,356	6,360	7,311	7,638	
William McGoon	NFP	938	939	940	1,240	1,840	1,860		
Jone V Navakamocea	SDL	8,537	8,538	8,546	8,545	8,553	8,610	10,143	
Viliame Bale	NAPF	346	347	347					
Informal		2,581							
Total votes		20,362							
Total valid		17,781							
Turnout (per cent)		89.9							
Total registered		22,642							
67. Bua/Macuata West Open									
Josefa Cavu	NAPF	939							
Hazrat Ali	NAPF	48							
Vitori Cavalevu	NAPF	30							
Tuvuki Isireli B	Ind.	235							
Lemeki Qalibau	FLP	4,618							
Josefa Dimuri	SDL	8,307							
Josefa Rusaqoli	NFP	565							
Suliasi Saraqia	Ind.	528							
Informal		1,297							
Total votes		16,567							
Total valid		15,270							
Turnout (per cent)		92.4							
Total registered		17,925							

	Party				Totals Counts					
		1st	2nd	3rd	4th	5th	6th	7th	8th

68. Labasa Open

Mohammed Sharif	SDL	80
Gonelevu Siteri Nai	NAPF	273
Koresi Matatolu	NAPF	5
Sailosi Semi Lutua	SDL	265
Poseci Bune	FLP	8,066
Timoci Bulitavu	SDL	3,015
Raman Pratap Singh	NFP	1,266
Informal		925
Total votes		13,895
Total valid		12,970
Turnout (per cent)		88.8
Total registered		15,651

69. Macuata East Open

Agni Deo Singh	FLP	8,357
Parmod Chand	NFP	1,669
Iliesa Seru	SDL	3,343
Informal		1,580
Total votes		14,949
Total valid		13,369
Turnout (per cent)		91.7
Total registered		16,306

70. Cakaudrove West Open

Gilbert Vakalalabure	Ind.	511
Tuikoroalau Aporosa	Ind.	540
Ratu Osea Vakalalabure	SDL	8,409
Naulu Peni	Ind.	1,544
Inia Poate Tubui	SDL	698
Saliceni Tulevu Gonelevu	FLP	2,359
Solomone Catarogo	PANU	91
Informal		1,128
Total votes		15,280
Total valid		14,152
Turnout (per cent)		86.2
Total registered		17,717

71. Lau/Taveuni/Ratuma Open

Fani Tago Vosaniveibuli	NAPF	2,553
Ilisoni Taoba	Ind.	204
Savenaca Uluibau Draunidalo	SDL	10,888
Pio R Naiqama	Ind.	223
Informal		1,705
Total votes		15,573
Total valid		13,868
Turnout (per cent)		92.1
Total registered		16,906

Index

www.ingramcontent.com/pod-product-compliance
Lightning Source LLC
Chambersburg PA
CBHW050810270326
41926CB00045B/4558